PUBLICATIONS

OF THE

STATE DEPARTMENT OF ARCHIVES AND HISTORY

THE PAPERS OF
WILLIAM ALEXANDER GRAHAM

Will H. Graham

The Papers of

William Alexander Graham

Edited by

J. G. DE ROULHAC HAMILTON

VOLUME ONE

1825-1837

RALEIGH

STATE DEPARTMENT OF ARCHIVES AND HISTORY

1957

iii

iv

CONTENTS

FOREWORD

In publishing the papers of William Alexander Graham, the Department of Archives and History is continuing its policy of publishing materials which have not been published and which are not generally available to the research student and to the public. The law of 1903 establishing the Department (formerly the North Carolina Historical Commission) definitely charged the Department with the duty of publishing and making available to the public the unpublished materials pertaining to the history of the State. During the years the Department has issued many volumes thereby enriching the holdings of university, college, school, and public libraries throughout the State and making its history more accessible to the general public.

In 1940 the Department invited Dr. Hamilton who had previously edited *The Correspondence of Jonathan Worth* (two volumes), *The Papers of Thomas Ruffin* (four volumes) and *The Papers of Randolph Abbott Shotwell* (three volumes), to edit the papers of Governor Graham. Dr. Hamilton accepted the invitation, but due to his obligations to the University of North Carolina and to The Southern Historical Collection, the work was delayed.

Later Mr. John W. Clark of Franklinville, a grandson of Governor Graham, became interested in the Graham papers. Dr. Hamilton then asked the Department to relieve him of his obligation to prepare these papers for publication by the Department. This the Department agreed to do.

In 1950 Dr. Hamilton approached the Department about publishing these papers and reported that both he and Mr. Clark wanted the Department to undertake the publication of these papers, and to this the Deparment agreed.

This is the first volume in a series of approximately seven volumes. The papers cover the period before, during, and after the Civil War. Graham was active in this period and these papers add much to the available information of North Carolina history.

The Department plans to proceed with the publication of the other volumes as soon as the funds are available.

D. L. Corbitt, *Head*
Division of Publications

January 30, 1957

EDITORIAL INTRODUCTION.

The editing of the following portion of the correspondence and other papers of William Alexander Graham has been sponsored by his grandson, Mr. John W. Clark, of Greensboro, N. C. Mr. Clark's deep interest in the life of this distinguished ancestor, combined with his keen historical interest, has inspired in him a worthy desire to make available, not only to Governor Graham's descendants and to historical investigators, but to general readers as well, so valuable a picture of the man, and also of the life and thought over half a century in North Carolina and in the nation, as is contained in these papers.

They have a wide interest. They throw light upon life all the way from the frontiers to the capital of the nation. They touch on family and social life, on business, the professions, and politics, on agriculture and slavery, and on state and national government. They are revealing as to numerous well-known persons, as well as to even more who are little known. They throw much light on two wars with which Graham was intimately concerned. And, finally, they give an excellent picture of Graham himself.

Naturally their most intimate relationship is with the man himself. The most distinguished figure in the history of North Carolina,[1] as measured by his ability, his learning, particularly in the fields of law and government, the high public offices he filled with honor and distinction, his wide acquaintance in the state and elsewhere, and his tremendous influence upon his contemporaries, his correspondence furnishes a very unforgettable picture— and a very inspiring one—of the man.

It is fortunate that this is so, for, with all the wide recognition of his qualities of greatness, he deserves a more human portraiture than later generations have seen. Many have regarded him as cold, detached, and even austere, but no one who reads the family letters herein contained, or those written to him by his contemporaries, ranging from the highest in the land to the humblest

---

[1] The following sound analysis in the address of Frank Nash seems convincing as to the accuracy of this estimate: "Judge Murphey was a greater genius but he was not so practical; Judge Badger had greater intellectual endowments, but he was not so industrious; Judge Mangum was a greater popular orator, but he was self-indulgent; Judge Ruffin was a greater lawyer, but his life ran in a narrower channel; Judge Gaston was a greater lawyer, and orator, and as pure in heart and life and conduct as he, but he was not ambitious."

members of society, without realizing that it is an inaccurate picture which has come down to us. Reserved and dignified, he was never austere or other than entirely human, devoted to his family and numerous friends, and keenly interested in all the life about him. Possibly the fact that he applied his intellect, much more than did those around him, to public and private problems, has contributed to the popular conception of him. He was judically-minded, but it is also true that upon occasion emotion— and temper—could betray him into feeling, utterance, and action more characteristic of lesser men. And when he was thus moved— sometimes to error—his human stature is not diminished, but is just better understood by the average man. There is abundant evidence in the letters of his intimates that he was, with all of his dignity, a loveable person.

His statesmanship, viewed with detachment, was greater than that attained by any of his North Carolina contemporaries, and by few elsewhere. Based upon intellect, learning, study and reflection, it was moulded by his passion for law, and for the larger public good. He was far-seeing and wise, and, consequently, somewhat lonely, and to him, as to all others of his type, came much of disappointment, not so much personal but chiefly in relation to the public weal, for he was a large-minded man in his view of life. But he never sulked in his tent, and to the end of his life, even in weakness and suffering, he continued to labor and strive for the common good.

The letters and papers here published are drawn from a variety of sources, but chiefly from the large collections in the Southern Historical Collection of the University of North Carolina and the North Carolina Department of Archives and History. Letters written by him have been chiefly drawn from other personal collections in the same two places. Unfortunately the papers of most of those with whom he corresponded have been destroyed, or are not available today.

The papers printed have been selected with great care from a much greater number. I have attempted in the selection to present, so far as possible, every type of correspondence, other than which relates to his practice of law, including examples which show his many interests, his problems and policies while in public office, his tremendous public influence, his wide contacts and reputation, his way of life, and the many interesting people with whom he was more or less intimately associated. I have selected all letters which seem valuable for historical information not particularly connected with him. And I have also included samples of letters from cranks of greater or less degree, who, then as now, attempt to prey upon public men. If relatively unimportant, they are interesting.

Of necessity the individual letters required editing to the extent of eliminating much casual matter of little or no interest today, as well as much touching upon professional and business matters. If I have erred, it is in the direction of inclusion rather than of exclusion.

The question of how far to go in the inclusion of Graham's writings other than letters, offered a rather difficult problem which I have solved by a compromise. I have included all un-published writings of his that could be located, as well as all published only in newspapers. I have included a number of im-portant speeches and reports which, although they were separately printed, are rare and difficult to locate. I have not included his messages as governor, his reports as secretary of the navy, partly because they include much technical matter, and partly because they are fairly easily available. I have not included his long and powerful speech in the impeachment trial of Governor William W. Holden, because it was a definitely assigned portion of the argument of the prosecution, and not easily understood apart from the context of the whole case. Nor have I included his long and elaborate address of 1875 on the subject of the Mecklenburg Declaration of Independence, which was printed in at least one periodical, and also published in a large edition.

I have not attempted to write any biographical sketch, but have, instead, republished the two best sketches of his life that have yet been written. They are the extensive address by the late Frank Nash, delivered at the unveiling of a bust of Graham in the state capitol by the North Carolina Historical Commission, and the elaborate memorial address by his contemporary and intimate friend, Montford McGehee. If there may appear in each of them a touch of hero-worship, it must be remembered that the authors lived in a period and in communities and families where their subject was so regarded. But it must also be remembered that one of these authors knew him intimately over many years, and that the other was a life-long student of North Carolina history and, as well, a capable historical investigator. It is to be hoped that with the publication of these papers an adequate biography of Graham will follow in due course.

The letters are printed as written with spelling unchanged and unnoted except where it seemed necessary to clarify the meaning. It must be remembered in reading them, that spelling in those days was a much more subjective matter than it is today. Punctuation is treated, in the main, in the same way, except that where a dash was employed for all punctuation, then simple points replace the original. Omissions from the text are indicated with the customary asterisks * * * * * for entire paragraphs, and periods . . . for a portion of a paragraph. Where periods are lacking at the close of a sentence, a space indicates the end. I have omitted in general the opening and closing salutations from the letters, including them only when they are indicative of relationship with the correspondent.

Footnotes are used only sparingly with respect to matters discussed in the text and only where necessary for clarification. On the other hand, they are numerous for persons mentioned. I have tried to make them as complete as possible, realizing that information of this sort is one of the important contributions of a publication of this kind. Unfortunately there are numerous names in the text that cannot now be traced. In such cases I have omitted mention in the notes. Also I have not thought it necessary to make notes for Presidents of the United States and numbers of other well-known figures in and out of the country. In the footnotes I have omitted after the names of North Carolina counties any mention of the state. When the word university appears without designation the reference is to the University of North Carolina.

I find it an impossible task to mention every one of a host of persons to whom I am indebted for aid in the joyful task of preparing the papers for publication. I shall have to content myself with naming a group who have been of great and constant aid to me. First of these is my devoted friend and adviser of nearly half a century, the late Robert D. W. Connor, who was unsparing of time and thought in the solution of innumerable problems, great and small, which arose in the work. My friends and colleagues, Professors Hugh T. Lefler, Fletcher M. Green, and James W. Patton, have been no less generous. Dr. Elizabeth G. McPherson, of the Manuscript Division of the Library of Congress, and the staff of the Naval Division of the National Archives have given me valuable assistance. I acknowledge with gratitude and appreciation the assistance and unfailing helpfulness of Dr. Christopher Crittenden, Mr. D. L. Corbitt, Mr. W. F. Burton, Mrs. Mary Jeffreys Rogers, Mrs. Julia C. Meconnahey, and other members of the staff of the North Carolina Department of Archives and History who have in every way facilitated my work. I owe no less a debt—and probably a greater one because of my being more constantly under foot—to my associates in the Southern Historical Collection, Mrs. J. P. Watters, Miss Anna B. Allan, and Mrs. Carolyn Wallace. As always in such work I owe thanks to my wife for constant aid in the verification of the manuscript and in the reading of the proof. And, finally, to give due acknowledgment of my greatest indebtedness, I mention Mrs. Mary Patterson Fisher, who, not only with remarkable accuracy transcribed all the papers herein included, but through her genius for deciphering difficult and often otherwise unreadable handwriting, has made possible the inclusion of much important material that might otherwise have been omitted. Also, as editorial assistant, she has given me invaluable aid in countless ways.

To these, all and singular, I render thanks.

J. G. de Roulhac Hamilton.

Chapel Hill, North Carolina.
January 30th, 1957

LIST OF LETTERS

Letters Written By William A. Graham Printed in This Volume

Place	Date	Written to
Lincoln County	July 15, 1834	James Seawell
Raleigh	Dec. 20, 1834	William Gaston
Raleigh	Jan. 25, 1836	Thomas Stamps
Greensboro'	Oct. 25, 1836	Susan Washington Graham
Hillsboro'	Nov. 2, 1836	William Gaston
Raleigh	Nov. 20, 1836	Susan Washington Graham
Raleigh	Feb. 12, 1837	Susan Washington Graham
Hillsboro'	Feb. 17, 1837	Susan Washington Graham
Hillsboro'	Feb. 25, 1837	Susan Washington Graham
Hillsboro'	March 3, 1837	Susan Washington Graham
Hillsboro'	March 11, 1837	Susan Washington Graham
Hillsboro'	March 17, 1837	Susan Washington Graham
Lincoln County	March 23, 1837	Susan Washington Graham
Salisbury	April 1, 1837	Susan Washington Graham
Greensboro'	April 24, 1837	Susan Washington Graham
Greensboro'	April 29, 1837	Susan Washington Graham
Caswell Court House	May 8, 1837	Susan Washington Graham
Hillsboro'	May 20, 1837	Susan Washington Graham
New York	June 14, 1837	Susan Washington Graham
New York	June 22, 1837	Susan Washington Graham
New York	June 28, 1837	Susan Washington Graham
New York	July 3, 1837	Susan Washington Graham
Balston Spa	July 5, 1837	Susan Washington Graham
Greensborough	Oct. 21, 1837	Susan Washington Graham
Hillsboro'	Nov. 10, 1837	Susan Washington Graham
Hillsboro'	Nov. 11, 1837	Joseph W. Evans
Hillsboro'	Nov. 22, 1837	Susan Washington Graham
Hillsborough	Dec. 2, 1837	Susan Washington Graham
Vesuvius Furnace, Lincoln	Dec. 16, 1837	Susan Washington Graham
Raleigh	Dec. 30, 1837	Susan Washington Graham

Letters Written to William A. Graham Printed in This Volume

Place	Date	Written by
Vesuvius Furnace (Lincoln)	August 2, 1825	Alfred Graham
Rutherfordton	August 27, 1825	James Graham
Lincoln	June 14, 1826	George F. Graham
Rutherfordton	March 21, 1827	James Graham
New Bern	August 31, 1827	Matthias E. Manly
Near Charlotte	Sept. 12, 1827	Robert Hall Morrison
Gallatin, Tenn.	Sept. 15, 1827	David M. Saunders
Gallatin, Tenn.	Oct. 1, 1827	David M. Saunders
Gallatin, Tenn.	Oct. 2, 1827	David M. Saunders
Rutherfordton	Nov. 9, 1827	James Graham

Vesuvius Furnace [Lincoln]	Nov. 9, 1827	Alfred Graham
Raleigh	Nov. 30, 1827	Hugh Waddell
Gallatin, Tenn.	Dec. 10, 1827	David M. Saunders
Gallatin, Tenn.	April 6, 1828	David M. Saunders
Brookland, Ala.	April 14, 1828	Sophia Witherspoon
Vesuvius Furnace [Lincoln]	April 27, 1828	Alfred Graham
Mocksville	June 30, 1828	Richmond Pearson
Shelby City, Tenn.	July 8, 1828	Joseph Graham, Jr.
Vesuvius Furnace [Lincoln]	July 14, 1828	Alfred Graham
Newbern	Dec. 23, [1828]	Matthias E. Manly
Vesuvius Furnace [Lincoln]	March 31, 1829	Alfred Graham
Vesuvius Furnace [Lincoln]	Dec. 6, 1829	Alfred Graham
Vesuvius Furnace [Lincoln]	March 19, 1830	Alfred Graham
Newbern	Aug. 31, 1830	Matthias E. Manly
Vesuvius Furnace [Lincoln]	Oct. 29, 1830	James Graham
Columbia, S. C.	Dec. 19, 1830	James Graham
Vesuvius Furnace [Lincoln]	Jan. 1, 1831	Alfred Graham
Rutherfordton	Feb. 2, 1831	James Graham
Vesuvius Furnace [Lincoln]	March 13, 1831	Alfred Graham
Rutherfordton	May 23, 1831	James Graham
Rutherfordton	Sept. 14, 1831	James Graham
Cambridge, Mass.	Oct. 4, 1831	Jo. Seawell Jones
-----	Jan. 12, 1832	James W. Osborne
Vesuvius Furnace [Lincoln]	Jan. 22, 1832	James Graham
Warrenton	Feb. 20, 1832	Jo. Seawell Jones
East of Memphis, Tenn.	Feb. 20, 1832	Alfred Graham
Charleston, S. C.	Feb. 29, 1832	James Graham
Warrenton	June 4, 1832	Jo. Seawell Jones
Rutherfordton	June 18, 1832	James Graham
Elm Wood Farm	Nov. 16, 1832	John D. Graham
Cambridge, Mass.	Nov. 30, 1832	Jo. Seawell Jones
Washington	Dec. 21, 1832	Daniel Moreau Barringer
Cambridge, Mass.	Dec. 31, 1832	Jo. Seawell Jones
Cambridge, Mass.	Jan. 12, 1833	Jo. Seawell Jones
Memphis, Tenn.	Jan. 15, 1833	Alfred Graham
Rutherfordton	Feb. 7, 1833	James Graham
Oxford	March 9, 1833	George E. Badger
New York, N. Y.	April 3, 1833	Jo. Seawell Jones
Rutherfordton	Aug. 12, 1833	James Graham
Memphis, Tenn.	Sept. 6, 1833	Alfred Graham
Rutherfordton	Sept. 8, 1833	James Graham
Cambridge, Mass.	Nov. 18, 1833	Jo. Seawell Jones
Hillsborough	Dec. 15, 1833	Hugh Waddell
Washington, D. C.	Dec. 16, 1833	James Graham
Vesuvius Furnace [Lincoln]	Dec. 22, 1833	Joseph Graham
Raleigh	Dec. 30, 1833	David L. Swain
Washington, D. C.	Jan. 2, 1834	James Graham
Washington, D. C.	Jan. 3, 1834	James Graham
Washington, D. C.	Jan. 5, 1834	James Graham
Hillsboro'	Jan. 7, 1834	Hugh Waddell

Raleigh	Jan. 17, 1834	William H. Haywood, Jr.
Washington, D. C.	Jan. 19, 1834	James Graham
Washington, D. C.	Feb. 23, 1834	James Graham
Washington, D. C.	April 1, 1834	James Graham
Washington, D. C.	April 16, 1834	James Graham
Mobile, Ala.	April 22, 1834	Frederick S. Blount
Gallatin, Tenn.	April 26, 1834	David M. Saunders
Washington, D. C.	May 28, 1834	James Graham
Washington, D. C.	June 26, 1834	James Graham
Leasburg	July 30, 1834	Jacob Thompson
Greenbrier Co., Va.	Aug. 11, 1834	James Graham
Mobile, Ala.	Sept. 17, 1834	Frederick S. Blount
Raleigh	Oct. 20, 1834	David L. Swain
Newbern	Nov. 12, 1834	William Gaston
Lincolnton	Nov. 17, 1834	James Graham
New York, N. Y.	Nov. 21, 1834	Jo. Seawell Jones
Raleigh	Nov. 22, 1834	George W. Freeman
Greensboro'	Dec. 3, 1834	John M. Dick
Hillsborough	Dec. 6, 1834	Hugh Waddell
Washington, D. C.	Dec. 8, 1834	James Graham
Person County	Dec. 13, 1834	M. McGehee
Hillsboro'	Dec. 18, 1834	Hugh Waddell
Washington, D. C.	Dec. 20, 1834	James Graham
Raleigh	Dec. 25, 1834	Lawrence and Lemay
Moore Fields	Dec. 27, 1834	Hugh Waddell
Edenton	Dec. 30, 1834	Robert H. Booth
Brookland, Ala.	Jan. 1, 1835	Eliza Witherspoon
Washington, D. C.	Feb. 13, 1835	James Graham
Spring Hill Forge	Feb. 25, 1835	Alfred Graham
Huntsville	Mar. 10, 1835	Thomas L. Clingman
Salisbury	April 9, 1835	Hugh Waddell
Brook-Land, Ala.	April 16, 1835	Eliza Witherspoon
Newbern	April 19, 1835	Matthias E. Manly
Wake Forest	May 18, 1835	James D. Dockery, et als.
Newbern	May 20, 1835	Matthias E. Manly
Spring Hill Forge	May 29, 1835	Alfred Graham
Charlotte	June 3, 1835	James W. Osborne
Brook-Land, Ala.	July 26, 1835	Eliza Witherspoon
Hillsborough	Aug. 6, 1835	Victor Moreau Murphey
Spring Hill Forge	Aug. 25, 1835	Alfred Graham
Warm Springs	Aug. 26, 1835	James Graham
Portsmouth, Va.	Sept. 7, 1835	James Murdaugh
Milton	Oct. 6, 1835	Calvin Jones
Raleigh	Oct. 13, 1835	William H. Haywood, Jr.
Asheville	Oct. 26, 1835	James Graham
Paris, France	Nov. 5, 1835	George S. Bettner
New York, N. Y.	Nov. 13, 1835	Jo. Seawell Jones
Charlotte	Nov. 16, 1835	Robert Hall Morrison
Petersburg, Va.	Nov. 20, 1835	Jo. Seawell Jones
Hillsboro'	Nov. 21, 1835	Hugh Waddell

Danville, Va.	Nov. 27, 1835	Robert B. Gilliam
Hillsboro'	Dec. 2, 1835	James S. Smith
Hillsboro'	Dec. 13, 1835	Alfred Moore
Lincoln County	Dec. 15, 1835	Joseph Graham
Washington, D. C.	Dec. 18, 1835	James Graham
Washington, D. C.	Dec. 22, 1835	James Graham
New Bern	Jan. 1, 1836	Jo. Seawell Jones
Washington, D. C.	Feb. 7, 1836	James Graham
Washington, D. C.	Feb. 25, 1836	James Graham
New Bern	Feb. 28, 1836	Jo. Seawell Jones
Washington, D. C.	Mar. 30, 1836	James Graham
Washington, D. C.	April 1, 1836	Lewis Williams
Raleigh	April 3, 1836	William Gaston
Washington, D. C.	April 4, 1836	James Graham
Greensboro'	April 8, 1836	James Graham
Huntsville	April 29, 1836	Thomas L. Clingman
Rutherfordton	May 7, 1836	James Graham
Charlotte	May 10, 1836	Robert Hall Morrison
Chapel Hill	May 30, 1836	David L. Swain
Algiers, Africa	June 9, 1836	George S. Bettner
Statesville	June 15, 1836	James A. King
Alexandriana	July 8, 1836	Moses W. Alexander
Pensacola, Fla.	July 8, 1836	John Cameron
Rutherfordton	Aug. 20, 1836	James Graham
Chapel Hill	Aug. 26, 1836	David L. Swain
Lincoln County	Aug. 30, 1836	Joseph Graham
Chapel Hill	Sept. 28, 1836	David L. Swain
Salisbury	Sept. 28, 1836	Thomas G. Polk
Elm Wood Farm	Nov. 17, 1836	John D. Graham
Charlotte	Nov. 17, 1836	Robert Hall Morrison
New Bern	Nov. 22, 1836	Susan Washington Graham
Newbern	Nov. 22, 1836	Robert H. G. Moore
Hillsboro'	Dec. 9, 1836	John W. Norwood
Rockingham County	Dec. 14, 1836	Thomas Settle
Raleigh	Dec. 18, 1836	David Outlaw
Washington, D. C.	Dec. 29, 1836	James Graham
Raleigh	Jan. 13, 1837	George W. Mordecai
Chapel Hill	Jan. 20, 1837	David L. Swain
Washington, D. C.	Jan. 29, 1837	James Graham
Raleigh	May 2, 1837	Charles L. Hinton
Rutherfordton	May 8, 1837	James Graham
Raleigh	May 23, 1837	Weston R. Gales
Roxborough	June 20, 1837	Giles Mebane
Hillsborough	June 23, 1837	John W. Norwood
Person County	June 27, 1837	M. McGehee
Davidson College	Aug .7, 1837	Mary G. Morrison
Raleigh	Aug. 11, 1837	Charles L. Hinton
Raleigh	Aug. 12, 1837	Charles Manly
Rutherfordton	Aug. 15, 1837	James Graham
Steamboat "Kentucky"	Sept. 1, 1837	James W. Bryan

GRAHAM PAPERS,

PRINTED ELSEWHERE AND NOT HERE INCLUDED.

Willie P. Mangum Papers

To Willie P. Mangum:

Jan. 6, 1834, Dec. 8, 1834, Feb. 4, 1835, Nov. 4, 1836, May 25, 1837.

From Willie P. Mangum:

Dec. 16, 1834, Dec. 17, 1834, Nov. 23, 1836.

To Thomas Ruffin:

Oct. 5, 1825, Jan. 6, 1827, Nov. 7, 1827, Aug. 10, 1829.

CHRONOLOGY OF WILLIAM ALEXANDER GRAHAM

1804-1874

1804	September 4. Born in Lincoln County, North Carolina.
1816-19	Attended school in Lincolnton and Statesville.
1819-20	Attended Hillsboro Academy.
1820	Entered the University of North Carolina.
1824	June 10. Graduated with first honors.
	Began the study of law under the direction of Judge Thomas Ruffin.
1826	Completed his law course and settled in Hillsboro.
	December Term of Supreme Court, received County Court license.
1827	February. Sworn in at Orange Court.
	September Term of Supreme Court, received Superior Court license.
1828	March Term Orange Superior Court, admitted to Bar, and began regular practice.
1833	August 15. Elected to House of Commons from Borough of Hillsboro.
1834	August 14. Re-elected to House of Commons.
	December. Speech against instructions to Willie P. Mangum.
	December 29. Elected a Trustee of the University of North Carolina.
1835	August 13. Re-elected to the House of Commons.
	November 16. Whig candidate for speaker of the House.
1836	June 8. Married Susannah Sarah Washington, of New Bern, North Carolina.
	August 2. Elected to House of Commons from Orange County.
	November 21. Whig candidate for speaker.
1837	July 27. Defeated for Representative in Congress by William Montgomery.
1838	August 2. Re-elected to the House of Commons.
	November 19. Elected speaker.
1840	August 4. Re-elected to the House of Commons.
	November 16. Unanimously elected speaker.
	November 24. Elected United States Senator.
	December 10. Took seat in Senate.
1841	January 7. Speech on Pre-emption Bill.
	June 2. Elected Chairman of the Committee on Claims.
1842	April 13. Speech on the Loan Bill.
	June 3. Speech on Distributing Clause of the Apportionment Bill.
	December 20. Defeated for re-election to the Senate.
1843	December 7. Nominated for Governor.
	December 18. Accepted the nomination.
1844	August 1. Elected Governor.
1845	January 1. Inaugurated Governor.
1846	January 12. Re-nominated for Governor.
	August 16. Re-elected Governor.
1847	January 1. Inaugurated Governor.
1849	June. Offered mission to Spain and declined.
	June. Elected a Trustee of Wake Forest College.
	June 6. Address to the Literary Societies of the University of North Carolina.
1850	June 21. Appointed Secretary of the Navy.
	August. Wrote opinion on the power of the President with respect to New Mexico.

November 30. **Report recommending fundamental re-organization of the Navy.**

Memorandum on Presidential Elections.

Planned expedition to Japan, and the exploration of the Valley of the Amazon River.

1852   January 28. Graham, the county seat of Alamance, named for him.

June 21. Nominated for Vice President.

June 24. Accepts nomination.

June 28. Resigns as Secretary of the Navy.

November 2. Defeated for Vice President.

1853   January 19. Address on the British Invasion of North Carolina, before the New York Historical Society.

1854   August 3. Elected to state Senate.

December 14. Speech on amendment of the state constitution.

1856   January 15. Legal opinion on the "Legacies of Maxwell Chambers."

September 17. Speech before Whig convention in Raleigh.

1860   January. Active in organization of Constitution Union Party.

January 16. Appointed to National Executive Committee.

February 22. Endorsed for Presidential nomination by Constitutional Union convention in Raleigh.

December. Address at Greensboro on Life and Character of General Nathanael Greene.

December 26. Wrote resolutions of Hillsboro Mass Meeting.

1861   January. Declined to be considered for a post in Lincoln's Cabinet.

February. Opposes call of state convention.

February 28. Elected a delegate to the convention that was defeated at the polls.

April 27. Speech in Hillsboro on political situation.

May 17. Elected to secession convention.

May 20. Nominated for president of the convention. Defeated by Weldon N. Edwards.

June 20. Appointed with Thomas Ruffin on Commission to confer with Confederate authorities in Richmond on acceptance of troops from the state.

December 7. Speech in convention on the Test Oath.

1862   May 9. Declined to be a candidate for Governor.

August 7. Elected to state Senate.

November 27. Elected to Confederate Senate, Second Congress.

1864   January 6. Declined appointment to fill vacancy in Confederate Senate.

May 2. Took seat in Confederate Senate, Second Congress.

May 24. Speech in Senate on Habeas Corpus.

December 14. Speech in Senate on exemption of state officers.

1865   January 30. President *pro tempore ad interim* of the Senate.

March 2. Elected by Senate in executive session on committee with R. M. T. Hunter and J. L. Orr to confer with President on state of the country and his plans.

March 3. Presented in executive session a verbal report of the conference with the President. Gave notice that he would presently offer a resolution for opening negotiations for peace with the United States on the basis of the return of the seceded states.

March 20. Had interview with Governor Vance concerning a called session of the General Assembly.

April 6. Had a second conference with Governor Vance, again advising call of General Assembly.

April 9. Interview with David L. Swain. They agreed that General Assembly should be called to elect commissioners to treat with the United States and report to a convention which should be immediately summoned.

April 12. After conference with Governor Vance, appointed with David L. Swain commissioner to arrange with General William T. Sherman for the surrender of Raleigh.

July 25. Petitioned for pardon.

October. Influential in the movement to elect Jonathan Worth Governor.

October 16. Discussion of the "Iron-clad Oath," in letter to William E. Pell of the Raleigh *Sentinel*.

November 9. Elected to state Senate.

Novmber 27. Presented certificate of election to Senate, but because unpardoned did not take seat.

December 4. Elected United States Senator and resigned from state Senate. Pardon signed but not delivered.

1866   March 16. Published in *National Intelligencer* letter on the Reconstruction Committee.

July 19. Delivered Memorial Address on George E. Badger.

1867   February 7. Appointed Trustee of the Peabody Education Fund.

May 2. Pardon delivered.

1868   February 5. Speech at Conservative convention in Raleigh.

February 29. Declined to be considered for gubernatorial nomination.

September 3. "Judge Pearson's Letter," published as an editorial in the *Sentinel*.

1870   July and August. Active as counsel for Kirk's prisoners.

October 21. Memorial Address on Thomas Ruffin.

December 23. Appointed counsel for the managers in Holden impeachment trial.

1871   March 15. Speech in the Holden impeachment trial.

May 1. Elected Trustee of Columbian College (now George Washington University.)

1872   January 30. Graham County established and named for him.

1873   February 5. Disabilities removed.

1874   May 28. Appointed as an arbitrator in the Virginia-Maryland Boundary case.

December 15. Published an appeal for the call of a constitutional convention.

1875   February 4. Address in Charlotte on the Mecklenburg Declaration of Independence.

March 20. Elected member of the commission to build the Western State Hospital.

July 17. Address to the People of Orange County.

August 5. Elected to the constitutional convention.

August 11. Died at Saratoga Springs, New York.

August 15. Buried at Hillsboro.

SYMBOLS USED TO DESIGNATE DEPOSITORIES
OF GRAHAM PAPERS

A   North Carolina Department of Archives and History.

U   The Southern Historical Collection of the University of North Carolina.

G. P.   Governors' Papers.

G. L. B.   Governors' Letter Books.

A MEMORIAL ORATION [1]

By MONTFORD McGEHEE

Gentlemen of the Judiciary and Bar:

When I learned that, under a resolution adopted by the Bench and Bar of the Supreme Court, I had been appointed to deliver an "Address on the Life and Character of the Hon. William A. Graham," I stayed not to question my own sufficiency for the duty to which you assigned me. Coming from such a source the appointment had to me somewhat the force of a command. No command, however, could have been more grateful, since it had for its object to do honor to one for whom I have ever cherished a veneration and affection which hardly knew a limit.

One word will be permitted me as to the manner in which this duty has been performed. It will be seen that my sole object has been to present a faithful sketch of the life of this illustrious man, together with such reflections as naturally arose out of a study of his career—such as were suggested by a consideration of his labors, his motives and his aims.

I have adopted this course from a profound conviction that the truest narrative of his life would be his best monument; that the highest eulogy that could be pronounced upon him would be to present him just as he was.

In the execution of this design I have been led to touch, at one point, upon that period of our own history when the existing political parties of the day had their origin, and when political feeling was very much embittered; at another, to a somewhat extended examination of a statement contained in a recent address published in *Our Living and Our Dead*. In the former will be seen, I trust, no trace of partisan feeling; in the latter no purpose other than to elucidate the truth of history.

William Alexander Graham was born on the 5th day of September, 1804, in the county of Lincoln. He was fortunate alike in the race from which he sprang and in his own ancestry. The race was that which by a change of residence from Scotland to Ireland, anterior to its emigration to this country, acquired, as it

[1] This oration was published with the following title: *Life and Character of the Hon. William A. Graham. A Memorial Oration* by Montford McGehee, Esq., delivered before the Bench and Bar of the Supreme Court, in the Hall of the House of Representatives, in Raleigh, June 8, 1876. It was published in Raleigh by News Job Office and Book Bindery, 1877.

were, a double nationality and name, to-wit: Scotch-Irish. It was a people of marked characteristics. By their residence among the Irish they seemed to have added somewhat of the fervor of mind and feeling which distinguishes that race, to the clear intelligence, strong will and shrewd sagacity of their mother country. They were noted for their unconquerable attachment to the great principles of liberty. They speculated with the coolness and sagacity of the Scotchman upon the functions and limitations of government, and, like the Irishman, then kindled into flame upon any invasion of their rights. They were Presbyterian in their tenets, and devoted to that form of worship. Wherever they went the minister went with them; amid all the chances and changes of life he was there to instruct, to encourage and console. The polity of that church demanded a learned ministry, and the minister was almost always a secular as well as sacred teacher; hence, wherever they established themselves, liberal education was fostered and classical learning taught. In Mecklenburg and the neighboring counties they earnestly sought, while North Carolina was yet a colony, to found a college. Twice was a charter granted by the Legislature, and twice disallowed by the King. Charters were granted to institutions the instructors of which were members of the Church of England; they were denied where the instructors were of the Presbyterian faith. "The faith of Calvin," says Bancroft, "has ever been feared as the creed of Republicanism."

Early in our colonial history they signalized their zeal for civil and political liberty. The political disturbances anterior to the Revolution, which issued in the Mecklenburg Declaration of Independence, were the outgrowth of this spirit. This spirit was not the offspring of a vague enthusiasm. No people ever had clearer conceptions of the objects they sought to compass. "The genuine sense of America at that moment," says the elder Adams, speaking of the Mecklenburg Declaration, "was never so well expressed before nor since."

The ancestry of Mr. Graham were deeply imbued with the spirit of this people. His maternal grandfather, Maj. John Davidson, was one of the signers of the Mecklenburg Declaration, and acted a conspicuous part in the Revolution. The name of his father, Gen. Joseph Graham, is one of the best known in our Revolutionary annals. The biographical sketch incorporated into Wheeler's History is a brief but noble record. He entered the army at nineteen years of age. At the end of two years of arduous and responsible service he was stricken down by a severe and lingering illness, but returning health found him again in the field. When the war invaded his own section, and the army under Gen. Greene withdrew towards Virginia, to him was assigned the command of those troops which sustained the rear-guard under Gen. Davie. For many miles he was confronted with the troops of Tarleton, the best body of calvary in the British service. The obstinate resistance which he opposed to their intrepid advance had nearly closed his career. After many gallant but ineffectual attempts to drive back the enemy he at length fell, literally covered with wounds. When his wounds were healed he again took the field. The service which now fell to his lot was one of peculiar privation, suffering and sacrifice: commissary stores, his command often had none; nay, were sometimes under the necessity of supplying their own horses and purchasing their own equipments. But his patriotism was entire and uncalculating, he recked not of means, health or life itself in the cause to which he had devoted himself. Suffice it that he continued in the field as long as there was in the country an enemy under arms; and though he had, when peace was declared, but entered on the threshold of manhood, he had commanded in fifteen different engagements.

In civil life he was scarcely less distinguished; the many important positions filled by him afford the highest testimony to his capacity and character. It is to be regretted that we have no extended biography of one who so well illustrated the character of the soldier and the citizen.

His mother was distinguished for her personal beauty—distinguished as well for her sense, piety and many amiable virtues. But death deprived him of her fostering care before he had attained his fourth year, and he was then consigned to the care of an elder sister. The tender affection and respect with which he always referred to this sister, attests how fully she discharged a mother's duty.

He received the rudiments of his education in the common schools of the country. He commenced his classical education in the Academy at Statesville, then under the care of the Rev. Dr. Muchat, a scholar of good repute. Mr. Graham verified the apparent paradox of Wordsworth,

"The child is father of the man."

He was noted, from his earliest years, for his industry, his thirst for knowledge, and his aptitude to learn. One who knew him well,[2] testifies that from his childhood, he was no less remarkable

---

[2] Rev. R. H. Morrison.

for his high sense of truth and honor than for his exemption from the levities and vices common to youth. At this Academy he applied himself to his studies with the most exemplary diligence. A classmate [3] at that time says of him, "he was the only boy I ever knew who would spend his Saturdays in reviewing the studies of the week."

An incident which occurred about this time affords a striking proof of his early force of character. Gen. Graham was a pioneer in a branch of industry, yet but little developed in this State—the manufacture of iron. Upon his removal to Lincoln he established a furnace and forge, which, at the time now spoken of, had become quite extensive. From some cause the works were left without a Superintendent. The General installed his son William, though then but a boy, and wholly without experience, at the head of the establishment; and the energy and judgment with which he conducted it, obtained his father's entire approval. The old gentleman often recurred to it with great satisfaction.

He was next sent to the Academy at Hillsboro. This institution, subsequently under Mr. Bingham, acquired a renown in the South and Southwest, not inferior to the renown of Rugby, in England, under Dr. Arnold. It was then under the direction of Mr. Rodgers. He had been educated for the Catholic Priesthood, and for accurate scholarship and capacity as a teacher, had few superiors. Here Mr. Graham was prepared for College.

From this Academy he went to the University of the State, where he was matriculated in the summer of 1820. His course throughout his college life was admirable in every way. He appreciated the scheme of study there established, not only as the best discipline of the intellect, but as the best foundation for knowledge in its widest sense. He mastered his lessons so perfectly, that each lesson became a permanent addition to his stock of knowledge. The professors rarely failed to testify by a smile, or some other token, their approval of his proficiency. On one occasion, a professor,[4] who has achieved a world-wide reputation in the field of science, remarked to one of his classmates [5] that his lecture on Chemistry came back as perfectly from Mr. Graham as he had uttered it on the previous day.

Some thirty years after, the same professor in a letter to Mr. Graham, (then Secretary of the Navy,) uses this language: "It

---

[3] Judge Brevard.
[4] Professor Olmstead.
[5] John W. Norwood, Esq.

has often been a source of pleasing reflection to me, that I was permitted to bear some part in fitting you, in early life, for that elevated post of honor and usefulness to which Providence has conducted you."

His high sense of duty was manifested in his conscientious deportment under the peculiar form of government to which he was then subject. His observance of every law and usage of the College was punctilious; while, to the faculty, he was ever scrupulously and conspicuously respectful.

His extraordinary proficiency was purchased by no laborious drudgery. The secret of it was to be found in the precept which he acted upon, through life: "Whatsoever thy hand findeth to do, do it with all thy might." His powers of concentration were great, his perceptions quick, his memory powerful, prompt, and assiduously improved. By the joint force of such faculties, he could accomplish much in little time. Hence, notwithstanding his exemplary attention to his College studies, he devoted much time to general reading. It was at this time, no doubt, that he laid up much of that large and varied stock of information upon which he drew at pleasure, in after life.

Intent upon availing himself to the full, of every advantage afforded him, he applied himself assiduously to the duties of the Literary Society of which he was a member. He participated regularly in the debates and other exercises of that body. For all such he prepared himself with care; and it is asserted by the same authority,[6] to which I have already referred—a most competent judge—that his compositions were of such excellence that, in a literary point of view, they would have challenged comparison with anything done by him in after life.

His engaging manners brought him into pleasant relations with all his fellow students. He lived with them upon terms of the frankest and most familiar intercourse. In their most athletic sports, he never participated, but he was a pleased spectator, and evinced by his manner a hearty sympathy with their enjoyments. His favorite exercise was walking, and those who knew him well, will recollect that this continued to be his favorite recreation while health was spared him. With his friends and chosen companions he was cordial and easy, and always the life of the circle when met together.

The class of which he was a member was graduated in 1824. It was the largest up to that time; and, for capacity and proficiency,

---

[6] Mr. Norwood.

esteemed the best. It was declared by Professors Olmstead and Mitchell, that Yale might well have been proud of such a class. It embraced many who afterwards won high distinction in political and professional life. One, who divided the highest honors of the class with Mr. Graham, attained the highest judicial station in the State—a seat upon the Supreme Court bench.[7]

No one could have availed himself to a greater extent than Mr. Graham did, of the oportunities presented in his collegiate career. "His College life, in all its duties and obligations," says the gentleman before quoted [8] "was an epitome of his career upon the stage of the world." He adds that on the day when he received his diploma, he could, with his usual habits of study, have filled any chair with honor to himself and acceptance to his class. Such is the emphatic testimony, of one who himself graduated with high distinction in the same class. Might we not subjoin, building upon the above remark, that his career in after life was, in great part, the logical result of the discipline and training to which he submitted himself, so conscientiously, in his college life?

After graduation he made an excursion to some of the Western States, which occupied a few months. While at Lexington, he heard Mr. Crittenden address the jury in a great slander or libel case. Of all intellectual displays, there are none so dazzling as those of the great orator or advocate. There are none, the triumphs of which are so palpable and so intoxicating; none so calculated to excite the enthusiasm of a young and ingenuous mind. The speech, which was worthy of the great advocate's fame, made a profound inpression upon Mr. Graham. It may have had some influence in determining his choice of a profession, or in fixing it if already made. We shall see in the sequel that to the youth, who, unknown to him, listened with such admiration to his speech that day, Mr. Crittenden many years after appealed for the use of his name, and the weight of his influence, at a crisis of great peril to their common country. From this tour he returned in 1824 and entered upon the study of the law in the office of Judge Ruffin.

The opinion of Judge Ruffin, as to the course proper to be pursued with a student of the law, was somewhat peculiar. He held that he should have little assistance beyond that of having his course of study prescribed. He must, as it were, scale the height alone—by his own strength and courage; availing himself of a guide, only at points otherwise inaccessible. His brother, the Hon.

---

[7] Hon. M. E. Manly.
[8] Mr. Norwood.

James Graham, in a letter written at this period, made mention of this opinion, and urged him to adopt the expedient resorted to by himself: "When he would not examine me, I took," said he, "the liberty of questioning him very frequently, and by drawing him into conversation on legal subjects, my own ideas were rendered more clear, correct and lasting." It is not likely that counsel so judicious, and from such a source, was neglected.

He obtained his County Court license in the summer of 1826. At August term of the Court he appeared at the Orange Bar. The rule then required between the admission to practice in the County Court, and the admission to practice in the Superior Court a novitiate of one year. This period he spent in Hillsboro, that he might continue to profit by the instruction of his learned precepter. At the end of the year he received his Superior Court license. It was now a question where he should establish himself for the practice of his profession. The counties of Mecklenburg, Cabarrus, and Lincoln were filled with his blood relations, connections and friends. They were among the most distinguished for their wealth, intelligence and Revolutionary fame. Their combined influence would give him command of all the important business of those counties, and place him at the outset in the position of a leader of the Bar. The prospect in Orange and the adjoining counties was widely different. In these latter counties he would have no adventitious advantages. The business of these counties, moreover, was engrossed by an able and a numerous Bar. At the first court which he attended after he obtained his Superior Court license they mustered the number of twenty-six. A large portion of these were young men recently admitted to practice; but after deducting these, and many more of longer standing and respectable position, there still remained a Bar which for learning, abilities and eloquence was never surpassed in this State. Of resident lawyers there were Thomas Ruffin, Archibald D. Murphy, Willie P. Mangum, Francis L. Hawkes and Frederick Nash; of lawyers attending the court, from other counties, there were George E. Badger, William H. Haywood and Bartlett Yancey. What recollections of renown connected with the forum, the Senate and the church flood the mind as we recall these names! Fain would I pause to contemplate the career of these illustrious men, by which the character of North Carolina was so much elevated in the consideration of the world, and so much of honor brought to the State. But other subjects press upon me— subjects of more immediate interest.

Notwithstanding this formidable competition—a competition which might well dismay one at the outset of professional life, Mr. Graham resolved to fix his residence at Hillsboro. Two reasons were assigned by him for this conclusion: first, an unwillingness to relinquish the foothold he had gained in the county courts of Orange, Granville and Guilford; second, a reluctance to sever the associations formed with his professional brethren at those courts. Another reason, quite as potent, probably, was a well-grounded confidence in his own abilities, and in his knowledge of his profession. Against such men he entered the lists, and against such he had to contend; not indeed all at the same time, but all within a period of two years. It may be mentioned as an instance of the vicissitudes of human life, that five years from the August of that year—1827—not one of those illustrious men remained at that Bar.

His first case of importance in the Superior Court was one which, from peculiar causes, excited great local interest. It involved an intricate question of title to land. On the day of trial, the court room was crowded and the Bar fully occupied by lawyers—many of them men of the highest professional eminence. When he came to address the jury, he spoke with modesty, but with ease and self-possession. His preparation of the case had been thorough, and the argument which he delivered is described as admirable, both as to matter and manner. When he closed, the Hon. William H. Haywood, who had then risen to a high position at the Bar, turned to a distinguished gentleman, still living, of the same profession, and inquired who had prepared the argument which Mr. Graham had so handsomely delivered. The answer was, "It is all his own;" to which Mr. Haywood replied with the observation, "William Gaston could have done it no better."

Mr. Graham knew none of that weary probation which has been the lot of so many able men. His argument in the case just mentioned at once gave him a position of prominence. It was not long before he attained a place in the front rank of his profession. Here, with the large stores of professional knowledge which he had laid up, it was easy to sustain himself. His high mental qualifications, his habits of study, his perseverance, his unutterable faith in his cause, brought to him a constantly increasing business, and a constantly widening reputation. He was early, for so young a man, retained in the most important causes in the courts in which he practiced, and his associate counsel generally gave him the leading position in the trial.

For forty years and more he maintained his high pre-eminence in his profession. His name appears in the Reports, in nearly all the appeals from his own circuits, and in many of the important cases from the other circuits of the State. It would be impossible, in the compass of this Address, to present any view, however brief, of the nature and variety of the causes in which he was employed. They will be found to embrace nearly every principle known to the common law and to equity jurisprudence, applicable under our system of government, and to our changed condition of society. To his clear, penetrating, masculine intellect, both systems were alike adapted; but the system of Equity seemed, to me, to offer to him the most congenial field. Thoroughly versed in the learning of this branch of jurisprudence, his fine, natural sense of right had led him to the study of the best ethical writers. He had thus rendered still more subtle his native perception of those more recondite principles of justice which it is the object of that science to administer. And though the system of equity has for a long time been little less circumscribed by known rules and precedents than the system of law, yet his mind found a grateful occupation in tracing those rules and precedents back to the great principles from which they were deduced, and vindicating their authority upon the ground of reason.

Not, however, in courts of Equity did he establish his great reputation in his profession. The fame acquired in this branch of practice is limited almost entirely to the Bench and Bar. It admits of none of those intellectual displays of which the trial by jury is so well adapted. It is to the Law side of the court that we must repair, if we would see him in that sphere, in which, professionally, he was best known, and where his most signal triumphs were won. But of his distinguishing characteristics as a lawyer, I propose, hereafter, to speak.

In 1833 he was elected a member of the General Assembly from the town of Hillsboro. His first appearance on the floor has an interest from the relations subsequently existing between him and the distinguished man to whom the motion submitted by him had reference. He rose to move the sending of a message to the Senate to proceed to the election of a Governor of the State, and to put in nomination Gov. Swain. A day or two after, he had the satisfaction of reporting that that gentleman—who was ever afterward united to him in the closest bonds of friendship—had received a majority of votes, and of being named as first on the committee to inform him of his election. He took, from the beginning an active part in the business of the House relating to Banks Law Amendments and Education. A few days after the session commenced, he was appointed chairman of a special committee, and submitted an adverse report upon the petition of certain citizens of France, praying that they might hold and transfer real estate. Near the end of the session he was chairman of another special committee, to which was referred a question, then much discussed. The question was, whether a person holding an office of profit or trust under the State government could, during his term, hold a like office under the government of the United States. The question arose under the Constitution of '76, and is of no practical value now. But it was a question of interest at the time, and possesses an interest for us, as the first work of any kind done by Mr. Graham which has come down to us. He disposed of the question in a report clear and well reasoned, and marked with great precision of language.

He was a member from the same town in 1834, during which session he appears to have discharged the duties of the chairman of the committee of which he was a member, the Committee on the Judiciary.

I record an incident which attests the high consideration which he had already acquired in the country, and the importance attached to his opinion. Judge Gaston had been elected in 1833 to a seat on the Supreme Court Bench by a majority of two-thirds of the General Assembly. He had been brought up in the Roman Catholic faith—the faith of his fathers—the faith in which he died. The thirty-second section of the old constitution declared incapable of holding office all those who "deny the truth of the Protestant religion." Some dissatisfaction had been expressed at his accepting a judicial office under a constitution containing this clause, which in the opinion of some, excluded him. For some time he did not deem it necessary to advert to the matter. In 1834—Nov. 12—he addressed a letter to Mr. Graham, enclosing a written paper, in which he stated succinctly, but with great clearness and irrestible force, the reasoning by which his acceptance had been determined. In the conclusion of his letter he referred it to Mr. Graham's judgment, to determine what degree of publicity should be given to the paper. Whether it was ever published we do not know; but when we consider Judge Gaston's high station and great name in the country, and that the purity of that name was in a measure at stake, the incident must be regarded as a singular tribute to the character which Mr. Graham had thus early established. It is well known how Judge Gaston availed himself of his place in the convention of 1835 to set forth to the world the reasons by which his decision had been influenced—reasons so cogent and conclusive as to satisfy every mind. It is known, too, that the object of the great speech delivered by him then—an object happily accomplished—was to bring about such a modification of the obnoxious clause as to deprive it of all sectarian intolerance.

Mr. Graham was again a member from Hillsboro in the year 1835. In the organization of the committees the post of Chairman of the Committee on the Judiciary was assigned to him, and the journals bear testimony to the diligence with which its duties were discharged. It was through him, in his capacity of chairman, that the various reports of the commissioners to revise the Statute Laws of the State—the Revised Code being then in progress— were submitted to the House.

From the ability displayed and the high position held by him in the Legislature, we should naturally expect to find him in the Constitutional Convention of 1835. It has been well said that the county of Orange has been to North Carolina, what Virginia has been to the Union, the mother of statesmen.[9] On this occasion, by one of those caprices which sometimes seize upon communities as well as individuals, the noble old county seemed to care little for her ancient renown. There seems to have been no action by the county to secure delegates worthy of her former reputation. We learn from the remarks of one of the delegates[10] in the Convention, that there were ten candidates in the field, and that the successful candidates were returned by so small a vote as to call forth a taunt from a member of the Convention. In such a contest Mr. Graham had no desire to enter the field; indeed, whenever he offered himself for the suffrages of his countrymen, it was as the chosen champion of the principles of a great party.

He again represented the county of Orange in the Legislatures of 1838 and 1840, in both of which he was elected speaker. This withdrew him from the arena of debate, and we learn little more of him from the journals of those sessions, than the uniform punctuality and universal acceptability with which he discharged the duties of that high trust.

We take leave for the present of Mr. Graham's legislative career. His talents were soon to be exerted on national subjects, and on a grander stage. It needs but a cursory glance over the journals

---

[9] Maj. Gales' sketch of Gov. Graham, in "Illustrated Age."
[10] Dr. Smith, "Debates" p. 307.

during the time he was a member to observe the extent of his labors. The bills introduced, and the reports submitted by him embrace every great interest of the State. They embrace the subjects of banks, finance, education, internal improvements, and measures relating to amendment and repeal of statutes. Here will be seen the causes of his pre-eminence among the statesmen of North Carolina. That pre-eminence was the fruit of a careful study of the State in all her resources and in all her interests.

A revolution in the politics of the State brough about a vacancy, in 1840, in the representation from North Carolina in the Senate of the United States. Mr. Strange, under instructions, had resigned his seat. The term of the other Senator was near its end. There were thus two terms to be filled by the legislature of 1841. Mr. Mangum was elected for the full term, Mr. Graham for the unexpired term. This election was considered by Mr. Graham as the most emphatic testimonial of the confidence and favor of the State which he received during his life. Mr. Mangum and he were residents of the same county, and of the many able men who might justly advance claims to the other seat, Mr. Graham was the youngest. Certainly an election under such circumstances constituted a tribute of peculiar significance and value.

He was among the youngest members of the Senate when he took his seat; but he soon commanded the esteem and respect of the entire body. That, it has been truly said, was pre-eminently the age of great men in American parliamentary history, and of such he was regarded as the worthy compeer. "He never rose to speak," says a distinguished gentleman[11] who was himself a member of Congress at that time, "that he did not receive the most respectful attention. When the Senate went into Committee of the Whole he was usually called upon to preside. Reports from him as chairman of a committee almost invariably secured the favorable consideration of the Senate." From the same authority we learn that the relations existing between him and Mr. Clay were of the most kindly and intimate character, and that Mr. Clay "regarded him as a most superior man, socially and intellectually."

The period during which Mr. Graham was in the Senate was one of the most stormy in our political annals. The Whig party had just achieved a great victory, and Harrison and Tyler had been elected by an immense majority. That party reckoned confidently, that it would now be able to carry out those great principles of government, for which it had so long contended, and which

---

[11] Hon. Kenneth Rayner.

had been so signally approved in the recent election. In the midst of these patriotic anticipations, General Harrison died, and Mr. Tyler succeeded to the Presidential chair. Mr. Tyler had adopted the platform of the Whig party, and in his address, upon assuming the duties of his high office, he did not intimate the least change of policy from that which his predecessor had announced in his inaugural. He had, moreover, retained the same constitutional advisers. The statesmen of the Whig party now set to redeem the pledges which had been made to the country. A great financial measure was passed; this was vetoed by the President. A second measure of the same kind, framed in conformity to the views indicated in his veto message, was passed, which was vetoed in like manner. A tariff bill was passed, but this shared the same fate. Efforts were made to pass these bills over the President's veto, but in every instance the veto was sustained by the opposite party. The results of these repeated disappointments was, that all hope of united and efficient action in carrying out the great principles of the Whig party was finally abandoned.

The administration of Mr. Van Buren had largely exceeded the revenues. Provision for this deficiency had to be made by the incoming administration. To meet an emergency so pressing, a bill was introduced, known as the "Loan Bill." It was strongly opposed, among others, by Mr. Calhoun in a speech of characteristic force and compass. So far as the Whigs were concerned it was an appeal by the administration for aid, to a party which it had betrayed. Mr. Graham only recollected that the good of the country was involved, and gave it his support. "I will not," said he, "stop the action of the government by denying it the means of going on, no matter who may be in power." The speech which he delivered on this bill was eminently able and statesmanlike. He demonstrated the necessity of the measure; he traced out the cause of the deficiency, and pointed out the remedy. The subject has little interest to the general reader at this day, yet in that speech there are passages of such profound reflection and philosophic scope as will give it a value to the political student at all times. Of the three propositions which he laid down as applicable to the emergency then existing, the two latter comprehend the highest wisdom in our own day: "Reduce the expenditures to the lowest point consistent with an efficient public service;" "Levy such duties as are necessary for an economical administration of the government, and no more."

When the Apportionment Bill in 1842 was under consideration, very strong opposition, headed by Mr. Buchanan, of Pennsylvania, and Mr. Wright, of New York, was made to the Districting clause. Mr. Graham, on June the 3rd, addressed the Senate in support of the clause. In a calm, condensed, weighty and conclusive argument, he demonstrated that the District system of electing Representatives to Congress, was in conformity to the true theory of Representative Government, and was the one contemplated and expected by the framers of the government; that it was sanctioned by usage almost unanimous in the old States, and by the usage of two-thirds of the new; that the general ticket system was fraught with evils, public and private; nay, with dangers to the Union. There was a passage in that debate which so forcibly illustrates the high moral plane upon which he discussed public affairs, that I cannot pass it by. It was objected by Mr. Woodbury, of New Hampshire, that if the Act were passed by Congress, it had no means of enforcing it. He wished to know whether an armed force or a writ of mandamus would be sent to the State Legislatures to compel them to lay off the Districts. In reply, Mr. Graham showed that if, notwithstanding the law, a State should return members according to general ticket, the House of Representatives, as judge of the election of its members, could pronounce such election a nullity. "But the duties of the States under our Constitution," said he, "are not to be determined by their liability to punishment, but by the covenants into which they entered by that instrument. It is faith, honor, conscience, and not the 'hangman's whip,' on which, at last rest the blessings of this noblest human institution which has ever been devised for the security, the welfare and happiness of man." In this exclamation, he unconsciously announced those great principles by which his own conduct through life was regulated, and to whose slightest behest he ever yielded an unhesitating obedience.

A short time after—July 25, 1842—he received the following letter from Chancellor Kent: "I thank you for your speech on the Districting clause of the Apportionment Bill. I have read it carefully, and I deem it in every respect logical, conclusive, and a vindication of the power assumed by the Bill, in language clear and specific, tempered with due moderation and firmness. The District System is essential to check and control the cunning machinery of Faction."

After the expiration of his term—March 3, 1843—Mr. Graham resumed the practice of his profession.

In 1844 he was nominated by the Whig party of North Carolina for the office of Governor. He had not sought the nomination;
nay, would have declined it if he could have done so consistently
with his high conceptions of the duty of a citizen. In 1836 he had
married the daughter of the late John Washington, Esq., of
Newbern, a lady of rare beauty and accomplishments—a union
which brought to him as much of happiness as it is the lot of man
to know. From this union a young and growing family was gathering around him. His patrimony had not been large, and the
requirements of his family demanded his constant professional
exertions. He was now at the summit of his profession, and his
emoluments would be limited only by the nature of the business
in an agricultural State, where commerce existed to only a small
extent, and manufactures were in their infancy. His attention had
been much withdrawn from his profession during his Senatorial
career, and besides the expense and loss of time in a State canvass,
he would, if elected, be entirely precluded from the exercise of
his profession during his term of office. The salary of the office
was small, and a residence in the capital as Chief Magistrate,
would render necessary an increased scale of expense. On the
other hand, were considerations of great weight. Letters came to
him from many gentlemen of high standing in various parts of
the State, pressing his acceptance by every consideration that
could be addressed to an elevated mind. Moreover he was not
unmindful of the honors which had been conferred upon him,
and not ungrateful. He held, too, that the circumstances must be
very exceptional, which could justify a citizen in withholding
his services when called to a public station by the general voice
of the people. To determine his duty, cost him much anxious
reflection; but the latter consideration proved decisive. The decision once made, he acted with his accustomed energy.

His nomination was hailed with satisfaction throughout the
Union. Among other letters which he then received giving expression to this feeling, was one from Mr. Clay. In conclusion he
thus expressed himself: "Still, I should have preferred that you
were in another situation, where the whole Union would have
benefitted by your services."

His opponent was Col. Mike Hoke. He was born in the same
county with Mr. Graham, and was nearly of the same age. He
was a gentleman of fine person, of fine address, of considerable
Legislative experience, and of high position at the Bar. The canvass was well contested on both sides; on the part of Mr. Graham

it was conducted with surpassing ability. When it came to the vote he led his competitor by several thousand majority.

He was inaugurated on the 1st of January, 1845, the oaths of office being administered by Chief Justice Ruffin. The Raleigh *Register* of that date remarks, that "the audience which witnessed the ceremony, for everything that could make the occasion imposing, has never been surpassed within our recollection. The lobbies and galleries were crowded with strangers and citizens, and a brilliant assemblage of ladies."

The Inaugural Address was worthy of the speaker. It is full of lofty thoughts and wise suggestions. It is pervaded throughout by that philosophic tone which belonged to whatever he wrote or spoke. The earlier part contains political reflections of such weight and value, that I would gladly present them if they could be condensed into a less space. In this address, as always, he held up the State as the worthy object of our best affections. His glance at the working of our State government since its organization, was calculated to exalt to the highest degree the popular estimate of the Constitution. Some of the noblest institutions of our State had practically their inception in the recommendations of that Inaugural—as the Asylum for the insane, and the Asylum for the deaf and dumb.[12] Here, too, practically dates the origin of that great measure of scientific progress—the Geological survey, by which North Carolina stands so enviably distinguished among her sister States immediately around her. He gives just prominence in this address to the Common School System, which then had been just introduced. The University, which always commanded the entire homage of his heart has its due place here. In the latter half he takes a survey of the State—her physical condition and her needs—and suggests from the resources of political economy, the true principles of her future progress. He dwells, toward the conclusion, with just exultation upon the high character which our people enjoyed for honesty and fidelity. "Thus far," said he, "our escutcheon is unstained—the public faith has been kept; the public honor inviolate." History will record that it was always so, while North Carolinians had the control of their

---

[12] The Act for the charter of the Institution for "The Deaf, Dumb and Blind" was passed in 1846. In 1848 were passed Acts for the charters of the North Carolina Railroad, the Fayetteville and Western Plank Road, the Slackwater Navigation of the Cape Fear and Deep Rivers, and, prospectively, of the Yadkin, with a portage railroad connection with Deep River. This Legislature also made an appropriation for the erection of a Lunatic Asylum. The Act authorizing a Geological Survey was passed in 1850—the year after the expiration of his term—but the Act was mainly due to the influence exerted by his Inaugural address and other Messages.

State. The last sentence is characteristic of the man; it breathes a devout invocation that our beloved State should not outstrip her sister States in the career of ambition and of glory, but "that she may be permitted to 'walk in her integrity,' the object of our loyalty and pride, as she is the home of our hearts and affections." I have dwelt upon this address because it epitomises the measures, and exhibits the spirit of his administration. It would be impossible to present here any view of the progress of the State during his administration. His first term was so acceptable that he was elected for the second by a largely-increased vote. His two terms embrace that period during which North Carolina made the greatest progress in all her interests. The messages of his very able predecessor, Gov. Morehead, followed up by his own, drew the attention of the whole State to the subject of Internal Improvements, and a powerful impulse was given to that great interest. Space would fail me for a separate notice of each of the great interests of the State. To sum up in brief, whatever could tend to her material or intellectual progress was duly fostered and encouraged. His messages were regarded as among the best State papers of his day. Of this I could cite many proofs; I must content myself with one. In a letter Mr. Webster writes as follows:

"The tone which your Message holds, in regard to the relations between the State Government and the General Government is just, proper, dignified and constitutional, and the views which it presents on questions of internal policy, the development of resources, the improvement of markets, and the gradual advancement of industry and wealth, are such as belong to the age, and are important to our country in all its parts."

His earnest recommendation of a Geological Survey elicited from Prof. Olmstead, a letter commending his views expressed in that regard, in which he said: "There is no State in the Union which would better reward the labor and expense of a Geological Survey than North Carolina."

In 1849 he delivered the Address before the Literary Societies at Chapel Hill. His subject was a cursory view of the objects of liberal education. This Address stands out in wide contrast to those which have been customary on such occasions, and is solid, sterling, practical. It is a vindication of the University curriculum. Subjects of highest interest are discussed, and with all due attractions of style. It concludes with brief, but weighty suggestions to the graduating class, calculated to stimulate to high aims in virtue, knowledge and patriotism.

Public honors have been coy to most men; it was the reverse in his case. They waited around him with perpetual solicitations. In 1849, Mr. Mangum, one of the confidential advisers of the President, wrote to Mr. Graham that he might make his election between the Mission to Russia and the Mission to Spain. Subsequently the Mission to Spain was tendered to, and declined by him.

Upon the accession of Mr. Fillmore to the Presidency, a seat in the Cabinet was tendered to Mr. Graham. In the letter addressed to him by the President, informing him of his appointment, he said: "I trust that you will accept the office, and enter upon the discharge of its duties at the earliest day. I am sure that the appointment will be highly acceptable to the country, as I can assure you, your acceptance will be gratifying to me." In a letter couched in proper terms, dated July 25, he communicated his acceptance.

His first report as Secretary of the Navy is dated the 30th of Nov. 1850. His diligence, during the two months which had elapsed from the time when he assumed office, is attested by the comprehensive nature of that report. It embraced a review of the whole Naval establishment, accompanied by recommendations, which, in many particulars, went to the extent of a re-organization of the Navy. The recommendations involved, especially, great changes in the *personnel* of the Navy: such as the retirement of officers, promotions on a new system, and other changes equally great, and it is with pleasure we observe the spirit of equity and the sense of delicacy which pervade these recommendations— equity in providing compensations for retiring officers; delicacy in the manner in which the changes are to be carried into effect. The subject matter of this, and subsequent reports, lies beyond the domain of our observation. I therefore subjoin a few testimonials from many at hand, to assist our judgment of this part of his career.

A distinguished Senator of great experience and wide national reputation wrote as follows of his first report: "You had a new field opened to you and well and ably have you occupied every portion of it. The report is to be properly characterized by a bold originality of conception, and a fearlessness of responsibility, too rare in that class of State papers.

"You have had to grapple with a system built up by a series of abuses, and to use the knife—that fearful and unpopular instrument—somewhat unsparingly.

"If I do not greatly err, it will give you more reputation in the country than anything you have hitherto produced before the public."

In a letter dated the 19th of February, 1851, Mr. Benton wrote as follows: "I have just read a second time, your report on the Coast Survey Subject. I consider it one of the most perfect reports I ever read—a model of a business report and one which should carry conviction to every candid, inquiring mind. I deem it one of the largest reforms, both in an economical and administrative point of view, which the state of our affairs admits of."

His administration of the Navy Department was signalized by an enterprize, which, for the completeness of the success with which it was crowned, was one of the most remarkable of the age—the Japan expedition. A brief retrospect will assist us to appreciate its difficulties and triumphs. In the year 1637 was consumated a revolution in the Empire of Japan, which resulted in the banishment of the Portugese, the only European people who had free access to that Empire, and who appeared to have firmly fixed themselves there. While the merchants of that nation succeeded in possessing themselves of nearly the whole foreign trade of the country, its missionaries had exerted, not less activity in the conversion of the natives to the faith of Rome. The secular rulers, with most of the Princes, had accepted the christian religion; it was reckoned that, about that period, one half of the inhabitants were christians. The new revolution re-established the ancient religion. In the forty years persecution which succeeded, many millions of lives were sacrificed, and the christian religion, it was supposed, extinguished there forever.

In consequence of this revolution all trade and intercourse with civilized nations were cut off, except with the Dutch, and as to them, was limited in amount, and circumscribed to one place. This concession, moreover, was purchased by the most abject submission, and was attended with the greatest humiliation. A very limited trade was likewise permitted to China. With these exceptions the Japanese had withdrawn from the world. The settled feeling of the people was one of unmixed hostility to all nations professing the christian religion; the settled policy of the government, one of non-intercourse with such nations, diplomatic or commercial. Within the century preceeding that expedition, the English had made many efforts, as had also the Russians since 1792, to establish intercourse with a country abounding with so many objects of desire to civilized man. All of these efforts had failed in turn. In 1846 an attempt to accomplish the same object, was made by the United States. A fleet was sent under Commodore Biddle, which came to anchor at Jeddo, in July of that year. It remained ten days, but no one was permitted to land, and nothing was accomplished. In 1849 the Preble, under Commodore Glynn, was sent out to Japan to demand the release of sixteen American sailors who had been wrecked on one of the islands, and who had been detained in prison many months—an imprisonment, the hardship of which was aggravated by great cruelty and inhumanity. After various resorts, intended apparently to test the temper of the Commander and the government which he represented; after various delays, occasioned by the evasive diplomacy of Japanese officials, the prisoners were, at length, delivered up and brought home. The duty of giving adequate protection to American citizens, thus added another motive for opening up intercourse with Japan. In the mind of Mr. Graham the obligation of this duty was supreme. A government which failed to give protection to its citizens on every part of the earth's surface, and among every people was, in his opinion, a government but in name. He therefore resolved, in which resolution he was strongly supported by the President, to send an expedition to Japan and bring that empire within the pale and comity of civilized nations. The command was assigned to Commodore Perry. The event showed what statesmanlike sagacity was exercised in planning the expedition and in the selection of its leader. Everything that was contemplated was accomplished. The success of that expedition constitutes one of the principal claims of Mr. Fillmore's administration to the admiration of the country and of posterity. Its success constitutes, indeed, an era in the history of the world. Its results have been great and cannot but be enduring. It has placed our relations with Japan upon a just and honorable basis. It has given a new direction to much of the commerce of the world—pouring its fertilizing tide throughout the heart of the American continent. Its effects upon Japan are but beginning to be seen; yet already they exceed what would have been brought about in the ordinary course of affairs in a thousand years. No people have ever availed themselves of the light of a superior civilization as the Japanese have. In that light they have seen the unfitness of many of their old institutions and have abandoned them; they have seen the unfitness of their language for foreign intercourse, and are preparing to substitute the English language. The changes thus made are harbingers of progress which will justify the most lively anticipations for the future. The friends of humanity and religion, especially, hail the prospect with delight. They see in what has been already done, the prospect of an entire change in the institutions of that land. They hope, at no distant day, to see liberal institutions introduced there. They hope to see a universal recognition of popular rights, where the bonds of caste have been so inexorable; to see equal laws take the place of a despot's will, and to see the Christian religion again introduced, never more to be disturbed in its peaceful reign.

Another expedition was sent out in 1851 under the direction of the Navy Department. The object was the exploration of the Valley of the Amazon in the interests of commerce. The instructions to Lieut. Herndon—to whose charge the expedition was confided—contained in the letter of Mr. Graham, of February 15th, were full and particular. They embraced the position of the country—the navigability of its streams—its capacities for trade and commerce—and its future prospects. In February, 1854, the report was published by order of Congress. It contains the most ample information upon all the points embraced in the instructions. In the "Westminster Review" of that year, it was noticed with just credit to the author, and due recognition of the enlightened policy which projected the expedition.

In the year 1850, were passed those great measures of national healing, known as the Compromise Measures. These constituted a part of a series of measures resorted to at short intervals in our history, to give peace to the ever recurring agitation on the subject of slavery. This question had been a disturbing one from the commencement of our national existence. It had presented a formidable barrier to the formation of our federal constitution; this was removed by an adjustment, based upon suffrage. It obtruded itself upon Congress in 1790 in a petition for the abolition of slavery, headed by Dr. Franklin; this was put at rest for a time by a resolution of that body, disclaiming any authority to interfere with the emancipation or with their treatment in any of the States. It emerged again in 1820 in a more menacing form than before, startling the country, as Mr. Jefferson expressed it, "like a fire-bell in the night;" it was now quieted by the Missouri compromise—long regarded as a "solemn compact and covenant" upon the basis of a fair division of the public domain between the free and slave States. The question was put at rest for a long time, and it was hoped that the rest was final. It sprung up again in 1846 in connection with the vast territory acquired by the conquest of Mexico, to which it was proposed to apply the "Wilmot Proviso," which restricted slavery in any newly acquired territory without regard to the Missouri compromise line. The old settlement being thus repudiated, the country was given up to agitation, in which every turbulent passion seemed let loose. This agitation raged with increasing violence through every session down to the administration of General Taylor and of his successor Mr. Fillmore. With the progress of the discussion the sessions grew longer and the passions of men more stormy. It was a time of profound anxiety and apprehension. The imminence of the danger brought back Mr. Clay to the Senate. His great compeers, Mr. Calhoun and Mr. Webster, were already there. To Mr. Clay, more than any other, the eyes of the country were turned at this crisis. He had once before quieted the storm which threatened the country from the same quarter; it was believed that all men would listen to him now. It was believed that the winds and waves of faction would still obey his voice. He was in the fulness of his fame. In abilities he had no superior, in eloquence he had no peer; in patriotism he ranked with the Revolutionary sires. The country did not look to him in vain.

On the 29th of January he brought forward his celebrated measures of conciliation and adjustment. They encountered great opposition. In their progress they were altered in form; but in substance they were finally passed. These measures were approved everywhere, and gave satisfaction to an overwhelming majority of the country.

We, standing amid the wrecks and ruins, in which that agitation finally resulted; taught, alas! by the most mournful of all wisdom, that which comes after the fact accomplished, know that this healing was but a delusion. We know that this slavery question was a cancer, which though it might heal over and wear the external appearance of health, struck deeper in with each specific, to re-appear with increased virulence. Yet it was for a time a miracle of healing. The measures themselves were eminently wise; nay, the utmost that human wisdom could do. They gave peace to the country—a profound peace of many years. A part of that triumph belongs to North Carolina. Her favorite statesman was then in the cabinet, and shared in the counsels by which these results were brought about. During the progress of these measures he was in constant conference with their author, and to the opinion of none did their author pay greater deference.

His labors as Secretary of the Navy were brought to a sudden termination. The Whig party met in convention on the 16th of June, 1852 and put in nomination for the Presidency General Scott, and for the Vice-Presidency Mr. Graham. Mr. Graham's preference for the Presidency was in favor of Mr. Fillmore, and without a distinct declaration of principles, and an approval of the course of his administration, he would not have permitted his name to be placed on any other ticket. This declaration was made, and in terms as explicit as he could wish; with that declaration, it became a mere calculation of chances which was the candidate the most acceptable to the country. Under these circumstances he accepted the nomination. Immediately on his acceptance, with a view as he expressed it, "to relieve the administration of any possible criticism or embarrassment on his account in the approaching canvass," he tendered his resignation. The President "appreciating the high sense of delicacy and propriety" which prompted this act, accepted his resignation with expressions of "unfeigned regret."

In Mr. Stephen's History of the United States, it is said that in accepting the nomination tendered him by the Whigs, General Scott "cautiously avoided endorsing that portion of the Whig platform which pledged the party to an acceptance of, and acquiescence in the measures of 1850." If avoidance there was, it was because he deemed it unnecessary to pledge his faith to measures with which he was so intimately identified. He was acting Secretary of War during the pending of these measures. "No one," says Mr. Graham in a letter to a friend, "more deeply felt the importance of the crisis, or co-operated with us more efficiently in procuring the passage of the Compromise Measures, or rejoiced more heartily in the settlement thereby made." With a soldier's sentiment of honor, General Scott rested on his record, which was open to all the world. But the charge of unfaithfulness to those measures was made against him, and urged with fatal effect. And so it came to pass that the two candidates who had exerted all their abilities, and used all their influence official and other, to secure the passage of the compromise measures, were beaten upon the charge alleged against one of them of unfaithfulness to those measures.

After his retirement from the cabinet and in the same year—1852—he delivered the sixth lecture in the course, before the Historical Society of New York, in Metropolitan Hall, in the city of New York. "The attendance," we are told in the "Evening

Post" of that date, "was exceedingly numerous." Ever anxious to exhalt his State, and set her before the world in her true glory, his subject was taken from the history of North Carolina. It was the British Invasion of North Carolina in 1780 and '81. It is known what scant justice has been done to our State by the early Historians of the country.

This injustice, Mr. Graham, as far as a lecture would admit, undertook to redress. Though his subject confined him to the events of less than two years, and took up the story five years after the first blood had been shed at Lexington, and four years after the Declaration of Independence, he presents a rapid and graphic sketch of what was done in North Carolina down to the year 1780. He depicts the advanced state of opinion in North Carolina before the war; he recounts the military expeditions sent out by her in support of the common cause; and shows that "from New York to Florida, inclusive, there were few battle fields, on which a portion of the troops engaged in defense of the liberties of the country were not hers." He then places before us in strong colors, the period just before Lord Cornwallis commenced his famous march—that period so justly designated as the dark days of the Revolution; when Georgia and South Carolina had been over-run and subjugated; when the army of the South had been nearly an-nihilated by the disastrous battle of Camden and the catastrophe of Fishing Creek. He relates the bold measures—measures which call to mind those of Rome, at similar crises of peril—with which the State of North Carolina prepared to meet the impending shock. He then enters upon a narrative of the different operations of the American and British armies under their respective com-manders, Greene and Cornwallis, and a finer narrative it would be difficult to point out. A bare recital of the incidents of that campaign could not want interest in the hands of the driest his-torian, but in this narrative it is brought before us in vivid colors. By his brief but striking delineation of the principal actors; by his rapid touches in which the relative state of the Whig and Tory population of that day are brought to view; by his sketches of the scenery of the Piedmont country—the theater of that campaign; by his notices of individual adventure; above all, by his masterly recital of the incidents of the retreat of General Greene and the pursuit of Lord Cornwallis—a retreat in which the hand of Provi-dence seemed from time to time, so visibly interposed—the grand procession of events pass before us with the interest of an acted drama. We experience a feeling of deep relief, when at length, the army of Greene is placed in safety. After taking breath, which we had held as it were, during the quick succession of events in that celebrated retreat, we retrace our steps and the interest culminates in the battle of Guilford. "The philosophy of history," says Mr. Benton in his 'Thirty Year's View,' has not yet laid hold of the battle of Guilford; its consequences and events. That battle made the capture of Yorktown. The events are told in history, the connections and dependence in none." The future historian will find the task done to his hand in this Lecture. Its decisive character is there appreciated and set forth.

In the remainder of the Lecture he glances at the minor invasion of Col. Craig, and the operators under his command from the valley of the Neuse to the highlands of Chatham, and at the romantic career of the vile but intrepid Fanning. He gives us a sketch of Gov. Burke, his capture and escape. He presents a brief view of the expedition of Gen. Rutherford against the British post at Wilmington, who after many skirmishes, drove and kept the British and Loyalists within the lines of the garrison, until the evacuation of the town, and the retreat of the enemy to Charleston. He sets out the forces sent forth by North Carolina, under Gen. Sumter, which forces formed a conspicuous part of Greene's line at Eutaw, and followed the flag of the Union until the disappearance of the enemy's sails off the harbor at Charleston.

The Lecture closes with some reflections on the "Act of pardon and Oblivion" passed by the Legislature, after the proclamation of peace, at its first session in 1783. "An Act," says Mr. Graham, "of grace and magnanimity, worthy of the heroic, but Christian and forebearing spirit which had triumphed in the struggle just ended." The words have a peculiar and melancholy significance to us, who recollect how long after the war, he stood among us as an alien and a stranger, deprived of the commonest right of citizenship; and how by mistaken party spirit he was debarred the enjoyment of those Senatorial honors, with which a grateful people would have cheered and crowned the evening of his life.

This Lecture will, I think, be regarded as the maturest of his literary efforts. It presents the events of the time of which it treats in new combinations, and sheds upon them new lights from original investigations. The style is always clear, forcible and harmonious. Classic ornament is introduced to an extent rare for him; for though he retained his classical learning to the end of his life, his sense of fitness led him to employ very sparingly, what one might be disposed to attribute to ostentation. Altogether it is the most valuable contribution yet made to the history of North Carolina at that era. It sets the State in a juster light than any thing on record. It particularly commends itself to all who cherish in their hearts the sacred flame of State-love and State-pride; to all who hold in honor the renown of their ancestry; to all who would catch

"Ennobling impulse from the past"

Mr. Graham was again a member of the Legislature in 1854-'5. The great question of that session was what was popularly known as "Free Suflrage." Its object was to abolish the property qualification for the Senate, and extend to every voter the same right of suffrage, whether for the Senate or the House. To this extension of suffrage *per se* he made no objection. He contended, however, that the constitution was based upon carefully adjusted compromises of conflicting interests, and that an amendment of the constitution confined to this single point—as it must necessarily be if carried out by the Legislative method—would disturb those compromises and thus destroy or greatly impair the harmony of that instrument. He, therefore, advocated the calling of a convention, that all the questions embraced in these compromises might be duly considered, and other parts re-adjusted to suit those which might be changed. These views were presented in a speech, memorable for its ability. In the former part he discusses the question at issue, and here will be found some of the finest examples of his skill as a dialectician; in the latter part he gave an exposition of the subject in all its constitutional bearings—an exposition learned, lucid and conclusive.

The administration of Mr. Buchanan drew to its close amidst signs ominous for the future tranquility of the country. These signs awakened the fears of all who loved and valued the Union, and the trusted statesmen of the country made arrangements to meet for conference, and to give expression to their views. The Executive Committee of the Constitutional Union party determined early in January, 1860, to issue an address to the people of the United States upon the grave exigencies in national politics. A committee of seven, all men of the highest national distinction, among whom was Mr. Graham, was appointed to prepare the address. Mr. Crittenden notified him of his appointment in a letter of January 24th, and urged his attendance at the meeting of the committee. In his answer, Mr. Graham had left it doubtful whether the pressure of his engagements would permit his attendance and requested that another might be appointed in his place. Accordingly Gov. Morehead was appointed. But Mr. Crittenden wrote again, and to show the importance attached to his judgment and action I subjoin an extract from his letter: "The crisis is important, and fills the public mind with expectation and anxiety. It is earnestly to be desired that the character of our convention should be conspicuous and equal to the occasion. We have good reason to feel assured of the attendance of many of the most eminent men of the country, and it is by the great weight of the moral and public character of its members that the convention must hope to obtain for its acts or counsels, whatever they may be, respect and influence with the people. We cannot do without your *assistance* and *name*. All the members of the committee, who were present when your letter was read, united in wishing me to write and to urge your coming to the convention. Your absence will be a positive *weight* against us."

A number of eminent statesmen, among whom was Mr. Graham, met in Washington City in February to consult together upon the dangers which menaced the country. The result was the convention which nominated the Constitutional Union ticket for the Presidency, in behalf of which he canvassed the State. Upon the election of Mr. Lincoln he made public addresses and exhorted the people to yield due obedience to his office.

But the tempest had long been gathering, and was now ready to burst. No human power could avert it. The people of South Carolina and of the other States of the far South had been educated in the doctrine of secession, and there were few in those States who did not hold that doctrine as an undeniable article of political faith. The time was come when this doctrine was to be tested. The election of Mr. Lincoln constituted the cause in the minds of the people of South Carolina. On the 20th of December, 1860, that State held a convention and declared her connection with the United States dissolved, and proceeded to put herself in an attitude to make good her declaration. In this action she was followed by the States to the South of her, and on similar grounds.

The doctrine of secession met with little favor in North Carolina. As a right deduced from the constitution, and to be exercised under its authority, it was believed by Mr. Graham and the school of statesmen to which he belonged to be without foundation. The Legislature of North Carolina directed the question of a convention to be submitted to the people. The question was discussed, in the light of recent events, by the Press of the State, and num-

erous meetings of the people were held in every part. These
meetings were addressed by our ablest men. Amongst these a
monster meeting was held at Salisbury which was addressed by
Gov. Morehead, Mr. Badger and Mr. Graham, who, as well for
the exalted positions they had held as for their commanding
abilities, were looked to for counsel in this emergency. The people
at the polls pronounced with great unanimity against a convention.

But events were marching on with rapid strides. On the 13th
of April, 1861, Sumter surrendered to Confederate guns. On the
15th Mr. Lincoln issued his call for 75,000 troops. This call was
made without authority, and was the first of that series of public
measures culminating in the unauthorized suspension of the
Habeas Corpus Act on the 10th of May, under the shock of which
the public liberties of the North for a time went down.

By these events the aspect of things was wholly changed. The
question of secession as a right, whether the election of Mr.
Lincoln was a just cause for the exercise of the right, had drifted
out of sight. War was inevitable. Virginia had followed the example of the Southern States, and North Carolina was now girdled
with seceded States. All that was left her was a choice of sides.
The language of Mr. Graham at this crisis was the language of
all thoughtful men; nay, it was the language of the human heart.
And looking back upon all that we have suffered—and there are
none even in the Northern States but say we have suffered enough
—if a similar conjuncture were to arise, the heart would speak
out the same language again. Speaking the voice of the people of
North Carolina, as he, from the high trusts confided to him in his
past life, and from the confidence always reposed in him, was more
than any other commissioned to do, in a public address, at Hillsboro in March, 1861, he expressed himself as follows:

"Ardent in their attachment to the Constitution and the Union,
they, had condemned separate State secession as rash and precipi-
tate, and wanting in respect to the sister States of identical interests; and as long as there was hope of an adjustment of sectional
differences, they were unwilling to part with the Government,
and give success to the movement for its overthrow, which appeared on the part of some, at least, to be but the revelation of a
long cherished design. But the President gives to the question
new alternatives. These are, on the one hand, to join with him in
a war of conquest, for it is nothing less, against our brethren of
the Seceding States—or, on the other, resistance to and throw-

ing off the obligations of the Federal Constitution. Of the two, we do not hesitate to accept the latter. Blood is thicker than water. However widely we have differed from, and freely criticized the course taken by these States, they are much more closely united with us, by the ties of kindred, affection, and a peculiar interest, which is denounced and warred upon at the North, without reference to any *locality* in our own section, than to any of the Northern States."

Under the influence of these counsels so wisely and temperately expressed, a convention of the people of North Carolina was called. On the 20th of May, a day memorable in the annals of the State and of the world, the convention passed the ordinance of secession.

For this ordinance the vote was unanimous. But though the vote indicated an entire unanimity among the members it was unanimity only as to the end to be accomplished. The views of Mr. Graham, and the statesmen with whom he acted, had in regard to secession as a Constitutional remedy undergone no change. To set forth their views, Mr. Badger offered a series of resolutions in the nature of a protestation—an exclusion of a conclusion. These resolutions asserted the right of revolution, and based the action of the convention on that ground; but the minds of men had been wrought to such a pitch of excitement that the distinction was unheeded, and the resolutions failed.

On the 20th of June the convention passed the ordinance, by which the State of North Carolina became a member of the Confederacy. To this measure Mr. Graham offered a strong but fruitless opposition. In the perilous career upon which we were about to enter he was unwilling to surrender the sovereignty of the State into the hands of those whose rash counsels had, in the judgment of the people of North Carolina, precipitated the war. He wished the State to hold her destinies in her own hands, that she might act as exigencies might require. Those who realize the delusive views under which the government at Richmond acted during the last months of the war will see in this opinion another proof of his wise foresight.

The progress of the war which now broke out with such fury demonstrated that there were here, as at the North, those who conceived that the public peril had merged the constitution and the laws. Early in the session "an ordinance to define and punish sedition and to prevent the dangers which may arise from persons disaffected to the State," was introduced.

On the 7th of December Mr. Graham addressed the convention in opposition to this ordinance. The speech which he delivered on this occasion was, perhaps, the noblest effort of his life. It breathes the true spirit of American freedom. It is the product of a mind deeply inbued with the great principles of civil liberty, and which had devoutly meditated upon all those safeguards which the wisdom of successive generations had thrown around it. His wide acquaintance with history had made him familiar with every device by which liberty may be sapped and undermined; his exalted estimate of its value and dignity had developed this acquaintance into a special sense by which he could detect any design hostile to it, under any pretence or subterfuge, however specious or skillful. This special faculty is strikingly exhibited in this speech in tracing and laying bare the dangerous tendencies which everywhere lurked under this ordinance. It abounds with historical illustrations and allusions. It contains passages of graphic eloquence—that, among others, in which he sketches the settlement of the Society of Friends in this State, and with a few touches depicts the genius of that sect. It is pervaded by a warmth and animation unwonted in his speeches, sometimes, indeed, bordering upon enthusiasm. In none of his parliamentary efforts does he seem to have yielded so freely to his native impulses and feelings. It is strictly logical in its structure and advances by regular progression. In its style it is nervous and idiomatic, and the thoughts are often expressed with the highest degree of energy and terseness. Like all great leaders he had the power of clothing popular thoughts in brief, pithy expressions, which at once become current like stamped coin. One such, uttered by him on that occasion, was worth many speeches: "We are resolved to be independent and free, not only in the *end*, but in the *means*." From the commencement to the conclusion of this speech he moves with equal freedom, grace and power.

From the beginning of the war the current of power set steadily from the Confederate States to the Confederate government; and with each year of the war, the current flowed on with increasing tide. Within its just bounds, no man yielded a heartier allegiance to that government than Mr. Graham; but on the other hand, no man stood ready to oppose a firmer resistance when that government overstepped those bounds. The war had been begun and was then prosecuted for the maintenance of great principles, and it was his fixed purpose that civil liberty should not, at the South as at the North, be engulfed in its progress. In the year

1862 a Minister of the Gospel—a man of learning and of irro-proachable character—was arrested in the county of Orange, under a military order, sent to Richmond and cast into prison. He was not in the military service of the Confederate States, and therefore not amenable to military law. As a proceding against a citizen, such an arrest, without charge made on oath and without warrant, was in violation of all law; while his deportation beyond the limits of the State, for trial, by military tribunal, was in contempt of the dignity and sovereignty of the State. Mr. Graham, being then Senator from Orange, introduced a resolution demanding a return of the prisoner to the State, which was passed at once. On introducing the resolution, he expressed the opinion that the proceeding was without the sanction of the Confederate Executive, or of the Secretary of War. The sequel proved this supposition to be correct; the prisoner was sent back with a disavowal of any knowledge of the proceeding on the part of the President or the Secretary, until the confinement of the prisoner in the military prison at Richmond. The Secretary frankly admitted the erroneous nature of the arrest and imprisonment, and disclaimed all intention to interfere with the rightful jurisdiction of the State. On the 22nd of January 1863—upon the incoming of the message with the accompanying documents, touching the case —Mr. Graham paid a merited tribute to the enlightened comprehension of the relations existing between the Confederate government and the States, evinced by these sentiments, and in the further remarks submitted by him, he took occasion to restate the great principles of personal liberty—daily more and more endangered in the course of the war—and to impress them upon the public mind by apt comments upon the case to which the pubilc attention was then so strongly directed. This was the first, and is believed to have been the last case, in which military power was used to override civil law.

In December 1863,* Mr. Graham was elected to the Confederate Senate by a majority of two thirds of the Legislature. He took his seat in May 1864. There was then need of the best counsel. The brilliant successes which had crowned our arms in the early years of the War, had been replaced by a succession of disasters. The battle of Gettysburg and the fall of Vicksburg had brought us apparently to the brink of fate. As the year 1864 rolled on the prospect became darker and darker, and at the end of the year the situation was to the last degree critical. Our territory had been cut in twain, and we were beleaguered by land and by sea. With-

* This is an error. He was elected November 27, 1862.

in the area which acknowledged the Confederate Government, there was great exhaustion of all kinds of military supplies, and a like exhaustion of all the elements for the support of human life. Gen. Lee was only able to oppose the front of Gen. Grant by extending his lines until it was ready to snap from excessive tension. To strengthen his force from the white race was impossible; conscription there had reached its limit. Gen. Sherman had swept through Georgia and the broad track of desolation which he left behind him too truly told the story of our helplessness. It was known that each Confederate soldier was opposed by as many as five Federal soldiers; the former scantily fed, clothed and shod; the latter supplied with every comfort and many luxuries.[13] It was plain there was no longer any hope of a successful prosecution of the war. In the midst of the dense gloom which shrouded the country on every side, a ray of light dawned in the proposed peace conference at Hampton Roads. Mr. Graham had endeavored to reach this form of intercourse from the commencement of the session. He was not without hope of a peaceful termination of hostilities; not so much from his estimate of the statesmanship of President Davis and his Cabinet, as from the extremity of the case which left no other alternative. The conference took place on the 3rd of February, 1865. The terms offered by Mr. Lincoln were, that the seceded States should return to the Union under the Constitution, in the existing state of affairs, with slavery as it was, but liable to be abolished by an amendment to the Constitution. He pledged himself to the utmost exercise of the Executive powers in behalf of the South. The demand of the Commissioners was for independence. There could be no middle ground, and the conference ended. Upon the return of the commissioners, Mr. Davis and Mr. Benjamin made public speeches in Richmond, to fire the Southern heart anew; but the event proved how little sagacity they brought to the direction of affairs at that supreme hour. The speeches fell still-born.

One principle had actuated Mr. Graham from the beginning of the war; to sustain the Government in its struggle for independence until it should be demonstrated that our resources were inadequate for that end; and when that should be seen and acknowledged, to seek, if possible, a peaceful solution. How well

---

[13] The odds were exactly 7 to 1. The whole number of Confederates surrendered, including Lee's and all, amounted to about 150,000 under arms. The whole number of Federals, then in the field, and afterwards mustered out of service as the records show, amounted, in round numbers, to 1,050,000. Stephen's *History of the United States*, p. 466.

he sustained it, is matter of history. He sustained it in every way in which his talents and his means could be made available. He sustained it by his counsels in the State and in the Confederate Government. He sustained it by blood more precious in his eyes than his own, all his sons, five in number, who had attained the age of eighteen, entered the army, and were in the army to the end.

The inadequacy of our resources, particularly of the population from which our soldiers were drawn, had now been demonstrated. It was known to Congress; it was admitted by Gen. Lee in his proposition to conscribe slaves; it was proclaimed from the steps of the Capitol by Mr. Benjamin: "Unless the slaves are armed," he said, "the cause is lost." Every expedient had been tried; the extremest measures had been put in operation; "by means of conscription, impressment laws and the suspension of the *habeas corpus*, the whole population and all the resources of the country had long before been placed at the command of the President for prosecution of the war." All had been found unavailing.

One resource, in the opinion of some, remained—the conscription of negroes. A bill for this purpose was introduced into Congress. It was opposed by Mr. Graham upon the ground, that it was unconstitutional, as well as inexpedient and dangerous. His sagacious mind saw that this was a measure, not of safety, but a measure born of the wild promptings of despair. On the 21st of February it was indefinitely postponed, though it was subsequently taken up and passed.

If ever negotiation was to be resorted to it was clear the time had come. We know but little of what passed in the Confederate Congress at that time. Its proceedings were had in secret session; nor is it now known whether the journals of the body escaped destruction. All that we know is derived from what was published by the members after the fall of the Confederate Government. Among these publications is a paper contributed by Mr. Oldham, then Senator from Texas, to DeBow's Review, in Oct. 1869, which gives us some information of the proceedings of the Senate at that time. A few days after the conference at Hampton Roads, he informs us, a committee consisting of Messrs. Orr, Graham and Johnson, was appointed to confer with the President, and ascertain what he proposed to do under the existing condition of affairs. In a few days they made a verbal report through Mr. Graham. "Among other things," I quote his words, "they stated that they had inquired of the President his views and opinions in regard to proposing to the United States to negotiate for peace upon the basis of the Confederacy returning to the Union, and that he had answered that he had no power to negotiate a treaty upon such a basis; that his authority to make treaties was derived from the Constitution, which he had sworn to support and that such a treaty would operate as an abrogation of the Constitution, and a dissolution of the government; that the States alone, each acting for itself, in its sovereign capacity, could make such a treaty. Mr. Graham said that he gave notice that he would, in a few days, introduce a resolution in favor of opening negotiations with the United States upon the basis of a return to the Union by the States of the Confederacy; that he did not give the notice at the instance or under the instruction of the committee, but upon his own responsibility. The notice was received in such a manner that he never offered his resolution."

I never saw the paper from which the foregoing quotation is made, and was a stranger to this passage of Mr. Graham's life until within the last forty days. I read it with a feeling of profound relief. I have ever regarded him from my earliest years, with the warmest admiration and the most affectionate respect; but his failure, as I thought, to take some action looking to peace after the Hampton Roads conference—when the plainest dictates of humanity so clearly demanded it—left upon my mind the painful impression that he had been wanting to himself in that, the most important, crisis of his life. There is a deep seated conviction that the blood which was shed after that conference might have been saved. That the waste of the fruits of past centuries of toil— a waste which consigned so many of the present and future generations to want and misery—might have been avoided. It is with gratitude I reflect that not a tittle of responsibility for this bloodshed and waste lay at his door. And when the inevitable hour came to him, I doubt not the thought that he had done what he could to arrest a war attended with such terrible and useless sacrifice, was one of the sweetest reflections of his whole life.

The position assumed by President Davis, that he had no authority to make a treaty upon the conditions proposed—since that would amount to an abrogation of the Government which he has sworn to support—had, no doubt, a great influence on his mind; but it is clear that it did not express the whole case. If the oath was binding upon him to that extent, it was binding upon Congress to the same extent. Such a construction abnegates one of the highest functions of government, the power of peace and war.

It nullifies the treaty making power *"quoad hoc,"* and transfers it from the council chamber to the field, from the Cabinet to the General. And if that oath bound him to hold out to the end, unless the Confederate States prevailed, it equally bound Gen. Lee to continue the struggle as long as a company could be brought into the field. A surrender by Gen. Lee was tantamount in all its most dreaded effects, to such a treaty by the President, with none of the beneficent results which might have been secured by treaty. There is no principle upon which a General is justified in surrendering an army to avoid destruction, which does not apply with tenfold force to the surrender of a State to avoid destruction. The State embraces, beside the army, all the helpless population of both sexes, and by so much the case is the stronger.

The difficulties connected with the abrogation of the Government, especially by those appointed to administer it, are undeniably great; but they cannot be allowed to be conclusive against the interests of human life; such a theory cannot be maintained. If the condition of things be such that the Government or the people must be sacrificed, there cannot be a doubt where the sacrifice must fall. All would say that the Government was made for the people, not the people for the Government.

The strongest reason for the action of Mr. Davis, at that time, action so long an impenatrable mystery, is now made clear from the most authoritative source. In a recent number of the "London Fortnightly Review," is a review, by the first English Military critic of the age, of the works of Gen. Johnson and Gen. Sherman, giving the history of their several campaigns. Speaking from information derived from one "who was daily in the Council Chamber at Richmond," he says that during the latter stages of the war, Mr. Davis and his Cabinet acted under "thoroughly false views of the military situation." "The Richmond Cabinet was perfectly blinded," says he, "by certain successes of the earlier part of the war; and its military adviser lacked the insight or the honesty to explain to it, that the disproportion of fighting power which had certainly at one time existed, whatever its cause, had passed away." The source from which this information was derived could be no other than a member of the Confederate Cabinet, for none other could have had "daily access to the Council Chamber at Richmond." This information, then, is to be regarded as entirely authentic; and it is fully sustained by the spirit and tenor of the speeches made by Mr. Davis and Mr. Benjamin at the time referred to above, and those made shortly afterwards.

The writer continues, "it"—the Cabinet at Richmond—"could not realize the facts of the case." With reference to General Sherman and his army, he says: "Sherman's reputation, and the immense strength of the army he commanded, were well known at that era even on this side of the Atlantic, and ought not to have been ignored at Richmond." Mr. Graham did realize the facts of the case. His letters published in "The last ninety days of the War," show with what clear vision he swept the horizon. Hence his movement looking to negotiations "to ascertain for the States what terms would be yielded, provided they consented to re-adopt the Constitution of the United States."

Congress adjourned about the 16th day of March. Impressed with the imminence of the emergency, Mr. Graham stopped but one day at home—that day being the Sabbath—and on Monday proceeded to Raleigh to confer with the Governor. The conference was long and earnest. Mr. Graham laid before the Governor, the views of the President, the state of the armies and earnestly recommended that the Legislature should be convened. He sustained his advice by the opinion of General Lee and that of many good and able men with whom he had been associated. He ended by telling him that Richmond would fall in less than thirty days, and that event would be followed probably by a rout or dispersion of General Lee's army for want of food, if for no other cause. The Governor was surprised by his statement of facts, and incredulous in some degree as to his conclusions. He agreed to consider the subject and convened the Council on that day week. Hearing nothing of their action, in a few days Mr. Graham visited Raleigh again. The Governor informed him that on the day appointed, a bare quorum of the Council attended and being equally divided, he had not summoned the Legislature. He said that Mr. Gilmer, with whom Mr. Graham had advised him to consult, had suggested to him to solicit an interview with General Sherman on the subject of peace. Mr. Graham remarked that if such an interview were held, Mr. Davis should be apprised of it. To this, the Governor at once assented. Mr. Graham suggested further that if that course were taken, he, (the Governor) should be in a condition to act independently of the President, and convene the Legislature. To this proposition the Governor manifested reluctance; but finally agreed to call the Council of State again. But while negotiation halted, the march of Gen. Sherman's army decided events. In a few days no resource was left, but an unconditional surrender. With the part borne by Mr. Graham at that trying time, a gifted authoress of North Carolina has made the public already familiar in the captivating pages of her work. "The Last Ninety Days of the War."

There is no part of Mr. Graham's life in which the calm wisdom for which he was so distinguished, shone more conspicuously than in the closing months of the civil war. When independence was demonstrated to be hopeless, he sought peace; but even then, only in channels admitted to be in accordance with the great principles of our Government.

In his opinion, that peace ought to be sought by the State after the failure of the conference at Hampton Roads; he was sustained by our entire delegation in Congress, and a large proportion of the leading citizens of the State. Yet so anxious was he not only to avoid any appearance of conflict among the Confederate States, but to conform to all that the most punctilious deference for the Confederate Government might require, that he did not move in the matter until after a conference with the President, and then only in the track pointed out by him. The President disclaimed all power of making a treaty, which would abrogate the Government, and declared that the "States alone, each acting in its sovereign capacity, could make such a treaty." In the line of action here indicated the State could not be put in a false position; nay, her honor would be put beyond all cavil. It was known that we had no power to arrest Gen. Sherman's march. Gen. Johnson confronted him, and all felt convinced that whatever his great military genius could accomplish would be done. But it was also known that his gallant army was out-numbered six to one. A surrender in a few days would be inevitable. Burning capitols, desolated homes, famine and destruction of life, followed Sherman's march. Was it not worth the effort to put a stop to such frightful calamities? What Mr. Graham urged, was that the people might be allowed to determine their fate for themselves. Such a course was in strict conformity to the fundamental principles of our Government. A convention of seven Governors at Altoona had precipitated the war when peace counsels seemed to be in the ascendant. Was not Mr. Graham justified in the opinion that executive powers which had been so destructively exerted in the beginning, might be beneficently exerted in the end?

In an address delivered by Gov. Vance before the Southern Historical Society, at White Sulphur Springs, West Virginia, August 18th, 1875, occurs the following statement:

"Soon after the failure of the Fortress Monroe or Hampton Roads conference, I was visited by Gov. Graham (whose death we so recently deplore) who was then a Senator of the Confederate States. After giving all the particulars of that conference which had not appeared in the papers, and the prevailing impressions of Congressional circles about Richmond &c., he informed me that a number of leading gentlemen there, despairing of obtaining peace through Mr. Davis, and believing the end inevitable and not distant, had requested him to visit me and urge me as Governor of North Carolina, to take steps for making separate peace with Mr. Lincoln, and thus inaugurate the conclusion; that he agreed to lay their request before me without promising to add his personal advice thereto. I asked who those gentlemen were, and, with some reluctance, he gave me their names, chiefly Senators and Representatives in the Confederate Congress. I asked why these gentlemen did not begin negotiations in their own States with the enemy, and if they would come out in the papers with this request to me. He said they could not take the initiative, they were so surrounded at home, and so trammeled by pledges &c., as to render it impossible- I declined the proposition of course."

It is with reluctance that I advert to this statement. Had it been given to the press with a sponsor less entitled to consideration, I should have been disposed to let it float with the tide. But it presents itself under imposing circumstances; it proceeds from one who at the time referred to, was at the head of the Government in North Carolina; it is contained in an address made before a society whose object it is to preserve the memorials of that time. The statement thus passes into history. It will not be waived. It peremptorily challenges attention.

The address had for its object the vindication of North Carolina, and the vindication was complete, upon the facts and figures presented. It was made in reply not to any recent strictures upon the State, but to strictures made during the war. Ten years had elapsed from the end of the war to the date of that address. But the *statement* was made, not in the way of vindication, but in the way of recrimination, and Mr. Graham's name was used as the instrument of recrimination. Now it will be regretted by all who love the State, and the fair fame of her statesmen, which forms her highest glory, that such a use of his name was not made till the grave had closed upon him, and his voice was mute forever.

Had this statement been delayed to make avail of facts which came to light afterwards, the cause of the delay would be apparent, but every fact used in defense of the State was as available at any time during those ten years, as it was on the 18th of August when the address was delivered. The effect of that statement was, in the judgment of a large portion of our people, to put Mr. Graham and the Senators and Representatives alluded to, in false relations to the Confederate Government. It excited a deep feeling in this State, and called out acrimonious comments from the Southern Press. Governor Vance perceived at once the light in which it would be regarded. His language is emphatic, "I declined the proposition of *course.*"

There are some reflections which arise, spontaneously, in the mind of every one who reads this statement, and who was acquainted with Mr. Graham.

According to this statement, Mr. Graham came charged with a momentous proposition from parties whose names, at first, he did not disclose. It will be admitted by all, that it would be hard to conceive a situation more at variance with the tenor of his life than that in which this statement places him. He was a man of a lofty, fearless and commanding spirit. In action he was one of the most independent of men. He opposed secession when fealty to the South was measured by zeal for that doctrine. He opposed the extreme measures of the Confederate Government when the temper of the times scarcely tolerated any dissent. He opposed the Johnson Constitution; he opposed the Reconstruction Constitution. In the latter instances he brought himself into conflict with those who wielded the powers of the Federal Government; and that too when he was already under the ban of that Government. He had a just sense of his own dignity. He had a just sense of his own weight in the country. His conduct had always been so high and clear that never, during a life of three score years and ten, was he once called upon for an explanation. Not a single lineament of his character do we recognize in the bearer of such a proposition from nameless men.

We are told that, though the bearer of the proposition, he refused or declined to express any opinion in regard to it. This reticence is unaccountable. On public affairs Mr. Graham had no concealments. His opinions as a private man could be known by all who sought them; as a public man he never hesitated to proclaim them. There was no feature of his character which impressed his opponents more than this. A distinguished Republican,[14] who knew him well, gave it as one of his most character-istic traits, that "he had eminently the courage of his opinions." Would such a one withhold his opinions when the fate of his country hung in the balance, and when the high position which he occupied made it his duty to express them?

The alledged proposition involved the destruction of the Con-federate Government, and the transfer of the allegiance of its citi-zens to the Federal Government. Could he have so entirely lost that political sagacity which made him a light and a guide to the generation in which he lived, as to suppose such a proposition would be listened to, coming from nameless men? If such a course had been necessary to escape ruin, otherwise inevitable, it could only have been taken by the concerted action of those who were strongest in the confidence of the country. That, no one knew better than he. Further, he knew that to secure for the proposition a favorable hearing, it must appear that it was a movement which enlisted able and patriotic men. To suppress their names, then, argues a degree of simplicity which would be unaccountable in the weakest of men, and seems impossible in one of the strongest.

Mr. Graham has left on record, in a letter to Gov. Swain, a full and minute account of this interview. That it was the same is proven by reference to the time. Gov. Vance says it was after the Hampton Roads conference. Mr. Graham, as we have seen, reach-ed home from Richmond on the 19th of March, and went to Raleigh on Monday the 20th. It is proved to be the same by the identity of topics discussed or referred to, as far as those topics are alluded to by Gov. Vance. It is proven by the identity of words, one of them used, not in its plain and obvious, but in its remote and secondary sense.

That letter and the circumstances under which it was written thus become of interest. On Saturday, the 8th of April, Gov. Swain wrote to Mr. Graham urging that he would go with him to Ra-leigh to confer with Gov. Vance upon the state of public affairs. He pictured in strong colors the imminence of the dangers which beset the country. He told him that the State looked to none of its citizens for counsel and guidance as it did to him. He told him the Governor would give as favorable consideration to his sug-gestions as he would yield to any citizen or functionary in the Confederacy. To this letter Mr. Graham replied on the same day at considerable length. He wrote that he left Richmond thorough-ly convinced: 1st. That independence for the Southern Confed-

---

[14] Hon. S. F. Phillips.

eracy was perfectly hopeless. 2nd. That through the administration of Mr. Davis we could expect no peace. 3rd. That the State Government should make a movement in behalf of peace. He then proceeded to give in detail what had occurred on the occasion of his visit to Gov. Vance. This account was written for the purpose of putting Gov. Swain in possession of what had passed, no doubt with the expectation that it would be used by him in the interview with Gov. Vance, and also show how frankly he had expressed his views upon the state of the country. On the Monday following, Gov. Swain went to Raleigh, and the conference between him and Gov. Vance was long and full. It may, I think, be assumed as certain, from the importance attached by Gov. Swain to the opinion of Mr. Graham, and from the weight which he thought those opinions would have with Gov. Vance, that the contents of that letter were made known to Gov. Vance, and formed the basis of their conference. An account of the interview was furnished by Gov. Swain to the author of "The Last Ninety Days," together with the letter in question. The inference is clear that Gov. Swain understood that letter as containing a true narrative of what passed between Mr. Graham and Gov. Vance. Further, the "Ninety Days" has been for years before the world, and the correctness of that narrative has been unchallenged. That narrative has thus the direct sanction of Gov. Swain, and by acquiescence during Mr. Graham's life, it has the sanction also of Gov. Vance.

Now compare the narratives and note the difference. In Gov. Vance's version, Mr. Graham comes to him from third persons whose names were not disclosed; in Mr. Graham's, he went unprompted by anybody; unprompted save by his own high sense of duty. In Gov. Vance's version, he came the bearer of a proposition from others; in Gov. Graham's, he went to submit his own views. In Gov. Vance's version, the proposition is to "make separate terms with Mr. Lincoln;" in Mr. Graham's, to call the Assembly. In Gov. Vance's version he withholds his advice; in Mr. Graham's, he went for no other purpose than to give his advice, and did give it at length. The only reference in Mr. Graham's narrative to any third person, is when he reinforces his advice by the opinion of Gen. Lee, and by the opinions of those considered by him as the wisest and best men with whom he had conversed. It is absolutely certain that what is alleged in the "statement," as having occurred, did not happen before the 20th of March, because between the Hampton Roads Conference and that time, Mr. Graham had not been in Raleigh. It is morally certain that it did not occur after that time; because if Gov. Vance rejected Mr. Graham's advice to call the Legislature, and thus allow the representatives of the people to decide their own fate, the latter would not have submitted a proposition that the Governor should, at the instance of nameless men, decide their fate for them. Whence, then, the irreconcilable discrepancy between the two versions? The explanation lies in the fact that Mr. Graham's narrative was penned a short time after the interview occurred, when the facts were fresh in his mind; while Gov. Vance's was not written until over ten years had passed away.

In a note appended to the address, in the November number of *Our Living and Our Dead*, Gov. Vance says: "Since the synopsis of this was published I have received a letter from an esteemed friend in Hillsboro, who says he had had a conversation with Gov. Graham on the same subject, and his recollection is that the proposition made to me was, that I should take steps to withdraw the North Carolina troops from General Lee's army, which would force him to surrender and thus end the war. It may be that my friend's recollection is correct."

The inference of the reader of this note would be that the letter from Hillsboro sustains Gov. Vance's recollection in every particular, except the manner in which peace was to be brought about; the writer's understanding being, that it was to be accomplished by withdrawing our troops. I subjoin the clause of the letter of which the "note" is intended as a summary. The author of the letter, in writing to Gov. Vance about the statement in the White Sulphur Springs address, says: "You state that the purpose of persons whose message Gov. Graham delivered to you was to make 'separate terms with Mr. Lincoln, and thus inagurate the conclusion.' This announcement surprised me, because Gov. Graham stated the same thing to me, and I understood the purpose to be that North Carolina should withdraw her troops from Gen. Lee's army, and thus compel a surrender and end the war."

The letter undoubtedly bears the construction put upon it by Gov. Vance, nay, I think it is the most obvious construction; yet nothing was farther from the intention of the writer. The single point intended to be made by the writer, as is shown in a subsequent letter, was as to "separate terms." It was to the alleged proposition looking to "separate terms," that he alluded when he wrote this announcement, "surprised me." Mr. Graham's position in regard to peace was known to him, and it was to Mr. Graham's purpose to inaugurate a movement in favor of peace that he alluded when he wrote, "Mr. Graham stated the same thing to me." The writer of the letter alluded to in the "note" had no thought either of confirming or controverting Gov. Vance's recollection of what transpired at the interview between him and Mr. Graham, because he had not heard from Mr. Graham that he had any interview with Gov. Vance. In the subsequent letter, just referred to, he says, "Mr. Graham made no mention"—*i. e.* in the conversation alluded to —"of his having been charged with any message or communication to Gov. Vance about ending the war; indeed, he made no mention of his having had any interview with Gov. Vance on the subject."

It will be observed that the writer of the letter to Gov. Vance, in speaking of withdrawing our troops, says nothing of any communication made by Mr. Graham of such a purpose: his language is "I *understood* the purpose to be;" it was a conclusion of the writer, deduced from what he heard around him.

It is very apparent that this letter was thrown off in great haste, and without a moment's thought as to the construction which might be put upon it. Hence the erroneous implication conveyed, and hence the erroneous construction of Gov. Vance.

That letter changed the opinion of Gov. Vance, and left him in doubt as to what was the proposition submitted. "It may be," says he, "that my friend's recollection is correct." Upon this point, no doubt, I think, can exist, if we refer to Mr. Graham's recorded opinions. In his letters, given at length in the "Ninety Days," he lays open all his thoughts without reserve to his life-long friend, Gov. Swain. In them is to be found no hint of any other measure than that of calling the Legislature and allowing the people to consult together for their common safety in this unparalleled strait. These letters show further that he never contemplated separate action by the State of North Carolina.

After the Hampton Roads Conference he had no longer any hope of a peaceful solution through the action of President Davis; from thenceforth he turned his thoughts to the accomplishment of the same end, through the action of the States. The subject is often recurred to, but not an intimation can be found of any plan, except that of the States acting in conjunction. Very soon, united action on the part of all became an impossibility; conquering armies had dismembered the Confederacy—had left indeed but two States that could act in concert. But his plan still embraced these two. March 26th, he writes as follows to Gov. Swain: "I went to

Raleigh to have an interview with the Governor on the subject matter referred to in your letter. The result was a convocation of the council of State to assemble to-morrow. The Legislature of Virginia has taken a recess until the 29th instant, and I think it very important that that of North Carolina should be in session as early as possible. The war is now nearly reduced to a conflict between these two States and the United States!" In his letter of the 8th of April, which contains, as I think has been shown, the true account of the interview between Mr. Graham and Gov. Vance, Mr. Graham says: "I told him I should attend the session of the General Assembly, and, if desired, would address them in secret session; that I had confidential conversations with a committee of the Virginia Legislature, which had taken a recess for ten days, and that it was important to act in concert with that body."

The surrender left the State under the control of the Federal Generals and under the military law. According to the theory of the Administration, all civil government had ceased; all the offices were vacant. The government, for a time, was such as a conquering army administers in a subjugated country. At length to inaugurate a civil government, the precedent for the admission of territories was partially adopted. A provisional Governor was appointed with power to call a convention. In execution of his powers, the Governor appointed to the vacant offices and issued a call for a convention. Mr. Graham was nominated for the convention; but it being announced by the executive, that persons unpardoned would not be allowed to take their seats, he withdrew from the canvass.

A Constitution—the old constitution—with some alterations, was adopted. Mr. Graham opposed its ratification. From his action at this time many of his best friends dissented. They admitted with him, that a convention called, not by the people, but by a power *ab extra* and under limitations of suffrage unknown to the constitution, was an anomaly in American institutions. But certain changes were regarded as inevitable after the war, and if the Administration, then wielding supreme power over us, should rest satisfied with the changes thus made, it was conceived by them to be the wiser course to raise no question as to the manner in which the convention was called. But in Mr. Graham's view, many of the ablest men in the State concurred, and the constitution was defeated. Certainly it seems more in accordance with the spirit of a great patriot to make continual claim, even if ineffectual, in behalf of the principles of Government established by our fathers. Any mitigation which an abandonment of those principles might have obtained would have been but temporary; the principles themselves were for all time.

The reconstruction measures were now passed. The former government was swept away. The whole power over the question of suffrage, that question which lies at the foundation of all representative government, and which under the old constitution belonged to the States, save that Congress might pass uniform naturalization laws, was assumed and exercised by Congress. Suffrage was adjusted upon a new basis; all the black race was enfranchised, and a large portion of the white race was disfranchised. Under this adjustment, a new convention was called, and a new constitution adopted, the constitution under which we now live.

These measures, so extreme in their nature, were regarded while they were yet in progress by a large part of our people with a feeling little short of consternation. The government seemed wholly changed; the constitution irrevocably wrenched, if not destroyed. A profound apathy fell upon the minds of the people. A vast number ceased to take any cognizance of public affairs. They seemed to regard them, as removed forever beyond their control. In this state of things a convention of the conservative party of North Carolina was called. It met on the 5th of February, 1868, in Tucker Hall in the City of Raleigh, and was presided over by Mr. Graham.

Upon taking the chair, he spoke at length upon the state of the country. The scope of that speech is summed up in the conclusion which I give in his own words: "I have detained you thus long, but to brief and state our case as it is, against the thousand misrepresentations with which the ear of the authority is vexed, for the consideration of yourselves, of our own people, of our fellow citizens of North and West and the calm judgment of the world at large." It was thus a broad appeal to the judgment of mankind, embracing in its ample verge all the issues evolved by our situation; and I think whatever may be the party affinities of men at this day, all will allow that it was worthy such an audience. He placed himself at the very start upon the highest ground by showing that the struggles in which the party there represented was then engaged, was not the offsring of resentment or contumacy, but only for the preservation of the rights of American citizens. A few strong sentences suffice to paint the condition of the Southern country at the close of the war. He refers in eloquent terms to the civil war, and to the profound submission then, three years after its termination, everywhere manifested to the authority of the United States. He refers to the Reconstruction measures and sharply presents the spirit of those measures. He contrasts the spirit of English statesmanship at the era of the Restoration, an era analagous to our own after the conclusion of the war. He showed that the evils under which we were laboring were the result of political enthusiasm. He dwelt upon the truth impressed by the great historian of the Restoration, the feebleness of reason to oppose this passion, whether in religion or politics, and that there is but one safeguard against its fatal consequence "in religion, never to lose sight of morality; in political speculation, never to depart from the forms and maxims of the Constitution." By the forms and maxims of the American Constitution, and by the precedents of our own history at its best eras, and under our Presidents the most renowned in peace and war, he proceeded to test the Reconstruction measures. The framers of those measures admitted that they were "outside of the constitution." Mr. Graham demonstrated with boundless wealth of learning, and with resistless logic, that they were in conflict with the constitution and with the spirit of American liberty. There are many who differed in opinion from him upon the topics proper to be discussed, and the course of action recommended by him on that occasion; but, I think, that even they would allow, as he spoke that day on the great doctrines of civil liberty, so Somers and Camden would have spoken; and that the constitutional doctrines which he then laid down would have received the sanction of Madison and Marshall. I have read that speech recently and with care. I was impressed anew with its wide range, and its deep and mature learning; with the skill with which the topics are arranged and discussed; with the admirable temper which he preserves on the most exciting subjects; with his familiarity with the writings of political sages, whose weighty apothegms are scattered through it; with the high finish of certain passages; but above all with the dauntless spirit with which he maintains what, in his judgment, are the true principles of our Government.

The effect of this speech cannot be estimated. It aroused the people from their despondency; it animated them to new efforts; it went further, it infused into them the spirit with which the speech itself was instinct. From that day the Conservative Democratic party dates its existence in this State, as a regularly organized party; within a short time thereafter, it gained possession of the Legislature and has held it to the present time.

The Convention had directed that the Legislature should be convened. An election was accordingly held and the Legislature met in the winter of 1865. Mr. Graham was unanimously elected for the county of Orange, but, being unpardoned, he did not offer to take his seat. It was the universal desire of the people that he should represent the State in the Senate of the United States, when restored to its old relations. It was felt that North Carolina had no one more competent to vindicate her action or represent her interests. It was felt that she had no one who, by his balanced judgment, his temperance of feeling, his urbane bearing, would do more to mitigate the asperities which had been provoked by civil strife. He was elected by a large majority. Upon his election he repaired to Washington and presented his credentials. They were laid upon the table. He presented to the Senate a manly and respectful memorial; but he was never permitted to take his seat. The spectacle presented by the exclusion from public affairs of a man of his antecedents, while so many who had an active agency in bringing on civil strife, had been promoted to high station, arrested attention everywhere. Many of the most eminent men in the Northern States, used their best efforts for the removal of his disabilities, without effect. Political persecution, set on foot by parties in his own State, pursued him until it was placed beyond all human probability that he should ever enjoy the honors for which the State had destined him. When that had become a certainty, to wit, in 1873, his disabilities were removed. What reflections arise, as we recur to this passage of his life! Mr. Graham had clung to the constitution until the rising tide of secession had flowed around and completely insulated his state; to this ancient ark of our fathers he again clung when after the war the waves of political enthusiasm inundated the country and the constitution. Yet he was left stranded, while many of those who had fanned the tempest of both, found secure anchorage. But we look beyond today. The things seen are temporal in more senses than one. The impartial tribunal of posterity rises up before us. Then, when the actors of to-day are weighed in even scales; when the influence of passion and prejudice is unknown, then will the consistent devotion to principles by which his conduct was always actuated, receive its due meed of admiration and applause.

The State of North Carolina was, in 1870, the scene of events without a parallel in American history. The reconstruction government had then been in existence for two years; and though it introduced many changes in the organic law, changes repugnant to the great body of the people, it was now in quiet operation. Its authority was everywhere acknowledged; submission to it was universal. In the counties of Alamance and Caswell, acts of lawlessness, startling and exceptional, had occurred; but they nowhere took the form of resistance to law; they rather indicated the temper of a people driven to phrensy by actual or anticipated outrage. These acts were deeply deplored by all thoughtful men, who earnestly exerted themselves to put an end to them. At length, by their efforts, seconded by the presence of a company of United States troops in each of those counties, order and quiet were restored. It was now that the Governor, under authority of an act passed at the previous Legislature, declared by proclamation these counties in a state of insurrection. He then proceeded to levy troops, which, when raised, were marched into those counties. Here arrests were made of leading citizens, without charge and without process. When arrested, most of them were held in strict confinement; some were thrown into close prison. In some instances torture was resorted to, to extort accusation against themselves. To crown all, measures were being taken to organize courts-martial for the trial of the citizens thus arrested. To put a stop to proceedings so unexampled, recourse was had to that great birthright of English speaking people, the writ of Habeas corpus. Application for the writ was made to the Chief Justice, who promptly ordered the writ to be issued; but owing to the action of the Governor the benefit of the writ could not be obtained. A number of motions was submitted by the counsel for the prisoners, but each in turn proved nugatory. Finally a motion was made for a precept to be directed to the Sheriff—the precept to be executed by the power of the county. This the Chief Justice declined to grant, stating that in the then condition of things, such a proceeding "would plunge the country into civil war."

Hopeless now of obtaining any relief from the courts of the State, recourse was had to the courts of the United States. A petition for redress was made to his honor Judge Brooks of the District Court. The question of jurisdiction was argued by Mr. Graham, and other eminent counsel. The Judge at length, ordered the writ to be issued. The prisoners were brought up, and after the hearing, were discharged. It may be safely said that nothing has occurred since the war, which did more to rekindle the affections of the people of North Carolina toward the Government of their fathers, than the action of Judge Brooks in these cases.

The events thus briefly referred to, occurred in the midst of a profound peace. The courts held their regular sessions at the appointed times in the counties of Alamance and Caswell; and the processes of law ran unobstructed to every part of those counties. Political proscription there was none. The party of which the Governor was the head, held undisputed sway in those counties. The negroes voted at pleasure for the object of their choice. The public mind was profoundly moved by these proceedings. The sense of injury was deep; yet there was no open resistance—no tumultuary assemblages. The inborn reverence for law, which has prevailed in this State since the Revolution—since the adoption of popular institutions—everywhere asserted itself. The people waited to see what course two or three eminent citizens, who had been honored and trusted by them, would advise at this crisis. To Mr. Graham first and foremost, they instinctively turned. He advised a resort to none but constitutional remedies—first, an appeal to the people at the ballot-box; secondly, an arraignment of the Executive at the bar of the people. The success of such an appeal, he did not doubt. No statesman ever reposed greater confidence in the capacity and patriotism of the people. The result vindicated his judgment. The canvass of that summer turned upon the ursurpations and high-handed proceedings of the Governor. The election resulted in the return to the Legislature of a majority of two-thirds of the Conservative-Democratic party.

The adoption of the second step was more difficult. A vague but deep-seated dread, growing out of a recent experience of the power of the Federal Government, which had not returned to the old constitutional channel, from which it had been diverted by the war—pervaded the State. The Reconstruction Government, which owed its origin to the Federal Congress, had been recently established here. The Republican party had established that government,, and that party swayed the powers of the Federal Government in every department. Any action toward removing the highest official in the State, might be construed by that party into a menace against the Reconstruction Government, and lead to a speedy and decisive interposition. Mr. Graham did not participate in these apprehensions. His views are best expressed in his own words. "I do not believe," he said, "the Congress of the United States will depart from that Constitution under which we are now

living in harmony; and that when the State of North Carolina renewed her constitutional relations to the Federal Government, she
came back with all the rights and privileges of a sovereign State;
and that her State Senators and Representatives, when charged
with duties by the people, are to perform their functions under
the same responsibilities that belong to the Senators and Representatives of any State of the Union." These weighty views, in
which there was a general concurrence among the ablest and most
trusted public men of the State, prevailed. On the 14th of December, 1870, a resolution was adopted by the House of Representatives of North Carolina, that the Governor of North Carolina be
impeached of high crimes and misdemeanors. On the 23d of
December, the Court of Impeachment was duly organized, and
sat forty days. The judgment of the court was, that the Governor
be deposed from office, and forever disqualified from holding
any office of profit or trust in this State.

Mr. Graham was the first counsel named among the eminent
gentlemen of the Bar selected to assist the managers appointed
by the House; and he bore a principal part in the management
of the trial, and in the discussions of the various questions of evidence which arose in its progress. It was assigned to him to make
the first of the speeches in the final argument. In his exordium,
he used the language quoted above—language which embodied
the advice which he had given to the members of the Assembly
by whom he had been consulted when the impeachment resolution was pending. The passage which follows, addressed to the
Senators sitting in their judicial capacity, evidently lays down the
rule by which his own public life had been guided:

"For my own part, I have to say to every public man, in regard
to his public life, what the great poet represents the angel as
having said to our first ancestor:

'Nor love thy life, nor hate; but what thou livest
Live well, how long or short permit to heaven?' "

The feelings with which he approached this trial were in part
those of an elder generation. He was born and brought up among
a people conspicuous for their gallantry and sacrifices in the
Revolutionary War. The section in which they lived was singled
out by the British historians as that which was the most active
and inveterate in its hostility. His own ancestry in that section
had given the best years of their life—had offered their means

without limit—had shed their blood on many fields for the assertion of the great principles of liberty. The establishment of a
free government was to him the dearly bought acquisition of his
patriotic sires, to be transmitted to children's children. The great
principles of liberty embodied in the Bill of Rights and in the
Constitution were a part of his personal inheritance. Any usurpation of power by the government, any encroachment upon the
rights of the people, he regarded as an invasion of his own birthright—as a personal wrong and grievance.

All such usurpations and encroachments he brought to a standard, just, if severe. Political science had been one of the favorite
studies of his life. In the history of government of every kind he
was well versed. He regarded a well ordered State as the highest
achievement of man. He knew that two thousand years ago, man
had carried the arts and many branches of science to the highest
pitch of perfection. He knew that no free government could boast
an existence of more than two hundred years. As well regulated
liberty was the latest gift of time, so its value was above all others
to be prized. It was that which gave value to everything else; since
upon that value of everything else depends. A blow in this direction, involving all that men prize and cherish, was to be redressed
by the heaviest and most lasting of civil penalties.

The speech of Mr. Graham in this trial was one of very great
ability. With the feelings to which I have referred, it might have
been anticipated that he would occasionally launch out into
denunciation and invective against one who had trodden under
foot the Constitution and laws, and defied the Chief Justice of the
State. But amidst the intensity of his feelings, his wonted self-
command did not for a moment desert him. It was a trial of one
who had been charged with the grossest violations of the highest
of human rights; and it was plainly his purpose that no sentence,
phrase or word of his should afford ground for the assertion that
political animosity or prejudice had aught to do with the judgment, which he believed would be pronounced by the high court
before which the Executive was arraigned. That judgment should
be the irresistable dictate of reason, one in which the feelings
should have no share. This occasion admits of no extended analysis of that speech; but I cannot refrain from saying that, for
clear and masterly statement of the several charges embraced in
the articles of impeachment; for skillful analysis of the testimony,
and of the specious pretences urged in defence, which, combined
with a dextrous array of facts and authorities, seemed to promise

immunity to the accused; for the force and power with which all these were sifted, exposed and refuted; above all for the constitutional and common law learning, so apposite, so conclusive, poured forth in the course of that speech, it deserves a high place among the best efforts of that kind. So completely was every point of law and fact covered by Mr. Graham, that the eminent counsel who concluded on behalf of the managers, confined himself to a re-statement of the positions taken by him, and to such further discussion as was rendered necessary in reply. That speech will not fail to be studied, whenever the great principles of government then involved, shall come to be again defended here.

As has been said, he was not permitted to take his seat in the Senate of the United States. But while he was debarred the enjoyment of those honors which his State would have conferred upon him, he was the recipient of other honors of the highest kind—honors which the highest in earthly estate might have envied.

Mr. Peabody, whose great heart had been moved by the misfortunes of the Southern people, conceived the idea of employing some portion of the princely fortune with which providence had blessed him for the permanent benefit of that people. He was a Northern man by birth, and as such had little sympathy with the ends which the South sought to accomplish by the war. But he knew that our fathers had fought for an idea in the war of independence, and that the South had fought for an idea in the civil war; he could not recognize that as guilt in us, which was a source of pride and boast in our common ancestors. He contemplated no mere eleemosynary institution; a people who had exhibited such constancy and valor as they had displayed during the war—though great suffering among them was inevitable—could not long want aid of that kind. But the interest of education at the South had not kept pace with the same interest at the North, where the people were homogeneous, and where the efforts of all were directed to that end. The apprehension felt—too surely justified by the result—was, that when the people of the South came to estimate their losses by the war, the sense of these losses, coupled with their poverty, would lead to still further neglect of that most important interest. It was to the interest of education, then, that the great philanthropist resolved to address his beneficence. His plan required the interposition of trustees, and it was necessary that they should be men eminent for abilities and virtue and of national reputation. Mr. Graham, in whom all these requisites met, was one of the three or four trustees selected from the South. Through a common friend, the Hon. Mr. Winthrop, of Massachusetts, Mr. Graham was invited to meet Mr. Peabody and two or three other gentlemen in February, 1867, in the city of Washington. The result is well known. The beneficent plan was put in operation, and now yields its valuable fruits to thousands of the children of our land. Mr. Graham entered warmly into Mr. Peabody's views. He attended with great regularity the meetings of the board of trustees, and participated in all its counsels. He seconded the resolutions which were adopted by the board upon the death of the great Philanthropist, and then gave expression in fit and eloquent words to the sense of his loss here felt. The South has no means to commemorate her gratitude to this illustrious man in "statues, storied urns or animated busts," but his benefactions have sunk deep into the hearts of our people, and the honor with which his name is everywhere mentioned among us, is, perhaps, the noblest monument to his fame.

Sometime after, he received another marked testimonial to the high esteem in which he was held by States as well as individuals. The boundary line between the states of Virginia and Maryland had long been undefined, and had produced embarrassment in the administration of the laws within the disputed limits, and, in some conflicting interests, had nearly led to a collision between citizens of the two States. It was determined to adjust the matter by arbitration. The grand old Commonwealth of Virginia—grander in the virtues which she has displayed in her misfortunes, than those which she exhibited in her prosperity; insomuch that we check the current of compassion for her misfortunes, in the thought that the world will be the better for the example which she has afforded under adversity—confided her interests to Mr. Graham. Some meetings took place between him and the arbitrator selected by the State of Maryland; but no award had been rendered at the date of his death, and the matter was left unadjusted.

In the year 1875—upon the 4th of February—he presided over a meeting held in Charlotte, to take steps for the proper celebration of the Centennial of the Mecklenburg Declaration of Independence. Some writers of ability had seized upon that event, and in that spirit of historical skepticism so rife in our days, had undertaken, out of a few minor discrepancies, to deny the genuineness of the Declaration, or that any meeting was held on the 20th of May. Mr. Graham had been often solicited to place that event upon its proper basis. He had heard it often talked of at his father's fire side; he knew all the traditions connected with it; he had known and talked with many of the subscribers of that Declaration; he was well acquainted with public opinion regarding it, in that section where the event occurred, down to the date of its publication in 1820. For a long time, motives of delicacy, growing out of his connection with some of the principal actors, restrained him. But, at that time, all the actors had passed away; they could no longer be heard; and a just regard for their fame urged his acquiescence. He embodied his vindication in the form of an address which he delivered on this occasion. No fair synopsis of that address is possible; it is a solid, compact argument which would be greatly impaired by any attempt at abridgment. Let it suffice to say that the evidence is arrayed in the spirit of the philosophical historian, and with the skill of a consummate lawyer. It will not put to silence the mere caviller; no amount of evidence will, on this or any other subject; but the candid inquirer will rise from his perusal with the conviction that few events in history rest upon a firmer foundation than the Mecklenburg Declaration of Independence.

Mr. Graham left behind many literary essays, but none which were prompted by mere desire for literary distinction. His efforts of this kind were all the result of passing events; all the fruit of hours snatched from an absorbing profession. Yet if collected together they would form a considerable volume; and if we consider their contents they give a high idea of the intellect which could find its relaxation in such labors. The dominant feeling of his life was loyalty to the State and her institutions; hence the subjects usually selected by him were drawn from her history.

Among these was a lecture delivered at Greensboro in 1860. The citizens of that section of country, of which Greensboro, is the centre, contemplated the erection of a monument to commemorate the services of Gen. Greene in the Revolutionary struggle. This lecture was delivered in aid of the enterprise, and embraced a life of Greene and a history of Revolutionary events in this State. A copy was solicited for publication, but from some cause it was never published. It remains in manuscript, full and entire, as if prepared for the press. Here may be mentioned the two Memorial Addresses—the one upon the life and character of Hon. George E. Badger, and the other of Hon. Thomas Ruffin. These fine Addresses, which have received the commendations of many of the most competent judges, North and South, are too fresh in the recollection of all to need any comment.

This record would be most imperfect, did it fail to bring into the most prominent relief, the services of Mr. Graham in his office of trustee of the University. He regarded the University as the best ornament of the State, and no one of all its sons nursed it with a more devoted or wiser care. He attended all its commencements, and was most active in watching over all its interests. No one labored with more zeal for its restoration to the control of the true sons of the State. For many years he was a member of the Executive Committee, and at the time of his death he was the Chairman of that Committee. It was to him, finally, that Gov. Swain in the last years of his successful administration, looked for direction and support in all its trials and embarrassments.

"It is not unusual for men of eminence," said Judge Story[15] "after having withdrawn from the Bar, to find it difficult, if not impracticable, to resume their former rank in business." Mr. Graham experienced no such difficulty. Though often called from his profession to public station, at the first court at which he appeared after his term of office expired, he was retained in all important causes, and business flowed in upon him thenceforth as if he had never been absent. In common with all the people of the South, his resources had been somewhat impaired by the war, and when civil Government was restored, he resumed the practice of his profession with more than his wonted ardor. He returned to all the courts of his former circuit; the business of which had greatly increased by the general settlement of all previous transactions which took place after the war. The business of the circuit and district courts—both which he regularly attended—had been greatly enlarged by the new system of revenue laws and other changes introduced by the war, but, above all, by the bankruptcy laws then recently enacted. These with appeals to the Supreme Court of the State, and appeals to the Supreme Court of the United States increased his labors, protracted his absences from home, and left him few intervals for repose. It was felt by his friends that he was overtaxing his strength by these great exertions, but there was no abatement of his energies until about a year before his death. Symptoms then appeared which inspired deep apprehensions. It seemed but too certain that disease had fixed itself upon some of the great organs of life. He

---

[15] "Miscellaneous Writings" Sketch of Hon. Samuel Dexter.

now gave up attendance upon courts, but still watched over the progress of his causes, and labored in the preparation of briefs— the causes themselves being argued by his son Maj. Graham. He was pre-eminently a worker and he continued to work to the end. At length the symptoms became more distressing, and he repaired to Philadelphia to consult the eminent physicians of that city. The result confirmed the opinion before entertained, that his malady was disease of the heart. Upon his return home he continued his labors in his office. It was only under physical exertion that his malady gave him trouble; when in repose he was capable of as great mental efforts as ever.

At this period of comparative inaction, that fortunate destiny which presided over his life was constant to him still. The pain, which was incident to his malady, was only felt at intervals, and then was not severe. Apart from this, there was every possible compensation. Besides the department of professional labor still left to him, he had the boundless resources of literature, ancient and modern, which in the busiest periods of his life he had always cultivated and justly prized. Every day, moreover, brought to him in the visits of friends, or through the mails, in newspapers and letters, some new testimonial of esteem and regard, public or private. But above any and all of these, he could now enjoy without interruption those pleasures, in which, amidst his most brilliant successes he ever found his chief happiness, the pleasures of home and its sweet endearments.

Mr. Graham had been nominated by acclamation by the people of Orange for the Constitutional Convention which sat in September, 1875, but the state of his health rendered it impossible for him to undergo the labors of the canvass. This was not needed on his own account, but his absence from the hustings was regretted on account of the Convention cause. He published, however, a strong address to his constituents; which was widely circulated, and had an important influence on the result.

A meeting of the boundary Commissioners had been arranged to take place at Saratoga Springs, in the State of New York, in the month of August, 1875. Thither Mr. Graham accordingly went, accompanied by Mrs. Graham and his youngest son. For many days he appeared to be in his usual health; but a great change was at hand. After an evening spent with his friends, whose society he enjoyed with more than his wonted zest, he retired a little beyond his accustomed hour. Soon after, the symptoms of his disease recurred in aggravated form. Physicians were summoned who ministered promptly, but ineffectually. Meantime the news of his situation spread, and messages of inquiry and offers of personal services testified to the general and deep concern. But all that science and the most affectionate solicitude could suggest proved unavailing. He expired at 6 o'clock on the morning of Wednesday, the 11th of August, 1875.

It had long been believed, by those who knew him best, that Mr. Graham was at heart a Christian. It is with inexpressible gratification, I am able to add, that when approached on this subject during the last days of his life, he freely expressed his hope of salvation through our crucified Redeemer.

The intelligence of his death was transmitted by telegraph to every part of the country. All the great journals responded with leading articles expressive of the national bereavement. Numerous meetings were held—meetings of the bar, meetings of citizens, meetings of political opponents—for political enemies he had none —to give their estimate of the illustrious deceased, and to speak their sense of his loss. The states of Virginia and Maryland, with that high sense of delicacy which marks all their public acts, took care that the remains of one who had stood in such honored relations to each, should be conveyed with due honor across their bounds. At the borders of our State they were received by a committee appointed by the Bar of Raleigh; by a committee appointed by the Mayor and common council of that city, and by a committee from Hillsborough, and conveyed by special train to Raleigh. There they were received by appointed committees—by the Raleigh Light Infantry, by the Raleigh Light Artillery—of both of which companies he was an honorary member—by the United States troops from Camp Russell, and accompanied by a great concourse of the citizens, conveyed to the capitol. There the remains were deposited in the rotunda, which was draped in mourning for the occasion. Late in the afternoon of the same day they were conveyed with similar ceremonies to the Central Station. From thence, attended by the Raleigh companies, and by special guards of honor, appointed by cities and towns of the State, and by the family of the deceased, they were conveyed by special train to the station at Hillsboro. From thence they were escorted, with the addition of the whole population of the town, to his mansion, where they lay in state till the noon of Sunday the 15th. At that hour they were conveyed to the Presbyterian Church, and after appropriate funeral services, were interred with solemn ceremony amid an immense concourse gathered from many counties, in the grave-yard of that Church.

The intellect of Mr. Graham was of a rare order. For the business of life, public and private, it may be said to have been perfect. Though in the endowments of genius—taking that word in its extended sense—he assuredly was not wanting; yet, like all who have accomplished much, he trusted little to its unaided impulses and suggestions. Very seldom did he call to his aid the powers of imagination in his speeches or writings. The bent of his genius did not lead him to indulge in vivid painting, glowing imagery or bold contrasts. With this faculty so restrained we would not seek in his speeches for passages of the highest oratorical merit. In them will be found none of those high-wrought appeals, invocations or adjurations in which the orator gives utterance to excited feelings; nothing which would show the man possessed and transported by his theme; nothing of that passion which passes by electric communication from the speaker to the hearer and bears him along by a force that is irresistible. It was in the resources of a clear, capacious and powerful understanding, sustained and enlarged by a special and inborn capability for labor, that he centered his strength. In him was seen, not one possessed by his theme, but one who was master of himself and his theme; not one who would hurry his hearers along despite themselves, but one who by persuasion would lead, and who by argument would convince his audience.[16] If then, his hearers missed some of those more striking forms of thought in which imagination delights, they were more than compensated [16] by the freer play and wider scope thus given to the powers of reason. In this respect the demands of the judgment were completely satisfied. In truth, for the purposes of the lawyer and the Statesman, he was all the better for this abstinent use of a faculty which, while it brightens and adorns, too often misleads—too often presents truth through a colored and false medium. Truth took no color in his mind from false lights, intellectual or moral. It was this constitution of mind—this habitual ward and absolute control over every faculty that could mislead—which, united with a singular equanimity of temper gave him a power in which he was surpassed by no one; the power of seeing things in their true proportions—of seeing things precisely as they are. It was this moral and mental equili-

---

[16] This was in strict observance of one of the rules enjoined by the severe taste of the Attic orators. "The orator must always show that he was master of himself, and never was run away with by the vehemence of the moment."—*Lord Broughton's Dissertation on the Eloquence of the Ancients.*

brium which gave him a judgment which, in the affairs of life seemed never to err. Hence it was that he was the trusted counsellor of every friend in difficulty; often of the Executive and of the Legislature of the State in cases of doubt and embarrassment; always of the people in every time of political trouble.

The place which will be awarded him in the ranks of orators will not be the highest. Indeed at oratorical effects, purely as such, he never aimed. There is no doubt, but that he might have employed the resources of oratory, other than the very highest, to a much greater extent than he did. All who have heard him in capital trials and on other occasions when great interests were at stake, were persuaded that he possessed reserved resources of this kind to which he did not give play, and which he could have called into requisition at will. That he refrained was matter of deliberate judgment. He preferred to address himself to the understanding. He relied wholly upon argument, disdaining the adjuncts of mere rhetoric. He knew that the triumphs of reason are more durable than those which are the offspring of excited feeling. Reaction and change follow the latter: the former leave full, permanent conviction.

As a parliamentary speaker and as an advocate he stood in the first rank. His style was that which finds so much favor among eminent English Statesmen, that style in which the results of thought and research are given with the warmth and ease of animated and unpremeditated conversation.[17] In this style of speaking, supreme excellence is more difficult to attain than in any other. It demands a perfect mastery of the subject; entire possession of all the faculties of the mind; and a command of language copious, pure and idiomatic. Such speakers address themselves professedly to the judgment. They challenge criticism, and seek no protection from those fervors of feeling which it is the object of the orator to excite. In this style of speaking he was a model.

In addition to his high intellectual endowments, nature had to him, been profuse in external gifts. In person he was the ideal of the patrician. His features regular and classic in their outline, would have satisfied a sculptor. The habitual expression of his face was one of blended thought, refinement and quiet will. His form was noble and commanding; cast, indeed, in nature's finest mould. These advantages were set off by a dress always scrupu-

---

[17] Sir James McIntosh remarked, that "the true light in which to consider speaking in the House of Commons was as an animated conversation on public business, and that it was rare for any speech to succeed which was raised on any other basis. Canning joined in this opinion. *London Quarterly Review,* April, 1858.

lously neat, and sufficiently conformed to the prevailing mode to escape observation. The advantages, thus slightly touched upon, were singularly calculated to impress favorably the mind of any audience. If we add that he appeared before every audience with the prestige of a character, which calumny itself would own to be without a blemish, the causes of his uniform success are easy to discern.

In his discussions whether of the Senate or of the Forum, no man was ever freer from any of those intellectual artifices to which speakers sometimes resort. He approached his adversary's stronghold by no circuitous lines; he practiced no feints to draw off attention from his own weak points. Indirection of any kind was foreign to his nature. There were no bold attacks, no sudden onsets. His speeches were always clear, strong, convincing; on great occasions they resembled a triumphal march—a quiet but imposing display of strength. In intellectual conflicts his self-possession never failed him. If his antagonist, in his assault upon his position, chanced to carry any of his out-works, he referred to it, with an easy, careless indifference that impressed all hearers with the idea that his opponent had misdirected his attack, and thrown away his strength. The effect of this temporary advantage being thus weakened or destroyed, he threw out some brief, pregnant suggestion, which served to fortify anew the damaged point. At the Bar his case was always presented in its strongest aspect. The leading principles of law were clearly enunciated. His discussions of them were clear, pointed and full. He then proceeded to support the case from the testimony adduced. In this respect he was unsurpassed. His mind had been subjected to such thorough discipline, that it worked with mechanical ease and accuracy. The evidence, however multifarious, fell at once into due order and compact array. His vast acquaintance with the business of life in every phase, enabled him to see in facts a significance and bearing that would be perceived by few, and to use and apply them in a way at once ingenious, startling and legitimate. His insight into character—originally keen, and so improved by contact with men in every class of life that it had grown into an intuition—was brought to bear with decisive effect in every case of conflicting testimony. In such cases he reasoned upon the motives of men with almost irresistible force and power.

He cherished the highest idea of the dignity of his profession, and his practice of it was regulated by the most exalted principles. The rule of professional conduct laid down by Lord Brougham, as counsel for Queen Caroline, it will be remembered, was as follows: "An advocate, by the sacred duty which he owes to his client, knows in the discharge of that office but one person in the world, and none other. To save that client by all expedient means—to protect that client at all hazards and cost to all others, and among others to himself—is the highest and most unquestioned of his duties; and he must not regard the alarm, the suffering, the torment, the destruction which he may bring upon any other." This rule he condemned and repudiated. His own conduct was conformed to the principles laid down by Lord Langdale in Hutchinson *vs.* Stephens: "No counsel supposes himself to be the mere advocate or agent of his client to gain a victory, if he can, on a particular occasion. The zeal and arguments of every counsel, knowing what is due to himself and his honorable profession, are qualified not only by considerations affecting his own character as a man of honor, experience and learning, but also by considerations affecting the general interests of justice." Within the domain of the principles here announced, there never lived a counsel who exceeded him in zeal, fidelity and constancy to the interests of his client, or in unflagging hope in his final triumph.

He possessed in many respects the temperament of a great commander. As difficulties thickened around him, his courage seemed to rise, and his resources to develop. No man ever fought a losing cause with more courage and constancy. When in important cases the tide of testimony unexpectedly turned and flowed dead against him, there was nothing in his look or manner that betrayed the change. His attention would be redoubled, but in all else there was so much of calm composure, that lookers on, inattentive to the evidence, have left the Court House under the impression that he would gain the cause. He preserved under all circumstances in the trial of causes, the lofty tenor of his bearing.. He was never betrayed into an altercation with witnesses. It may be that awe of his character, and a consciousness of his practiced sagacity and penetration constrained witnesses, when in his hands, to an unwonted utterance of the truth. This impression may have been assisted, and probably was, by the fairness and integrity observable in his whole bearing. But whatever the cause, it is certain he never resorted to boisterous tones or a brow-beating manner. Equally removed was his manner from all the arts of cajolery. In his examination of the most refractory witness, his mien was calm, his look observant and penetrating, his voice never or but slightly raised above its ordinary tone. In such a contest, the contest between acute, disciplined reason, and cunning or obstinate knavery, the victory was always on the side of the former.

In his moral constitution he was complete on every side. All his conduct in life was regulated not only by the highest sense of honor, but by the most scrupulous sense of duty. This supreme sense of duty in everything that he did, whether great or small, was his distinguishing characteristic. From his cradle to his grave, not a shadow of a shade ever rested upon him. Esteeming a stainless character as the highest of all earthly possessions, he exercised the most scrupulous caution in his judgment of others. Few men were more often in the public arena. He took part in all the political canvasses of his time; in many of which partisan feeling was inflamed to the highest pitch. Yet he never assailed the motives of his opponent and never left any feeling of personal injury rankling in his bosom. He always contended for principle, and disdained to use any argument which reason would not sanction.

In debate, he was a model of candor, and whoever might be his opponent he would always accept Mr. Graham's statement of his position. In all his intellectual conflicts, whether at the Bar, on the Hustings or in the Senate, under no provocation was he ever excited to an unseemly exhibition of temper. "Although," said a gentleman of high distinction who knew him long and well:[18] "Although I have been present at the Bar and upon other public occasions when he must have been greatly tried, I have never seen his countenance degraded by an expression of passion. His look may at times have been stern and high, but at all times it could with advantage have been committed to marble or canvass."

It was the opinion of that eminent lawyer, Archibald Henderson, that public men should mingle much with the people—that there is to be found the true school of common sense. Either because he held the same opinion, but more probably from inclination, his intercourse with the people was constant and cordial. When in attendance on his courts it was his custom when the day was fine to repair, after the adjournment of court, to the portico of his hotel, or the lawn in front of it, and sit for an hour or two. This was often his custom after the evening meal, usually served in his circuit at hours primitively early. Here he

---

[18] Hon. S. F. Phillips.

became the centre of a group of citizens all of whom he received
with courtesy. The talk on such occasions was free and general;
and whatever the topic, he listened to their views with attention,
and in turn frankly gave his own. Thus his information in regard
to all matters of general interest was minute and particular. It
was thus too that he became informed as to the current opinion
in regard to public men and public measures. This intimate
knowledge of the people was one of the great sources of his
strength, it rendered his judgment of the probable fate of State
and National questions of great value. His judgment upon such
matters, in the counties in which his circuit lay, was almost infallible.

In his social relations Mr. Graham was one of the most attractive of men. Few had so wide a circle of friends, or friends so
attached. His manner to all men was urbane; to his friends cordial and sincere. There was, except to a very few, and at times
even to them, a shade of reserve in his manners; but there was
nothing of pride, nothing expressive of conscious superiority.
There was great dignity, tempered by unfailing courtesy. Perhaps this tinge of reserve made his subsequent unbending the
more agreeable. In his social hours, in the long winter evenings
at Court, with the circle gathered around the blazing hearth—it
is as he was then seen, that his friends love best to recall him. For
many years, there met together at one of his courts a number of
gentlemen of high intellectual gifts and attainments. These were
the Hon. Robert Gilliam, the Hon. Abram W. Venable, the
present Judge of the 7th circuit, and others less known. With
such men there was no need that any limitations should be imposed on the conversation. Except in the field of exact science
they were very much at home in all. The conversations ranged
wide, law, cases in court, history, biography, politics—largely
interspersed with anecdotes—formed the topics. But rich as the
repast was in all respects, the part which possessed the highest
interest was that which was individual to each; the wit which
flashed and faded away; the humor which played so felicitously
in its legitimate sphere; reminiscences of personal incidents, reminiscences of celebrated persons and events—the latter so invaluable to the historian and biographer. Of the latter kind the contributions made by Mr. Graham were of pre-eminent interest
and value, since his theatre of action had been higher and wider.
Had those conversations been taken down as they occurred, they
would have formed a work, which, beside the exquisite charms of

wit and humor, for the light which it would have thrown on life and manners, for shrewd observation of character, for striking remarks upon subjects, moral social and political, would have been surpassed by few in English literature.

I have thus placed before you a brief and imperfect sketch of this illustrious man—how imperfect no one knows better than myself. It is a sketch of one eminently favored of nature in his personal and intellectual gifts; of one upon whom fortune delighted to bestow her choicest favors. He was the recipient of every honor, except those voluntarily declined, which his state could confer. He received high honors from the National Government, and was designated by all but a majority of his countrymen for the place second in rank in that Government. He was one of the few selected out of forty millions of people, to carry out the most comprehensive scheme of benevolence, that individual philanthropy ever framed for the human race. And when a controversy arose between two great States, second in lustre to none in the Union, it was to his arbitrament and that of two others that this quasi-national question was submitted. To few of the sons of men have been allotted so splendid a career. There is enough here, and more than enough to satisfy the aspirations of the loftiest ambition. But in the contemplation of that life he must be blind indeed who does not see that the moral rises high over the intellectual grandeur. The moral dignity of man never received a higher illustration than in the life before us. We admire the pure Patriot in whose thoughts the State—her weal and her glory—was ever uppermost; the learned Jurist who from his ample stores informed and moulded the laws of his own commonwealth; the eloquent Advocate who stood always ready to redress the wrong, whether of the individual or the community at large; the wise Statesman who swayed the destinies of his State more than any of his generation. But we render the unfeigned homage of the heart to him, who by the majesty of his moral nature, passed pure and unsullied through the wide circles of trials and conflicts embraced in his life; and who, in his death, has left a fame that will be an incentive and a standard to the generous youth of North Carolina, through all the ages that are to come.

WILLIAM ALEXANDER GRAHAM [1]

By FRANK NASH [2]

INTRODUCTION

"Office is the most natural and proper sphere of a public man's ambition, as that in which he can most freely use his powers for the common good of his country." — Lord Palmerston.

In recent years it has been the endeavor of some writers to strain the facts of history a little in order that North Carolina may appear to have been first in some great political, or other, movement. This not only makes our State motto an hypocrisy, but it has no sound moral basis, is untrue in fact, and is foolish from the standpoint of philosophy. That she was first at Bethel was an accident; that she was farthest at Gettysburg and last at Appomattox, means daring, but steady, courage and staunch unfailing fidelity. Indeed the things in which she was last have done her more credit than those in which she was first. I do not like to think of her as a meretricious, volatile, impulsive figure, but as a noble, steadfast one, unadorned (certainly by gewgaws and jim-cracks), and like the Mother of the Gracci pointing to her sons as her jewels. Certainly she has a right to be proud of them, for, at no time from the days of Glasgow to the days of the Carpetbagger and from the days of the Carpetbagger to the present, did any of these sons prey upon her. Peculation and fraud in public life may have existed elsewhere, but not in North Carolina.

In this paper I try to depict one of those sons as the most prominent figure amid the scenes in which he lived and worked, and in the company of those who lived and worked with him. I want, too, to show what he was and what he stood for, as well as what he did, for it is not so much the material as it is the spiritual, that gives to men real power and renders them immortal. Not that activity and energy are to be contemned, far from it—slothful

[1] *Address at the Unveiling of the Bust of William A. Graham, by the North Carolina Historical Commission, in the Rotunda of the State Capitol, delivered in the Hall of the House of Representative, January 12, 1910.* (Raleigh: Edwards and Broughton Printing Co., 1910. pp. 94.) (The footnotes in this original publication have been renumbered so as to run consecutively. Ed.)

[2] Frank Nash (1885-1932), lawyer, author, State Senator, 1915, Assistant Attorney General, 1918-1931.

in business can never be predicated of the truly great and good—but because it is the subtle and silent, but pervading, influence of character, only, that gives action, force and efficiency for good.

The story of William A. Graham's life is well worth the telling for what he did, but much more for what he was. The writer is very conscious that it has not been told adequately in the following pages. The final word about him cannot be said until his literary remains are collected and published with his correspondence.

HIS ANTECEDENTS

William A. Graham was no less fortunate in the race from which he sprang than in his immediate ancestry. The Scotch Presbyterians, located in Ireland by James I, and the English by Cromwell, made that composite race which has been for some time known to history as the Scotch-Irish. During three or four generations they lived in Ireland among a people hostile in faith and differing in language, in ideals, in aims and in temperament. The Saxon was the representative of a stern, unyielding, but essentially uplifting Calvinism, while the Celt was the representative of all the superstition and ignorance of an unenlightened Romanism. The one had a faith so clear, so earnest, so vital that, in his worship he discarded nearly all symbol, while the other's faith was so obscured by false conceptions that only a sensuous and symbolic worship could appeal to his inferior nature; the one, even in his superstitions, dealing only with things supernal, while the other made to himself graven images, likenesses of things in heaven above and in the earth beneath, and bowed down to them and worshiped them; the one industrious and thrifty, doing with all his might what his hands found to do, the other thriftless, industrious only by fits and starts, content, in the midst of degrading poverty, to live among swine and fowls; the one sensitive about his rights, and ready in the fear of God to defend them with a calm, cool, unflinching courage; the other, a serf to his lord, a child to his priest, a willing servant to his friend and a savage to his foe, his emotions a sensitive harp that responded to every wind of passion.[3]

---

[3] It must be remembered that the Irish of the 17th century had only reached a stage of racial development, through which their Saxon foes had passed 200 years before. So this parallel has to do only with such developments, and not at all with racial capabilities.

What wonder that the contact of two such races should result only in an antagonism which manifested itself, on occasions, in murders, in riots and in relentless warfare! But all this was to the Saxon a tonic, stimulating his intellectual, moral and physical development, making him the bolder, the more watchful, the more self-reliant. He was a minority of the people of Ireland, but it was a militant and dominant minority. So little brought in contact with the English government was he, that he was fast becoming republican in his political ideals. Kings and governors were kings and governors to him only so long as they obeyed the laws and were faithful to the rights of the people. Otherwise he cared nothing for them. His liberty consisted in laws made by the consent of the people, and the due execution of those laws. He was free not from the law but by the law. So these English and Scotch Protestants in Ireland, these Saxons in Celt land, were, in their dealings with the Irish unconsciously fitting themselves for their greater work in America. It was, so to say, a forty years sojourn in the wilderness in preparation for the land of Canaan, and they entered that land strong in the holy confidence that, "the Lord, He it is that doth go before thee; He will be with thee; He will not fail thee, neither forsake thee; fear not, neither be dismayed."

Of this sturdy and virile race was James Graham, who at the age of nineteen years, in 1773, migrated from County Down, Ireland, to Berks County, Pennsylvania. He was twice married, his second wife being the widow Mary Barber, and died in 1763. By the last marriage there were five children. In 1768 Mrs. Graham, with her children, coming by sea to Charleston, S. C., thence across country, located in Mecklenburg County, N. C. In 1771 she purchased a tract of land containing two hundred acres within three miles of the then little hamlet of Charlotte. Most of these Scotch-Irish, and there were many of them, migrated from Pennsylvania south in search of fertile lands in a milder climate. It is probable that this was Mrs. Graham's motive, induced thereto also by the fact that many of her neighbors and friends had preceded her. She must have been a woman of remarkable courage and strength of character to undertake this long, tedious and dangerous journey with six young children, the youngest scarcely more than four years of age. No doubt she selected the actual location with a view to the religious and educational priviledges convenient to it. John Frohock, Abraham Alexander and Thomas Polk had already laid off the town of

Charlotte into 360 half-acre lots, and on some of these good, habitable houses had been erected. Eighty lots had been sold and must be built upon within three years, under pain of forfeiture. [4] So with the court-house, prison and stocks there, with tradesmen and artisans plying their trades, and lawyers locating to practice their profession, Charlotte at the time of its incorporation, November, 1768, must have been attracting some attention as a place with a future. Many of the settlements about the county, too, were fertile, fruitful, well tended farms. The rule, however, was here, as it was in all these Scotch-Irish communities, the man to the plow, the woman to the distaff and the child to the school. Mrs. Graham, though of limited means, after giving her children such instruction as she was capable of doing, sent most of them to the best school in this section, Queen's Museum, afterwards Liberty Hall. She instilled into all of them a love for learning and a desire to acquire knowledge. Her sons were among the most prominent men of their time, and probably came into public notice at an earlier age than any other youths of the county. Her daughters were the heads of families whose descendants are known for their virtue and intelligence, and have ever been prominent in the communities in which they lived on account of their worth and public spirit. She was, herself a faithful Presbyterian, member of Sugar Creek church, and her children were noted not only for their intelligence and activity in worldly matters, but were also earnest supporters of morality and religion. [5]

Her third son, Joseph Graham, was born in Chester County, Pennsylvania, October 13th, 1759. He assisted in cultivating his mother's farm and attended school in Charlotte. He was distinguished among his fellow-students for talents, industry and manly bearing. The mere schooling, though, was not the most valuable training that he had at that period. In the political ferment of the time, 1768-1776, the minds of men were expanding. At every church gathering, at every county court, they discussed the power of parliament, the rights of the colonies, and how best to preserve those rights. These discussions were going on throughout all the colonies, making every intelligent man a politician, and causing the patriots in the face of threatened danger to draw closer together in sympathy, thus paving the way for future organization. Patrick Henry, in Virginia, was but

---

[4] State Records of North Carolina, XXIII, 772-3.
[5] Graham: Revolutionary Papers of General Joseph Graham, 16.

giving eloquent utterance to the aspirations and hopes and ambitions of the people, unexpressed, or inadequately expressed, by themselves. He was, in other words, but the mouthpiece of, and interpreter for, the people. The intelligent boy or youth, standing about in these crowds, listening to these discussions among his elders, was having his own ideas enlarged, his patriotism aroused and his mind trained for his future work. Joseph Graham was interested in all these discussions and attended many of these public meetings. He, as a boy in the 16th year of his age, was present at the adoption of the Mecklenburg Resolves of May, 1775. Fifty-five years later he gives an account of this meeting and testifies that it was held on May 20th. At this distance of time, without any contemporary record to verify his memory, there are errors in his statement which subsequently-discovered records show. In several instances, he mistakes the time of events that he undertakes to narrate, but he and others have so completely identified May 20th as the date upon which some resolutions were adopted, that, in the absence of better evidence we may assume that a meeting was held on that day, in order to take some action upon the news of the Battle of Lexington, which, we know, arrived that week, the 20th occuring on Saturday. And it makes no difference whether they met on Friday the 19th and continued the meeting over until 2 a. m. of the 20th, or met on Saturday morning the 20th, so far as the essential fact is concerned, that a meeting was held at that time and that certain resolutions were adopted. Confining the issue to this essential fact, I have seen nothing that contradicts the testimony of the many eye-witnesses on that point. We can imagine the excitement and anger among these descendants of the bold defenders of Londonderry and Enniskillen at the news of Lexington, how they would hold a public meeting as soon as the crowd could gather, how in the anger and excitement of the moment they should adopt resolutions, which on calm second thought they would realize were premature and unwise. That there were two meetings at least, is perfectly apparent from the fact that the papers of which J. McKnitt Alexander had the custody were resolutions adopted at a public meeting of which he was secretary, whereas those of the 31st were adopted at a committee meeting, Ephraim Brevard being the secretary of that committee. The resolutions of the 31st, too, necessarily presupposes a previous meeting, or meetings. They are not the product of a day or of a week. They were not devised by one mind or written by one hand. They show calm deliberation, and not emotional excitement or sudden anger, such as that provoked by the news of the Battle of Lexington. It seems to me, with deference, that the modern historians have taken issue on immaterial facts and have obtained a verdict on those issues alone. Captain Jack did not take the resolutions of the 20th to Philadelphia; he did not take those of the 31st. Admitted, because proven. Governor Martin sent those of the 31st, and not those of the 20th, to London. Admitted, because proven. There was no contemporary record, or allusion to those of the 20th; there were both to those of the 31st. True, also, so far as discovered. The resolutions written down from memory by J. McKnitt Alexander in 1800, show in their verbiage the influence of the Declaration of July 4th 1776. This, too, is probably true. We have been mistaken heretofore in regard to these matters, it is true, yet after all, none of them is essential to the determination of the true issue—was there a meeting held on the 20th with resolutions which amounted to a Declaration of Independence adopted? And to this there are a cloud of witnesses. The writer, when not more than half as old as was General Graham at this time, was told of General Lee's surrender by a lady, while we were near an osage orange hedge, and while she was talking a raccoon came from under the hedge. If he should live a thousand years he will never forget the fact of the coon, the expression of his countenance, and his connection with General Lee's surrender. Now, the news of the Battle of Lexington was to Joseph Graham what this coon was to myself,—a fact indelibly engraved upon his memory. It seems, therefore, reasonably certain, though there are many conflicts in the testimony of the various witnesses, that the resolutions of the 20th were real, but having been adopted in a moment of anger and excitement, the sober sense of the people prevailed in those of the 31st, and the latter were published, while the former were permitted to slumber undisturbed, in the possession of Alexander, as a folly to be regretted rather than a matter of supreme importance.

It was amid scenes such as these, among men such as these, that young Graham worked studied and thought, his character under the control and guidance of a wise mother, developing into an almost perfect type of the noble race to which he belonged—bold, self-reliant, earnest, God-fearing.

He was eighteen years of age when he took up arms for his country and fought valiantly, successfully and faithfully, until his services were no longer needed. He was just twenty-two years of age at the close of the Revolutionary War. "He entered the army as a private, passed through the grades of orderly sergeant, quartermaster sergeant, quartermaster, adjutant, captain, and major. * * * He commanded in fifteen engagements with wisdom, calmness, courage and success to a degree perhaps surpassed by no other officer of the same rank. Hundreds who served under his command have testified to the upright, faithful, prudent and undaunted manner in which he discharged the duties of his responsible stations. Never was he known to shrink from any toil, however painful, or quail before any dangers, however threatening, or avoid any privation or sacrifice which might promote his country's cause." [6]

The every qualities that made him successful as a soldier — courage, alertness, intelligence—made him successful in civil life, as legislator, as member of two Constitutional Conventions, as iron miner and founder. I may not pause over the stirring incidents of the military service of this excellent man and soldier, nor can I tell more fully of his great usefulness to church and state in the quieter walks of his civil career. Suffice it to say that he loved and served his state and church faithfully and well, that in all that concerned their welfare, he was not only interested, but active, not only intelligent but wise. "His life was a bright and illustrious pattern of domestic, social and public virtues. modest, amiable, upright and pious, he lived a noble ornament to his country, a faithful friend to the church and a rich blessing to his family." In 1787 he married Miss Isabella Davidson, a daughter of Maj. John Davidson, and of a family distinguished alike for intelligence and patriotism. It was in consequence of this marriage that, forming a business connection with his father-in-law, he moved to Lincoln County in 1792, and became an iron founder and monger. Mrs. Graham is said to have been the most beautiful of Major Davidson's handsome daughters, and her character corresponded in loveliness and goodness to her personal appearance. It was from her that the subject of this sketch derived so much of the manly beauty that was one of his distinguishing characteristics during his long life. At the residence of his father near Vesuvius Furnace in Lincoln County, he was born, September 5th, 1804.

---

[6] Revolutionary papers of General Joseph Graham.

Childhood, Youth And Young Manhood

William Alexander Graham was the eleventh child and youngest son of General Joseph Graham and Isabella Davidson Graham, his wife. Mrs. Graham died January 15th, 1808. The eldest sister, Sophia, who afterwards married Dr. John Witherspoon, of South Carolina, but was then only seventeen years of age, assumed the care of the younger children of the family. She performed the duties with faithfulness, consideration and affection. She was regarded as a typical older sister and daughter and was remembered with great love and pleasure by those to whom she had given her attention and love. Young William was, too, an object of especial solicitude and care to his father. He made him his companion by day and by night, and instilled into him lessons of virtue, piety and patriotism. This constant association with so excellent a man and so good a Christian as General Graham was one of the strongest influences in shaping the boy's life. For years he lived the happy, free life of the country boy in a household where there was competence if not wealth. When he was older he was sent to a neighborhood school, very much against his will, for he hid under a bed and had to be dragged out by the heels. There he acquired the rudiments of learning. His first school away from home was in Mecklenburg County, where he lived with his mother's brother, Mr. Robin Davidson. The school-house being three miles distant, he rode to it on horseback, generally accompanied by James W. Osborne, of Charlotte, who, being the younger, rode behind. His uncle became very fond of the motherless lad, and the boy reciprocated so heartily, that he later named one of his sons for this uncle. From this country school he was sent to the Pleasant Retreat Academy at Lincolnton, of which his father was one of the trustees. His room-mate was his cousin, Theodore W. Brevard, who afterwards became distinguished in the State of Florida, where he held several important offices. Next he was sent to the classical school of the Rev. Dr. Muchat at Statesville. He was noted for his industry, his thirst for knowledge and his aptitude to learn. One who knew him well, (Rev. Dr. R. H. Morrison), testified that from his childhood he was no less remarkable for his high sense of honor and truth, than for his exemption from the levities and vices common to youth. At this academy he applied himself to his studies with the most exemplary diligence. Judge Brevard, a classmate, said of him: "He was the only boy I every knew, who would spend his Saturdays in reviewing the studies of the week." [7] This habit he kept up, too, during his subsequent school and college course. When he was fourteen or fifteen years of age, he, for a time, probably during a vacation, superintended, on the advice of his brother John, Spring Hill forge. General Graham was much pleased with his work in this capacity, saying that it was one of the most successful seasons in the history of the works. His final preparation for college was obtained at the Hillsboro Academy, an uncommonly good classical school. The Rev. John Witherspoon had the general supervision of this school, but the active teacher was Mr. John Rogers, who had distinguished himself in his profession at Wilmington. President Caldwell induced them to agree that their institution should be preparatory to the University. Members of the faculty could participate in the periodical examinations of the pupils, and those passing the examinations of the highest classes had a right to enter the University on certificate of the fact. [8] Mr. Rogers had been educated for the Catholic priesthood, and for accurate scholarship and capacity as a teacher, had few superiors. [9]

Young Graham matriculated at the University in the summer of 1820. Says Mr. McGehee in his very admirable memorial oration: [10] "His course throughout his college life was admirable in every way. He appreciated the scheme of study there established, not only as the best discipline of the intellect, but as the best foundation for knowledge in its widest sense. He mastered his lessons so perfectly, that each lesson became a permanent addition to his stock of knowledge. The professors rarely failed to testify by a smile, or some other token, their approval of his efficiency. On one occasion a professor (Olmstead), who has attained a world-wide reputation in the field of science, remarked to one of young Graham's classmates (John W. Norwood) that his lecture on chemistry came back as perfectly from Mr. Graham as he had uttered it on the previous day. Some thirty years after, the same professor in a letter to Mr. Graham, (then Secretary of the Navy) says: "It has often been a source of pleasing reflection to me, that I have been permitted to bear some part in fitting you, in early life, for that elevated post of honor and usefulness to which Providence has conducted you."

[7] McGehee: Memorial Oration on Life and Services of William A. Graham.
[8] Battle: History of the University of North Carolina, 283.
[9] McGehee: Memorial Oration.
[10] Pages 8-9.

His high sense of duty was manifested in his conscientious deportment under the peculiar form of government to which he was then subject. His observance of every law and usage of the college was punctilious, while to the faculty he was ever scrupulously and conspicuously respectful. His extraordinary proficiency was purchased by no laborious drudgery. The secret of it was to be found in the precept which he acted upon through life - "whatsoever thy hand findeth to do, do it with thy might." His powers of concentration were great, his perceptions quick, his memory powerful, prompt and assiduously improved. By the joint force of such faculties, he could accomplish much in little time. Hence, notwithstanding his exemplary attention to his college duties, he devoted much time to general reading. He participated regularly in the debates and other exercises of the Literary Society. For all such he prepared himself with care; and it is asserted upon the authority of Mr. John W. Norwood - a most competent Judge - that his compositions were of such excellence that, in a literary point of view, they would have challenged comparison with anything done by him in after life.

His engaging manners brought him into pleasant relations with all his fellow students. He lived with them upon terms of the frankest and most familiar intercourse. In their most athletic sports he never participated, but he was a pleased spectator, and evinced by his manner a hearty sympathy with their enjoyments. His favorite exercise was walking, and those who knew him well will recollect that this continued to be his favorite recreation while health was spared him. With friends and chosen companions he was cordial and easy, and always the life of the circle when met together.

He graduated in the class of 1824, he being one of the four first honor men, the others being Thomas Dews, afterwards a very able lawyer, but dying early, Matthias Evans Manly, afterwards state senator, judge of the Superior and Supreme Courts, elected United States Senator in 1866, but not allowed to take his seat, and Edwin D. Sims of Virginia, afterwards tutor in the University, and professor in Randolp-Macon College and in the University of Alabama. To young Graham was assigned the classical oration. It has been the privilege of the writer to see this. It is a pleasant and orderly resume of the history of the preservation of the classics, and an argument for their continued usefulness in the training of the mind and their giving breadth to one's culture. His style at that early period had not become individualistic, but was rather a reflection of his own training at the University, so was a little stiff and formal.

Other noted graduates of 1824 were Daniel B. Baker, judge of the Superior Court of Florida; John Bragg, member of Congress and judge of the Superior Court of Alabama; James W. Bryan, strong lawyer, trustee of the University and state senator from Craven; A. J. DeRosset, physician and merchant of Wilmington, treasurer of the Dioceses of North and East Carolina and often deputy to the general Conventions of the Episcopal Church; Augustus Moore, judge of the Superior Court; John W. Norwood, able lawyer, member of the legislature and senator from Orange; David Outlaw, member of Congress, state solicitor, state senator and delegate to the convention of 1835, and Bromfield L. Ridley, chancellor of Tennessee.[11]

After his graduation, he visited his sister, Mrs. Witherspoon, at Lexington, Ky., and while there he made the acquaintance of John J. Crittenden, and had an opportunity to hear him in a great slander case.

On his return from this tour he began the study of law in the office of Judge Ruffin at Hillsboro. The opinion of Judge Ruffin as to the proper course to be pursued with a student of law was somewhat peculiar. He held that he should have little assistance beyond that of having his course of studies prescribed. He must, as it were, scale the height alone, by his own strength and courage; availing himself of a guide at points otherwise inaccessible. Young Graham's brother, James Graham, in a letter written at this period, made mention of this opinion, and urged him to adopt the expedient resorted to by himself: "When he would not examine me, I took the liberty of questioning him very frequently, and by drawing him into conversation on legal subjects, my own ideas were rendered more clear, correct, and lasting." [12]

We may be sure that the contact of two such minds - the one young, ardent and acquisitive - the other mature and vigorous, the mind of a master in his particular calling, could result only in good to the younger, whatever the method of instruction might be. As a matter of fact young Graham came to the bar remarkably well prepared. The points he made were substantial and well sustained, and six years afterwards he was in the full tide of a successful practice. He obtained his county court license at

[11] Battle: History of University, 296.
[12] McGehee, 10 and 12.

the December term, 1826, of the Supreme Court, and was sworn
in before the County Court at Hillsboro in February, 1827. His
first litigated case in that Court was at the August term, 1827,
Charles Allison v. Samuel Madden, Judge Nash, who had recently resigned from the Superior Court bench, appearing with him
for the plaintiff.[13] At the ensuing November term he had two
other cases on the trial docket, and three on the appearance.
He obtained his Superior Court license at the December term,
1827, of the Supreme Court, and took the oaths at the March
term, 1828, of the Superior Court of Orange County. His first
litigated case was at the same term of that court,—Doe and John
Dunn, executor of William Keeling, v. James Keeling; A. D.
Murphey and Willie P. Mangum for plaintiff, and Frederick
Nash and W. A. Graham for the defendant.[14] His first case of importance in the Superior Court," says Mr. McGehee, "was one
which from peculiar causes, excited great local interest. It involved an intricate question of title to land. On the day of trial,
the court-room was crowded and the bar fully occupied by lawyers—many of them men of the highest professional eminence.
When he came to address the jury, he spoke with modesty, but
with ease and self-possession. His preparation of the case had
been thorough, and the argument which he delivered is described as admirable, both as to matter and manner. When he
closed, the Hon. William H. Haywood, who had then risen to
a high position at the bar, turned to a distinguished gentleman,
still living, of the same profession, and inquired who had prepared the argument which Mr. Graham had delivered so handsomely. The answer was, 'It is all his own,' to which Mr. Haywood replied, 'William Gaston could have done it no better.'"

At the time he determined to locate at Hillsboro, young
Graham had already spent several years there; first, as a student
at the Hillsboro Academy; second, as a student of law under
Judge Ruffin, and third, as practitioner in the county court. It
was centrally located, convenient to the State capital. It was the
county seat of a large county, with a population of about 25,000,
and there was much litigation. It was then, as it had always been,
the foster mother of great men. There was no town in the State
that contained so much that was best of the public life of the
State, though it had then only about four hundred white inhabitants. There was Murphey, perhaps the greatest genius in its

[13] County Court Records.
[14] Superior Court Records.

history; Ruffin, the greatest lawyer and Judge; Mangum, one of its greatest popular orators and statesmen; Norwood, the elder, able lawyer and upright Judge; Nash, whose excellencies as an advocate, said Mr. Abraham W. Venable, were equaled by few and surpassed by none, attaining later the highest honors of his profession; Dr. James Webb, distinguished physician and business man, and others too numerous to mention, while Duncan Cameron, George E. Badger, William H. Haywood and Bartlett Yancey, were intimately associated with the place. Among men of his own age, were Richard S. Clinton, Dr. Edmund Strudwick and John W. Norwood, his college-and-class-mate. The pastor of the Presbyterian Church at that time was the Rev. John Witherspoon, grandson of the signer, an able man, and, though unequal, on occasion eloquent. He was afterwards moderator of the Presbyterian General Assembly. The rector of the Episcopal Church was the Rev. William M. Green, afterwards Bishop of Mississippi and chancellor of the University of the South. Mr. Dennis Heartt was successfully editing and publishing the *Hillsboro Recorder*. The social advantages of the place, too, were very great. It was full of cultivated men and women, none very wealthy, but all having an abundance of the comforts of life, and many of its luxuries, and they were hospitable without stint. This society, though somewhat formal, was wholly delightful. Nor was the competition at the bar so stringent as appears on the surface. Judge Norwood was at that time on the Superior Court bench, and so continued until 1836. Judge Ruffin was on the Superior Court bench, resigned that year, 1828, to accept the presidency of the State Bank, and the following year was elevated to the Supreme Court. Judge Mangum was elected to the Superior Court in 1828, and to the United States Senate in 1830. Judge Nash was left, but he returned to the Superior Bench in 1836. Judge Cameron lived out in the country, and presided occasionally over the county court. Judge Murphey's health was failing, and he died in February, 1832. Of the visiting lawyers, Bartlett Yancey, who did a large business in Orange, died in 1828. There is no wonder then that so able a young lawyer as Mr. Graham should locate under these favorable conditions at Hillsboro. Nor is it any wonder that he should be cordially received there, and in a few years should be at the head of its bar, a preeminence which he maintained for forty years. Few young men have commenced the practice of the law with greater natural and acquired qualifications than had he. In him a remarkably handsome and dignified presence was united to the highest character, excellent mental endowments, untiring industry, kind, courteous and elegant, rather genial manners and thorough conscientiousness. He was fully six feet tall, very erect, and had hazel eyes, dark hair and clearcut features. His action in speaking was easy and graceful, sometimes warming into energy and force when the subject demanded it, and the tones of his voice were mellow, harmonious and well modulated. He was ambitious and self-reliant, so all that was best in him came at his demand. Success and complete success to such a character was only a matter of time, and one could predict it for him with absolute confidence at the outset of his career.

Legislator, 1833 To 1841

Hillsboro, enfranchised by Governor Tryon in 1770, continued to be one of the borough towns of the State under the Constitution of 1776, and until borough representation was abolished by the convention of 1835. The qualifications for voters in these towns were: First, possession of a free-hold in the town, whether the proposed voter was a resident or not; second, freedom, coupled with residence in the town for twelve months, next before and at the day of election, and payment of public taxes. The election for borough members were annual. Mr. Graham represented Hillsboro the last three years of its existence. At that time there were about 85 qualified voters in the town, and the elections were generally close, and conducted amid great excitement with the free use of intoxicants. Though William Norwood, Thomas Ruffin, John Scott, and Frederick Nash had at intervals of time represented it, its member was often some tavern-keeper, or one of the lesser lights of its citizens. At Mr. Graham's first election he was vigorously opposed. He was thereafter, however, elected with little opposition.

At the time he entered public life, North Carolina was on the whole retrograding. Its soil, moderately fertile, yielded remunerative returns only to intelligent and persistent labor. It contained a great variety of minerals; generally enough in a single locality to attract the adventurous prospector, not enough to prevent disappointment to his hopes. There was vast wealth in its forests, but there was little capital to exploit it, and no accessible market for it. Away from the cotton section, in its midland and west, it was a country of small farmers, a majority of whom had their material wants well supplied from the products of their farms, but again there was no adequate market for any excess. Without this market, there was no hope that they could improve their condition, and without this hope, they toiled on, generation after generation, quite often the laborious father being followed by the shiftless son. In consequence of this occasional retrogression in families, there were whole communities, not numerous, or large in themselves, scattered here and there throughout this section, plague spots upon the body politic, in which the men were without God and without hope in the world, and the women were without decency and quite frequently without virtue—communities, whose fragmentary remains are with us to this day, fast disappearing, thank God, under more hopeful conditions. The opening of the West, too, with its inviting opportunities for the adventurous and bold, was carrying away more and more the brawn and sinew of the State. Those who owned slaves might, year by year and generation after generation, tend their ancestral acres on or within reach of the navigable streams of the East, and live in ease and comfort while they educated their children, but to the small farmer of the West was lacking that contact with the world which brings enlightenment and hope, and stimulates ambition and effort. What wonder then that North Carolina was retrograding and that the pall of ignorance, instead of receding, was extending wider and wider over its people!

It is natural that under such narrow conditions the people themselves should become narrow, and should think that the whole science of government must expend itself on a pennywise pound foolish economy, and that the two great evils in the world were death and taxation. There are two remedies for such a condition that are perfectly obvious to us and were no less obvious to the great men of that period : First, bring the people in contact with the world by opening highways of trade and commerce through their borders; second, place a free school within reach of every child in the State. That was Murphey's program, that was Graham's program, that was the program of nearly all the Whigs of the period. Some talk nowadays of the ante-bellum aristocracy standing in the way of the people's enlightenment, of their progress. No so. The aristocrats (if I may use so false a term to designate the better educated class) were the progressives; the reactionaries, with a few exceptions, were the neighborhood political bosses, whose principal stock in trade was an attack upon the kid-gloved aristocracy, as they dubbed

the Whigs of the towns. These Whigs, with some notable exceptions, built the railroads of the State. They, again with some
notable exceptions, laid the foundations of our public school
system. In both these enterprises, Mr. Graham was a leader. His
temperament peculiarly fitted him to be a pioneer in this great
work. The influence and training of his father, and of Dr. Joseph
Caldwell, supplemented by association with Judge Murphey,
made internal improvements, the education of the people and the
preservation of the history of the State the three great ends that
he set himself to secure in his public life. With him it was a
calm, set purpose, to be worked out through the means and instrumentalities which the times provided. Those means were
small, and the instrumentalities often perverse and blind and
stupid, yet with a self-reliance that came from self-knowledge as
well as knowledge of the subject, with a self-control that prevented
any irritation, he pursued his ends with a placid, but firm persist-
ence which was not checked by any rebuff nor daunted by any
defeat.

Throughout his legislative career, during his incumbency of
the gubernatorial office, he was constantly stimulating the ambition and State pride of the people by telling them of the great
deeds of their sires, constantly in season and out of season, striv-
ing to enlighten them by diffusing the blessings of education
among them and to arouse them to effort and industry by bringing the highways of commerce to their doors. Early in life he
learned the great lesson, that in a democracy, where so many adverse minds are to be convinced, the progress of any great reform is necessarily slow, that often it is the work of more than
one generation, that he and his contemporaries must be content with line upon line and precept upon precept, here a little
and there a little, leaving to the future the fruition of their
hopes. Very, very, often the ideals and aspirations of the great
men of the past have been realized in the everyday life of the
commonalty of the present. To them the days that were to come
are the wisest witnesses.

In the Legislature of 1833-4 he was placed upon the Judiciary
Committee and the Committee on Education.[15] The House of
that body was of average ability, its ablest members, David Outlaw, D. M. Barringer, W. H. Battle, Charles B. Shepard, J. R. J.
Daniel, James Seawell, Charles Fisher, Daniel W. Courts, and
the Speaker, William J. Alexander. It was in session fifty-five days,

---

[15] House Journal, 142.

including Sundays, enacted 184 laws, only twenty-four of which were public. Nineteen academies or schools, including the predecessors of Wake Forest College, Guilford College and St. Mary's at Raleigh, two libraries, three gold mining companies, one manufacturing association and twelve railroad companies were incorporated. This indicates the drift of public sentiment at that time. The Bank of the Cape Fear was rechartered, and the Bank of the State of North Carolina, the Merchant's Bank of New Bern and the Albermarle Bank of Edenton, were chartered. Mr. Graham was the author of a bill, afterwards enacted into law, which corrected a gross inequality in the criminal laws as then administered, making one guilty of grand larceny as infamous upon conviction as one convicted of petty larceny.[16] He was on a committee to inquire into the right of Romulus M. Saunders to continue as Attorney-General of the State after having accepted a commissionership from the Federal Government on the French spoliation claims. He wrote the report in favor of Mr. Saunder's right.[17] His argument is based on the wording of the Constitution of 1776 — "No person in the State shall hold more than one lucrative office at any one time," and also upon the fact that the offices were not inconsistent. The constitutional prohibition seems upon its face to apply only to State offices. Especially is this true when it is remembered that the Federal Government was not in existence when the State Constitution was adopted. The Legislature of 1833-4 adopted the report thus made by Mr. Graham, but that of 1834-5, repudiating that view, passed a joint resolution that the office of Attorney-General had been vacated by Mr. Saunder's acceptance of the Federal Commissionership, and Mr. Saunders, to avoid controversy, but protesting against the accuracy of this legal conclusion, resigned as Attorney-General. Mr. Graham adhered to his opinion and voted against the resolution.

He was sent again as representative from Hillsboro to the Legislature of 1834-5. By that time the demand for an amendment of the Constitution of 1776 had become so insistent that it could no longer be disregarded with safety to the peace and welfare of the State. Mr. Graham supported the convention bill very heartily. During its consideration he voted against the provision allowing the convention to submit the election of governor to the free white vote of the State,[18] though he afterwards voted

[16] House Journal, 182.
[17] House Journal, 252.
[18] House Journal, 1834-5, 220.

for the bill with this provision in it. This vote was afterwards remembered to plague him in his canvass with Mr. Hoke for the
gubernatorial office in 1844. He explained that he was never opposed to the provision, but voted against it while the House was
considering the bill, section by section, because he was informed
by Mr. Outlaw of Bertie that the eastern members, without whose
vote the bill could not become a law, would not vote for it with
that provision in it, so he voted against that to save the bill itself,
but afterwards finding that the bill could be passed with that
provision in it, he followed what was his inclination all the time
by voting for it. To show the attitude of some members of the
House on this provision and others, at first its advocates could
muster but thirty-five votes, while there were ninety-four against
it.[19] On the proposition to submit the election of Supreme and
Superior Court Judges to the popular vote, there were twenty-
two ayes to one hundred and three nays.[20] On the proposition
to debar lawyers, pleading under a license, from membership in
the Legislature, the vote was twenty ayes to one hundred and
ten nays.[21] At this session Mr. Graham was again on the Judiciary
Committee, and was Chairman of the Education Committee. In
the latter capacity he made a report January 3, 1835, on the resources of the Literary Fund, and the best means of improving
the same, and accompanied the same by a bill to authorize the
Literary Board to sell certain portions of the swamp lands belonging to it.[22] This bill passed the House, but failed in the Senate.
Mr. Hugh McQueen, of Chatham, at this session also introduced
a bill in the Senate, to provide a fund for the establishment of
free schools. This passed its first reading, and was then laid on the
table. By joint resolution of the General Assembly, however, it
was afterwards ordered to be appended to, and published with,
the laws of the session. The Literary Fund amounted to about
$180,000, with the hope that it would enlarge at the rate of
$15,000 or $20,00 per annum, through the sale of swamp lands
and the receipt of dividends from investment of its capital. This
sum was wholly inadequate to establish any general system of
public schools, so the efforts of legislators were directed, for the
present, wholly towards increasing it. In the state of public
sentiment, they did not dare levy additional taxes. Indeed con-

[19] House Journal, 220.
[20] Ibid, 221.
[21] Ibid, 221.
[22] Coon: Public Education in North Carolina: A Documentary History, 1790-1840,
II., 683 et seq.

ditions among the people were so wholly adverse to increased taxation, that a plan that involved such increase would have proven utterly futile.

On December 29, 1834, Mr. Graham was elected by the Legislature a trustee of the University,[23] and he continued until his death to be actively interested in all of the affairs of that institution. An interesting political event occurred at this session. Judge Willie P. Mangum and Bedford Brown were the senators from the State in the Federal Congress. Mangum voted for the resolution of censure on Jackson for removing the deposits, passed March 28, 1834, and refused to vote for Benton's resolution to expunge the censure. The Legislature of 1834-5 was Democratic, or pro-Jackson, and hence opposed to Mangum. It instructed Mangum and Brown to vote for the expunging resolution. While the House was considering these instructions, Mr. Graham delivered a speech of remarkable power against them.[24] He had just passed his thirtieth birthday, yet this speech made him a leader of his party, the Whig, only second to Mr. Mangum in influence and power. It had so great an effect upon his fortunes and is so characteristic, that these alone would justify my giving it in full, if space permited. It, too, gives a remarkably clear and just view of the conditions as they were in North Carolina at that period, and of the political issues that confronted the people.

Mr. Graham was again member of the House of Commons, from Hillsboro in the Legislature of 1835-6. Among the other able members of that Legislature, were Matthias E. Manly, Kenneth Rayner, Thomas L. Clingman, and Michael Hoke, the first three being Whigs, and the latter a Democrat. Mr. Graham was his party's candidate for speaker, but was defeated by William H. Haywood, the vote being fifty-four to sixty-eight. He was again on the Committee on Education, and was chairman of the Judiciary Committee. He introduced a bill incorporating the Raleigh and Gaston Railroad, and defended it during all the stages of its enactment into a law against a vigorous opposition. It was the first railroad built in the State.

There was much discussion of the division of the proceeds of the sale of public lands by the Federal Government among the states, and a resolution was adopted by the Legislature that they ought to be so divided, the vote being seventy ayes to fifty-four nays, the division being not along party lines, Mr. Graham

[23] House Journal, 223.
[24] House Journal, 97.

voting aye. Judge Martin, having resigned as one of the judges of the Superior Court, Romulus M. Saunders was elected by a vote of ninety-seven to succeed him. On the last ballot Mr. Graham received sixty votes, and the *Register* of November 22, 1835, commenting on this, says : "It is due to Mr. Graham to state, that though strongly solicited, he refused to suffer his name to be put in nomination. Had he consented, he is so deservedly a favorite, that the contest would have been a very doubtful one. Mr. Graham is a young man, and the flattering vote which he received, under the peculiar circumstances of the case, is conclusive evidence of his elevated standing in the State."

The New Constitution, having gone into effect on January 1, 1836, and boroughs having been thus abolished, Mr. Graham was a candidate before the people of Orange County in the summer of 1836, to represent that county in the Legislature of 1836-7. He, for the first time, canvassed the county for internal improvements and for the distribution of the land proceeds. He was triumphantly elected, carrying with him also, two out of the other Whig candidates for the House, Orange being entitled under the new Constitution, to four representatives. He, however ran one hundred and twenty-one ahead of his ticket.

The House was again Democratic by a small majority; Haywood received sixty votes for Speaker, and Graham fifty-three.[25] He was on the same standing Committees as at the last session, and was again chairman of the Committee on Judiciary.[26] He was also chairman of the Committee on the Revised Statutes, which were then to be enacted into a law, and looked carefully, painstakingly and ably after their progress through the House. He was also chairman of a joint committee of both Houses on the funds to be received under the Deposit Act of Congress, and as chairman pro tem. of the committee made an able and lucid report upon the disposition of that fund, accompanied by bills to carry the suggestions of the committee into effect.[27] In pursuance of the act for the distribution of the surplus revenue, nearly $28,000,000 were deposited with the states, by three equal payments in January, April and July of 1837. North Carolina's share was $1,433,757.39. The Graham report contemplated an equal division of this fund into two : one, to constitute a fund for common schools, and the other, a fund for internal improve-

[25] House Journal, 243-4.
[26] House Journal, 268.
[27] Legislative Documents, 1835-9, No. 15.

ments. It very strongly reprehended the diversion of any portion
of this fund to meet ordinary State liabilities. The legislation,
however, did not follow this report in its entirety. $100,000 were
diverted to the payment of the civil contingent expenses of the
State Government, $600,000 were used in purchasing bank stock,
$200,000 were appropriated to draining swamp lands, and $533,-
757.39 purchased stock in the Wilmington and Raleigh Railroad.

The General Assembly of 1835-6 had enacted a law to regulate the mode of passing private acts. After the enactment of this
law, the Constitution of 1835 went into effect. A new provision
was incorporated therein that the General Assembly shall not
pass any private law, unless it shall be made to appear that
thirty days notice of application to pass such law, shall have been
given under such directions and in such manner as shall be provided by law. Upon this state of things two questions were submitted by the Assembly of 1836-7 to its Judiciary Committee,
of which Mr. Graham was Chairman : First, was the Act of 1835
superseded by the Constitution, which went into effect January
1, 1836, in such way as to render it inoperative upon the present
and future assemblies, without its reenactment; second, what is
the line of demarkation between public and private acts? Mr.
Graham replied to these questions in a very able and luminous
report. Except as restricted by the State and Federal Constitutions,
the authority of the General Assembly to legislate is plenary,
and its legislation binds its successors unless altered or repealed
by them. The Act of 1835 was obnoxious to no provision of the
Constitution of 1776, and being in entire accord with the provision of the new Constitution, quoted above, it is still in full
force and effect. Upon this point, among other things, he said :
"The convention has not only not taken away the power to enact
such a law, but virtually ordained that it should be passed. It
is supposed that the right to pass it is derived from the amendment, and it could only be passed by a Legislature convened
under the new Constitution. It must be observed, however, that
the paragraph of the amendment now under discussion, confers
no new power on the General Assembly, but forbids the exercise
of an old one, except on certain conditions. The legislative power
of the General Assembly extends not merely to the present time
and events, but may prospectively embrace any future contingencies. The law in question might have provided that in the event
of the adoption of the amendments to the Constitution, adver-

tisement of application for private acts should be made for thirty days, much more, when it was authoritatively announced that the amendments had been adopted, might it provide to give them practical operation. A wise lawgiver will endeavor as well to prevent grievances as to administer remedies for them. To have enacted no law in reference to private acts at the last session of the Legislature, would have been to exclude any private bill from consideration for at least the first thirty days of this session. Your committee, therefore, deem the passage of the said act to have been both constitutional and expedient."

In answer to the second question he said : "On the one hand your committee felt that by a too strict interpretation of the term, private law, much useful legislation might have been prevented at the present session, whilst on the contrary the salutary operation of this section of the Constitution would be wholly abrogated and annulled, unless the General Assembly shall affix a proper construction to this term, and insist on its enforcement in every instance. It can hardly be supposed that the judiciary branch of the government will have either the disposition or authority to look beyond the enactments of the Legislature, to ascertain whether they were passed with, or without legal notice of their introduction. This clause of the amended Constitution is binding therefore only on the conscience of the legislator, and is dependent upon this alone for its observance. Its true meaning is for that reason to be sought with greater diligence and adhered to with more vigor. * * * In some statutes special clauses have been inserted declaring that those statutes shall be held and deemed public acts, but this, as your committee believe, has been properly construed not to change the character of the acts, but merely to determine the manner in which they shall be alleged and proved in courts of justice. Whether a statute be public or private, must depend on its nature and object. If those be private, the statute itself can not be public, notwithstanding the declaration of the Legislature to the contrary; nor should the evasion be allowed of inserting provisions of a public kind for the mere purpose of dispensing with the necessity of advertising, where they do not belong to the general scope of the particular bill. The general description of public acts is, that they relate to the interests of the public at large; and private, that they relate to individuals and their interests only. This vague description which pervades all the elementary books and has by many been mistaken as a definition, affords but an un-

certain test for discrimination. Your committee believe that the
following points are settled by adjudication or by common consent, to wit, that all acts are public:

"1. Which concern all persons generally.

"2. Which affect the sovereign in any of his rights of sovereignty
or property. Hence any act which gives a penalty or fine to the
State is, on that account, public.

"3. Which concern the officers of the State, whether civil or
military.

"4. Which concern the Legislature.

"5. Which relate to trade in general, or the public highways
or navigable rivers.

"And of these some are termed public local acts, and others
public general acts, according to their respective spheres of operation. The foregoing summary may not embrace all acts of a
public nature, but is supported by authority so far as it extends,
and may be useful in drawing the line of distinction. Private acts
embrace all those not falling within any of the descriptions aforesaid. An attempt to define them more particularly is unnecessary.
Your committee are aware that the precise boundary between
public and private acts can not in every instance be determined
by the rules here furnished, but they are gratified by the reflection that in a great majority of bills there can be no question as
to their character, and in any particular case where difficulty may
arise, the foregoing classification may be found useful if not
decisive. To the wisdom of the House it will belong to apply
them with proper discrimination, in each case in which the application becomes necessary."

I reproduce this long extract, not so much because it is an
admirable statement of the legal principles involved, as because
it throws light upon the stage of mental development at which
he had arrived when he was only thirty-two years of age, and
also upon his character. This constant sense of the eternal fitness of things, this assumption that because power is irresponsible,
it is the more incumbent upon those who exercise it, to exercise
it with the utmost circumspection and caution, characterized all
his utterances and actions throughout his whole career.

While on his way to one of his courts, in 1836, he was so injured
by an unruly horse, that he was compelled to go North for treatment in the summer of 1837. Before the accident, it was understood that he or Judge Mangum was to have been the Whig

candidate for the Federal House of Representatives. Judge Mangum, however, positively declined, and insisted that Mr. Graham should be nominated, and he was nominated without a dissenting voice. He was absent at the North until a few days before the election. He could make no canvass. Instead he addressed an open letter to the voters of the district, in which he discussed the issues of the day and offered himself as a candidate for their suffrages. Martin Van Buren had been President only a few months, and the country was in the throes of a severe panic, largely induced by the arbitrary measures of his predecessor, General Jackson. Mr. Graham, in this letter, thus rapidly describes conditions as they then were:

"Our public moneys amounting to many million dollars have been paid into banks which are unable or unwilling to repay the government, and much it is feared will never be repaid at all. Bank notes which constitute by far the largest portion of our currency are no longer convertible into specie. Exchanges are destroyed, so that it is difficult, if not impossible, to make remittances from one part of our country to another, to carry on the necessary commerce between it and foreign nations. Many of our merchants and other citizens, both the judicious and prudent as well as the reckless and speculating, have suddenly and unexpectedly, both to themselves and others, become insolvent. Pecuniary confidence between man and man has been greatly abridged, and in many places destroyed. The great staple productions of the country have fallen in price, and agricultural as well as mechanical labor meets with insufficient reward. Our immediate section of the country, from its interior position, as well as other causes, is happily exempt in a great measure from the calamities which oppress others; but no section can long escape unless a remedy is speedily applied. Every section is interested in the safe-keeping of the public moneys, the soundness of the circulating medium, the facilities of domestic trade and the prosperity of our foreign commerce."

His remedy was a national bank, such as that which was chartered during the Washington and Madison administrations. "I believe", said he, "that Congress has the constitutional power to establish such a bank, and I, at present perceive no measure better calculated to relieve our distresses. I am aware of the danger of moneyed power, and if such a corporation can not be so restricted as to be incapable of wanton injury, either to the public or individuals, it should not be allowed. But the legislative power must be lamentably impotent if it can not fashion the creation of its own hands that it shall be accountable to the law for its conduct and thus prevent its abuses."

And he concludes thus: "It is known to many of you that I did not concur in the election of the present chief magistrate, and should a competitor be presented whom I prefer, I probably shall not do so at the next election. I will endeavor, nevertheless, whether in public or private life, to do justice to his measures, and should deem myself altogether unworthy of your confidence, were I capable of opposing or supporting any measure on account of the sources from which it springs. My first wish is that the country should be well governed, rather that it should be governed by any particular set of men."

The *Raleigh Register* had the following on his candidacy, issue of July 17, 1837: "We do not believe there lives a man who can with truth allege aught against the character of Mr. Graham. We say of our own knowledge, that he is as pure a public man as we ever saw, and if elected, will add greatly to the learning, talent and eloquence of the House of which he is a member." In the issue of July 31, 1837, he is designated as follows: "A man whom even his political foes respect for his acquirements, and honor for the irreproachable purity of his private character."

The *Standard* of July 19, 1837, took a somewhat different view: "In him the bank Whigs and Wall street brokers will have as warm a friend and as ardent a champion as they desire.— As to Mr. Graham's private character we know nothing and have heard nothing against it. He is a man of talents, but he can never be great among great men.*** Though he may be looked upon as estimable as a man, he is dangerous as a politician."

At almost exactly the same time and in England another newspaper writer wrote of Mr. Gladstone: "He is a man of very considerable talent, but has nothing approaching to genius. His abilities are much more the result of an excellent education, and of mature study, than of any prodigality on the part of nature in the distribution of her mental gifts. I have no idea he will ever acquire the reputation of a great statesman." [28]

Mr. William Montgomery was elected by 191 majority, the only instance in Mr. Graham's long public life in which he was defeated in an election before the people of North Carolina.

He was again a commoner from Orange County in the Legislature of 1838-9, the only Whig elected in that county, all his

---

[28] British Senate, Vol. II, 54.

colleagues being Democrats. The House, however, was Whig, and he was elected speaker over Michael Hoke, the vote being sixty-one to forty-nine. This General Assembly is distinguished by its enactment of the first comprehensive school law. Says Mr. Coon:[29] "Early in the session of the Assembly of 1838-9, Mr. Dockery repeated his resolution relative to the establishment of public schools. H. G. Spruill presented a resolution and a plan which contemplated dividing the counties into school districts and holding an election in each district on the question of school or no school. The district was to be empowered to levy a tax to pay one-half the teacher's salary, the other to be paid out of the income of the literary fund. A notable feature of this plan was the suggestion that every district refusing to establish schools should be required to vote on the question every year until they were established. The plan submitted by the Literary Board recommended the division of the State into 1250 districts, estimating the average school population for each district of 108 children between the ages of five and fifteen; the establishment of normal schools after the fashion advocated by President Caldwell some years before; the holding of an election in each county to determine whether it was willing to levy a tax for schools in amount to twice the sum expected from the literary fund; and the appointment of a state superintendent of public schools. It was estimated by the board that the income of the school fund was then about $100,000. This amount, added to $200,000 proposed to be raised by county taxation, would pay the 1250 teachers each a salary of $240 a year. The suggestions of the board were received with considerable interest. Bills to carry out its plans were introduced in the Senate by William W. Cherry, and in the House by Frederick J. Hill. Mr. Cherry's bill did not contemplate establishing schools until another meeting of the Assembly; Mr. Hill's bill provided for their immediate establishment.— The net results of the education efforts of the Assembly of 1838-9 was the passage, on January 7, 1839, of a law submitting the question of schools or no schools to a vote of the people of several counties in August, 1839. A favorable vote meant a tax levy of one dollar for each two dollars to be received from the income of the literary fund. The schools established were to be under the control of five to ten county superintendants; the whole territory of the county was to be divided into no more districts than one for each thirty-six square miles, and the first term of the schools

---

[29] Coon: Public Education in N. C., I, xliii.

in each district was to be conducted on $20 of county taxation and $40 income from the literary fund."

No member of the Assembly took a more active interest in the enactment of this law, than did the speaker, Mr. Graham. Four out of the nine sections of the original House bill were in his handwriting, and two of the bills finally adopted by the Conference Commitee were also in his handwriting.[30] It is said to have been adapted from the New York law on the same subject.

Mr. Coon very finely says of this act:[31] "While the school law of 1839 was not a very satisfactory measure, it marked the beginning of a new era. Individualism was now gradually to give way to community spirit; selfishness and intolerance, which only desired to be undisturbed, must now needs give place to measures devoted to the welfare and uplift of the people; hatred of taxation for schools must now begin to disappear before the dawning of that wiser policy that no taxation is oppressive which is used in giving equal educational opportunities to all."

Mr. Graham was reelected a member of the House of Commons from Orange in 1840. He was accompanied by two Whig colleagues too, and Mr. Willie P. Mangum was senator in the General Assembly of 1840-1. So fair and impartial as speaker was he the preceding session that he was reelected unanimously at this. The meeting of the Legislature was immediately after the triumphant election of Harrison and Tyler. The State, falling in line, had given the Whig ticket a large majority. The Democratic Legislature of 1835-6 had instructed the then Senators in Congress, Bedford Brown and Willie P. Mangum, to vote for Benton's expunging resolution. Mangum, denying the authority of the Legislature to instruct him how to vote, voted against that resolution, and refused to resign. In the campaign of 1836 he and Brown, who took the affirmative of the right of the Legislature to instruct, discussed the matter largely before the people of the State. The General Assembly, elected that year, was Democratic by a very small majority, and Mangum, interpreting this as a rebuke of his own course, by the people themselves, resigned and was succeeded by Robert Strange, a Democrat. In 1838-9 conditions were reversed. The Benton resolution was passed by the Senate January 16, 1837, both Brown and Strange voting for it, The General Assembly of 1838-9 was Whig by a substantial majority. Kenneth Rayner, on December 4, 1838, introduced

---

[30] Pub. Ed. in N. C., II, 881 and 890.
[31] *Ibid*, I, xlvii.

in the House of Commons a series of resolutions that in the aggregate amounted to a condensed but definite statement of the Whig faith, the first resolution containing a simple allegation that the present Senators had not truly represented the people of the State in voting for Benton's expunging resolution, and the last, being as follows: "That our Senators in Congress will represent the wishes of a majority of the people of the State by voting to carry out the foregoing resolutions." There is no doubt that these resolutions were drawn up at a conference of the Whig leaders, for the *Register,* in its issue of November 26, 1838, said: "That course is not to instruct them as their party instructed Mangum to do a particular act or resign, but to give so decided and unequivocal an expression of the opinions of their constituents, that they can not disregard it, unless they are determined to set at naught the popular will and practically assert their independence of it." So every amendment in the House and in the Senate was voted down, and the resolution passed the former body, without dotting an *i* or crossing a *t,* December 25th, and the latter, December 27, 1838, in each instance by a strict party vote, so far as their essential features were concerned. Senators Brown and Strange, protesting that when positive instructions were given them they would either vote as the General Assembly commanded them, or resign, by a letter to that body, dated December 31, 1838, asked for more authoritative instructions. These the Legislature never gave. Messrs. Brown and Strange, still treating these resolutions as an expression of opinion on the part of the Legislature, which did not concern them, refused to resign until June 30, 1840. Their resignations were accompanied by long explanations, the gist of which may be found in the following: "My resignation is not prompted by a belief that the resolutions imposed on me any such obligation, but from an anxious desire to submit my public course to the decision of the people of the State, which would have been done sooner, if an election had sooner intervened." As I have already said, the General Assembly, elected the second Thursday in August, 1840, was Whig by a large majority. These vacancies were to be filled by it at its coming November session. Bedford Brown's term was to expire March 4, 1841, Willie P. Mangum was elected to fill the unexpired term, and also for a full term commencing at that date. Robert Strange's term was to expire on March 4, 1843, and William A. Graham was, on November 24, 1840, elected to fill this by a vote of ninety-eight for himself and sixty-four for

Strange. Both candidates were selected by the Whigs in caucus, out of some five or six names. Mr. Mangum was at the time the leader of the Whig party in the State. By general consent of the Whigs at large he was to be Mr. Brown's successor, and he was unanimously so named by the caucus. It was a very great and unusual honor that the Whigs conferred on so young a man as Mr. Graham to choose him out of five candidates as United States Senator, when he was a resident of the same county as Mr. Mangum. It is, too, the strongest testimony to his ability and his private and public worth. His selection was received with great satisfaction by the Whigs. Said the *Register* of November 27, 1840: "He is a statesman of high order, is a powerful debater, and combined with these qualifications has indefatigable application. His virtues and amiable qualities endear him to all who know him." The Democratic comment, however, was rather caustic, on his age, his lack of experience and his geographical situation.

UNITED STATES SENATOR

It was the second session of the Twenty-sixth Congress that the new Senators first attended. Mr. Mangum was sworn in on December 9th, and Mr. Graham, December 10, 1840.[32] That Congress was Democratic, both in the House and in the Senate. The Senate was composed then, of the ablest men in public life throughout the country. From Alabama there were William R. King and Clement C. Clay; from Deleware, Thomas Clayton; from New Jersey, Samuel L. Southard; from Kentucky, Henry Clay and John J. Crittenden; from Missouri, Thomas Benton; from Georgia, Wilson Lumpkin; from New York, Silas Wright and Nathaniel P. Tallmadge; from Massachusetts, Daniel Webster and John Davis; from South Carolina, John C. Calhoun and William C. Preston; from New Hampshire, Franklin Pierce; from Vermont, Samuel Prentiss; and from Virginia, William H. Roane. Martin Van Buren's term as president was expiring, and his last annual message was a defense of the policy of his adminis-tration.[33] Especially did he congratulate the country that in the midst of the very trying conditions which confronted it at the outstart, a panic and the stoppage of specie payments by the banks and the consequent loss of revenue from such a condition, compli-cated by large expenditures in the removal of the eastern Indians,

---

[32] Senate Journal, 1840-1, 22.
[33] Senate Journal, 6, *et seq.*

appropriations for which had already been made, every demand upon it at home and abroad, had been promptly met. "This has been done not only without creating a permanent debt, or resort to additional taxation in any form, but in the midst of a steadily progressing reduction of existing burdens upon the people, leaving still a considerable balance of available funds, which will remain in the treasury at the end of the year.— The policy of the Federal Government, in extinguishing as rapidly as possible the national debt, and subsequently in resisting every temptation to create a new one, deserves to be regarded in the same favorable light. Coming into office the declared enemy of both [a national debt and a national bank,] I have earnestly endeavored to prevent a resort to either."

Mr. Graham was placed on the Standing Committee on Revolutionary Claims at this session.[34] From that Committee, on January 13, 1841, he reported a bill to cause monuments to be erected in honor of Brigadier-Generals Francis Nash and William Davidson, favorably.[35] He accompanied the bill with a special report which was ordered printed. It being his first attendance, and at a short session when the Democrats had a majority, he does not appear to have taken any part in the larger debates, contenting himself with a constant attendance, voting generally with his party.

The Senate of the Twenty-seventh Congress, at the call of the President, met in special session on March 4, 1841. Mr. Webster, having been nominated as Secretary of State by Mr. Harrison, had resigned and was succeeded by Rufus Choate. Levi Woodbury, who had been Secretary of the Treasury under Van Buren, appeared as one of the Senators from Vermont. John J. Crittenden, who had been appointed Attorney-General, was succeeded by James T. Morehead. John McPherson Berrien appeared from Georgia, and Richard H. Bayard from Delaware. The leaders of the Democrats were, Thomas H. Benton, William R. King, James Buchanan, Silas Wright and Levi Woodbury; of the Whigs, Henry Clay, Thomas Clayton, Samuel Prentiss, William C. Rives and Willie P. Mangum. The Whigs had a majority of seven. This, however, was merely an executive session to confirm the nominations of the new president, Harrison.

The new Cabinet was: Daniel Webster, Secretary of State; Thomas Ewing, Secretary of the Treasury; John Bell, Secretary

---

[34] Senate Journal, 23.
[35] Senate Journal, 101.

of War; George E. Badger, Secretary of the Navy; John J. Crittenden, Attorney-General, and Caleb Grainger, Postmaster-General—
a very able company of counselors. At Mr. Clay's suggestion,
President Harrison called the Twenty-seventh Congress to meet
in extra session on May 31, 1841. Unfortunately for the country
and fatally for the Whig party, Mr. Harrison died, after a short
illness, on April 4, 1841, and was succeeded by John Tyler, the
Vice-President, a Democrat, misplaced in the Whig party, to the
confusion and dismay of all who wished it well. The extra session
began at the time appointed, the House being also Whig by nearly
fifty majority. The program of the Whigs as announced by their
leader, Mr. Clay, was:[36]

1. The repeal of the sub-treasury law.
2. The incorporation of a bank adapted to the wants of the
   people.
3. The provision of an adequate revenue (there was a deficit
   at that time, estimated, of $14,000,000), by the imposition
   of tariff duties, and a temporary loan.
4. The passage of the necessary appropriations.
5. The prospective distribution of the proceeds of public land
   sales.
6. Some modification of the banking system of the District of
   Columbia.

Of the general legislation involved in this program, all was·
frustrated by the veto of President Tyler, except the repeal of
the sub-treasury law, and the temporary loan.

The chairman of the standing committees of the Senate were
chosen by the ballot of the senators. Mr. Graham was elected
chairman of the Committee on Claims,[37] a very important position
for so new and so young a senator. He was also a member of the
Committee on Revolutionary Claims,[38] and was appointed a member of a select committee on so much of the President's message
as related to a uniform currency, and a suitable fiscal agent,
by Mr. Southard, president pro. tem. of the Senate.[39] Remember-
ing that one of the greatest evils of the times was the wholly inadequate currency system, this was one of the most important
committees of the Congress, and it was composed of very able
senators,—Mr. Clay, chairman; Mr. Choate, Mr. Wright, Mr.
Berrien, Mr. King, Mr. Tallmadge, Mr. Bayard, Mr. Graham and

[36] Senate Journal, 1841, 24.
[37] Senate Journal, 1841, 18.
[38] Senate Journal, 1841, 20.
[39] Senate Journal, 1841, 20.

Mr. Huntingdon. As above said, however, all the measures of this committee were made futile by the veto of the President.

At the second session of the Twenty-seventh Congress, Mr. Graham was continued as chairman of the Committee on Claims, but was transferred from the Committee on Revolutionary Claims to that on Pensions.[40] He presided over the Senate as president pro tempore on February 17, 1842.[41] He was appointed second on the special Committee on Retrenchment, on February 28th.[42] On March 31st.[43] Mr. Clay retired from the Senate, and was succeeded by his friend and follower, John J. Crittenden, who, with all the rest of the original cabinet except Mr. Webster, had resigned the preceding September. "I want rest," wrote Mr. Clay, "and my private affairs want attention. Nevertheless, I would make any personal sacrifice, if by remaining here I could do any good; but my belief is, I can effect nothing, and perhaps my absence may remove an obstacle to something being done by others."

As I have said, the administration of Mr. Van Buren had left to the administration of Mr. Tyler an inheritance of debt, and the compromise tariff measure of 1833, working automatically, had reduced the revenues below the necessary expenses of the government. There was an annually increasing deficit. The special session of 1841 had authorized a temporary loan of $12,000,000, to tide over immediate embarrassments. Coupled with that measure was one requiring the distribution of the proceeds of the sale of public lands among the States, this distribution, however, to be suspended whenever the necessities of the treasury required an increase of the tariff duties above the twenty per cent fixed by the compromise of 1833. To raise the duties above this twenty per cent level was absolutely necessary to secure an adequate revenue for the expenses of the government. Thus any further distribution of these funds among the states could not be made. Indeed such was the condition of the treasury, that Congress was compelled at the ensuing session to extend the loan of 1841 and add $5,000,000 thereto. The Democrats wished to devote the proceeds of the sale of the public lands to the gradual liquidation of this temporary loan. This the Whigs opposed, and, having a majority, defeated. It was while the bill authorizing this loan was pending that Mr. Graham made his first set speech, April 13, 1842. He first shows that during the four years of the

[40] Senate Journal, 1841-2, 22.
[41] Senate Journal, 1841-2, 173.
[42] Senate Journal, 1841-2, 188.
[43] Senate Journal, 1841-2, 262.

Van Buren administration, the expenses of the government exceeded its revenue by $31,000,000; that this defecit was reduced to $5,500,000, by the application of $26,000,000 of extraordinary funds, $17,000,000 of surplus at the beginning of the administration, $9,000,000 of which should have been the fourth installment of the deposit of land prodeeds with the states, and $9,000,000 were received from debts due the United States, principally for the sale of its stock in the late Bank of the United States; that they not only diverted this capital to the payment of the ordinary expenses of the government, but they were compelled to borrow $5,500,000 more by the issue of treasury notes to meet their extravagant expenditures, and this legacy of debt they have left the Tyler administration. "To meet this deficiency, what have we? Instead of surplus, we have debt. Instead of extraordinary means falling in, we have a daily increasing charge of interest. Instead of a tariff of forty per cent, we have one nearly approaching 20 per cent, and that upon little more than half the imports. What then is to be done?*** Mr. President, our whole duty in this emergency seems to be comprehended in three propositions:

"1. Borrow such sum, upon the best terms we can obtain, as will relieve our present necessities, and save the public honor from disgrace.

"2. Reduce our expenses to the lowest point which is consistent with an efficient public service.

"3. Levy such duties upon imports as are necessary for an economical administration of the government, and no more."

The Democrats had suggested that the Tyler administration could relieve itself of all its financial difficulties by demanding the return of the $28,000,000 of land proceeds already distributed among the states. Mr. Graham proceeds in a calm, courteous and well-reasoned argument to show that such extraordinary funds were not to be devoted to the ordinary expenses of the government, according to the scheme of the Constitution itself, even if they could surmount the impracticableness and injustice of the scheme of taking back from the states the money which had been so recently deposited with them. "I have said, Mr. President, that the authors of the Constitution did not rely upon the public lands as a means for the ordinary maintenance of government, and, in my humble opinion, to effectuate their design to make this a government of limited powers, confined to comparatively few objects, it ought to be restricted to those modes of supply pointed out in the Constitution. All history will verify the fact, that those nations have been most remarkable for purity and correctness of administration, for the strictest accountability of public agents, and have longest preserved their liberties, who have kept their ruling powers constantly dependent upon the contributions, direct or indirect, annually levied upon the people. As a certain writer has remarked, 'They who would trample on their rights are restrained by the want of their money.' This general truth applies with tenfold force to a government like that of the United States, far distant from the great mass of the people whom it affects, and so complicated in its structure and so diversified in its operations, that, to keep up a minute knowledge of its details of administration, federal politics must be made, to a great extent, an exclusive profession. That period of our history, when peculation and embezzlement were most rife, when the responsibility of public officers was least rigid, when salaries were unregulated and the gains in many offices were almost what their holders desired, and when appropriations were most extravagant, was the period which I have reviewed in the part of these remarks (Van Buren's administration), when revenue was not redundant but grossly deficient, but there were surpluses and extraordinary means in your coffers, which the administration had nothing to do with, but to expend. Think you, sir, that in any other state of the treasury, a district attorney would have been allowed to receive emoluments greater, by more than one-half, than the salary of the President of the United States—greater according to his own declaration when about to leave office, 'than any citizen of a free republic ought to receive'; that marshals, collectors of customs and postmasters, would have been permitted, like Roman proconsuls, to enrich themselves to immense fortunes out of the offices created for public benefit alone, and oftentimes, by like instances of official abuses—abuses to which no corrective was applied until the third of March, 1841, the very last day of the late administration, when a clause was inserted in the appropriation bill—a kind of bequest to pious uses upon the deathbed repentance, spoken of by the senator from South Carolina (Mr. Preston), restraining the compensation of these functionaries to $6,000 per annum, for the future."

On May 31, 1842, Mr. Mangum was elected president pro tem. of the Senate in the place of Mr. Southard, of New Jersey, who had resigned, thus making a vacancy on the Finance Committee.[44] Mr. Graham was appointed to fill this vacancy.[45] A question about which there was much discussion at this session was the redistricting of the country according to the census of 1840. The Democrats were in favor of leaving the matter of electing members of the House of Representatives by districts or by a general ticket to the legislatures of the various states. Mr. Graham was in favor of Congress determining this question for itself and of requiring the legislatures to lay off contiguous districts containing a certain number (70,680) of voters, thus in effect prohibiting the election of representatives by general ticket. On June 3, 1842, he made a very able speech sustaining this view. He discusses it, first, from the standpoint of expediency and, second, from the standpoint of its constitutionality. In concluding the latter branch of the discussion, he said: "But we are told we have no power to pass this law, because we cannot enforce its execution by penal sanctions; and an urgent appeal is made to us by the senator from New Hampshire (Mr. Woodbury) to know whether an armed force or a writ of mandamus is to be sent to the state legislatures to compel them to lay off the districts. No, sir, neither. No one ever conceived the idea of compelling a free legislative assembly to do, or not to do, anything by physical force, or the precept of a court of justice. The crime of omission or commission in their constitutional duty, like that of parenticide among the Athenians, is provided with no legal sanction, but left to the oaths and consciences of men, to an accountability to public opinion, and to that constituency whose rights have been outraged or neglected. The preservation of this government greatly depends on the faithful fulfillment of the duties imposed by the Constitution on the state legislatures. If a majority of them shall fail to elect senators (as one has done), if five or six of those in the largest states shall fail to make regulations for choosing electors of president and vice-president, in conformity to the laws of Congress, the Union would be as effectually dissolved as if we who are sent to the legislative halls of the capitol should obstinately refuse to attend in our places and pass the laws annually necessary for the support of the government. It is faith, honor, conscience, and not the hangman's whip, on which at last rest the blessings of this noblest human institution which has ever been devised for the security, the welfare and the happiness of man. The duties of the states,

---

[44] Senate Journal, 1841-2, 366.
[45] Ibid, 377.

under our Constitution, are not to be determined by their liability to punishment, but by the covenants into which they entered by that instrument."

At this session of Congress a tariff bill was passed.[46] It represented fairly the Whig idea of a tariff, *i.e.* for revenue with incidental protection. The President had already stated his objection to a bill [47] that contained a provision continuing the distribution of the public land sales. Mr. Graham was with the Democrats in nearly all the reductions proposed by them during the consideration of the bill, and voted against it on its third and final reading. He was very earnestly in favor of continuing the distribution of the proceeds of the sale of public lands, and this bill being a surrender to the President on this subject, he could not vote for it without stultifying his own record. Compared with the present it was an exceedingly moderate protection measure, not averaging more than thirty per cent. Moderate, however, as protection was at that period, he, being a southerner, was even more moderate. He said himself in his letter accepting the Whig nomination for governor, December 18, 1843 : "I have no hesitation in saying, that whilst I think the government should collect the least amount of money, which may be necessary for an efficient public service, in laying duties to raise such sum, I would incidentally afford protection to American interests, when they were deemed of sufficient importance to deserve it, as well as counteract the effects of restrictive regulations on our trade by foreign nations wherever it should appear expedient to do so.***

"I did not vote for the tariff now existing. Some of its duties were higher than I approved, but in the vacant condition of the treasury, I would not have withheld from it my support had an amendment which I offered, proposing a distribution of the proceeds of the public lands among the states, been incorporated in the bill."

At the third session of the Twenty-seventh Congress, 1842-3, he was again Chairman of the Committee on Claims, second on the Committee on Finance, and second on the Special Committee on Retrenchment.

When it is remembered that Mr. Graham was only thirty-eight years and five months old when his term as United States Senator expired in March, 1843, and consider the influential position he

---

[46] Senate Journal, 1841, 251.
[47] *Ibid*, 643.

had taken in that august body, we need no stronger evidence of his ability, his faithfulness and his industry.

The functions of the Chairman of the Committee on Claims, at that time when there was no court of claims, were very much like that of a chancellor presiding over a court of equity. Many important matters were presented to that committee while Mr. Graham was chairman, matters which involved the reading and digesting of a great mass of written evidence, the application of the principles of law and of justice to the case under consideration, and finally the rendering of the written opinion in such form as to carry conviction to the minds of the great lawyers and eminent statesmen, who constituted the body to which the report was made. None of his reports was perfunctory, and some of them show such industrious mastery of detail, such capacity for shifting out the strong from the weak, the true from the false, from a great mass of conflicting, or obscure, or false testimony, such clearness in statement of conclusions of fact and enunciation of legal and constitutional principles applicable to them, that we are convinced he would have made a great chancellor as well as a great senator, if fair opportunity had presented itself.[48]

The Legislature elected in North Carolina, in 1842, was largely Democratic in both branches. Mr. Romulus M. Saunders and Mr. Bedford Brown, both Democrats, were candidates to succeed Mr. Graham, and divided the votes of that party between them, while the Whigs voted to a man for Mr. Graham. On December 20, 1842, Mr. Graham's name was withdrawn from the ballotting, and the next day Mr. William H. Haywood, Jr., was elected senator. Says the *Raleigh Register* of December 23, 1842: "The elevation of this gentleman over the head of all of the leaders of the genuine Democracy is a strong exhibition of political legerdemain, in which, however, we believe he, himself, had no hand. (As a matter of fact he was not in Raleigh at the time.)— At the beginning of the session, Judge Saunders was taken up as a representative of the Calhoun wing of the party, while the Hon. Bedford Brown, being the beau ideal of pure locofocoism, was the nucleus about which the elements of Van Burenism rallied. It was in vain that caucus after caucus was held. The friends of Saunders, regarding his success as a matter of vital importance to Mr. Calhoun, would not give way, though in a

---

[48] See his Report, Harris-Farrow Claim, 3 Senate Doc., 27th. Cong., 3d Session, No. 157.

minority. On the other hand, many of Brown's friends at an early period declared that they would prefer Mr. Graham to Judge Saunders, and some of them affirmed that in no event could they be brought to the support of any man tainted with nullification."

After Mr. Graham's withdrawal on the 19th, the Whigs had no candidate, but voted, some for Saunders, and others, scattering. When the Democrats, however, centered upon Mr. Haywood, they again voted as a body for him, the final ballot standing Haywood ninety-five and Graham sixty-nine, with two scattering.

First Term As Governor

At the end of his term of service in the United States Senate, Mr. Graham returned to the practice of the law at Hillsboro. But the people of North Carolina were not willing that he should remain long out of their service.

The Whigs throughout the State, while they were intensely indignant at what they regarded as Mr. Tyler's treason to their party, were not discouraged by it. They turned as one man to Mr. Clay, as their candidate for the presidency in 1844, and to Mr. Graham as their candidate for governor. The Whig State Convention was held in Raleigh December 7, 1843, and Mr. Graham was unanimously and with great enthusiasm chosen as its candidate for governor. It was with some sacrifice of his financial interests that he accepted this nomination. He said in his letter of acceptance, December 18, 1843: "But, however gratifying to an honorable pride, your communication awakens feelings also of a different character. It breaks in upon my plans of life, my professional and agricultural pursuits, and demands a sacrifice of interests which can not well be spared from my family. I have therefore most earnestly and anxiously hoped that the choice of the convention would have fallen on some one of those able and virtuous citizens, whose names have been connected with this subject and whose disinterestedness and zeal in the Whig cause, is only equaled by their devotion to its principles. Nevertheless, with my conceptions of duty, (however much I had wished it otherwise) I have no alternative but to accept the nomination. Without stronger reasons than any I have to urge, I could not hold any other person justified in refusing a call from such a source, to lend his name and his efforts to the support of principles, which, I verily believe, lie at the foundation of the enduring prosperity and happiness of the country." [49]

Mr. Graham's opponent was a personal friend and fellow country-man, Michael Hoke, of Lincoln. Mr. Hoke was young, (only thirty-four years of age), ardent and able. He was considered the most promising of the younger Democrats of the State, had great personal magnetism, was a fine debater and universally popular. He was a man of irreproachable character and had a great deal of humor, but it was a kindly, genial humor that left little sting behind it. His death, on September 9, 1844, from a fever contracted in the eastern part of the State during this campaign, was a great loss to the State, and it was deplored scarcely less by his political opponents than by his party associates. The campaign was arduous, the candidates occasionally meeting in joint discussion. Graham, more learned, more experienced, calmer, more dignified and impressive; Hoke, more nimble, quicker, brighter, and more entertaining. The Graham-Hoke campaign was long spoken of in the State in very much the same terms that we speak of the Vance-Settle campaign of 1876, as one of the most remarkable in the history of the State. Mr. Graham was elected by 3,153 majority.

Here is a contemporary estimate of Mr. Graham which I give. It is that of a political follower, but allowing something for natural partiality and exaggeration, its essential features present him very near as he was: "Governor Graham dignifies and adorns everything he touches. Such grace, such elegance, such ease, such candor and so much placid eloquence, were never seen before concentrated in one man. He can not fail to acquire the attention of his audience, and when acquired, he keeps it chained with a magic spell. We have seen speakers who seemed as if they snatched the very lightenings and thunders of heaven to assist them in overpowering the senses and arousing the passions of their hearers; we have seen those who appeared to make the very walls laugh with anecdote and the air boisterous with mirth; we have seen those whose plain, matter-of-fact statements fell with convincing force upon the judgment, but in so cold and formal a manner that, although we were compelled to acknowledge the force of the argument and the solidity of the facts, we could not forget the repulsive manner of the speaker; but never have we seen so

---

[49] Note.—He was urged very strongly by Senator Mangum and Mr. James W. Osborne not to accept this nomination, that his proper place was in the U. S. Senate, and this would prevent his being considered for that place.

due a degree of the excellencies of a public speaker united in one man as in Governor Graham. He is possessed of a lofty dignity without haughtiness, ease without affectation, talent without vanity, and principles which have the respect of even those who entertain others."

Of course the tone of this is exaggerated, but after all it is simply truth somewhat colored. Governor Graham had a very fine and noble presence. He was at this time the handsomest man in public life in North Carolina. The tones of his voice were mellow and harmonious, and, though not strong, well modulated. His action was free, easy and graceful, on occasion warming into energy. His matter was carefully arranged so as to give his argument the effect of cumulation. He was fair in statement, and perfectly honest and sincere in the positions he took. His public addresses, though always orderly arranged, are never closely reasoned. He knew the danger of the logical short cut in dealing with public questions. Its beauty and force could be appreciated only by the initiated, and such were not his fellow-citizens whom he was addressing. He very seldom dealt in sophistry. Indeed so practical a mind as his could rarely do so. In short the matter of his public speeches was interesting and instructive, while his manner was always attractive.

On January 1, 1845, he was installed as governor, the oaths of office being administered by the Chief Justice, Ruffin, in the Commons Hall, in the presence of both houses. He then delivered his inaugural address. After a merely cursory glance at the relations of the State to the Federal Government, in which he condemned the practice of devoting so much of our public discussions to Federal topics, he confines himself to the problems which were to confront him in his coming administration.

"That these important concerns of the nation should be objects of constant observation and active vigilance is to be expected and desired; but that they should be so to the exclusion of those immediate interests which come to our homes and our firesides, and which are wisely retained under state jurisdiction, is a misfortune to be deprecated. If we glory in the name of American citizens, it should be with feelings akin to filial affection and gratitude, that we remember we are North Carolinians; and that the preservation and prosperity of our system and its ability to secure the permanent and habitual attachment of the people, depend quite as much, nay much more, upon an enlightened policy and a correct administration in the state governments than in that of the union. * * * North Carolina, possessing a soil, upon the average not above the medium grade of fertility, but yielding fruitful returns to patient toil, in our generally salubrious climate; excluded by the nature of our sea coast from any enlarged share in the commerce of the world, her people have been inured to self-reliance, industry and economy. The natural fruits of this situation have been personal independence, unostentatious self-respect, habits in general of morality, obedience to the law, fidelity to engagements, public and private, frugality in expenditures and loyalty to the government, the offspring of the simple manners and honest and manly character of its citizens." He then proceeds to show the necessity for continued efforts to provide an adequate common school system, and the means for creating an adequate market for the products of the people: "If we can not, without too great a loss of profits, send our staples to existing markets, we must endeavor to bring a market nearer to them, by inducing capital to come to the State, by utilizing local capital in the establishement of various industries for which the State could provide so much raw material, by the building of more railroads and better local highways. Our country must be made to hold out the hope and expectation of acquiring the means of comfortable livelihood and a reasonable accumulation, or its population can not be expected to remain, nor its resources to increase. While labor is the true foundation of national wealth, it may be, much aided in its efforts by the kind and upholding hand of government." He concludes thus: "In our past history we have gained a high character for the virtues of honesty and fidelity. Thus far our escutcheon is unstained, the public faith has been kept, the public honor is inviolate. And whatever tests may await us in the future, let us fervently unite our invocations to that good Providence, who has so signally upheld and preserved us heretofore, that our beloved North Carolina may still be permitted to walk in her integrity, the object of our loyalty and pride, as she is the home of our hearts and affections."

The *Register* of January 8, 1845, commented on this address as follows: "We have never seen a larger or more intelligent assemblage on a similar occasion in our State; and we can say without disparagement to others that the address of Governor Graham on the occasion was decidedly the best inaugural we have ever heard, or have ever seen from any of the state executives of the union. It speaks the words of truth and soberness to our sister states and counsels our own in a language of the soundest wisdom."

One of the first problems with which Governor Graham had to deal was the foreclosure of the State's mortgages on the Raleigh & Gaston Railroad. The building of railroads was, of course, a new thing in North Carolina. The lack of experience in such work, as usual, wrought its own penalty. It cost more than it should, and was operated badly—expensively and inefficiently. The State had made itself liable as surety on $787,000 of its bonds. The company had failed to pay even the annual interest on these bonds, and the State was forced to pay both interest and a part of the principal. Legal proceedings were instituted for the foreclosure of all the mortgages on all the property of that Company at the Spring term, 1845, of the Wake County Court of Equity. But owing to the resistance made by the company, and the decision of the Superior Court in their favor, an appeal was rendered necessary to the Supreme Court, and the decree of foreclosure was postponed to the fall term of that year. The cost of the road was $1,500,000, and it brought at the foreclosure sale, on the bid of the State, through Governor Graham, $363,000.

The Legislature of 1844-5, also, made it the duty of the Governor to collect the memorials of the Revolutionary history of the State. In pursuance of this, Governor Graham wrote to Judge Francis Xavier Martin, of Louisiana, on February 8, 1845: "Presuming that your researchers when engaged in writing the history of the State put you in possession of many of the letters of these early governors (Caswell, Nash and Burke), as well as other documents of great interest to our people, I have to request as a special favor to North Carolina that you will be kind enough to communicate to me any of our public documents of the description desired, which may be under your control; or that you will inform me as early as your convenience will permit, where copies of them may be procured." But Judge Martin, as he wrote Governor Graham on March 29, 1845, had collected no material so late as the administrations of early governors. He corresponded also with Miss Mary Burke, the only surviving child of Governor Burke, and it was by her consent that the Burke papers, then in the possession of Dr. James Webb, of Hillsboro were turned over to Governor Swain.

On March 5, 1845, he issued a circular letter to the people of the State, reciting the resolution of the Legislature and giving in detail the public documents already discovered in the capitol and describing those missing and desired, and requesting them to cooperate with him in the preservation of the memorials of the Revolutionary period. The early part of his first administration, too, was much occupied with the preliminaries to the establishment of a school in Raleigh for the deaf, dumb, and blind.

He met his first Legislature in November, 1846, with an elaborate and very able message, dealing largely with the finances of the State. The average expenditure for the ordinary support of the government at that time was $67,500 per annum. At the same time the income from ordinary sources of revenue averaged $83,000, the excess of which, over and above ordinary expenses, was devoted to the account of rebuilding the capitol, interest on the State's debt until it was liquidated in full and to liabilities of the railroad companies. After showing that the income could be largely increased by an adequate assessment of the lands and polls in the State (there had been no reassessment of lands in ten years), he proceeds: "No valuation can continue to be a just criterion of worth for any considerable period, and a reassessment should be provided for once at least in five years, if it be not annually. By adopting these measures of fairness and justice, to collect what is now imposed without increase of taxes, it may reasonably be expected that the public revenue from present sources, now equal to about $86,000, may be raised to $100,000 per annum." He then recommends a specific tax upon pleasure carriages, gold watches kept for use and other articles of luxury, to go into operation at once, and to continue in force until the expiration of the next session of the General Assembly. "In advising therefore but a temporary provision for extra taxation, I am influenced by the consideration, that possibly it may not longer be required, rather than a fear of any aversion of our constituents to contribute whatever may be needed to redeem the public obligations, however incautiously or unfortunately entered into. The odious doctrine that a State may refuse or postpone the fulfillment of contracts guaranteed by her public faith and sovereign honor, has no resting place in all our borders, and I am yet to hear of a single exception to the unanimity of our people upon this subject."

There were at the time many railroad schemes. Among others were two proposed railroads into South Carolina, one from Wilmington, which was by this Legislature incorporated as the Wilmington and Manchester, and one from Fayetteville. Governor Graham, while not opposing these projects, was very much in favor of a railroad from Fayetteville to Salisbury or Charlotte, and thence into South Carolina. And the Legislature did grant a charter to the Charlotte and South Carolina Railroad.

At that time our common school system was in its infancy, only $95,578 being distributed by the State for its support. Governor Graham recommended that the office of Commissioner of Common Schools be created, and that it be filled by one charged with the superintendance of the system throughout the State, and devoting his whole time and attention in imparting to it vigor and usefulness. "The subject is of sufficient weight, especially in the infantile stage of these institutions, to engage the best talents and most exalted patriotism of the country."

In May, 1846, the President, Polk, called for one regiment of volunteer infantry, to be enrolled and held in readiness to aid in the prosecution of the existing war with the Republic of Mexico. Governor Graham, in response, issued his proclamation, and with a most commendable promptitude, said he, more than three times the number required tendered their service. Capt. S. L. Fremont, the army officer appointed by the Federal Government to muster this regiment into service, wrote, after he had performed this service and was leaving the State : "Public men may differ about the justice of the war, but the good people of the Old North State have shown that in a foreign war, they know no party but their country, and no country but their own."

Governor Graham's attitude towards the Mexican War was that held by most of the leading Whigs of the period, i. e. it was unnecessary, if not criminal, and was brought on, not by the annexation of Texas, but by President Polk's precipitancy in sending General Taylor to take possession of the territory in dispute between the State of Texas and the Republic of Mexico. War being flagrant, however, everything must be done to make the arms of the United States successful.

To some degree Mr. Graham's first term as governor was devoted to carrying out the plans of the previous administration (Morehead's) or those inaugurated by the General Assembly of 1844-5, such as, for instance, saving the State harmless from the bankruptcy of the Raleigh and Gaston Railroad and the Club-foot and Harlows Creek Canal, and directing the settlement of the accounts between the State and insolvent purchasers of the Cherokee lands and their bondsmen. In all these matters he demonstrated his very superior ability as an administrator. Especially was this the case in his management of the Raleigh and Gaston

Railroad. Had it not been for a fire in February, 1848, by which the machine shops and engine house were destroyed and its stationary engine and four locomotives were seriously damaged, it would in the course of a few years been made a profitable investment.

There had been occasional discussions of amendment to our penal code which would moderate its harshness and provide a penitentiary for a certain class of offenders, from 1791 on, notably so in 1817 and in 1822, but nothing definite had been done until the General Assembly of 1844-5. The governor was directed to secure statistics from States in which the penitentiary system then prevailed and submit the same to the people before an election to be held under the Act. Governor Graham, through an extensive correspondence, did collect the data desired and publish the same in the newspapers of the State in the early Summer of 1846. Under the act, the question of a penitentiary or no penitentiary was submitted to the people at the time of the election for governor in August of that year. The election seems to have gone by default against any change, the vote for it being very small.

So satisfactory to his own party and to the people of the State was his first term as governor, that in January, 1846, Governor Graham was nominated for a second, by a largely attended and very enthusiastic Whig convention, and the following August was reelected by a great majority (7,850), over his Democratic opponent, James B. Shepard. Mr. Shepard was a man of fine ability and was a good speaker, but he had inherited wealth, so was disinclined to the drudgery of politics and of the bar. His candidacy and canvass against so popular and efficient a governor as Mr. Graham was, of course, a forlorn hope. Mr. Graham, had, by this time, become unquestionably the leader of the Whig party in the State. He practically dictated the policy of that party. I do not use the term dictate in an offensive sense, for he was too courteous a gentleman and too wise a public man ever to assume a dictatorial manner. His knowledge of the people was so extensive and so accurate, that his party associates had the utmost confidence in the soundness of his judgment in all matters of policy, and so almost invariably adopted his views after a conference, or if on rare occasions they overruled him, had cause to regret it, as subsequent events showed their wisdom. As a party leader, it is quite probable that he was never excelled by any man in the history of the State.

In the General Assembly of 1848-9, the two parties were tied in both House and Senate, so a compromise was made by which R. B. Gilliam, Whig, was elected Speaker of the House, and Calvin Graves, Democrat, was elected Speaker of the Senate. The principal subjects for consideration by this Legislature were the establishment of a State Hospital for the Insane at Raleigh, the disposition of the Raleigh and Gaston Railroad and the charter of the North Carolina Railroad. Governor Graham gives his views at large on all these topics in his last biennial message. He concludes his recommendation of a State Hospital as follows: "A distinguished person of the gentler sex,[50] who has devoted much of her life to the pious duty of pleading the cause of the lunatic before States and communities, has recently traversed a considerable part of this State in search of information respecting these unfortunates among us, and will probably ask leave to present their cause to you at an early day. I cannot too earnestly commend the cause itself, or the disinterested benevolence of its advocate."

There is no more dramatic incident in the history of the State than Miss Dix's appeal to this Legislature, Mr. Dobbin's great speech, and the passage of the act on January 29th, 1849, but it is without the scope of this paper.

Governor Graham's views in regard to the disposition of the Raleigh and Gaston Railroad were so interwoven with those on the charter of the North Carolina Railroad, that I discuss them together. He said in his message that there were only three modes of disposing of the former road : 1st, a resale to existing stockholders by compromise of the suits now pending, if suitable terms be offered; 2nd, retain it as a permanent property of the State after repairing it in the best manner; and 3rd, to unite it with another work through the interior of the State. The last was the plan which he urged very forcibly upon the Legislature in his regular message and in two special messages sent to the Senate. His idea was to fill in the missing link between Raleigh and Columbia, S. C., in the great chain of railways from New York to New Orleans by incorporating and building a railroad to be called the North Carolina Railroad, from Raleigh to Salisbury, and thence on to Charlotte, where it would connect with the Charlotte and Columbia road, already chartered and then being built. The details of his plan may be summarized thus : Private individuals to subscribe $500,000. As soon as the Board of Internal Improvements should be satisfied that these subscriptions were

---

[50] Dorothea L. Dix.

in good faith and solvent, the suits then pending against delinquent subscribers to the stock of the Raleigh and Gaston road should abate, the new corporation was to be formed and the State to convey that road to it. He estimated that the cost of the new road would be not more than $2,500,000, and of this the State was to assume half, but the conveyance of the Raleigh and Gaston road was to be in lieu of $500,000 of the State's subscription. The $500,000, subscribed privately as above said, were to be used first in putting the Raleigh and Gaston road in thorough repair and good condition, and the balance was to be expended in building the new road toward Salisbury from Raleigh. He estimated that there would be about forty miles thus completed. After so much of the work should be done, then the State was to advance such further sum as might be necessary to complete the road, the amount paid by the State, however, to be always in equal proportion to those paid by private stockholders. His scheme also comprehended the building later a railroad from Raleigh to Goldsboro and one from some point east of the Yadkin to Beaufort. As is well known this scheme was not adopted in its entirety. As a matter of fact, it was only through many concessions and compromises in the face of very determined opposition that the North Carolina Railroad was chartered.

The Democratic Speaker of the Senate, Calvin Graves, fully aware of the consequences of his act, committed political suicide when he broke the tie in the Senate in favor of the Railroad. Governor Graham supported this measure sincerely, though it was some modification of his own. He is said to have drawn the whole bill, which was introduced in the Senate by Mr. William S. Ashe, of New Hanover, and was certainly the author of section 45 to the end of the act. (Laws 1848-9, chapter 82.) If any one could be said to have been the father of the North Carolina Railroad, where there were so many taking an active and efficient part in its inception, certainly it was Governor Graham. Ground was broken for the new railroad by Calvin Graves in the presence of a large crowd at Greensboro, on July 11th, 1851. Governor Graham was then in Washington City, as Secretary of the Navy, so could not attend this meeting, but he wrote a letter, which was read to the assembly and from which I extract the following: "To the friends of this enterprise, with whom I have been proud to cooperate in the darkest hours of its fate, as well as to all the good citizens of the State, who shall participate in the celebration of its happy commencement, I offer my hearty congratulations and good wishes. * * * I look forward to the day of its final completion, as a time of deliverance not merely from the shackles of commercial bondage, but from the dominion of prejudice and error, which, however, honestly entertained, have been the bane of our prosperity."

There were three measures that he repeatedly urged upon both of his Legislatures, but in vain : 1st, the appointment of a state commissioner of education; 2nd, the abolition of the jurisdiction of county courts over pleas, and 3rd, a more modern and more efficient system for the maintenance of public roads.

This summary of the leading events and measures of Governor Graham's two administrations shows how wise and practical he was in dealing with the affairs of the State. Adopting a phrase of his own, "he devoted himself to those noble studies, by which States are made prosperous and their people happy," and the knowledge thus acquired he applied wisely to the service of his native state. His messages, addresses and other state papers were systematically arranged, businesslike and practical, indicating hard, intelligent, apprehending and appreciative labor. Their style was pellucid, flowing and attractive, yet dignified and impressive. In the weight of their matter, in the orderliness of its arrangement and in the attractiveness of their vehicle, they compare well with the state papers of any man at any period.

To The Civil War

At the end of his last term as Governor, in January, 1849, Mr. Graham returned to the practice of his profession at Hillsboro and in the adjoining counties.

General Taylor was inaugurated as President in March of that year. The end of the Mexican War, with the cession of a vast territory to the United States, presented many serious problems to the Taylor administration. That, however, which assumed an exceedingly threatening aspect and absorbed most painfully the attention of the whole country, was what was and should be the legal and constitutional status of slavery in the newly acquired territory. The North, speaking generally, was determined that there should be no extension of slave territory, while the South, standing upon its clear rights under the Constitution, was equally determined that the new territory should be open to settlement by slaveholders if they so desired, without any interference with their slave property. Never in the history of this country has there appeared in the Senate of the United States so splendid an array of talent, of statesmanship and ardent patriotism as in the Senate of the Thirty-first Congress at its first session, yet never was there so plain an illustration of the futility of all the wisdom of the wisest of men when set in opposition to that march of events, which is controlled only by the infinite wisdom of Providence. These wise men could bring about a compromise which could postpone for a moment the final catastrophe,—that is all.

Mr. Graham was a very much interested and sympathetic observer of all the events which led up to Mr. Clay's famous compromise, and was in frequent communication with the senators from North Carolina, Messrs. Badger and Mangum. He, himself, supported that measure without reserve. In the summer of 1849, President Taylor offered him his choice of the missions to Russia and to Spain. Fortunately for his State and country, he had no inclination to a foreign appointment. On July 4th, 1850, the President was much exposed to a hot sun, and contracted a fever from which he died on the 9th. The Vice-President, Millard Fillmore, qualified the next day as President. It has been the habit to speak of Mr. Fillmore as man of only moderate ability, dominated and controlled by his very able and experienced cabinet. The truth is, he had already as chairman of the Ways and Means (then also Appropriations) Committee of the Twenty-seventh Congress, shown his unusual ability as a practical, conservative, laborious legislator. Without being at all brilliant, he had in full measure the capacity for labor, for calm, sane, unimpassioned investigation, and for firm, consistent action, when once his course of action had been determined upon. He was a man of high character and indubitable patriotism. Had not the majority of both Houses of Congress been averse to him during the less than three years of his administration, that administration would have been noted for its constructive statesmanship. Many useful and salutary measures advocated by him were disregarded by Congress, but his administration has to its credit cheap postage, the extension of the Capitol, the Perry Expedition, the exploration of the Amazon and, to some extent, (he and his advisors being in sympathy with it, whereas General Taylor was lukewarm, if not opposed to it), the compromise of 1850.

Soon after General Taylor's death, his cabinet resigned. Mr. Fillmore selected as their successors: Daniel Webster, Secretary of State; Thomas Corwin, Secretary of the Treasury; Charles M. Conrad, Secretary of War; William A. Graham, Secretary of the

Navy; James A. Pearce, Secretary of the Interior; Nathan K. Hall, Postmaster-General, and John J. Crittenden, Attorney-General.

To this important office, Mr. Graham, though comparatively a young man, only 46 years of age, came in the full maturity of his powers. His diligence in mastering detail, his capacity for labor, his accessibility and courtesy to competent advisers and his sound and well-balanced judgment, soon made him an exceptionally efficient Secretary. The measures with which he was especially identified were four:

1st. Reorganization of the coast survey, making it more practical and useful.

2d. Reorganization of the personnel of the navy, providing for the retirement of officers, etc.

3d. The exploration of the Amazon.

4th. The expedition to Japan.

On the first of these measures Mr. Benton commented as follows in a letter to him, dated February 19th, 1851: "I have just read a second time your report on the coast survey subject. I consider it one of the most perfect reports I ever read,—a model of a business report, and one which should carry conviction to every candid, inquiring mind. I deem it one of the largest reforms, both in an economical and administrative point of view, which the state of our affairs admits of."[51]

A gentleman, still living and who has a very accurate memory, reports a conversation had with Com. M. F. Maury long after this period, in which he spoke in the highest terms of Secretary Graham's efficiency, and his own sense of gratitude to him for giving him opportunities to set out on his own distinguished career.

On the second of these measures, Mr. McGehee quotes a letter of another distinguished Senator: "You had a new field opened to you, and well and ably have you occupied every portion of it. The report is to be properly characterized by a bold originality of conception and a fearlessness of responsibility too rare in that class of state papers. You have had to grapple with a system built up by a series of abuses, and to use the knife—that fearful and unpopular instrument—somewhat unsparingly. If I do not greatly err, it will give you more reputation in the country than anything you have heretofore produced before the public."

The third great measure of his Secretaryship was the exploration of the valley of the Amazon by Lieutenants Herndon and

[51] McGehee, 26.

Gibbon. This was suggested by Lieut. M. F. Maury. Seeing the importance of this venture, both as adding to the world's knowledge of that remote and little known country, as well as the possibilities for trade with its inhabitants, Secretary Graham readily adopted the suggestion. His letter of instruction to Lieutenant Herndon, February 15th, 1851, is characterized by that familiarity with the details of the project and that clearness as well as largeness of view which are found in all his important papers.

Of all the great measures with which he was identified as cabinet official, that which was most fruitful in results was the Perry Expedition to Japan. There had been many disasters among the fishing vessels of the United States on the uncharted, or insufficiently charted, seas of the northeast coast of Asia. A fishing vessel had been cast away on the coast of Formosa, and all of its survivors had been massacred. Another vessel had been wrecked off the coast of Japan, and the fifteen survivors had been cast into prison and treated with great cruelty. The settlement of the Oregon boundary dispute, the cession of California by Mexico, the discovery of gold there and the completion of the Panama Railroad, had aroused the people of the United States to the promising aspect of trade on the Pacific coast and to the far East. Japan was at that period one of the hermit nations of the world. As early as December, 1850, Commodore Perry suggested to Secretary Graham the project of an expedition to Japan. Mr. Graham, at once impressed with the hopefulness of the scheme and its far-reaching consequences if successful, encouraged the commodore to confer confidentially with Mr. Aspinwall, of New York, who had experience in trade to the East, and had recently completed the Panama Railroad, and certain mariners in Boston, and collect such facts and statistics as might throw light upon the subject, and report to him. At this time the discussion was kept from the public, because it was feared that England or France might forestall this country, if information of these proposals should reach either of those powers. Mr. Graham, upon receipt of the information desired, seems to have laid the matter before the cabinet, but without their coming to any definite conclusion at that time. Soon after it was the fortune of an American vessel to rescue a number of Japanese in the Pacific about six hundred miles from Japan, and to bring them into the port of San Francisco. The administration, upon hearing of this, quickly realized its importance as giving an opportunity to establish friendly relations with

Japan. Preparations were immediately made to return these Japanese to their home on a man-of-war, which, leaving San Francisco, was to join the Eastern Squadron at Macao or Hong Kong. Meantime Com. John H. Aulick was dispatched, with additional vessels, to take command of the Eastern Squadron, bearing with him from President Fillmore a letter to the Emperor of Japan. The instructions to Aulick, May 31st, 1851, drawn by Secretary Graham, do not on their face contemplate a special mission to Japan. When the shipwrecked Japanese reached their home escorted by the American war vessels, the natives refused to permit them to land, or to supply the American vessels with food or water. Early in the year 1852, no doubt under the urging of Commodore Perry and Mr. Graham, the plans of the administration underwent a change. It was then determined that Perry should be given the command of the Eastern Squadron and that he should go with very considerable reenforcement of vessels upon a special mission to Japan. He was commissioned on March 24th, 1852, preparations were begun immediately to fit out his squadron, and he sailed on November 24th, 1852, Aulick having in the meantime, July 10th, been relieved of the command of the Eastern Squadron. The results of this expedition are before the world. There can be no doubt that Governor Graham was the prime mover, in the cabinet, of this epoch-making adventure.

His services as Secretary of the Navy showed the country that he was a fine administrator as well as an able statesman, as much master of detail, as he was capable of taking whole views of great public questions. The Whig National Convention met in June, 1852. President Fillmore, who was supported very earnestly by Mr. Graham and who, according to all the rules of the game, should have been nominated, led on the first ballot, but Mr. Clay, who was still all-powerful, threw his influence to General Scott, and nominated him. Mr. Graham was nominated for the Vice-Presidency on the second ballot, receiving 232 votes against 52 for Bates, of Missouri.

Never was a weaker nomination made for an exhalted office by any party than that of General Scott by the Whigs. He was an able and virtuous man, but many of the salient features of his character approached so near being ridiculous in themselves and lent themselves so readily to caricature, that his candidacy, though a tragedy to the Whig party, became a comedy to a large majority of his fellow-citizens. There was defection, too, among the Whigs of the South, because he was thought to be tainted with freesoilism, and among the Whigs of the North, because he was thought to be under Southern influence. The result, of course, was foredoomed. He received only 42 out of a total of 296 electoral votes.

Whatever expression of dissatisfaction there may have been at the head of the ticket, there was none at the nomination of Governor Graham. His personal worth, his ability and his usefulness were freely admitted by every one. In Pennsylvania, however, party capital was made against him on account of his votes on the Whig tariff bill of 1842. He generally voted with the Democrats for lower rates when the measure was up in the Senate and against the bill, when completed, because provision for the distribution of the proceeds of the sales of public lands was omitted. Notwithstanding the evident failure of the Scott campaign, Pierce and King carried the State of North Carolina by only 603 majority. This, under the discouraging conditions for that party then existing in the State, was a Whig victory, or rather a Graham victory, for it was his popularity and influence only that reduced the Democratic majority of a few months before of 5,564 to 603. The disintegration of the Whig party, the symptoms of which were very marked in most of the other States, had also begun in North Carolina. David S. Reid, Democrat, had been elected Governor in 1850. Renominated by his party in 1852, he and the very eloquent and accomplished John Kerr, the candidate of the Whigs, had canvassed the State on Governor Reid's proposition to remove the freehold qualification from voters for State Senators, and in August of that year Governor Reid had been reelected by the largely increased majority stated above. This free suffrage program was not alone in undermining the Whig strength in the State, for voters were coming more and more to realize that the only safety for slavery was the continued ascendancy of the Democratic party in national affairs.

Governor Graham seems to have had no substantial objection to the extension of the suffrage. He was so much absent from the State after the subject was introduced in the General Assembly of 1850, that he gave the matter only casual consideration until 1853. Then he was opposed, not so much to the policy as to the method of incorporating it in our fundamental law. "A constitution of government for a free people," said he, "is a complicated machine, like a steam engine or the human frame. It consists of various parts adjusted to one harmonious whole. In other or more familiar language, it is a system of checks and balances, one article of which would not have been inserted without another on kindred subjects, and one of which can not be removed without carrying with it others, or deranging and destroying the balance of the whole." He happily illustrated this idea, as follows: "It might be supposed by a superficial observer that the human hand would be improved by cutting off the fingers to equal lengths, and the operation would be so simple that any child who could handle an axe could perform it. And yet we know that the curtailment of an extremity would wound nerves and blood vessels connecting with the brain and heart, the very vitals of the system."

The freehold qualification for voters for Senators was incorporated in the Constitution of 1776 and retained in that of 1835, as a measure of protection to the landed interest against those who owned no land, yet as free men voted for members of the House of Commons and so were represented there. Land was much the more valuable part of the possessions of the citizens of the State who lived in its midland and its west, whereas slaves constituted a large part of the wealth of the east. By a compromise between these conflicting interests, the land was given this measure of protection in return for that given slave property by forbidding any other taxation than the poll tax, (the same as that of the whites), on all slaves between twelve and fifty years af age,—much less than this property would yield if taxed *ad valorem,* as land was. Yet the Democrats proposed to strike down the protection to land, while leaving slave property still protected, and paying an inadequate tax. He, then, met the plan to enact the suffrage amendment only, by a bill to submit to the people the question of a convention to amend the Constitution, not only in this regard, but in others where it required amendment.[52] As a sort of forlorn hope that he might stem the tide setting so strongly against the Whig party, he was elected to the Senate from Orange County in 1854. On December 14th of that year he made a very able speech in the Senate elaborating the above ideas. That the Democrats, themselves, split a few years later on the question of *ad valorem* taxation of slaves, and were finally forced to adopt it as a party measure, is very strong evidence of Governor Graham's political acumen.

The immediate effect upon the South of the compromise of 1850, was quieting. The love of the Union, that had been weakened by the agitation which induced that measure, became once

---

[52] Senate Journal, 1854, 70.

more an active principle in that section. The failure of some States in the North to enforce, or permit to be enforced, in their borders, the fugitive slave law, (the only thing which they yielded in the so-called compromise), in good faith, the Kansas-Nebraska agitation and the Dred Scott decision, however, soon aroused both North and South as they had never been aroused before. It became daily more and more evident that Mr. Seward's irrepressible conflict was not an oratorical exaggeration, but a stern reality. Men, wise men, patriotic men, continued in the midst of the turmoil to cry peace, when there was no peace and could be no peace. We, from the vantage ground of the present looking back upon the past, can only wonder that the final catastrophe was postponed so long. That it was, is due in large degree to the wisdom and moderation and patriotism of the dwindling band of Whig leaders in the South and of their sympathizers in the North. There is something very admirable in the character and pathetic in the history of the Old Line Whigs of the South. In politics they were conservative, but in all that concerned the industrial interests of the country they were progressives. They were as incorruptible as a Roman senator in the palmiest days of Rome. Their public life was as clean and immaculate and as far above suspicion as Caesar would have had his wife. To them patriotism was more than a sentiment, it was almost a passion. To them the Federal Constitution was not a compact, but the great charter of an indestructible Union, the repository of the political wisdom of the ages, by which America was to be made great and kept great throughout all time. Patriotism to them, then assumed a twofold aspect—love for their native State, and love for the Union. This blinded them to that fact of facts, which is written all across the history of the period immediately preceding the Civil War, namely, that it was either slavery *or* the Union. There was no other alternative. If slavery was to continue, then the Union must go; if the Union was to continue, then slavery must go. The vision of the secessionist was clearer. He saw that he could not long hold on to his slave property in the Union, so he prepared himself to hold on to it out of the Union. To him, to use the sharp and cutting characterization of Henry A. Wise, there were only three parties—the Whites, the Blacks and the Mulattoes: the Whites, the secessionists; the Blacks, the Republican party North; and the Mulattos, the union men of the South. It was the day of the extremist. Events moved too rapidly for the moderates. They could not stem the tide; they must move with it, or be overwhelmed. It was a choice between loves, and, in agony of soul, they chose the greater, their homes, their firesides and their neighbors, and ever after their faces were to the foe. Governor Graham was one of the wisest and noblest of the moderates. He loved the Union scarcely less than he did his native State. He thought the Southern agitator only less to blame than the Northern abolitionist. He condemned secession with all the earnestness of his nature, not only as a political heresy, but as essentially suicidal to the best interests of the South. So strong was his position before the country at large, so great was the confidence in his ability, his moderation, his probity and his patriotism that he was supported by North Carolina, Georgia and several district delegates for the nomination for the presidency by the Constitutional Union party in 1860. And after the popular election of Mr. Lincoln in the fall of that year, the New York and Pennsylvania electors were strongly urged to cast their ballots for him in the electoral college, as the only means to avert the impending dissolution of the Union.

Even after the secession of South Carolina and the Gulf States, Union sentiment in North Carolina continued very strong. Governor Graham could see no reason for secession, (or revolution, as he preferred to call it), in the bare fact of Mr. Lincoln's election. He regarded the strong expressions of the campaign used by Mr. Lincoln, Mr. Seward and others, (i. e., that the government could not endure half slave and half free, that the question was whether freemen should cultivate the fields of the North or slaves those of the South, etc.) as mere oratorical exaggeration, rhetoric of the hustings on which they were canvassing for free-soil votes. He, therefore, very consistently opposed the calling of a convention in February, 1861, and his course therein was sustained by a majority of the people of the State. After Mr. Lincoln's inauguration, he hoped that he might let the seven "erring sisters go in peace," that he would convene Congress in extra session, acknowledge the independence of these States, grant guarantees to the other slave States, which had adhered to the Union, that slavery would not be interfered with within their borders, and thus maintain a happy and connected Union of twenty-seven States, instead of precipitating the country into a bloody and destructive Civil War. This seems to have been Mr. Lincoln's program at the time he offered a seat in his Cabinet to Mr. John A. Gilmer, but later, his views no doubt modified as well by the current of events as by the urging of more bloody-minded advisers, he adopted what historians now call the bolder policy; he called for troops to crush the rebellion, as he called it. Thenceforward Governor Graham saw clearly that there was no other alternative but Civil War, and that North Carolina must take part with the other Southern States. He had no illusions about its extent. He knew that it was to be long drawn out, destructive and agonizing, with the South's only hope a desire for peace at the North, or interference from abroad. He was sent as a delegate from Orange County to the secession convention of May, 1861, and after strenuous efforts to change its phraseology so as to make it an appeal to the ultimate right of revolution, instead of to the constitutional theory of secession, he, with all other members, signed the secession ordinance, after it had been adopted by the convention.

THE CIVIL WAR AND AFTER

Governor Graham's training, his temperament and his habit of thought, would necessarily make him a moderate in any acute crisis, so though he sincerely desired the success of the arms of the Confederacy, (he devoted five of his seven sons to the cause, all that were old enough to bear arms), he was in opposition to the government. In the State Legislature, in 1863-4, when he was Senator from Orange, in the State Convention, and in the Senate of the Confederate States, he uniformly opposed all propositions to abridge the freedom of the press or of speech, to suspend the privilege of the writ of habeas corpus, to substitute military for civil tribunals, or otherwise impair the common rights of the people. The disastrous defeats of Vicksburg and Gettysburg, and the consequent declension of the fortunes of the Confederacy, made the people of North Carolina turn more and more to the original union men. Governor Graham was elected to the Confederate States Senate by a more than three-fourths majority in February, 1864,* and took his seat in May of 1864. At this session he, in conjunction with other members of Congress, labored to procure the opening of negotiations looking to peace, but unsuccessfully. For the same object he labored at the ensuing session, and the Hampton Roads Conference was, to some extent, due to his counsels. After the failure of that Conference, he insisted that a new commission should be sent without limitation of powers; for the independence of the Southern States it was evident was not obtainable, and if the administration scrupled

---

*This is a mistake. He was elected November 27, 1862. *Ed.*

to treat on the basis of the annihilation of their own government, that commission might, nevertheless, ascertain what terms would be yielded by the United States to the States concerned, and communicate the same to them for their action; but his exertions in this behalf were of none effect. When he became satisfied that it was the fixed purpose of the administration to make the recognition of independence the basis of any peace, he lost no time in counseling the Governor of North Carolina (Vance) to interpose promptly for the termination of the war. The rapidity of military operations on the part of the troops of the United States did not allow adequate time to render such interposition effective, had Governor Vance been complaisant, as he was not, and it is perhaps fortunate that such was the fact and that the war closed when and in the manner it did. Had the State intervened at this, or some former period, the disaster to the cause would have been imputed solely to that reason, and ill blood and angry feeling, crimination and recrimination, would have been the consequence. As it is all are convinced that the result is to be ascribed to the exhausted resources of the country and its entire inability longer to maintain the struggle against such fearful odds. There was left, therefore, no jealousy or controversy among States or individuals, but a general disposition to submit as to a decree of fate. This is, substantially, Governor Graham's own account of these transactions in his petition to Andrew Johnson for pardon, dated Raleigh, July 25th, 1865.[53] His course shows his calm, unimpassioned wisdom in the midst of the most exciting circumstances in a very remarkable light. If his course at the end of the war, set out above, was erroneous, it was a virtuous error, founded upon the highest of motives, the desire to stop the further effusion of blood and to save the people of his own State from the horrors which marked the course of General Sherman's army through the other States of the South; this too when there was not the slightest hope for a successful issue to the contest.

He was elected to the United States Senate by the General Assembly of 1866, but was not allowed to take his seat. For the remainder of his life he was a loved and trusted adviser and leader of the people, without being allowed to serve them in any public office, for rancorous politicians in North Carolina prevented the removal of his disabilities before his health had failed

---

[53] See also his letters in Spencer's "Last Ninety Days of the War in North Carolina," pp. 112-120.

—a very marked instance of the small things of this world confounding the great.

In 1867 George Peabody established a fund of $2,100,000, increased in 1869 to $3,500,000, to be devoted to education in the Southern States. This fund was placed under the control of fifteen trustees, of whom Robert C. Winthrop of Massachusetts was chairman, and they were to meet annually. At the suggestion of Mr. Winthrop, Governor Graham was selected by Mr. Peabody as one of the original trustees. Among his associates in the management of this fund were, besides Mr. Winthrop, Hamilton Fish, General Grant, Admiral Farragut, Bishop McIlvaine, of Ohio, W. M. Evarts and William C. Rives, and later, to fill vacancies, Bishop Whipple, A. H. H. Stuart and Chief Justice Waite.

Governor Graham was wholly in sympathy with the attempt to reorganize as a political force the better element among the white voters of the State, regardless of their former political affiliations. He was one of the fathers of the Conservative-Democratic party—a flexible and convenient designation, which could be reversed in Democratic communities, while it remained steadfast in Whig. He presided over the political convention that met in Raleigh, February 6, 1868, and made a notable speech defining his position, and later canvassed the State for Ashe against Holden.

He recognized fully the brutal folly, if not criminality, of the reconstruction program of Congress; he was opposed to negro suffrage, because he knew the negro was not fitted for the ballot, yet he believed in strict obedience to the law and a patient biding the time when the extent of the evil should, itself, work its own remedy in the awakening of the public conscience North, and the arousing of the people of the South to the necessity for firm, consistent, united action against the vandals and corruptionists who were preying upon them. He condemned the Ku Klux organization, not only as unwise, but as criminal, as a resort to extra-legal remedies, that could be justified by no concatenation of circumstances. Applying Bacon's definition of revenge a species of wild justice, to their deeds, he did not hesitate in his great speech as leading counsel for the managers in the impeachment trial of Governor Holden, to describe the hanging of Wyatt Outlaw "as an atrocious act of assassination." It is difficult, if not impossible, for human wisdom to devise a formula beforehand, that will fit abnormal and unforseen conditions, which may arise in the future. In this assertion, Governor Graham was applying this formula in all its damning quality, disregarding the abnormal conditions which rendered it not strictly applicable. But this illustrates his remarkable moral courage. Never in his long public life did he hesitate to do or say anything, which he thought wise or true, on account of any supposed bad consequences to himself.

His health commenced to fail the latter part of 1872, and in 1873 it was apparent to his physicians that he was suffering from a heart disease that might end his life at any time. In 1874 he was selected by Virginia as one of the arbitrators between that State and Maryland. He concurred fully with the public sentiment in North Carolina, which enabled the Legislature of 1874-5 to call a Convention to amend the Constitution of 1868. He thought that Constitution too cumbersome, too minute in its provisions and too restrictive upon the Legislature while placing too much patronage in the hands of the Governor. Orange County elected him its delegate to the convention of 1875, but on August 11, 1875, while at Saratoga Springs, New York, in the performance of his duty as one of the arbitrators of the boundary dispute, he expired in the 71st year of his age.

"The intelligence of his death was transmitted by telegraph to every part of the country. All the great journals responded with leading articles expressive of the national bereavement."[54] In North Carolina all the people grieved at the death of its greatest and most honored citizen. At the border of the State his remains were met by many of its prominent men, and escorted to Raleigh where they lay in state in the rotunda of the Capitol, guarded by State and National troops, for hours as they were viewed by crowds. Late that afternoon they were conveyed to Hillsboro, attended by the militia and special guards of honor from the towns of the State, where they lay in state at his own house until the noon of Sunday, August 15th, when funeral services were held over them at the Presbyterian Church, and in the presence of an enormous concourse, collected from many counties. They were interred in the graveyard of that Church.

There has lived in North Carolina no public man, whose life was a greater force for good than was that of Governor Graham. It was, and is, an exemplification of all the virtues that a public man should have—intelligence, industry, courage, unselfishness, devotion to the public welfare and to duty. Ingrained into his nature too was that respect for religion, without which no man can be good, as well as a definite faith in Christ, not only as a great moral teacher, but as the Redeemer of mankind. He was a

---

[54] McGehee, 75.

Presbyterian by inheritance and by choice, though for reasons satisfactory to himself, he did not enroll himself as a member of that Church. During the last few years of his life (the writer, as a boy had personal knowledge of this), no one in the community in which he lived, ever spoke of him without the very tones and inflection of his voice showing the deep respect and admiration and regard he had for him. The feeling with which a North Carolina Episcopalian thirty years ago spoke of Bishop Atkinson, more nearly expresses the regard of the people of Hillsboro and Orange County for Governor Graham, at that period, than anything else. He was endowed by nature with an excellent mind, and a noble and very handsome presence. His mind was assiduously cultivated and trained. He had the religious and moral instincts by inheritance, and these grew and strengthened in the environment in which his life was placed. He had no bad habits as a boy, none as a youth and none as a man. Instead, the habits of thrift, of industry and thoroughness became a second nature to him. He was ambitious, but it was with a guided and controlled ambition, which sought place and power for larger spheres of usefulness. All these when he came to face the world enabled him to conquer a place for himself second to no North Carolinian. Judge Murphey was a greater genius, but he was not so practical; Judge Badger had greater intellectual endowments, but he was not so industrious; Judge Mangum was a greater popular orator, but he was self indulgent; Judge Ruffin was a greater lawyer, but his life ran in a narrower channel; Judge Gaston was a greater lawyer and orator, and as pure in heart and life and conduct as he, but he was not ambitious.

Yet if the capacity for taking pains should be the test for one's greatness, Governor Graham was greater than any of these. He was many sided, and a great deal of his work remains, and there is none of it that is not far above the average. He is entitled to very high rank as a lawyer, as a public speaker, as a statesman and as a writer, and the highest rank as a faithful, as a thorough and as a conscientious public official. There was never a more diligent and faithful legislator, never a more diligent and faithful Governor.

> He labored, day and night, in little things,
> No less than large, for the loved country's sake,
> With patient hands that plodded while others slept,

* * * * *

Doing each day the best he might, with vision
Firm fixed above, kept pure by pure intent.

His addresses on subjects connected with the history of North
Carolina, have the same qualities of accuracy and thoroughness
that all his work has, and his memorial orations on Murphey,
Badger and Ruffin are classics in their perfection of form and
taste, and in their combination of ease and grace with accuracy,
strength and dignity.

On June 8, 1836, he married Susannah Sarah, daughter of John
Washington, Esq., of New Bern, and by her had ten children.
She was a lady of rare beauty and accomplishments, and the union
brought to him as much of happiness as it is the lot of man to
know. Mrs. Graham survived her husband fifteen years, and their
descendants, as well said Governor Kitchin, "in the State to-day,
represent the highest type of culture, patriotism and citizenship
in the records of both their private and their public life, having
the same devotion to their country and fidelity to their country's
call as the illustrious William A. Graham."

As a fitting close to this paper, I give the estimates of Governor
Graham by others, most capable judges, residents of other States
and associates with him in the management of the Peabody Fund.
In the resolutions reported by Mr. W. M. Evarts, and evidently
written by him, occur the following:

"The distinguished public character of Governor Graham, and
his strong hold upon the confidence of the people of the North
and of the South alike, have been of the greatest value and importance, to this board in securing the sympathy and cooperation
of men of credit and of influence in the country, in furtherance
of the beneficial system of education at the South, which Mr.
Peabody's munificent endowment has so greatly aided in developing. That our personal intercourse with Governor Graham in
the discharge of our common duties, has shown us his admirable
qualities of mind and character; and we lament his loss, as of a
near friend and associate, as well as an eminent public servant
and benefactor."

Hon. John H. Clifford, of Massachusetts, wrote: "I should not
fail to bear my testimony to his thorough fidelity, his manly
frankness and his amiable temper, which had made him one of
the most agreeable, as he was one of the most useful, members
of the board."

Said the Hon. Robert C. Winthrop, of the same State: "He has held, as you all know, many distinguished offices in the service of his State and country. In all these relations he had won for himself a widespread reputation and regard, which any man, North or South, might have envied. I knew him intimately, and have always cherished his friendship as one of the priviledges of my Washington life. * * * No one of us has been more punctual in his attendance on our meetings, or has exhibited a more earnest and intelligent interest in all our proceedings, while his dignified and genial presence has given him a warm hold on all our hearts."

Said Mr. A. H. H. Stuart, of Virginia: "He possessed a sound and vigorous intellect, which enabled him to grapple with the most difficult questions; and he was singularly free from all those influences of passion and excitement, which too often disturb the judgment. His views of every subject were clear, calm and well considered. He possessed that happy balance of the intellectual faculties, which is the parent of wisdom. Although he has for more than forty years occupied a prominent position in public life, and has filled many important offices during times of high party excitement, no man has ever ventured to question the integrity of his motives or conduct; and up to the hour of his death he enjoyed the unlimited confidence of all who had the happiness to know him. * * * I have rarely met a wiser man, and never a better man, than William A. Graham."

THE PAPERS OF
WILLIAM A. GRAHAM

An Early Composition.[1]

Was it expedient in the State of North Carolina to expend so large a sum in procuring the Statue of General Washington?

To perpetuate the fame, to record the actions, to applaud the virtues and admire the abilities of the good and great are objects that justly claim the undivided attention of genius and literature.

To the hero, the statesman, the patriot, who has been emphatically styled our bulwark in war and guide in peace we are compelled by the obligations of gratitude and affection to give imperishable honours. But in performing this incumbent duty we should use those means which seem best calculated to effect this object without incurring an unnecessary expence or bestowing superfluous labour.

Were the heroic deeds of this chieftain nowhere represented, were his memorable actions about to be forgotten, then it would be expedient in us to adopt this measure. But since the pages of Ramsay, Marshall, and numerous other literary authors teem forth in his panegyricks since the name of Washington is inseparable from that of the American people, it was altogether unnecessary for our Legislature to take this method to preserve his fame.

Before the days of Dr. Faust such an expedient might have been adopted with propriety; but in this enlightened age our citizens can read the achievements of their heroes as portrayed to them in their true colours by the most eminent authors. There then being no necessity for this statue either to preserve from oblivion the actions of this great man or to impress them more forcibly on the minds of his countrymen, the expense of it next deserves our attention.

The Legislature of North Carolina has ever been remarkable for their parsimony except in this single instance; in which, unwisely and unaccountably, they have gone to the opposite extreme and from the sparing Miser become the profuse spendthrift. Would it have not been better for this money to have been spent in aiding the cause of learning and internal improvement through-

---

[1] From a typescript. Place and date unknown.

out the State? Does the magnificence of this statue which is a fragment of ancient ostentation, at all correspond with the known plainness and simplicity of North Carolina?

Our seminaries of learning, our internal navigation and various other institutions first demand our attention and even then it would be throwing away money to expend it procuring an useless piece of marble.

Will A. Graham

1823

Speech to Dialectic Society.[1]

Should the United States assist Spain in her present struggle with France?

Mr. President:

The charges which have been prefaced against the allied sovereigns we will neither attempt to dispute or extenuate. We acknowledge that their principles are despicable—that their conduct during the last half century has been infamous to an excess. But it is one thing to execrate and another to chastise—it one thing to sit peacefully down in our happy homes and give vent to indignant feelings and another to reform the European world.

Though we most cordially join the gentleman who has just addressed you in loathing that confederation of tyrants which now infests Europe yet we are far from believing that a declaration of war would ever be politic under circumstances like the present. If there be any treaty of alliance existing between this country and Spain—if their interests are in any respect coincident—or if past conduct has been such as would give her a just claim on our assistance then we are bound to participate in this struggle. But here our obligations end. Among nations there can exist no such thing as a perfect disinterestedness. Though the benevolent genius of christianity may teach us as individuals to sympathise with the unfortunate and extend a helping hand to the miseries of mankind yet this can never obtain among nations. Such are the evils of modern politics—such the direful consequences which await the slightest error in diplomatic concerns that interest must ever constitute the grand incentive to national exertion. Censurable as such principle may appear in an individual it is sanctioned by the practice of all nations. If we examine the book of time we will find it to have constituted a distinguishing feature of every government which has secured duration to itself and happiness to its subjects. But what advantage are we to receive for an interference in the contest between the Spanish nation and the allied powers?

---

[1] Delivered in the Dialetic Society, at the end of his Junior year at the University of North Carolina.

Can distracted bankrupt Spain make any remuneration? Can she solace the widow and orphan? Can she replenish an exhausted treasury? When the autocrat of Russia and his despotic coadjutors shall have forgotten their antipathy to the Spaniard and begun to pour their "fierce Hussurs" upon our north western frontier will Spain step forth the defender of our cause? Let her remote situation her destitution of moral virtue her woful inability answer. But we are told that in fighting for Spain we are combatting our own enemy—that if we suffer the abettors of despotism thus openly to violate the law of nations the period is not far distant when this country will be invaded by these subverters of liberty.

Grant that this imaginary danger is real. How are we to provide against it? Will we prepare for the storm while we are yet blessed with the sunshine of peace? Will we collect our strength and remaining in our native land—where every arm can be raised where every nerve can be exerted in defense of our native common country receive the shock with a fixed determination to conquer or die; or will we transport a force into Europe and vainly indeavour to contend with the innumerable myriads which the allies can muster? An invasion from the forces of combined Europe is greatly to be deprecated by our country; but if ever that unhappy day shall arrive when we will be called upon to repel such an invasion our whole support will depend on an unanimity among our citizens an abundant treasury a vigorous and active soldiery. With these advantages we may hope for success. But let us make Europe the theatre of war waste our armies exhaust our resources in attempting to chastise her oppressors and we invite the enemies of our country to visit us "with fire and sword." The gentlemen next tells us that Spain is defending her unalienable right and for this reason she is justly entitled to our aid. Whence Sir does he derive this conclusion.

If all nations which are engaged in procuring liberty may rightfully demand our assistance why has it not been discovered long ago? Why have we not assisted the Frenchman? It has been Sir because our wise politicians foresaw the danger of such a procedure. They wept for that nation which had so gallantly fought and bled in defense of our liberties — they sympathised with our brethren of the South — they commiserate the unfortunate subjects of Turkish despotism but a regard for our vital interest has proved them to do no more. The great end of human learning is to instruct us "in the way we should go" to teach us to avoid the errors of former times and pursue that course which has led others to success. Notwithstanding this the gentleman urged us to tread those very steps which brought unhappy France to her tremendous downfall. The famous decree of the national convention which "declared to all nations who were desirous of liberty that France was ready to furnish the requisite aid" was the signal for the destruction of this illfated republic. No sooner was it rumored abroad than the whole of Europe came pouring forth and well nigh terminated her national existence. Without however dwelling longer on this argument which might be more properly addressed to chivalrous spirit of the fifteenth century than the cool dispassion of the present age let us come to his last consideration. The pending contest he asserts must witness the overthrow or triumph of constitutional liberty throughout the world. Yea Sir that to raise our puissant arm in the cause of the Spaniard is all that is requisite to make the world free. This Mr. President is an extravagant conjecture. Does our opponent think that a country which embraces the human race in all its variety from the rude unlettered barbarian to the most enlightened nations in the world can ever be subjected to one form of government? Has he forgotten that intelligence is the life of liberty and that ignorance and despotism are inseperably connected? Can he believe that while the shades of so many martyrs in the cause of freedom still hover o'er the Englishman while the eastern continent can boast of those philosophers who have so ably defended the rights of man or that while science continues to erradiate the mind of the European the flame of liberty can ever be extinguished? And on the other hand it is rational to suppose that the oppressed Russian the degraded Austrian or the lethargic German is qualified to govern himself? No Sir it is impossible. Give them a free constitution and you give them an instrument for their own destruction. No political maxim is more clearly demonstrable that in all nations the government will conform to the peculiar condition of the people; and if the regions of despotism which we are told are now pregnant with liberal principles are capable of maintaining free governments they will work out their own salvation without any assistance from this country. No effort of ours can prepare the minds of these ruthless savages for the maintenance of a constitution such as we enjoy. Nothing is more certain that under existing circumstances revolution cannot ameliorate their unhappy situation and that the political milleneum which Mr. Booth anticipates from assisting Spain is the child of his own imagination.

Thus far we have considered the nation which it is proposed to succour as possessing a negative merit; as one which we ought to assist if to any our assistance be granted. Our information concerning Spain I confess is limited. Such are the restrictions to which her press has been subject such the ignorance which has uniformly pervaded that bigotted country that her government like her religion is involved in mystery. But the conduct of the nation is a sufficient index to the government. Let the tumult which attends the session of the Cortes the contending factions which agitate the country the scenes of bloodshed which are daily exhibited tell what kind of order exists in the peninsular. The crown appears to have been lifted from the head of the embecile Ferdinand and placed on that of the most despicable of all tyrants the swinish multitude. Nothing is stable nothing regular. Well has it been denominated by the poet "the land where law secures not life." Yet Mr. President this is the government which we are told we should cross tempestuous seas to defend — this is the shrine at which we are invited to sacrifice the prosperity of this rising republic. Again — does the new order of things in Spain promise any advantage to our country? No Sir. On the contrary have we not in the very infancy of her present constitution seen her overthrowing the landmarks of international law and unprovoked taking part with our avowed enemies? Call to your recollection the eventful period of 1813. Remember that while clothed in the garb of neutrality she was slyly and secretly like the midnight assassin murdering our unsuspecting countrymen. Forget if you can that while the Spaniard and the citizen of the U. S. reciprocally saluted each other with the appellation of friend the former was sheltering in his Florida territory the British soldier that he was arming and encouraging the merciless Indian to commit depredations on our frontier. These were the first fruits of that government for which Spain is now contending; and will we embark in this portentous conflict to defend a constitution which suffers the faith of treaties to be violated with impunity? Will we quit our happy homes to assist a nation by which we have been so heinously maltreated—a nation which if it does not fall prey to the rapacity of the allies will ultimately sink under the weight of accumulated depravity? Will we contrary to the last parting request of our beloved Washington contrary to the advice of the sage Hamilton, send our own to stand on a foreign land to fight a foreign enemy in alliance with a foreign friend whose amity is more to be dreaded than her enmity? Let your good sense Sir and the judgment of this assembly answer. Let lawless Spain and the rapacious allies fight their own battles; whilst they squander their resources in bloody contention our flag will ride over sea enriching our country from the calamities which afflict agoniseing Europe. And when that dark cloud which now lowers over Spain shall have spent itself and the trumpets clangor and the cannons roar shall have ceased we will have acquired a strength which will enable us to set at defiance all the efforts of despotic rapacity and punish with due severity all the encroachments of Spanish perfidy.

Will A. Graham,

May 20, 1823.

An answer to the speech of W. R. H. Booth.

1824

Graduation Oration.[1]

June 10, 1824.

Oration on Classical Literature

The productions of genius like the character of individuals have been subject to the opinions and prejudices of man-kind. They have had their days of triumph and degredation, of prosperity & depression. At one time they have been cherished, caressed and admired, at another neglected, persecuted and despised. Now the favorites of princes and fostered by national patronage; now mendicants at the door of royalty or outlaws from human society. Nor have they been uninfluenced by those political revolutions which have so often desolated nations and destroyed empires. The same hands which have overthrown governments have not unfrequently superinduced the most direful disasters on the offspring of the mind.

Literature like the rest has been exposed to depredations from these various sources and like them too has suffered losses, but it is something anomalous in the history of the intellect that although most of its early productions have scarce outlived those from whom they emanated, many of the most ancient literary monuments have survived unimpaired the various changes in the condition and manners of men. "Time which wears the marble down" has made no impression on the adamant of these geniuses of antiquity. To these writings which have borne the brunt of time, which have defied so many, powerful efforts to destroy them, and which after the lapse of so many ages are held in the highest estimation wherever they are read and understood, to these we apply the epithet of Classical.

Kingdoms have risen and flourished and fallen, generations have passed away since they first appeared, but these remain unaltered by the change of man's moral condition, and unaffected by the increasing lights of philosophy and experience. The clue which history affords to direct us through the period of alternate light and darkness which has intervened since the introductions of Egyptian and Phoenician learning into Europe exhibit an

---

[1] From a typescript. The original has not been located.

impressive representation of the fortunes of Classical Literature; of its rise and decline; its accession and deprivations how it has been sometimes cloven down by the ravages of war and again risen in triumph ascending over the conqueror. And if we be prepossessed in its favor how readily does this prepossession strengthen into an attachment, when we perceive that our opinions accord with those of mankind in all enlightened nations, The difficulties which they have encountered and the dangers of annihilation which they have escaped, together with the evidences which these authors present on the slightest acquaintance convince us unavoidably of their superior excellence.

When the infant muse first appeared in Greece and Homer's song was rehearsed to the listening multitudes of his countrymen, learning was a stranger in the European world. The heroic Grecians were versed only in the arts of carnage and bloodshed, and Troy's unhappy fate had just made a brilliant accession to that glory which they revered as the reward of man's noblest efforts. But so captivating were the strains of this divine poet that the chivalrous virtue of the warrior soon became less estimable than poetic skill; and war-like Greece forgetting the trophies of her victories began by gradual advances to approach that height of literary fame which has acquired for her history an imperishable remembrance. Then arose those poets, historians and orators who attained the admiration of their contemporaries in their own country and who together with the ancient bard formerly mentioned are venerated as the fathers of Classical Literature.

On the transfer of the destinies of Greece into the hands of the Romans by the victories of Armilius, learning seems to be doomed, to an early grave. The proud mistress of the world had scarce excelled the neighboring barbarians in the productions of mind, the genius of her government had been adapted to war and conquest, and though in fields of blood she had gathered many laurels, but few of her citizens had designed to pluck the flowers of literature. But after the subjection of Greece her authors though the offspring of a different clime and though degraded as captives, soon acquired a high repute and triumphed over the rudeness of their conquerors. The sons of Mars began to prefer the prospects of reaping the fruits of genius to the more laborious and hazardous employment in which they had been recently engaged, and, the literary spirit continued to increase until that bright day of literary glory which attaches a greater esteem to the

Roman name than the heroic fortitude of her warriors, the devotedness of her patriots, or the splendor of her conquests. The Grecian Classics saw their numbers greatly augmented by the cultivation which they introduced, and the Romans though they continued to conquer and subject, rivalled their polished masters in the excellence of their literature.

Under the tyranny of the later Caesars learning began gradually to decline and at length sunk in the gloom of universal night which was brought on by the conquest & division of Roman empire by the Goths and Vandals. From being the darling of a monarch and the foster child of the greatest political power then existent, it now became an object of odium and persecution, and while the sword of the barbarian was employed in retributing Rome, with the wounds which she had recently inflicted on her less powerful neighbors, his sacrilegious hand was not less industrious in devoting to destruction the relics of her intellectual grandeur. But notwithstanding this humiliating reserve it was the fortune of by far the more eligible part of the Grecian and Roman authors to escape the fury of the savage hordes. Buried beneath the rubbish in ancient architecture or preserved in secrecy by some remaining votary they slept in quiet retirement through those days of murderous barbarity of which little more is known than that in them the most highly cultivated portions of the globe returned to worse than primitive darkness.

Nor were the conquerors of Rome the only enemies of literature in this inauspicious period. On the establishement of Christianity by Constantine many transcripts which had found refuge in Constantinople from the destruction which was overspreading the Western regions fell victims to the misguided zeal of the early Christians. Elated with the idea of diffusing universally the Christian faith they sought to inter in one common sepulchre all that remained of superstition and heathen genius. Accordingly the inestimable writings of antiquity were wilfully destroyed by fanatic rage or erased to afford materials for conducting those violent disputes which at that time agitated the christian world. The rapine and conflagrations of the Saracens gave another destructive blow to the literary monuments of Greece and Rome. All denominations of men no matter how rancorous were their political or religious hostility, seem to have denounced ancient learning and to have conspired for its utter extermination.

But though mutilated by these multifarious attacks, it continued nevertheless to drag on a slender existence. Preserved in the silence of the cloister by a few monks who were less enthusiastic zealots than their contemporaries, the musty manuscripts of antiquity lay concealed from their vindictive destroyers until the cloud of ignorance and barbarism began to vanish and the slumbering muse awoke under the happy administration of Pope Julius the second. Literature began to regain somewhat of its former estimation, and in the succeeding reign of Leo Xth the Greek and Roman Classics were revived and admired with the same rapturous attachment as in the days of Augustus. From this era learning began to be more extensively diffused over the continent of Europe and Classical Literature emerging from its dark retreat and finding its way into more extensive circulation fell in with the taste of the Northern European and has ever since been studied with an increasing assiduity.

As there is implanted in our nature by the hand which framed us a conscience which fixed the standard of moral rectitude, so also we are gifted with a faculty which decides on the merit of the productions of genius. It may lie dormant during a state of barbarism—it may be blinded by prejudice—or warped by envy, but when illuminated by reason and influenced by no unhallowed motive it candidly discriminates between what is excellent and defective in the products of the mind. This principle constitutes the tribunal of literature. On its slow verdict depends the fate of authors; and if we would pronounce him excellent who has merely endured the dilapidations of time, what shall we say of those who in addition to this have undergone so many perils? Who converted the rude warrior into the scholar; who turned the proud conquerors of the world into the polished votaries of the muses, who defying the savage violence of the Goths and Vandals the ill directed zeal of the early christians, and the fire of the bloody Saracen, have corresponded to the natural taste of mankind wherever they have been thoroughly understood. Nor do they require any superior degree of sagacity to discover the charms by which they have captivated the scholar in all enlightened nations.

To pass over the melody and harmony of those languages in which they are written—to say nothing of the influence which they are found to exert in strengthening and perfecting the various faculties of the mind, their unaffected simplicity and elegance of style—its superiority over the hyperbolical manner of the Orientals, and the turgid pompousness of those literary ephemera which are sometimes foisted into a momentary favor, together with their happy effect in cultivating and fixing the standard of taste, are sufficient allurement to the student of literature.

Would we write with the hope of being known to posterity what better manner can be adopted than that which has already secured immortality to the writings of others. If we turn over the biography of the British compositionists and examine from what source certain of her writers obtained that matchless superiority which has distinguished them by the appelation of the modern classics, we find that their earlier days have been spent in the closet with Caesar and Sallust, or that they have been nurtured by the precepts of Cicero and Quintilian. The prose writer may indeed be more obnoxious to this remark than the poet, the offspring of nature and creature of fancy, yet few who are gifted with the ethereal fire of poetry may not peruse with advantage these models of antiquity.

If we admire the productions of the native genius of Shakespeare in all their rank luxuriance in what an extraordinary degree would our admiration be enhanced were they pruned by that classic taste which Milton derived from the ancient authors.

But the mighty allurement which has secured to Classic writers, such ready and fond admiration wherever they have become thorough acquaintances, is the variety and extensiveness of their intellectual pleasures. If in the successful prosecution of scientific investigation, we experience a triumphal delight, there is something in the perusal of these memorials, of antiquity more mild and temperate, but of a far more durable character. What a fund of enjoyment through life is prepared for him, who in his youth has become thoroughly conversant with these masters of learning. They dwell habitually in the memory and are ready at all times to fill up the interval of severer employments; and in our homes of rural retirement and leisure, warm the mind with the fire of ancient genius and animate every scene we enter with the offspring of Classic fancy. The meandering rivulet, the hum of the cascade, the customs and labors of rural life, the variegated scenery, administer additional pleasure to the reader of Classical Literature. They are to him hallowed by their connection with a thousand remembrances on which the mind dwells with peculiar delight.

When overwhelmed by misfortunes or tortured by care how pleasant is the change to turn from the passing scene, and live with the genius of antiquity in the sweet communion of studious retirement.

When all that is mortal turns to dross around us these writers retain their steady value. When friends grow cold and the converse of intimates languishes into vapid civility, these continue the unaltered countenance of happier days, and cheer us with that true friendship which never deceived hope nor deserted sorrow.

Will A. Graham.

Chapel Hill, May, 1824.

1825

From Alfred Graham.[1]

Vesuvius Furnace, August 2, 1825.

Some time has passed since I have received a Letter from you though you are still one in my debt if you have received my last. I have been closely confined at home since I saw you and of course will have but little news to tell you. Our Furnace continues Blowing.

We had Mr. Olmsted [2] with us a week or 2 ago. Father and him spent a day riding about the little mountain examing the Rocks; he discovered nothing valuable except Iron Ore. they also discovered and analized a Spring of mineral water similar to that of Reads Spring only contained more sulphur.

We have lately purchased 2 Negroe men, Bradshaws Terner and a nother negroe man. We now carry on the Furnace with more ease since this addition to the present Hands.

We had a considerable parade and a ball at our fourth of July though I suppose Davidson has given you an account of it as he was present. Our Candidates in this Country all came forward for the Legislature week before last. They are Danl Forney[3] for the Senate without opposition, Conrad,[4] Holland,[5] & Shipp[6] for the Commons. When they declared themselves, Conner[7] and Shipp had a Warm debate on internal improvement; both got mad I was told; one opposed to it, the other in favor of it. Shipp

---

[1] Alfred Graham (1803-1835), the youngest of William A. Graham's six elder brothers. He became dissatisfied with his prospects in Lincoln County, and in 1830 made a trip to Memphis, and to Alabama. Later, he moved to Memphis, where his brothers, Dr. George Franklin and Joseph resided, but returned in 1834 to join his brother, John Davidson, in operating Vesuvius Furnace.

[2] Denison Olmstead (1791-1859), scientist, author, and teacher, born in Connecticut, educated at Yale, professor, University, 1817-1825, state geologist, 1825; professor at Yale until his death.

[3] Daniel Monroe Forney (1794-1847), born Lincoln County, educated at the university; major in the War of 1812; M. C., 1815-1818; commissioner to the Creek Indians, 1820, state senator, 1823-1826; member council of state, 1830-1831.

[4] Daniel Conrad, who represented Lincoln County in the house of commons, 1819-1820; 1822-1825; 1827.

[5] Oliver W. Holland, member of the house of commons, 1821, 1823, 1825-1826, 1836-1840.

[6] Bartlett Shipp (1786-1869), lawyer, soldier of the War of 1812, represented Lincoln County in the house of commons, 1824, 1826, 1828-1830, in the state senate, 1834, and in the Convention of 1835.

[7] Henry W. Connor (1793-1866), a native of Virginia, educated at South Carolina College, a planter in Lincoln (now Catawba) County, major and aide to General Joseph Graham in the Creek campaign of 1814, was a representative in congress, 1821-1841, and senator from Catawba County, 1848-1850.

it is said was a little drunck which caused him to proceed Farther than he would have done, And I suppose his talk on that day will cause him to loose his Election. Several persons who had supported him last year were swearing they would not vote for him on account his personal abuses to Conner in their debate before the Grand Jury.

Sister Violet [8] and W Alexander[9] were with us 4 or 5 days ago, they have returned to Mecklenberge. The Camp Meeting at Robies will take place on the day of Election, the Methodists are already preparing for it. Theadore Brevard [10] and William Hane[11] have lately came up from Columbia, they intend setting out to morrow for Tennessee and expect to visit Memphis in their Tour.

We have not received any Letters from our friends in the West lately. I wrote to Joseph[12] by Theadore. I intended visiting Memphis myself this fall but I fear the long Blast of the Furnace will put it out of my power, however I intend making the proposition to Father and if he can any how do without me I will go and see that Country this Fall. We had preaching at Unity on Sunday a great many people attended among the number Sophia Forney just from Raleigh I returned from Chappelhill directly home in company with 8 or 10 students. We had a great deal of sport by the way. Though I took very sick at Lexington and could scarcely get on to Salisbury, I detained a day at Salisbury, got better and set out for home the next morning but continued unwell a week after my arrival home.

Sadler brought on Peter quite esily, he has been at work very well since he arrived. We did not confine him any after he arrived but give him a Thrashing and set him to work.

Brother James[13] I here is hard Electioneering in the mountains,

---

[8] Violet Winslow Wilson Graham (1799-1868), eighth child and third daughter of General Joseph Graham, who, in 1821, had married Dr. Moses Winslow Alexander (1798-1845), of "Alexandriana," Mecklenburg County.

[9] Dr. Alexander was usually called by his middle name.

[10] Theodorus (later Theodore) W. Brevard (1840-1877), was the son of Alexander Brevard, a partner of General Joseph Graham, who married Mrs. Graham's sister, Rebecca Davidson. After studying law, he moved to Tuskegee, Ala., where he became a judge. He later moved to Florida, where he was State controller. After the Civil War, he returned to Lincolnton, where he taught school until his death.

[11] Hayne.

[12] Joseph Graham, Jr., (1797-1837), the sixth child, and fourth son of General Joseph Graham, moved early to Memphis, where he was engaged in planting and business enterprises until his death.

[13] James Graham (1793-1851), the fourth child and second son of General Joseph Graham. He was educated at the university, studied law under Judge Thomas Ruffin, and began practice at Rutherfordton. After service in the house of commons, 1822-1823, 1828-1829, he was elected to congress, where he served 1833-1843, 1845-1847. As his letters indicate, he was the devoted guide and mentor of his brother William.

old Felix[14] has withdrawn, and it is thought now the contest will be between him and Carson[15] he has not been here since I saw you No more but remain your

Brother

Write shortly

From James Graham.   A.

Rutherfordton,

August the 27th, 1825.

I received your Letter some time since, inclosing the note I sent by you to Judge Ruffin[16] and I should have answered you sooner but for the pressing engagements preceding the Election.

The Election having terminated I am once more at liberty to resume my professional pursuits and attend to the social intercourse of my friends and relations.

When I became a Candidate for Congress Walker, Vance[17] and Carson all became fearful that they would be defeated and that I would succeed; hence each of them determined to exert themslves directly against me apprehending no danger from each other and if they could not secure an interest or vote to their own advance-

---

[14] Felix Walker (1753-1828), a native of Virginia, and a farmer and merchant there for some years. Later, he moved to North Carolina, went with Daniel Boone to Kentucky, was clerk of court in Washington County, (now Tennessee), a revolutionary soldier, clerk of Rutherford County, and a Republican member of congress, 1817-1823. He moved to Mississippi in 1825, and died there. He is remembered chiefly for a reference to Buncombe County, which gave a new meaning to the word.

[15] Samuel P. Carson (1798-1838), of Burke County, state senator, 1822-1824, 1834. Democratic member of congress, 1825-1833. His opponent at his first election, and also in 1827, was Dr. Robert Brank Vance, the incumbent. The latter campaign was bitter, and was followed by a duel, in which Vance was killed. Carson was defeated in 1833 because of his support of Nullification, but he was a delegate to the constitutional convention of 1835. The following year he moved to Texas, where he was at once elected to the constitutional convention. He was commissioner to the United States, 1836, and secretary of state of the republic, 1836-1838.

[16] Thomas Ruffin (1787-1870), born in Virginia, who, after graduation from Princeton, studied law under David Robertson, of Petersburg, for a year. He then followed his father to North Carolina, and continued his study under Archibald D. Murphey. Admitted to practice, he quickly acquired a reputation. He was borough member of the commons from Hillsboro, 1813, 1815-1816, and speaker, 1816. He was superior court judge, 1816-1818, 1825-1828; a justice of the supreme court, 1829-1833, 1858-1859; and chief justice, 1833-1852. He was a delegate to the peace conference, and the convention of 1861. He was also a successful planter in Orange (later Alamance) County. James and William Graham both studied law under his direction.

[17] Dr. Robert Brank Vance (1793-1827), of Buncombe County, physician, member of congress, 1823-25.

ment individually, then an exertion was made to withold it from me.

Thus we progressed until Walker discovered I was about to take his whole interest and he withdrew from the contest alledging publickly & voluntarily he would take no part in the Contest but at the same time secretly and privately had made his arrangement with Carson to transfer his interest and influence to him and some entertain the opinion for a valuable consideration (of this however I wish you to say nothing as I hope the truth will develop itself in a short time, tho' Report speaks frequently on this subject) at all events while Walker pretended to be nutral he was writing Letters through the district and Riding through his own County—& Haywood County. The Presidential Election was pressed into the Election by all my opponents, and indeed through out the district Demagogues have used the name of Genl Jackson as a passport to political promotion and the county Candidates in this district were loud in the praises of Genl Jackson. The people are told by promoting Jackson men they can elevate the Genl. four years hence to the presidential chair.

I faced the current and independently mentaned my privilege and right to think and choose for myself. In Rutherford, I Recd 1073 votes, Carson, 453 Vance, 201. In Burke, Carson got 907, Vance, 545 I, 308. In Buncombe Vance, 976, Carson, 271. I got 262. In Haywood Carson, 448. I got 265, Vance 202.

I hope Judge Ruffin's promotion to the bench will give an opportunity of devoting more time to your examination I believe the profession are much pleased with the appointment and I presume there is no doubt of its confirmation by the Legislature. I expect to spend the ensuing winter in close study having rather neglected my profession for some time.

You state in your letter that Judge Ruffin expresses the opinion that a student has little more assistance than that his course of studies should be prescribed. I know that was the Judges opinion formerly, but still if he would not examine me, I took the Liberty of examining him very frequently and by drawing him into conversation on legal subjects my Ideas were more clear correct and lasting. Conversations on legal subjects sharpens the intellect and makes the impression more lasting. I would recommend that you, frequently after reading on any subject, should throw your book one side and then collect and embody your ideas in writing.

I have not been at Fathers for some time but will soon go on to Sister Mary.

I hope you will call and cultivate an acquaintance with Judge Paxton[18] by whom I will send this Letter, he can inform you of occurrences in this quarter.

I have no news worth your attention and I hope you are patiently persevering in your studies as your future prospects in Life must mainly depend on your present exertions.

Mr. Roane and a servant of Jo Wilsons were shot lately in this county on the place where Allen Twitty lived by David Twitty, son of Allen; they are pronounced out of danger and fast recovering.

The particulars of the affair are known to Judge Paxton.

Your affectionate brother

---

[18] John Paxton, of Rutherford County, a native of Virginia, who, after failing as a merchant in Morganton, became a successful lawyer. He served with distinction as a judge of the superior court from 1818 to 1826.

1826

From George Franklin Graham.[1]

Lincoln, June 14th, 1826.

Your letter dated 27th Ult. was recd. by Mail before the last. When it came to hand I was truly glad to learn you intended to visit Father this Summer as I thought it probable at that time I should be here on your arrival, but must now inform you I shall set out alone next week for Memphis Ten. It would afford me great pleasure to see you I do assure you. From report you must have completely out-grown my recollection. Since I left this Country seven years ago, Alfred, who was then scarcely half grown, has attained features, size, etc., which give him quite a different aspect. And had he not been pointed out as my brother I should never have recognized him as such.

On my arrival in this Country, the Old Mansion-house, fields, trees &c. for a time had a novel and strange appearance, but a few cursory glances of the eye and a few moments reflection, presented everything in its natural order, save the house which appeared empty and waste, and abandoned by those brothers and sisters who were often gathered together at this Old spot *called sweet Vesuvius* where we happily spent our days of youth and enjoyment; but have rambled and roamed thro' many regions and are now scattered and settled in the East and West. Never Never shall we be all again convened at the same time in the land of our nativity; Nor should we look for such a thing, according to the common course of human events. The tide of time flows briskly on, we grow up in years, and descend the hill of life governed by those motives which direct us to our interest, without often giving one thought to those who stood near and dear to us in former days. Sic transit gloria mundi.

I did intend soliciting a visit from you previous to my departure for the West, but was informed you had last Fall paid a visit to Father and it would be inconvenient for you again to come to this section of country in so short a time. My stay here has been

---

[1] George Franklin Graham (1794-1827), was the fifth child and second son of General Joseph Graham. After graduation from the university in 1815, he obtained his medical degree from the University of Pennsylvania. He settled in Memphis, and there and in the surrounding country, built up a large and lucrative practice. He died of fever contracted on a Mississippi River boat, where he was called to treat a passenger with the disease.

longer than I anticipated, owing, as you I presume have understood, to a Connubial engagement and the delay which necessarily follows such matters. I am now compelled to give an eye to my interest in the West where I shall remain till Fall—say Oct—at which period I calculate on returning here for the purpose of removing out my family.

Shall I hope to see you here in the Fall?

A few days since I recd. a letter from Alfred, he was at the date of the letter at Josephs near Memphis, expected to set out for Carolina first of this Inst. was well pleased with the Bluff, tho' said but little respecting the Country generally. He stated a species of Insect called Buffalo-Gnat had produced great destruction among the horses of that Country, particularly in Memphis and its vicinity Something like 52 horses were killed by them in about 48 hours. Such a Plague has never before been known there, and I hope will never occur again.

Our relations in this section of Country are generally well. Father looks quite firm and stout We have but little news here, except Wm Davidson, son of Geo Lee, and Camilla Byers will be married to-morrow evening and that Clayton Abernathy, the polite merchant of Lincoln, has failed and ran off. Several persons have gone in pursuit of him. I have not heard whether they have overtaken him as yet or not.

Your Brother

P. S. I am informed the Stage from Salisbury to Lincolnton will commence running about 1st. of July.

1827

From James Graham.   U.

Rutherfordton, March 21st, 1827.

I am gratified to learn you have obtained a country court License and when I was in Lincoln a few days since Father informed me you had written him on the subject of your location and permanent residence and that you suggested an idea of establishing yourself at Hillsboro, to which he remarked he would be satisfied you might settle wherever you thought you could do best and he desired me to write you concerning it.

I believe I stated to you my impressions with regard to it last summer. I believe Hillsboro unites more advantages and inducements for a settled residence than any other point in the state; it combines health, wealth, and intelligence and interesting society. These I conceive to be the "Sine qua non," to the enjoyments of life, to the fortune and fame of those whose aim and object is usefulness and happiness. I know the opinion is common that it is imprudent for a young lawyer to settle among old and experianced and learned Lawyers, but sir this [is] a mistake, when a young man learns the rules of Practice and the practical principles of the Law from an intercourse with profound and eminant Lawyers he learns them correctly and scientifically and the Law is demonstrated to be, what it ought to be, The Science of Reason and common sense, founded upon the immutable principles of natural Justice, and accomodated to the frailty of Human nature and the circumstances of Society; correct first principles, Right views and clear conceptions in this noble science are much more easily and accurately acquired by a free and frequent intercourse in the transaction of business with an able and highly distinguished Bar, than "by the blind leading the Blind."

These distinguished men are as apt to die as any one, and they are always fair candidates for promotion; upon the whole I give a preference to H,boro over any other place in the State.

I never have considered my self located but *pro tem* and I am much perplexed to know where to make a favorable residence. If I remain in this section of the State I have been thinking *but saying nothing* of Lincolnton and Charlotte but I am not pleased with either place. If I were married I believe I should not encounter this perplexity and If I could see some fair one whose beauty and many virtues attracted my eye, I do believe I should tell her my misfortune and ask comfort I am quite tired of this wandering life. My poverty brought me here and my *will* will not permitt me to tarry much longer tho I do not wish my intention known untill I resolve where to fix my ultimate destination. I am doing all I can to prevail on Father to Sell his Works and I hope a purchaser may be found; at all events no exertions on my part shall be spared and if needful I will go on to the North and endeavor to make the Sale; his interest and the interest of his family require it. But if he cannot sell in 12 or 13 months he ought to dispose of his works to some of his children and relieve himself from a burthen he is not able to bear. Perhaps you had better not finally determin where you will ultimately reside untill you obtain superior court License but at any rate I would advise you to continue in H, boro until that time by which your mind may become decided.

You should take *every opportunity to talk* with Judge Ruffin on legal subjects and you should not wait untill he began the conversation because he might be unwilling to commence it yet very willing to carry it on. This Practice will enable you to read with pleasure and profit and set adrift errors which may have lodged in your mind. I saw F. Davidson at Iredell Court he is at his fathers and says he will attend Iredell, Lincoln, & Mecklenburg he appears in fine health and spirits. Present my respects to my friends and write me to Lincolnton shortly.

From Matthias Evans Manly.[1]   U.

New Bern, Aug. 31st, 1827.

Your good, long, very acceptable, and interesting letter was duly received and certainly deserved a speedier answer. Merit, however, does not always meet with its proper reward else we should not now have to lament the defeat of Judge Murphey[2] in the late

[1] Matthias Evans Manly (1801-1881), a native of Chatham and a classmate of Graham at the university. A successful lawyer, he represented the borough of New Bern in the house of commons, 1834-1835. He was also a delegate to the convention of 1835. He served as a judge of the superior court, 1840-1860, and as associate justice of the supreme court, 1860-1865. He was elected United States senator in 1866, but was denied his seat. He served in the state senate, 1866-1867.

[2] Archibald De Bow Murphey (1777-1832), a native of Caswell County, graduate of the university, and later briefly a professor. He became a distinguished lawyer, and a state senator from Orange County, 1812-1818. He formulated policies for

elections. But joking apart, and I must think with you, that few things have occurred in our history more mortifying to state pride. We would be more respectable were the state disfranchised entirely and partitioned, like Poland, between New York Virginia and S. Carolina. These parts would make very convenient plantations for New York—the North and Northwest might go to Virginia—the South and West to South Carolina. In this way we might be instructed in our true policy, in good morals and good manners. Standing alone and consulting for ourselves, I fear we are doomed to insignificance. The Presidential question, as it is commonly called, is the subject of much general conversation in this section. This town is about equally divided; if inclined any way, 'tis in favour of the administration—the district is Jackson, John Bryan,[3] our representative, is administration, tho' very reserved and cautious in all his talks.

I received a letter from Robert Ogden[4] on Wednesday last. He is well, in health and spirits, but has his head chock-full of old Hickory—makes many enquiries about his prospects in this State, etc.

A tremendous storm happened here and on all our coast last Saturday—much loss of life and property. Parts of vessels, articles of merchandise, mangled corses and human limbs are constantly floating ashore. Besides all this there are seven wrecks between and near the Capes Lookout and Hatteras. Our merchants are down at the bar, looking sharp for a speculation. The people on the N. Carolina coast are perfect Harpies and consider these storms in the light of true Godsends. Yesterday I went to ride in my sulkey—the horse ran away with me—I stuck to him for about half a mile—then jumped and cleared myself without any injury. The Sulkey was broken into atoms and the horse injured so much I apprehend he will never recover. But to return to the storm; it has done a good deal of damage to our town by driving the vessels into the streets, washing up the wharves, blowing down the

public education, and internal improvements that made his name immortal in North Carolina. He was a judge of the superior court, 1818-1820, was reporter of the supreme court, and agent of the state and the university for claims on lands in Tennessee. He planned an elaborate history of North Carolina, but did not live to write it, and most of the material he gathered was lost.

[3] John Heritage Bryan (1798-1870), of Craven, graduate of the university, a distinguished lawyer. He was a member of the state senate, 1823, 1825, and a Whig member of congress, 1825-1829.

[4] Robert Nash Ogden (d. 1859), of New Orleans, a graduate of the university. He served in the legislature, and was a justice of the supreme court of Louisiana. He was a descendant of Governor Abner Nash of North Carolina.

sheds and trees and scattering the china berries about without the least discretion. Miss Simpson's dwelling and the houses and contrivances thereunto appertaining and belonging are unhurt; I watched them in storm and thought they stood sublimely erect and firm during the wild uproar of winds and waters. 'Twas a proud spectacle; Her spirit surely actuated the whole. How does Simpson get along with you? How often does her dad say 'yes sir' when you are talking to him? . . .

I had a heap more to say but I have been so long writing this I've forgotten the rest. Write me a long letter about everything—who is that, that is such an ungentlemanly unfeeling fool as to criticize Murphey's speech in the Register? Is it Prof. Mitchell? [5].

John Stanly's[6] health continues to improve. James Bryan[7] has issued proposals to publish a new manual of the statute laws of the state. It is to be gotten up on Judge Haywood's[8] plan precisely, with the addition of such decissions of the supreme court as affect the construction of acts. These are to be inserted in the body of the work, under the statutes to which they relate, in small print. The work will be printed and bound in Philadelphia; provided always a sufficient number of subscribers can be obtained to defray the expenses. Dr. Camey is still here, "cracking jokes." I am in good health—prospects *middling*.

Your Friend Forever.

---

[5] Elisha Mitchell (1793-1857), born in Connecticut, graduate of Yale, professor in the university, 1818-1857, author and scientist. He located the mountain which bears his name, and identified it as the highest peak east of the Rocky Mountains. He was killed while remeasuring it to settle a controversy with Thomas L. Clingman.

[6] John Stanly (1774-1834), of New Bern, who was educated at Princeton, and became a distinguished lawyer. He represented the borough of New Bern in the commons, 1798-1799, 1812-1815, 1818, 1823-1826, and was a member of congress, 1801-1803, 1809-1811. An intense and bitter Federalist, he was forced into a duel by Richard Dobbs Spaight, who was killed.

[7] James West Bryan (1805-1864), a lawyer, planter and business man, a classmate of Graham at the university. Their close friendship and intimacy was presently strengthened by their marriage to sisters. Bryan was state senator from Carteret, 1835-1838, and a delegate to the convention of 1835.

[8] John Haywood (1762-1826), eminent lawyer and judge, author, a native of Halifax County, who in succession was clerk of court of Hillsboro district, solicitor general, attorney general, and judge of the superior court. He resigned his judgeship to defend James Glasgow, and then moved to Tennessee, where he resumed practice. In 1816 he became a justice of the state supreme court, serving until his death. His legal writings were voluminous, but his best known works were *Natural and Aboriginal History of Tennessee,* and *Civil and Political History of Tennessee.*

From   Robert   Hall   Morrison.[9]   A.

Near Charlotte, Sepr. 12th, 1827.

*   *   *   *   *

Our family for the last few weeks has been much afflicted with sickness. About three weeks since Mary[10] was taken violently with the fever and for 8 or 10 days was extremely ill. Since that time she has been recovering *slowly.* She is now able to sit up some, but is still very weak and far from being well. I trust in a few days she will be able to travel by short stages towards Lincoln.

Our little Isabella has also been very sick for several weeks, but is now better.

A number of our servants have shared in the sickness prevalent.

The health of the people generally in this section of Country is much better than during last fall; but still there are scattered cases and some mortality.

Rev. Mr. Hunter[11] of Steel Creek died suddenly a few weeks ago.

Your Father was down during Mary's confinement and was in good health. Mary recd. a letter lately from her sister Mrs. Witherspoon—Family in good health—Not fully satisfied with their move. Prospects of a crop gloomy, etc.

We have our dwelling house finished, except plaistering. It is small but comfortable—two rooms below & 2 above. I have built 4 good outhouses, cleared 16 or 18 acres of Land, and hope by next Spring if spared & prospered to be comfortably fixed. I am altogether satisfied with my change of residence.

I am glad to perceive that you enjoy with so much apparent fervour of health the company of the *fair ones* now giving animation to your town. Marriages with us are somewhat rare of late. Rev. Mr. Pharr[12] of Unity is to be married next Tuesday to Miss

---

[9] Robert Hall Morrison (1798-1889), a native of Cabarrus County, Presbyterian minister, a graduate of the university, the founder and first president of Davidson College. He was Graham's brother-in-law, and the father-in-law of Generals T. J. Jackson, D. H. Hill, and Rufus Barringer.

[10] Mary Graham Morrison (1801-1864), the ninth child and fourth daughter of General Joseph Graham.

[11] Humphrey Hunter (1755-1827), a native of Ireland, who came to Mecklenburg County in 1759, attended Dr. James Hall's famous school, "Clio's Nursery," and Queen's Museum in Charlotte, leaving to become a soldier. He was captured at Camden, but escaped. After the Revolution he was again a student in South Carolina, finally becoming a Presbyterian minister. He was pastor in Lincoln (now Gaston) County, for a time, and later was pastor of Steele Creek Church in Mecklenburg.

[12] The Rev. Henry N. Pharr, pastor of Unity Church.

Amanda King of Iredell Co. Miss Palina Byers lately made the bold attempt of running away with a carpenter from Salisbury. He was working at Jno. Graham's house and she, during the sickness of her Sister, was there considerably. They there made known their feelings and matured their plans. Set off on the Sabbath from Unity Church during preaching and were 7 miles above Mr. Byers' when he overtook them and cooled down the marriage fever by bringing Palina home behind him. You may guess the tumult it made among the *talking ones* and especially in Mrs. Byers' bosom.

As it regards your permanent settlement I have nothing to suggest upon which you have not doubtless duly deliberated. It is a decision which every man must make for himself. Ours is a poor, contracted, and ungrateful State. It neither fosters genius nor rewards virtue.

And this very consideration, although a strong temptation for youth of aspiring views to leave it, is in my opinion one strong reason why they should not do it. I think we are justified in looking forward to a better state of things, and it will rest on those now coming on the Stage of action to exert a mighty efficiency in bringing it about.

Although as an individual I would rather live between the Catawba and Yadkin rivers than in any other part of the State, yet were I in your profession and looked forward to eminence in conjunction with profit I would prefer Hillsboro'. That place is distinguished for its intercourse with other parts of N. C. Talents and attainments there displayed are known and more apt to be rewarded. It is more in contact with Raleigh and the Legislature than any other town.

And what is more than all, the members of the Bar there lay out for themselves a higher Standard and exert themselves to come up to it. It is an saying the truth of which is easily accounted for *that men of eminence flock together.*

Your residence in Hillsboro. has given you already facilities in obtaining business which it would take some time to gain in any other situation. The Society there is very good and the place healthy.

I trust the great Disposer of events will guide you in this and in all your other decisions for the advancement of your greatest good and your consequent happiness—Not simply temporal which must vanish away, but supreme and eternal.

From David Mitchell Saunders.[13]   U.

Gallatin, [Tenn.] Sept. 15th, 1827.

My Friend Graham

Your very friendly communication came to hand today after a considerable detention on the road I suppose from its date, and gave me much pleasure, as indicitive of that esteem and regard which have always marked our intercourse. It is on feelings as landscapes that distance spreads its magic influence. It is the absent friend that has our highest and holiest regard. Intercourse from day to day becomes familiar, and friendship is degraded to a level with ordinary feelings.

Since my departure from N. Carolina and settlement in this place, I have had but little or no intercourse with my old friends and acquaintances in Hillsboro or indeed in any part of the State. This has been to me a source of much regret. My chief pleasure is in corresponding with my old Class mates and college friends, and keeping a line on recollection of those halcyon days which are now gone, never to be recalled; I often think with "fond regret" of the various events that are interspersed in the short history of my life, and which though they give pain are nevertheless pleasant to dwell upon. My love *amours* and *masterly* defeats are all green in my memory, and though for a time there was Much regret yet no "pain and anguish now wrings the brow" by their rememberance. The name of *Julia* carries along with it something sweet, yet painful—I once loved her, and loved her ardently; I loved her for herself alone, and in the anguish of my soul repined at my lot. But it is well that it has so happened, and I have ceased to think of her only with esteem and respect. If she should be still in Hillsborough present my best respects to her, and tell her that I wish her a *husband,* much peace and much happiness, with all the comforts and none of the wants of life. As for myself tell her that I have ceased to frequent from all society and have lost for them my usual fondness. And from the present state of my feelings it is uncertain whether I shall ever marry. I say so because every variety of beauty, of talent and wealth in the sex passes every day in review before me, without exciting a momentary reaction. The rigours of *age* and *interest* are daily pressing the siege of the heart, and I fear a few more years will still

---

[13] David Mitchell Saunders, of Tennessee. A classmate of Graham's at the university.

its emotions forever, and memory will be left to flit a lonely spirit o'er their tomb, and tell us of their departure.

I would indeed my friend be more than pleased at the idea of being in Hillsborough in the fall if I thought there was the least probability of realizing it. I know of no spot that I hold in such fond rememberance as the borough; the dark walk, the sulphur spring and third mountain all have charms for me, and I am determined at no distant day to visit them; when that time may arrive however I fear that for me they will have lost half their interest, the friends both male and female with whom I was in the habit of spending so many pleasant hours may then be gone, and those several spots which best recall the most pleasant period of my life, and I will be left without the possibility of enjoying them. I know no spot, or situation that I would desire to spend my life in preference to Hillsborough; the climate, water, and above all the society renders it preferable to any place that I have ever resided at. A young man in situating himself for life should take all these things into consideration and although a few years at the commencement of his career is a matter of great importance yet I would nevertheless be willing to contend against them before I would be willing to desert them, save the frowns of poverty. You consider your residence in Hillsborough merely temporary, and to what spot you will next stear your course is uncertain. The state of Tennessee holds out many inducements to men of enterprise and *legal* learning. It is true that our bars are crowded to overflowing by lawyers, and to the eye all the avenues to success are completely stoped, The most of them however are of a character not much to be dreaded, and who stand in their places from year to year without employment, and who at length retire with great disgust. The states however still west of this, offer still greater inducements to men of such character. Illinois, Indiana and Missouri as well also as Mississippi are fine theatres to insure a success. If you should emigrate to either of these states you would necessarily have to contend against many difficulties which tend for a time to alarm or intimidate, a smokey cabbin, the manners of the aborigines, and are uncultivated as but fire charms, but they will all soon give a way before the approach of civilization. You would necessarily have to be deprived of many of the comforts and even necessaries of life, notwithstanding all this success would be certain. Our friend Blum[14] wrote me some time

---

[14] Probably Benjamin Byrum Blume, of Stokes County, a classmate of Graham. He later moved to Petersburg, Va.

since, and spoke of moving to this state, I am in hopes that he will not decline the idea. N. Carolina in her Congressional elections as well as state elections seems disposed to keep within her territorial limits all the talent that she possesses. From your district I expected better things. I had contented myself with the idea that that great and good man, A. D. Murphey, would most certainly be elected, that ere this they had learned how to appreciate his intellectual and moral worth. Our Representation in the next Congress will be characterized by dullness, imprudence and blackguardism. There but two or three respectible men in point of talents in the whole delegation. You have heard of the celebrated Loco Crockett [15] "who can whip his weight in wild cats," "jump up higher, fall down lower and drink more *liquors* than any man in the state," he is returned now a very gentle and respectable man. To give you a correct idea of the man, I will repeat the sentiments that he gave at our last national Anniversary. Says loco Crockett, "Jackson is a hero, *but* Crockett is a [page torn] by the same, Here is to General Jackson in the next presidents chair, loco Crockett in his seat in Congress, and loco Alexander [16] in the corn field," loco Alexander was his opponent, and the last man to be in Congress from the district. I regret that Mr. Hawks [17] has so far forgotten the situation in which I was placed, and the situation in [illegible] planned to send an order out against me for 200 dollars. You know my friend that not many months after I came to Hillsborough I became indisposed and continued so nearly the whole of the time that I remained previous to my departure for Baltimore; that early in June I left Hillsborough and did not return any more to spend any time until some time in July or August. From the first of June I hardly considered myself a member of his office, I received from him no instruction and he gave me none. When I left N. Carolina for Baltimore I did not calculate that Mr. Hawks would consider me as a member of his office and hence the reason that I did not tell him so. I remained in Baltimore some time, became a member of Hoffmans

---

[15] David Crockett (1786-1836), native of Tennessee, major under Jackson in the Creek campaign of 1813-1814, member of state house of representatives, 1821-1823, Democratic member of congress, 1827-1831; as a Whig, 1833-1835. Killed at the Alamo, 1836.

[16] Adam Rankin Alexander, a native of Virginia, who removed to Tennessee. He served in the state senate in 1817, was a member of congress, 1823-1827, and of the state lower house in 1841 and 1843.

[17] Francis Lister Hawks (1798-1866), born in New Bern, graduate of the university, and of the Litchfield Law School. He was for some years the supreme court reporter, but abandoned law, and became a distinguished Episcopal minister. He was the author of many historical works.

law school, and paid him 50$ for legal instruction. Doubtless I am indebted to Mr. Hawks something, and if I thought that my friends could believe that Mr. Hawks had any claims against me founded either in law or in equity I would satisfy the demand unhesitatingly. At all events Mr. Scott [18] shall not loose any thing.

. . . Present me to friend Scott and his daughter Nancy and wife.

Go in *proper person* to John Scotts and present my best respects to Miss Julia Miner and Mrs. Scott—You know that the family, Miss Miner in particular, was one of my warmest friends. Tell Jno Kirkland [19] if he courts that Girl any more he will make a *Cad* of himself—and that all the good or harm that I can wish him is that she will not have him. Tell John to Miss Julia M. to play for me "Oh! tell me how from love to fly" and that he must accompany her with his truly melodious voice.

My compliments and respects to My friends (you know who they are) both male and female.

From David M. Saunders.   U.

Gallatin, Oct. 1st, 1827

Since the date of my last communication to you, several circumstances of interest to myself have transpired, which from the publicity that has been given to them, requires from me a statement to my friends, who will without an explanation understand my motives. A few moments after my letter to you was sealed, and before it was deposited in the post office, I was attacked in the public square in this place by Willis Alston[20] formerly a member of our class to know whether or not I had ever used expressions calculated to injure him. He presented himself with his hand on a pistol for the purpose of alarming me, and to force me into an unqualified denial of the remarks I had made. It seems that about two months since while in Nashville I had in an incidental conversation observed that Mr. Alston was a gambler, and for using that expressing he alleged that I had slandered him.

---

[18] John Scott, a resident of Hillsboro, who represented the borough 1818-1820, 1824-1827, was solicitor general, 1827-1834, when he moved to Texas, where he became a judge.

[19] John Umstead Kirkland, of Hillsboro, a merchant and planter.

[20] Probably Willis Alston (1803-1840), a member of the same class at the university with Graham and Saunders. Though registering from Georgia, his name would seem to indicate a connection with the Alston family of Halifax and Warren counties.

A few days later I went to Nashville for the purpose of coming to more deffinate understanding with Mr. Alston, and after remaining several days I ascertained that Mr. Alston after having treated me in the most unauthorized and ungentlemanly manner and after having bound himself to assume the authorship of the report if no responsible author could be found, and after having circulated reports altogether unfounded, I addressed him a note admitting what he accused me of saying for the purpose of eliciting from him a challenge. This he avoided by a publication in which he used the epithets of coward scoundrel and liar in reference to myself. I met his publication and satisfied the Citizens of Nashville that from the course he had pursued and the manner he had acted that he was no longer worthy to be noticed as a gentleman. Shortly after my publication made its appearance he by the assistance of some one or two made another publication, and immediately after its appearance he made his exit for Georgia for the purpose—he alledged—of bringing his Brother to fight me. Previous to his departure and after I had satisfied my friends and the public that he was unworthy of my notice, I challenged his friend and advisor. The Challenge was presented on Wednesday about one oclock and excepted on the next day about the same time. It was stipulated that we should meet on Friday about five oclock P. M. that the arms should be rifles, and distance forty yards. We accordingly met about two miles and a half below Nashville and fought agreeably to the stipulations. My Antagonist, James Collinsworth, Esq., was shot throu his left hand, the ball cutting the two fore fingers of the right hand, glancing from his gun and striking him on his chinn, then in his shoulder a little above his niple and has there lodged, and I have since understood that it can not be extracted. I received merely a slight tuch on my right rist without doing me any injury. I will send you by the next mail a copy of the correspondence between myself and Mr. Collinsworth together with the stipulations by which we fought. I had made preperation to start to N. Carolina but have learned that my Antagonist will unquestionably recover. This is for you and the rest of my Hillsboro friends.

In speaking of this matter I do not wish you to give any one to understand *except a few of my friends* that I have written to you on the subject. It is too delicate a matter for me to talk or wright character. I have met them on their own ground, and have main- about. There was a desperate effort made to ruin me and my tained my *honour* and my *character*.

From David M. Saunders.   U.

Gallatin,

Oct. 2nd, 1827.

I promised in my letter of last week that by the next mail I would send you a copy of the correspondence between Mr. Collinsworth and myself, and the stipulations by which we faught.

Nashville, Sept. 19th,

Wednesday Evening,

Mr. James Collinsworth

Sir,

I have satisfactory evidence to convince me that you are acting as the aider, abetter & assistor of Willis Alston by exciting and encouraging him in his attempts to ruin my character. He sir as I have satisfactorily proven to the world, is a man unworthy of notice. But you sir can be recognized in the light of a gentleman, though by identifying yourself with him, you are equally deserving of contempt. I call on you, sir, to unmask yourself and render me that satisfaction which one gentleman is bound to render another.

Yours etc.,
David M. Saunders.

To which I received the following reply:

Nashville, Sept. 20th.

Thursday Evening.

Sir your impertinent note of yesterday was handed me by Capt. Peyton.[21] Your wishes can be gratified, let me know what you want.

Yours &c.
James Collinsworth.

----

[21] Balie Peyton (1803-1878), a native of Tennessee, lawyer, Whig member of congress, 1833-1837; moved to Louisiana in 1841, and served as federal district attorney, on staff duty in the Mexican War, minister to Chile, 1849-1853; lived in California, 1853-1859, and then returned to Tennessee, where he was a Bell and Everett elector, 1860, and state senator, 1869-1870.

David M. Saunders, Esq.

To which I made the following reply, Nashville Sept. 20th Thursday Evening. James Collinsworth, Esqr., Sir. Your note of this date has been received by the hands of Mr. Washington, in which you pretend not to understand the exact import of a note sent you on yesterday. I will explain it. You have been instrumental in attempting to do me an injury. I therefore demand of you satisfaction in the manner that is resorted to by gentlemen.

Yours etc.,

D. M. Saunders.

To which he answered:

Nashville, Thursday Evening,

Sept 20th.

Sir. Your note of this evening has been handed me by Capt. Peyton & I am willing to give you the satisfaction you require. My friend Mr. Washington is authorized to make arrangements for that purpose.

Yours etc.,

Jas. Collinsworth.

David M. Saunders, Esquire.

The following are the stipulations by which we fought: In the affair of honour now pending between David M. Saunders & James Collinsworth, we, the friends, agree to meet on the 21st. of Sept. at 5 o'clock P. M. one half mile below David McGavock's ferry on the south side of Cumberland River.

Stip. 1st. The arms to be used by the parties are doubled triggered rifles, not to exceed three feet 10 inches in the barrels. Stip. 2nd The principles to stand back to back 40 yards apart, with their heels to a line, their rifles to an order, triggers sprung but not cocked. Stip. 3rd. The friends of the parties shall throw up for the word, and the gentlemen winning the word shall repeat it an audible distinct voice, three times before the parties take their stands, so that each principal may understand the manner of giving it, & it shall be repeated in the same manner and tone of voice while the parties take their stands as he did before. Stip. 4th The manner of giving the word shall be make ready—fire. And neither party shall change his position, or move his gun from an order until the word fire is given. Stip. 5th. Each principal shall load his own gun with one smooth round leaden ball, in the presence of the friends of both parties. Stip. 6th. The principals to be in their shirts and pantaloons, and each principal to be examined by the friend of his antagonist, to see that there is nothing about his person to impede the progress of the ball. Stip. 7th If either party change his position, or move his gun, he shall be shot down by the friend of the other party. 8th. After the word fire is given the parties shall be allowed six seconds to each and fire. 9th. There shall be a person selected by each party to keep the time, who shall at the expiration of six seconds cry *halt*. If either party fire after the word *halt,* he is to be shot down by the friend of the other party. Stip. 10th. A snap or a flash is to be considered a fire. 11th. The seconds shall stand half way between the parties face to face, each having a loaded pistol. 12th. We are under a pledge of honor that no person shall be present or in sight, with our consent, except the time keepers. 13th. The parties when firing shall stand erect—there shall be no stooping. 14th. We pledge our honours that every stipulation in this article shall be faithfully adhered to, under the penalty that the party violating any of them shall be shot down. Sept. 20th, 1827.

Balie Peyton
Wm. Washington.

These stipulations were presented about half after 10 o'clock on Thursday night, and signed by the seconds on the next morning and the meeting took place about 5 o'clock of the evening of the same day. This communication with the enclosed document you must preserve. Show it to some few of our friends.

I see that *Cups* has married Miss Taylor; Can you not furnish Mr. Heart[22] with a simular notice? Your old law preceptors daughter is a fine fat healthy lass. The objection that I should have to her is that she looks to be too prolific. In the Old North State Corn is scarce and the fewer to eat the greater the abundance.

Present me to my friends. Tell John Kirkland to ask Miss Julia Burgwyn to play *for me* "Oh tell me how from love to fly."

I have troubled you too much of late. You must write me. Tell William Murphey[23] his friend *Look* Lewis is dead.

---

[22] Dennis Heartt, editor of the *Hillsborough Recorder.*
[23] William Duffy Murphey (1802-1831), eldest son of Judge Archibald D. Murphey, a graduate of the university. He had visited Tennessee in August, 1827.

[*Enclosure*]

TO THE PUBLIC

On Wednesday evening the 12th of this month, Mr. Willis Alston, accompanied by Mr. Wm. B. Miller, arrived in Gallatin for the purpose of ascertaining from me whether or not I had ever used expressions calculated to injure him. Previous to Mr. Alston's departure from Nashville, a friend of mine understanding the object of his visit, addressed a communication to a friend in Gallatin, which enclosed a note to me, informing me of Mr. Alston's intention. The communication was placed in Mr. Miller's hands, with a positive understanding that he would deliver it, so soon as he saw the person to whom the letter was directed. The attack was made upon me on Thursday morning, about 9 or 10 o'clock. Mr. Miller had put up at the same house with the gentleman for whom he had the letter, breakfasted with him, was introduced to him, and remained conversing with him for some time. Mr. Miller did not deliver the letter until after the interview between Mr. Alston and myself, and just as he was about to leave Gallatin, he delivered the letter, and on his return to Nashville he told my friend, that his reason for detaining the letter was a suspicion, that it might inform me of the intended attack. I did not know Mr. Alston was in Gallatin until the very moment the interview commenced. Mr. Alston charged me with having slandered him, by saying he was a gambler, or a professed gambler. After some conversation, I told Mr. Alston that if had approached me as one gentleman ought to have approached another, I would have given him entire satisfaction; that he had proceeded in an unauthorised manner; that he came upon me in the street with his hand upon his pistol, doubtless for the purpose of shooting me. I told Mr. Alston, that I had said, he was fond of playing cards; that if I had ever said he was a gambler, or a professed gambler, I did not at that time recollect it, but if any gentleman would come forward and say I had made such a statement, I would admit the fact, and that I was responsible to him for the assertion. I told Mr. Alston in an audible and distinct tone of voice, that if any man had said that I should have said he went to New Orleans and Mobile the last winter ostensibly for the purpose of playing cards, upon my own responsibility, or without having authority for the assertion, told a damned lie. I then demanded of Mr. Alston his author; he said he did not know whether or not he was at liberty to give up his author; that he would go to Nashville and see, and return again to Gallatin on Saturday; that if he did not give up the author he would assume the authorship himself. I told him it would be unnecessary for him to return to Gallatin, that I should be in Nashville on Saturday. I accordingly came to Nashville on Saturday, under the expectation that Mr. Alston would give me up his author or assume the authorship himself. Believing Mr. Alston did not intend taking any further steps in the matter, and having become convinced that I had used expressions from which no inference might be drawn of an intention on my part to injure Mr. Alston, I addressed him the following note.

Nashville, Sept. Monday morning

Mr. Willis Alston,

Sir: When you were in Gallatin on Thursday last, I said to you in the presence of several gentlemen, that I did not at that time recollect that I had ever said that you were a gambler, or a gambler by profession, but that if any gentleman would come forward and say to me that I had made that statement, that I would admit the fact. Since my arrival here, I am induced to believe that such an inference may have been fairly drawn from a conversation I had with one or two persons on that subject. Any opinion that I may have formed or expressed in relation to your being a gambler, or a gambler by profession, I have no reason to alter on a further consideration. Yours, etc.,

David M. Saunders.

I delivered a true copy of the above to Mr. Alston about 6 o'clock on this morning.

Balie Peyton.

Monday evening, Sept. 17, 1827.

After the above note was handed to Mr. Alston, I anticipated and hoped that we would be fully at issue, and believed that there was but one course for an honorable man to pursue. He however avoided it by a publication which has been freely circulated. It can now be satisfactorily ascertained whether I have slandered Mr. Alston by saying that he was a gambler, or a professed gambler. If the statements here made are not sufficient to prove to the world that Mr. Alston is even more than I have said, I pledge myself to produce other testimony.

Since Mr. Alston arrived in this place, he won at a match game a small amount of money, (I will not undertake to say how much) of a Mr. Joseph Morris. Mr. Morris states that he soon discovered he was not able to play with Mr. Alston, and broke up the game. This Mr. Morris will not deny when called upon. Justice to myself and my friends, require of me this statement, to counteract the impression that he has endeavored to make by indulging in epithets, which are in the mouth of every black-guard and black-leg in the country. I trust that there will be no difficulty in making a correct application of the language which he has made in reference to myself.

DAVID M. SAUNDERS.

Having been requested by D. M. Saunders, Esq., to state a conversation which took place between himself and a Mr. Alston at the door of Mr. Crockett's tavern in Gallatin on the 13th instant: we state as follows; That Mr. Saunders told Mr. Alston that he did not at that time recollect of having called him a gambler, or a professional gambler, that his recollection of what he had stated about Alston, was, he was very fond of sporting, but if any gentleman would say that he had called him a gambler, or a professional gambler, he would acknowledge or admit the fact and hold himself responsible to Mr. Alston; Mr. Alston said he did play cards sometimes, but he was no gambler. Mr. Saunders demanded his author; Mr. Alston hesitated, and observed he did not know whether he was at liberty to give up his author, that he would go to Nashville and return by the day after to-morrow, and if he did not give up his author he would assume the authorship himself; Mr. Saunders replied, you need not return as I will be in Nashville on Saturday next, and you can there see me. After Mr. S. had pledged himself to admit he had called Mr. Alston a gambler if any gentleman would state he had said so. There was some conversation about Mr. Alston's going to Mobile and New Orleans last winter for the express purpose of gambling, and it was to this part of the conversation that Mr. Saunders gave the lie. We have seen the statement made by Mr. Saunders about this part of the conversation, as well as the previous part of it, and believe that to be correct. From what passed we distinctly understood that no further steps would be taken in the matter until

Mr. Saunders should come to Nashville on Saturday, and then the issue was to be between Saunders and Alston, by Saunders admitting what Alston charged him with, if any gentleman would state he had said so. We will farther state that Mr. Saunders' conduct on that occasion was firm and gentlemanly. Given under our hands this 17th Sept., 1827.

> Balie Peyton.
> Matthew Jones.
> Elm. Douglass.

Being called on by Mr. David M. Saunders, to say what I know of Mr. Willis Alstons being a gambler, state as follows:

In the month of July I was in the Mansion House in this place, when I heard Mr. Bradley of Cahawba, say in a public company, that Mr. Willis Alston had swindled Mr. Davis, and that he, Alston, was not only a gambler, but a *damned swindler*. Alston was in Nashville at the time, and was informed of it. I will further state, that I believe Mr. Bradley to be a man of truth. Given under my hand this 17th Sept. 1827.

> Franklin Saunders.

In a conversation with Mr. Tompkins yesterday morning, he informed me that whilst in Alabama last fall or winter, Mr. Alston came there in company with Davis, (now in this place) who had some three or 4 race horses, that Alston was pretty generally in the company of Taylor and Crittenden, celebrated faro dealers; that he, (Mr. Tompkins) was inclined to view Mr. Alston as a sportsman. If Mr. Tompkins was not absent he would no doubt make this statement. Given under my hand this 17th Sept. 1827.

> E. Douglass.

From James Graham.   U.

Rutherfordton, Nov. the 9th, 1827

It is with heartfelt sorrow and regret that I communicate the *death* of our brother G. F. Graham. He died of a bilious fever at Memphis on the 27th. Sept. You know I presume he left one child. The situation of his wife is truly distressing. I have not learned whether she desires to return or not: but at all events, it is too late in the season to return before spring by which time she can make up her mind and inform her friends.

On Monday last a *Duel* was fought between Samuel P. Carson and Robt. B. Vance near the Saluda Road in Greenville So. Carolina. The particulars I have not learned. Vance however was shot in the Abdomen and the wound is said to be mortal. Carson had his *belt* cut by Vance's ball. The friends of Vance were Franklin Patton,[23] Genl. P. Brittain[24] and Dr. Phillips;[25] the friends of Carson were a Mr. Davis[26] & Thompson and Dr. Sheiflin.[27] Carson, report says for I am not a confident on either side, challenged Vance after having received infinite abuse.

*   *   *   *   *

I wish you to spend a week or two in Raleigh just before the Assembly Rises; it will extend your acquaintance and give you a more correct notion of Legislation for however improper it may be for a young gentleman to embark in political pursuit in early life still he ought to understand not only the Theory but practical details of Legislation.

Before you return to Lincoln I should be glad to know that I may meet you at the Furnace.

From Alfred Graham.   U.

Vesuvius Furnace, Novem. 9, 1827.

I received your Letter 8 or 10 Days ago and must acknowledge I have been neglectful of late in writing to you. I have just recovered of a long spell of the Fever and ague. I was attacked the latter part of September and only got rid of it a few days ago. This will appear somewhat strange as their was never a case of it on this place before; it has been quite Comon all around here this fall, their was scarcely a family within 5 Miles of here but had more or less of it. I am a good deal reduced and look as yellow as a Low Country South Carolinian, however I thinck I am recovering rapidly.

---

[23] Franklin Patton, a member of a numerous family of Buncombe County.

[24] Philip Brittain of Buncombe, house of commons, 1810-1811, 1816-1817; state senate, 1823-1824.

[25] Dr. George Phillips was Dr. Vance's surgeon.

[26] Warren R. Davis (1793-1835), of South Carolina, a cousin of John C. Calhoun, a graduate of South Carolina College, M. C. 1827-1835, and an active Nullificationist. Alney Burgin, of Burke, was also one of Carson's seconds.

[27] Dr. Shuflin was Carson's surgeon.

I suppose you have heard before this will reach you of the Death of Brother Francklin; lest you have not I will give you the acount as stated in Letter rec. from Joseph. He states that he expired of a Billious Fever in Memphis on the 27th of September, he had been a little unwell from the last of August but was not confined to bed untill seven days before his Death. Joseph states that he had him brought to his Farm and burried there, and that Martha was living with him. Father and H. Conner has not yet concluded whether it will be best for her to return or not but I thinck she will return.

Our Furnace has been in Blast since the last of Septem We expect to Blow untill Spring if possible. The Ballace of our Hands are pulling and halling in our Crop of Corn. We shall make a larger Crop of Corn this year than we have done for several years and I thinck will not be under the Necessity of purchasing any. John Sadler our Manager at the Forge Died with the Consumption night before last he has been incapable of attending to business for some weeks shortly before his death; we got a man in his place by the name of Lumroe from near Lincolnton; he is unacquainted with the Iron business but is highly recommended for his integrity and has no family. Brother James was with us last week but has returned again to Rutherford. Sister Mary was also with us 3 or four weeks ago. Theodorus Brevard and his wife set out last week for S. C. Joe and him and their Wives have been here and took dinner with me twice this Summer. I thinck them both Plain Friendly Women and tolerably handsome. I have had two sheets made for you but do not know what opportunity I will have to send them to you but will try to send them the first Chance that offers.

*   *   *   *   *

M. Polk[28] had considerable Wedding I am informed including ladies and gentlemen he had 10 attendants.. Sophia Forney was one of them, John Henderson[29] and Tom Smart were two others. I dont know who were the rest. They gave them a Ball in Charlotte the night after the wedding. I understand Polk will set out with his wife for Tennessee immediately. No more Marriages are spoken of in this part of the County. You mentioned you had heard of Polina Byers night adventure; it caused a great

---

[28] Probably Marshall Polk, of Columbia, Tennessee, a graduate of the university in 1825.

[29] Probably John Caruth Henderson (1801-1833), a son of Lawson Henderson, (q. v.) and brother of James Pinckney Henderson (q. v.).

deal of talk in this part of the Country. I was at preaching at Unity when they attempted to run away first, but they were over-taken by Byers and brought back; the second time she run away from Byers House and was recd by Lemlys Party at Dark on the river Banck and embarked in a canoe and sailed 2 Miles down the River, landed on the Lincoln side and was married by Bob Abernathy the next day, set out for Salisbury and there remains. Byers and the old Lady are in great wrath say will never receve her again and will not give them any thing. This is the effect of suffering men of the lower order to associate in genteel Houses. Mrs. Byers might not have expected any thing more.

From Hugh Waddell.[30]   U.

Raleigh, Novr. 30th, 1827.

My dear Graham!

I had intended dropping you a line for some days past, but we have been *turning over & over* so fast that I hardly knew whether my head or my heels were uppermost.

The Western men are divided & subdivided in such a manner that we can agree on no one to run as Senator. Old Stokes[31] you know won't do & my excellent friend James (yr. brother) being pushed by him to say what he would do, to use his own expressive phrase, being penned, "he reared up." Stokes has been this day withdrawn & we learn that Mr. Fisher[32] will be nominated. This likewise will not do: the *Gentlemen* of the West are disposed to take Iredell[33] as they have no Western man whom they can present to their Eastern brothers as worthy of support. God knows what will be done but I hope Iredell may be elected; the

[30] Hugh Waddell (1799-1878), of Orange, a native of Bladen, graduate of the university, lawyer and planter. He was prominent in the Whig party, and was a member of the house of commons in 1835, and of the state senate in 1836, when he was speaker. He was again a member 1844-1846.

[31] Montfort Stokes (1760 *ca.* -1842), of Wilkes County, a Revolutionary soldier, clerk of court of Rowan, clerk of state senate, 1803-1816. Elected to the United States senate, he declined, but accepted a second election in 1816 and served, 1817-1823. He served in the state senate 1826, in the commons, 1829-1830, when he was elected governor, and served two terms. He was Indian agent in Arkansas from 1834 until his death.

[32] Charles Fisher (1789-1849), of Rowan, a prominent Democratic lawyer, who served in the state senate in 1818; in the house of commons, 1822-1823, 1833; in congress, 1819-1821, 1839-1841; and in the convention of 1835.

[33] James Iredell (1788-1853), of Edenton, a graduate of Princeton, lawyer, soldier in the War of 1812, who had served in the commons, 1813, 1816-1820, 1823-1827. He was governor, 1824-1828, and was United States senator, 1828-1831.

West has great claims, but we must forbear to press them at present. Genl. Saunders[34] was elected Atty. General on Friday & so soon as we get through these fermenting elections we shall proceed to business.

You may see that Mr. Potter[35] has introduced his Retrenchment Bill, but the common opinion is, that it will not pass; God grant this! the Bank Committee are in daily Session & we hear they are likely to have enough labour; but so far it seems the calculations of the Chairman (Potter) have not been realized, for it is said the Banks have not issued as much paper as they were authorized by the Charter to do, & more, that there has been twice as much specie paid in by the Stockholders as was supposed by Potter & his friends. Whether these examinations will bring to light any malfeasance or not we cannot tell, as they have not progressed sufficiently in the examination. the Judiciary Committee have this day had, for advisement, Mr. Nash's project to amend the Supreme Court system. What will be done with this plan I know not. Mr. Gaston[36] said today in Committee that "he had heard no suggestion yet, which met his approbation," & I am satisfied he will oppose the Bill of Mr. Nash.[37]

On the Bank question, or rather a motion in relation to the powers of the Committee, a day or two since, yr. brother made

[34] Romulus Mitchell Saunders, (1791-1867), of Caswell County, was educated at the university, and studied law under Hugh Lawson White. He was a member of the commons, 1815, 1818-1820, speaker, 1819-1820, member of congress, 1821-1827, 1841-1845, attorney general, 1828-1833; judge superior court, 1835-1840, 1852-1867; author of the two-thirds rule in the Democratic convention; minister to Spain, 1845-1849, represented Wake in the commons, 1850-1852; and at various times was candidate for governor and senator.

[35] Robert Potter (1800 ca.-1842), of Granville, a native of Halifax. He was a midshipman in the navy, and then became a lawyer, member of the commons, 1828-1829, member of congress, 1829-1831, again in the commons in 1834, where he made a violent attack upon the banks of the State, which aroused bitter hostility. He had recently been guilty of mayhem, and while in the legislature he engaged in a fracas over a card game, and was expelled from the house. He went at once to Texas, served in its constitutional convention, and later became secretary of the navy of the republic. He was a man of great brilliance and power.

[36] William Gaston (1778-1844), a native of New Bern, was educated at Georgetown and Princeton. He studied law under Francis Xavier Martin, and was immediately successful, becoming one of the most learned and brilliant lawyers in the history of the state. He served in the state senate in 1800, and represented the borough in the commons, 1807-1809, 1827-1829. He was a Federalist member of congress, 1813-1817, and a delegate to the convention of 1835. He served as a justice of the supreme court from 1833 until his death.

[37] Frederick Nash (1781-1858), a native of New Bern, educated at Princeton, began practice in New Bern, which he represented in the commons, 1804-1805. He moved to Hillsboro in 1807, and represented Orange in the commons, 1814-1817, and the borough, 1828-1829. He was speaker in 1814. He was a superior court judge, 1836-1844, associate justice of the supreme court, 1844-1852, and chief justice, 1852, until his death.

a most excellent speech of which I heard Mr. Gaston speak in high terms; his remarks had their weight & on the question being proposed, his views prevailed: He is one of that Committee.

Blackledge[38] has given us his Shff's Bill & it will be called up in a day or two; the Senatorial ballot has been deferred to Monday next & all the Legislature is in *Caucus*.

* * * *

From David M. Saunders. U.

Gallatin

December 10th, 1827.

Friend Graham.

After an absence of 10 or 15 days I was gratified on my return to find a communication from you, in which you acknowledged the receipt of my several letters detailing the result of my differences, produced by the unauthorized and ungentlemanly conduct of Willis Alston. I have just learned that he is to be in Nashville in a few days, with his Brother Augustus who is take upon himself the *onus probandi* of defending Willis. What will be the result of his visit circumstances must determine. From my acquaintance with the *par nobile fratrum* I should judge that the young is the best man, possessing however a warm and impetuous disposition with great confidence in his bravery, and skill in the use of fire-arms. The elder of the two is a man devoid of honorable feelings, and destitute of any noble and enviable trait of character. He is in truth no better than an assassin, and like a cunning and unfeeling savage he will strike only when his enemy has his back turned to him.

It would afford me much pleasure if I could be in the burrow to be an eye witness of the various matrimonial connections between my old and much esteemed friends. So William James, my son, I heartily tender my earnest wishes for an uninterrupted and undisturbed series of years of peace, happiness and quiet. May they both prosper, fructify, and be abundantly fruitful. But has our friend *Ben* entered a *retraxet* to Miss Ames hand, or has he been driven from the field *vi et armis*? I sympathise with *Ben*— Lord God how the *smoke* will fly and Scotts Brandy suffer!

---

[38] Thomas Wharton Blackledge (1793-1857), of Beaufort County, a native of New Bern, a graduate of the university, member of the commons, 1820-1823, 1827-1828.

I have had the pleasure of seeing Marshall Polk and his lady since their return. She is not so beautiful as I expected, but upon the whole an interesting and engaging woman. During his visit to N. Carolina he seems to have met with *my friend Miss Susan Nash,* and with an inventive genius, and predisposition to jest even though it may be at the expense of his friends, he claimed a licence never extended to him by me, of saying to Miss Nash in answer to certain interrogatories that I had spoken of Miss Burgwin in the following terms: "That I did not care any thing about the poor thing." If Miss Nash should ever mention this observation of Marshall's you will correct it. Although my feelings toward Miss Julia are not of so warm and ardent a nature as they once were, yet even at this distance of time they are far from being lukewarm. I should be doing an injustice to so amiable and lovely a female, and laying myself at the same time liable to the severest reprehension, if I was to speak of her in terms *other* than those of the greatest respect. I have thought her like most women who had been flattered and caressed not sufficiently attentive to a maxim peculiarly applicable to women that the surest and greatest preservation of *love,* friendship and esteem is to treat all men with becoming respect, none with marked and pointed neglect. She is beautiful, and a consciousness of the fact leads her into frequent errors which a close and minute observer and critic of her sex would unsparingly condemn. I deny without equivocation the language attributed to me by Marshall and I depend upon your *offices,* & Miss Susan's sisters, and intercede for me with Julia. Tell me my friend whether the suspicions as to your intentions are true; Are you my real successor or not? I have just learned that my old flame Miss P. is married. Would to God that he who has married her may be worthy of her hand and heart. She had many faults, and she had too many redeaming qualities. The mention of her name will even unto death produce sensations pleasant yet mournful to the soul. The recollection of events connected with my intercourse with her presents a picture the outlines of which are beautifully delineated by a master's hand surrounded by and embellished by the most beautiful [illegible] of roses, and flowers beneath which lies artfully concealed briars, thorns and prickels. The history of my life, though short, is checkered with various events, none of which is truly hideous to the sight save that one. If in it however I have erred I appeal to God for the rectitude of my intentions and the honesty of my motives. I did perhaps treat her very wrong, and what my experience may now condemn, my youth sanctioned and approved. I am gratified to learn that the prospects of our friend A. Rencher[39] present so flattering an aspect May heaven speed him in his career, and may he attain the highest object of a virtuous ambition. We in Tennessee begin to think from the "signs of the times" as made manifest by the late elections in New York that the old Chief is to be our next President. Come my friend ground your opposition and *holler* for old Hickory. Present me to Scott and tell him that I propose dining at his house; (the bugle *tonens*) next fall God willing.

Present me indiscriminately to all my old friends. What is James and John Norwood about? remember me to them.

I remain your friend,

Truly.

---

[39] Abraham Rencher (1798-1883), native of Wake County, student at the university, lawyer, planter, Democratic member of congress, 1829-1839, 1841-1843, minister to Portugal, 1843-1847. He declined appointment as secretary of the navy. He was governor of the territory of New Mexico, 1857-1861.

1828

From David M. Saunders.   A.

Gallatin, April 6th, 1828.

Your last letter to me has been on hand for some time, and aught according to my usual custom of doing business especially wen my friends are conserned to have been answered some time since. It should have received the notice to which it was entitled but for a variety of circumstances which surrounded me, and for a time threatened the most important consequences. It is indeed a situation of all the most unpleasant to be annoyed by a vindictive and insidious enemy who would without remorse of conscience stoop to do an act of war with every honorable feeling, and ennobling quality of our nature. Such an enemy I have in the person of Willis Alston who has again been seeking a controversy with me. I treated him and his emissaries with marked contempt, and abruptly refused to notice him in any way. He is still in Nashville and for aught I know contemplates an attack on me. I have determined, and I will not shrink from my determination to kill him whenever the least cause from him will justify so desperate an act. It is true that I should dislike above all things to stain my hands with the blood of despicable a character, and but for the great law of self preservation should most certainly avoid it. Whether the affair is finally terminated I cannot at present say I hope however it is.

I presume you consider yourself permanently located in Hillsborough. I wish I had taken up residence there. It may not present as fine an opening to you as other places that might be selected yet your situation will be comfortable and the prospect of success not very distant. If I could be permitted to express my opinions on the subject I should say that I should prefer seeing you settled in some place were the prospect of success would be more immediate. Three or four years in a young man's life is off the greatest importance. And you will excuse me when I say that although I am convinced that land your bark on whatever sea you may, you will triumphantly overcome every obstacle that presents itself, and finally attain the highest goal of your ambition, yet the object might be attained elsewhere where your services would be more needed and your labours crowned with equal honor. Industry and perserverance conquers all things, and you have only to *will*, and you will find all your wishes more than realized.

You never say anything to me about our old friend Mat E. Manly, Where he is, what he is, and what he is likely to be. I feel interested in his future prosperity, and should be so sorely agrieved if he should meet with any reverse of fortune. I hope that fortune will smile upon him, and make him one of her favorite sons.

But you will allow me a little scrap for the girls. Julia Burgwin is going to Europe. Why dont you tell her to turn over the last *page* in the history of her fathers life, and that there she may find an instructive lesson. The old man if I am not mistaken took an English woman to wife. Tell her Englishmen dont suit the family and she had better not risk the "billowy deep" as old Stewart would say. Miss Anne Nash is married; present my congratulatory respects to the Dr. and his lady. Tell Miss Susan that I hope she will not think me capible of using the remark which Marshall Polk was so ungracious as to ascribe to me.

Poor John Kirkland he had better run from the hurry and bustle of life and harmoniously chant "Oh! tell me how from love to fly," the Still Small remnant of his days, or move with Dr. V. Ferrell to "A nother government" w[h]ere the ladies will know how to appreciate mail, and extol true worth.

From Sophia Witherspoon.[1]   U.

Brookland, [Hale Co., Ala.], April 14th, 1828.

I recieved your affectionate letter by Mrs. Strudwick & her daughter; they arrived in the neighborhood the week before christmas tho I did not see them for several weeks after. I am much pleased with them. Mrs. Ash & Mr. Sam Strudwick are among our most respectable neighbors.[2] Our family are in the enjoyment of health as we have generally been since our arrival in this state, we have another daughter now 5 months old which we call Mary Sophia, this makes 4 sons & 2 daugters all healthy & promising. Thomas Franklin, our youngest son, is the largest of his age. Elisa is also large of her age; she bids me say for her

---

[1] Sophia Graham Witherspoon (1791-1865), the third child and second daughter of General Joseph Graham. She married in 1815 Dr. John Ramsay Witherspoon (1774-1852), of Charleston, S. C. They moved to Kentucky, and later settled near Greensboro, Alabama.

[2] Both Mrs. Ashe and Samuel Strudwick were originally from North Carolina.

she thanks you very kindly for her ring. I believe I have not written to you since we moved to this state; we are indiferently setled as yet, that is in comparison with what we were in Kentucky; this I do not mind if we had our farm open & our Mills in opperation we could soon get better improvements. the last summer was the driest that has ever been known since the first settlement of the state. there is great scarcety here; corn selling 1 dollar pr bushel & very scarce at that price. the wheat has been killed by a late frost. it is thought by many that there will not be seed raised in this part of the state. our corn crop the last season only served us till christmas & we have been buying since. it is particularly hard on us having provisions to buy for 2 years & our cotton crop light also. our land is good, that is the low ground, I am under the impression that it will not stand drought, the contrast is great with us, all that we could get when we sold out in Kentucky for our corn was 9 cents pr bushel. we sold 3 thousand bushels at that price, still I will hope for better time. our family white and black have been so much more healthy that if we could have seasons I do not regret our move. We have paid 5000 dollars for the farm 1000 is still due the next year. we expect to live very economical until we can get thro with the land. our difficulties are greater in respect to mony matters than they ever have been. I still hope we will get thro without a sacrifice of property, it appears to be a general thing in this state to be in debt; I do not know an acception in this neighborhood. I received a letter lately from brother John also one from Mary; they both mention their having had sickness at fathers the last fall tho no deaths nor none among the relatives accept Elisa Maclean or Carmel since Brother Franklins. this my dear Brother is a solemn warning to us all to be ready when the messenger comes. often have I thought of our Brother, if he thought he would die, if he was resigned, if he was prepared, for that change. these are very important considerations. I have never heard the name Martha has given her daughter. I hope you will write often & not think any thing about my not writing often; it is not for the want of affection that I do not write oftner, it is more a lazy habit that I have got into togather with my domestic engagements. it always gives me pleasure to hear from any member of my family, more I think since I have come to this state than formerly. the Doctor also writes less, he is so much engaged building mills & so much concerned lest they should not do well. he has a cotton Gin in opperation & comenced a grist mill & saw mill. the grist

mill we expect to start in 2 or 3 days. do write soon & let me hear all about Miss Ruffin,[3] what you are about. I think your setling in Hillsboro looks a little suspicious, the Doctor & each of the children joins with me in love to you & believe as ever your
affectionate sister
P. S. When you write diret your letters to Greensboro, it is a handsome little town 4 miles from us, the county seat is Erie 18 miles distant.

S. W.

From Alfred Graham.   U.

Vesuvius Furnace, April 27, 1828.

I received your Letter about a week ago in which you mention you have got round the Circuit of Courts and have got back to Hillsborough. Our Court at Lincolnton is just over 2 Criminals were tryed for Murder but were both acquitted. Brother James is now with us, he will set of this evening for Iredell C; after it is over he will set out for Tennessee. He has business at Nashville after attending to that he will go on to Brother Josephs and if Martha wishes to return he will bring her back with him in to this state. I received a Letter from Joseph last week; all are well, but he tells me his Negroes have been doing very badly lately Ned he says run away and joined 8 or 10 other runaways and assisted in Robing Houses and Waggons and armed themselves with Guns and attempted to go the Ohio, Wash and a Negro man of Franklins are Indicted for breaking a Trunck and stealing money in Memphis. He stated that he had got Ned and to save his Neck employed W. Thompson to run him down to Natches and sold him.

*   *   *   *   *

Our furnace has blown out we made a blast of 6 months and 2 weeks the longest we have ever made since my recollection We made a great deal of Pigmetal but not many Castings; the sale of them is so dull it was not worth while. Our Horses and Oxen held out very well and the Furnace Hearth also, we might have blown 2 months longer had not it interfered with the Crop season. Robert Davidson is still here reading and attends to some little business when I am away.

*   *   *   *   *

[3] Catherine Ruffin, later Mrs. Joseph B. G. Roulhac, the eldest daughter of Judge Thomas Ruffin, of Hillsboro.

The Presidential Election is the general subject of conversation here at this time. Adams is gaining ground I thinck. Though the Majority of this Electoral District will be I thinck in favor of Jackson. Jos. Brevard [4] is in favor of Jackson and it is believed he will be left at home this year in consequence of it. His friends are pretty generally Administration men. Forney it is said will not offer this year Reinhardt will be out again.

A Letter arrived here for you the week after you set off for Hillsborough I opened it, it was from M. V. Murphey [5] and gave the history of his excursion to the Wilmington Wedding, also some instruction relative to Lottery Tickets that were in your possession. We have had no Letters from Doct Witherspoon lately.

From Richmond Mumford Pearson. [6]   U.

Mocksville, June 30th, 1828.

I arrived here on friday and I assure you it is with great pleasure I again endeavour to settle down upon matters purely *legal.* I say pleasure because I am tired of skimming over the surface of things; and am perfectly convinced that the happiest life is one of business, variegated now and then with a short indulgence in lighter pursuits.

I cant say I have entirely got over the effects of my visit to Hillsboro, I frequently find myself carried back to the presence of — and cant help thinking that the reality is better than the precious pleasure of dreaming of such an — (shall I in real noble style) say, *angel,* and perhaps thoughts of that kind as the object is in Hillsboro, by that strong principle of association, propinquity, made me lay aside a long bill of equity that I have

---

[4] Alexander Joseph M. Brevard, Graham's first cousin. He represented Lincoln in the commons in 1827.

[5] Dr. Victor Moreau Murphey, (1805-1862), second son of Archibald D. Murphey, after graduation at the university, studied medicine in Philadelphia, and then settled in Mississippi. He served in the legislature in 1838, and was clerk of court, 1859-1862. He served briefly as a Confederate surgeon in 1861.

[6] Richmond Mumford Pearson (1805-1878), a native of Rowan, after graduation from the university, studied law under Chief Justice Leonard Henderson, and quickly acquired reputation at the bar. He represented Rowan in the commons, 1829-1832. Elected a judge of the superior court in 1836, he became in 1848 a justice of the supreme court, and from 1858 until his death, was chief justice. A staunch Whig in politics he strongly opposed nullification and secession. Bitterly opposed to the Confederate Government, he became a Republican after the war. For many years he conducted a large private school at "Richmond Hill" in Yadkin County.

been engaged at all morning, and made me think of think of you and your question of the sale of a bailer, — you see it requires an exertion to settle down, — three months ago, and your question would have been attacked in the first line, now, I have written a whole page and more, without saying *"bailer* ! but once.

* * * * *

I am in such a talking humour, that I can't leave all this white paper and will fiill it up by the news of the day, giving you the privilege of doing the same. rumour says that James Morehead [7] is making a severe push at J. H.. I found him in Salisbury, where he had been for a week with no ostensible excuse except to court, and he had not the same advantage that we had in Hillsboro, unluckily, there was no other girls to create a diversion, and set the good folks to conjecturing, it was *point blank* J. H., and he could not get around it at all; he has visited Salisbury twice in two months, and he never was there before; if he comes again, he will be engaged — if he dont come, he will be kicked ! and if he comes again and dont afterwards continue his visits, he will be blown, *"sky high.* I think the youth has got into a difficulty I could have given him my experience ! but he did not ask it, and I shall retreat from publick rumour, under the smoke he will raise, as I now have something else to think about; he may be courting in earnest, he had better do so now, he will have the credit of it any how.

From Joseph Graham, Jr.   U.

Shelby City, Tennessee.

July the 8th, 1828.

It has been some time since I received your last letter. I would have written you before now but not knowing certainly whether you were in Lincoln or Hillsborough.

Brother James has lately payed us a visit tho he only remained here twelve days oweing to his business at home being urgent. Sister Martha and her Child has gon with him to Carolina, and I think it doubtful whethre they will return to this country again. Since they have left me I have been very lonesome; indeed

---

[7] James Turner Morehead (1799-1875), of Greensboro, a graduate of the university, a lawyer and planter, and a younger brother of John M. Morehead. He served in the state senate, 1835-1843, and was a Whig member of congress, 1851-1853. The courtship alluded to was unsuccessful.

I miss the company of the Child more than the others as it was very lovely and playful and afforded me a grate deele of amusement. I think the onley way that I can remedy my lonely situation with any kind of conveneance is either to get married or to Sell my farm and commence the mercentile business, at this time I have it in view to doe one or the other in the cource of the next year and I am not determined on which yet; the farming business is a verry slow way to accumulate perticularly at the presant prices of Cotton which is the only artickle that the farmer can make here that will command Cash. Our Crops in this section of Country are flattering tho we have had a remarkable wet Spring. the Mississippi River has been very nearly stationary at high watter mark from the Month of December last till June; it has now gotten within its banks again.

* * * * *

. . . Memphis is improving rapidly, its population now is 8 or 9 hundredred Soles thare are two News papers published thare, last Season thare was about 1500 bales of Cotton Shipped from that port. Our most unhealthy season here comences on in this Month after the Spring freshet begins to Swage and leve exposed to the rays of the sun that wide and Filthy Swamp from the Mississippi to the highlands of St. Francis River, a distance of thirty five miles.

Thomas Reed & W Thompson [8] I believe are the only acquaintances you have in this section, they and thare familyes and my self and the Negrows have enjoyed good health, thare has beene but *one* case of the Fever, on my Farm in four *years* past.

* * * * *

From Alfred Graham.   U.

Vesuvius Furnace, July 14th, 1828.

I received your Letter about 10 Days since and have just taken my seat to write you in turn, Though I am as usual nearly barren of News. Sister Martha [9] arrived here from Tennessee 4 or 5 days ago in Health. her and her Child left Joseph well. James came in with her as far as Rutherford; from their she came alone here. She brought with her 2 Horses and a Carrial, young Stephen

---

[8] Possibly Dr. William Henry Thompson, a classmate of Graham, who was a resident of Chapel Hill before his graduation.

[9] Mrs. George F. Graham.

and a Nurse called Chance; the rest of her Negroes are hired in Tennessee. I do not know where she will live yet but suppose she will remain with us for some time. We expect Brother James here at our County Court next Week, After Which I shall be able to answer your enquiry relative to our Candidates for the Assembly. Reinhardt [10] as yet has no opposition in the Senate. Conrad, Holland, Shipp, Brevard, and Loreto [11] a Ducchman near Lincolnton, are Candidates for the Commons again and I am told will declare themselves as such next week. It is said Harry [12] will not offer this year. The people appear very indifferent about it Much more is said about the Presidential Election at present here. Alexander Colwell is a Candidate for the Comons in Mecklenburg and I am told will stand a very good Chance of being elected. Julius Alaxander [13] and Blackwood [14] are only other Candidates for the Commons. W. Davidson [15] of Charlotte and a man by the name of Mussa [16] are for the Senate. Bergin [17] and Colonel John Kincade of Buck are candidates for the Senate and Newton, Old Brice Collins,[18] and some 4 or 5 others I dont recollect are for the Commons. I have not heard who are out in Iredell. Our friends in this section are as usual. Rufus Reid [19] is to be married in a week or 2 to Miss Nancy Latta. Franck Henderson and Sarah Johnson are also said to be engaged. Theadorus Brevard and Isaac Hayne [20] were with me all Day one day last Week. Theadore is very much distressed and looks very unhealthy. him and I Hane are to set of for Reynoldberg in Tennessee in a day or 2 to attend some business of Unclle

---

[10] Michael Reinhardt, one of a numerous and important family of Lincoln County, who was state senator 1827-1828, 1836-1838.

[11] Andrew H. Loretz represented Lincoln in the commons, 1828-1830.

[12] Probably Major John B. Harry, a prominent citizen of Lincolnton who was state senator in 1835.

[13] William Julius Alexander (1797-1857), a native of Salisbury, a graduate of the university, lawyer, represented Mecklenburg in the commons, 1826-1830, 1833-1834 (speaker, 1828, 1833-1834). He was made superintendent of the Charlotte mint in 1846.

[14] Joseph Blackwood represented Mecklenburg in the commons, 1827-1828, and was state senator in 1829.

[15] William Davidson (1778-1857), of Mecklenburg, a native of Charleston, state senator, 1813, 1815-1818, 1825, 1827, 1830, and a member of congress, 1827-1829.

[16] Henry Massey, state senator, 1831-1832.

[17] Merritt Burgin served in the commons, 1820 and 1822, and in the state senate, 1827-1829.

[18] Brice Collins served in the commons, 1805-1807, 1813-1817, 1819, 1821, 1823.

[19] Rufus Reid (1789-1854), moved to Iredell, and represented that county in the commons, 1844-1846. He lived at Mount Mourne.

[20] Isaac W. Hayne became a brilliant, noted, and successful lawyer in Charleston, and was attorney general of South Carolina from 1848 until the close of the Civil War.

Brevard [21] and try if it will improve his Health and spirits which are much depressed. Brumby[22] is still at Brevards since his Marriage and intends living somewhere in this County Robert Davidson is here yet and speaks of remaining untill fall; he is a great deal of company for me and attends his studies very attentively. Mary nor Robert have not been to see us lately. I suppose they will be here as soon as they here of the arrival of Martha. James Osbern[23] has arrived from Chapelhill also Torrents.[24] Matthews Davidson is still bent on Florida in the fall, he has all ready made sale of some of his furniture, and & Uncle Jack[25] has given out moving untill next fall. I thinck it doubtfull whether he will go. Sylvester has been there for some time preparing for the reception of his and Mathews Familys again Fall. We have the best prospect of Crops in this section of Country we have had for several years. We have just finished ours And will commence getting Timber for our Furnace Wheel next Week which will have to be built entirely new and a new Shaft also before we commence again blowing. Castings remain dull as usual almost impossible to affect sales for Cash at any price. Iron some little brisker Though we cannot make sales of $\frac{1}{4}$ of what we manufacture As to the result of [torn] killing adventure in the South I can give you no information as yet. The People know more about it than I do myself. We have had no Balls or any amusement on the furth of July here except firing some Guns and drincking Grog. Henry Fulenweder[26] has lost his Child and four of his Negroes lately with Typhus Fever and is sick himself; his Mother also has had a sever attack.

Your Brother

N B Will you return this summer here or not?

---

[21] Alexander Brevard, a Revolutionary soldier, iron manufacturer, the brother-in-law of General Joseph Graham.

[22] Richard Trapier Brumby (1804-1875), a native of South Carolina, a graduate of South Carolina College, who had his preparatory training in Statesville and Lincolnton. He read law under Stephen D. Miller and William C. Preston, and moving to Alabama, edited the *Expositor*, a Nullification newspaper there. He became a professor in the University of Alabama, and is credited with first discovering the coal and iron resources of the state, on which he published an important report. He was later professor at South Carolina College.

[23] James Walker Osborne (1811-1869), of Charlotte, a native of Rowan, graduate of the university, a lawyer and Graham's close friend. He was superintendent of the Charlotte mint, 1850-1853, a judge of the superior court, 1859-1866, and a delegate to the convention of 1861.

[24] Hugh Torrence of Mecklenburg, then a student at the university.

[25] John Davidson, brother of Mrs. Joseph Graham.

[26] Henry Fulenwider, member of a prominent Swiss family, a business man, engaged chiefly in iron manufacturing, and in mining.

From Matthias E. Manly.   U.

New Bern,

Decr. 23rd, [1828.]

My dear Graham

I hate all apologies from the bottom of my soul; but such is the situation in which I am often placed that one becomes of primary necessity.

What account shall I render you for not writing long ago?

How satisfy a mind, even so much disposed by friendship to be satisfied, that this neglect of you has not proceeded from indifference? ————— I must make a plain and honest confession.

————— An almost incorrigible *laziness* is the cause ——— You can bear me witness that my habits are averse to exertion whether mental or corporal. *Poverty* alone can move me ——— Poverty *has* impelled me to labour industriously in my vocation. And the same cause I earnestly hope will make industry a habit —business a pleasure—my profession a profit and honor.

Our legislature has done little or nothing yet. The project to incorporate a new Bank is immensely important to this section of country. It seems to me upon the whole, to be the only feasible plan of averting the wide-spread calamity which the late resolutions of the State Bank must superinduce. The people cannot possibly be prepared to pay more than one instalment of a tenth upon a debt of six millions. Where is the money to come from? The United States Bank will only lend upon a prompt payment of one-third every ninety days. This, then, the only resource, will increase the pressure. You may depend upon it, debtors will not sit still when they see such ruin impending; they will take their negroes and other moveable property, pull up stakes and run over the mountains. Principals and securities all will dodge and leave the Bank to make the most of their lands. Such an issue as this would be deplorable both in its effects upon the interest of the stockholders and the general wealth and prosperity of the State.

The bill providing for the election of the sheriff by the people, I observe is about to pass. I do not know what will be its effects, but it appears to me to be an idle, not to say dangerous experiment. The evils complained of under the present system are frequently fanciful; where they are real, the change will hardly obviate them. And innovations upon established customs, we say in politicks, ought never to be made except for the soundest reasons, under urgent necessity.

Potter's retrenchment resolutions[27] seem to have met the fate they deserved, an ignoble and noiseless death. He notwithstanding seems to be much concerned about every thing in the house, indefatigueable at least in his enmity to the banks. Upon an inquiry of his made two or three days ago, it was reported to the legislature by the officers of the State bank that there was in the vault at Raleigh only about $350 in specie! Molly, what a bank!! Guess they will soon have to stop specie payments sure enough.

*   *   *   *   *

---

[27] Robert Potter introduced resolutions for an investigation of the State Bank. Certain statements in the preamble were immediately declared to be "a violent and vindictive assault" on the banks of the State, and his name, already under a cloud, was henceforth anathema to all the monied classes of the State, and their followers. The resolutions, themselves, do not seem highly objectionable today.

1829

From Alfred Graham.   U.

Vesuvius Furnace, March 31, 1829.

I know not what excuse to make you for not writing long before this only that I have not written. We are all as usual here and our friends all well except Brother James. He met with an accident last week a little similar to yours in Rutherford. He was travelling in Fathers sulky in a storm and a Tree was struck with lightning very near to him, part of the Tree fell on the sulky and Horse and Injured the sulky a little. He was very much stunned by the shock and fell from the sulky. The Horse also fell and as soon as he recovered run off and tore the sulky to pieces. We understand James was able to get on to Burk Court this week but still feels the effects of the lightning. Our Furnace is in blast at present; we are making mostly Pigmetal as Castings are so remarkably dull of sale. Bartholomew Thompson is still our overseer. I suppose you have heard before this of the marriage of Brother Joseph. He was married to Miss Kimbrough of his County in November last. She was formerly from Wake County in this state and is some relation of Ned Jones.

* * * * *

There will be a Meeting of Presbytry in Lincolnton next week we expect Mary and Mr. Morrison here at that time and probably Violet. Theadorus Brevard has gone to Charleston and has again commenced the study of law; he intends practicing in Columbia when he obtains license. Joe is in bad health and his wife is said to be very much dissatisfyed living up here. He says he will not go to S. Carolina. Marshall Polk is practicing law here and is living with Joe Willson at Charlotte. His wife is determined not to go go back to Tennessee. They still continue finding Gold very fast in Mecklenberge. I was at Bysels mine about 2 weeks ago and went 140 yards under Ground up one the Tunnels where they are at work with Candles. He gets on an average 1½ lbs of Gold per week He has some spaniards working at the mine from Mexico that cannot speak English. He is concerned with a very rich Company in Charleston; last week they sent up 60 Negroes to work the mine. Jack Davidson and Joe Alexander have a mine that they are making money at very fast.

Will you return home this summer or not report says you are very attentive to Miss Ruffin; is it a fact or are you in earnest about the business.

From Alfred Graham.   U.

Vesuvius Furnace, Decem 6, 1829.

Your Letter was received about 2 weeks since I have neglected writing to you so long that I am almost asshamed to write. However I hope you will not think the reason any other than neglect. We are all in health here and since the Cold weather has set in the neighborhood has again become healthy. I suppose you have had an account from James of the sickness and Deaths this Fall in our neighborhood. Robert Brevard has not yet recovered altogether And his constitution is so much shattered that I dont thinck he will ever be healthy again. Ephraim[1] has recoverd again and has returned from D. M. Forneys to their Furnace. Uncle Brevard[2] directed in his will the Negroes 9 in number and the other property he had reserved for himself to be sold at Vandue. They are to be sold in February. . . . The People here still search a little for Gold. Several have found it in small quantities in the Branch. Father and Isaiah Abernathy found a Branch Mine last week on our Land above Canselers on Lickrun that he thincks will be worth working Isaiah found 2 Pieces att as large as a Grain of Wheat, and several small Particles. Father spent 2 days making further search there with 3 hands digging on the hills about it; in all the Pans of Earth they washed they found more or less of the Blacksand at Bottom you described in your Letter. He has never made any Further search beyond the little mountain since you were here. There has been a branch Mine found near Baussels 6 Miles below here which they are doing a good business at.

*   *   *   *   *

You have heard from James I suppose of Fathers purchasing the Arehardt[3] Place below; he still speaks of building a small Forge there but I cannot think the water sufficient for the purpose at that place not even for one Hammer. Whether he will give it out or not I dont know but if he builds atall he cannot do any thing at it untill next Summer. We have just finished putting in the Hearth of the Furnace Though we shall not be ready to

---

[1] Son of Alexander Brevard.
[2] Alexander Brevard (1755-1829), a Revolutionary soldier, who married Rebecca Davidson, a sister of Mrs. Joseph Graham. With Joseph Graham he engaged in iron manufacturing and became wealthy, and was a man of much influence in Lincoln County.
[3] Earhart.

Blow before February. Our Negroes are Ditching the Creek on the Arehardt tract and Clearing a little above Bradshaw's Place on the Creek also.

1830

From Alfred Graham.   U.

Vesuvius Furnace,

March 19, 1830.

*   *   *   *   *

Our Furnace has been in operation since the first of January; we expect if no accident takes place to blow untill the latter part of May. We are making very few Castings on accounte of the dullness of the sale of them. So far we have made a large quantity of Pigs and once in a while do some Casting for the Gold Mines. I made a search for Gold this Winter near the Forge on a small Branch that runs into Mississippi Branch and found 2 pieces as large as Grains of Wheat. We can also find it at Cretens old Musterfield on the Branch and the Hill both. I thinck if Machinery was put in operation it would be worth working. Our Hands are so engaged about the place that we have not time to do any thing at the business untill the Furnace is out of Blast. The Mines is assisting the Iron business a good deal this Spring and Winter. We have sold more than usual for the time principally for Cash. None of the Worcks in the County have much on hand. Henry Fulenweder[1] is driving away on a great scale, Heals over head as usual. With his Nail Factory, Forge, and Goldmine. He is involving himself very much from want of system in business and extravagant dealing. It is believed by Numbers in the County that he will break in 8 or Ten years. He was sued lately for a Debt of 900 Dollars and report says 8000 would not Clear him at this time. We have during the Winter been Ditching and Clearing a little on the Earhart Place, Have Built a House there and I expect as soon as the Furnace Blows out We will commence building a Forge there. Father still keeps every thing secret as usual about it so far but keeps preparing about it in way that his intention canot be Mistaken. I thinck the stream to small for constant Worck even for one Hamer. . . .

---

[1] Henry Fulenwider.

From Matthias E. Manly.   U.

Newbern, Aug. 31st, 1830.

It has been a long time since I did a thing so sentimental as writing to a friend. As the world goes a few only have capacity or taste for such exercises and I am not one of that few. After the interesting realities of life have once passed across the mind, abstractions, whether upon politicks religion or law have no attraction for it; and sentimentality and professions of friendship are vain and suspicious

I was in Hillsboro and remained a day not long since. How immensely stupid it was! Of all the dull places for dullness it excels—I had the horrors—and they now, God deliver me, seize upon my reminiscence with a most pervading and resistless avidity. Its effects upon a fair townswoman of mine (Miss J. B.) I was edified to observe—she has improved in good manners with such amazing velocity—by associating, I dare say, with the swine and wallowing in the mud puddles. Get out of it my dear Will an' you love me! If you have any of the siberian in your nature who loves his country for her very infirmities I recall what I have said and present a description of the other side of the picture—dwell with delight upon the hour I spent in the company of Messrs. H. Waddell, J. Norwood,[2] W. E. Anderson,[3] to whose politeness I feel much indebted and upon the pleasantness of the landlady whose good humored face was a true oasis in the desert.

My journey was a rapid one which afforded me small opportunity to make observation on the way except at Geo Whitfield's[4] where we staid 3 days and the only conclusion I drew there was that we had pretty well consumed his entire stock of patience and food. He is a gentleman whom you know and lives in the most hospitable abundance of any one in the low country. But the journey was upon the whole a pleasant one with five ladies of full pattern in one stage in warm weather! How could it be otherwise—there was such interesting and imminent danger of vertigo, apoplexy, or syncope.

I think you will find the ladies referred to pleasant company; we board in the same house and are quite infamous.

---

[2] John Wall Norwood (1803-1885), of Orange, a graduate of the university in Graham's class, lawyer, member of the commons, 1856, 1858; state senate, 1872-1874.
[3] William Edward Anderson (1805-1852), who after graduation from the university, taught for some time in Hillsboro, and then became a merchant and banker in Wilmington.
[4] George Whitfield was a wealthy planter of Lenoir County.

Eliza is said to be engaged to A. Gaston[5] who by the by is with you attended by Burgwyn who acts as his groom and will I suppose *pet him* when the time arrives. Frances is courted by a young doctor named Borden who accompanied her a part of the way to Hillsboro. James Rowe is also said to be pleased with her. . . . Julia is engaged to Edward Stanly,[6] John's son, Harriet is being engaged to C Hawks[7] and the other in order to dispose of her I'll must take myself and be the younger brother.

I have been this particular because I deem it meet when I introduce persons into new society to give them histories and a woman's history is a recital of her loves—when they are told you have it all

We have had a great storm in these parts; the crops of corn it is estimated have sustained much damage.

I have written this epistle in the midst of company which however much it may evidence my industry does not prima facie speak favourable of my politeness; they are friends who know how to excuse a case of necessity however.

I don't know what I have written for it is late and the mail goes before I get up in the morning. I'll write to enquire ere long.

With constant wishes for your success and happiness.

---

[5] Alexander F. Gaston, a son of Judge William Gaston, of whom little is known today, save that he was a son of his father's second marriage. After engaging for a time in planting, he moved first to Lincoln, and then to other western counties, prospecting and mining. He was active in the militia, and attained the rank of major general. His son William lived for a time with Judge Gaston, but I have not been able to trace his, his brother's, or his father's later history.

[6] Edward Stanly (1808-1872), of Beaufort County, a native of New Bern. Educated at Norwich University, he studied law, and was quickly successful. But his ambitions lay in the direction of politics. He was brilliantly able and eloquent, but arrogant and quarrelsome. He was a member of congress, 1837-1843, 1849-1853, a member of the commons, 1844-1846, and speaker at his first session, attorney general, 1846-1848. He was bitterly opposed to secession, and in 1853 he moved to California, and while still a slave owner, was the Republican candidate for governor in 1857. In 1862 Lincoln appointed him military governor of North Carolina, but his mission was a failure. He violently opposed the policies of the Radicals, had an unpleasant row with Charles Sumner, and finally resigned. He coined the phrase "unterrified democracy."

[7] Cicero Stephens Hawks (1812-1868), of Craven, brother of Francis L. Hawks (*q. v.*), graduate of the university, Episcopal bishop of Missouri.

From James Graham.   U.

Vesuvius Furnace, October 29th, 1830.

I have this moment arrived here from Lincoln Court and there are no white persons but Thompson and Jesse Saunders. Father has gone to Church, and Alfred accompanied sister Sophia about ten days since to Alabama, he does not expect to return before Christmas. The old mansion looks like some deserted Castle and calls to recollection manny a scene which can never be acted over again but upon which the memory delights to dwell.

A few days after you left us I set out with brother Joseph and went with him to the top of the Blue Ridge and I have not been here since. I went to the Warm Springs, spent a week and saw that far famed Belle, Miss Champion, or as she was more generally called there that *rich gall.* Our friend Washington Alexander[8] was her shadow there. He had Tom Smart in company to make necessary arrangements and tell the folks that that noble man whom you see is Mr. *Lawyer Alexander*—However Miss C. has so strangly thundered in the Lawyers Ear and thereby impaired his vision and rendered him so blind that he could not tell a Mountain from a Mole hill, and he and his Aid-de-camp Maj. Smart both *turned over* their Sulkies at one time and their horses run and broke every thing into fragments.

On my return from the Springs I spent a few days in the Southern part of Buncombe among some of the most wealthy, fashionable and literary people from the lower part of South Carolina, who are building stately mansions and improving their summer seats in the most tastful stile.[9] Thence I travelled over to Greenville in Company with Chancellor Dessasure[10] and his daughter and eight or ten others; upon our arrival at Green-

---

[8] Washington Clay Alexander was at a later date sheriff of Gaston County, which was cut off from Lincoln. It is possible it was he who is referred to.

[9] The reference is to the development of Flat Rock by the Charleston colony.

[10] Henry William deSaussure (1763-1839), of South Carolina, a revolutionary soldier, studied law under Jared Ingersoll, and began practice in Charleston. He was a member of the constitutional convention of 1790, and of the lower house, 1790-1794, 1796-1798, 1800-1802, 1807-1808. In 1808 he was elected to the court of chancery, and during the years which followed published four volumes of Chancery Reports, from the Revolution to 1817. The equity system of the state owed to him "its shape, form, and existence." He was intendant of Charleston, 1797-1798, and was an ardent defender of Low Country supremacy in the state. As director of the United States mint in 1795 he brought about the first coinage of gold. He was prominent in the founding of South Carolina College.

ville we found the present Governor Miller,[11] Mr. Hugh Legree[12] of Charleston confessedly the first literary gentleman in So. Ca., and a large portion of the talent, wealth, fashion and beauty of South Carolina. I spent a week there very pleasantly in eating good dinners and *nullifying good wine,* and must say no people can be more polite, kind, and hospitable. They really study how to make you happy by every means in their power. I did not see much beauty the females have a sort of Beeswax complexion, the Rose on the cheek is the production of Art not nature; however they are sprightly and intelligent. From Greenville by a forced march I returned to Burke Court and have been closely engaged ever since. Next week will terminate my circuit. I then go to my plantation to see about gathiring and selling my cotton & corn. I propose going to Columbia about the 1st. week in Decm. and after staying a short time to return to my Circuit as I design to read more closely than heretofore.

Judge Mangum[13] has done a great quantity of business on our Circuit and given much satisfaction; although not a profound Lawyer he is prompt and quick to decide and right or wrong you know where he is and what he means. Our friend R. H. Burton[14] speaks of being a candidate for public treasurer in case Robards[15] declines, and think him admirably well quallified to fill that appointment. We have no prommant man who aspires to the Senate of U. S. Tis understood though that neither Genl Stokes nor Sam Carson would decline that distinguished honour; be-

[11] Stephen Decatur Miller (1787-1838), of South Carolina, a graduate of South Carolina College, lawyer, and planter, was a member of congress 1817-1819, of the state senate, 1822-1828, governor, 1828-1830, United States senator, 1831-1833, delegate to the Nullification Convention. He moved to Mississippi, and was a cotton planter until his death.

[12] Hugh Swinton Legare (1789-1843), a native of Charleston, graduate of South Carolina College, studied law at home and abroad. He was a member of the assembly, 1820-1822, 1824-1830, attorney general, 1830-1832, *charge d'affaires* at Brussels, 1832-1836. He opposed Nullification, was a Unionist member of congress, 1837-1839, and attorney general of the United States from 1841 until his death.

[13] Willie Person Mangum (1792-1861), of Orange County, a graduate of the university, had a long and varied public career. He was a member of the commons, 1818-1819, a judge of the superior court, 1819-1820, 1826, 1828-1829; presidential elector 1828, United States senator, 1831 to 1836, (when he resigned because of legislative instructions); state senator, 1840 United States senator, 1840-1853, and president *pro tem,* 1842-1845.

[14] Robert Henderson Burton (1781-1842), of Lincoln County, a native of Granville, was a student at the university for a short time, studied law, and was a successful practitioner. In 1818 he was elected a judge of the superior court, and, after riding one circuit, resigned. In 1830 he was elected state treasurer, and declined.

[15] William Robards, of Granville, member of the commons, 1806, 1808, state treasurer 1827-1830.

tween Owen[16] and Donnell [17] I presume the West will have but little preference. I am inclined to think if Seawell [18] ever hopes to be a Senator his prospects would be good. He is no favorite with me but we ought to have a man of talents in the Senate.

* * * * *

From James Graham.   U.

Columbia, So. Ca., Decm. 19th., 1830.

I have been here two weeks and been much gratified with my visit. I have formed many acquaintances and heared the great debate on the great question of convention. It was discussed ten days and terminated on friday last when the question was decided and the vote stood in the house of Representatives 60 for Convention and 56 against it—The Constitution of the State requires a majority of 2/3 to call a Convention so that the friends of Convention are frustrated and foiled for the present. Judge Huger[19] was the prominant man against this measure and Wm. C. Preston[20] its able advocate. I have been much disappointed in the Talents of the most distinguished men in So. Ca. Declamation is indulged in here more than any place I have ever been. However the debate was conducted with the utmost propriety and Dignity and fore-

[16] John Owen (1787-1841), of Bladen County, studied at the university, and became a planter. He sat in the commons, 1812-1813, in the state senate, 1819-1820, 1827, and was a delegate to the convention of 1835. He was governor, 1828-1830, and refused re-election. He was president of the Whig convention at Harrisburg in 1840.

[17] John Robert Donnell (1789-1864), of Craven, a native of Ireland, a graduate of the university, was a state solicitor, 1815-1819, and a judge of the superior court, 1819-1837. Retiring, he devoted his attention to his large planting interests.

[18] Henry Seawell (1772-1835), a native of Franklin County, who spent his life in Raleigh, "a man of strong intellect and little education," who served in the commons, 1797, 1799-1802, 1810, 1812; in the senate, 1821-1826, 1831-1832; and was a delegate in the convention of 1835. He was a judge of the superior court, in 1811, 1813-1819, 1832-1835. He was a member of the commission appointed under the Treaty of Ghent.

[19] Daniel Elliott Huger (1779-1854), of Charleston, a graduate of Princeton, served in both branches of the legislature, was a distinguished judge, a Unionist leader in the Nullification controversy, and United States senator, 1843-1845. He offered amendments to resolutions introduced by William C. Preston, and defended them in a speech which lasted nearly twelve hours.

[20] William Campbell Preston (1794-1860), of South Carolina, a Virginian, born in Philadelphia, a graduate of South Carolina College, a lawyer, a leader in Nullification, served in the legislature, and was United States senator, 1833-1842, when he resigned. He was president of South Carolina College, 1846-1851. He offered a set of resolutions on Federal relations, chiefly dealing with the tariff, and endorsing the doctrine of Nullification, and defended them with eloquence equal to that of Judge Huger.

bearance until the last day when some offensive expressions were used by a Mr. Smith[21] towards Judge Huger; the latter challenged him in ½ an hour and the mutual friends of both gentlemen interposed and prevailed on Smith to make a public apology in the House.

Theadore and Joseph Brevard are both here on yesterday I dined with them at Mr. Hopkinses They are both much esteemed here. Theadore is about to settle in Camden and practice the Law. He begins to manifest a strong disposition to marry again and think will marry well. Isaac Hayne and his sister are both here. Isaac is esteemed one of the most talented and promising men in the state. There have been a great number of strangers in Columbia from all parts of the State, and many of So. Ca's. fairest and most beautiful flowers. Miss Champion is here and her name is used here as senonymous with *money*. She has not attracted the attention that was anticipated. I have mingled a good deal in the gay circle but have been more struck with the fine manners of the Ladies here than their superior beauty. As soon as I put this letter in the P. office, I expect to leave for N. Carolina By way of Catawba Cottage to Rutherfordton.

I have just seen that D. L. Swain[22] is elected a Judge, that R. Burton is Treasurer, and Mangum, Senator, and that the governors election is closely contested. I am more and more convinced that poleticks is a Lotery with many blanks to a prise.

* * * * *

---

[21] Robert Barnwell Smith, later Robert Barnwell Rhett, (*q. v.*) an active Nullificationist.

[22] David Lowry (originally Lowrie) Swain (1801-1868), of Buncombe County, after a good academic preparation, spent a part of 1821 at the university. He served in the commons, 1824-1826, 1828-1829, was a judge of the superior court, 1830-1832, governor, 1832-1835, a delegate to the convention of 1835, president of the university, 1835-1868. Able and progressive, he popularized the university. A Whig, he had contacts with men of all parties, in and out of the state. He rendered valuable service in locating historical manuscripts, and in arousing popular interest in the history of the state. Displaced by the Republicans in 1868, he died soon afterwards as the result of an accident. He and Graham were devoted friends over many years.

1831

From Alfred Graham.   U.

Vesuvius Furnace, January 1, 1831.

I have at length arrived here again after a long and lonesome ride of about 600 Miles from Alabama.

I left Dr. Witherspoon on the 7th December and returned by Montgumery, Alabam, Milledgeville, Georgia, and Abbeville, S. C. on home. We had fine weather going out not one day of Wet weather on the way Sister Sophia and the Children stood the Journey very well although we past over some as bad road as ever a Carriage or waggon did pass in the Cherockee Nation a distance of 160 Miles; the Indians have quit worcking on their Roads for the last 3 years, owing to their difficulties with Georgia and the General Government, and the Road is almost impassible. We found the Doctor and McCalla[1] at Home living in as rough Batchelor style as any men; it put me in mind of home when there is no one there but Father, myself and Thompson. They were very much rejoiced to see us particularly the Doctor; it was amusing to see his meeting with his little Children. He is making the best Crop of Cotton which he has made since he has been in the state on his Cane Break farm; he had picked when I left there 130 Bales and expected to make altogether 155 or 60. Cotten Crops are very fine generally in that part of Alabama. I was in Tuscaloosa 2 Days during the Session of the Legislature. McCalla and I went up to see and here the news among them and spent our time very pleasantly. We were all at a ball there and saw the Races on 1 and 2 of December. They were attended by nigh 1000 People 2 men from old Kentucky took the Purse both days. There were Gamblers and Horse racers from nearly all the Western States south of Ohio. Charles Conner[2] was there, a member of the House of Representatives and rancks among their most intelligent in the House. I heard him make 2 speeches in the House; 1 in Favor of an appropriation of 8000 Dollars for finishing the statehouse, and the other on the subject of a Contested Election which

[1] McCalla Witherspoon, probably a brother of Dr. Witherspoon. There are several allusions in the Graham papers to McCauley Witherspoon, but I have not been able to identify him.

[2] Charles Conner, presumably, was one of the Lincoln County families of that name. He represented Marengo County in the legislature.

was before the House. Crawford [3] who married Aunt Margaret Davidsons Daughter is also a member of the Senate there and is a Judge of their County Court.

I am much better pleased with alabama than when I saw it in 1826 and if Land Could be got at a fair Price would like to live there.

I was compelled to part with my fine Bay Horse on the way out; he became lame in both his Fore Legs so that he could not travel, owing I thinck to his Jumping over the stone wall below the House before I started from home. I lost Considerably in the swap gave $20 to Boot and got a much less valuable Horse but there was no other Chance but to swap; I Could not get on with him. McCalla would have come with me to this state if he could have got a good Horse. He is coming to Charleston this Spring and told me he would return this way home and spend a week or 2 here.

Nothing new has taken place here since I set out for Alaba. The Furnace has been in Blast about 2 weeks. Father employed Elisha Saunders to stay here untill I returned. He has given out doing any thing more at the Arehart Place for the present.

*   *   *   *   *

From James Graham.   U.

Rutherfordton, Feb. 2d, 1831.

I received your letter written at Raleigh by Judge Swain, and also yours of the 1st. Jan'y at Hillsboro by mail. I very much regretted to learn that our friend Scott is embarrassed with debts and difficulties. I make it a rule myself never unnecessarily to incur professional responsibility. I collect every mans money as soon as I can, and put it in a parcel to itself, labelled, of whom Rec'd, how much, and to whom due, and pay it over the first opportunity. If poor Scott once gets down he never can rise. I was surprised to her of Miss T—s' excentrick movements, though perhaps we should not when we remember a young female is a brilliant constellation of fanciful aberrations and Romantic frenzies. The Whitaker family passed this village about ten days before my return from Columbia; and if the present administration were about to ascertain the quallifications of a Foreign-minister,

---

[3] The name does not occur in Thomas M. Owen's lists of members from the several counties of Alabama.

they could not have exercised their inqusitorial talents more than my good friends did concerning me. My acquaintances thought it "very misterious" and "passing strange" that such particular inquiry should be made about any body. Upon their arrival here, a negro boy went into the Bar room and asked if Mr. Graham lived here? he was told yes and asked if he knew him, the boy said "he is a sweet heart of my young Mistress, ah says the barkeeper and what luck, oh says the boy "I bleve she pends pun him yet" The Barkeeper left the Whisky runing and went right into the room to look at Mr. W. the *news* spread and the whole town were putting on their "tother clothes" to see what sort of creature she could be when she departed on her journey. I did not hear of her again untill you mentioned they were in Hillsboro. Brother Alfred has just returned from Alabama and speaks of removing next spring to the Missippi State. You can readily perceive this will leave Father in a deplorable situation. Alfred is resolved at all events to do something for himself and father will be obliged to curtail his business and change his complicated pursuits. I have endeavored to pursuade Alfred to postpone his departure untill next Autumn though he appears reluctant to do so. I saw Treasurer Burton at Lincoln *Co Ct,* and although I never felt colder weather, he was in Court all week arguing six-penny cases, he is so fond of money that I believe his conscience would take *the cramp* on a sixpence. As last Session of the Legislature was *Resolution Session,* they ought to have passed one more: "Resolved that Rob Burton be compelled to wear a Petty-coat and bed-gown the residue of his life and that said garments be made up out of the ragged treasury Bills instead of burning them"— he is politically dead and d—d too. Our friend Dick Pearson[4] passed through here about the *middle of January* on his way to the *Warm Springs.* He will return the last of this week and report the Degrees of heat in Tennessee according to Hymen's Thermometer. John Hall, son of the Judge,[5] has removed to Buncombe to take charge of Swain's business. . . . I design next fall to take Mecklenburg into my Circuit and leave Haywood and perhaps Burke. I must be at my plantation occasionally and I will take fewer Courts and

---

[4] Not identified, but probably Richmond M. Pearson, (*q. v.*).

[5] John Hall (1767-1833), of Warrenton, a native of Virginia, and a graduate of William and Mary, was a judge of the superior court, 1800-1818, where he acquired a fine reputation. When the supreme court was established in 1818 he was elected to it. He resigned in 1832 on account of bad health. He was grand master of Masons, and notwithstanding his judicial position, a Democratic elector in 1828. His son, here referred to, has not been further identified, beyond his having been appointed a superior court judge and failing of election by the legislature.

give them more attention. Charlotte *is growing rapidly* and promises to be the 1st. town in the western part of the State. I think you would do well to visit the North next Summer. I think your health would be improved, at all events you must take more exercise *every day.* Ride, walk or chop wood until you begin to sweat, eat but little and chew that little *a great deal,* drink Porter or light wine. I believe a little reflection bestowed upon our own constitutions and a fixed Resolution to adhere to the dictates of nature and nature's Law, which is always simple and generally sure and efficacious, would, in nine out of Ten cases, insure the health & happiness of the human race.

Our Post Coaches have just commenced runing from Salem by this place to Greenville So. Ca. and from Lincolnton through this to Asheville. The tide of travelling begins to set strongly through this ugly Town and business is looking up for larger profits & and brighter prospects.

From Alfred Graham.   U.

Vesuvius Furnace, N. C., March 13, 1831.

*   *   *   *   *

You mentioned in your Letter that you had heard of my intention of removing to the West I will now inform you that I have determined on going and expect to set out the last of this month or first of Aprile. If you can arrange your affairs I would be glad to see you here before I set of. I have everything ready now except one more Horse and some money to Collect. I would have set out early in the Spring but could not Collect Money in time. I do not expect to make a Crop this Season; I thinck of hiring the Negroes out untill the first of september or putting in with Brother Josephs and let them make provisions to do them during the winter; in the meantime I will look out a suitable place and purchase land early in the Fall. I have remained here so long doing nothing for myself that I have become impatient to get away Though I dislike the thoughts of leaving Father and my Friends behind, but I cannot waist my time as I have done without a compensation. What Father intends doing with the Worcks here I can give you no information but thinck he will carry them on 8 or 10 years longer as he is now doing. . . .

From James Graham.   U.

Rutherfordton, May the 23rd, 1831.

I received your last letter of the 23d. ult, by the hand of Mr. Cowan[6] at Iredell Superior Court and I am gratified to learn you intend visiting Father early in June. On tomorrow I will set out for Vesuvius and spend one or two days there, and then go on to the Catawba-Cottage where I design taking a Negro boy that I have just bought, and where I wish to sell the residue of my corn, which is now a cash article in that neighbourhood, at one dollar per bushel. Fortunately for me last season I raised a good crop of corn and but little cotton. I was in Charlotte about twelve days since and was surprised to see the whole face of the town and adjacent country growing and improving so rapidly; the strangers or recent settlers are becoming so numerous as to give a tone and new direction to the manners and customs: and instead of the notions and habits of the Scotch-Irish, (which were about as stiff and unyielding as the *black-Jacks* of their own soil), You now begin to look upon the polish and refinement of a French Society. If Charlotte can acquire a character for health no one can doubt its prospects are quite flattering. Washington Morrison is to be married in next month, says the report of Charlotte, to Miss Rosanna Patton of Asheville. Our friend and relation Theodore Brevard has just been married the second time in Columbia to a Miss Mays, a very beautiful girl, and is already keeping house in Columbia. Eaphraim Brevard, Daniel Forney, and Genl George Lee Davidson and his son, set out to explore Florida, Alabama, and Western Tennessee. I believe their views are not ascertained, though it is presumed they are dissatisfied in No. Ca. and are desirous of removing. We understand in this quarter that Seawell in the Libel at Salisbury annihilated Judge Martin[7] and crippled Julius Alexander very badly. The Fisher party claim a triumphant victory over the Alexander connextion. When Martin heard the result of the trial and the liberty Seawell took with his name, he was at this Court and he was obviously much chagrined and looked very much like an Indian who had resolved to kill the next white man he could see, so that the legal-sinners feared and trembled

---

[6] Probably J. C. Cowan of Rutherfordton.
[7] James Martin (d. 1846), of Stokes County, a graduate of the university, state senator, 1823. He was a judge of the Superior Court, 1827-35, when he resigned, and moved to Mobile.

for their fate. You have heard I presume that Dick Allison[8] of Iredell was indicted for a Libel on Pinkney[9] and Hiram Caldwell and after the failure in Salisbury was promulgated the prosecution against Dick was dismissed.

There was lately a grand Washington City wedding in this vicinity, Samuel P. Carson to a Miss Wilson, a cousin of his own, and the sister to two of his brothers wives. I believe they have been courting one or two years and in the mean time *Sam-Patch* was trying his fortune in Washington; but learning that the fates had decreed against him, he resolved if he could not get Honey he would take Molasses. My particular friend John Hall whom I mentioned to you last winter had removed to Buncombe has returned again to this place, . . . he and a Doctor Miller of this County are now gone into So. Carolina to court the first two Pritty galls they meet. They have gone in good stile and will make a favourable impression until the *brandy* washes it out—Hall, upon his parting grog, declared "he was Rattle-snake and Miller was his pilot: and he'd be damned if they didn't bite some one before they came back." Brother Alfred has gone and the old mansion looks lonesome indeed, but Father gets on as usual, he has now blown the Furnace out and is working the Earhart place chiefly. I do hope he will either sell or give up his iron works to some of his children or lease them as it is out of his power to manage at his time of life so complicated an establishment. I confess when I go to see him I am *grieved* to see the negligence, confusion, waste, and indolence and stealing which are apparent and which I fear will be increased since Alfreds departure. I believe Father is like most old men; they dislike the thought of abandoning business, it looks to them, too much like the final exit were approaching and we are, disposed to hide that event from our view. I have not yet determined to go to Nashville tho' I think I may during the summer if I do not will see you when at Fathers. I hope you will not abandon your Northern tour as I know you will derive unspeakable gratification from such a Jaunt, and if my western business were settled I would accompany you. Present my respects to enquiring friends in Hillsboro and accept the best feelings of your brother.

[8] Richard Allison, of Iredell, a graduate of the university, member of the commons, 1826, 1828, 1830.

[9] Pinckney Cotesworth Caldwell (1802-1865), of Lincoln (now Gaston) County, a graduate of Transylvania, and a prominent physician. He represented Mecklenburg in the convention of 1861.

The Journal of

William A. Graham.[10]

June 20, 1831.

Having made due preparation, I left Hillsboro' for Roxboro' at 6 a. m., and passed rapidly on to the latter place, which I reached before the session of the county court. The country is so familiar between these towns that it provokes no particular remark.

June 21st. and 22.

I attended the court, and on the 23rd. set off with A. W. V. (Venable),[11] Esq., and came as far as his house, Brown's store Granville, N. C., 27 miles. The country lying near Person Courthouse on this road is miserably poor, but as we approached Grassy Creek the soil was more fertile. * * * The agriculture along this road is in a low state. The crops of wheat which were being gathered, were moderate, though somewhat injured by rust. Spent a pleasant evening at Mr. V's, with his relatives, Reid, Cabell, etc., who arrived after us.

(June) Friday 24th.

Took leave, and got fairly under way on my journey. A ride of 21 miles brought me to Haskin's Ferry on Roanoke. The farms in Granville from Grassy Creek to the Virginia line are of good soil, particularly on Nutbush, which is crossed on a bridge, and many of the buildings are in good taste, and the farms handsomely improved.

(June) Saturday 25th.

Traveled over a tolerable road, rather a poor soil.

---

[10] From the *North Carolina Review*, Aug. 6, Sept. 3, and Oct. 8, 1911. The asterisks appear in the *Review* copy.

[11] Abram Watkins Venable (1799-1876), of Granville, a native of Virginia, who was educated at Hampden-Sidney and Princeton, and a graduate of both. After two years' study of medicine, he turned to law, and, after some years of practice in Virginia, moved to Oxford. He was a Democratic elector in 1832, 1836, and 1860, a member of congress, 1847-53, and a member of the Confederate Congress from 1861 to 1865. He was widely popular, respected for his high character and purpose, and beloved for his personal charm and his bubbling and infectious humor.

(June) Sunday, 26th.

Journeyed by Dinwiddie Courthouse to Petersburg, 30 miles. Many parts of this road are very bad, causeways, mud-holes, etc. The geology is primitive as all the preceding, until after passing Dinwiddie Courthouse, when sands and long-leaf pines occur anon, until you reach Petersburg. Petersburg is on the south side of the Appomattox, a river about 150 yards wide, has been a place of considerable commerce, but has declined of late from the resort of the country merchants to New York. It has considerable expectations from the railway now in progress from that town to the Roanoke at Weldon, 60 miles. No part of that road is completed, but it is all under contract; cost of the whole is estimated at $380,000. No steamboat ascends the Appomattox above City Point. The principal business is done on Sycamore, Banks, and Bollingbroke streets. It contains four churches, which are numerously attended. The lower part of the town is called Blansford, and on the opposite shore, Chesterfield. There are some highly improved private residences.

(June) Monday, 27th.

After exchanging money with the Messrs. Dunns, I set out in the stage at 8 o'clock a. m. for Richmond, which I reached by 11 o'clock. Twenty miles of the road is a fine turnpike, and passes through a miserably poor district. Half a mile from Manchester it passes over the new railroad, from the coal pits to the James River, which is now completed, and cars will start upon it on the 4th. of July.

Manchester. Richmond approaches more nearly to a city than any town in the South, except New Orleans and Charleston. Visited the dock-yard, commerce, etc. Streets straight and regularly built. Capitol. Governor's house and City Hall fine buildings. Penitentiary, 176 convicts who work together under overseers for each squad; four or five females (only one white); shaving of heads once a week. Armory owned by the State, where are 256 pieces of ordnance. Here the guard, 68 in number, who protect the Capitol, Petersburg, etc., rendezvous. Spent a pleasant evening at the house of Mr. Campbell. Many buildings here are very fine, banks, etc., musical clock. The Eagle Hotel affords good accommodations.

(June) Tuesday, 28th.

I left Richmond during a rain which had been falling all night, at 5 o'clock in the morning, in company with two other stage passengers.* * * Passed Bowling Green, Caroline Courthouse, dined on the way, and reached Fredericksburg, 60 miles from Richmond, at 4:30 p. m. Fredericksburg is well built and seems to be a place of considerable commerce. Steamboats ply to Baltimore, Washington, etc. There is a good bridge across the Rappahannock. After remaining half an hour, we set out in two stages for Potomac Creek, which we reached over a bad road of nine miles, at 6 p. m. Supped at the tavern on shore. The rain ceased before sunset, and we had a beautiful view of the sun going down beyond the creek, which is here one and one fourth miles wide, as also of a rainbow. Went aboard, and got under way immediately after the appearance of twilight, and proceeded down the creek 4 or 5 miles, when we entered the great Potomac, which in the dim light seemed shoreless as the ocean. The tide was at flood, and as we passed down the creek I mistook it for the river, which we seemed to be ascending in a swift current. The wind was a head, and blew so as to give motion to the boat, but we took our berths at about 9 o'clock, and all was silence until about 5 a. m., when the passengers for Alexandria were called to go ashore. We again slept until daylight, when our arrival at the Federal City was announced, and the passengers for Baltimore notified to rise.

(June) Wednesday 29th.

The light of the morning showed us the Potomac, one and one-half miles wide, surmounted by a bridge which had been in many places broken by the ice last spring, and was not yet repaired. Steamboats and square-rigged vessels lying above and below us, and a small portion of the city. After some delay for the ladies on board, we all passed in one stage to Gadsby's National Hotel, an extensive and splendid house. After breakfast I walked to the Capitol with the two fellow passengers from Richmond. We were conducted through it by an individual whose business it seemed to be. Passed the rotunda containing the four paintings of Trumbull, the Hall of Representatives, and Senate Chamber, Supreme Court rooms, ascended to the summit of the dome, 190 feet from the foundation, and 250 feet above Pennsylvania Avenue; extensive and sublime prospect. The Capitol is by far the most splendid architecture which I have even seen, and amply compensates for a journey to it. We then walked to the President's house, but as he was absent on a visit to Old Point Comfort, we did not enter; viewed the improvements, inclosures, offices of the departments situated on each side of it, etc. Messrs. Livingstone[12] and Woodbury[13] were the only cabinet officers in the city. Great indignation prevailed against Mr. Eaton,[14] late Secretary of War, for his attack on the character of Mrs. Ingram.[15] In the evening I visited Thompson's book store, purchased some caricatures, and rode over to Georgetown Catholic College, nunery, etc. Returned to tea, and engaged a seat for Baltimore.

(June) Thursday 30th.

I was roused at 4 a. m., set out in the Phoenix line of Post coaches with four other passengers. The road is an excellent turnpike, which we passed at 7 or 8 miles an hour. Passed by Bladenburg, the scene of battle before the burning of the Capitol in the late war, (1812), and of the duels between the members of Congress and others. * * *

The trip was enlivened by the jests of Captain Phillips, of Baltimore. Having dressed, I walked to view the city of Baltimore, and found it superior in extent, population, and commerce to any town I had yet passed. After dinner, I rode on the celebrated railroad to Ellicott's Mills, 13 miles, in a horse car, (the steam cars not being in operation this evening). This road is a stupendous work. Carrollton bridge, the deep cut. Patterson's bridge, viaducts, etc. Cost of the road more than $50,000. per mile thus far, though the expenditures of a great part was useless, as no inconvenience arises for an ascent of 25 feet per mile; part of the

---

[12] Edward Livingston (1764-1836), of Louisiana, a native of New York, graduate of Princeton, lawyer, Republican member of congress, 1795-1801, and U. S. district attorney, 1801-1803. He moved to Louisiana in 1804, and was the author of the state code. He served on Jackson's staff in 1815, was a member of congress, 1823-1829, and U. S. senator, 1829-1831 and secretary state, 1831-1833. He was minister to France 1833-1835, and upon his return moved back to New York.

[13] Levi Woodbury (1789-1851), of New Hampshire, had served as governor, 1823-1825, speaker of the state lower house, 1825, as U. S. senator, 1825-1831, and was now secretary of the navy. He was secretary of the treasury, 1834-1841, Democratic senator, 1841-1845, and associate justice of the United States supreme court, 1845-1851.

[14] The reference is to the cabinet quarrel which spread to the whole country, about Mrs. John H. Eaton, born Margaret (Peggy) O'Neil, which led to the break-up of the cabinet. Eaton, a native of Halifax County, who was senator from Tennessee, before he became secretary of war, was later minister to Spain and territorial governor of Florida. Mrs. Eaton's reminiscences were published after her death with an introduction by the Rev. Charles F. Deems who was her earnest defender.

[15] Samuel Ingham, the secretary of the treasury, and his wife were bitterly hostile to Mrs. Eaton, and Eaton, writing to Ingham, reminded him that even Mrs. Ingham had not escaped rumor. He later challenged Ingham who fled.

rails of wood, and part stone, both laid with iron. The iron is brought from Liverpool, ready to be laid. A single horse has pulled on the road 200 barrels of flour. The steam cars run 20 or 25 miles per hour.

The road was completed for 20 miles, but the workmen on the further extremity having failed to get their wages by the absconding of the contractor, on this day destroyed four miles of the finished road, and the material for laying 6 miles more. There are considerable factories of iron, cotton, etc., on the Patapsco, owned by Ellicotts, Gray, and others. We returned in a shower of rain to Baltimore at 7 p. m. Found the city in a tumult about the riot on the railroad, and the military from Fort McHenry and the city, collecting to quell it. At 9 o'clock they marched, and took the cars for the scene of the riot.

(July) Friday, 1st.

Rose to breakfast, walked to the Washington Monument and ascended it, 178 feet. It is a perfect piece of art, on the summit is a statue holding a scroll. In the evening walked to the docks and saw the operations of the dredging and discharging machines. The city had been full of reports on the subject of the expedition against the rioters, all the morning. At 5 p. m. the military marched in, bringing with them 40 of the rioters prisoners, and committed them to jail. There had been 370 engaged in the work of destruction, they fled on the approach of the armed force, and only those were taken. One, Hugh Riley, the leader, was marched in front with his lieutenant. None were killed, and but one wounded. There was but little resistance. A force was left to guard the road from further violence. On my return ascended a shot tower, and saw the mode of manufacturing them. Height of tower 180 feet. In the evening I was visited by Mr. Russell,[16] of North Carolina, midshipman, who remained with me until 10 p. m.

(July) Saturday, 2d.

* * * I took leave of Barnum's splendid hotel with regret, as it affords the best accommodations I had ever received. At 12 and one half o'clock we sailed on board the George Washington steamboat, for Philadelphia; down the Patapsco to the bay, thence

---

[16] Possibly William Russell, who became a midshipman in 1826 and resigned in 1832.

across to the mouth of Elk river, up the river and Back creek to Chesapeake village. The only interest I felt in our voyage, was in examining the rapidity of the boat's motion, and in viewing the scenery we passed. There were no passengers on board whose appearance or conversation were attractive. Judge Glenn, of the United States District Court, was along, but I opine is not a Mansfield. We met the Charles Carroll boat on the way, and reached Chesapeake village about 5 p. m. Here we took a canal boat, drawn by five horses, along in Chesapeake and Delaware canal thirteen and a half miles. This canal is well described as the "Traveler's Guide." The deep cut, summit bridge, the hand bridges, and one lock are the most conspicuous objects. * * * This canal is a stupendous work, and cost two and one-half millions of dollars. We passed up the Delaware on board the "Robert Morris," in the night, and arrived at 1 a. m. at Philadelphia. * * *

(July) Sunday, 3rd.

At 5 a. m. I entered the city, and took lodgings at the City Hotel, Nible & Heiskie. Being somewhat fatigued, and meeting no acquaintance, I did not go to church. Read part of Croly's "Life of George IV." After dinner, called on some comrades at Congress Hall. The citizens appeared generally to attend church, and behaved with much propriety during the day. In the evening I strolled on the wharf, and witnessed the arrival of the Baltimore boat.

(July) Monday, 4th.

The ringing of bells and beat of drums announced the anniversary of Independence. Called on Mr. C. G. Bancker, in Chestnut St., with a letter of introduction from Mr. Campbell. To his kindness I was indebted for many favors. Went in his company to hear Mr. David P. Brown, orator of the young men's celebration, but failed in producing an entrance to the church; proceeded thence to dinner at the "Musical Fund Hall." Six hundred persons were present, and part could not be accommodated with seats. The President of the day, John Sergeant,[17] Esq., before reading the

---

[17] John Sergeant (1779-1852), of Pennsylvania, a Princeton graduate, lawyer, who, after holding a number of minor offices, and serving in the lower house of the legislature, 1808-1810, as a Federalist, was a member of Congress, 1815-1823. He was named a delegate to the Panama Congress in 1826, and was returned to the house of representatives in 1827 as a Whig. He was defeated for vice president in 1832, and was again in congress, 1837-1841.

toast in honor of H. Clay, delivered an animated address on the present state of the administration of the Government. Alleged that the recent dissolution of the cabinet was owing to the imbecility of the head, (Andrew Jackson) however it might be attributed directly to the malign influences of male or female, that the President had been lauded for his skill in judgment of men, but there were some other people of whom he was perhaps not so good a judge; that he had greatly misconceived the moral feelings of the matrons of our country, and with all his ability to discern the qualifications of men, it was somewhat remarkable that, in the whole United States, he could not get five men whom he could keep from fighting in his presence. He said the history of the resignations of Van B. (Buren) and Eaton, as given by themselves and the President, was similar to that of John Brown's two little Indian Boys.

"One ran away,
And the other wouldn't stay."

Said that all the operations of the Government were concealed, that no one but the President and a few friends knew anything about it. He was in many instances happily sarcastic, and was cheered with great acclamation by the crowd. His delivery is distinct and plain, though he has somewhat of a tone, and appeared to labor much. Mr. Chambers,[18] the Senator from Maryland, when the toast was read in compliment of himself and his State, addressed the assembly, but in a clumsy manner and with but little else to recommend his remarks. Colonel McKinney (dismissed Clerk of the War Department) told the story of "Old Billy" upon the request of the President, with considerable effect. After tea, I visited with a friend, West's picture of "Christ Rejected;" a most excellent specimen of the limner's art. On this day I saw a caricature of Mrs. Eaton as a slut, Eaton as a gallant mastiff, and Timberlake a sneaking hound. The old bell which proclaimed the independence of our country, was rung at assembling of the citizens today, as it is kept for holidays only.

---

[18] Ezekiel Forman Chambers (1788-1867), a graduate of Washington College, Maryland, lawyer, brigadier general in the War of 1812, state legislator, Whig senator, 1826-1834, judge, 1834-1851. He declined the post of secretary of the navy under Fillmore.

(July) Tuesday, 5th.

* * * Visited the hall where independence was declared; found workmen engaged in refitting it. The State had modernized its architecture in the interior, about fifteen years ago. It has been since given to the corporation, who have pulled down the modern work, and are endeavoring to fit it up precisely as it was at the time of July, 1776.

(July) Wednesday, 6th.

Visited the Navy yard, and saw the immense vessel on the stocks, to be called the Pennsylvania. She has four decks, and will carry 160 guns. The Government has 60 marines in the navy yard to guard it, and provided extensive buildings to secure the ship stores. Commodore Barron[19] is now in command, and has his residence in the city. From the navy yard, I rode to the Arcade, and visited the museum, which contains an extensive collection of curiosities, the skeletons of the mammoth elephants, animals, birds, minerals, optical illusion, Washington's sash, etc. Went thence to the Mayor's court, held by the recorder and two aldermen; trial of a culprit for selling strong drink without a license. Walked next, to the Mint, and saw the process of coining. The precious metals are first melted with a proper degree of alloy, and beaten in bars, these are passed through several sets of rollers until they are reduced to the proper thickness, then, by a machine worked by hand, the bars are cut into dollars, halves, quarters, etc. They are then placed in a small cylinder, and by a machine, are dropped one by one under a stamp, where they receive the impression, and are thrown out into a box. * * *

(July) Saturday, 9th.

I bade adieu to Philadelphia at 6 a. m., took the steamboat for New York, passed by Burlington, Bristol, Bordentown, where I saw the residence of Joseph Buonaparte.[20] He has an observatory

---

[19] James Barron (1769-1851), a native of Virginia, who after service as a sailor on merchant ships, entered the navy in 1798 as a lieutenant. He was promoted captain the next year. He served in the Mediterranean from 1800 to 1805. He commanded the "Chesapeake" in 1807-1808, and was wounded in the affair with the "Leopard." He was tried by court-martial and suspended for five years, during which time he was a high officer in the French navy. He came back to the navy in 1813, fought a duel with Stephen Decatur in which the latter was killed, and he himself was wounded. He was on "waiting orders" for the rest of his life.

[20] Joseph Bonaparte (1768-1844), born in Corsica, elder brother of Napoleon, king of Naples, 1806, and of Spain, 1808-1813. He came to the United States in 1815, and had homes in Philadelphia and New Jersey. He moved to Italy in 1841.

on the shore of the Delaware, which commands a view of Trenton above, and an extensive prospect below. Trenton is a considerable place, has a handsome bridge across the river, State House, etc. * * * From Trenton we set out in coaches, passed through a level country, pretty well improved, to Princeton, saw the Theological Seminary, the college, Alma Mater of so many distinguished men; thus passed to Kingston on the Raritan, from which a canal is being dug to the Delaware, thence to New Brunswick. Here again a steamboat (Swan) was taken for New York. * * *

New York, (July) Sunday 10th.

The City Hotel is an extensive building, and a highly agreeable house. After breakfast, and reading the news, I went to the Roman Catholic Church in Prince Street. A large crowd was gathered about the door, and many kneeled, both without and within. The priest was engaged in the celebration of high mass, and the kneeling posture, the devout appearance, the solemn chant, accompanied by music, and the lighted tapers and georgeous decorations of the cathedral united to give a most imposing appearance to their worship. The organ was finely toned, and a lady's voice who sat near it, was exquisitely fine. After the celebration of mass, a priest appeared in a clerical dress, but without the gaudy decorations of his reader of prayers, who delivered a handsome declamatory sermon against drunkenness; after which he of the rich dress resumed reading and chanting, in concert with the music. Lighted tapers in a vessel which was brought in by four boys who attended, and strewed the smoke of the incense on the altars, etc., before him, after which it was handed to one of the boys, who strewed it on the priest in like manner. The sacrament was given to two females by the priests putting into their mouths a small wafer. Upon the whole, the ceremony was well adapted to give solemnity to their devotions, and must operate to produce much practical morality among the ignorant, but the more intelligent will look on a great part of it as idle pomp. In the evening, I walked on the shore of the North river, and saw Jersey City and Hoboken ferries, as also the tomb of Hamilton in Trinity Church yard. Saw several merchants from the South. Walked to the Battery and Castle Garden. This is a most delightful pleasure ground, and much frequented in the warm season by the citizens for the air in the evening.

(July) Monday 11.

Went out among the merchants, * * * called at the office of the Courier and Enquirer, visited the Exchange, which is a fine edifice in which is kept a register of the vessels arriving and departing from the port, to which merchants go and learn the state of trade. Post Office in the same building. Arcade is better filled than at Philadelphia, though many of the apartments are unoccupied. Went to the American Bible Society House, which I found to be a large establishement. Numerous copies of the Scriptures were here packed up, to be sent abroad to different parts of the Union. The printing is done by a steam press, which in addition to the fireman and engineers, employs twenty or thirty hands, chiefly women and children. The binding, etc., is all done in the same house, and under the direction of the society. Richard Varick, president.

(July) Tuesday 12.

Presented my letter to Charles Baldwin, Esq., who politely showed me much attention. At 11 a. m. I went with Mr. Baldwin to City Hall, where the Courts of Chancery and Comman Pleas for the city and county of New York were in session. McConn, Vice-Chancellor, president of the former, and Jones, the late Chancellor, of the latter. In the Court of Chancery a bill for separation, and to have guardianship of a child, filed by a wife against her husband, was under discussion. Mr. Ogden[21] for the complaint, and Mr. Griffin for defendant; the former is now at the head of the city bar, is of an ungainly form, and without much literary polish, but speaks very sensibly, and in a manner which commands attention. The latter is very precise in everything, from an argument in Court down to the trying on of his Cravat. The bar is much crowded, but is composed principally of young men, many of whom are Irish imigrants. * * *

(July) Monday, 18.

Paid my bill, and set out for West Point on board the Constitution. * * * Reached West Point to dinner. It is a beautiful place, and consecrated by many historic recollections. Fort

[21] Daniel Byrd Ogden (1775-1849), of New York, an eminent lawyer, who won his chief fame before the supreme court of the United States. John Marshall said, "When he stated his case, it was already argued." His most celebrated case was *Cohens* v. *Virginia,* but he appeared in many other noted ones. He was a Federalist, and then a Whig. His only political appearances were as member of the state assembly in 1814, and in 1838.

Putnam, Monuments of Kosciosko. Col. Wood, and the cadets. The public buildings. Visited the Monument and Garden of Kosciosko, saw Brumble and others from Carolina. The cadets were in camp. drilled in the evening, and had a beautiful parade at sunset. A soldier with his arms received our names, both on arrival and departure. * * * * *

(July) Wednesday, 20.

* * * Reached Albany at 8 a. m., took breakfast, walked up to the Capitol. * * * Albany presented an appearance of much business, and is more modern in the appearance of its buildings than I had supposed. Its public buildings in good taste. Stages in great number at this season, run to Saratoga Springs, one of which I took at 11 a. m. At six in the evening we reached the Springs, and found a large assemblage of guests, who eyed us with much scrutiny on our arrival. There was at the Congress Hall when we took up a large proportion of ladies who were not without the curiosity of the sex. After tea the amusement was promenading the Piazza, and a ball at U. S. Hotel.

(July) Thursday, 21.

Walked to the Congress Spring, whither a vast multitude assembled, and drank two glasses of water. The water is dipped from this, and all the other springs, by little boys, to whom it is expected the visitor will make compensation. After breakfast. I strolled to the various hotels to search for acquaintances, but found none. Found at the upper end of the village a Rowlett table, nine-pin alley, and mimick circus flying horses, visited the reading room. The company at the Springs was gathered from all parts of the world. There was no general acquaintances, and not so much conversation as in similar parties in the South. At dinner I subscribed to a hop, (dance), to which I went in the evening, but finding no beauty, and nothing else to attract, I made no effort to extend my acquaintance. The dancing was altogether cotillions, which were executed with but moderate skill by the company.

(July) Friday, 22.

Drank four glasses of water before breakfast, strolled to the reading room, and stayed till 12 a. m., rather a dull morning. Dined at 2 p. m., large company. Another hop subscription, but I refused. * * * They are sadly in want of a beau Nash, who could afford facility to enjoyments which are now only denied by the distance which the laws of fashion have imposed on the intercourse of entire strangers. There were visitors from Maine to Louisiana, and I believe from each of the intervening States, as well as from Russia, France, Scotland, England, Spain, and South America.

(July) Saturday, 23.

I set out for Lebanon at 9 a. m., and crossed the North river on a bridge at Waterford, passed Lansingburg, a flourishing village, to Troy, which is a considerable town, has a large manufactory of rolled iron, and a foundry, mills, etc. Here I took another stage, passed several mills and factories, the villages of Ransselsersville, once famous for its glass factory, but has been ruined by its burning. Nassau to Lebanon. * * *

(July) Sunday, 24.

Made an excursion in a chanderdan to the Shaker village of New Lebanon, two and one-half miles from the springs, to see the worship. Many of the visitors went out from the springs, and a considerable company came from the neighboring towns. On approaching the village, which we reached at 10 o'clock a. m., I was struck with the neatness and marks of industry which distinguished the houses, gardens, yards, etc., of the Shakers. The houses are considerably scattered, and this singular people are divided into families of one hundred each, who sleep under the same roof, eat together, etc.

In a neat yard, handsomely paled in, and covered with grass, stood the meeting house. A white building, which may be 90 by 70, with an arched roof, covered with tin. At the south end is a projection containing a room which opens into church by two doors, on the east side are two doors, at one of which the males, and the other females, enter. Immediately on entering on the east side are seats raised one above another, for the accommodation of spectators. The gentlemen and ladies, not of the society, walked in at these respective doors, and took seats in the places assigned them. In a short time a door on the north was opened, and the female Shakers began to enter, attired in white dresses of the plainest style, and white caps of like simplicity. They took off their bonnets, (which were after the Quaker fashion) and hung them on pegs, three rows of which were fixed around the room at suitable distances to be reached. This done, they seated themselves on plain benches without backs, which were placed in that part of the room appropriated to worship. Each had a white napkin, or handkerchief thrown over the arm, and sat with the fingers of each hand clasped in those of the other. A part of the females afterwards came in from one of the doors at the south side, and walked across to join those of their own sex on the other. Whilst these were coming in, the males began also to enter by the other door at the same end. They were clad in shirts of plain cotton, striped homespun pantaloons, and a kind of vest, remarkably long, with the two front skirts extending so far back as to give them somewhat the appearance of goatees. Over these a few had coats of plain drab, and a few without coats had the arms bound above the elbows with green tape, but the great majority were dressed in the simple manner first stated. They also wore broad-brimmed hats, which on their entrance they hung on the pegs before described, and then seated themselves with their hands clasped in like manner with the females, and in the opposite end from them.

They sat in deep silence for some minutes, and the pure white dresses of the females, and their pale, wan, faces, added to the solemn aspect of the greater part of the men, and made a solemn and interesting spectacle. There were among them several children of both sexes, who seemed to go through the forms of worship with as much exactness as their elders. Suddenly, without speaking a word, they rose from their seats, and the benches were carried back and set against the wall. The two sexes formed lines fronting each other, similar to those which they had occupied when sitting, and commenced singing with great rapidity some song, the words of which I could not understand. This being finished, they loosed their hands from the grasp which had been continued all the time, let them drop to the natural position, and immediately clasped them again. One of the elders now stepped forth and made a short address to the spectators, in which he exhorted them to the observance of good order during the worship. The females then hung up their napkins, and the men with coats stripped them off, they then commenced to sing rapidly a brisk tune, and danced back and forward in the lines which they occupied, now advancing towards the spectators, and now retreating to the opposite wall. They kept time well, and went through the evolutions with the regularity of soldiers. This was continued until they all were somewhat fatigued.

They then ceased, the females took the napkins which they had brought, and wiped the perspiration from their faces. The benches were restored, and they resumed their seats in the order first occupied. An old man rose and made a short discourse on the enjoyment of holiness, another followed, who eulogized Ann Lee, the mother of the society, and said she was greatly slandered as a drunken old woman, that she was his mother, etc. Another followed, who said that in former time when a man or woman intended to preach they had need to study what to say, but in our times the themes were so abundant and so prolific, that there existed no such necessity. If we looked to our own country, the late dissolution of the cabinet, the head of the Government, the confusion growing out of it, or to the scenes acting in Europe, Polish war, etc., there were ample subjects. The burthen of the speech was that the Shaker faith produced no such calamities as these, and was therefore preferable to any other, etc.

When he had concluded they rose up, removed the benches again, the females hung their napkins, and resumed the lines fronting each other. Eight persons of each sex formed themselves into a ring, in the middle of the floor, commenced a brisk tune, and the congregation, in sections of five, began to dance about the ring, so as to form a procession around it. At intervals in their song and dance they smacked their hands simultaneously, with great violence, beating time to the music, now and then they halted and struck a different tune, which again set them in motion. At length the two persons nearest the ring of chorist-ers, in each section, began to countermarch, the others still pur-suing their course, and this motion was continued for some time, they then halted, the females resumed their napkins, the benches were placed again in the positions, and the company seated. An elder then rose, and made a short address, hoping that the opportunity of worship might be improved, etc. The audience meeting was dismissed, they then went out by couples, in families, and marched to their different houses, the two sexes keeping dis-tinct from each other. There were among them three negroes, two men and one woman, who stood on an equal footing in all respects with the white. As they marched off, a gentleman from Philadelphia pointed out to me a Shaker, who had been a citizen of that city, and had brought to the society more than $100,000. I regretted that I could not have a conversation with one of them, but as it was Sunday, and I was to return in the carriage which took me out, there was no opportunity.

Monday, 25th. (July).

Left Lebanon Springs in company with nine passengers in a stage for Northampton, Mass. * * * Rough as it is, this country is thickly settled, and the inhabitants generally live in comfort, some of them in apparent splendor, and none of them in abject poverty; their agriculture is confined to corn for their own use only, Irish potatoes, but principally grasses, which enable them to raise sheep and cattle, which with their products, wool, butter, leather, etc., are the chief articles for market. The sheep do not appear to be very superior, but the cattle are all of one breed, (red color), and are remarkably fine. Many of the milch cows seemed to have an unnatural swelling of the bag. The principal timber trees of this region are white pine, and hemlock, these they cut into lumber by saw mills, which are profusely scattered, in the mountain streams. Tanneries are common, the bark of the hemlock being used instead of oak. The scenery is grand in the whole route, but chiefly in the Green Mountains, many of the summits over which the road passes are very high, and overlook a vast extent of country. On one of the highest, I saw the sugar maple, and a small furnace for boiling. The road is generally macadamized, is smooth, but badly laid out. At some places, (Snake Hill) we were obliged to get out and walk. Along the entire road, at short intervals, churches with steeples, and sheds for the horses of the congregation, presented themselves, and that glory of New England, school houses, with their teachers and the children of the township. This was the season of mowing, which was being done at almost every farm. I was much surprised to see the grass growing on the steep hill sides, and the mower felling it with his scythe. They obtain but one crop of hay annually. Oats were still green in the fields, the corn was generally indifferent.

Tuesday, 26th. (July).

Northampton is probably the most beautiful village in New England. It rained so much in the morning that I was unable to walk much over it, but by the assistance of a fellow traveler, I gained an entrance to the steeple of the Congregationalist Church, from which I had a view of the village and surrounding country for many miles. * * *

Wednesday, 27th. (July) (Brookfield).

* * * We also visited a school kept by Miss Lucy Haile, an intelligent and polite young lady, who showed us her modes of
instruction, and apparatus adapted to the simple comprehension
of small children. At nine we set out, passed still through a graz-
ing country, where fine cattle, neat houses, churches and schools
still continued in view, to Leicester, which is situated on the
highlands which separate the waters of the Connecticut from
those which are discharged into the Atlantic to the east. It has
large manufactories of woolen cards. Thence we passed through
some smaller villages to Worcester, a considerable town, at the
head of the Blackstone Canal; from that place to Providence, R. I.
Worcester is the residence of the present Governor, Levi Lincoln,
whom we saw at his door in passing. It contains some most splendid edifices, and rivals Northampton in beauty. On the hill east
of it, a lunatic hospital is rearing. After dinner here, we departed
for Boston at 2 o'clock, over a turnpike road, there being another
route called the old road. A railroad is about to be commenced
between the two places. We entered Boston over the mill dam
bridge, at half past eight p. m.

Boston
Thursday, 28th. (July).

After writing a letter, I walked to the north wharf, market,
etc. There was not much shipping in port, but commerce was
tolerably brisk. The market is a beautiful building, appears to
be too much confined. I next visited Faneuil Hall, in the second
story of a house. It is not very spacious, is adorned by a portrait
of J. Hancock, and a bust of J. Adams, over the president's chair.
Stuart's painting of Washington on the right, represents him
standing by his horse. On the right also, nearer the chair, is a
likeness of Warren. On the left, is Commodore Preble. It had
also some ornaments lately put up for the Jackson dinner on the
4th. Above the hall are the rooms of divers volunteer companies,
in which their arms and equipment are handsomely arranged.
After dinner I walked on the mall, a shaded walk which surrounds the common pleasure ground of five or six acres, bordering on the mill pond.

Thence went next to the State House, a tasteful building with
a portico in front, on which is a colonnade on the second story;
the entrance to house leads through to Chantry's statue of Wash-

ington, which is placed in a low addition to the house that seems to have been erected for it. The location I think unfortunate. The statue is of full length, and on a pedestal about six feet high. The dress is the continental uniform, but is almost concealed by a cloak, which is thrown around the person. One hand holds the cloak on the inside, and the other hangs by the side, holding a scroll. Tout ensemble, it is much inferior to Canova's late at Raleigh.

I was next shown into the Senate room, a small but handsome apartment, in which forty members convene. Over the door are two muskets, a drum and cap, which were taken at the battle of Bennington. The colonnade in front gives a beautiful view of the lower part of the city, of South Boston, Dorchester, Roxbury, etc. The Commons Hall is large, and is occupied by five hundred members. It is ornamented by a cod-fish, a collection of implements of war, of agriculture, of commerce, and a chair representing the Union, all in stucco. From the dome of the State House I had a prospect of the city, the harbor, the forts, the neighboring towns and country. The towns, beginning in the north, are Salem, Charlestown, Lachmere Point, Cambridge and port, Brighton, Roxbury, and Dorchester. The Dorchester Heights are conspicuous, also Port Independence, on an island and port.

Friday, 29th. (July).

Took a horse and chaise and went to Cambridge to present a letter to J. S. Jones,[22] Esq., who received me kindly, and showed me the University of Cambridge. The Library is the largest in the United States, contains 25,000 volumes, many of them extremely rare. Some manuscripts were exhibited to me of Greek, which were elegantly executed, although a few had been done in the 9th. century. The library is arranged in alcoves, each of which has the name of some benefactor of the University, and is adorned with many paintings. Mr. Folsom, an acquaintance,

---

[22] Joseph Seawell Jones (d. 1855), familiarly known as "Shocco" Jones, from his place of birth in Warren County, was a student at the university during 1824, and a law graduate of Harvard, after three separate periods of attendance there. He wrote "A Defence of the Revolutionary History of North Carolina," "Memoirs of North Carolina," and, many years later, "My Log Cabin in the Wilderness." He is supposed to have coined the term, "Old North State." His work is marked by intense hostility to Virginia and Virginians, Jefferson and John Randolph being especially selected as targets for the vitriolic product of his pen. His numerous letters to Graham will give a fair picture of his qualities and personality. He moved to Mississippi, and never returned. An excellent and humorous sketch of him by Marshall DeL. Haywood is in Ashe, ed., *Biographical History of North Carolina*, Vol. VI, pp. 329-34.

was there, and took much pleasure in exhibiting the curiosities of the Library to me. Among the other rare works were two copies in English of Lawson's History of North Carolina, and one in German. I also visited the Halls of Lectures, and the philosophical apparatus, cabinet of minerals, etc. There are five college buildings, enclosed in a handsome yard. Dined with Jones, and went in the evening to Jamaica Lake, and the house of his friend, Mr. Bussey, who has a most splendid establishment, ornamented by a large number of marble statues before the door, and by beautiful walks, etc., in the rear and front. The old gentleman was extremely hospitable, kept good cheer, talked much in favor of the American system, etc. He is engaged in a wool factory, and insisted that sheep is the peculiar production for North Carolina. Returned by Roxbury and Boston Neck; after went with Jones to visit Miss Marshall, and spent an agreeable evening.

Saturday, 30th. (July).

Went after breakfast to Nahunt Point, by steam boat. * * * The amusements at Nahant, like those of other watering places, are billiards, nine pins, riding on the beach, dancing, etc. There is sea bathing, but not very commodious, and a sea breeze, which always produces a pleasant atmosphere. I strolled on the seashore in the morning, and rolled nine-pins in the afternoon, until the boat returned. A great many passengers. The sea was somewhat rough, and a constant breeze produced a great degree of coolness. On the way we saw a porpoise, and a seal. Arrived at sunset, and found H Webb,[23] and Dickens, from North Carolina.

Sunday, 31st. (July).

Attended church in morning at the new Gothic Church. Mr. Hopkins. The church is superb architecture, and the sermon was good. Jones dined with me, in the evening went with him by Boston Neck to Cambridge. After tea, we made a visit to Mr. Davis, Solicitor General of Massachusetts, and his two daughters. The old gentleman is quite a veteran in the practice, and is said to have a book on the criminal law in press. He was attentive and polite, the young ladies were quite agreeable. I was surprised

---

[23] Henry Webb (1808-1878), of Hillsboro, a collegemate of Graham. He later moved to Alabama.

at one custom of the Puritans which I witnessed there, to-wit, that the Sabbath ended at sunset. We were not only hospitably received, but one of the young ladies gave us divers love ditties and sentimental songs, accompanied by her piano-forte, this violation of the Sabbath might have been permitted to her, however, as I have never heard so divine a voice.

Monday, August 1st.

By invitation of Judge Story,[24] through Mr. Jones, I called on him. He was very kind, and entertained me with much legal conversation, and remarks on the legal talent of our country, in the first rank of which he placed Messrs. Webster, Mason[25] of New Hampshire, Wirt, Gaston. I was sorry to find that he attended but little to the jurisprudence of North Carolina. He expressed great satisfaction at seeing me, and was complimentary to our bar. We then called on Mr. Everett,[26] of Charlestown, but did not find him at home. Went to Bunker Hill, (Breed's Hill), and saw the unfinished monument. The view from it is beautiful. The association for erecting it have lately been much agitated, and divided on the subject of anti-Masonry, but on today the Masonic party prevailed in the election of managers. Went next to the Navy Yard, saw the dry dock, a stupendous work of Quincy granite. Vessels were being built, and the Constitution and another were lying in the harbor. In the afternoon, we called at Judge Fay's in Cambridge. Spent the evening with Messrs. Gilchrist, Hutchinson, and Dubignon, law students.

Tuesday, 2nd. (August).

Went to Boston, visited the Atheneum, which contains the largest library I had even seen, except that at Cambridge. And numerous specimens of painting, sculpture, etc. It was founded by private contributions, and affords ample opportunities to the

---

[24] Joseph Story (1779-1845), jurist and prolific legal writer, a native of Massachusetts, and a graduate of Harvard, state legislator and member of congress, associate justice of the United States supreme court.

[25] Jeremiah Mason (1768-1848), a native of Connecticut, a graduate of Yale, a lawyer. He moved to Vermont and then to New Hampshire, was state attorney general, 1802-1805, U. S. senator, 1813-1817, and president of the branch bank of the United States. He moved to Boston in 1838.

[26] Edward Everett (1794-1865), of Massachusetts, a graduate and later professor and president, of Harvard; Unitarian minister, Whig member of congress, 1825-1835, governor, 1836-1840, minister to Great Britain, 1841-1845, secretary of state, 1852-1853, U. S. senator, 1853-1854, candidate for vice president, 1860.

studious and tasteful; thence I went to the Court of Common Pleas; Judge Ward on the bench; he seemed to be antiquated and dull, and the bar did not impress me very favorably.

Wednesday, 3rd. (August).

Called at Mr. Buckingham's and read the Raleigh Register. The rain prevented me from walking much, though I strolled out to look for Hancock House, but did not find it. In the afternoon, I went by invitation to Cambridge, to spend the evening at Judge Fay's. Went first to the private library of Mr. Dowse, a currier and tanner of leather, who has exhibited a strong passion for letters, and a refined taste, by collecting at great expense all the standard works of English literature, together with a great variety of fine paintings, engravings, etc. He still works at his trade, and bestows his leisure hours on books. There I was introduced by Jones to Miss Fay, an intelligent and agreeable lady, who was very conversant with the library, and very politely attended there to exhibit it to us. Spent the evening at Judge Fay's, where I again met the Misses Davis. Walked into Boston, paid my bill, and packed up for departure.

Thursday, 4th. (August).

Took leave of J. S. Jones, to whose kindness I am much indebted, and set off for Providence, R. I. I left Boston with regret, my acquaintance was beginning to be agreeable. I had been shown some hospitality and was pleased with the courtesy and exact gentility of the citizens. For cultivated mind and taste, and for all the points of substantial character, it is perhaps unequalled by any town in our country. * * * 9 o'clock p. m. set out in the stage for Hartford, Conn., 70 miles distant.

Friday, 5th. (August).

Arrived to breakfast at Windham, saw Hartford from high grounds 12 or 14 miles east. We passed over a poor but well tilled country, through East Hartford, and arrived at Hartford at 1 p. m. The Connecticut river is here surmounted by a fine bridge. After dinner visited the Capitol; in the Senate Room here the Hartford convention sat. Both this and the Hall of Representatives has a full length portrait of Washington over the Speaker's chair. In the first story of the building I found the Supreme Court sitting.

Judge Haseur was Chief Justice, but Daggett [27] is said to be the ablest lawyer. The last has a dignified and imposing appearance. Hartford, like Providence, has many elegant churches, with lofty steeples, visited two of these, but did not ascend them; went to see the famous "Charter Oak," in the south part of the city. It is large around the trunk, but low, and the hollow, if it ever had one, has grown up.

Saturday, 6th. (August).

Left Hartford in the stage. * * * Arrived at New Haven at 1 p. m., dined, and called on Reinhardt, who was there in the law school. At 7 p. m. I sailed in the steamboat for New York. New Haven is a most beautiful town. The six or seven colleges are in a row, and make a front of at least 200 yards. In the face of them is a green square, in which stands the State House, and three churches of fine architecture. The Legislature here sits alternately at New Haven and Hartford, as in Rhode Island at Providence and Newport. * * *

7th. 8th. 9th. 10th. (August).

I spent in New York, the weather was bad, and I could not extend my observations much. Visited Thorburn's Garden, store and aviary, saw also Chancellor Kent,[28] at the office of his son, Wm. Kent,[29] Esq. His appearance is not very striking, his speech quick and rapid. He spoke of the loss of the Washington statue, (by Canova) and expressed much disgust at the negligence which had caused it, of Captain Hale, Frederick the Great of Prussia. Visited the New York Museum, which occupied four rooms, and contains many rare curiosities. Called on Mr. S. Cambreling, but had not the pleasure to see him, also on R. Donalson,[30] Esq., but did not see him. Through the politeness of Mr. E. C. Bettner I was

[27] David Daggett (1764-1851), of Connecticut, a graduate of Yale, lawyer, state legislator, Federalist United States senator, 1813-1819, professor at Yale, and judge of the state supreme court.

[28] James Kent (1763-1847), of New York, jurist and legal commentator, a graduate of Yale, Federalist legislator, delegate, constitutional convention of 1821, professor in Columbia, supreme court judge, and chancellor, 1814-1823. He was the author of the famous "Commentaries on American Law."

[29] William Kent (1802-1861), son of Chancellor Kent, was a graduate of Union College, a judge, and professor of law at Harvard. He was a member of the American Philosophical Society.

[30] Presumably Robert Donaldson, of Cumberland County and New York, lawyer and banker, who was a graduate of the university. He married a daughter of Judge Gaston.

conducted to see my friend, Miss Jones, who had just arrived from New Bern. Mr. Van Buren, the Minister to England, was at the City Hotel, where I lodged, but kept out of public view.

Thursday, 11th. (August).

I left New York in company with J. Reed, Esq., for Philadelphia. We had a pleasant passage, arrived at 7 p. m. The Secretaries of the State and Navy, Livingstone and Woodbury, and Commodores Rogers[31] and Stewart,[32] were at the Madison House, where we lodged, but were not visible.

Friday and Saturday, 12th. and 13th. (August).

I spent in Philadelphia, called on my former acquaintances, but made no new ones. * * *

Sunday, 14th. (August).

Left Philadelphia at 7 a. m.

Monday, 15th. (August).

Sailed (from Baltimore) in the old boat "Constitution," Capt. Turner, with few passengers on board, for Norfolk. * * * Arrived in Norfolk at six in the morning, and immediately took passage in "The Richmond" for City Point. Reached City Point at 4 p. m. saw a fortification just below which was erected during the late war, and Bermuda Hundred, just above; passed in a stage to Petersburg, over an uninteresting road.

Wednesday, 17th. (August).

Left Petersburg, took my horse at Mrs. Lamb's, and came to Scoggins. This evening the sun was again of a green color, the season had been unusually wet, and the roads in many places boggy. It is indeed surprising that the trade of Southern Virginia and North Carolina should have gone so long to Petersburg on no better roads. After the lapse of a century and a half from the settlement of the country, and more than half a century from its independence, there are no facilities for transportation which did not exist at either of these periods. Indeed, the country seems exhausted, and the inhabitants cannot be said to have more substantial wealth than they had fifty years ago. * * *

---

[31] Probably George Washington Rodgers (1787-1832), of Maryland, who was, however, not a commodore but a captain.

[32] Charles Stewart (1778-1869), of Pennsylvania, was also a captain, but had been previously acting commodore. He became a rear admiral in 1862.

Saturday, 20th. (August).

Completed my journeying, arrived in Hillsboro' at 12 o'clock, found my friends in health, and received their kind greetings, felt much gratified that I had performed my whole journey without any injurious accident, or one hour's sickness, and returned to my labor, renovated by improved health, and animated by an ardent desire for the prosperity and the glory of my country.

From Frederick S. Blount [33]   A.

to J. Seawell Jones.

Philadelphia,

July 7th., 1831.

Permit me to introduce to you my friend William A. Graham, Esq., a member of our Bar, and a resident of Hillsboro', and to request from you an extension of those kind and friendly civilities to him, which I received at your hands.

You will perceive from the date of my letter that I am jogging on gradually to the South, and I shall expect to receive a letter from you on my arrival at home.

I remain respectfully
and truly your friend

Arbitration Statement   U.

Whereas we Hugh D. Waddell & William A. Graham both of the town of Hillsborough & State of North Carolina have been mutually agreed upon & chosen by the parties to arbitrate and settle a certain matter of controversy which hath lately arisen between James Jones of the town aforesaid and George Wm. Gronlund and it having been alleged before us that the said Geo. W. Gronlund had made certain accusations against the said James Jones impeaching his character for honesty and truth. We have heard the evidence pertaining to the matter and have requested the said Geo. W. Gronlund to appear before us who acknowledges that he did speak harshly of the said James Jones, when

---

[33] Frederick Swann Blount (b. 1807), a native of New Bern, who was at the university with Graham. He was a lawyer in Mobile.

under the excitement of anger, but that he has no deliberate belief that the said Jones is properly subject to such imputations, and that he has no design to injure the reputation of said Jones. We do therefore award that all rights or causes of action and all dispute and controversy touching the premises shall hereby cease and determine.

Given under our hands this 31st. Augt. 1831.

H. Waddell.

Will A. Graham.

From James Graham.   U.

Rutherfordton,

September 14th., 1831.

Dear Brother

I rec'd your letter written in New York, and the next day, the 1st. of August, set out for Nashville, Ten., and returned on Sunday last. I have instituted suit for the recovery of the Nelson Land in the Western District, and employed Thos. Washington to attend to it.

I was much gratified at the kindness and attention I rec'd from the citizens of Nashville. It is a gay, fashionable and commercial town, and growing rapidly.

*   *   *   *   *

I spent a few days very pleasantly in Buncombe, on my return from Ten'. Morrison, of Charlotte, married Miss Patton the week I was there, and there was merry times, and great joy. Maj. Smart and Lawyer *(Wash)* Alexander were his aids in matrimonial manoevers—

I have seen but little of No. Ca. elections since my return, but that little is discouraging. I may possibly be in Raleigh a week during the Session, but am not positive.

I hear the Horn blowing and the Mail coming, and must close my letter. Do write me soon, and let me know all the news in that quarter.

I have just heard that Bob Potter has turned Surgeon, and is a bold operator.

Your Brother

From Jo. Seawell Jones.   U.

Cambridge, October the 4th, 1831.

Your much esteemed favor of the 4th of Sept reached me more than a week since and nothing but the most indespensable engagements prevented an immediate reply. I however dispatched a number of an Eulogy delivered by John Q. Adams on Mr Monroe to assure you of my very sincere regard.

I am sorry I cannot write you what I will venture to term a "local" letter—as they are always more agreeable to read and less difficult to write—for here I live like Pyrrhs on a sea of speculation, not much matter of fact entering into my daily duties—unless my dreams, wishes, and prayers for the welfare of old Carolina & her people may be thus denominated. I had hoped ere this to be on my way to the shores of Europe but unexpected but not unsurmountable obstacles have for the present arrested my adventure so I am here until the month of January at all events and design at that period making my bow—my farewell goodnight to my "native Land."

I am at present devoted to the Study of Spanish Literature and history. My opinion of that people has been very much exalted by an insight into their true and ancient character. The creations of the human mind are not more splendid in any other Empire of the Globe and the ferocity of character which has been attributed to them is the offspring of English rivalry and envy. It is curious to remark the various elements entering into the composition of the Spanish character, for it is the most interesting and pleasing duty of the Student of history to observe not only "the dates and events" of a people but to look even into their original formation and establishment. In the earliest ages of Antiquity a race of people called the Iberians were the occupants of the whole Peninsular—a sample of that people may be found at this day in the "fastnesses" of the Pyrinnees—and they are remarkable for speaking the oldest living language. The Hebrew, the Greek, and the Latin have long since ceased to be the medium of communication but their ancient neighbour and contemporary, the Iberian, still lives and animates a whole nation of Spanish Biscayans. The old Spanish Iberian character was the first diluted by an association or rather communication with the Phenicians and of course the Carthaginians whose commercial enterprise penetrated into every nook of the then habitable world. A consolidation of the Iberian and Phenician character had scarcely taken place when the Romans by the downfall of Carthage became undisputed Lords of Spain. Only a few years elapsed when a Law was passed at Rome legalising the marriages of Romans and Iberians or Spaniards and long before the downfall of that empire a native of Spain sat on the throne of the Empire of the World. This singular compound of Iberian-Phenican and Roman character was next diluted by the torrents of Goth or Visigoths which by infusing into the Luxury of Spanish life the rugged spirit of nature, contributed to strengthen and renovate the whole nation when the second and third generation became Spanish citizens. The sixth and last element of the Spanish character was contributed by the Arabs, to whom we are indebted for what may be called the Romance of Spanish character —the wild and chivalrous spirit which for many ages distinguished the nation and even the light—the light Guitar is the offspring of the Spanish Arabians. You will perceive from this how various and suitable for purposes of Literature were the materials which such a "compounded character" would produce and I am anticipating much pleasure in the Study of the history of such a people. I do not know what has led me to give you this account; my mind has been so much absorbed on the subject that I could not abstain from a few remarks.

If you are curious in politics, it may perhaps be amusing to you to hear that Mr. Adams has determined to cut the Clay party of this State and was yesterday nominated for the office of Governor in opposition to Lincoln the present officer and the candidate of the National Republican party. Adams is the candidate of the Antimasonic party.

*   *   *   *   *

1832

From James W. Osborne.   U.

Jan. 12, 1832.

I had intended by the close of the present month to be with you in Hillsborough. But as Unkle Robert is without a suprintendant on his farm I have determined to remain here until the commencement of spring. This arrangement will not interfere materially with the attention required by my studies. The work in which I am at present engaged will as you are aware afford me employment for the greater part of the time. And a friend has kindly offered me the use of such books as I may desire. The advantages of retirement are as complete as could be wished while the attention which I shall bestow on the concerns of the farm will be nothing more than such exercise as health and pride demand.

I am sorry to inform you of the death of your venerable grandfather.[1] He died on tuesday the 10th inst. His friends had hoped that his life unusually extended as it was would have been still longer spared. And his illness at its commencement was of such a character as to occasion no serious alarm. But a stroke of the palsy, which occurred a short time after he was taken, destroyed every hope of recovery. He lay, such was the strength of his constitution—bearing the weight of 97 years, with a blighting paralysis, nearly two weeks. He retained full possession of his faculties until within a few hours of his death. I visited him while he lay, and he inquired with solicitude after your welfare.

* * * * *

I must request you to inform Col Anderson[2] of my intention to remain longer than I had expected, and present him with my respects. I shall be happy to hear from you in my solitude & receive such information as to my studies as you may think necessary. Unckle thinks favorably of my going to Cambridge during the next year. The opportunity in the Circuit at present is however more favorable than I will most probably enjoy again, and it may be questionable whether I should forego the advantages I

---

[1] Major John Davidson (1735-1832), a native of Virginia, a Revolutionary soldier, and father of Graham's mother.
[2] William E. Anderson.

might derive from that cause, in the way of getting into business. There will be time enough to consider the matter when I see you. You will oblige me by writing as soon as is convenient.

*   *   *   *   *

From James Graham.   U.

Lincoln, Vesuvius Furnace, January 22d, 1832.

Two days since at Lincolnton I received your letter written from Hillsboro just after your return from Fayetteville and Raleigh. I presume from the occasion of your visit to Fayetteville and from the gay season which overtook you at Raleigh, that the jaunt was a very pleasant one. I did not visit Columbia in December last, as I contemplate going to Charleston in February next and will probably leave my plantation about the 8th of next month and will be absent about 30 or 40 days which will embrace the Races and the Gay season in Charleston. I anticipate much pleasure in my absence as I have a numerous acquaintance in that City and the middle Country. I regret that I must loose Iredell and Mecklenburg county courts—however he who lives in my circuit must make some sacrifices or he never can cammand time enough visit any City. This trip I have proposed to myself for the last three years. I have not yet got company tho' hope to find some in Yorkville or Camden. I saw several members of the Legislature on their return from Raleigh but had a very limited opportunity of learning much of the proceedings of the Assembly. The intelligence of the west appear anxious to throw their most talented men into the next Legislature and arrangements are now in progress to accomplish this object and I hope most fondly the west and the Cape Fear will be united as one man and that they will take a sailors pull against the Roanoke, that is, "a fair pull, a strong pull, a long pull and a pull *all-together*" on the subject of Convention. I have recived numerous solicitations to become a candidate. I have not consented as the period is yet distant and I wish to be untramelled for a while. I presume you have heard Grand Father Davidson died on the 16th of this month—he was about 97 years old. He appeared satisfied to go, and fully sensible of approaching death. Father's health and spirits are very fine. He has Thompson, Saunders and young Henderson (son of Wm) near uncle Robts. with him. The Furnace is blowing and will continue doing so untill perhaps the middle of March.

We had a very merry Christmas at Rutherfordton. A wedding and two large dancing parties. The Gold Miners are continuing to flow in and are about to make permanent locations. Judge Forman[3] has married an old maid the daughter of Nelson at the Warm Springs. The old fellow has been all but crazy for a wife but declared after Miss Brown of Caswell discarded him that he would never cease his Fire until someone surrendered.

* * * * *

From Jo. Seawell Jones. U.

Warrenton, Feb 20th, 1832.

I have for some time cherished a hope of visiting Hillsboro before my return to Boston, but the moment is so near at hand that I am compelled to abandon it altogether. And yet I do not hail any hour so unwelcome as that which hurries me from old Carolina; no matter to where it may start me it is still an hour of grief and gloom.

I have (I suppose in common with yourself) to lament the death of Judge Murphey who at one period of his life was certainly one of the Stars of our State. His thirsting enterprise was perhaps his great misfortune and even this was a forcible illustration of the vigour of his mind. Whatever faults he may have had—I have never learnt but the sooner to be forgotten—and with the deepest sympathy for the misfortunes of his old age I retained to the last a most profound admiration for his talents and the principles of his life. I suppose it is very generally understood that he had on hand many valuable materials for a history of the State—a task which he had in contemplation and which no one was more competent to perform.

I am curious to know what disposition will be made of whatever manuscripts or other materials he may have collected. His library I suppose will be sold, and it has been suggested to me his papers on our history might share similar fate. Can I get the favour of you to ascertain as far as you can what direction they will probably take, and particularly whether they *could be bought.*

---

[3] Joshua Forman (1779-1848), a native of Duchess County, N. Y., the founder of Syracuse, and backer of the Erie Canal, who spent his last years in Rutherford County.

I have never thought he had either arranged or composed his papers with a view of submitting them immediately to the press, for if they are in such a state the best and most profitable disposition of them would be immediate publication. His collection of facts relative to the Regulation must be very extensive and authentic and will be found perhaps to constitute the most valuable portion of his materials. I should be glad to hear from you on this subject as soon as is convenient.

*   *   *   *   *

From Alfred Graham.   U.

At my Plantation 8 Miles East of Memphis,

February 20th, 1832.

Your Letter was received a week or 2 ago And as delays are always uncertain with me I have concluded to give you an answer immediately. I had heard most of the news it contained from Letters received from our friends in Mecklenberg before it reached me. After arriving in this Country I hired out my Negroes untill last fall and after examing the Country a little during the Summer I purchased a small Tract of Land one Mile east of Joseph. Commenced building and Clearing on it the last of September. It was an unimproved Tract, not a Cabbin on it. I got it lower considerably on that account I paid $2.50 per Acre. I should have commenced on it sooner but was attacked with the Billious fever on the 10th. of August and did not recover sufficiently untill the latter part of September I now have all my Cabbins done and about 30 Acres of Land Cleared and fenced. This I thinck sufficient for Simon and his family to worck in Corn. The other 2 Boys I intend hiring to Joseph who will move into Memphis in 2 or 3 weeks and intends engaging in a Brickyard. There will be great demand for them the approaching Summer. We think it much more sure and profitable a business Than making Cotten at the present price. Jos. has employed an Overseer to take Charge of his farm where he will leave his Negroe Weomen and Children to make Corn enough to do him. Memphis is improving faster considerably at this time than any Town in the district. Merchants, Mechancks, Lawers, and Doctors, are flocking in there very fast. Among others General Gaines lately. He intends making it the Headquarters of the Army from this on. I am much better pleased with this Country than when I saw it comparatively a Wilderness to what is now, Though most Persons who emigrate here have to undergo a Climatising before they enjoy good health.

The society of men in Memphis is equal I expect to that of any where else. Respectable young Ladies are scarce. What few arrive get married immediately as there are about 15 young men to one respectable Lady. They are quite a Gay People frequently have Balls and smaller Parties, are very social and friendly. I have attended 2 Balls there And a Pleasure Party up the Mississippi on a steam Boat, All of which I enjoyed myself very well. About 100 of us Went on Board the Boat by invitation of the Capt. Who agreed to give them a Dinner and drincks free besides the Days ride for nothing, His object being to get the Custom of Memphis. in preference to other Boats. We had a pretty good Band of Musick and as soon as the Boat started commenced Dancing this was kept us untill she run 30 Miles up the River when we eat dinner wheeled about and returned to Memphis, landed about sunset all well pleased with the ride. We have had a very cold winter here The Icce was running at one time in such large Pieces in the River that the Boats all has to Land to prevent being stove. It has all disappeared and the weather has been warm and wet for near 3 weeks. The River is now rising rapidly which we expect will continue untill spring. You would be astonished to see this immence River whirling and foaming when the spring freshet is coming down. Jos, and his wife are both well; he has a Daughter lately that looks as unlike him or his wife and his other Boy as any person can look. She has a very fair skin and Blue Eyes and is much handsomer than Cavallo[4] Who I thinck gets Darcker and uglier as he grows older. I have seen none of your acquaintances spoken of in your Letter in this County; should I see them they will be receved with respect. I can give you no information when I will be in N. C. again, though I doubt very much indeed if my visit will be in search of a wife when I do come unless prospects are 10 to one better than when I took leave, In the Circle of my acquaintance at least. I received a letter from Winslough Alexander by the last Mail he mentions the death of Grandfather Davidson and tells me of a number of weddings which have taken piace about Charlotte since I last heard from there; surely leap year must have some affect in making People Marry. there has been a number of Wedings here, I have attended two myself one of them as attendant. A Merchant in Memphis was married to a

---

[4] George Cavallor Graham, the son of Joseph Graham, Jr.

young Lady at Lagrange 30 Miles from here and invited me to stand on his right There were several respectable Ladies there but unfortunately they were not very beautifull. We were very kindly received and spent our time very agreably during our stay there. I suppose you were very much gratifyed with your Northern Tour. In a few years if I do not get married and my purse will admit of it I thinck I shall take a similar Tour. We can go from here to New York in 15 Days by steam and stage by Wheeling and Baltimore. I shall be glad to receive a Letter from you when ever you have Leisure to write.

From James Graham.   U.

Charleston, So Ca., Feb. 29th, 1832.

I have been here about two weeks, have seen the great match Race between *Clara Fisher* and *the Bonnets o' Blue* and other fine sport on the turff.

The number of strangers was never so great in Charleston; every public house was full to overflowing and indeed some were obliged to continue on Board the Steam Boats in which they came for the want of accommodations.

This city presents a rather gloomy appearance when compared with northern cities. The houses are inferior and look dark coloured or dingy, the streets are narrow and dirty, though the Bay is most beautiful and extensive. The shipping here is much greater than I anticipated. I have been present at two large meetings of the Nulification party, at one of which they done me the honour to give me a seat on the floor. I have never heard the General Government so much abused and vilified, and Genl. Jackson came in for his full share of left handed compliments. As for instance Mr. Preston the champion orator of the party said "Mr. Chairman I have heard lately Calhoun, called a *fool,* Hamilton[5] *a Knave;* Genl. Jackson *a wise man,* and Mr. Van Buren *an honest one,*" Indeed the whole party are much embittered with Genl. Jackson.

---

[5] James Hamilton, Jr., (1786-1857), a native of Charleston, lawyer, rice planter, major in the War of 1812, intendant of Charleston, member of assembly, 1817; member of congress, 1822-1829; at this time serving his second term as governor. He was the organizer and practical political leader of the Nullification movement. Later, he was to be president of the Nullification Convention, brigadier general, commanding the state troops. He served in the state senate in 1836, was prominent in Texas affairs, and was the diplomatic agent of the republic to Great Britain, France, Belgium and Holland. He was drowned in the Gulf of Mexico.

The Theatre is open and has been attended by fine lace but not with fine beautiful ladies though the crowd has been quite great. Miss Clara Fisher is the favourite and deservedly so. I met her at a large party at Workman Connor's,[6] she is quite modest and retiring and is well received here. I have met a great number of acquaintances here, among them of your acquaintance Wm. Mares[7] and Walker of Wilmington, and McCauley Witherspoon returning from Washington city to Alabama. I have visited and dined with Mr. Haynes family; and learn cousin Harriet is about to be married to Pickens Butler[8] a very respectable lawyer from Edgefield.

I am building a Cottage house on my plantation and take this opportunity to purchase my Nails, locks, glass, etc. I have just heard from W. Connor that our common friend Richd Allison died a few days since in one of the West India Islands.

I shall leave tomorrow for No. Ca. and must be quite industrious to make up my lost time.

The Strangers are nearly all gone and the Theatrical amusements will terminate next week.

I have visited the Court of Appeals two or three times and seen and become acquainted with some of their most distinguished men. I have had a ride on the Rail Road 12 miles and back. I was delighted. * * *

From Jo. Seawell Jones.   U.

Warrenton, June 4th, 1832.

Your recent esteemed favour of date the 5th of March last has (I am sorry to say) but just come to hand. I notice what you say of Judge Murphey's progress in composing a history of the State with surprise as I had been induced from what I had seen and heard to suppose a good deal of the labour of composition completed. I am now eager to know if I can at *this time* by a visit to Hillsboro have

---

[6] Henry Workman Conner (1797-1861), a native of North Carolina, who settled in Charleston, where he became a prominent banker. He was intendant of the City, and a member of the secession convention.

[7] William Belvidere Meares (1787-1841), of New Hanover, a student of the university in 1802, lawyer and planter, who served in the commons, 1818, and in the state senate, 1828-1830, 1833.

[8] Andrew Pickens Butler (1796-1857), of South Carolina, a graduate of South Carolina College, member of both houses of the legislature, judge, 1833-1846; United States senator, 1846-1857.

an opportunity of inspecting the papers to which you allude, and find from them whether those papers relate to anything else than the affairs of the Revolution. By the way, he had an invaluable copy of a most valueless work: "The Biography of the Signers of the Declaration of Independence," the margins whereof are some times adorned by notes—and important notes too—from his own hand. For instance—at the close of that of Hooper[9]—there is in pencil hand an extract from a letter of Hoopers to old Senator Smith[10] near Wilmington, which is the strongest evidence to establish the charge of Toryism which Jefferson imputed to him. When I first saw that unfortunate publication, The Works of Jefferson, and in the course of a perusal found that mere assertion, "I foamed at the mouth," and went about to do what Jefferson should have done, viz. to see what reasons there could be for such a gross charge, and after a great deal of scouting I am forced to say that Hooper was not at heart, a Representative of the people that sent him.

The letter—the extract whereof the Judge quoted below the high sounding peroration usual and perhaps proper on all such occasions—was dated I think the Spring previous to the 4th. July 1776, and the tenor of the epistle is entirely too tame (and indeed conciliatory and servile) to come from the pen of the Representative of No. Ca.—a state which instructed her Representatives to make unqualified independence the only terms of a peace or a reconciliation. I have some knowledge of the conduct of Hooper's relatives in Massachusetts during the war of the Revolution, and am sorry to say they were Tories of the worst stamp. Still I am opposed to the denunciation of Jefferson and I can abduce at least twenty reasons to vindicate the accused and snatch his fame from the dark grave to which the popularity and not the genius of Jefferson has consigned it.

If you have paid a very minute attention to the history of our state and some little to that of So. Carolina you will remember that Sir Walter Raleigh endeavored to raise up a great people on the Island of Roanoke, and that Admiral Coligny, the great leader

---

[9] William Hooper (1742-1790), native of Massachusetts, signer of the Declaration of Independence. The reference by Jefferson to him is in a letter to John Adams, discussing the authenticity of the Mecklenburg Declaration.

[10] The reference may be to Benjamin Smith (1756-1826), of Brunswick County, a Revolutionary soldier, state senator 1783, 1792-1800, 1804-1810; member, commons, 1789-1791; governor 1810-1811, benefactor of the university, but it seems unlikely.

of the Hugonot party during the reign of Charles 9th. of France, endeavored to found a Colony in or near the present *scite* of Beaufort, So. Carolina, which latter colony was however afterwards removed to the mouth of the St Marys. I have been studious on these two points of our history and have in my possession something like two hundred sheets of paper, closely written, on this subject. If I should become crazy during the coming twelvemonth you may expect something like a book of 3 or 4 hundred pages, tinctured too with a little romance. I found the original documents on the subject of these two colonies in the Cambridge Library.

I have visited Newbern too, and found myself in your tracks, particularly at Miss Washingtons. During my stay I searched into the clerks office and was gratified with "old things"—they go back as far 1730—and are uninterrupted to this day. The clerk, J. S. Stanly, is however better on the subject than any documents I have ever seen—he is a complete Antiquarian as well as a very clever and polite gentleman. I saw too the ruins of the old Palace and the *Treaty tree*— (live oak).

I may be in this state for some three or four weeks to come and possibly visit your city if I can be accomodated with an insight into those papers. So let me hear from you as soon as is convenient. Manly seems happy beyond "any sort of right." I saw much beauty —and fell in love of course—Miss Burgwin, has no right to look so beautiful, and I shall have her before my friend Alfred if she does not take care.

Van Buren is all the go here; this county is litteraly putrid with it. An Anti Van Buren Meeting is to be held in this place on thursday and although it will be very thin I intend to go and be one of them. I have to day writen to J. S. Campbell at Wilmington; is he there?

With every assurance of my regard.

From *James Graham.*   U.

Rutherfordton, June the 18th, 1832.

* * * * *

The Electioneering campaign is beginning to wax warm in this county. Thomas Dews,[11] Dr. Irvin,[12] James Webb,[13] and John Bradly are announced in the commons and Jos. Carson[14] is expected to be out in the Senate, as yet the opposition to Carson is not known; in the neighbouring counties the political excitement is beginning to arouse the feelings of the people; still however very few able men are before the people. The state convention attracts some notice though the people do not seem to be sufficiently alive to the importance of the question; our members last year with the exception of Dr. McEntire[15] who declines a reelection, were dull and stupid men who could not infuse any political information among the people.

A new Bank on some plan (not Bob Martins[16]) seems to be desired, *a seventh circuit* is also "most devoutly wished for" and I think will be attempted. I have refused to become a candidate myself as I have found it heretofore to interfere so much with my professional business and mainly with my reading. I have now purchased a Lott here with an office and stable upon it, and I hope to read much more attentively and understandingly than heretofore as well as to live more cheaply. Dr. Scheiflin, a distinguished surgeon of this town, on yesterday made an attempt to committ suicide by taking Laudanum but did not quite succeed, he is a very intemperate and reckless man who might have been one of the first men of the age in his profession, but habitual intoxication has rendered life burthensome to him and he has

---

[11] Thomas Dews (1808-1838), a young lawyer of considerable brilliance and promise, a graduate of the university in Graham's class, dividing first honors with him and Matthias E. Manly. He was clerk and master in equity of Rutherford, and was a member of the commons, 1832-1833.

[12] Dr. Osmyn B. Irvine (1802-1880), who served in the commons, 1832-1833. He later moved to Greenville, S. C.

[13] James M. Webb, of Rutherford, sat in the commons, 1828, 1830-1831. He later became a prominent Baptist minister, was a newspaper editor, and clerk of the superior court.

[14] Probably Joseph McDowell Carson, a distinguished lawyer, a member of the commons, 1812-1814, 1835; of the state senate, 1832, 1836-1840. He was also a delegate to the convention of 1835.

[15] Dr. John McEntire, state senator, 1829-1831.

[16] Robert Martin, of Rockingham County, a member of the commons, 1822-1825, and of the state senate, 1830-1834, in the preceding session of the legislature, had introduced a bill to charter a bank, with a capital consisting entirely of state funds. His daughter married Stephen A. Douglas.

firmly resolved to terminate his own existance. Soon after the Dr. has swallowed the Laudanum, the whole village assembled at his room and among others an old prostitute called Caty Dean. The Dr. lay quite torpid some time, at last he opened his eyes and saw this old woman and instantly said "Well Caty I expect to be at Hell in a few hours, *when shall I tell them you'll be there?* However the Dr's prevented him from setting out on his Journey for a while.

The country people are somewhat alarmed at the expected appearance of the Comet and all the supersticious predictions of Ignorance and credulity are in frightful anticipation before the multitude. Buncombe is expected to be the scene of more fashion and gaiety this summer than it has ever been; several have already [torn] Gavin Hogg[17] and his brother of Raleigh passed [torn] week on their road to *Ten.* He informed me that Mr. Badger[18] would probably be a candidate for a seat on the Supreme Court Bench in the event that Judge Hall left it. Last week we had two marriages in this town; next week we expect three—Ned Davis is living in this county about 10 miles off, he is the *master-man* already in his neighbourhood and has some fine fellows around him. I am going to see him next week. The mining prospects are improving *rapidly here.* Wm. McGee[19] of Person bought a mine a few days since at $8,500 and is in treaty for another.

---

[17] Gavin Hogg (1788-1835), of Bertie, and, later, a lawyer of distinction, a graduate of the university, a captain in the War of 1812. The brother mentioned was either James, or Richard, of Raleigh.

[18] George Edmund Badger (1795-1866), of Raleigh, a native of New Bern, educated at Yale, member of the commons, 1816, a judge of the superior court, 1820-1825; secretary of the navy, 1841, United States senator, 1846-1855, one of the greatest lawyers in the history of the State. He was nominated to the Supreme Court of the United States, but was, for party reasons, not confirmed. He was an anti-secession member of the convention of 1861.

[19] William McGehee was probably a son of Thomas McGehee, and a brother of Montford McGehee, of Person County.

From John Davidson Graham.[20]   U.

Elm Wood Farm,

November 16th. 1832.

Dear Brother

*   *   *   *   *

The lawers told a good jocke on James Graham at Rutherford Court; the Honl. L. Carson made a Speech on Nulification & stated the meetings in his district had been got up by James to nulify him, that Judge Smiths[21] Grand Daughter and Sugar plantations made him a Union man. Jas. reply that the salt works in Virginia & the lady that owned them had not detered Mr. Carson from being a nulifier these are not perhaps the exact words but the Substance.

The Furnace commenced Blowing a few days Since. Father & all well. I expect you must of heard before this that Major Forney lost his 2d boy Macon, Killed by a Kog wheel, Skull broke all to pieces. I suppose he did not live a moment after caught. Our Crops of Cotton very bad in this section of Country. I will not make a ¼ crop. . . .

From Jo. Seawell Jones.   U.

Cambridge, Nov. 30, 1832.

I have on divers occasions by mail posted to you one or two pamphlets of a general interest by way of a token of my remembrance. I beg leave now to give you the more solid assurance of a letter.

There is nothing talked of here among the knowing ones but Nullification and its awful consequences. All are opposed to it, but all I find are still more opposed to any force on the part of the general government. The matter is gravely debated with a view

---

[20] John Davidson Graham (1789-1847), planter and iron manufacturer, the second child and eldest son of General Joseph Graham.

[21] The reference is clearly to Judge William Smith (1762-1840), of South Carolina and Alabama, a native of North Carolina, who was about to close a distinguished public career as state legislator and judge, and United States senator, during which he changed from a violent defender of state sovereignty to an even more violent nationalist. When Nullification won, he shook the dust of South Carolina from his feet, and moved, first to Louisiana, where he had large plantation interests, and later to Huntsville, Alabama. He was a member of the legislature, 1836-1840. He twice declined a seat on the United States supreme court.

to Disunion and the Yankees are ruminating on their existence as a separate New England Confederacy. In the midst of these gloomy forebodings I am carried back to the days immediately preceeding the adoption of the Federal Constitution as detailed by the letters and histories of that day. I hope old N. Carolina will act nobly on this occasion for if So. Carolina goes out of the Union, she will in the course of time follow her.

When I was in Hillsboro I copied from the papers of Judge Murphy two letters of Alexander Elmsley's,[22] which were lost on their passage, viz. so damaged by sea water as to be illegible. One of them was a long discussion of the great disputes in the days of Jo Martin[23] about the Courts and the Attachment Law. The other gave an account of the reasons why No. Carolina was expcected out of the Restraining act. This however I can read.

This letter on the attachment Section of the Court Law I am obliged to have, and if you will be so good as to select it from the papers and get *Bruce*[24] to transcribe it, I shall be much your humble Svt. Tell Mr. Bruce I will send five dollars (5) for the service when ever I shall hear from you that he has performed it. When he has finished, enclose it well and "Sans ceremonie" direct it to me by *mail*. I want it copied *exactly*, not omiting the most trivial word or circumstance. I do not mind the postage of a document which I want as much as I do *that*, and Mr. Bruce can copy it close and thus make but a small packet. Of course I mean that my most respectful compliments should be presented to Dr. Murphy and his permission asked.

I am up to the ears in a book on the history of No Carolina which I hope to publish the ensuing spring. It is a vindication of the State from the aspersions of Jefferson in his letter to Mr. Adams on the Mecklenburg affair. I have contracted for the printing of it which is to be on the type of the No. American Review. It embraces in three (3) chapters the whole scope of that letter. The first being devoted to the history of the State immediately preceding the National Declaration, which will clear the State

---

[22] Alexander Emsley represented the borough of Halifax in the colonial assembly in 1762. He was later an agent of the assembly to promote the acceptance by the governor of a court act.

[23] Josiah Martin (1737-1786), the last colonial governor of North Carolina, who had a struggle with the assembly over a court bill, with the result that North Carolina had no courts from 1773 until 1776, when the state courts were established. After he fled the colony at the outbreak of the revolution, he co-operated with the British, returning to England in 1781.

[24] Probably Alexander B. Bruce, clerk of the court of Orange County, a native of Halifax County, Virginia, and a former student at the University of North Carolina.

of any suspicion of doubtfulness. The Second discusses the Mecklenburg Declaration, and the third vindicates Hooper from the charge of Toryism. I have offers of assistance from many eminent gentlemen and by the kindness of Mr. Sparks[25] I have an opportunity of seeing the whole of Gen Washington's papers, which, you will be surprise to hear, are abridged in two hundred Vols. of manuscript; worse than Vineas abridgement.

I shall expect an immediate answer to this, and there is one thing I want to know. Is it your Father who dates from the Vesuvius Furnace in the little pamphlets of the Legislature signed *J. Graham*. I shall hang a considerable argument on his letter, although I shall use it as circumstantial—being determined to prove nothing by the depositions of my fellow-citizens unless in a circumstantial way. Judge Story has a new work in the Press—four large Volumes—of Constitutional Law. Exactly three volumes too much. It is full of a great deal of valuable information, but does not contain much learning. All the Constitutional Law in it is the political stuff of the day. Nullification is discussed at length, and a great many principles which are too ultra for the Ghost of Hamilton are put forth. The Judge you may know is a new convert to these doctrines, and has run away with them with the zeal which new and fiery converts feel!!

Such things do not look well—such clothes do not fit him. In early life he was an absolute leveller; he idolised Jefferson and even in 1828 swore he was infallible. In 1829 the works of Jefferson came out and revealed to the eyes of the worshipper the contemptous opinion of the God. Webster it is said is writing a book on Nullification too. My respects to Mr. Ellinwood.[26] Where is Campbell? tell him if he will not come here to take up arms and turn General.

With every assurance of my regard and affectionate esteem.

---

[25] Jared Sparks (1799-1866), then engaged in editing (and revising to his own notions!) the letters of George Washington. He was a graduate of Harvard, an extensive traveller, a Unitarian minister, editor of the North American Review, and president of Harvard, 1849-1853. In addition to the garbled edition of Washington's writings, he collected and published "The Diplomatic Correspondence of the American Revolution."

[26]. Henry S. Ellinwood (d. 1833), came as a teacher to North Carolina, and became an editor, finally going to Wilmington as editor of the *Advertiser*. He was an educated and scholarly gentleman, and seems to have been quite widely popular.

From Daniel Moreau Barringer.[27]   A.

Washington, 21st Dec., 1832.

. . . As you are in the regular recpt. of The Intelligencer, you have the regular Details of news here, to which I can add nothing worth your attention.

The crisis on which we have been precipitated by the sudden and violent action of So. Ca. is the topic of most Interest and conversation; and the appearance of the proclamation has added no little to the intense excitement which pervaded the public mind; You will have seen by quotations from Northern prints, that that important instrument has been well recd. in The middle and Northern States, And with many qualifications in the South; from the West we have yet no accounts. *Here* it has produced a perfect ferment; those who have been touched by a smack of Nullification are uttering deep denunciations of all Its doctrines, others, are speculating upon The abstract propositions therein set forth, whilst another class of politicians, and not the smallest number—for the end it proposes— (the preservation of the Union) and care little about its abstractions upon The whole. The President is sustained in his course by a decided majority of both houses. I fear however any agitation of the topics embraced by the proclamation at this time, But would prefer decidedly that Congress should enter at once, & vigorously upon a redress of all real grievances, which I think they are inclined to do; and of which I should have no doubt, but for the unwillingness manifested, to seem To yield to the swaggering and bullying of So. Ca.

I believe that the protective system, as a system, Is falling into disrepute in the north, and That, if this Congress does not, the next will bring it down to a mere revenue standard; and I verily have seen nothing to cast The shade of a doubt upon such a consummation, but the violent course of the So. Ca. Hot Spurs. I hope our Legislature will Take some steps to mollify and recall that Refractory State to moderation and forbearance; backed by Va. she will have a decided influence. I desire to see the Union preserved and preserved without bloodshed. You know my sentiments and feelings In regard to that absorbing subject, and The mere prospect of civil commotion inhances my estimate of its value many fold.

* * * * *

[27] Daniel Moreau Barringer (1806-1873), of Cabarrus County, a graduate of the university, member of the commons, 1829-1834, 1840-1842, delegate to the convention of 1835, Whig member of congress, 1843-1849, minister to Spain, 1849-1853, delegate to the peace conference, 1861.

From Jo. Seawell Jones.   U.

Cambridge, Dec. 31, 1832.

A few days since I received your much esteemed favour and am in hopes to get in a few days the copied letter of Elmsley by Mr. Bruce. I thank you for your kind agency in this matter. I find you say in your letter, Speaking of Nullification, that you are sorry to hear Judge Story has given his countenance to the doctrine. Did I write you this? If I did I meant some other Judge or some other story. Just before the Presidential election however, the Judge as well as Webster and others did favour the doctrine—as far as it was opposed to Jackson. Mr. Webster particularly in his Worcester Speech a copy of which I sent, predicted as a great calamity the present State of things— (which I a few days since heard him rejoice in as an unexpected blessing). I have—as the Englishman in the play says—no national prejudices, but I have not much confidence in some (Frenchmen) Yankees. Myself indifferent to the political feuds of the day, I admire honesty and steadfastness more than I applaud eloquence and zeal. The Judge is actually publishing a book against Nullification. He was once in early life a Stamp Nully, but he has been gradually seeping off, and when Jefferson's work was published denouncing him as a *pseudo democrat,* he cut the whole party in a tangent. It is bad enough to have been such a democrat as he was in *1806*—but even then to have been *pseudo* was too much.

Paulo Majora canamus—My copied letter of Elmsley's giving the real reason why No. Carolina was excepted out of the restraining Statute, is too much defaced for an entire publication which I have been persuaded to do. If it is not troubling you too much I will get you to search it out and hand it over to Bruce for copy. Tell him he shall be paid, but not five dollars, more, but as much more than five as it is worth. My great anxiety for the Attachment letter was the inducement of the high offer I made him. I hope you will direct them both and be particular in giving the whole of my name and the word, Massachusetts, as letters have gone to Cambridge, Md. which were intended for this place. I have a printed copy of the journals of the Congress of the 20th of August, 1775—I should like to have before me such a copy of any other Congress or Assembly before the National Declaration of Independence. If you have one—or can get one—suppose you lend it to me by mail. I will return it when I come to Carolina in May safe and sound. I had a letter from Governor Swain this morning. He informed of a bill in the Legislature to incorporate an Historical Society. I hope you are one of the corporators. I feel flattered to hear that I am to be one. When I am again in No. Carolina I shall travel over the hills and far away to see your Father. I gave up the story about the Tarboro Convention while in Philadelphia in September. I found there an extract from the journal of Fayetteville Convention and a long string of resolves by a Mr. Gallaway.[28]

How difficult it is to write with freedom the history of that period of time embraced from 1760 to the National declaration. I have concluded to commence my volume with a chapter on the advance of liberal or Whig principles in North Carolina. The famous controversy in 1760 between Gov Dobbs[29] and the popular House, arising out of his Veto on the Court laws I have always thought to be the starting point of such principles. I say it is difficult to write the history of that period because there are so many families in N. Carolina still enjoying the greatest respectability, whose ancestor I should be obliged to place in an odious and unpopular view. This would give pain to them and mortification to me. The family of Spaight, of Waddel, and of many others were abused by Bury, Childs, and Swain as traitors to the society in which they lived as early as 1760. From that period however I have concluded to start and serve up a Chapter of a hundred pages. I shall treat of the Regulation and I shall endeavour to give it a better name than Martin or public opinion. By the way, I have a letter from that old sloth—Judge Martin[30] —which is of no value as an historical document. I have no room to say anything about the Proclamation. Haynes[31] reached Boston last night. It is spoken well of to day.

[28] James Galloway, who represented Rockingham County in the state senate for the first four years after its establishment, was a delegate to the conventions of 1788 and 1789. In the latter he took a prominent part in the discussion of the necessity for a Bill of Rights in the Federal Constitution.
[29] Arthur Dobbs (1689-1765), a native of Ireland, colonial governor of North Carolina, 1754-1765, whose administration was notable for controversies between him and the assembly.
[30] Francois Xavier Martin (1762-1846), eminent jurist, prolific legal and historical writer, editor, publisher, a native of France, who settled in New Bern about 1782, as a printer. He studied law, and represented the borough in the commons, 1806-1807. Appointed a territorial judge, first in Mississippi, and then in Orleans, he was appointed to the supreme court of Louisiana in 1815, and chief justice in 1836. He wrote histories of North Carolina and Louisiana.
[31] Robert Young Hayne (1762-1839), of South Carolina, lawyer, soldier of the War of 1812, member and speaker of the state commons, state attorney general, governor, and president of the Nullification Convention, succeeding James Hamilton, Jr. As governor, he issued a counter-proclamation to Jackson's famous blast against nullification. He was the chief promoter of the Charleston and Cincinnati Railroad.

Tell Campbell there is a gentleman here by the name of *Chaplain* from Maryland who is an acquaintance of his. My love to the excellent youth.

I predict that the doctrines of the Proclamation will not go down, and that they will injure the cause of the Union in Va.

1833

From Jo. Seawell Jones.   U.

Cambridge, Jan. 12th, 1833

Enclosed is five (5) dollars for Mr. Bruce. If it were not for the above exordium I should scarcely trouble you with a repitition of my epistolary. I am perfectly confounded with the intelligence in the papers from Raleigh. Daniel [1] elected Judge of the Supreme Court; I swear it is the grossest act that ever was perpetrated by a party. Knowing the man as well as I do, I am ashamed that such a creature should be lifted above the heads of his Superiors (in every thing except ignorance and impudence) in a state which I am proud to claim as my birth place. Why it is actually worse than before the resignation of Judge Hall—for Daniels debility of mind is after all greater than Halls debility of body.

The consequence of his election will be the downfall of the court. Already I see the salaries are to be reduced and that is half the deed of death. Whenever I settle permanently in North Carolina, which will shortly be I hope, I shall go for an entire revolution of every principle of government. None of your Conventions to amend but actually to destroy the Constitution; I do not believe we can be worsted. What is the Judiciary worth if the Judges are to be elected by a party? — however I will not rave after such a manner, as my Uncle [2] was a contending candidate.

The letter of Elmsley's copied by Mr. Bruce, I should have said before, has come to hand and is copied in a manner highly satisfactory. I wrote you a few days since and troubled you with another commission. I had a letter of Elmsley's, accounting for the circumstance that North Carolina is excepted out of the general law of Parliament, restricting the trade of the colonies to Great Britain, etc. It was injured as the other was destroyed by sea water, and grows worse every day. I must have a copy of it from Bruce and must trouble you to search it out and hand it over to him. I will pay him for it whatever it is worth. In that same letter I asked of you the favour of a loan of any of the old

---

[1] Joseph John Daniel (1783 *ca.* - 1848), of Halifax, attended the university for a short time, and then studied law under William R. Davie. He was a member of the commons, 1807, a judge of the superior court, 1816-1832, and a justice of the supreme court, 1832-1848. He was eccentric, volubly profane, and learned.

[2] Judge Henry Seawell.

Journals of the Congress in *No. Car.* before the Revolution. I have two, the one which contains an account of the abduction of Booth and Dunn, and which assembled in Hillsboro on the 20th August, 1775. The other which I have is the one republished by the Legislature. Now if you have or can get one anterior to that of the 20th of August 1775, have it by mail I must, and have it again during the summer you shall by my own hands. I wish I was in Hillsboro for a week or so. I see our Legislature will adjourn without even incorporating the Historical Society.

I have hopes of being the owner of a copy of Lawson's History of the State before I see you again.

I am leaping on like an antelope with my book and think of scarcely any thing else save its advancement. I am if well enough (for I have lately been confined with a fractured leg) going to N. York next week to see that creature, Doct. Hosack [3] about old Williamson's [4] papers, having an order on him from Hugh Waddell for his quarters. I could not keep off the Regulation and so my book as at present arranged will open with about forty pages on that rebellion. I espouse the cause of the Regulators—vindicate them—and sanctify them with the title of real Fire Worshippers. Such a thing will do for an *"overture"* to the main body of the volume which I am afraid will be more than 250 pages, the limit which I allowed myself. The second Chapter I shall deal with *Jo Martin* and his Secretary Mr. Biggleston,[5] and with the history of those days up to the 4th of July 1776. The third Chap. will choke the Ghost of Jefferson on the Mecklenburg affair, and the fourth and last *Chap.* I shall vilify the aforesaid Ghost for his vilification of Billy Hooper and others.

Tell Campbell I shall expect him here soon and shall be prepared for his reception. I have several numbers of Ellinwood's paper and shall write a letter of subscription shortly.

---

[3] David Hosack (1769-1835), of New York, a distinguished physician and medical author, professor in Columbia College, and the College of Physicians.

[4] Hugh Williamson (1735-1819), a native of Pennsylvania, graduate and professor of the University of Pennsylvania, student of medicine at Edinburgh, London, and Utrecht, who practiced briefly in Philadelphia, and then went into business, and engaged in the study of astronomy, and other scientific subjects. He settled at Edenton in 1777, and entered the West India trade, and resumed the practice of medicine, becoming surgeon general of the state troops, in which position he anticipated many of the practices of modern military medicine. He was several times a member of the commons, served in congress, 1782-1785, 1787, and was a member of the Annapolis convention, and of the convention of 1789. He was a member of congress, 1790-1793. He spent the remainder of his life in New York. His profuse writings included a history of North Carolina.

[5] James Biggleston, secretary of Governors Tryon and Martin, and judge of the court of admiralty of the colony of North Carolina.

From Alfred Graham.   U.

Memphis, January 15, 1833

Your Letter has been receaved long Since and ought to have been answered before this, howeverer I thinck it not to late. I have rented out my Farm near Brother Jos, and have purchased a Lot in this place and expect to live here this year. I made Corn enough last year to do me this, and have halled it here. I am running a Dray with one Hand, the ballance of my People I hire by the month here, and so far as I have tryed it thinck it a much more profitable way than farming.

Henry become such a Rogue that I determined not to be bothered with him any longer And last month swaped him to a Negro trader for a Woman and Child. the Weoman is 22 years old the Child 1. I received $50 to boot. Brother Jos. and Family are well. he is living on his Farm in the Country at present but once in a while brings his family here and stays a week or 2. Is still carrying on his brickyard here and improving some lots. We are all here getting alarmed again about the return of the Cholera; last Fryday night the Steamboat Polander from Orleans landed one Case here and had burried 4 or 5 with it on her passage. The Lexeton passed yesterday with one Case on board and burried 2 the day before. The Crews said it had broken out at Natches very severely.

Since moving to Memphis I spend my time much more pleasantly when I have time to spair; there is always something new to be seen passing on the river—besides the society of young men here is equal to almost any where else. I have built a Negro House and Crib and stable on my Lot and stay myself on one of Josephs which there is a very good House on The Mississippi has been rising very fast for the last 3 days; a great many Flat boats are coming down with the rise The Winter has been unusually warm here so far untill within a few days it has been as warm as May. There is a great deal said here at present about the late Proceedings of the South Carolina Convention Jacksons Procklamation and its reception in S. C. As Nullifyers are very scarce here all are in favor of putting them down by force. I received by the last Mail 2 Papers from you the Register and Watchman. They were late coming to hand. I had seen all the News they contained before in Papers taken here, The Election of D. L. Swain Governor and Hamiltons adress to the S. Carolina Legislature. I have received no Letters from N. C. Lately, the last from Doctor Joe Alexander. He mentioned that Winslough had gone on to Alabama to see the Country; if he is pleased I suppose will move there. I should be glad to hear whether he will move and to what part of Alabama, whether in Doctor Witherspoons Neighborhood or not. In the Month of Novem. and December we were crowded here with the Choctaw Indians moving west; more than 2000 arrived here in one day; some were carried from here on the steamboats, others were ferryed over the River and went on by land. You have no doubt seen an account of the Treaty with the Chickasaws; if it is approved by Congress we expect they will commence moving next Fall. Memphis will then become a Place of Double the business as there will be a very extensive Country to support it And no prospect of a Landing anywhere on the Mississippi for a great distance south. We had a fire here last week and one of the most valuable steam mills entirely destroyed. Situated at the Mouth of the Wolf river, a Drunken fellow had built up a fire in it to sleep by in the night and it caught from that. The owners of the Mill gave him nigh 100 Lashes put him in a Canoe without a Paddle and let him go down the Mississippi. We understood a few days ago he landed safe 20 Miles below.

From James Graham.   U.

Rutherfordton, February 7th, 1833

I received yours of the 6th ult. and would have answered you forthwith but for a short yet severe attack of the Cholera-Morbus which entirely prostrated me; however I have now recovered my usual health and strength again. After finishing my circuit last week at Burke I went to Lincolnton to attend the Methodist conference where I found between 80 and 100 of the Revd. Clergy assembled and I was surprised to find so much talent and Learning and Eloquence among them. Bishop Andrew [6] of

---

[6] James Osgood Andrew (1791-1871), a Methodist bishop, a native of Georgia, who served there, and in the Carolinas until his election as bishop. At the General Conference of 1844 it was voted that he should desist from the exercise of episcopal functions until he ceased to be a slave holder. He was willing to resign, but the other Southern delegates bitterly opposed such action, although many were individually opposed to slavery. The final result was the division of the Methodist Church.

Augusta and Mr. Capers [7] of Charleston would be distinguished ornaments in any Church. Lincolnton during the conference presented a most animated scene; it was crowded with strangers, male and female; the dashing of carriages and the Beaus and Belles, arm and arm marching to Church and to the Shops and Stores presented an imposing scene and indicated the march of Improvement and refinement. . . . The people of this County were greatly surprised and are equally dissatisfied with the views and votes of our late members of Assembly on the subject of Nullification. Our County Court was in session on the return of some of our members and the People called upon them all to make a public declaration and account for their votes on the Nullification Resolutions. The Excuse rendered was that the subject was one on which the Legislature had no right to act, alleging that the general Government had exclusive power to express an opinion thereon and in the next place that the Resolutions were too violent and tended to exasperate So. Ca. The people were not at all satisfied with the reasons assigned for the vote and although both the commoners utterly deny being Nullifiers, they can't induce the people to think so. You mention in your letter that it is reported I am to be a candidate for Congress. I have been generally solicited from all parts of the District to do so but have not consented. I dislike to abandon my profession at this time, and my unfinished business in Tennessee renders it inconvenient for me to enter the list of Candidates. I think it absolutely certain Samuel Carson cannot be reelected. I am informed there are several persons in keeping for the race.

Maj. Forney has gone with two thirds of his slaves to Alabama to purchase and settle a plantation. Dr. Winslow Alexander has returned from Alabama. I have not seen him but hear he has not purchased because of the high prices at which Land sold there. . . . I am strongly inclined to go and see Alabama next Fall and perhaps the Mississippi State. We anticipate much confusion in this quarter next summer from the increased number of Elections created by the last Legislature. I believe all the old clerks

---

[7] William Capers (1790-1855), of South Carolina, a graduate of South Carolina College, a Methodist minister, who had served in the Carolinas and Georgia, had been superintendant of Indian missions, and had done notable work among the negroes on the South Carolina plantations. He had a wide reputation as a preacher, and on the separation of the Methodist Church, was elected bishop. He was the father of Ellison Capers (1837-1908), Confederate general and Episcopal bishop, and the grandfather of Bishop William T. Capers, of Texas.

will submitt to the new law, but Maj. Henderson,[8] I learn, intends to dispute the Power of the Legislature to vacate his office and present the question to the Court. . . .

We were all very much surprised to learn that Judge Swain was elected Gov. and yet those who know him best ought not to be surprised as popular preferment is the ruling passion of his soul.

I think Judge Daniel ought to have been bound over for his good behavior before he took his seat on the Supreme Court bench as he will curse *there* if things don't go right. He and Seawell must have formed a coalition or public opinion predicated on strong circumstances is much deceived. I shall be at Iredell on the 3rd week and the 4th week of this month at Mecklenburg so that if you come up to Fathers I hope to see you there. The Furnace is still blowing and doing well and Fathers health is excellent.

Our Merchants and planters are trading now chiefly with Augusta in lieu of So. Ca. and much fear is entertained here that So. Ca. money will depreciate.

*   *   *   *

From George Edmund Badger.   A.

Oxford, 9th March, 1833

Considering the character of the agent to whom you intrusted the charge of bringing to you the 2nd. Gallison, you could not have been surprized that it was forgotten. What Winston [9] with his usual negligence omitted, *I* with my *habitual* accuracy and attention have performed & 2nd Gallison under the charge of the Solicitor General is now on its way to you.

A short time since I accidentally observed in an old Newspaper late in May or June last, a very fulsome advertisement announc-

---

[8] Lawson Henderson (1774-1843), of Lincoln, sheriff, 1796-1801, superior court clerk, 1807-1837, an influential citizen, and a man of fine mind. When the selection of clerks was transferred by legislative act to the voters for a specified term, he declined to surrender his office. John D. Hoke, who had been elected, brought suit, and the case went finally to the supreme court, which decided, Judge Ruffin writing the opinion, (*Hoke* v. *Henderson*, 15 N. C., 1) which was at variance with all the federal and state decisions on the subject, that Henderson had an estate in the office of which he could not be divested by statute. Many years later, this doctrine was dissented from by Chief Justice Walter Clark, in *Abbott* v. *Beddingfield*, (125 N. C., 256,) and was overruled by the court in *Mial* v. *Ellington*. (134 N. C., 136.)

[9] Patrick Henry Winston, of Rockingham County, student at the university, 1818, lawyer.

ing to the publick that Mr. Gaston was to deliver the then usual evening annual address at Chapel Hill. As I very sincerely detest and abhor all such stuff which must be offensive to every man of the least pretensions to taste, and should be deeply mortified to see any such announcement of myself in the publick prints, I must beg the favour of you (and a favour it will indeed be) in such way as you may think most proper and delicate, so to manage as to prevent *any notice whatever* (no matter what may be its shape or character) of my appointment to deliver the next address.

From Jo. Seawell Jones.   U.

A Work will be published, during the ensuing Fall,
Entitled [10]
A VINDICATION
OF THE CHARACTER OF THE
STATE OF NORTH CAROLINA,
From the
ASPERSIONS OF MR. JEFFERSON,
As contained
In his Letter to the late JOHN ADAMS,
published in the 4th volume of the
Boston edition of his Works, pp. 314-15.
By Jo. Seawell Jones,
of North-Carolina.

———————

Subscriptions are solicited for the proposed work, returnable to Messrs. Turner & Hughes, of Raleigh, by the first of October; and the author embraces the opportunity to remark, that his work will comprise a History of the Revolution in North-Carolina, from the year 1771, to the fourth of July, 1776, as well as the other matters embraced in the title of the book. It will be published in one octavo volume, of about 270 pages. Price, $2.

March 27th, 1833.

———————

[10] As published, the title reads; "A Defence of the Revolutionary History of the State of North Carolina from the Aspersions of Mr. Jefferson," etc.

N. York, April 3d, 1833.

I regret very much to inform you—that—from circumstances beyond my control I have been compelled to defer the publication of my work until the period limited for the return of these papers, viz. 1 October. I had progressed even in the printing a considerable number of pages when I was informed by the Hon. Lewis Williams [11] that a letter; written by the late John Adams to his brother, John Williams [12] of Tennessee, controverting the aspersions of Mr. Jefferson against Mr. Hooper was either lost or mislaid. I cannot consent to publish immediately without so valuable a document, and am determined to discover its hiding place if possible.

I am on my way to Washington City and am in hopes to hear from the letter through the agency of The Hon. J. Quincy Adams. I am moreover anxious to read several letters in the State Department of which I have heard since my arrival in this City. I have all the Manuscript of my work with me and, should I not obtain the letter of John Adams, shall come directly on home. There are several portions of it I should like to correct with the papers of our No. Ca. State Department before me.

From Robert Potter to William Swaim.[13]   U.

Hillsboro, 11th. Augt., 1833.

Dear Swaim,

I send you above a copy of *the* indictment, it is a *volume,* and abounds in terrific and awful epithets, well calculated to shake the nerves of novices; but you will find when matters are brought to the *test* I shall cover the conspiracy of villains who hatched it with confusion—the law of libel in No. Carolina allows *the truth* to be given in evidence, and I am prepared to maintain by proof the truth of the allegations so awfully denounced in the

[11] Lewis Williams (1786-1842), of Surry, a graduate of the university, member of the commons, 1813-1814, member of congress, 1815-1842. At his death, he had served longer than any member up to that time, and was called "The Father of the House." He was one of the founders of the Whig party.

[12] John Williams (1778-1837), native of Surry, and brother of Lewis Williams, a lawyer of Knoxville, Tennessee, colonel under Jackson in the War of 1812, United States senator, 1815-1823, charge' d'affaires to the Central American States, 1825-1826.

[13] William Swaim (d. 1835), of Greensboro, founder and editor of the *Greensboro Patriot,* a prominent Quaker, and a leader in the North Carolina Manumission Society.

indictment as false malicious etc., etc., etc., give yourself no un-
easiness therefore, nor incur the *unnecessary* expense of retaining
counsel. I would write you more at large, but I understand from
Mr. Young you will be here next Sunday, and I have moreover
fatigued my fingers just now by the tedious process of copying
the bill, a labour which I did not feel at liberty to devolve on
Mr. Young. You have probably heard by this time that they man-
aged contrary to expectation to juggle me out of my election by
11 votes. from what I can understand there can be no doubt that
in fairness and according to the intentions of the people I was
elected, but was juggled out of it by the foul and dishonest conduct of the poll keepers and this I understand is the general
opinion in Granville; however the matter sits lightly on me.

Mr. Young tells me you have a dozen or so of *the* pamphlets
on hand—let me request that when you come down you will bring
them to me. I have none left, and they would be *useful* in my
hands, many people from *below* are frequently applying for them,
and they might *there* have a salutary action on public opinion.
I have no time at present to say more than to renew to you the
assurances of my *lasting* respect and regard.

Rob. Potter

[Enclosure ¹⁴]

State of North Carolina	)	Superior Court of Law
	)	
County of Orange	)	Begun and held on the second
	)	
	)	Monday of March A. D. 1833

The Jurors for the State upon their oath present, that long
before, and at the time of composing, printing and publishing
of the several false, defamatory and malicious libels hereinafter
mentioned; and at the several times and occasions in and by the

---

¹⁴ A portion of this document is published, because of its own historical im-
portance. In addition, it illustrates the absurdities of many legal documents of
that day.

said libels mentioned and alluded to, Robert Strange[15] Esquire was, and still is, one of the Judges of the Superior Courts of Law and Equity in and for the State of North Carolina aforesaid, and that before the time of composing printing and publishing the several false defamatory and malicious libels and libellous matters hereinafter mentioned, towit, at a Superior Court of Law begun and held for the County of Granville in the State aforesaid at the Court House in Oxford on the first Monday of March in the year of our Lord one thousand eight hundred and thirty two by and before the aforesaid Robert Strange Judge as aforesaid an Indictment charging one Robert Potter, Attorney at Law, with an assault and battery on the Reverend Lewis Taylor[16] by beating stabbing and castrating him, came on to be tried; and that the said Robert Potter being then and there put upon his defence pleaded "Guilty" to the said charge, and witnesses were thereupon examined as well for the said Robert Potter as for the State. Whereupon the said Robert Strange Judge as aforesaid upon consideration thereupon had gave as the Judgement of the Court, that the said Robert Potter for the said offense should be imprisoned for the space of two years and at the expiration of such imprisonment that he enter into Bond with security in the sum of two thousand dollars to keep the peace for one further year thereafter, and that afterwards and during the said Term of the said Court on motion of the Solicitor General, and for good and sufficient reasons appearing to the Court, it was further ordered by the said Robert Strange Judge as aforesaid, that the said Robert Potter be removed to the jail of the adjoining County of Orange to undergo his imprisonment agreeably to the Judgement aforesaid: Nevertheless the said Robert Potter late of said County of Orange attorney at law and one William Swaim late of said County of Orange printer well knowing the premises and unlawfully wickedly and maliciously devising contriving and intending to scandalize vilify and defame the said Robert Strange Judge as aforesaid, and his conduct and acts as such Judge and

---

[15] Robert Strange (1796-1854), of Fayetteville, a native of Virginia, a graduate of Hampden-Sydney, who represented the borough in the commons, 1821-1823, 1826, was a judge of the superior court, 1827-1836, and United States senator, 1836-1840, succeeding Willie P. Mangum, who resigned under instructions. Mangum succeeded him in 1840.

[16] The Rev. Lewis Taylor, a relative of Mrs. Potter, one of the persons upon whom Potter committed mayhem.

as much as in them lay to cause it to be believed and thought that on the trial and proceeding aforesaid before the said Robert Strange Judge as aforesaid, he the said Robert Potter was cruelly unlawfully and unjustly deprived of the liberty of speech in defending himself; and that during and throughout the said trial and proceeding the said Robert Strange, Judge as aforesaid, abused the powers of his office to the great oppression and injury of the same Robert Potter and thereby to bring the said Robert Strange as such Judge as aforesaid into great hatred and contempt to and amongst all the good citizens of the State, afterwards, towit, on the first day of November in the year of our Lord one thousand eight hundred and thirty two with force and arms in the said County of Orange falsely wickedly and maliciously did compose print and publish and cause and procure to be composed printed and published of and concerning the said Robert Strange Judge as aforesaid and of and concerning his conduct and acts as such Judge in and upon the trial and proceeding aforesaid a certain false scandalous malicious and defamatory libel in the form of a pamphlet entitled "Address &c to the People of Granville County" in which said libel were and are contained divers false scandalous malicious defamatory and libelous charges and matters of and concerning his the said Robert Strange Judge as aforesaid and of such concerning conduct and acts as such Judge upon trial and proceedings aforesaid, in one part thereof to the tenor and effect following, that is to say—When I, (meaning himself the said Robert Potter when on the trial and proceeding aforesaid) rose to speak I was not allowed to proceed without interruption (meaning that he the said Robert Potter was so interrupted by the Said Robert Strange Judge as aforesaid) I (meaning himself the said Robert Potter) was checked—restrained—constantly reminded that I (meaning himself the said Robert Potter) was in the presence of *power;* by the active and oppressive exercise of which they (meaning the said Robert Strange Judge as aforesaid and certain other persons named and alluded to in said pamphlet) were determined to disable me (meaning himself the said Robert Potter) from doing myself (meaning himself the said Robert Potter) justice. My condition (meaning his the said Robert Potter's) was that of a man under the agonies of moral suffocation. I (meaning himself the said Robert Potter) had been buried more than six months in a dungeon. My case (meaning the charge in the Indictment aforesaid) in the mean time had employed every tongue. Yet when after all this, I came into Court (meaning when put on his trial as aforesaid) *where alone* I (meaning himself the said Robert Potter) could be heard in my (meaning his the said Robert Potter's) defence the Judge (meaning the said Robert Strange Judge as aforesaid) had the brutishness to deprive me (meaning himself the said Robert Potter) *of liberty of speech.* He (meaning the said Robert Strange Judge as aforesaid) tied down my (meaning his the said Robert Potter's) hands when battleing for life—he (meaning the said Robert Strange Judge as aforesaid) stifled my (meaning his the said Robert Potter's) voice when pleading for moral existence. He (meaning the said Robert Strange Judge as aforesaid) stood ready at every turn of the proceedings (meaning the trial and proceedings aforesaid) to jump with the whole force of his (meaning the said Robert Strange's Official weight upon my (meaning his the said Robert Potter's) shoulders."

Every body knows how difficult it is to *wring* the truth from a dishonest witness even with the utmost latitude of examination; but when such a witness sees *the Judge* ready to take sides with him, whenever he is pressed, he will easily put you at defiance, and in fact assume the airs of a commanding integrity. Such was the conduct of Judge Strange (meaning the aforesaid Robert Strange Judge as aforesaid) towards those (meaning the witnesses offered and examined on behalf of the State on the trial and proceedings aforesaid) who came into Court, to bear me (meaning himself the said Robert Potter) down *by perjury.* He (meaning the said Robert Strange Judge as aforesaid) seemed quite anxious to protect everybody but me (meaning himself the said Robert Potter) was in his (meaning the said Robert Strange's) *custody* Yet he (meaning the said Robert Strange Judge as aforesaid) even permitted me (meaning himself the said Robert Potter) *to be dogged in his* (meaning the said Robert Strange's) *presence;* and though a pistol was fired in the scuffle *under his* (meaning the said Robert Strange's) nose he (meaning the said Robert Strange Judge as aforesaid) took *no notice of it.* Yet he (meaning the said Robert Strange Judge as aforesaid) was so zealous to enforce the law against me (meaning himself the said Robert Potter) that

after sentencing me (meaning himself the said Robert Potter) to
two years imprisonment he (meaning the said Robert Strange
Judge as aforesaid) ordered that at the end of that time I (meaning himself the said Robert Potter) *should give security for keeping the peace.*" And in a certain other part of which said pamphlet
there were and are contained certain other false defamatory
malicious and libellous matters and words of and concerning the
said Robert Strange Judge as aforesaid according to the tenor
and effect following, that is to say; Another incident will serve
to show the spirit in which he (meaning the said Robert Strange
Judge as aforesaid) presided (meaning on the trial and proceeding aforesaid) I (meaning himself the said Robert Potter) had
Seawell (meaning Henry Seawell Esquire attorney at Law and
now one of the Judges of the Superior Courts of Law and Equity
in and for the State aforesaid) summoned as a witness and when I
(meaning himself the said Robert Potter) remarked that I (meaning himself the said Robert Potter) wanted *"that man sworn."*
Seawell (meaning the aforesaid Henry Seawell) appealed to the
Judge (meaning the said Robert Strange Judge as aforesaid) and
asked "if his honor (meaning the said Robert Strange Judge as
aforesaid) would permit him (meaning the said Henry Seawell)
to be insulted by that individual," (meaning the said Robert
Potter) Whereupon *his honor* (meaning the said Robert Strange
Judge as aforesaid) at once declared that if Mr. Potter (meaning
the said Robert Potter) had not already suffered so much that he
(meaning the said Robert Strange Judge as aforesaid) knew of no
way in which he (meaning the said Robert Strange Judge as
aforesaid) could add to his (meaning the said Robert Potter's)
sufferings he (meaning the said Robert Strange Judge as aforesaid) certainly would punish him (meaning the said Robert
Potter) for the insult he (meaning the said Robert Potter) had
offered to Mr. Seawell (meaning the aforesaid Henry Seawell)—
Surely his honor (meaning the said Robert Strange Judge as
aforesaid) must have taken this complaint of Seawell's (meaning
his the said Henry Seawell's appeal to the Judge as aforesaid) into
consideration when he (meaning the said Robert Strange Judge
as aforesaid) sentenced me (meaning himself the said Robert
Potter) *to two years* imprisonment (meaning the aforesaid Judgment of imprisonment) What chance had I. (meaning himself the

said Robert Potter) for justice under such circumstances." And in a certain other part of which said pamphlet that were and are contained certain other false defamatory malicious and libellous matters and words of and concerning the said Robert Strange Judge as aforesaid according to the tenor and effect following, that is to say "But he (meaning the aforesaid Henry Seawell) is a great man in *North Carolina;* and by his (meaning the said Henry Seawell's) influence with the *great* men (meaning among others the said Robert Strange, Judge as aforesaid,) who controul her laws (meaning the laws of North Carolina) he (meaning the said Henry Seawell) has contrived to have me (meaning himself the said Robert Potter) *transported* out of my (meaning the said Robert Potter's) county (meaning the county of Granville aforesaid) certainly one of the most unauthorized acts of tyranny ever perpetrated under *color* of Law was the order (meaning the aforesaid order of removal of the said Robert Potter from the jail of Granville aforesaid to the jail of Orange aforesaid) procured by Seawell (meaning the said Henry Seawell) from Judge Strange (meaning the said Robert Strange Judge as aforesaid) to have me (meaning himself the said Robert Potter) transported to the prison in Hillsborough (meaning the jail of Orange aforesaid). And in a certain other part of which said pamphlet that were and are contained certain other false defamatory malicious and libellous matters and words of and concerning the said Robert Strange Judge as aforesaid according to the tenor and effect following, that is to say, "But this (meaning the kindness of the jailor and others to him in Hillsborough) does not excuse the tyranny of the Judge (meaning the said Robert Strange Judge as aforesaid) or his (meaning the said Robert Strange's) subserviency to the views of Seawell (meaning the said Henry Seawell and that the said order for removal to the jail of Orange was made by the said Robert Strange Judge as aforesaid to subserve the views of the said Henry Seawell) my (meaning the said Robert Potter's) treatment here (meaning in the jail of Orange aforesaid) was not forseen or cared for by them (meaning the said Robert Strange Judge as aforesaid and the said Henry Seawell) Their (meaning the said Robert Strange Judge as aforesaid and the said Henry Seawell) object was to *transport* me (meaning himself the said Robert Potter) out of the county of Granville) to the great scandal injury and disgrace of the said Robert Strange Judge as aforesaid in contempt of the laws of this State to the great offence of all civil Government to the evil and pernicious example of all others in like case offending and against the peace and dignity of the State.

* * * * *[17]

John Scott
Sol. Gen'l.

From James Graham.   U.

Rutherfordton, August 12th, 1833.

I have not written you for some time in consequence of my absence from this place in the political bustle of the Election; That event is just over. In this County the vote was for Graham 1381. for Carson 553.
Newland 298. In Buncombe for G __ 1018 for C __ 316 N __ 670. In Burke G __ 458 for C __ 900 N __ 700. A Gentleman from Buncombe arrived last night who says he learned before he left home that I was elected by eight hundred votes in the district; the exact vote of Haywood and Macon he could not state, but that was the result. I am gratified that I am elected and exceedingly glad that the contest is over, as both my competitors made a direct push at me, believing me to be the strong candidate and of consequence I laboured under every disadvantage. In this county the candidates for the senate were Martin Shuford [18] Jos. Carson [19] Genl. John Carson [20] and one Hicks; Shuford was elected by a large Majority. In the Commons, Irvin and Moore [21] (the young lawyer) were elected, they both protest they are not nullifiers, still the intelligence of the county believe they are, but their opponents were in favour of removing the Court house and that prostrated them. Our old Supr. Court Clerk was beaten by James

<hr/>

[17] The portion omitted is an identical repetition of the preceding portion.
[18] Martin Shuford (1794-1836), was state senator from Rutherford, 1825-1829, and 1833.
[19] Joseph McDowell Carson (1779-1860), of "Pleasant Garden" and "Green River," in Burke (now McDowell) County, served in the commons, 1812-1814, 1829; in the state senate, 1832, 1836-1840; and in the convention of 1835.
[20] John Carson (1766-1846), a native of Virginia, an outstanding citizen of Rutherford, represented it in the commons, 1815-1816, 1819-1826. He was defeated in this election.
[21] Alanson W. Moore, member of commons, 1833; state senator 1835.

Webb, the old member. The County Court Clerk, Mr. Birckett,[22] was elected by a large majority. In Lincoln Danl. Hoke[23] is elected in the Senate, Cansceller[24] and Perry Robarts[25] in the Commons. J. D. Hoke[26] Supr Ct Clerk, and Miles Abernathy[27] Co Ct Clerk. I am informed you are a Candidate for the Town of Hillsboro and I feel a deep solicitude for your election but as your competitor Smith[28] is *great in small things* I am fearful the result is doubtful. Let me know as early as possible what is the event. I never had my office so much like a lumber house before; I presume I have 15 or 20 letters unanswered and as many papers not issued. I hope in a week or two to bring up the rear and prepare for my Fall circuit. . . . I have not been at Fathers since May last, and I have received no letters from our western friends, but brother Joseph for 3 months. My Plantation I have not seen since May, and I begin to conclude Popular favour is not a money making business. There are but few persons in Buncombe this season attending on the Springs, I believe the want of Funds has prevented many from visiting the up country.

I hope to spend a few days in Orange in the fall and see some of my old and valued friends.

* * * * *

[22] Theoderic F. Birchett, a native of Raleigh, held many local offices in Rutherford County, and was a delegate to the convention of 1835.

[23] Daniel Hoke (b. 1773), native of Pennsylvania, a captain in the War of 1812, had represented Lincoln in the commons, 1809-1813, 1815-1816, and in the state senate since 1829. He was now elected for his last term. He soon after moved to Alabama.

[24] Henry Cansler, who represented Lincoln County in the lower house, 1831-1836, 1854-1855.

[25] Peregrine Roberts, who served this one term only.

[26] John D. Hoke, who was elected clerk of the court, and was prevented from taking office by the decision in *Hoke* v. *Henderson,* above referred to.

[27] Miles W. Abernathy, a Democrat, represented Lincoln in the commons, 1831-1832, and was clerk of the county court, 1833-1837. He later moved to Alabama, where he was a state senator.

[28] William A. Graham was successful in his candidacy for the commons over Dr. James Smith (1790-1859), for the borough of Hillsboro, and thus entered upon his long, honorable and brilliant career in public service. Dr. Smith, a native of Orange, a graduate of Jefferson Medical College, had been a member of the commons in 1821, and had been a member of congress, 1817-1821. He was later a delegate to the convention of 1835. He moved to Chapel Hill a few years later.

From Alfred Graham.   U.

Memphis, Ten., Septem. 6, 1833.

Having heard no news of you for some time I have taken my
seat to try the effect of a Letter In order to bring something of
the sort in turn from you. Perhaps you have been too busily
engaged Electioneering of late to attend to absent Friends. I
see in the Register taken by a Gentleman in this place that you
have been elected from your Town by one Vote. Also in the
same Paper the Election of James to Congress by a handsome
Majority over Carson and Newland.

Our town has been quite healthy since the Midle of June. We
have had not one Case of Cholera among the Citizens since that
time and not more than 3 or 4 from the River. The Place has
never been known to be as healthy at this season of the year.
In fact since the disappearance of the Pestilence we have had
scarcely any sickness atall. In Counting up the deaths by Cholera
since the first of February we make between 80 and 90. At least
one half were of the Crews of Boats and the remainder Citizens.
The greatest number of Deaths in one Day was 8 persons; from
3 to 5 was very comon about the 1st of June. I remained here all
the time though I sent the Negroes to the Country and was about
to leave myself when the disease began to abate. Brother Joseph
and Family are well. We have all enjoyed excellent Health for
some time. I still keep my negroes emplyed here though I have
become quite tired of it, On account of the bad habits they are
getting into in town which they would have no opportunity of
in the Country. I can still employ them more profitably here than
farming, But have determined to place them on my farm again
in the Fall rather than run the Risk of having them exposed
runing about at night drinking, etc. The Man that has my Place
rented has raised an excellent Crop of Corn and some little
Cotten He is to give me 10 Bushels per Acre rent which will be
more than will do me next year. Generally the Crops are pretty
good in this Country though latterly they have suffered with
Drouth and the Rust in Cotten. The Mississippi is very low at
present and an extensive Mudbar is to be seen in front of the
Town 150 yards wide and half mile long. This keeps forming
wider every year and baffles all hopes of ever having any permanent Wharfs except Floating ones. At present they have two old
Steamboats that Rises and Falls with the water which affords a
very safe landing at all times for steamboats by night or Day. . . .

Our Elections here are over we elected to Congress a Lawyer by the name of Dunlap [29] not celebrated for Talents but a very clever fellow. The election was pretty close between him, Williams,[30] and Alaxander.[31] Col Crocket is elected over his opponent Fitsgerald [32] by 160 votes.

I witnessed a very severe rencountre about 3 weeks ago here between 4 of our most respectable Citizens or as much so as any. Some anonamous Letters had been written by the Mrs. Hulls two Brothers Ridiculing the Dress of a Doct Christian and Robeson and their wives. They were ascertained to be the authors and were attacked with Pistols. One of the Hulls was shot under the Arm and the ball lodged in his breast. The other was shot through the Body below the breast with shot. Robeson was severely stabed in the Body with a large Dirck by one of the Hulls. Christian was the only one engaged who was not Hurt. The Wounds were all believed to be Mortal at the time yet all are getting well. No man interfered though 30 or 40 were present.

I have attended 2 Camp Meetings lately, one in this County and one in Fayette. The Methodists here are very much like those of N. C. in making Noise, But are much more hospitable in hunting out strangers and providing for them something to eat.

I should be glad to hear from as often as convenient; the longer I remain away from my native state the less frequent I discover I receve Letters, Though it is a good deal the case with me in writing.

From James Graham.   U.

Rutherfordton, September 8th, 1833.

I received yours of the 14th ult. and am much gratified to learn you have succeeded in the election; and I am the more pleased as I had anticipated your defeat and as I knew your competitor was thoroughly versed in all the little tricks of Electioneering. A few days after the election was over I wrote you concerning my

---

[29] William Claiborne Dunlap (1798-1872), of Tennessee, studied at Maryville College, and became a lawyer. He served in the Indian campaign of 1818-1819, and as a Democrat was in congress, 1833-1837. He moved to Texas in 1838, and was minister of the republic to Mexico.

[30] Christopher Harris Williams (1798-1857), of Lexington, Tennessee, a native of Hillsboro, N. C., M. C., 1837-1843, 1849-1853.

[31] Adam Rankin Alexander, of Memphis, a native of Virginia, state senator 1817, a Federalist member of congress, 1823-1827, delegate to abolitionist convention of 1834, state house of representatives, 1841, 1843.

[32] William Fitzgerald, a lawyer, Democratic member of congress, 1831-1833.

own triumph. Mr. Carson is much mortified at the result and presume will now drink to a great excess as he has heretofore indulged quite freely with the French Brandy. Report informs me that he has just sold his plantation in Burke for $12,000 and is about to move to the Mississippi State. He is intemperate and unhappy and often chagrined at his overthrow. Since I am successful and have been making my arrangements to go abroad I percieve distinctly I have *gained a Loss*. However the Die is cast and I must abide the throw. About ten days since I saw Genl. Newland [33] at Ashville dressed cap a-pie in true military style. His long boots, white stockings, and short buff britches, white vest, and buttoned Coat tied on with a red sash glittered to such a degree that it would hurt your eyes to look at him in the sun and in this dress he rode off from Ashville towards Macon with *a large Bandanna handkerchief* tied up full of clothes *suspended on his Arm* and dangling from his side; after he descended beyond the Western hill we fancied his brilliant Robes still illuminated the vallies and reflected light on the neighbouring nobs.

Our village begins to grow and we have had several families from So. Ca. spending a part of the Summer here. I flatter myself that this village will hereafter receive a liberal portion of encouragement from the low country as we have an easy and quick intercourse with Charleston by stage and rail road in 3 days travel. I will set out this week to my plantation and stay there until the 18 or 19 when I shall go to Fathers and hope to meet you there. . . .

I have recd 2 late Treatises on Chivalry from Salisbury—one from Caldwell [34] and one from Fisher.[35] I think the state of society about Salisbury must be more embittered than any section of the State known to me. I think however they are much more apt to raise the price of Ink than Powder.

---

[33] David Newland, of Burke, member of the commons, 1826-1829, state senator, 1830. Defeated by Graham in this election, he was again a candidate in 1827. James Graham was declared elected, and Newland contested. Graham was unseated, but was immediately re-elected.

[34] David Franklin Caldwell (1790-1859), of Iredell, attended the university for one year, and then studied law under Archibald Henderson. He was a member of the commons, 1816-1819, from Iredell, and of the state senate, from Rowan, 1829-1831, (speaker, 1831), a judge of the superior court, 1844-1859.

[35] Charles Fisher (1789-1849), of Rowan, a Democratic leader, was state senator, 1818; member of congress, 1819-1821, 1839-1841; of the commons, 1822-1823, 1833, 1836; and a delegate to the convention of 1835.

Give my respects to my friends in Hillsboro. I hope to see them in Nov. The death of Judge Henderson [36] induces many conjectures who may be his successor and opens the door for much log rolling in the Legislature.

From William Gaston[37]

to Thomas P. Devereux.[38]   A.

Baltimore, Novr. 3rd, 1833.

I avail myself of a moment of rest on my journey to New York to submit a short view of a subject which for some time occasioned me doubt and gave me difficulty. I am bound as a Citizen, and am bound by oath, to support the Constitution of No. Carolina. I am avowedly a believer in the doctrines of the Catholic Church. If that Constitution disqualifies a believer in those doctrines from holding office, it would be dishonorable and wicked in me to accept it. If it contains no such disqualification, and my Country calls on me to render important services which I am able to perform, it is my duty to obey the call. As the Constitution is based upon the general principle of Civil and religious liberty all Citizens of the State are competent to take & hold office whom the Constitution does not *clearly* disqualify. Penal incapacities it was in the power of the People to create, but they must be unequivocally declared before they can take effect. The only part of the Constitution which can be supposed to contain such a disqualification is that part of the 32d. Section which declares incapable of office those who "deny the truth of the Protestant Religion." It is very possible that some of the framers of this section intended to exclude R. Catholics from office, but can this clause of the section be judicially interpreted as imposing this degradation and disability? It seems to me that it cannot.

1st. what is "the Protestant Religion?" If we had a religious establishment and some ecclesiastical tribunal, or other legal in-

---

[36] Leonard Henderson (1772-1833), of Granville, studied law under Judge John Williams, was clerk of court for the Hillsboro district, clerk of the superior court, 1808-1816, associate justice of the supreme court, 1818-1829, and chief justice, 1829-1833.

[37] Copy.

[38] Thomas Pollock Devereux (1793-1869), a large planter, distinguished lawyer, supreme court reporter, Federal district attorney, a man of many friends and great influence.

stitution, to determine the tenets of that Religion, and to pronounce what is schism and heresy, there would be some means of ascertaining what is the Protestant Religion and what is a denial of its truth. But this cannot be, for it is expressly forbidden by the Constitution. There being then no Church with lawful authority to establish creeds, and such being forbidden in the Constitution—and the Constitution having failed to define the Protestant Religion and not having excluded the Catholics or any other denomination of Christians *io nomine* from office—we are obliged to hold that clause in the Constitution ineficient and unmeaning, or incorporate into the text the multitude of new notions theological, metaphysical, etc., as parts of "the Protestant Religion."

Again. R. Catholics do not *deny* any of the doctrines which other Christians believe; but they believe doctrines which Protestants deny. For instance. In the Episcopal Protestant Church of this Country the two Creeds usually called the apostles creed and the nicine Creed, are the standard symbols of faith. These are also the standard symbols of the R. Catholic Faith. I do not know a single affirmative dogma which the Episcopal Church teaches, which is not also taught in the Catholic Church. Is then a belief in the latter a necessary denial of the truth of the doctrines of the former?

Again. When the Constitution was formed test laws and disqualifying enactments were familiar with our ancestors. R. Catholics were well known, and long had been the subjects of political proscription in England and in her Colonies. In these acts of disqualification & proscription there was no room left for doubt. "Papists" *io nomine* were excluded from all places of Civil trust, and care taken to make the exclusion effectual by imposing oaths which no Catholic could take.

If this system of proscription were intended to be preserved under the new order of things—under that republican Constitution based on the principles announced in the declaration of rights—can it be questioned but that the intent would have been unequivocably manifested?

This is necessarily but an *outline* of my views on this Constitutional question. My conclusion is that the Constitution does not disqualify me because of my religious opinions from taking or holding office—that I have no right by any over nice scruples to be instrumental in *practically* interpolating into that instrument an odious provision which it does not contain—and that as on one hand I do not seek office so on the other I should not decline it when honourably tendered to my acceptance and when I can reasonably hope to discharge its duties with advantage to my country.

I pray you to believe me very
truly your affect. friend.

From Jo. Seawell Jones.   A.

Cambridge, Nov. 18, 1833.

I hope I have not gone out of your memory during the long silence which the most urgent engagements doubtless on both sides have produced.

It occurred a few days ago to Campbell and myself that you were on this day to take upon your maiden shoulders the high and responsible duty of a Legislator and upon such a circumstance I would congratulate both my friend and my country. I rejoice you are in politics and implore you to legislate for the honor and interest of the Rip-Van-Winkle of the South *exclusively*. I have no question but that you and Dave Barringer [39]—one of my best and most beloved friends—must often walk side by side in the party conflicts of the State, and wish you both success and comfort in your political schemes. I do not believe we agree on the subject of Internal Improvements, for I am for building a Chinese wall around the State and forcibly restricting the trade of the people to home markets. I hate Virginia and her dominant school of politicians so bitterly—so reverently eschew the memory of her *trans Roanoke* influence and so sincerely deprecate the extensive influence and circulation of the Richmond Enquirer—that I am all for stoping all commercial intercourse with so insolvent a neighbour as the first step towards independence. I should not be surprised if Barringer agreed with me, although I have not heard from him on this or any other subject for nearly a year. While on the subject of Internal Improvements I beg leave to mention to you the name of a very distinguished Engineer now engaged in this part of the world, but who is a native

[39] Probably with characteristic inaccuracy, Jones referred to Daniel M. Barringer.

of our State. Wm. Gibbs McNeill [40] of Bladen originally and now a Major in the Army and one of the head-men on the subject of Rail Roads in Boston. He is at present employed by three distinct companies and cannot be in the receipt of less than $10,000. for his various services.

Now if you all are in earnest on the matter of Rail Roads, for heaven sake, at every hazard, procure the services of an able and practical engineer, and when the thing is possible, at an equally great hazard and rate, let that officer be a Native of the State. I do not know that it would be practicable to obtain the services of Major McNeill at present, but I do know that he is proud of his Nativity and a defender of the State in all table chats and fire side arguments. He is in the confidence of all the Capitalists of Boston and is the Agent of an extensive family, who are deeply engaged in the various stocks in the country. I should like to have some of this Boston Money expended on North Carolina rail roads and if McNeill would recommend any particular project in the State over which he was or might be Engineer, I will venture to say a large quantity of stock could be disposed of on Boston Change.

Paulo Minora Canamus. My book, though nearly through the press, is going on slow, I think. I have to be very cautious in all corrections and intend it shall be more elegant in its Mechanical than in its literary execution. I am sorry to say, however, that I see no chance to escape a considerable loss in a pecuniary way; for this getting up a book in fine Stile is more expensive than I had calculated and I have increased its size one hundred pages. I have printed *1500* copies and even if all of them should be sold, the publishers and booksellers commissions will eat up too much of it to leave any thing like an adequate compensation. These book-sellers charge from 20 to 33 pr. cent for selling and distributing and this percentage is on the price and not the profit of the book.

I hope to be home by the month of January and shall spend as much as six months in the State. During this time I design, by the permission of the Assembly to examine by detail the papers

---

[40] William Gibbs McNeill (1801-1853), a native of Wilmington, graduate of West Point, who rose to the rank of major, was aide to Jackson in 1817, and later to General Gaines, and an eminent engineer. He was lent by the Army for survey and construction work in Massachusetts, Georgia, New York, Kentucky, and Ohio. He resigned, and became president of the Chesapeake and Ohio Canal Co., built a large part of the Baltimore and Ohio Railroad, and was major general of state troops during the Dorr Rebellion. Some time after the date of this letter, he was employed for several important surveys in North Carolina.

in the office of the Secretary of State. When I was in Raleigh last Summer although I was at all times priviledged by the Secretary to ask for and then copy or read over any specified document, yet the old gentleman [41] who is extremely ignorant of the proper use of the papers in his office, was not at all disposed to permit me to search for myself, and would *squire* me about from Shelf to Shelf and say, "here are the patents for the year 80," and so on. Now I want to go into that office on my hook and give those papers a thorough overhauling and see what is in them of historical value, and for this purpose I must beg you or Barringer to bring in a bill to this amount. "An act to authorise Jo Seawell Jones to examine the papers in the office of the Secretary of State and take with him into the said office one or more assistants." In case I should obtain such permission, I design taking Mathew, Lt. Clarke, and Peter Force [42] into the office as assistants in case they should come along as I expect they will. I am very anxious to go through those papers and see what is in them and I should take great pleasure and pride in returning them to order and a better State of preservation. By the way, there is one subject connected with that office which the Legislature ought to take up. The Journal of the Assembly of the year '65—one of the most important Sessions in the history of the State—is gone. I could not find it, *high* nor *dry*, and as Judge Martin in his history quotes from it, he must know where it is—if *it is* at all. I have a note in my book accusing him of having carried it off, to which I intend to call his notice. If such a thing was practicable I should like to see those old Journals republished, but I tried last year on Barringer, Judge Seawell, and Gov. Swain, and they thought the thing impossible as it would cost money.

I shall let you have a copy of my book as soon as it shall see day light—which I hope will not be longer than a fortnight.

Campbell is siting by the fire with both legs reared up on the fireside reading a review of the old English Writers out of the Edinburgh Review; he sends his hearty love to you and says he will be Southwards shortly, probably with me. He is much abdicted to Miss Marshall—so am I.

My love to all the ladies and my compliments to the State.

Ever your friend

Raleigh.

---

[41] William Hill.

[42] Peter Force (1790-1868), archivist, collector, and historian, was born in New Jersey, educated in New York, was a soldier in the War of 1812, and then became a printer in Washington. He was alderman and mayor. He is best known for his "American Archives," and similar historical publications.

From Hugh Waddell.   A.

Hillsborough, Decr. 15, 1833.

Owing to the Jackson derangement of the mails your favour of
the 8th. was not received by me for several days after its date &
I fear this reply to it will seem negligently slow from the same
cause; however if the effect of the reply be the same with that
produced by the letter, the longer it is deferred the better. For
you will stare when I tell you that the instantaneous effect was
to put me into a passion & produce some oaths to the great
astonishment of my family. the anger as you well know was not
with you, but *for* you; It arose from the conduct of your Speaker.[43]

At the beginning of the Session I was much astonished at your
name's not appearing on all the Committees of importance, but
thought it was possible that they were selected by the different
Judicial Districts as they were in my day & that you were not
known personally to many of the representatives. But I knew
that this applied only to the standing Committees & not to those
specially raised by the House, & was therefore offended that the
"Currency Committee," the "Amendment of the Constitution
Com." & another, did not contain your name; still I was at a loss
to account for it, except by referring it to your *criminal* back-
wardness. When the "Memorial Committee" was raised, I was
no longer in doubt as to the motive of the Speaker; it is the
"Herens lateri lethalis arundo" of your brothers opposition to
him as Solicitor. No doubt he is prostituting his place to secure
future favour, & this may be part of the reason of his neglect of
you; but that the first is the principal reason I feel satisfied.

How bitterly does an honorable mind scorn such a course. I
know nothing which so bespeaks the corrupting effect of place
in our Country, as that, the moment one is elevated to a station
of dignity he does something to forfeit the esteem of honorable
men, in order to secure a continuance in his "bad eminence."

However let this poor tool of the rabble be dropped, you
despise the impotence of his malice as much as I do. Where God
and Nature have placed you, is as much beyond his wrath, as to
attain it is beyond his reach. My friends from Raleigh all tell
me that you are. where you ought to be, in the public estimation, the Speaker "to the contrary notwithstanding." I sometimes

---

[43] William J. Alexander, of Mecklenburg.

wish I were with you, as I believe my greater pliability (you call it by a worse name, courtierism, hypocrisy,) would be of service to us both & I know you stand in need of such a friend, upon the principle that the late Judge Moore [44] refused to go to Congress unless Gen. Davie [45] would go too; the Judge like you said, "he did not know how to mix with those fellows to any purpose," but that Davie did, & together they might do something; perhaps I overvalue my skill in that way, but my experience in 1828 raised my estimate of it.

I see by the last paper that a Bill was reported by the Judiciary Committee, of course with your approbation, to erect a 7th Circuit. Will it succeed? I suspect not, for it will require an alteration of several Circuits & this will generally kill any Bill. I should be pleased to know the fate of this project & who may fill the office if created.

Some days ago I sent you by Turner [46] a hasty memorial for the renewal of the Charter of B. C. Fear. I hope it may be re-chartered for several reasons public & private.

We have nothing here of the smallest interest as *you* know who have dragged through December in H. so often. We look to Washington & Raleigh for all stirring news & at the former place they seem to be carving out work that old Hickory with Major Downing's assistance will hardly be able to go through. The new Secretary of the Treasury's reasons are the lamest I have ever seen for so important an act as removing the deposites.

---

[44] Alfred Moore (1755-1810), of Brunswick, son of Maurice Moore of colonial fame, educated in Boston, a Revolutionary soldier, was state senator, 1782, 1784, attorney general, 1782-1791, a judge of the superior court, 1798-1799, and associate justice of the Supreme Court of the United States, 1799-1805, when he retired because of ill health. He was appointed attorney general before he had ever opened a law book.

[45] William Richardson Davie (1756-1820), a native of England, grew up in South Carolina, and was a student at Princeton when the Revolution began. He at once went into service, but received his degree between campaigns. He had rather a brilliant career as a commander, rising to the rank of colonel, but his most useful service, perhaps, was as commissary general of Greene's army, and, later, of North Carolina. He settled at Halifax, quickly became one of the leaders of the state bar, represented the borough in the commons 1786-1787, 1789, 1791, 1793-1794, 1796, 1798. He was a delegate of some influence in the Federal Convention, and was a Federalist delegate to the state conventions of 1788, and 1789, where he worked for the adoption of the Federal Constitution. In the Legislature of 1789 he introduced the bill to charter the University of North Carolina, which act, combined with his later leadership in the actual establishment of the institution, won him the title, "Father of the University." When the threat of war with France came, Washington appointed him brigadier general, and the same year he was elected governor, but resigned after a few months to become commissioner to France. He was defeated for congress in 1803, and in 1805 moved to South Carolina.

[46] Probably Thomas Turner (d. 1870 *ca.*) of Hillsboro.

Norwood & myself will certainly think of your proposition to become Cotten's[47] aids de Camp if the office had been that of Major Gen. in the Wars of Venus & not those of Mars, the present Maj. Gen. would have been singularly qualified to fill it. Heavens what are we coming to? O, that Deveraux Delacey[48] were here to be run for next Senator! Your body is a singular one, liberal enough to elect *Gaston,* & *Swain,* & *save the Sup. Court* & then after all, turn about and elect Cotten! ! !

Write me as soon as possible what you are doing. On the 20 I go to Pittsboro' at which place I shall remain 4 or 5 days & would be glad to hear there from you also.

Ask Moseley[49] what he is thinking of, that he has not written me a word? I take it unkindly of him.

*   *   *   *   *

Raleigh.

From James Graham.   U.

Washington City, Decm. 16th, 1833.

On the same day I took my leave of you I felt some what indisposed from cold but determined to come on here and procure a good seat in the H. of R., and I found all the members with whom I met making a great rush for the same purpose.

My fellow travelers from Raleigh were Genl. Blair[50] of So. Ca. and Gov. Murphy[51] of Alabama; we took in Mr. Archer[52] on the way. I came here without stoping and took a most violent and dangerous cold which settled in my head and after being in the house

---

[47] Richard Carney Cotten, of Hadley's Mills, Chatham County, served in the commons, 1816-1818, 1822, 1824, 1833-1836, 1850-1856. He was active in the militia and attained the rank of major general. He entered the Civil War as a captain in the 44th N. C. Regiment, of which he was later lieutenant-colonel.

[48] John Devereux De Lacey came to North Carolina for Robert Fulton in 1813 to make surveys and organize steamship companies. The Neuse Navigation Company employed him later. He was in Raleigh until his death in 1837.

[49] William Dunn Moseley (1795-1863), of Lenoir County, a graduate of the university, state senator, 1829-1836, (speaker, 1833-1835), moved to Florida later, and was the first governor of the State.

[50] James Blair (d. 1834), of South Carolina, Democratic member of congress, 1821-1822, 1829-1834.

[51] John Murphy (1786-1841), a native of South Carolina, and graduate of South Carolina College, moved to Alabama in 1818, became a lawyer, and was governor, 1825-1829, and a member of congress, 1833-1835.

[52] William S. Archer (1789-1855), of Virginia, graduate of William and Mary, member of the house of delegates, 1812-1819, member of congress, 1819-1835, United States senator, 1841-1847. He was a devoted Whig.

two days I have ever since been confined to my room and a part of the time to my bed. I hope I am now out of all danger and improving; my breast has escaped unhurt but my head is still affected slightly. I cannot give you scarcely any of the news of the city; on the evening preceeding the meeting of Congress I had the honor of a special invitation from the President to take Tea with him at the government Mansion. Mr. Senator Rives [53] of Virginia and my travelling companions Blair and Murphy were also of the party. Mrs. Donalson [54] done the honours of the Tea table in very neat stile. Genl. Jackson is more like Genl. John Moore [55] of Lincoln than any other man I know, and his manners are remarkably easy and elegant. I have never seen a good likeness of him; he is quite slender and tall and the expression of his face has nothing of that Roughness or savage expression which are presented in his portraits. The only defect on his face is that it is not quite *broad enough*. His diction and expression and pronunciation are just like our Scotch Irish kin in Mecklenburg; firmness and decission of character stand out in "bold relief" on the old veterans face.

I have not seen any of the other great men yet, however I have seen enough to satisfy me that among manny of *our great men* a great manny of them are *greatest a great way off.* There are a great number of young men in Congress and the Ladies I am informed say they never saw so manny young Ladies from a distance and others are still coming in. Genl. Hawkins [56] says he will produce at Christmas the prittiest and richest gall Miss Falkner of Warren that ever walked over the *Washington turf.*

*   *   *   *   *

[53] William Cabell Rives (1793-1868), of Virginia, who, after attending William and Mary, studied law under Jefferson. He quickly became active in Democratic politics, was a member of the house of delegates, 1817-1819, 1822, member of congress, 1823-1829, minister to France, 1829-1832, United States senator, 1833-1834; 1836-1845, again minister to France, 1849-1853. He was a member of the Confederate congress from the secession of Virginia, to the end.

[54] Emily (Mrs. Andrew Jackson) Donelson, Mrs. Jackson's niece, who was hostess at the White House.

[55] "General John Moore" (1759-1836), a native of Lincoln (now Gaston) County, member of the commons for seventeen terms, between 1782 and 1806. He was speaker, 1806. He was also a delegate to the conventions of 1788 and 1789.

[56] Micajah Thomas Hawkins (1790-1858), of Warren, a Democrat, served in the commons, 1819-1820; in the state senate, 1823-1827; and was a member of congress, 1831-1841. He was a member of the council of state in 1854.

From Joseph Graham.[57]   U.

Vesuvius Furnace 22 December 1833

We are in usual health here. The Furnace blowing, it works as well as common but owing to the Cold and severe weather is some what dificcult keeping a regular supply of Stock to keep going tho have not had much snow, still some on the ground since the 15th Instant and the Thermometer in the morning commonly ranges from 12 to 20°. About 10 days past Col. J. Davidson and family, Joseph Alexander (Beans son) & Family, Major Forney & Family, Doctor Winslow Alexander, and William Lee Davidson started to Alabama; had with them near 100 Negroes. Their views were on their Arrival to hire their Negroes to pick out Cotton, were advised they could get 75 Cents pr. Day for them. As soon as that arrangement could be made they would take Horse and cross the Tombigbee and explore the Country in the Chocktaw purchase if they found or could obtain any place to send them would return for their hands and begin improvements they all appeared to be undecided whether they would finally move, the whites expect to return in March. I availed myself of the oppurtunity of sending by Doctor Winslow Alexander Doctor Witherspoons proportion of the cash about dividing and wrote my views of the arrangement intended against next July or August. I have likewise written to Joseph and Alfred stating what measures are intended that their proportion of Money is ready if they can send for it by a safe hand.

In October I went to Salisbury to settle for the Iron I furnished for the Jail at the time the Convention on internal improvements were in Session. I heard their discussions on hat subject stated my views to some of them relative to Brunswick. from Colo. Dudley[58] (of Wilmington) I learned that tho the Channells both

---

[57] Joseph Graham (1759-1836), of Lincoln County, William A. Graham's father, was a native of Pennsylvania, who was brought as a child to Mecklenburg County. He had a long and distinguished career. He rose to the rank of major in the Revolution, and took part in fifteen engagements. After the war, he was sheriff of Mecklenburg, a delegate to the convention of 1788, where he voted against ratification of the Federal Constitution, and to the convention of 1789, where ratification was secured. In the same year he was elected to the original board of trustees of the university. He was a state senator, 1788-1792, was a brigadier general in the War of 1812, and took part in the Creek campaign. From 1791 until two years before his death he was, with great success, engaged in iron manufacturing, and planting.

[58] Edward Bishop Dudley (1787-1863), of New Hanover, a native of Onslow, which he represented in the commons, 1811, 1813, and in the senate, 1814. Moving to Wilmington, he represented the borough in the commons, 1816-1817, 1834-1835. He was a Whig member of congress, 1829-1831, and declined re-election, declaring that congress was no place for an honest man. He was the first governor elected by the people, and served from 1837 to 1841. Deeply interested in internal improvements in general, he was the first president of the Wilmington and Weldon Railroad.

at the Cape and New Inlet are somewhat altered in their Position yet as much depth as was upwards of half a Century past when Sir Peter Parker was there, the New inlet some deeper. He believes that Vessels of the same Class that comes into Charleston could come there, but his objections are that Brunswick is unhealthy surronded with Ponds. Query could not they be drained? that in the summer Vessels there or at Smithville were liable to be eaten with Worms or Barnacles on acct. of the Salt water as at Charleston from such injuries they are Exempt at Savanah & Wilmington having Fresh water to lye in. But admiting the advantages are susceptible of improvement at Cape Fear & merchants could ship direct to Europe they could not do it as Cheap as carry them to New York there is so much Shipping and packets and such Competition in the Carrying business. the price of Freightage is reduced so low that any Southern Merchant finds it more to his interest to employ them than do it himself—if so that part of the business must Regulate itself. Mr. Henry [59] of Fayetteville described the rates and Convenience of Transportation on the Cape Fear River I am satisfied it would be improper to have a Rail Road below Fayette and think that the point at which to start.

Mr. McBee[60] called on me on his Return from the Convention at Raleigh and I have since seen their Report if I understand their recomendation is the State to pass a Rail Road through the State to the Tenessee line and Companis might be incorporated to execute other projects or branches from it. As the chief difference in the Expense of a Rail Road of one mile more than another is grading the Tract or bringing it to the Required level the wood & Iron being always near the same cost there ought to be the greatest pains taken to give a location that in whole length will be the Cheapest grading and likewise in such a direction as will be approved of by those who live a Century after us, there ought to be a Reconizance of different Routs by skilful Engineers before any actual survey.

[59] Louis D. Henry (1788-1846), of Fayetteville, a native of New Jersey, and a graduate of Princeton read law under his uncle, Edward Graham, of New Bern, served in the commons, 1821-1822, 1830-1832, was a member of the council of state, 1835, declined the mission to Belgium, but served on the commission on claims against Spain. He was defeated for governor by John M. Morehead, in 1842.

[60] Vardry McBee (1775-1864), of Lincoln, a native of South Carolina, a self-educated man of fine sense, ability, high character and tireless industry. Before coming to Lincolnton, he had lived in Kentucky and Tennessee. He was clerk of the county court for twenty-one years, and, becoming the owner and operator of flour, cotton, woolen and paper mills, amassed a fortune. He moved to South Carolina, and was the promoter of the Greenville and Columbia, and the Seaboard and Roanoke railroads. He had many prominent descendants.

The general plan of Celebrating matrimony now is by a License from the Clerk of the County supposing an Act of Assembly was passed making it the duty of the Justice of Peace or Clergyman [page torn] penalties to endorse on the Licence the day of Celebration and [page torn] 5 or 6 persons names who were present & that in a suitable time he make Return of said Licence so Endorsed to the Clerks Office from which the Licence was obtained there to be filed may be had recourse to at all time hereafter. a suit in Rutherford considerable property in Contest a marriage said to have taken place in Granville or Warren some 30 or 40 Years ago. my neighbour Robey Attends, is, I believe, the only witness. in Indictments for Poligamy it might be useful

I know it is a delicate matter for members to interfere with private Bills which suppose dont concern them in the Year I think 1790 Genl. Dickson[61] from Lincoln in the Senate introduced a Bill the first of the kind to Restore Frederick Ward [62] to Credit. I was about to oppose it on the ground of fixing a precedent in such case but he stated Ward was a notable hand at Elections with a Certain Class I let it pass and from that Session to the present you may see the result on your Statute Book. could not the Legislature by some Law place such power (if Needful) elsewhere without deciding themselves on exparte Evidence?

The papers Recd. at this office gives but little accts. of your proceedings be pleased after Reading your Register to send me one giving the proceedings more in detail

Your affectionate Father

From David L. Swain. A.

The GOVERNOR
presents his respects to Mr. Graham
and requests the pleasure of his company
to tea, at 8 o'clock,
on the eve of the new year.
December 30, 1833

---

[61] Joseph Dickson (1745-1825), a native of Pennsylvania, who came to Rowan County, and was a member of the committee of safety there in 1775, and rose to the rank of brigadier general in the Revolution, settled in Lincoln, where he was clerk of court, 1781-1788, state senator, 1788-1795, and delegate to the convention of 1789. He was a member of congress, 1799-1801. He moved to Burke, and then to Tennessee, where he became a member, and speaker, of its lower house.

[62] No mention of Frederick Ward's name appears in the journal of that session.

1834

From James Graham.   U.

Washington, Jan'y 2d, 1834.

I received your letter of the 25th. ult. and learn this morning
in a letter from Guinn that the Resolutions instructing Mangum
had passed the Senate. I am well convinced Branch[1] and Carson
have injured Mangum's cause. Nullification is so odious in the
minds of the People in No. Ca. that it will injure any cause that
its leaders advocate. I feel not much solicitude about the result;
Mangum is a nullifier and only wanted an opportunity to denounce the President because of his determination to put down
Nullification, and the Bank question was selected for that purpose. I am satisfied I voted right, but I confess I was in bad company. The Raleigh Resolutions have been dictated by Demigogi-
cal office hunters and supported by men, by timid partisans whose
principals are governed by loaves and fishes. You ask my opinion
with regard to nominating Judge White[2] for the Presidency at
Raleigh. I believe from present appearances he will be in the
field with Van Buren and *no other candidate.* The Tennessee
Delegation (with 2 or 3 exceptions) are pledged for him and
active. One of them told me White's friends would be much
gratified at a nomination in No. Ca. *where he was born.* I feel
indifferent myself about the matter. Van Buren is a talented,
polished man. White is a plain honest man of fine talents but has
not that courtly polish of Van B. I incline to White. I believe he
is one of the most honest public men at Washington. If however
the Nullifiers come out for him they will *nullify him.* If White
is to be nominated at Raleigh or in primary assemblies, he ought
to be nominated by *original Jackson men,* and prevent the cry

---

[1] John Branch (1782-1863), of Halifax County, a graduate of the university, who
studied law under Judge Henderson, but never practiced. He was state senator, 1811,
1813, 1817, 1822; governor 1817-1820; United States senator, 1823-1829, when he
became secretary of the navy, but resigned when the cabinet broke up in 1831. He
was defeated for governor in 1838, and in 1844-1845 was governor of the Territory
of Florida.

[2] Hugh Lawson White (1773-1840), of Tennessee, a native of Iredell County, N. C.,
began the practice of law in Knoxville, was a justice of the supreme court, 1801-
1807, 1809-1815; state senator, 1807-1817; Federal district attorney, 1808; president
of the state bank, 1815; United States senator, 1825-1833, (president pro tem., 1832),
1836-1840; Whig candidate for President, 1836.

that he is brought out by his enemies. Judge McLean[3] of Ohio is out of the question, he is not talked of here. The Virginians & Georgians here are very generally for White. Old White is becoming very polite and is much gratified at the manifestations developing in his favour. My feelings are kind to Van Buren, and if it were not for that New York damnable principle of the Rober that "the victor is entitled to the spoils," I would be satisfied with him. My opinions are to yourself alone, to no one else. J. Q. Adams delivered an oration (to both branches of Congress, the President and an immense crowd) on the Life and Character of Lafayette that excells any thing of that sort in the last half Century. When published I will send it to you.

This City is becoming very gay. I was at a splendid square at Forsyth's on the night before new year. The parties will continue now for 5 or 6 weeks. I will go to about half; I don't like to dissipate too much in this climate.

I think the chances for a war with France decidedly preponderate towards Mars. I think the French Minister here so regards it. We shall be actively employed now every day late & early at the Capitol. It is difficult to say which of the numerous questions will claim most attention.

We have a deep snow here, the Slays are runing in every direction.

From James Graham.   U.

Washington, Jan'y 3d, 1834.

I wrote you yesterday but omitted to bring to your notice one subject that I conceive to be of importance to No. Ca. I suggest and propose to you to present some plan to the Legislature to perpetuate the Declaration of Independence in Charlotte, Mecklenburg County. This may be done by having an appropriate Painting in the Capitol at Raleigh, or a suitable marble monument at Charlotte. If No. Ca. does not do something to indicate her claim to this high distinction the other States will never believe in the daring Deed. Perhaps a committee appointed at this Session to propose a Plan to the next Legislature to hand down

---

[3] John McLean (1785-1861), of Ohio, a native of New Jersey, member of congress, 1813-1816; judge of State supreme court, 1817-1823; commissioner United States Land Office, 1823, postmaster general, 1823-1829, associate justice United States supreme court, 1829-1861, and supposedly a continual candidate for President.

this noble deed to posterity would be sufficient. Think about it—
and at all events bring it before the State. If the people of No. Ca.
are willing to surrender that *political Immortality* to which their
ancestors are justly entitled, they deserve the cold contempt of
all pure patriots.

From James Graham.   U.

Washington City, Jany 5th, 1834.

I received a letter from you about ten days since and would
have answered you fourthwith but my indisposition threw me
behind in my business and I have been exerting myself to get even
again with my engagements. On Wednesday last, being new years
day, I in conformity to the Custom of the City visited the President, his mansion was full to overflowing. The President stood in
one corner of the room receiving the congratulations of the season
and bowed for three hours from 12 until 3. Mrs. Donalson (attended by the maids of honour,) stood in another corner congeeing
and hearing all the soft sentiments and congratulations which hol-
liday hilarity so liberally bestow. All the Heads of Department,
the foreign Ministers and the officers of the Army and Navy in
full dress mingled in the crowded scene; you might tread on the
toe of a Secretary or Senator, or press a lady's leg without stoping
to ask pardon. Indeed the squese was so tight that it was difficult
to elbow through the mixed multitude and reminded me more
of a country frolic than the President's Levee. This is the morning star of the days of feasting and the evenings of dancing which
will quickly succeed in the entertainments of the Secretaries and
foreign ministers which are now in preparation and coming on
this week. On yesterday I went round and was introduced to all
the Secretaries and the P. M. General. I am much pleased with
Lewis McLean [4] and Gov. Cass; [5] the former is somewhat in his

---

[4] Louis McLane (1796-1857), of Delaware, served in the navy in 1798, and in
the War of 1812, was a member of congress, 1817-1827, senator, 1827-1829; minister
to Great Britain, 1829-1831, 1845-1846; secretary of the treasury, 1831-1833, secretary
of state, 1833-1834; delegate to Maryland constitutional convention, 1850.

[5] Lewis Cass (1782-1866), of Michigan, a native of New Hampshire. He walked to
Ohio in 1799, became a lawyer; was United States marshal, 1807-1813; rose to brigadier general in the War of 1812; was governor of the Territory of Michigan, 1813-
1831; secretary of war, 1831-1836; minister to France, 1836-1842; United States
senator, 1845-1848, 1849-1857; Democratic nominee for President, 1848; secretary of
state, 1857-1860.

manners like John Stanly, and I am more pleased with him than any gentleman I have yet seen here.

Webster has the most intellectual face I have ever seen and the bigest head; his hair and eyes are as black as a Ravan, and his whole countenance reflects light and knowledge through every feature in his face. He has been thus far silent in the Senate, and there is great trepidation among the ranks of Clay and Calhoun lest he may support the administration. I anticipate a rich intellectual treat from Webster when Calhoun's Proposition to repeal the force Bill comes up for debate. Mr. Van Buren is a small man of modest unassuming deportment; I have not been nigh enough to him to deliniate his face. He called to see me in my absence and left his card. On tomorrow we expect to hear Mr. Binny[6] of P. on the removal of the deposits. His effort is looked to with deep interest as he comes from a city manifesting more feeling on this subject than any other and his talents are of the highest order. The deposit question will consume a great deal of time. Indeed at this time it is impossible to say how long it may consume as there are a great number preparing to hold forth upon it. Rumor says here Mr. Tany's[7] appointment by the Senate is doubtful but I have heard nothing said about who may next be nominated. In many *of the States* exertions are making to present their favourite Candidate for the next Presidency, and I think if *a respectable portion of the* members of the Legislature of No. Ca. would now hold a meeting and nominate Mr. T. Ruffin for that high office that he would succeed. Such a nomination could in no event injure Mr. R. or No. Ca. and might be serviceable to both. There is a strong prediliction in many influential gentlemen in the non-slaveholding States to take a President South of the Potomac, and South Carolina has lost her hopes by Nullification, and Virginia has by talking about Secession, while old No. Ca. has had an abiding confidence in the Constitution and been "good and true" to the Union; and if she would *now* come out from her retirement and present an unbroken front in behalf of one of her distinguished citizens I believe she might prevail— at all events there is much to gain and nothing to lose and a

[6] Horace Binney (1780-1875), of Pennsylvania, graduate of Harvard, lawyer, served in the state legislature and was a Whig member of congress, 1833-1835.

[7] Roger Brooke Taney (1777-1864), of Maryland, graduate of Dickenson College, Federalist member of the state legislature, but a Democrat after the War of 1812, was attorney general of Maryland, 1827-1831; attorney general of the United States, 1831-1833; Anti-Bank secretary of the treasury, 1833-1834, nominated to the supreme court, 1835, but not confirmed; chief justice, 1836-1864.

nomination at this early period would direct the public eye to the individual named, and prevent our State from being forestalled or pledged to another. Consult some of our common friends if you coincide in opinion and see what the sense of the Legislature may be. If the State will aspire to her rank and respect herself, then may she hope to command and enjoy the Respect of others.

*   *   *   *   *

From Hugh Waddell.   U.

Hillsboro', Jany. 7th, 1834.

I fear some of my friends must have told you that I expected to be in the City by this time or you certainly would have written me. I was at Pitts [boro] during the Xmas holidays but have been at home now some days. From the last advices you seem to be going back, as compared with the beginning of the Session, Postponing all propositions for Internal Improvement, etc.

I have been much gratified to see & to hear that you have met the expectations of your friends in several efforts; particularly that on the Bank of the State. I desire to see you that we may talk over all these things by the fireside.

As you are thinking of adjourning, I will not now talk of Legislative matters. The principal purpose of this hasty scrawl is to enquire whether you will leave Raleigh for 8 or 10 days to come as I wish to go down some day next week.

*   *   *   *   *

From William Haywood, Jr.[8]   A.

Raleigh, 17 Jany., 1834.

You are appointed on the Central or Executive Committee for writing address, etc., &c. on the subject of Convention. I have the honour to be Chairman & the address is written & now ready for the press. How shall I manage to submit it to your criticism; if that will delay the publication, will you object to its being printed under your joint signature even before you see it. Please

---

[8] William Henry Haywood, Jr. (1801-1852), of Raleigh, a graduate of the university, Democratic member of the commons, 1834-1837 (speaker, 1835, defeating William A. Graham); United States senator, 1843-1846, when he resigned rather than vote for the Walker tariff.

write me immediately for this cause will be again defeated if we
do not publish at once.

We propose to publish Tracts & pamphets to follow the address.
One is already in a state of forwardness & I have written to others
as I do now write to you to take subscriptions for it. Prices are

Single copy	10 Cents
12 Copies	100 Cents
50 Copies	$3 —
100 ditto	5
300 ditto	10. —

P. S. If you possibly can do so you must *write for your paper*
now & then. Can you not prepare a pamphlet? I have undertaken as much as my time will permit me to do.

[Enclosure]

Raleigh, Jan. 17, 1834.

The Executive Committee appointed by the Convention meeting to prepare an Address, &c. are ready to publish it.[9] Much time
will be lost by waiting for remittances of money to cover the cost,
and indeed, we doubt whether the delay would not defeat the object in a great degree. Unless a large number shall be printed
no good will be done. If the discussion is delayed even a month,
it is to be feared that the public mind will lose every thing that
we have gained from the impetus which has been given by legislative action. We must print 6000 copies. The Printer must be
paid something—at least, he must not lose by it. The collections
in the counties are very uncertain. Will you agree to be responsible for $20, in case the fund which is reckoned to cover ex-
penses, falls short of the objects? As many of the Committee as
are in reach do so stipulate, and I write to others besides yourself
a letter similar to this, and as soon as we can get answers which
"assume the responsibility" the address shall appear. We propose
likewise to publish the Essays of SENEX,[10] *revised and improved
by the author.* This may be done by subscription. Raise a subscription in your county at the following prices: single copy at 10 cents

[9] It was published in the Salisbury *Western Carolinian*, March 29, 1834.
[10] A series of communications, signed *Senex,* written in advocacy of a constitutional convention, appeared in the *Raleigh Register* in the latter part of 1832 and
the early part of 1833. I have not been able to identify the writer.

one dozen at $1.00; 50 copies at $3.00; 100 copies at $5.00. And let us hear from you on the first part of this communication by return of Mail; on the latter part, in one month.

Yours respectfully,

Wm. H. Haywood Jr

Chairman.

N. B. If you will not pledge yourself for $20, how far will you go?

I send you this from Newbern, but you will address me at Raleigh.

From James Graham.   U.

Washington City, January 19th, 1834.

* * * * *

The Deposite Question is still under discussion and likely to continue some time yet. Every thing which appertains to regulating or controuling the currency is difficult and delicate and but few of our most talented men understand it's practical operation and effects and therefore but few speeches are to the point.

Mr. Binny has made a very able speech, it was rather too prolix and he dwelt too much on details but he is a most able and amiable man.

I dined on Tuesday last with the President; a large company sat down to the table *at candle light,* and such a variety and profusion and costly table furniture I have never seen. On this evening I am going to take my dinner with Mr. McLean.

I have been 2 nights at the Theatre. Miss Fanny Kemble has commanded the whole city to witness her winning and bewitching manners and highly gifted powers.

* * * * *

Genl. Saunders[11] has returned and is much pleased that *the Prisoner* was acquited and that he still Atto. Gen.

---

[11] Burton Craige had offered a resolution declaring the office of attorney general vacant, because of the acceptance of Romulus M. Saunders of the federal post of commissioner for the French Spoliation Claims. Graham, as chairman of a committee to investigate the question, wrote the report declaring him entitled to his office.

Address to the People of North Carolina,
on the Subject of
Amending the Constitution of the State [12]

The general right of a Majority of the qualified voters in a State to alter their Constitution in any manner which may suit the pleasure of that majority, is, in our country, indisputable. But the practice of the American States has determined, that the most ordinary, and perhaps therefore, the appropriate, method of remedying Constitutional evils, is through the medium of a State Convention, authorized, and in its incipient steps, regulated by law. Accordingly more than 30,000 freemen of this State, petitioned the last General Assembly, to provide means for the cure of evils in their Constitution, against which they have been complaining for more than 30 years. This application was made under the additional sanction of your Bill of Rights, which reserves to the people a right *"to petition the Legislature for a redress of their grievances, and to instruct their Representatives;"* but it was rejected by the House of Commons, after having passed the Senate in the shape of the Bill which has been appended to this Address.

On the evening of the day when this Bill, for taking the sense of the people, was rejected, a meeting of the Representatives of a majority of the people took place, for the purpose of adopting such measures as were best calculated to meet the just expectations of the majority. The greater number of them believing that a fair and free discussion of the alterations to be proposed in your Constitution, and of the grounds upon which a change is demanded, would reconcile the minority to their adoption, were unwilling to recommend to their constituents an exercise of the right to proceed *without the sanction of legislative authority;* but hoping that a common interest, a sense of justice, a proper respect for the fundamental principles of popular governments, and a disabuse of the public mind as to the motives of a majority, may co-operate to secure the assent of all sections to this necessary reform, determined to pursue the course indicated by their proceedings now laid before you. The question is thus presented before the highest human tribunal. An appeal has been taken from the servants of the people to the sovereign people themselves, and to us has been delegated the trust of presenting it to you for determination. Our duty will be best performed by omitting every appeal to your passions and prejudices, and we content ourselves by laying before you FACTS, which make this appeal irresistable, if it is to be determined by the rules of *justice, patriotism,* and *candor.*

[12] From the Salisbury *Western Carolinian,* March 29, 1834.

I. UNEQUAL REPRESENTATION.

The first and prominent defect in your State Constitution, which it is proposed to correct, is that part which allows to each county *three members* in our General Assembly, without regard to its size, population, and taxes. This is the source of gross injustice, of loud complaint, and of great political evil. Aware how easily you may be deceived into a distrust of general statements made in a political Address, and desirous to advance none that can delude, we have carefully prepared, from the Official Reports of our Financial Officers and the last Census taken under the authority of the United States, a Table which exhibits, at one view, the annual public Taxes, *Federal* Population, and *White* Population, of each county in the State. It is here inserted and we beg you to examine it:

TABULAR STATEMENT of Taxes, and White Population, and Federal Population, of the Counties of North-Carolina, compiled from the Revenue List of 1832, and the Census of 1830.

Counties		Public Taxes	Federal Population	White Population
Ashe	— —	$ 450	6,800	6,400
Beaufort,	— —	1,080	9,300	6,300
Bladen,	— —	700	6,600	4,500
Brunswick,	— —	500	5,300	3,000
Columbus,	— —	300	3,700	3,000
Currituck,	— —	400	6,700	5,200
Camden,	— —	650	5,900	4,500
Chowan,	— —	1,000	5,200	2,700
Carteret,	— —	450	6,000	4,800
Duplin,	— —	980	9,600	6,700
Franklin,	— —	1,100	8,700	5,300
Gates,	— —	700	6,400	3,300
Greene,	— —	650	5,200	3,900
Hyde,	— —	400	5,400	4,000
Hertford,	— —	1,000	7,000	3,800
Haywood,	— —	360	4,500	4,200
Jones,	— —	500	4,400	2,300
Johnston,	— —	1,050	9,500	7,000
Lenoir,	— —	700	6,100	3,700
Macon,	— —	400	5,200	4,900
Moore,	— —	470	7,100	6,000
Martin,	— —	970	7,200	5,000

Nash,	— —	970	7,000	4,500
Onslow,	— —	700	6,600	4,500
Pasquotank,	— —	1,100	7,600	5,000
Perquimons,	— —	800	6,300	4,300
Person,	— —	850	8,300	5,400
Richmond,	— —	850	7.900	5,600
Robeson,	— —	650	8,400	6,200
Sampson,	— —	980	10,200	7,600
Tyrrell,	— —	430	4,200	3,300
Washington,	— —	600	3,900	2,700
Wayne,	— —	1,050	9,000	6,600
Bertie,	— —	1,500	9,600	5,300
Craven,	— —	1,800	11,900	7,200
Edgecomb,	— —	2,000	12,100	7,600
Granville,	— —	1,900	15,700	9,400
Halifax,	— —	2,100	13,800	5,800
New-Hanover,	— —	2,300	8,600	4,900
Northampton,	— —	1,800	10,300	5,100
Pitt,	— —	1,300	10,000	6,800
Warren,	— —	1,500	8,900	4,200
Wake,	— —	2,500	17,200	11,400
Anson,	— —	1,000	12,200	9,100
Buncombe,	— —	1,000	16,500	15,600
Burke,	— —	1,400	16,200	14,000
Chatham,	— —	1,300	13,500	10,100
Cumberland,	— —	1,860	12,800	9,000
Caswell,	— —	1,300	12,600	8,400
Cabarrus,	— —	800	7,900	6,500
Davidson,	— —	940	12,700	11,300
Guilford,	— —	1,400	17,700	15,700
Iredell,	— —	1,100	13,800	11,500
Lincoln,	— —	2,050	21,000	17,600
Mecklenburg,	— —	2,000	17,200	12,800
Montgomery,	— —	800	10,000	8,500
Orange,	— —	2,300	20,900	16,000
Rockingham,	— —	1,100	11,200	8,400
Randolph,	— —	900	11,800	10,600
Rowan,	— —	1,700	18,300	14,500
Rutherford,	— —	1,500	16,200	14,000
Stokes,	— —	1,300	15,100	13,000
Surry,	— —	1,000	13,700	12,300
Wilkes,	— —	600	11,400	16,300

Are your laws founded upon the public will? Make choice of the basis which accords best with your opinions of equal right and justice, whether it be taxes alone, white population alone, or federal population alone; or population and taxes combined—still, you will perceive that in this State, a minority of *one-third* govern and tax a majority of *two-thirds*. The 33 counties first named in this table, elect a majority of both Houses of the General Assembly, and yet, they pay no more than one third of the public taxes. They contain but very few exceeding one third of the *Federal* population, and not one-third of the *white* population of the State! Is this equal?

The necessary expenses of your State Government are about 80,000 dollars per year, and, according to its organization, each county is a source of precisely the same cost to the public revenue, and there being 64 [1] counties, the proportion of each is $1250. But the same 33 counties which contribute less than one-third of this revenue, do cost more than half of the total amount. By recurring to the table, you will perceive that they pay $22,790, while they cost $41,250, which is an excess of 18,460 dollars *cost*, beyond their aggregate *taxes*. Is it just, that they should elect a majority of the Legislature?

Some of these counties cost you four times as much as they pay; others three times as much; many others, twice as much. Is it just, or wise, that their representation should be equal to the others?

There are twenty-four counties whose aggregate expense to your Government is more than double their aggregate public tax; and twenty of these do not pay into the Treasury a sum equal to the wages of their own Members, added to a just proportion of the incidental charges of *Legislation* alone; and twelve of them pay an aggregate tax of $5,400 only, whose representatives alone receive back $8,000! Is this right? Is it just towards a people whose revolutionary struggle rested upon the basis "that taxation and representation should go together?"

There are forty counties in the State which do not pay taxes to cover their cost to your Government, and is it prudent to refuse your aid in correcting the rule which vests them with the power of electing two-thirds of your law-givers?

Do the counties, which are thus deficient in their contributions to your public revenues, and so onerous by their cost, contain a federal or white population which can make up their claims to

---

[1] A new county was created at the last session, but as its statistics have not been ascertained, it is impossible to take it into account. (This footnote and the following two are those of the committee making the address.)

the representation they have? Are they in a condition to give personal services, or to bear personal burdens, which justify this exemption from pecuniary burdens, while they have equal representation with the largest counties? A reference to the table of their population will determine this question beyond all contradiction. Look at it, and then let reason and conscience answer these inquiries. Their population is as disproportionate to the *power* they exercise, as their taxes have been shown to be.

One man, in one section of the State, has as much political weight as *seven* in another, or six in another, or *five* in another, &c. *Two-thirds* of the community pay *one-third* of the same community to be their masters. Disguise it as you may, this is the naked truth. We would not weary you by comparing the population and taxes of separate counties together, nor can it be necessary that we should.

Yet we must not omit to state, that this subject has brought into existence and fosters a spirit of sectional hostility, which mars the peace of your Legislature, and materially impedes the advancement of the common good. This is so plainly true, that none who has any regard for his character, will venture to deny it.

These are some of the reasons which sustain the demand that has been made for Equal Rights:

The largest vote ever taken in the State, at the Election for President of the United States, was 53,000. At the last August election, more than half that number voluntarily voted in favor of changing this feature of your Constitution; and if polls had been kept open in all the counties under the authority of law, there is no doubt that nearly two-thirds of the voters would have sanctioned it. A majority, then, demand this reform of their Government; and will the minority refuse to provide for it by the established forms of law? Can they do so, and be consistent in their attachment to Republicanism? Is the privilege too trifling to create such zeal and perseverance among those who ask it? Then the sacrifice will be less to those who yield up a power which they can lay no just claim to. But the right of representation—a fair and equal representation of the people—is now another name for civil freedom; and the struggle for it can never cease while the spirit of Liberty exists in our land. Freemen who resist it, do injury to themselves; they cannot enter upon such a warfare, without selling their principles as slaves to the spirit of party. Policy, patriotism, and self-interest, unite in requiring them to do *justice* and preserve equality in their Government.

II. THE LEGISLATURE.

By your present Constitution, the General Assembly meet *annually,* and it is proposed to alter it so as to have *biennial* sessions, except in cases of emergency; and, at the same time, to diminish the number of members.

This is a proposition in which *all* are interested, and the alteration is demanded as well by your *necessities* as by your *interest.* One portion of your Representatives have been engaged in excited strife against another, and the People have been agitated by these *sectional contests,* until both Representatives and People seem to have lost sight of the *Financial concerns of the State.* We propose to invite your attention to this subject—to point out, if we can, the main cause of evils which will be shown to exist, and disclose the remedy that is proposed.

In a time of profound peace; without any effort deserving the name of an *attempt* to carry on great public works, for developing the resources and improving the internal communication of the State; without any serious loss of public funds; nay, at the close of a most profitable speculation in the Stocks of Banking corporations, you will be surprized to hear that the *Treasury is wretchedly poor,* and that, in all human probability, the next Assembly may not find *unappropriated money in it sufficient to pay their wages! !* We have no desire to mislead, and no motive to deceive you; but to anticipate the attempts of those who may think it is their interest to do so, (if there by any such,) we will present you the official evidence in our reach:

The Comptroller's statement to the Legislature of 1833, puts down the balance of Cash in the Treasury, on November 1st, 1833, at _____ $57,877

A part of this, to wit: $17,970, was the unexpended balance of $50,000, appropriated by the Legislature of 1832, for re-building the Capitol, and which has been expended since the Report, _____ 17,970

Leaving in the Treasury, an unappropriated balance, November 1st, 1833, of _____ $39,907

Now the expenses of the Legislature for 1833, paid at the Treasury on the 14th January, 1834, were_____ $42,000

The sums paid, and to be paid, before the 1st of November next, for the salaries of Executive, Judicial, and other Officers of State, amount to _____ 30,000

The incidental charges of Legislation, and contin-

gent charges of the Government, to be paid in like
manner, will exceed 8,000
The appropriations made by the Legislature of
1833, for re-building the Capitol—for defending
suits—for compensating Commissioners to revise
the Statute Laws, &c, &c, to be paid in like man-
ner, will exceed 80,000
    Making an aggregate of $160,000
To cover these appropriations for necessary expenditures, the
following sums of money will be in, or receivable at, the Treasury,
on or before the 1st day of November, 1834, to wit:
Balance before stated, unappropriated on the 1st
November, 1833 .... $39,907
The ordinary revenue of the State not exceeding 68,000
The amount of 2nd dividend of *Capital* Stock in
the Bank of Newbern, being 20 per cent. on 1818
shares, payable 1st of March, 1834, ... 36,360
The amount of Bonds for sale, of Treasurer Hay-
wood's property, uncollected November 1st, 1834........ 2,500
    Making, together, the sum of $146,767
Or $13,233 *less* than the amount of indispensable demands upon
the Public Treasury, during the current year. [2]

Is this the result of accident? It has been foreseen and fore-
told. The Finance Committee of 1832 and 1833—The Treasurer
in his Reports to the Assembly, and the Governor by message
in 1833, have called upon the Legislature to anticipate these
things. The Committee of Finance proposed to submit a plan
for remedying this evil by "*increasing the Revenue;*" or, in plain-
er words, "*increasing the public taxes.*" But the people, by a vote
of 30,000 freemen, petitioned the same body to remove this
grievance by *diminishing their number and making their sessions
biennial.* The call of the people was disregarded, and the proposal of the Committee was never acted upon. Where will you
look for the causes of results like these? The answer is not difficult to be made.

The expenses of your Government have gone on to increase
with the multiplication of counties. When public convenience
made the erection of a new county *necessary* and *unavoidable* in
one section of the State, another has been frequently erected elsewhere without necessity, in order to preserve legislative *power*

[2] See note in next column.

among the latter. The recollection of men who have outlived their party feelings, will attest this statement, and if it did not, we are sustained by your Statute Book, and the recorded proceedings of the General Assemblies. Thus the State which was, in 1776, divided into 36 counties, (including the whole of what is now Tennessee) has ceded away the better half of her territory, and the remainder is cut up into 65 counties. The Assembly which was once composed of 115 members has gone on to increase to 202. Their sessions, which were once held 3 and 4 and 5 weeks only, are now held 8 weeks. Their sessions, which once cost $15,000, now cost the people $50,000; and a Government which once cost less than $40,000 annually, now costs $80,000 and upwards. Have these increased demands on the Treasury been caused by the expense of the Judiciary? Let any one point out the addition of a hundred dollars for the expenses of the Judiciary since it was placed upon a respectable basis, and suited to the absolute necessities of the State, and we will show him, in return, the addition of twice the amount to the Legislative department; although, while the latter has been growing less suited to its purposes, the former has been improved. Have they arisen from the expenditure of money for public work? Let the humbled pride of your State answer. Not one monument of public spirit is within your borders, unless it may be your University, and for that you are indebted to the patriotism and liberality of individual contributions. Are they the result of any unprofitable speculations or pecuniary loss? Far otherwise is the truth. The State, by embarking credit in the three old Banks, has realized a clear profit of *one million of dollars, and* (as we will show presently) has thereby not hastened on, but delayed, the day of her poverty, or, we might more correctly say, has postponed the day of its discovery; and yet the greater part of it has been already squandered, and the last dollar will soon be consumed unless some salutary reform can be introduced into the Government.

Whence, then, does it happen?—what is the real cause of this intolerable public evil?

1. "The ordinary revenue is between 12,000 and 15,000 dollars less than the *necessary* annual expense of the Government, and this has been the case for many years" — so say your public officers of Finance, and so have your Legislative Committees reported. The sources from which this deficiency has been supplied, (viz: the Bank Dividends and tax) are of late nearly discontinued, and will soon be exhausted. 2. The General Assembly

costs, yearly, *four or five-sevenths* of the revenue, in consequence
of their increased numbers and longer sessions. 3. These long
sessions are brought about by several causes; one is, that "large
bodies move slowly," and another, that sectional party strife has
grown up from the demands for reform of the Constitution on
the one side, and a determined resistance to it on the other;
another is, that the Legislature is clothed with the power of
electing Militia Officers, Justices of the Peace, and the *Governor,*
and these elections create contests and *electioneering;* another is,
that a system of *local* legislation for particular counties has become habitual, and is unchecked.

If the causes are here truly assigned, (and that they are, in a
great degree, none will doubt,) can you be at any loss for the
remedy of your condition? The expenses of the Legislature may
be diminished more than 25,000 per annum, by reducing the
number of members to 120 or 130, and by having *biennial* sessions. Thus, its annual cost may be reduced below one-third of
the revenue. By this means, and by transferring to the people
the right of electing their Governor, and by giving the appointment of Militia Officers and Justices of the Peace to some other
tribunal, its sessions will be shortened. You will be relieved from
the dishonor and expense which sectional controversies entail
upon the State, by giving equal representation to every part
of the community, according to a scale of population and taxation combined, and these together will furnish a salutary check
upon local legislation.

Can you call this question a *sectional* question? What portion
of the State—what *county*—is not deeply interested in its accommodation? There is no complete redress except by *reforming
the Constitution.* The censorious may set down the evil to a
want of public spirit and patriotism among your servants, but it
will not be just to do it. The Legislature might, it is true, increase your taxes, and thus alleviate the evils, by removing some
of their causes; but the effect would be temporary only; and,
were it otherwise, they have given the clearest proof that this
would be an unwelcome remedy, by declining for two years and
more to apply it. You can perceive how ineffectual it would certainly be as a relief to any, whilst it would be ungenerous to
some sections, and unjust to others. Those counties who pay
revenues beyond their expenses might unite in proposing a like
partial remedy by requiring each county to pay its own members out of the *county* Treasury; but it is vain to discuss a prop-

osition of this kind where two-thirds have a direct interest to oppose it. These, however, and all other legislative action unsanctioned by the sovereign will, would be temporizing expedients. The evil is a great one; its cause is the constitutional organization of the Legislature; the *People alone* can correct it.

True, there are 117,000 dollars in the hands of the Treasurer, which we have not reckoned in our preceding estimates, because the sum has been set apart by law to accumulate as a *School fund*, and is subscribed to the new Bank by the President and Directors of that fund, under the direction of our last General Assembly. True it is, likewise, that the State owns Bank stock to a considerable amount, diminished as it has been by a regular annual drain to supply these annual deficiencies. These stocks have been the means of creating false hopes, in many respects. They who used them for that purpose, have good reason to believe that no prudent State would permit her necessary expenses to exceed the ordinary revenue, and therefore may be entirely acquitted of blame. But, it has been said, with equal truth and force, that your affairs have "come to a crisis," when all your servants are bound to lay the truth as it is before the people, and leave the result to their patriotism and intelligence. Permit us, therefore, to give you some account of these funds, to show (as we can without doubt,) that more than half the amount is already consumed by the thriftless course of public proceedings, and to demonstrate how soon the other half will follow it, unless there is some efficient reform:

The State owns 2768 share of Stock in the State Bank, which this Bank is now dividing among the proprietors. The Stockholders valued it, by authority of law, at $80 per share; but the State received last year $50 upon the share at the 1st division of Capital. It is *expended - not re-invested.* Hence, the residue of Stock will be $30 per share, or _____$83,040 [3]

The State owns 1818 shares of Stock in the Bank of Newbern, in the same condition—valued by the Stockholders at $65 per share, (worth $70,) but the State received last year, at 1st dividend of Capital, $25 on the share, and receives this year, at 2nd dividend thereof, $20 on the share. The former is *expended,* not *re-invested*—the latter is included in the preceding estimates. Hence, there is a residue of Stock in the Bank of New-

---

[3] Since this Address was prepared, the State Bank has declared a 2nd Dividend of Capital, by which the State receives $20 per share the present year; but this can make no difference in the general result of these calculations, however it may relieve the present necessity of our Treasury.

bern, equal to $25 on the share, or_____$45,450

The aggregate of these two values of Stock is_____$128,490
But there is a deficiency already shown of _____ $13,233
There are about $70,000 Treasury notes re-
    deemable at the Treasury, (including
    10,000 which we have understood are
    redeemed and burned, but which come
    into next year's Treasury Report,)
    which notes were issued to pay for the
    Bank Stocks _____ 70,000
The Legislature have directed the whole
    Statute Laws to be digested for publica-
    tion, and at a very moderate estimate, it
    will cost $10,000 more to publish them_____ 10,000

These, added together, will make_____93,233
And being deducted from the above bal-
    ance of $128,490, the difference is the
    real amount of your State Bank and
    Newbern Stocks, which will be on hand
    at their close, viz: _____$35,527
A sum barely sufficient to meet the deficiency in your ordinary
revenue for two years; but which may not be received in time
to answer that object for the present year.

We wish to put the whole case before you. The State owns
also $200,000 worth of Stock in the Bank of Cape-Fear, not
taken into view by us, because the charter of that Institution is
extended, and therefore the Stock cannot be used unless it is *sold*
to meet the *wants of the Government,* and gradually consumed
by the same operations that have wasted the other Stocks. This
Stock is all that will be left in a few years, (with the addition
of a few Bank shares belonging to the School Fund,) of the Capital and profits derived by the state from Bank *Dividends,* and
taxes, and *Bonus* for charters. The amounts of these profits are
are thus stated in the official report of a Committee raised by
the Legislature of 1832, viz:

Dividends of profits to 1832, from the three Banks_____$860,000
Taxes paid by Bank of Newbern and Cape-Fear, 1832_____ 240,000
Bonus paid by Bank of Newbern and Cape-Fear,_____ 36,000

        Together, equal to _____$1,136,000

But, besides this, the State owned $125,000 in Government stocks, which the economy of earlier days had provided, and which were invested in these Banks, and it is sunk with the rest. Mark it! Here are one million and a quarter reduced to a fifth of that sum, and though the latter is diminishing every year, by the *necessary* expenses of the Government - by the expensiveness of legislation—you will be urged to withhold the instructions by which alone this can be effectually checked. Fellow-Citizens, will you listen to the counsels of mere sectional party-spirit under such circumstances? Or will you heed the calls of sacred justice, and enlightened patriotism, seconded as they are by the warnings of self-interest? Let not passion nor prejudice answer the inquiry.

This subject presents a forcible appeal to such among you as *desire* to see the State embark upon a scheme of Internal Improvements suited to her necessities, and calculated to elevate her character. Were a loan taken by the State, sufficient to commence operations in such a work, the funds must be under the control of a Government whose *necessary* expenses exceed the ordinary revenue $15,000 per year; and who does not know that the system would be a "scape goat" to the sin of all other expenditures, and become odious? Would the people at large be taught to discriminate, when it is notorious that few among you possess or have sought after any knowledge of our finances for many years? Depend upon it, you will never command money for the expenditure, or enterprise to pursue a system of great public works, if you are to rely upon an increase of taxes equal to the present deficiency of revenue for governmental purposes, added to the enlarged demand on it for the interest of a State debt. Far be it from us to damp the ardor of patriotism in the pursuit of an object so worthy of the State, so necessary to her prosperity and her character. But these are not times for concealing facts. The occasion requires of us to state without fear what we believe to be true. If, however, the State expenses can be diminished by a judicious reform, and harmony restored to her counsels, then the proceeds of your *Western Lands,* when disposed of, and your remnant of Stocks, will leave you the means to meet the interest of a loan for Improvements; and there cannot be a doubt of sucess, unless North-Carolina is destined to occupy in history the chapter of *exceptions* forever.

Tedious as we have been on this point, we feel constrained to add, that the expensiveness of your Legislature is not the only objection to its present organization. At an early period of our history as a State, the annual meeting of your Representatives was perhaps wise and necessary; but now it afflicts the country by too much legislation; it engenders two evils where it corrects one. The statute book is laden with laws which three men were permitted by *courtesy* to pass for the county represented by them, without debate among the rest of your representatives, merely because they were *local*. Unless some prudent check is applied, a few more years will give each county a code of its own. Local legislation "has increased, is increasing, and ought to be diminished." We may be deceived, but we think it proceeds from *County* representation in both branches of the Legislature. The people are not informed of the acts of one Assembly, before another Assembly has met and may have repealed or modified them. They are never able to test the sagacity of their Representatives by the results of experience, under the laws they have been the instruments for making, before a new election. Even the Sheriffs of the State are not unfrequently ignorant of material alterations made in the laws for collecting the revenue, until after they have incurred the forfeiture of neglecting their provisions. These, we confidently assert, are some of the legitimate fruits of *annual* Legislatures.

III

We have anticipated, by the preceding remarks, the statement of that basis of representation which is demanded, and the reduction of members, which is proposed. If there be any more just and republican standard, let it be offered. It is to regulate the scale of representation according to *Taxes* and *Population*. It is not proposed, by any, that your representation should be based on either of these separately. Such charges, are the pretexts of a prejudiced opposition to reform. But to meet, in a spirit of conciliation, even the prejudices, and to accommodate the habits and views of the minority, the majority, who ask this measure of justice, have pledged themselves that each *County,* no matter how small its population or taxes, must have the election of one member, whatever the ratio shall be which is fixed on. It is more than strict equality required of them, but we do not believe that any human power will induce this majority or their Representatives to disregard the pledge, if it is acted upon by the minority. The very small Counties in the State are peculiarly interested in embracing this conciliating offer, unless they have resolved to hazard the effects of additional exasperation, notwithstanding the certainly of ultimate success which awaits a cause resting upon the immutable principles of justice, and supported by a clear and unequivocal expression of the public will.

IV.

By the present Constitution, the election of your *Governor* is vested in the General Assembly, and it is proposed to transfer the exercise of this power to the people. It ought to be a sufficient reason for this change, that the Chief Executive is the officer of the People, and they desire to make the election themselves. Are *you* prepared to admit that this would be unsafe or unwise? The Governor has no power or patronage by which he can control or corrupt the election. According to the theory of free governments in this country, he is intended to act as a salutary check upon legislative encroachments. This is the great axiom of freedom, which your Bill of Rights affirms when it declares that the "Legislative and Executive Departments of the Government ought to be kept forever separate and distinct from each other;" and yet it is remarkable, that your Governor is kept in a state of absolute dependance on the Legislature. *They elect him annually, and regulate at will his salary.*

The Legislative Department of this State's Government, is, in practice, subject to little or no control. The Judges elected by them, 'tis true, hold their office by a permanent tenure, but even they are paid according to legislative pleasure, and the very nature of the judicial office excludes their interference with questions that are merely political. And if the *public will* were so effectual a check as political theorists say it is, the causes which have impelled us to address you would never have continued long enough to make this appeal necessary.

We have now laid before you the grievances which are complained of - the proof that they exist - the necessity for their cure by your own action - and, in part, the hazard of delaying it longer. The other parts of your Constitution which the advocates for Reform have proposed to alter, might give little cause for complaint, if these evils were removed. But the scrupulous performance of our trust requires that we should notice *all*.

V.

The proposition upon the subject of Slaves and Slavery, as it exists in this State, requires some explanation. The opponents of a Convention had repeatedly charged the advocates of the Reform of our Representation with a design to impose unequal burdens upon the Master, and, perhaps, interfere otherwise with his rights. The charge might have been repelled by a bare denial, and the absence of all proof to sustain it—or by the fact that *all* parts of your State contain a large Slave population—but the Representatives of a majority, determined to remove even a pretext for hostility against their just claims, consented to accept this modification, to put these things beyond the reach of ordinary contingencies.

VI.

It is also proposed to abolish Borough Representation, in whole or in part. If there be any towns in the State whose peculiar interests require, and whose population justifies a continuance of this privilege, it will be preserved by the Convention.

VII.

The present Constitution makes it *imperative* on the Legislature to elect Field-Officers of the Militia by *joint ballot,* and to nominate Justices of the Peace. It is believed that these powers might be more judiciously exercised, and certainly they would be more economically performed, by such tribunals as the Convention may think it best to invest with either or both. Whatever the theory of this provision may seem to be, the General Assembly is, in practice, a very unfit depository of these powers. The Officers of the Militia are elected without any previous knowledge of the qualifications of candidates, and a recurrence of the period at which your Constitution was framed, will show why it was *then* thought expedient to give your Legislature the exclusive right of electing these Officers. This was then a sovereign State, in the largest sense - maintained its own army, and organized its own forces. The war of the Revolution for Independence had begun and was urged with fury within your borders, and neither the Constitution of the United States, nor the Act of Confederation, had been ratified. As to Justices of the Peace, each county delegation do in *practice* make the nomination for their respective counties, and before the County Courts were divested of all their patronage, this privilege was not unfrequently abused.

VIII.

In the ninth section of the Preamble to the Bill which is appended, there is some obscurity in the words "to make some change in the requisite qualifications of *Members* and *Voters.*" It is to be regretted that these changes had not been specially pointed out. If, however, the measure meets with your sanction, your Representatives having entire control of it in the next Legislature, can make it more explicit. We are warranted in saying that nothing more was intended by these words, among the advocates of Reform, than to clothe the Convention with power to give to individuals, not owning 300 acres of Land, a right to be elected *Senators,* if they own a full-hold of less extent, though of equal value, and to clothe them with authority to divest *free negroes* of the right of voting at elections, or else to restrict this right to such of them only as have interests at stake in the country, and a character to deserve the privilege; and also to establish some constitutional rule by which these may be designated. It is not designed to limit the elective franchise of *free white men,* in any way, nor to alter the Constitution on these subjects, except as we have here explained to you.

IX.

The 32nd Article of the Constitution excludes from civil office all who may deny the truth of the Protestant Religion. This has no *practical* effect, for the plain reason, that there is no tribunal established by the Constitution to determine a man's faith. It is an odious badge of prejudice, which the enlightened liberality of the present day should scorn to wear. It is an unjust imputation against the Catholics of this State, to attach to them any such disqualification. The patriotism, personal virtues and ability, and the disinterested public services of a single individual, in the State, brand with falsehood the idle fears that are implied by this *paper restriction.* How far it is consistent with the spirit of Protestantism itself—how far it is compatible with the Bill of Rights, which declares "that all men have a natural and unalienable right to worship God according to the dictates of their own conscience," we leave to that bigotry which would perpetuate this stigma.

X.

Experience has taught us that some mode of amending the Constitution ought to be pointed out by the instrument itself. To prevent disorder, by a recurrence to fundamental principles, the mode of reform should be made practicable, and, to exclude a mere spirit of innovation, it must not be rendered too easy. This is all that the friends of the measure ask.

We have been necessarily prolix in the consideration of this important subject, and it is a source of regret with us that the compass of an Address like the present, will not allow us to discuss the modes in which these amendments to your Constitution might be effected. Let none, however, deceive you by his idle fears of a Convention. The delegates of the people, when elected, will have no *unlimited powers;* none such are desired. The act which your Legislature may pass, will be their sole warrant, its validity will be derived from the sanction of the People, who alone are sovereign. The act of the Legislature will become the act of the people whenever it is ratified by them, and is only a form by which the specific delegated powers are embodied and expressed. Delegates, clothed with like limited authority, have assembled in every State of the Union. They have assembled twice in this State—and an instance cannot be found in the history of the States, where they have undertaken to disregard the powers that were vested in them, or to pass the boundaries which a sovereign people had marked out. The indulgence of a suspicion which excites alarm at the organization of such a body, would subvert all the principles of action which arise from observation and experience, and would seem to be a mere pretext for opposition, really intended to mask a secret apprehension that an intelligent *people* are not competent to govern themselves.

We all claim to be Republicans—we profess to believe that the principles of a free government are established by the *practice* of the American States, and that they are no longer mere abstractions. But if injustice like that which we have shown to exist, if public evils like those we have pointed out to you, will not move into action the Legislative powers of the Government to provide some safe method of reforming the Constitution, so as to redress these grievances, to remove this injustice, to heal our divisions and give peaceable effect to the will of a majority of the People—*then* that Constitution is *unalterable except by a Revolution.*—It will be thus divested of the only criterion which distinguishes laws from dictates, rightful government from usurpation, freedom from servitude; and you, at least, will in effect declare that the great principles of a popular government are too dangerous to be practical—that they are no more than the mere ornaments of government—deceptive and useless in its administration.

FELLOW-CITIZENS: We know that these efforts to arouse the public mind to a consideration of State affairs will provoke a suspicion of motives among some, of censure from many, and a sneer of pretended scorn from others. In defiance of such obstacles, we have ventured upon the duty assigned to us by a respectable portion of your Representatives.

We are not sectional partizans. We "go for the State and the whole State." But we have seen her Legislature distracted by party spirit, and councils divided by sectional interests which are supposed to be different, but are in fact the same, until her name has become a bye-word of ridicule, and her own citizens become startled at the inculcation of principles asserted in their Declaration of Rights, and are growing too timid to advance one step in the race for honorable distinction and the fear of party reproach shall not drive us from the attempt to rescue her character, and re-animate her spirit.

We are not Alarmists! But we have observed the progress of causes calculated to stir into action a storm of popular indignation. We have seen the petition of 30,000 freemen, for redress of an admitted grievance, rejected by the Representatives of the people; and we have witnessed the excitement under which their immediate Representatives have returnd among them—we have ascertained, by impartial examination, the utter ruin which an uncorrected action of the present state of things must entail on our prosperity, and we will not timidly renounce the right to speak, or uncandidly conceal the furious agitations which threaten the peace and quiet of the State, in order to escape the passing censure of those who we think are misled from the course of true policy by their prejudices; or of those who are really indifferent to the condition of the Republic, while they flatter themselves that this ease is the fruit of a virtuous courage. We hold, that, in a free State, the will of the majority ought to be supreme. But we are not the advocates of licentiousness. It is because we would avert its evils, because we most sincerely deprecate its approach, that we invoke the people of every section and of every county to give this subject a dispassionate consideration—to remember that we can have no more wholesome legislation until it is de-

termined—to recollect that it is not a sectional question, when
properly regarded—to bear in mind that it has been pressed upon
the Legislature for more than 30 years, without any abatement of
zeal or determination among the people who have urged it—and
then to decide whether a cause resting upon clear principles of
truth and justice—which is commended by the interest of the
whole State, and enforced by her necessities—which is advocated
by the decisive voice of a majority of the people which connects
with it the great subject of State Improvement—whether such a
cause will not oblige them to instruct their Representatives in
the next Assembly to give to it their sanction, so as to make us
one people in feeling as we are already one in interest, and so
to do justice to a *majority* of the people, and remove the grievances of *all*. For ourselves we have so much confidence in the
straight forward integrity of the people, as not to hesitate in
believing that a fair, candid, free discussion, will lead to this happy
result in every county; and, in our judgment, *they* will assume a
heavy responsibility, who shall impede it by withholding correct
intelligence, or by appealing to the prejudices, or alarming the
fears, of a minority.

> WM. H. HAYWOOD, JR.
> WM. A. GRAHAM,
> R. M. SAUNDERS,
> WESTON R. GALES,
> JAMES SEAWELL,
> WM. R. HARGROVE,

Committee.

Raleigh, January, 1834.

From James Graham.   U.

Washington, Feb. 23d, 1834.

I have recd. yours of the 15th. inst. and I would have written you some time since but was doubtful where I should write. We have an animated scene going on here. Mr. Rives, the Senator of Va. recd. instructions from the Legislature of his State instructing him to vote for the restoration of the Deposites; having made a speech against the restoration he could not consistently vote against his own speech, and on yesterday *resigned* his seat in the Senate. Report says he will be offered a seat in the Cabinet. I spent last evening with him at Mr. V. Burens. I do not believe he will accept any appointment under the President at present. I regret the loss of Mr. Rives in the Senate, tho I think him wrong on the desposite question. He has followed the example of Mr. J. Q. Adams who *resigned* his seat in the Senate after receiving Instructions on the Embargo Question.

We have the prospect of a protracted Session and one in which little will be done. The Deposites will *not be restored* and no Bank will be Chartered this Session as I believe. Mr. Webster informed me he would make the attempt to extend the Charter of the present Institution. I believe it will fail at present. The opposition have been so violent and abusive that the friends of the Executive will sustain him at all hazards. I have not conversed with one member who thinks the original act was right, yet they say as it has been done, it is unnecessary to replace them.

You have seen the sudden deaths of Judge Bouldin [13] and Mr. Wirt [14] announced in the papers.

I have in the last fortnight been at numerous parties and become a good deal interested in the Society here. I very rarely meet any of my Colleagues at the parties. They appear to be afraid of the urbanity of City company.

Genl. Newland of Burke is here arranging his contracts in the P. O. Dept. He swells, like a frog at a fountain, and tells me he will be a candidate in the Senate for Burke County next Summer. He also desires to be appointed one of the Examining committee

[13] Thomas T. Bouldin (1772-1834), of Virginia, lawyer and judge, Democratic member of congress, 1829-1834. Wise had rebuked him in the house for failure to announce the death of his predecessor, and Bouldin, rising to reply, dropped dead.

[14] William Wirt (1772-1834), of Virginia, a native of Maryland, took part in the prosecution of Aaron Burr, was attorney general of the United States, 1817-1829, and was the Anti-Masonic candidate for President in 1832. He was author of a life of Patrick Henry, and of "Letters of a British Spy."

to go to West Point and examine the Military cadets at Wt Point. God save the State from this generation of hungry office hunters and deluding demagogues. Seven out of 13 of the Rep. of No. Ca. will vote for the restoration of Deposites, and a majority will vote the same way from here to Florida.

The Debate in the Senate is growing warm and somewhat personal. Forsyth [15] is a very handsome Debater and in skirmishing warfare excells anyone in the Senate. On yesterday he stated it was the intention of the Administration to put down the U. S. Bank now and the State Banks after a while. Webster asked him, very triumphantly, how this government would interfere with State Institutions. The Question could not be answered.

I presume the repeal of the force Bill will come up next after the deposites

From James Graham.   U.

Washington, April 1st, 1834.

My friend Genl. Blair of So Ca *has just* this day committed suicide by shooting himself in the head above the ear. Blair had been unwell and melancholy for some days and had just recd. a letter from his family which he asked Gov Murphy to read to him—and while the letter was reading by Murphy, Blair went to a drawer & secretly drew out a Pistol and instantly applied it to his head and blew out his Brains and fell a dead man without giving any notice.

Your friend Jos. S. Jones, Mr. Galloway, and a son of Cad. Jones are all here spending a week or two. The Miss Gastons are also here returning from N. York. I have been introduced to them. They appear to be fine girls, they will leave next week for No. Ca. I have lately been at a party in Alexandria, and one in Georgetown. They both have much beauty and fashion. But I have resolved not to acquire the name of a Gallant here, and therefore I shall prefer to make my entrance gradually into the gay circle. There is but little intercourse between Alexandria and Georgetown and this City. Our Merchants are passing daily from No. Ca. to the North. I learn from them that my constituents

---

[15] John Forsyth (1780-1841), of Georgia, a native of Virginia, was educated at Princeton, was state attorney general, 1808; Democratic member of congress, 1813-1818, 1823-1827; United States senator, 1818-1819, 1829-1834; minister to Spain, 1819-1823; secretary of state, 1834-1841.

generally approve my course on the deposite question. The debate is still progressing but will terminate this week, and I am glad of it. The vote will be a close one though I presume it will sustain the removal. Genl. McKay [16] is trembling in his skin and can't tell which will be the strong side. Mr. Choate [17] of Massachusetts made one of the best Speeches I have heard this Session, I will send it to you when published.

From James Graham.   U.

Washington, April 16th, 1834.

I received your letter a few days since. As to our friend Waddell's business with regard to Gov. or Gen'l. Nash, [18] I attended to that some time since, but he wrote to Mangum as well as my self and we both attended to it, and it was agreed that Mangum shoud write and send a letter from P. Hagner [19] stating the facts in relation to the matter. I hope you will state this to my friend Mr. Waddell. I much regrett the difficulties of his relations in the West India Islands, And will do what I can for them. You know that business belongs to the State Department and Mr. McLean has promised as soon as the U. S. will send a Minister to England that disgraceful scene shall be made the subject of immediate negotiation. Our Relations with England demand that we should have always a Minister at that Court, but the hostile attitude in which the President and Senate stand towards each other has prevented that desirable object.

You have seen from the N. Papers the lamentable condition of the local Bank in this quarter. The Bank of Maryland just failed, Two Banks in this City have stoped payment, one in Georgetown and one in Alexandria, and I am apprehensive a

---

[16] James Iver McKay (1793-1853), of Bladen County, state senator, 1815-1819, 1822, 1826, 1830, member of congress, 1831-1849.

[17] Rufus Choate (1799-1859), of Massachusetts, a graduate of Dartmouth, eminent lawyer, member of state legislature, M. C. 1831-1834, senator, 1841-1845, who refused all public office thereafter except membership in the constitutional convention of 1853.

[18] General Francis Nash (1742 *ca.* -1777), of North Carolina, who was killed at the Battle of Brandywine. Congress authorized the erection of monuments to him, and General William Lee Davidson (1759-1781), who was killed at Cowan's Ford, but never appropriated any money. William A. Graham endeavored all his life to secure the necessary appropriation. The monuments were finally erected at Guilford Battle-Ground, in 1903.

[19] Peter Hagner (1772-1850), a native of Pennsylvania, who was in the service of the federal government, chiefly in the treasury, for nearly fifty-seven years.

greater part of the State Banks throughout the Southern and Western country will stop pay't., and consequently their Notes will become greatly depreciated and the people much distressed. I think No. Ca. will sustain less loss and embarrassment than any other State in the Union, because she has fewer State Banks than her sisters, and because she (fortunately at this time) has but few State Bank notes in circulation. This Executive Experiment sickens the well and kills the sick. Some of the supporters of this measure begin to look pale and thoughtful, and I begin to hope if they can be furnished with a plausible pretext they will turn from the error of their ways and be willing to at least try and relieve the distress of a suffering community. The plain truth is, the excessive issues of Notes by the State Banks far beyond their ability to redeem or pay must have before long, without this improper interference of the Executive, produced great and general alarm in the Country and ruined thousands of People, and the President by his medling with a machine, the operations of which he did not understand, has hastened and aggravated a State of things which was obliged to burst upon the country. The State Legislatures have been running wild, yes mad, in multiplying Banks; they have been *minting Notes* and legislating value on paper and building charters and castles in the Air without looking to the solid foundations of the basement story; some of the State Banks have $10 in paper in circulation for $1 in Silver in their vaults; and if there be alarm in the country, the holders of the notes will forthwith return the Notes and demand specie. The Tempest, the Tornado has been raised by the President, unintentionally to be sure, and the hurricane is prostrating all the unsound State Banks as rapidly as though they were so many hollow rotten trees in the forest. If these rotten trees would fall only in the Forest and not in the husbandman's field upon the rich fruits of his labour and industry I should not regret the fall. But it is no respecter of Persons—and when or where, or how it will stop God only knows.

The Miss Gastons are still here or rather in Georgetown. I called over once to see them, but they were out, so I left my card. Jo. S. Jones, our historian, is still here, I have become acquainted with nearly all our great men here. Mr. Calhoun was lately delivered of his rickety Bantling speech on his proposition to repeal the Bill called the force Bill. It was a signal failure—metaphisacal nonsense and absurd abstractions. Clay followed him not in a speech, but in one of his happiest hits at *Ridicule* and *Sarcasm*.

He said good things and *looked bitter ones,* and confounded and annihilated Nullification. Calhoun looked like he was at a frolic where he was not welcome, and as though he was cursing himself for Intruding. Preston came to his aid, but the Gen'l was over powered and defeated and driven from the field before his *man Friday* could get his armour on, and I never saw two men so utterly unhorsed and unmaned, while the Senate and Spectators were delighted beyond description.

On this day we buried Mr. Denny [20] one of the Members of Maryland; this is the 3rd death in Congress this Session.

From Frederick S. Blount.   A.

Mobile, April 22nd, 1834.

The subject of the present letter has for some time occupied my mind, and after mature reflection, I have concluded to communicate with you thereon leaving it completely at your option, to act as may seem best to you.

Since I had the pleasure of seeing you in Hillsborough in 1831, I have been residing in this city in the practice of my profession the duties of which I find laborious and fatiguing. The confinement to the office during the *entire* day is exceedingly onerous; during the Session of the Courts I am frequently compelled to sit up until one or two o'clock in the morning making preparation for the succeeding day. Men among my professional brethren who have the largest show of practice have formed partnerships, thereby lessening the fatigue and labour of the profession, yet not materially diminishing the profits they would singly receive. My practice is not yet so extensive as that of a few, who have resided here for a long period of years previous to my arrival, yet it has exceeded my most sanguine expectations. During the last summer I visited all the Northern cities, and made extensive acquaintances in each among the merchants and others doing business with the city. At this time I am beginning to realize some of the benefits of the enterprize.

Mobile has a population of six thousand two hundred inhabitants, and it has increased twelve hundred in twelve months.

---

[20] Littleton Parnell Dennis (1786-1834), of Maryland, educated at Yale, served in the Maryland house of delegates, 1815-1816, 1819-1827; in the executive council, 1829; was a presidential elector, 1800, 1812, 1824, 1828, and a member of congress, 1833-1834.

I have not seen in any part of the Union in which I have travelled any town or city advancing so rapidly in wealth population and business. Its exports and imports are equal to about twenty millions. In addition to those branches of practice familiar to you in North Carolina, we have here a large share of Admiralty business.

The District Court of the United States holds a Session in this City semi-annually. The cases on its docket varies from one hundred to three hundred and fifty. The Circuit Court exercising similar jurisdiction to your Superior Courts, in Civil matters, and exclusive jurisdiction in Criminal matters, has likewise two terms during the year. The Sessions are limited by law to four weeks. We are now in attendance upon it, and the docket is scarcely entered upon; yet this is the fourth week of the term and the Chancery Docket will not be taken up at all. There are three hundred and fifty cases on this docket exclusive of Chancery & Criminal cases. The County Court has the same jurisdiction in Civil matters, but no Criminal jurisdiction. It is likewise a Court of Probate and Orphans Court. There are but two regular terms during the year. As a Court of Probate it is always open.

As to health, I know of no situation more salubrious, or any, where so little sickness has been experienced as in this city for the last four years. Every successive year adds many, to the precautions already taken to insure health.

I have thus succinctly stated to you some few inducements to the lawyers, to select our little city as a residence. There are perhaps considerations of a peculiar character which may affect in some degree the decision you may make on the proposition I shall submit to you. One of these is the circumstance of having a Sister resident in the State and only a short distance from you, the other, the present dilapidated and decaying fortunes of the good old State.

Will you permit me now to tender you the proposal of joining me in the practice of our profession in this City? I have no political aspirations to gratify and shall give and receive pledges (which will be unnecessary from you) not to intermediate with political parties. They are perhaps more virulent and bitter in this State, than in any portion of the world.

Be kind enough to give the matters and things contained herein your serious consideration, and advise me of your determination when your mind has made its conclusions.

With assurances of friendly regard

believe me dear Sir,

truly yours

Your classmate & friend Dr. Fearn [21] is now living in this City & begs to be remembered to you.

From David M. Saunders.   A.

Gallatin, April 26th, 1834.

. . . I have learned with much pleasure the success that has attended your political and professional efforts, you carry along with you my best wishes for your continued prosperity and future happiness and welfare.

I should be gratified to learn that you had determined to desert the shorn and bleak walks of celibacy and connect your destiny more intimately with the society in which you reside by making some woman a participant in your destiny. Be assured my Dear Sir that life is but a Barren heath without the genial influence which *a wife* has it in her power to impart to all that surrounds you. Life has no solid and enduring comfort; no substantial pleasure without *her*. Bind on your armour then prepare to attack some woman. Unless she is a *rara avis* she will take pleasure in surrendering herself a willing Captive to so meritorious a creature.

I intercepted a few days since in Nashville our old school fellow, Benj. Allston. [22] I accidentally met with him and although coy I brought him to bay and had a long interview with him; he is a farmer, cultivating the soil, a Cotton planter.

The old "Warrior Chief" has kicked up a h-ll of a dust throughout the nation. I see most of our friends of N. Carolina are against his "experiments." I should suppose however that the people of the State were for him; here you know that we all pull in the harness manfully—all are for him. I am no politician as "thou art Anthony" therefore I should not prognosticate as to the eventual result.

---

[21] Dr. Richard Lee Fearn, a native of Chatham, and a classmate of Graham at the university.

[22] Dr. Benjamin Hardy Alston (b. 1806), a native of Edenton, a classmate of Graham at the university.

From James Graham.   U.

Washington, May 28th, 1834.

I received your note by Mr. Waddell. He will leave in a few days having arranged his business and will leave it in charge of his brother, John. I have just returned from a very pleasant trip to Harpers Ferry by way of the Grand Canal. The distance is 62 miles, and the greater part of the way is a broken and mountainous country. The boat was drawn by three horses, and often changed. There are 34 locks on the Canal, each having a lift of 3 feet and being 100 feet long and 15 wide.

The Canal is 60 feet wide at top, and 42 at bottom and 6 feet deep. It is a magnificent work constructed through a rough country. We, (about 80 members of Congress and a few others,) made the trip in one day and a little of the night.

The United States Armory at Harpers Ferry is an important and interesting work. They make Muskets and Rifles in great numbers; I saw 70 thousand Muskets in one house.

The village is a small place, there being no room, that is, level ground on which to build. I saw no traces remaining that Mr. Jefferson's conjecture was true, to wit, that the Potomack and Shanandoah once formed an immense lake above the Blue Ridge and after the joint waters of the two Rivers rose to a great height they suddenly *burst* through the Blue Ridge.

There is not much company now here consisting of strangers. I am inclined to spend a short time at the Virginia Springs on my way home but I have not fully determined to do so. If any of the good people of No. Ca. are going there to the Springs in Virginia let me know. I will be at Fathers as soon as I can. I will write a circular letter and it will require me to stay here a short time after Congress adjourns to direct and distribute them.

I hope in No. Ca. gentlemen who are well quallified will become candidates for the Legislature. I look upon the next session to be one of a decided character, whether for weal or for woe, for good or for evil, remains to be determined.

From James Graham.   U.

Ho. of Rep. June 26th, 1834.

*   *   *   *   *

We are now treading on Ashes with fire Coles under them here. The political elements are quite warm in Washington. The Rejection of Stephenson [23] and Taney by the Senate have roused much bitter feelings. The Senate is a billious Body. They are excited & disposed to embarrass the administration. Louis McLane you perceive has resigned. I regret this, for I esteem him more than any man I have met here. He intended to leave the Cabinet when Duane [24] went out, but His friends interfered and importuned him to stay. I presume from Report Forsyth will go into the State Department. Polk [25] is talked of for the Treasury. The opposition are chuckling at the hope of destroying the administration. Their zeal and imprudence will defeat their desires. This Session of Congress will terminate on Monday next, and will long be distinguished for words, not works. I am rejoiced our session is coming to a close. I am much exhausted by incessant labour and hot weather. Judge Martin his wife, Miss Jane Henderson, Julius Alexander his wife, John Giles,[26] Franklin Smith and Wash Alexander spent a few days here lately on their way to N. Y. also Louis Henry, his wife, and Miss Ashe. They were all much pleased. I endeavoured to render their stay agreeable. I will not leave here for 8 or 10 days after Congress adjourns. I must write and distribute a circular before I leave, and then I will go, I think, by the Virginia Springs, to Fathers. I am desirous to get there as soon as I can for I am anxious he should make such disposition as he may think best of his property. His own Peace and comfort, as well as the welfare of his children require it, and he should be encouraged to persevere in doing it at once. I proposed to him if he found difficulty in division or distribution of any property, let him call

---

[23] Andrew Stevenson (1784-1867), of Virginia, who had a distinguished public career. After service in the legislature, he was a member of congress, 1821-1834; (speaker, 1827-1834); and had been appointed minister to Great Britain, only to have the senate refuse confirmation. He was, however, confirmed in 1836, and served to 1841.

[24] William A. Duane (1780-1865), of Pennsylvania, who, after appointment by Jackson, as secretary of the treasury, to "remove" the deposits, refused to do so, and was himself removed.

[25] James K. Polk, then a member of the house of representatives.

[26] John B. Giles (1788-1846), of Rowan, a graduate of the university, a delegate to the convention of 1835. Elected to congress, he did not qualify, because of ill health.

on such men as Alex McCorkle, [27] Maj. Henderson, [28] and Dr. Wm. Johnston, [29] and take their opinion as to the best course or rather let them put a value on any way no matter how, rather than permit things to remain in waste & Ruin. If you get to Fathers sooner than I do and he names the subject of division, advise him *at once to go on* and wait for no one. The property can be removed afterwards as [page torn] requires.

I will not be able to reach any of my County Courts this summer. A treaty is just made with the Cherokee Indians and now before the Senate.

From James Graham.   A.

TO THE FREEMEN [30]
OF
RUTHERFORD, BURKE, YANCEY, BUNCOMBE, HAYWOOD, AND MACON COUNTIES, NORTH CAROLINA.

FELLOW-CITIZENS:

The first session of the twenty-third Congress terminated its labors this day. The session opened with an animated and protracted discussion on the exciting and vexed question of the removal of the public deposites from the Bank of the United States. The investigation of this subject took a very wide range, and comprehended within its scope the whole currency of the country, and the complicated system of bank machinery. These are not surface questions; they are difficult, deep, and delicate questions, involving and sensibly affecting all the money, property, and business of the people throughout the nation.

The surviving soldiers of the revolution, and the history of that eventful period, inform us the currency of that day became greatly deranged and depreciated. Hundreds of soldiers were paid for their gallant services and sacrifices in continental money, which depreciated into worthless rags. Industry and labor had no sure

[27] Alexander McCorkle, of Lincoln, was held in high esteem throughout his community.
[28] Lawson Henderson.
[29] Dr. William Johnston (1790-1854), physician, iron manufacturer, one of the most influential men in Lincoln County. He served in the commons, 1820. He was the father of General Robert D. Johnston, C. S. A., and Governor and Senator Joseph Forney Johnston, of Alabama.
[30] Printed broadside.

reward—no certain standard of value; credit and confidence were destroyed; the prices of property and produce were as fickle and fluctuating as the wind. To avert these evils, and to restore a sound and uniform currency, the Congress of the United States, in the year 1791, composed chiefly of the patriots who achieved our independence, and of the sages who adopted our constitution, with General Washington at their head, established a Bank of the United States. The notes of that Bank were good, and equal to gold and silver coin; and the public revenue was ordered by law to be deposited therein. The charter of that institution expired in the year 1811. The public money was then placed in the State banks, and there kept until 1817. The State banks generally, iri the years 1813, '14, '15, and '16, stopped specie payments. They were unable to redeem their paper with gold and silver. The consequence was their notes immediately depreciated, and fell in the market *from five to twenty-five per cent* below their nominal value. A number of the banks broke, and failed entirely; so that the Government and the people both sustained large and heavy losses, amounting to several millions of dollars. In this wreck of business and crush of State banks, the republican Congress of 1816, with President Madison at their head, chartered the present Bank of the United States, to render the operations of the Treasury Department more simple and *safe;* and to restore a sound and uniform currency to the people. This fiscal agent is required to perform its public trusts under the orders of the Secretary of the Treasury and the laws of Congress. At the close of the late war in 1815, the General Government was indebted about one hundred and thirty millions of dollars; and its annual expenditures are fifteen or twenty millions besides. This institution has faithfully collected, safely kept, promptly transmitted, and honestly paid out all this immense amount of debt and expenditures without losing or costing the Government one cent. It has furnished the people with a sound circulating medium, equal to gold and silver, at every house in every State and Territory in the Union; and passes at par value in Europe and China.

By the sixteenth section of the Charter, the public moneys are to be deposited in this Bank, unless the Secretary of the Treasury shall otherwise order and direct; in which case, he shall immediately lay before Congress his reasons for such order and direction. The Secretary of the Treasury, on the first of October last, under the advice of the Executive, ordered the removal of the public moneys from the Bank of the United States, and deposited them in divers State banks, selected by himself, and not by Congress. Among the reasons rendered, he alleged the Bank was unconstitutional; that it had used its power to acquire political influence, and so on, but admitted that the public funds deposited therein were safe. After hearing and examining all the charges presented against the institution, I did not think the reasons of the Secretary sufficient to justify the interposition *of his authority.* As I understand his duties, he is the agent of the law, authorized by Congress to keep his eye constantly upon the safety of the public treasure, and see that the Bank promptly and faithfully perform its duties and services to the Government. He has no legitimate power to adjudge the law creating the Bank unconstitutional; that belongs to the Courts. He has no right to invade the province of Congress, and take under his care and keeping the conduct of the Bank in relation to its interference with politics, or any other subject not directly committed to his charge. Such improprieties and malpractices belong alone, and must be referred to, the Legislative Department; they cannot be delegated. The Secretary's reasons ought to have been entirely financial, and connected only with his official station; and not judicial or legislative in their character. I therefore think the Secretary mistook and transcended his duties (unintentionally, I presume) when he removed the deposites, for the reasons assigned by him.

A great and unexampled number of petitions and memorials, signed by upwards of *one hundred and twenty thousand freemen,* from all quarters, and of all parties, were presented to Congress, stating there was a remarkable scarcity of money and deep distress pervading the country, and *praying for relief* and the restoration of the public money to the United States Bank. I believe there were severe pressure and serious embarrassment felt in all branches of industry. Interest was high; property, produce, and labor were low; credit and *confidence* were paralyzed and prostrated; business lost its energy, and became nearly stagnant. This disastrous scene was soon succeeded by a great number of insolvencies and failures among persons of all classes and capitals; and some of the State banks took refuge from the impending storm by shutting their iron doors and stopping payment, while others were rendered bankrupt; and thus "the great storm which blows upon the coast will cast out whales on the strand as well as periwinkles." This scene of distress is attributable to the removal of the deposites. So large an amount of money, eight or nine millions of dollars, being *suddenly withdrawn* from the Bank of the

United States, compelled it instantly to collect its debts, and refuse loans and exchanges in a great degree. This source of supply and accommodation was nearly stopped and dried up—the public treasure having been deposited, without any law for so doing, in the custody of State banks which were much embarrassed with heavy debts, and, therefore, unable to swell the tide of trade and relieve the wants and distresses of the community. In this way the people were deprived of the use and enjoyment of their own money. Formerly the revenue had been collected and deposited in the United States Bank and its branches, and forthwith loaned out in each of the States among the people. In this way the current of commerce, like the current of life, (the blood in our veins,) was never still, but constantly circulating through all parts of the system. In this way too our taxes, never a blessing, were rendered something less an evil.

The State banks never can become convenient and safe depositories of the public treasure, or furnish the necessary facilities to distant dealings. There are about *five hundred local banks* in the different States, and no two of them are alike. They are as different in all useful and commercial purposes as the climates and crops of the States in which they are located. How can such dissimilar and discordant institutions afford secure depositories for the General Government, or "emit" a sound and equal currency to the people? You might as reasonably expect the cotton of Carolina to grow in Connecticut, or that birds of different kinds would have the same feathers. It is impossible. You cannot make State bank notes current and equal to specie in all the different and distant States: they must necessarily be local and limited in their circulation and character. The framers of the Constitution undoubtedly *designed* the General Government to control the currency of the country; and how can they effect this object through institutions over which they have no control? You perceive I decidedly prefer a United States Bank, and a new one if it can be had, to numerous State banks as depositories of the public money. I am not a very competent judge, yet I am a most impartial one, *never being interested in banks* of any kind as debtor or creditor, or in any way whatever. I am concerned only as every farmer and freeman is: when we sell a barrel of corn, a lot of cattle, a bale of cotton, or a wedge of gold, and receive bank notes therefor, we want the notes to be good, and passable at par value in any State, and convertible into gold and silver coin at pleasure. Such bank notes are "so like the truth, they serve the turn as well."

Some persons are utterly opposed to a United States Bank, and denounce it as dangerous, and liable to do much injury to the Government and the people, while they are loud in their praises of State banks. Now, to a plain man, like myself, this is incomprehensible reasoning. I cannot conceive how one bank is more dangerous than five hundred banks; neither can I understand why a United States Bank is obliged to be a sinner, and a State bank a saint. So far as their morality and religion are concerned, I believe neither of them have any souls to be saved, and, therefore, nothing to boast of. They are both cold corporations, legally constituted and associated to make money, and should always be guarded and watched with an eagle's eye. Experience, however, has taught me that State banks are often unsound; and he that holds the notes of some of them, holds his treasure in earthen vessels. Do you not remember the failure of the Cheraw Bank, in South Carolina, and the Macon Bank, in Georgia; and how many of our meritorious men suffered thereby? I remember them both, *to my cost.* Suppose you go now to the "far West," or to the North, on business, your Carolina State bank notes will not pass at par; and then you must be shaved, skinned, and hewed, in order to make your funds available. Now, sir, this is a right severe operation to a man who lives by the sweat of his brow, and, perhaps, sold his last summer's crop for such depreciated paper. I have said so much to briefly demonstrate and illustrate my general views and opinions in relation to the present critical condition of the currency.

In the early part of this communication, you are informed, I did not consider the reasons of the Secretary sufficient *for his* removal of the deposites. The reasons presented were sufficient to authorize Congress, not the Secretary, to institute an inquiry into the conduct and condition of the United States Bank; accordingly, I sustained a proposition to ascertain, generally, if the Bank had performed its duties or violated its charter. The committee went to Philadelphia, and attempted an investigation; but being divided among themselves with regard to their powers and mode of proceeding, and finding some obstructions thrown in their way by the Bank, they returned without effecting any useful purpose, and made two long reports, with neither of which am I satisfied. The conduct of the Bank in calling upon the committee for written charges and specifications, and resorting to technical entrenchments, meets my decided disapprobation and condemnation.

These reports, made just before the adjournment of Congress, were not acted on for want of time.

I very much regret we have not more gold and silver coin in circulation, and fewer and better bank notes. With a view to accomplish this desirable object, Congress has just passed a law fixing and regulating the value of foreign coins. It affords me *unalloyed* pleasure to inform you that Congress has now *raised the value of our own gold.* Heretofore, gold was more valuable in England and in Europe than in the United States; and as soon as our native gold was coined at the mint, it was immediately exported to foreign countries, where it commanded the highest price. By the act of Congress, just passed, gold will bear the relation to silver of one to sixteen; that is, one ounce of gold is worth sixteen ounces of silver. This valuation, I think, will convert all our gold into money, and prevent its transportation. I now fondly hope that our own precious metal will soon supercede the general use of printed rags, and that the *golden age* may return once more, to dispense choice blessings over the rich valleys, the green hills, and the blue mountains of North Carolina.

The Post Office Department is represented by a Committee of the Senate, charged to inquire into the administration of its affairs, to be in an irresponsible and insolvent condition. The majority of the committee report its indebtedness to be about $800,000; the minority say not quite $400,000 beyond its ability to pay. I do not know which statement is most accurate. However, both reports concede the department is greatly involved, and has borrowed large sums of money without the authority of law. We all have a direct and deep interest in this useful department; it is the main artery, through which facilities and conveniences are bestowed upon multitudes such as no man can number. Each branch of Congress has appointed a committee to sit in the recess, and examine into the alleged abuses.

Fellow-Citizens: It is a matter of painful reflection, that party influence so often warps and twists the deliberations and decisions of Congress. Verily, I believe, there is in the councils of the nation a greater love than love of country. Being myself upon a new theatre of action, and conceiving all my duties and obligations were due to my constituents and countrymen, and to no other power on earth, I resolved neither to approve nor to oppose any measure, until I had carefully examined and impartially investigated it; and then to pronounce that judgment which truth and justice dictated. The most engrossing subject is a very grave one, and paramount to all party feelings and preferences; it affects the labor and industry of the whole community; it touches the pockets, and pocket-books, and property of thirteen millions of people. My views and opinions are before the public. You are my triers. I hope you will put yourselves in possession of the facts, "the truth, the whole truth, and nothing but the truth", and to your candid verdict and better judgment I cheerfully submit.

Respectfully presented,

JAMES GRAHAM.

Washington, June 30, 1834.

Show this to your neighbors.

To James Seawell. [31]   U.

Lincoln County, July 15th, 1834.

Your letter of the 10th. inst. addressed to me at Hillsboro; was handed to me, after I had taken my seat in the stage for this place, whither I have travelled with the rapidity of the mail.

When the Bill to recharter the Bank of Cape Fair was before the House of Commons at the last session &, (I believe) after it had passed the second reading, & had been recommitted under special instructions to the committee, the subject was mentioned (I do not recollect by whom) at the table of Rigsbees Hotel where you and myself boarded, & frequently sat together. I remarked that in the existing condition of our currency, I believed a renewal of the charter of some one of the old Banks, to be almost indispensable; and so far as concerned the Banks I thought that of Cape Fear should be preferred, because it had not violated its charter, by buying in its own notes at a discount, & otherwise, as was said to have been done by the others. You replied that I was mistaken in supposing that the Bank had not shaved its own notes, for that Mr. Winslow [32] & yourself had been agents for the Bank in some transactions of the kind in one of the Northern cities, perhaps New York. I was somewhat surprised by the information. For although not very familiar with the history of the Bank I did not recollect to have heard the allegation before. As no secrecy was used in making the communication, & as I did

---

[31] James Seawell, of Fayetteville, borough member of the commons, 1833-1834. The letter is a copy.

[32] Probably John Winslow, of Fayetteville, member of the commons, 1815-1819.

not understand it to be confidential, I spoke of it, without reserve to others, probably to Mr. Jordan, [33] though I do not at present recollect to have done so. My own opinion of the propriety of the recharter was fortified by a Petition from my Constituents, which had been presented, a very short time before this conversation. I was anxious therefore that the Bill should pass, and desirous to know whether the transactions to which you had alluded, were capable of explanation. I accordingly made inquiries for the purpose of ascertaining, and in doing so, generally mentioned the source which I had derived my information.

I read no paper from Fayetteville, and have not seen any of the publications either of yourself or Mr. Jordan. The conversation before referred to, is all that I now recollect to have had with you relative to the violations of its charter by the Bank of Cape Fear. Upon my return from Raleigh early in the present month, I found a letter in the office at Hillsboro from Mr. Jordan, requesting a statement of my knowledge on this subject. I then respectfully declined to furnish it, as I supposed it was solicited for publication, and I was averse to an appearance in the public Gazettes. I recede from this determination now because the request has been repeated by you, and I learn from you that my name has been already introduced in one of the publications in the papers of your Town.

If you desire this communication for any other purpose than your own satisfaction, you will please to submit it to the perusal of Mr. Jordan as soon after its receipt as your convenience will allow.

From Jacob Thompson. [34]   A.

Leasburg, N. C., July 30th, 1834.

On my way to Raleigh two weeks ago it was my wish and expectation to have seen you in Hillsboro; but as I did not, and was informed that you would return from your visit to the mountains about this time, I take this means of laying before you a proposition which I hope will meet from you a favorable reception.

---

[33] Dillon Jordan, Jr., of Fayetteville, a member of the commons, 1833-1836.

[34] Jacob Thompson (1810-1885), of Mississippi, a native of Caswell County, N. C., graduate of the university, lawyer, M. C., 1839-1851, declined election to the senate, and was secretary of the interior, 1857-1861. He was inspector general, C. S. A., and Confederate agent in Canada.

I have now resolved, somewhat contrary to my previous expectation, to settle myself in this place and practice in or rather *attend* Caswell, Orange, Person, and possibly Granville County Courts. My object in taking this circuit is improvement rather than profit—my chief desire being to adopt such a course of legal reading as will enable me to take out superior Court license twelve months hence and to acquaint myself with that branch of science of Law in which I now feel the most embarrassing deficiency, *savoir,* the practical business part. In order to attain my end and remove the difficulty under which I labor, I feel that I must become the protege of one farther advanced, more experienced and more able than myself. It is therefore on you I wish to confer this charge. My request of you will be to direct me into a proper course of reading, to loan me such books as I may want and may not have, to examine me occasionally, if you should have leisure and inclination, for which purpose I can at any time visit Hillsboro, and to advise and instruct me at the different courts which we may attend together in all those little matters which, as you know, would perplex and puzzle a man who has spent the better portion of his life in poreing over books and discussing theories; and at which perplexity a man acquainted with the ordinary commerce of society would feel strongly disposed to laugh. These and other such favors as may be convenient will be gladly and thankfully received.

Please let me know by an early mail whether or not you would be willing to assume this relationship towards me; and if so, on what conditions, or vulgarly on what terms.

From James Graham. U.

Greenbrier County, Virginia,
White Sulphur Springs,
August 11th, 1834.

I am yet here and will leave tomorrow for the sweet Springs, stay a day or two, then to the Salt Springs, and then home. My health has become quite good.

There is much interesting company here some gentlemen of distinction and Ladies that are interesting but not pritty. The Miss Collins'es [35] of Edenton of whom there are three are the

---

[35] Daughters of Josiah Collins, of "Somerset Place," familiarly called "The Lake," because of its situation on Lake Scuppernong, (now Phelps), Washington County.

Bells. They are delightful girls having received high cultivation and charming accomplishments. Miss Henrietta is producing much sensation here. I regret I could not meet you at Fathers in July and it will be near the last of August before I return now. I will stay but a short time at Fathers then to my neglected plantation and then to my fall circuit. I will take no new cases as I had intended to do but will only attempt one thing at a time. I am not yet resolved whether I shall be a Candidate for Congress. I have no objection to the Honor but I don't like to lose the money. All the paths that lead to political preferment terminate in Insolvency and splendid misery. Mr. Simpson [36] of Newbern is now here and in a room with me, Deveraux [37] and Badger and their families have been here. G. Hogg and Mr. Boylan [38] & daughter are now here. This country is the Buncombe of No. Ca. except it is not so beautiful and romantic. These several springs in this region must receive near one million of Dollars annually, Upon my return home I will make a bold effort to animate those who own Watering places to improve their accommodations and induce the fashion and folly and disease of the Country to expend their substance among them.

I think the White Sulphur Springs of Buncombe and Rutherford are equal to the same kind of water in Virginia. Rencher who came with me here is still here. Conl. Benton [39] and Speaker Stephenson are here. McDuffie [40] who has just resigned his seat in Congress is also here; he is getting better and will be elected Gov. in So. Ca. next winter.

---

[36] Samuel Simpson, a merchant of New Bern, the father of Mrs. Matthias E. Manly, of Mrs. John Kirkland, and Mrs. Henry K. Nash.

[37] Thomas P. Devereux.

[38] William Boylan (1777-1861), of Raleigh, editor of the *Minerva,* president of the state bank, and one of the most prominent business men of the town.

[39] Thomas Hart Benton (1782-1858), of Missouri, a native of North Carolina, student at the university, who, after studying law at William and Mary, settled in Tennessee, where he was a member of the state senate, 1809-1811, colonel of volunteers, and aide to Jackson in 1812, lieutenant-colonel in the U. S. A. 1813-1815. He moved to Missouri, was elected to the senate, when it became a state, and served 1853-1855, when he became a candidate for governor.

[40] George McDuffie (1790-1851), of South Carolina, a native of Georgia, graduate of South Carolina College. He served in the commons, 1821-1834; was governor, 1834-1836; United States senator, 1842-1846. A fiery but impressive debater, he was continually in some sort of personal quarrel. He fought several duels, and was permanently injured in one of them.

From Frederic S. Blount.   A.

Mobile, September 17, 1834.

Your friendly favor of 24th ult. reached the city during my absence on the sea-shore of Mississippi, and I take much pleasure in devoting my earliest leisure moments to answer it.

I regret most sincerely the present unsettled state of your mind in reference to an emigration from North Carolina, and the indefiniteness of the time, which, if at all, will permit you to leave the State. I fully concur with you on the impracticability of your quitting it *now*, without manifest detriment to your private interests: and knowing the difficulties attendant upon the settlement of the business of a few years practice from personal experience, I did not think that you could so arrange matters as to remove immediately. These considerations offered themselves to my notice when my letter of 22nd April was addressed to you, and my impressions then were, that you might possibly accede to the propositions which it contained, and be enabled to remove by the Spring of 1835. The only supportable reason which I anticipated would induce you to decline the proffer which I made, was the prospect of *political advancement* which the State offers *now* to her talented sons. Knowing that you had served one Session of the Legislature, and would most probably be returned for the next, I was doubtful whether the allurements which political influence united with flattering prospects usually exercise, might not influence you in determining to remain permanently domiciled in North Carolina. There were considerations however of a serious nature affecting pecuniary interests which I presumed, if properly presented, would carry some weight with them in counterbalancing the benefits,—I would rather say, gratified ambition —arising from political distinctions. The latter, are at best, *profitless.*

The increasing depreciation in the value of real property, the emigration which is continually draining the State of its wealth, enterprise and business population and the spirit of lethargy which seems to paralyze all her efforts, and to render abortive every attempt to procure extensive benefits from a proper cultivation of her resources, and a judicious application of her means, cannot render a residence desirable merely for the honor of filling one of her public appointments. It is to be lamented that such an order of things should exist in any portion of our Union. To every North Carolinian it is a matter of deep regret that they should be found *alone* in his own native State.

By this time the distribution of property to which you allude has been most probably effected, and the disposition which you will be enabled to make of it, known to you. If circumstances have altered so as to render your emigration less productive of loss to you, during the next Spring, than you have hitherto supposed it to be; or if your business arrangements can be closed by the fall of 1835, the advantages which we may both derive from an association will still remain open for your acceptance. In making this offer I deem it due to you to say, that in looking over the list of my professional friends, I know of no one among them, with whom I would so readily accede to a connection in business as with yourself, nor one in whom the elements of success in the profession, united to moral and social worth of a high order, are so conspicuous. A proper regard for my health imperatively requires that I should obtain a partner. I would of course prefer one whose feelings, sentiments, and disposition were in unison with my own. Should circumstances still operate unfavorably, so as to prevent you from forming any decided opinion, will you be pleased to advise me thereof, so that I may consider of some proposition which have been submitted to me to this end.

* * * * *

The production of J. Seawell Jones to which you allude is, I understand, redolent of love for the Old State, and patriotic in the motive which led to the undertaking. I am under the impression, that however creditable the feelings which impelled the performance of, what he deemed, a duty to his native State as a literary production, subjected to the mature criticism of his own mind after the "nonumque prematur in annum" which Horace recommends, he will view it rather as the precocious offering on the altar of patriotism, than a sound and practical exhibition of the historical events, and political feelings of the period of which he writes. You, I know, will unite with me in expressing the wish, which friendly feelings on our part require in behalf of the author, that the work will be found to merit, that other, and to him more grateful expression of Horace, "Pope linenda cedro."

Drs. Fearn and Carter [41] were much gratified with your friendly remembrance, and desire me to express to you the assurances of their continued esteem and regard.

---

[41] Jesse Carter, a native of Caswell County, after graduation from the university, a year later than Graham, studied medicine in Philadelphia, and settled in Mobile.

Gift of Negroes to James Graham.   U.

Know all men by these presents that I, Joseph Graham, of the County Lincoln, North Carolina, for and in consideration of the natural love and affection, which I have, and do bear, to my son, James Graham. of the County of Rutherford, in the State aforesaid, & for divers other good causes and considerations, me thereunto moving. Have given, granted, confirmed and delivered, and by these presents do give, grant, confirm & deliver to my said son, James Graham, the following negro slaves, Towit,—Carter, aged 44 years & valued at $500. Harvey, aged 9 years, & valued at $375. Sam aged 8 years & valued at $300, and Mary aged 5 years & valued at $200. To Have and to Hold all the aforesaid negro slaves and their future increase to the said James Graham, his Executors, administrators & assigns forever.

In testimony whereof I have hereunto set my hand & seal this 23 day of September, A. D., 1834.

Test —
Alf'd Graham

Ackn'd —   (—)
            (Seal)
J. Graham   (—)

From David L. Swain.   U.

Raleigh, 20th. October, 1834.

*   *   *   *   *

We will doubtless witness a period of high and bitter excitement, next winter, which will command much interest as well without as within the State. Haywood will be decidedly at the head of his party, and you cannot but be aware, that you will be expected to lead the opposing division. National politics will be discussed pretty freely in my Message, and I am therefore very anxious to have a conference with you, on all the controversial topics

If an interview cannot be had, I will send you some days before the Session, of course in strict confidence, which will be reposed in no other member of your House, a copy of the Message itself.

*   *   *   *   *

From William Gaston   A.

Newbern, November 12th, 1834.

I have heard that some dissatisfaction has been expressed in certain parts of the State at my having accepted a judicial office under the existing Constitution. Perhaps the matter is not deserving of any notice on my part. But as next to the approbation of my own conscience I prize the good opinion of the upright portion of the Community; and as possibly some of these may have misconceived my motives in the act alluded to, I have concluded to make a short statement of them which you will find enclosed. I leave it entirely to your discretion to shew it to whom you think proper.

I beg of you to believe me with sincere respect and affection.
Your friend

[Enclosure]

The circumstances under which I was called upon to fill the vacancy on the bench of the Supreme Court, occasioned by the lamented death of Judge Henderson, rendered it in my judgment a *duty* to accept the appointment unless the Constitution excluded me from office because of my religious principles. Whether the Constitution did or did not thus disqualify me, became therefore a serious question and was deliberately considered.

The 32d Section of the Constitution declares "that no person who shall deny the being of God, or the truth of the Protestant Religion or the divine authority either of the old or new testament, or who shall hold religious principles incompatible with the freedom and safety of the State, shall be capable of holding any office or place of trust or profit in the civil department within this State." The whole difficulty was in fixing the construction of the phrase "who shall deny the truth of the Protestant Religion."

Not long after the great schism which arose in the Christian Church in the 16th Century, the term "Protestants" was used to designate all those denominations of Christians, however divided among themselves, which separated from the main body; while *these* claimed to be called *"Catholics"*, and because of their remaining in union with their visible head, the Bishop of Rome, were also called "Roman Catholics." The clause disqualifying those who deny the truth of the *Protestant* Religion may have been intended to embrace Roman Catholics, and this supposition is rendered more likely by the consideration that North Carolina had been settled almost exclusively by Protestants, at a time when bitter religious dissentions and prejudices prevailed, and that these religious prejudices had not entirely lost their force when the Constitution was formed. But the clause in question is part of the written, and fundamental law of the land, and is therefore to be expounded by the well established rules of legal interpretation. According to these unless it contains a *clear* disqualification, it must be understood as leaving unimpaired the right of the Citizen to hold and of the Country to confer office. The People of the State have a right to the service of every citizen whom they think worthy and capable of serving them, and there can be no restrictions on their choice except such as they have unequivocally imposed on themselves. The 19th section of our Bill of Rights proclaims "that all men have a natural and unalienable right to worship God according to the dictates of their own conscience" and every degredation imposed on a citizen because of his belief, unless clearly denounced by the Constitution, must be regarded as hostile to this great principle of Religious Freedom.

There is no ambiguity in other parts of the Constitution prescribing the qualifications and disqualifications for seats in the Legislature or for civil offices. *See sections 25, 26, 27, 28, 29, 30, 31,* and in this section there is sufficient explicitness as to the necessity of some Religious belief, and indeed of the Christian belief. He who denies a God, a future state of rewards and punishments, or the divine authority of the old *or* new testament, is distinctly and expressly disabled. But when we come to the other prohibitory clauses, there is a vagueness which defies a *satisfactory* exposition, and induces a conviction that while some of the Convention intended further exclusions from office because of religious belief, others, and those probably to whom recourse was necessarily had to draft the instrument, were equally resolved to extend the principle of religious disqualification no further.

Who shall judicially say what is *"the Protestant Religion"* or what is it *"to deny its truth?"* Who is to decide what religious principles are compatible with the freedom and safety of the State? If the Protestant Religion were made the religion of the Country, and there were organized some ecclesiastical Court, or other legal Tribunal to determine the tenets of that Religion and to decide on Heresy, there would then be the means of legally ascertaining what is the Protestant Religion. But it has not been made the religion of the State, and such a tribunal has not been and under the Constitution cannot be erected. "There shall be no establishment of any one religious church in this State in preference to an other." *Sect. 34.* Innumerable sects—differing each from the other in the interpretation of what all call the revealed Will of God—some holding for divine truth what others reject as pernicious error—are indiscriminately called and known as Protestants. The Constitution neither defines the Protestant Religion; nor fixes nor allows to be fixed any tribunal to define it; and excludes *by name* no sect of Christians from office. It seems impossible then to pronounce *judicially* what is the Protestant Religion or who are disqualified because of rejecting its tenets.

But if we could arrive at the clear meaning of the term "the Protestant Religion" what is to be understood by *"denying its truth?"* Protestants have separated from Catholics because, as they alledge the latter have added to the Christian Code doctrines not revealed. Protestants therefore *reject,* as error or as of human invention, more or less of what Catholics *receive* as divine truth. But I know of no affirmative doctrine embraced by Protestants generally which is not religiously professed also by Catholics. The latter hold that the former err not in what they *believe* but in what they *disbelieve.* The acknowledged symbol of Faith in the Protestant Episcopal Church in this Country is the Apostles Creed. This very Creed is the ordinary profession of faith in the Catholic Church and as such is always repeated at Baptism. Do Roman Catholics then come within the description of persons denying *the truth* of the Protestant Religion?

But again. Before the revolution R. Catholics laboured in the Mother country and in the colonies under grievous political and civil disabilities. These had been attached to them in precise and explicit terms. They were called by the legal nick-name of Papists and of Popish Recusants. At the Revolution the principle of Religious Freedom was proclaimed as a basis of the new Constitution. If the odious proscriptions against this class of Christians were *nevertheless* intended to be continued or renewed, this intention would have been expressed in unequivocal language. Before they shall be regarded as the victims of religious intolerance—and degraded from political rank—a distinct expression of Constitutional Law ought to be required.

Considerations like these brought me to the conclusion that, whatever reason there might be for suspecting that this clause might have been intended by a part at least of the Convention to impose political disabilities on Roman Catholics, it could not be judicially expounded as excluding them from office. A penal provision against a portion of the free-men of the State—a disabling provision against the whole community in its selection of civil officers—penal and disabling provisions because of religious principles which it was an unalienable and declared right to profess and to follow out in worship—could not be upheld and enforced unless *clearly* and *definitely* declared.

The question was purely one of legal and judicial exposition. It involved the construction of a written provision in the Constitutional Law of the Country. The construction which had been settled by Judicial Tribunals, or, where none such had obtained the construction which would be attached to it by Judicial Tribunals, according to the fixed principles of legal interpretation, *must be taken by all to be the true one.* Private Conscience was concerned so far only as not to violate the Law. But what the Law was, conscience could not determine, nor even private reason decide against either an official interpretation either actually made, or such as must result from the rules universally adopted by legal tribunals for their own government.

In this opinion of what must be the judicial exposition of this clause, I was confirmed by the highest legal authority within the State, and without the State. Moreover I had the written opinion given me more than thirty years ago when I first became a member of the State Legislature, of Samuel Johnston [42] who of all men then living best knew and was best qualified to expound the Constitution.

Under such circumstances to decline an office, which my conscience told me I was bound to take unless disabled by the Constitution, appeared to me an abandonment of duty. I had no well-founded scruple myself. To be deterred by the apprehension of what others might think seemed to me cowardice. Besides if from any mistaken notions of delicacy I could have consented

---

[42] Samuel Johnston (1733-1816), a native of Scotland, educated in New England, who came to Edenton in 1736, a lawyer, member assembly, 1760, provincial treasurer, delegate to the first four provincial Congresses, and president of the third and fourth. He was state senator, 1779, member of the Continental Congress, 1780-1782, and declined election as president. He was president of the conventions of 1788 and 1789, and the first United States senator elected under the Constitution, serving from 1789 to 1793. He was a judge of the superior court, 1800-1803. Gaston's tribute to his knowledge and wisdom is restrained, rather than otherwise.

to impose an interdict on myself—ought I by such conduct to have *practically* aided in interpolating into the Constitution a prohibition which I did not believe it to contain?—a prohibition insulting to the feelings and injurious to the rights of a portion of my fellow citizens; hostile to the principles of Religious Freedom; and abhorrent from all those sentiments of liberal toleration which at this day belong to enlightened Christians of every denomination?

My course appeared to me a plain one, and on mature reconsideration my conscience does not reprove me for having pursued it.

From James Graham.   U.

Lincolnton, Nov. 17th, 1834.

... We have now a great Flood here; at this moment the South fork is 6 feet over the top of the Bridge and the Banks and bottoms are covered with water.

* * * * *

I hope you will become acquainted and be civil to the Rutherford Members and to all the Members from my District. Dr. Perkins [43] of Burke is a very clever fellow and I think a little attention to the Yancy members will keep them right upon all questions that may come before the Legislature. A little civility that costs a man nothing is often regarded as an act of condecention and especial favour bestowed upon ordinary men.

I think there ought to be a 7th. Circuit created, and if that proposition were moved at an early period it might be adopted. I am for a Rail Road to Beaufort or Wilmington but not to Virginia or So. Ca. Bring the Rail Road from the Sea Board to Raleigh or Fayetteville and from these two points construct good turnpike Roads into the Interior and then all will be done that is practicable and useful. Let the Legislature instruct the Governor to ask the General Government for the Services of one of the ablest Engineers to examine the Country between Beaufort and Raleigh and Fayetteville and Report to next Legislature.

I hope the Convention may go on prosperously; but watch the disorganising distempers that are abroad in the Land and propose as few amendments as possible. I hope Gov. Swain may be elected to the Senate; I see no reason why he should denounce Jackson

[43] James H. Perkins, who represented Burke in the commons, 1834-1837.

or kiss the little toe of any would be President; let him stand erect and bear stifly up against party manoevers on one side or the other.

Gov. Burton [44] stayed with me at Father's 2 nights since. He told me he was inclined to run for Gov., supposing Swain went to the Senate. Burton is in Raleigh or will be soon.

Give my respects to Swain and Manly and Hinton.

From Jo. Seawell Jones.   A.

New York, Nov. 21, 1834.

I see in the Papers of our State the death of Colonel Martin, [45] and I have a great desire to obtain his papers if he has left any. It was the great Cherokee expedition of 76 upon which in the composition of my book I felt peculiarly ignorant, and as he was concerned in that I am the more anxious to have them. Will you do whatever you can for me in that way? Write or if you can speak to Judge Martin in my behalf and say to the holder of any such papers that I shall make a good use of them.

I have commenced the publication of another work on the history of our State which I have entitled "Curiosities of North Carolina," and the effort is to give general sketches of history, from the days of Sir Walter Raleigh down to the adoption of the Federal Constitution. I have got through one Vol.—which is now in type—and which comes down to the termination of the year 1775, and I have been to Boston and procured the suspension of the publication to see if I cannot do something in the way of collecting some interesting matter. When I shall come to the State, I shall be in Raleigh by the first of December, and shall rely on your valuable aid in the organization of the Historical Society.

I now begin to fear I shall never be able to make a visit to your venerable parent, General Graham, and even at this early day—a long time, I hope, before he is called away—I urge upon him through you to leave behind him some MS of reminiscences to guide me, at least, in whatever I may hereafter write on the annals of the State. You remember he was a member of the Convention

---

[44] Hutchins Gordon Burton (1782-1836), a native of Virginia, who settled in Granville. He sat in the commons, 1809; was attorney general, 1810-1816; moved to Halifax, which he represented in the commons, 1817; was a member of congress, 1819-1824, and governor, 1824-1827.

[45] James Martin (1742-1834), a native of New Jersey, who came to North Carolina in 1774. A colonel of Militia, he fought at Moore's Creek, took part in General Rutherford's expedition against the Cherokees, was at Guilford Court House, and was in service until the end of the war. He represented Stokes County in the commons, 1791-1792.

that rejected the Constitution—and that period of our history even now wants illustration. I hope to get some light on that subject when I examine the papers in the State Department, but private letters or semicircular would be most important help.

I believe you did not know The Hon. Joseph Pearson [46] of Rowan, who has for some years past resided in Washington and who lately died in Salisbury. He was one of the worthiest and truest sons of North Carolina; would that she had even a hundred such. He was so devoted to the old Mother of us all that I write no letter now without commemorating his worth. He deserves at the hands of the people of the State—I had almost said a day of general mourning—for he was proud of their fellowship—and the cry—I am a North Carolinian—was the highest introduction to the elegant hospitalities of his house.

I had known him somewhat intimately for some months past and had to mourn over the grave of a beloved friend as well as a distinguished countryman. If you create another new County —and I hope you will—adorn it with a name—"consecrated in the most unshaken public principle and the most undoubted and various talents."

There is a great deal of chit-chat among the politicians as to your Senatorial election. I have one word to say: elect a man of talents one who can make some stand—not so much against Jackson—or any body else—but for the character of the State. Van Buren says Brown [47] will be elected—the first ballot—and I made a bet of a dinner against him.

My compliments to Dick Alexander, [48] Barringer, Craige, [49] Long, The Governor, and all my friends.

---

[46] Joseph Pearson (1776-1834), of Salisbury, a lawyer, who was a member of the commons, 1804-1805, and a member of congress, 1809-1815. He fought a duel while in congress, with John J. Jackson, of Virginia, which undoubtedly contributed to the respect and admiration with which Jones regarded him, though he was entitled to both, as a man of ability, who possessed the confidence of his contemporaries. He was an uncle of Chief Justice Pearson.

[47] Bedford Brown (1795-1870), of Caswell County, after attending the university for a year, became a lawyer and planter. He served in the commons, 1815-1817, 1823; in the state senate, 1828-1830 (speaker, 1829); and in the United States senate, 1829-1840, resigning rather than obey instructions. He was state senator, 1840-1843, and having failed, after a long contest, of re-election to the United States senate, he moved to Missouri, then to Virginia, and finally back to North Carolina. He was state senator, 1858-1860. A Unionist always, he opposed secession, but was a member of the convention, where he voted for the ordinance of secession, and condemned it unsparingly thereafter. He was also a delegate to the convention of 1865.

[48] Richard Henderson Alexander, of Salisbury, graduate of the university, who represented the borough in the commons, 1833-1834.

[49] (Francis) Burton Craige (1811-1875), of Rowan, graduate of the university, editor, lawyer, served in the commons, 1833-1834, and was a member of congress,

From George W. Freeman. [50]   U.

SIR,

An Examination of the Pupils in the EPISCOPAL SCHOOL, will commence to-day, and be continued on the ensuing Monday and Tuesday. A regulation of the School requires that such Examination shall be conducted by a Committee, specially appointed for that purpose; and you have been selected as one of that Committee.

Your attendance is respectfully solicited.

By order of the School Committee
GEORGE W. FREEMAN, *Sec'y.*

Saturday, Nov. 22d, 1834.

* * * Hours of meeting, 10 o'clock, A. M. and 3 o'clock P. M.

From John M. Dick. [51]   U.

Greensboro, December the 3rd, 1834.

* * * * *

I have not heard a word from the City as to the probable results of your deliberations. As a Western man I would naturally enquire will you get a Convention this Session? Will the Legislature make any appropriation for a Central railroad?

If you have had the Greensboro Patriot you have seen the high ground we took on this subject at November Court. We had a very large & highly respectable meeting and there was great unanimity in our views on this subject; rail roads are becoming daily more popular & I hope the day is not far distant when all will unite and compel our wary politicians to do something for our State. But I still believe that but little will be effected until our Constitution is amended.

I would be gratified to hear from you if the affairs of State will afford you sufficient leisure to write to a friend.

1853-1861. An ardent secessionist, he was a delegate to the convention of 1861, and was selected by Gov. Ellis to have the honor of introducing the ordinance of secession. He was a member of the Confederate provisional congress.

[50] George W. Freeman (1789-1858), a native of Massachusetts, moved to North Carolina about 1822. He became an Episcopal minister, served in North Carolina, Tennessee, New Jersey, and Delaware. He was now rector of Christ Church, Raleigh. He became bishop of Arkansas in 1843.

[51] John McClintock Dick (1791-1861), of Guilford, state senator, 1829-1830, a judge of the superior court, 1835-1862.

From Hugh Waddell.   U.

Hillsborough, Decr. 6, 1834.

Your kind favour of the 20th. Novr. reached me some six days or more after it was written & I have been in the glooms ever since: have had no heart to reply to it. Poor Poor North Carolina! what depths are left yet to be explored by your Wittenagemote I will not hazard my character as a prophet by foretelling, but it must be something marvellous indeed. The boiling must have been over a *strong* heat, when B. B. [52] & Gin Allison [53] have got on the top. My first impulse is to "hang my harp on the Willows" & the next is, to give way to the ridiculous and seize the cap and bells of Momus, crying "vive le bagatelle."

Mr. Crain who reached here yesterday informed me, that the debate on the Mangum resolution was in progress & that he heard much anxious expectation expressed of a speech from you & I earnestly hope you have not disappointed the high anticipations which have thus been raised. I feel great confidence that you will not, & though the subject is hedged in by difficulties of an *intrinsic* nature & still more so by *popular* errors, which one would not willingly encounter, yet I think I hazard nothing in believing that you will take a statesmanlike view of it, regardless of the consequences to your own popularity. Would to God, we had more, who *thought* as you *think* and *feel* as you do.

Perhaps ere this you are bearing the laurel on your brow. you have made the speech and received the applause & I am preaching to you on the propriety of doing it.

I was pained & vexed to see that whenever the Speaker [54] (not Alexander the *great* God knows) had it in his power to appoint Committees, you were studiously excluded. He must have a poor spirit indeed, to sacrifice the public interest to his personal feelings. On the subject of my brother's [55] misfortunes, I was exceedingly anxious that you should be placed on the Committee & if I had seen you before you left, I would have asked that you would move a reference of that part of the Gov's Message (for I

---

[52] Bedford Brown.

[53] Joseph Allison, of Orange, a Democrat, who represented the county in the commons, 1830-1834, and in the senate, 1835, 1838-1839, 1842-1843.

[54] William Julius Alexander, of Mecklenburg.

[55] John Waddell had sailed from Charleston to New Orleans on the brig "Encomium," carrying with him twenty-five negroes whom he planned to place on a Louisiana plantation. They were wrecked and carried into Nassau, where the British freed all the negroes. The legislature passed a resolution redress through the agency of the Federal Government which, of course, was not obtained.

knew it would be referred to in the Message) & by this means you would have been on the Committee in spite of the Speaker. I fear the Report will not be a strong one & I am very anxious it should be. Gen. Dudley has written me to communicate the facts & I have thought it best to transmit them in the form of a Memorial from John & *it* may be referred to the Committee. Pray do what you can towards giving efficiency to the Report.

. . . Pray keep me informed of matters of interest which may arise, as you know it will always afford me real pleasure to hear from you.

*   *   *   *   *

From James Graham.   U.

Washington, Dec. the 8th, 1834.

I reached this City on the evening of the 2d day of the Session. Mr. Senator Brown joined me at his own house and came on with me. We had no other company until we arrived at Fredericksburg when many members joined us. The administration has increased strength in Congress. The house is now nearly full, the Senate is quite thin. The Committies have just been announced this day and are nearly the same as last Session. I have no opportunity yet to ascertain what will be the leading measures of this Session. The critical relations with France I presume cannot be definitely acted on this Session. The Presidents Message will be dissected on tomorrow and that will develop the tone and temper of the house. Judge Mangum is here and understands his conduct is under consideration before the Legislature by Resolutions. He appears quite calm on the subject and is prepared to hear Judgment of Condemnation from Raleigh. I have not asked him neither has he told me what he will do, though I presume he will resign.

I have never been in Mangum's political confidence; his attachment or association with nullification erected a sort of barrier in politicks between us. I fear however, that seems to be the opinion here, there are as many hungry office seekers and Senator seekers at Raleigh this Session of Assembly as were ever congregated in one Legislature.

There is a *bitter controversy* now going on in Tennessee between the friends of Speaker Bell [56] and Polk. The friends of the former are about to fix on Judge White for the Presidency and the latter are supposed to be with Mr. Van Buren. The President is in fine health. He told me on Saturday his health was better now than it had been in 10 years. The old man seems quite cool. The Post Office Committee will not Report before the 1st. or middle of January; of course I fear there will not be time this Session to act on the subject.

Connor appears to be much rejoiced at the election of Brown. Barringer [57] is here in *very bad health*. Many of us have the prevailing influenza, but keep our feet. Jessee Bynum [58] has not yet arrived. I presume a Caucus at Raleigh will nominate a Candidate for Congress in each district in No. Ca. where we have not sustained the Executive *in every act*. In My District the disposition is strong to run at me. The Aspirants are feeble men and they are anxious to jump on the tide while it is up.

I received a letter from Guin [59] yesterday informing me of the Introduction of Resolutions to Instruct Mangum. He thinks they will pass. He writes 2 of the Rutherford members voted against Swain for Governor. If I owed the Devil two fools, and he would not take either one of them and give a full receipt I would never pay. Guin professes feeling for me though is supposed to be one looking to a seat in Congress. My District is with me, although every Demaguge in it is yelping and barking at me. If they would be still I would like to abandon my seat and pursue one by which I could make some money.

*   *   *   *   *

---

[56] John Bell (1797-1869), of Tennessee, educated at the University of Nashville, state senate, 1817, member of congress, 1827-1841, (speaker, 1834); secretary of war, 1841; state representative, 1847; United States senate, 1847-1859; candidate for President, 1860.

[57] Daniel Laurens Barringer (1788-1852), of Raleigh, sat in the commons, 1813-1814, 1819-1822, and was a member of congress, 1826-1835. He was defeated for re-election, and moved to Shelbyville, Tennessee. He was member, and speaker, of the lower house of the legislature.

[58] Jesse Atherton Bynum (1797-1868), of Halifax County, attended Princeton, became a lawyer, was a member of the commons, 1823-1824, 1827-1830; and of congress, 1833-1841. He later moved to Louisiana.

[59] James Guinn (also spelled Guin, or Gwinn), of Macon County, state senator, 1830-1831, member of the commons, 1833-1836.

Speech on Instruction [60] *to Mangum.*

December, 1834.

Mr. Speaker:

I need not express my regret that these Resolutions have been introduced; that has been already done by my votes to lay them on the table. I trust, Sir, that I entertain all proper loyalty to the Federal Constitution, that I am duly sensible of the benefits which it has conferred on this, as well as the other states, and that no one more cordially desires its perpetual duration. But one consequence of its adoption has been most unfortunate for North Carolina. I allude to the effect which it has had, in withdrawing the attention of our people from our own domestic affairs, and fixing it almost solely on subjects of national concern. Like the anxious spectators at a theatre, who submit to be crowded and "bored with elbow points," and will bear patiently any degree of local inconvenience, that they may behold the grand pageant on the stage, in which they bear no part, so we appear altogether unmindful of what immediately concerns the state, but are keenly alive to the great affairs which pertain to the general government. Our decayed agriculture, our shackled commerce, the promotion of education, the improvement of our inland transportation, even the amendment to our Constitution, if they gain a temporary consideration, must all yield to whatever relates to national politics. A presidential election, like the rod of Aaron, swallows up all local controversies, and every plan of public benefit must be arrested until the result; and all for what? Why, Sir, that we may have our due proportion of cannon firing, huzzaing and grog drinking at the close of the contest. That has generally been

[60] As one of the issues which divided the Republican party in North Carolina into Democrats and Whigs, the right of the legislature to instruct United States senators was important. The Democrats, tending towards state rights, in spite of their support of Jackson, championed the right, while the Whigs in general bitterly opposed it. The legislature of 1834-35, on motion in the commons of John W. Potts, of Edgecombe, on Nov. 28th., 1835, by joint resolution instructed Willie P. Mangum and Bedford Brown to vote for Benton's famous resolution to expunge the vote of censure of Jackson, for his action in regard to the Bank of the United States. Brown, a Democrat, had no difficulty in obeying the instructions, and, voting to expunge, was re-elected to the senate. But Mangum had voted for the resolution of censure, and also denying the right of instruction, declined to resign. But, after a Democratic victory in 1836, he yielded. Graham's speech was the most important one in the instructions debate, and marked an important step in his own career. He became, as it were overnight, a leader of the Whig party, second only to Mangum. Strange to say, neither from the journal, nor in the newspapers, can the date of its delivery be asecertained. The speech was published in the *Raleigh Register*, Jan. 27, 1835, and in the *Hillsborough Recorder*, Jan. 30, 1835.

our share of the "spoils of victory." Whether it will be so again, may depend on the events of the ensuing campaign.

This undue preference of Federal affairs over those which immediately concern the state, deeply injurious as it has been to our prosperity, has not been less so to our intellectual character, and to the fame, influence and usefulness of our public men. No citizen of ours has ever aspired to the chief magistracy of the Union. Few ever sat in any of its high places. Those bitter controversies, which have divided us and absorbed all others, have been waged for the elevation of men belonging to other members of the Confederacy, who most of us have never seen, and who have been known here, only by a general reputation of their patriotic services. These have been so magnified and exaggerated by zealous partisans, that we have been taught almost from our infancy to look abroad for all the high exhibitions of human excellence, and of course to depreciate, if not to proscribe, our own brethren. It is a melancholy truth, which all who hear me will attest, that such is the deficiency of the state pride among us, that we not only neglect our own affairs to take care of those of the Nation, and undervalue our own citizens, in comparison of those of other states, but we are too ready, under the impulses of party passion, to offer up as victims to be sacrificed the most pure, the most useful, and patriotic sons of the state, upon a mere difference of opinion on an abstract question of Federal politics, or as to the character and qualifications of a favorite candidate for the presidency. Believing that these Resolutions have sprung from this diseased state of the body politic, and that their entertainment here would tend to aggravate it, I deprecated their appearance. It is too late, however, to indulge in unavailing regret. We are now "afloat upon a full sea," and I must take the current as it serves.

The questions involved in the Resolutions are chiefly questions of Constitutional Law. Before I proceed to their discussion, permit me to notice one or two remarks of the gentleman from Edgecombe, (Mr. Potts [61]) by whom they were introduced. That gentleman, towards the close of his address, unfurled the banner of party, and called on all those who had voted with him in the last Senatorial election, to stand by him in support of the Resolutions. Appeals such as this upon questions like these, are not only unfair in argument, but highly unfavorable to correct conclusions. Having sworn to support the Constitution, we must do.

<hr/>

[61] John W. Potts represented Edgecombe County in the commons from 1832 to 1835. He was a student at the university in 1820.

it at the peril of our oaths, and are not at liberty to give to it any interpretation which may happen to accord with the designs or prescriptions of the party which claims it as its property. The same gentleman informed us, with an air of triumph, that New York, on which he pronounced a high panegyric, and New Jersey also, had condemned the decision of the Senate of the United States, and expressed his confident belief that North Carolina would follow their lead. Sir, it is a rule of order in the Parliament of Great Britain, that neither the opinion of the king nor of the other House, shall be alluded to in the debates of either the Lords or Commons. It is also provided in all the Legislative Assemblies of this Country, so far as my knowledge extends, that the proceedings of one house of the legislature shall not be noticed in the discussions of the other. This salutary regulation of the wisdom of our ancestors, designed to secure deliberative Assemblies from any other influences than those of patriotism, justice and truth, must cease to be of any avail here, if we are to be swayed in our action by information such as this. Sir, there was a time when North Carolina could act for herself. When the men of that classic land (Mecklenburg) from which you came, met together to deliberate on the Independence of America, did they wait to ascertain what had been done, or was about to be done, elsewhere? or did they only inquire what it became freemen to do in such a crisis? They took council from their own strong heads, and their own stout hearts. Though the whole continent was uttering professions and making overtures for reconciliation —though New York (whose example is now presented for imitation) tamely kept her allegiance, was exempted from the restraining Acts of Parliament, and enjoyed all the priviledges of a free port, they resolved that the cause of their suffering brethren at Boston was the cause of the whole country, and that the injuries that they had endured demanded an immediate severance of the empire.

When again, in the Provincial Congress at Halifax, in April 1776, our delegates in the Continental Congress were instructed to vote for absolute and immediate independence, even before Massachusetts and Virginia had ventured to that desperate extremity, the spirit of the primary assemblies was embodied in the representative council, and our illustrious ancestors gave proof to the world that they were quite as well qualified to *lead* as to *follow*. But we petty men, in these degenerate days, to aid us in our determination, must be told of the "actings and doings" of other states, and calculate the chances of being in a majority. Sir, the matter before us arises in high preeminence above mere temporary party considerations.

It is not a petty controversy, only for the vacation of a place to be filled by some of ourselves, or some of our friends, or to influence the results of the next presidential election. The decision which we are about to pronounce is not only seriously to affect an able and honorable man, who is not here to be heard in his defence, but its correctness, under the lights which we possess, deeply concerns our consciences, and may, in future, vitally affect our liberties.

The instruction proposed to be given is, that our Senators shall vote to expunge from the Journals of the Senate a Resolution of the last session of Congress, in which it was declared that the President in certain executive proceedings in relation to the public revenue, had assumed upon himself authority and power not conferred by the Constitution and laws, but in derogation of both. These Resolutions then, assume that that of the Senate was false, and in substance affirm that the conduct of the President in the transactions referred to was authorized by the Constitution and laws, and was in derogation of neither. It therefore becomes important to ascertain, what had the President of the United States done? What were those executive proceedings in relation to the Revenue, complained of in the Resolution of the Senate? The facts may be briefly stated. Congress, by an Act of the year 1816, had directed the public revenue, when collected, to be paid into the Bank of the United States. The bank became bound by the same statute, not only to keep the revenue safely, but to transmit it to any point where it might be wanted for the disbursements of the government, and over and above to pay one million and a half dollars to the public for the priviledge of keeping and using their funds from the time of collection until the time of disbursement; and this disposition of the public monies, by depositing them in Bank, was to continue as long as the charter lasted, unless, "the Secretary of the Treasury should at any time otherwise order and direct," in which event his reasons were to be certified to Congress on the first opportunity. The arrangement provided by this act soon took effect, and for more than sixteen years the public treasure was administered by these means. In the autumn of 1833, the President of the United States, of his own mere notion, suspended the payment of the public monies into the Bank of the United States, removed that portion which it already held to the custody of other banks chartered by the different states (and employed an agent to inspect and superintend the newly selected banks, at a salary to be paid by them as one of the equivalents for the boon of using the public money. I say the President did these acts. It is true the orders for their immediate execution are all signed by a Secretary of the Treasury, but his predecessor had been displaced for refusing to do them, and he was brought into office for that purpose alone, and was the mere instrument of the President's will. To leave no doubt on this subject, I quote the words of the President himself, in which he avows the removal of the deposits as his own act, and relieves all others from responsibility. In his manifesto read to his Cabinet on the 18th of September, 1833, after enumerating the offenses of the Bank, the President again repeats that he begs his Cabinet to consider the proposed measure as his own, in the support of which he shall require no one of them to make a sacrifice of opinion or principle. Its responsibility has been assumed after the most mature deliberation and reflection, as necessary to preserve the morals of the people, the freedom of the press, and the purity of the elective franchise, etc. and proceeds "to name the first of October next as a period proper for the change of the deposits, or sooner, provided the necessary arrangements with the State Banks can be made." Now, by the oaths which we have taken in regard to the Constitution were these acts of the President authorized by the Constitution and laws! Those who support these Resolutions maintain that they were. I deny it. All here will concede, that the Government of the United States is a government of limited power—that neither all its departments together, nor any one of them singly, possess any authority or powers, but such as are given expressly or arise from a reasonable implication. Is the power of the President to remove the public revenue derived from the Constitution? If it be, I have a right to demand of those who affirm it, what clause of the Constitution, either by strict or loose construction, confers such a power? It surely is nowhere expressed; from what can it be inferred? The gentleman from Halifax (Mr. Daniel) has pointed us to three provisions of the Constitution, first, that which vests the executive power in the President; second, that which imposes on him the duty to see that the laws are faithfully executed; third, that one (merely implied) which allows him to remove incumbents from office. A power which claims as many parents, can hardly be legitimate to any of them; and he will scarce ask to be called a strict interpreter, who can deduce it, from any or all of these provisions. I shall speak of the last of them first, as it was by its exercise, that the removal of the public monies was accomplished And here it may be premised that it is somewhat remarkable that whilst the Constitution was under consideration previously to its adoption, the power "to displace officers" as well as to appoint them was represented as belonging to the President and Senate, (*Federalist*, No. 77.) And yet, that the first Congress conceded it to the President alone. This construction has been acquiesced in ever since, and it is not necessary for the purposes of this argument that I should deny its truth. Like all the other powers of government, however, it is a trust power, and can be legally exercised only with reference to the purposes for which it was granted. I speak of power in contra-distinction to right. By a dubious implication, the President has power to remove from office. This power is not given expressly and is implied from the duties which are imposed on that officer. If, for the performance of any of these duties, the removal of an inferior officer becomes necessary, it may be legally made; but if not so rendered necessary, it cannot be made without a violation of Constitutional duty. So, that although the President has power to remove from office *ad libitum* he has no right to do so, except in the instance before stated. The fact, that there is no authority provided to control him in the exercise of his official power does not license him to use them capriciously or wickedly. As he would grossly violate his duty, by the appointment of a fool or a knave to a responsible trust, so he would be equally delinquent in dismissing a public servant except for unfaithfulness or incompetency. A giant has power to take the life of a man; a trustee has power to convey away the legal estate and defeat the intention of those who confided in him; a jury has power to return a verdict against law and evidence; yet to enforce these, would be flagrant violations of their respective duties; when therefore, the power of displacing subordinate officers is admitted to the President, the right to employ it, save only with the qualifications before stated, is by no means conceded. But the power of displacing officers is not a substantive power to which others are incident, but is itself merely incidental to the authority conferred on the President in order to enable him to discharge the duties of his station. It draws after it, no other powers, and cannot therefore in the matter under consideration give to the President any control over the revenue of the Government. Nor can the power to remove from office be construed into a power to control the officer in the performance of his duties. All officers of the United States, below those of President and Vice President are created, and have their duties prescribed by the laws of Congress, and although liable to removal by the President; are the servants of Congress in the performance of these duties. If a specific act be required by an inferior officer, his superior cannot execute it, nor can the latter usurp what has been entrusted to the discretion of the former. Neither the Constitution nor laws will justify the exercise of a legal power, for the accomplishment of an illegal end; the President cannot therefore legitimately employ the power of displacing from office to compel an officer to violate the law. We have seen in the act of Congress before recited, that the public monies were to be deposited in the Bank of the United States, unless the Secretary of the Treasury should, at any time, otherwise order and direct. This power of suspending the payments in bank is in the nature of judicial discretion, which is incapable of being delegated either to a superior or inferior. To justify a removal of the Secretary from office, for failing to order the monies to be placed elsewhere, is to give the President, through the purely incidental right of displacing, a power not merely to suspend all law, but to dictate the action of government in every instance.

My honourable friend from Bertie, (Mr. Outlaw), illustrated this by stating the case of an individual who had obtained a judgment in one of the Courts of the United States, and has sued out execution. The President informs the Marshal that he shall not do execution—the Marshal remonstrates that he is bound by heavy penalties to perform the command of the Court; the President declares that it shall not be done—the Marshal proceeds in his duty, and is removed forthwith. All our civil laws are made to operate upon the insubordinate and delinquent, through the judgment of the Courts, yet the President, by this construction of his authorities, is invested with a right of pardon to all debtors and trespassers—yea, more, a power to prevent the enforcement of any law, no matter how long established, and to compel the officers of government under pretense of executing laws, to perform his arbitrary will. Allow me to add another example by way of illustration: The territorial Judges of the United States hold their offices for four years, and, I believe, are subject to removal by the President. Suppose that by statute that a criminal offence, counterfeiting the coin, for instance, is punishable by fine or imprisonment or death, at the discretion of the Court—that an offender has been convicted under this Act, and the judgment is about to be rendered—the President informs the Judge that the culprit must be cut off; the Judge believing that the case is not of high aggravation, certifies his opinion to that effect, and is about to punish by fine; the President dismisses him instantly and selects from the herd of minions, who throng the gates of power and patronage everywhere, an assassin who will do the deed of death.

Let me not be misundertood to impute such a disposition to the present incumbent of the Presidential office. But to such a tremendous extremity is it found necessary to extend his Constitutional powers, to vindicate his "proceedings in relating to the public revenue." Again, if the act of Congress before mentioned, instead of allowing the Secretary to countermand the payment of revenue into Bank, had directed them to be deposited there absolutely, the President's power of removing him would have existed in as full force then, as it does under the present provisions of the Act. Yet, none will be found hardy enough to assert, that in that event, the President could have been excused in turning out the Secretary for refusing to issue such an order at his command. The right to remove from office surely cannot be interpreted into a power of arresting all laws, and substituting the President's will as a rule of conduct for all officers. Nor can he derive any power over the public treasure from his duty "to take care that the laws be faithfully executed." In this province of his office, he acts merely as the servant of the Congress which made those laws, and must obey the rules which they have prescribed. The law had directed, as we have before seen, that the public money should be kept in the Bank, unless the Secretary should deem a different place expedient; that law was undergoing execution in the regular course pursued for 15 years, no complaint was made from any quarter that the money was unsafe, that the Bank had failed in its duties in paying it wherever and whenever required, nor that the Secretary was not executing the intention of Congress to its very letter. Such was the state of things when the President interposed and suspended the execution of the law, relative to the custody of the public funds, and loaned them to other Banks. To me, it is passing strange that from the duty of seeing that the laws are faithfully executed, the President should be supposed to be clothed with power to prevent their execution altogether. It remains to enquire, whether this power can be derived from the clause which vests in the President "the executive power". This deserves to be particularly considered, as it has not only been insisted on here, but is the chief ground relied upon, in support of the claim, in the Protest to the Senate. These words are found in the beginning of the second article of the Constitution, and so far from conferring the power in question really confer no power at all. They are a mere label on the door of the Presidential office, the duties and powers of which are in manner described by it, but are left to be defined in that the remaining sections of the same article. They mean no more than the phrase "there shall be a President of the U. S." His power and responsibility are to be looked for in the other parts of that instrument. If it be true, that by these vague terms, he is clothed with all powers which can possibly be denominated executive, then it was highly improper to have allowed him any share in legislation. And yet no act or Resolution of Congress, can be passed in the first instance without his assent. The first article of the Constitution as expressly gives all legislative powers to Congress, consisting of a Senate and House of Representatives, as the second confers the Executive on the President; but it never conceived, that by this they are authorized to legislate without his assent. This broad interpretation of general words would even exclude the Senate from any share in the conclusion of treaties with foreign powers, and in the appointment of officers both of which are admitted to be Executive powers, and are expressly granted. The Constitution of the United States not only consists of various articles, relating to different subjects; but of numerous sections in relation to the same subject matter. And as the whole Constitution is to be looked to, in determining the powers of that government in all its departments combined, so all that relates to any particular department must be reviewed in determining its limits. The President's powers we have already seen, are in part legislative. Those of the Senate are in part executive, and under a written Constitution which defines the spheres of each of the governing powers by its own positive injunctions. We are not allowed to give to the executive department a power, because in our speculations on the subject we deem it to be executive.

But why should I labor to prove that the words last quoted convey to the President no power over the public monies, whilst the affirmative of the proposition is with the other side, or whilst by express terms, all such powers are given to Congress. This is clear, not merely from their power "to lay and collect taxes," to pay the debts of the U. S., "to borrow money," "to coin money," etc., but they have also "power to dispose of, and make all needful rules and regulations respecting the territory or other property, belonging to the U. S." No people better understood the maxim that "Money is power," than the Anglo-American race, or more fully knew the dangers to be apprehended to liberty, from entrusting the public purse, either for the purpose of collection, custody or expenditure, to any other than the immediate representatives of the people. By means of this important power, their European ancestors had in a series of ages, extorted from the' grasp of executive usurpation the native liberties of man, and bequeathed them to them as a glorious heritage. Yet with the light of all this experience, and with the positive declarations of the Constitution staring them in the face, there are those who insist on the syllogism "all executive power is in the President"—to keep the public monies is an executive power—"therefore the custody of the public money belongs to the President." Yes, sir, the President himself, has been induced to sign a protest in which after stating that the custody of the public property has always been considered an appropriate function of the executive department, in this and all other governments it is declared, that "public money is but a species of public property." It cannot be raised by taxation or customs, nor brought into the treasury in any other way except by law, but wherever, or however, obtained, its custody always has been and always must be, unless the Constitution be changed, entrusted to the executive department.

No officer can be created by Congress for the purpose of taking charge of it whose appointment would not at once devolve on the President, and who would not be responsible to him for the faithful performance of his duties. Were the Congress to assume, with or without a legislative act the power to appointing officers independently of the President, to take charge and custody of the public property contained in the military and naval arsenals magazines and storehouses, it is believed that such an act would be regarded as a palpable usurpation of executive power, subversive of the form as well as the fundamental principles of our government. But where is the difference in principle, whether the public property be in the form of arms munitions of war and supplies, or gold and silver, or bank notes. None can be perceived—none is believed to exist. Congress cannot therefore take out of the hands of the Executive department the custody of the public property or money, without an assumption of executive power, and a subversion of the first principles of the Constitution." Sir, if these things be true, the awful prediction of Patrick Henry has been fulfilled, and your President—your Republican President, is "but a monarch in disguise." In disguise, did I say? The diadem and the purple are only wanting to constitute all the attributes of royalty. What bold usurpation is there in the assertion "that Congress cannot take out of the hands of the executive department the custody of the public property or money, without an assumption of executive power, and a subversion of the first principles of the Constitution!" Where were the eyes of the writer of that protest, that he failed to see the provisions of the Constitution before stated? That not only is no power over the public funds given to the President, but that to Congress is expressly granted, everything relating to the money as well as the "power to dispose of and make all needful rules and regulations, respecting the territory and other property belonging to the United States?" Can any one doubt for a moment, but that Congress may dispense altogether with the Treasury department as a branch of the Executive, and direct the public money to be kept in a strong box under the chair of the Speaker of the House of Representatives, and that drafts may be made upon it only by his warrant! Or that they may direct the revenues collected in each State to be paid to the Governor thereof? To be by him kept until disbursed by acts of Congress. These officers surely could not be removed by the President's executive power in any way contended by him. Sir, the Constitution of the United States places on the shoulders of the President no such Atlantean weight, it exacts from him no such responsibility, it confers upon him no such power. The executive department in every government of laws is merely ministerial to the legislative, and is but the executor of its will. This is particularly observable in the Constitution of the United States, which by its first article, vests "*All* legislative powers herein granted in a Congress, which shall consist of a Senate and House of Representatives." The second article declares that "The executive power shall be vested in a President of the United States." The question arises, what executive power? Why clearly, upon the supposition that this clause grants any power, only that which is necessary to the due execution of the legislative powers before granted. Until laws are enacted, there are none to be executed; and although our President has a share of legislative power, as we have before seen, he has no executive powers properly so called which are not dependent on the Legislature for their exercise. He is commander in chief of the army and navy, but until the Legislature has passed the laws creating these, he holds but a "barren sceptre in his grip." He may make treaties with the concurrence of two thirds of the Senate, and with their consent also, appoint ambassadors, ministers, consuls, judges and others; but all these powers require a previous action of the Legislature to enable him to fulfill them; Courts, whether supreme or inferior, must be regulated by laws, before judges are appointed. The offices, other than those connected with our foreign relations, must be first created by Act of Congress, before the President can appoint their officers. And an appropriation of money for their salaries, and the expense of treaties, will always be needed, before officers of the latter class can be brought into efficient action. He may give to Congress "information of the state of the Union"—recommend measures for their consideration— on extraordinary occasions he may convene, and in case of disagreement between two houses as to adjournment, adjourn them. But except so far as Congress wills, he has no military force, either land or naval, to command, no culprits to pardon, no treaties which he can fulfill, no officers to commission, and of course none to remove, no laws "to faithfully execute," no money to deposit or remove, not even a salary of a single dollar, to purchase his food or habitation.

Such are the humble powers of the President of the United States independent of, and prior to, the action of Congress. To such they may be again reduced, wherever it shall suit the good pleasure of the Legislature. Against such a reduction, the President can protect himself by no executive power, but only by his legislative negative. Among the axioms of freedom which our fathers incorporated into our Bill of Rights, it is declared "that a frequent recurrence to fundamental principles is absolutely necessary to preserve the blessings of liberty," and never has its truth or necessity been more clearly demonstrated, than by the alarming pretensions of executive power now set up for the first time. Accustomed as we are, almost at the end of the half century from the beginning of the Government, to view the President of the United States, exercising the authority and dispensing the patronage derived in consequence of more than a thousand statutes, we are apt to overlook the relation of the executive to the other departmenrts of the government, and to mistake derivative for an original power. Hence we hear in the protest to the Senate, of "original executive power," "left unchecked by the Constitution." And of analogies drawn from the powers of "the head of the executive department," "in the government from which many of the fundamental principles of our system are derived." Sir, the Constitution, as I stated in the beginning, conferred only specific powers on the President, as well as on the whole Federal Government, and did not "check" powers before possessed. He deduces from it his whole official existence, and I protest against his derivation of any power from a reference to the prerogatives of the king of Great Britain. We have also been told in this debate, by the gentleman who presented these Resolutions, in the excess of admiration for the executive, in disparagement of the legislative department of the government, that the latter had been always addicted to usurpation and the Senate of Rome was cited as an example. I thank God, that the liberties of my country are fixed on a basis more secure than those of any nation either of ancient or modern Europe. But for the sake of "setting history right," I would say a word in vindication of the law givers of other times. The Romans did not cease to be free, until the people had become thoroughly corrupted by their system of plundering the world and living on the spoils. From the influences of venality and corruption in the latter days of the Republic, no class was entirely exempt; but unless my recollection be untrue, the last flickering flame of Roman liberty expired in the Senate House. And even after all hope was lost on the fatal field of Pharsalia, and the darkness of military despotism had spread over the land, a lightening flash of the fire of freedom gleamed from the dagger of a patriot Senator. Those sturdy barons, who established the *Magna Charta,* the Hampdens, the Sidneys and Russels, who contributed so much to wrest absolute power from the hands of the king, and secure popular rights, the Parliament of 1688, and the American Colonial Legislatures, are surely exceptions to the general denunciations of the gentleman, unless, indeed, it be usurpation in the representatives of the people to deny slavish doctrines of non resistance and passive obedience to the divine right of Kings. Our predecessors too, in these halls, deserved no such imputation, since in the lapse of more than half a century, they have not enacted more than half a dozen statutes which the judiciary has declared to be beyond the limits of their powers.

But, Sir, I will not leave the subject before us to go into an examination of the comparative merits of the legislative and executive departments of government in other ages and countries; nor would I make an invidious distinction between those of my own, much less pass unrebuked an illegal exercise of power in either. I have been endeavoring to show that the President could derive no power over the public revenue from any of the grants in the Constitution, and as no law has been produced, bestowing such a power, the resolution of the Senate is taken to be true.

But suppose that I am deceived in all this, the demonstration of its truth is by no means necessary to the vindication of the resolution of the Senate,—from the very nature of government, the executive as such, is but the minister to perform the dictates of the legislature; and as the authority to command implies the right to obedience, it is at any time competent to the legislative power, to declare whether its will has been properly executed or whether under a pretense of its execution deeds have been done which it never authorized; this may be effected by a statute declaratory of what the law is, or by the expression of an opinion in the shape of a resolution. Where the legislative power consists in distinct bodies, either may make such a declaration, with or without the concurrence of the other. As both are charged with the responsible duty of examining the whole body of the laws, to ascertain what defects exist, and to provide suitable remedies, so both are equally bound to scrutinize the administration of the laws, and if they be found to be misunderstood or misapplied, to declare their true meaning and insist on their correct administration. Such declarations are not always made by the terms of enactment merely, but these are usually preceded by a preamble, reciting that "Whereas the judiciary has decided improperly," or whereas some executive officer has acted improperly. The terms of censure implied or expressed in such a preamble on the conduct of the officer in question, may be more or less severe. The right to use them is certainly unquestionable, and is under no other restraints than are attached to all the rights of a legislative body within the pale of the constitution,—their discretion and sense of propriety is their only guide. If the Senate of the United States had used the language of their resolution by way of preamble to a statute "declaring and enacting" that the Bank of the U. S. does and shall possess the right to the "custody of the public monies so long as they are kept safely and paid out faithfully," they certainly would have been within the limit of their powers, and yet the only effect of such an act on their part would have been the same with this resolution, that is, to express the opinion of that branch of the legislature on the illegality of the conduct of the President, that the act of 1816 ought to be executed, as it had always been heretofore.

It is likewise incident to every legislative assembly, as well as judicial tribunal, unless positively restrained, not merely to protect itself from interruption in the discharge of its duties, whence arises the power to punish for contempts, but also to resist any invasion of its rights by the other departments of government; and when the Constitution has provided no superior to determine such matters, it must be itself the judge on the question, whether such an invasion has been made. The mild and feeble mode in which only it is able to resist, can make no difference. It may not possess the power to compel the encroaching department to desist, but this does not prevent it from giving the alarm and rousing the vigilance of those from whom government has derived its existence. If the other house of the legislature should pass a resolution directing the public treasurer to pay a sum of money to an officer, without sending it here for our concurrence, it would not only be our right but our duty, to remonstrate against such a procedure. If his excellency the governor should draw a warrant on the treasury in favor of any individual under pretence or mistake that an appropriation had been made therefor by law, we should likewise resist that by protest or resolution. The governor of this state in 1818 appointed a Judge of the Superior Court to fill a vacancy which had occurred without the knowledge of the General Assembly, during their session. The letter of the Constitution authorized such an appointment only when the vacancy happened "during their recess." The legislature which next convened, probably concurred in the Governor's construction; but with all respect for that distinguished and patriotic magistrate (Gov. Branch), had the General Assembly or either House of it been of a different opinion, might they not have resolved that his Excellency in making such appointment has assumed a power "not granted by the Constitution and laws, but in derogation of both"? When such a declaration shall be made must depend solely on the opinion of the department or body which believes its rights have been violated. From the imperfection of man it may be inappropriately made, but the like result may happen in the exercise of any of its powers. The Senate of the United States therefore, being a legislative body, clothed with as full legislative powers as the House of Representatives, excepting in the single particular of being unable to originate revenue bills, had a perfect right whenever it was convinced of the fact, to declare that the President had invaded the province of the law-makers and under colour of executing his constitutional functions had assumed powers which belonged only to Congress. Though inferior in number and though chosen differently from the other House, they are with the exception before stated, equally charged with the high and solemn duties, not merely of enacting laws for this vast republic, but by perpetual vigilance of guarding from usurpation those inestimable rights, which it required ages and centuries, the blood of many martyrs, and the horrors of innumerable wars to rescue from the hold of executive power beyond the Atlantic. This ordinary incident of legislative power would never have been denied to the Senate but for the confusion of ideas arising from its also possessing judicial and executive powers; but it must be recollected that the two latter are in addition to, and do by no means abridge, its legislative authorities, because for one purpose, it is a judicatory and for another an executive council. It is not thereby the less a branch of the legislature, capable of framing and passing laws, of declaring their true meaning, of inquiring into the acts of all those entrusted with their execution and of asserting whether their intention has been fulfilled, or whether the conduct of any executive officer from the highest to the lowest has been in accordance with law, or in violation of it. The right of defending all its powers against infringement belongs of course to the Senate, if the President should appoint an officer "to fill up a vacancy," which had happened during their session, and not "during the recess," or if he should exchange ratification of a treaty with a foreign power, without consulting them, they would be authorized and bound to remonstrate against either, as an infraction of their executive power. The Constitution declaring that officers shall be appointed and treaties concluded by and "with the advice and consent of the Senate," if the House of Representatives should presume to pass judgment of removal from office against any individual or declare him incapable of holding office, the Senate may protest against that, as a direct encroachment on their judicial functions; so if the House of Representatives or President, or both, as coordinate branches of the law, in acting power shall assail its legislative rights, it may in like manner defend these, which are far more extensive than the two former, comprehending every legislative authority, granted to the other House, with the exception only before stated. It has been boldly promulged by the head of a department, during the present year, that the Senate has no right to investigate its affairs. If this indeed be true, then is the Senate deprived of half its efficiency in the enactment of laws; for how are they qualified to pass new laws, unless they can ascertain not merely how the old laws are written, but how they operate practically? And the people are robbed of one half of the sentinels whom they thought they had appointed to watch and to examine the administration of the laws, to commend the faithful and condemn the unfaithful ministerial servants. Shall I be told, as has been asserted before, that the Senate in such investigation, may conceive opinions and contract prejudices which may render them unfit to act as judges, if an impeachment shall be preferred against a delinquent officer thus detected?

This argument from inconvenience, if it be entitled to any notice, may be readily answered. Sir, postve stipulation, the observance of which is enjoined by oath, are not to be disregarded by individaul ideas of propriety and convenience, and that Senator would deserve and receive the severest reproof, who excused himself for a failure to sift the conduct of any public officer, by the fear that he would thus morally disqualify himself for the trial of an impeachment, should one be instituted by the other House of Congress. The same species of reason would forever forbid the Senate to vote for, or the President to approve, a declaration of War, lest they should in its progress so far lose temper as to be unfitted to negotiate a treaty of peace. A judge in like manner, would, by the acceptance of his office, surrender the power of self defense, being unable to deal any but judicial blows. It was the intention of the framers of the Constitution, that the Senators in Congress to whom these three-fold duties are confided, should possess the highest qualifications of mind and heart; but to guard against the frailties of human nature in its best state, when they put off the legislative to assume the judicial robe, they are required to take a new oath or affirmation, to direct their attention to the charges alleged and the evidence adduced by the other House, and as faithful triers to make their decision upon these only. It might possibly have been more proper to have given the judicial and executive powers of the Senate to some other body, but it is difficult to conceive how the super-addition of these should in any manner diminish its power of defending itself and the right of free examination into the execution of the laws and animadversion on the acts of executive officers of any grade, which, as I have endeavored to show, belongs to every legislative body—a right which has been nowhere exercised more freely than in the American Congress. In the year of 1793 Mr. Giles of Virginia, introduced sundry resolutions into the House of Representatives, casting the harshest censure on Alexander Hamilton, then Secretary of the Treasury, charging him among other things, with neglect of his office and indecorum to the House, *(Marshall's Life of Washington, Vol. 5).*

In 1796, a resolution passed the House of Representatives calling on the President (Washington), to lay before the House a copy of the instructions to our minister together with the correspondence and other documents relative to Jay's Treaty. The President in a written message refused to communicate the information desired, declaring that "to admit a right in the House of Representatives, to demand and have as a matter of course, all the papers respecting a negotiation with a foreign power, would be to establish a dangerous precedent." The message further proceeds, "it does not occur that the inspection of the papers asked for can be relative to any purpose under the cognizance of the House of Representatives, except that of an impeachment, which the Resolution has not expressed." And concludes, "a just regard to the Constitution and the duties of my office, under all the circumstances of this case, forbids a compliance with your request." Whereupon, Mr. Blount of North Carolina, in committee of the whole, moved the following resolutions which were adopted by the House:

Resolved, That it being declared by the second section of the second article of the Constitution, that "the President shall have power, by and with the consent of the Senate, to make treaties, provided two-thirds of the Senators present concur," the House of Representatives do not claim any agency in making treaties, but that when a treaty stipulates regulations, on any subjects submitted by the Constitution to the powers of Congress, it must depend for its execution as to such stipulations on a law or laws to be passed by Congress; and the constitutional right and duty of the House of Representatives in all such cases to deliberate on the expediency or inexpediency of carrying such treaty into effect, and to determine and act thereon, as in their judgment may be most conducive to the public good.

Resolved, That it is not necessary to the propriety of any application from this house to the executive, for information desired by them and which may relate to any constitutional functions of the house, that the purposes for which information may be wanted or to which the same may be applied, should be stated in the application. *(Journal Ho. of Reps. 2nd. Vol. 480, 488, 489.)*

These resolutions assert in substance, that the President in withholding the information sought by the house, on the ground that it had not been asked for, as evidence on an impeachment, had contravened their rights and violated his constitutional duty, yet they were adopted by a vote of 57 to 35. Among the former of whom are such names as James Madison and Nathaniel Macon. This censure of the House, however, drew forth no remonstrance from the President; he did not doubt their powers to express their opinions as to their Constitutional rights. A still stronger precedent is afforded by the case of Jonathan Robbins, during the administration of the elder Adams. A person of this name was in prison in South Carolina, for trial, on a charge of piracy and murder committed on board a British ship of war on the high seas. On a requisition of the British Government under the treaty of peace, the President informed the judge of that district, that he considered an offence committed on board a public ship of war on the high seas, to have been committed within the jurisdiction of the nation to whom the ship belongs, and requested the judge to deliver up the prisoner to the agent of Great Britain; *provided,* that the stipulated evidence of his criminality should be produced. The judge accordingly surrendered him, and he was tried and executed by a court martial on a charge of mutiny and murder. The House of Representatives called for the papers relative to the case, and resolutions were introduced reciting all the facts, and concluding "that the decision of those questions by the President against the jurisdiction of the Courts of the United States in a case where those courts had already assumed and exercised jurisdiction; and his advice and request to the Judge of the District Court, that the person thus charged should be delivered up; provided, only such evidence of his criminality should be produced as would justify his apprehension and commitment for trial, are a dangerous interference of the executive with judicial decisions; and that the compliance with such advice and request on the part of the judge of the district court of South Carolina, is a sacrifice of the constitutional independence of the judicial powers, and exposes the administration thereof to suspicion and reproach." These resolutions were not adopted because a majority of the House believed the conduct of the President to be legal. But, so far as I am informed, no doubt was expressed as to the right of the house to entertain them, and many distinguished names are recorded against the motion to discharge from their further consideration. Here then is a proposition for bitter censure not only on the President but on a judge of the United States in relation to their conduct in the construction of a treaty, in defining the limits between the executive and judicial powers, and on a difficult question of admiralty law, retained under consideration near twenty days, and finally rejected against the wishes of Albert Gallatin, Nathaniel Macon, John Randolph and others, who have been quoted here as proper expositors of the Constitution. I will only mention in addition to these the almost unanimous vote of commendation to President Washington, when retiring from office, (*Journal House Reps. Vol. 2, 619*), and leave to candor to say, whether if they have a right to praise they have not a right also to blame.

Is it objected, that these authorities come from the House of Representatives alone? My friend from Bertie (Mr. Outlaw) has adduced a precedent of a like proceeding in the Senate, (Gov. Branch's resolution 1826), which is too recent to require further comment now. The unanimous condemnation of the Postmaster General in the same body at the last session of Congress, demonstrates even to the unwilling that their right to do so is unquestionable. But what power has the House of Representatives to pass judgment on the acts of executive officers by resolutions which is not possessed by the Senate? By the Constitution, the house has "the sole power of impeachment" and the Senate "the sole power to try all impeachments." The power to impeach, however, does not give the right to censure, in any other way than by filing a criminal information to bring an offender to trial before the other body.

It is a power to indict an offender but not to find him guilty. Yet the resolutions before stated both begin and end the accusation, both charge and convict. They cannot therefore be traced to the impeaching function of the House of Representatives, but results as an incident from their legislative authority.

I regret, Sir, that I have felt obliged to detain the House thus long in endeavoring to demonstrate the right of the Senate of the United States to declare its opinion, whenever it shall judge it to be proper, of the official conduct of the President or of any inferior executive officer. I have been accustomed to consider this right of all legislative bodies as one of the elementary principles of freedom. The history of liberty for at least 800 years in Great Britain exhibits an almost constant struggle between the legislative and executive powers of the government—the Parliament insisting upon the rights of the people, and the king asserting the "original, unchecked executive powers" of monarchy. But ever since the assemblage of the inflexible barons at Runnymede, the right of the former to speak their minds freely of the conduct of their sovereign if it has been denied by the slaves of courts, has been exercised with the boldness which belongs to the votaries of freedom everywhere. As far back as the reign of Henry III, we are told by history, that "in full Parliament, when Henry demanded a new supply, he was openly reproached with a breach of his word, and the frequent violations of the Charter. He was asked if he did not blush to desire any aid from his people, whom he professedly hated and despised, and to whom on all occasions he preferred aliens and foreigners, and who groaned under the oppressions which he either permitted or exercised over them." (*Hume,* Vol. 2, 345). The famous *Petition of Right* was but a declaration in indignant terms, that the king had exercised prerogatives unauthorized by the British Constitution and in contravention of the rights of Parliament. In the latter years of Charles I, the preamble of a Bill to raise soldiers, denied the king's right to impress subjects into the military service. Charles came to Parliament and offered to sanction the Bill without the preamble, "by which means," he said, that "ill timed question with regard to the prerogative would be avoided, and the pretensions of each party be left entire." Both Houses took fire at the measure. The Lords as well as Commons passed a vote "declaring it to be a high breach of priviledge for the king to take notice of any Bill which was in agitation in either of the houses, or to express his sentiments in regard to it before it was presented to him for his assent." Such are the terms of denunciation in which the legislative assemblies of England were permitted to speak of their monarch before their rights were firmly established by the Revolution of 1688. Since that period, the most high prerogative Tory has never breathed a doubt of such a right in Parliament to its fullest extent. But it is vehemently contended here that one of the houses of the American Congress, the representatives of the whole 24 states, has no right to express its opinion, that the President of the United States had assumed powers which did not belong to him, but which were by the Constitution conferred on the legislature—that their mouths must be sealed as to all his acts, except when open for the ascription of praise, and that if, in an unguarded moment, under the impulse of the spirit of freedom, they have ventured to question the legality of a single one, the most honored sons of all the states must be humbled, not merely to confess their sorrow, but to undo the deed. Sir, I appeal to every American citizen to say whether the powers of their President are more absolute than those of a British king, or whether their Congress, in either house, has not a right, to speak of the former with a freedom at least equal to that of the Lords and Commons in regard to the latter. Why, Sir, the expression contained in the resolution of the Senate respecting the President is high commendation compared with the censure and animadversion which for centuries past, the two houses of Parliament have habitually passed on a king, who according to the theory of that government, "can do no wrong." The legitimate powers of the President are tremendous enough. To say nothing of the chief command of the whole military force and the negative on acts of legislation, the power to appoint 40,000 officers, compensated by salaries of many millions of dollars, and comprising the honors most grateful to ambition, the power to remove these again at will, and the power to conclude, with the concurrence of the Senate, all treaties with foreign nations, are quite as great as the jealous spirit of liberty will accord to any one man. Add to these the claims recently set up of controlling all incumbents while in office under penalty of removal, and thus to suspend any law, and to compel anything to be done under the form of law; of the entire custody and control of the public treasure; and forbid the Senate to question any executive act, and a perpetual Dictatorship is established "to take care that the Republic shall suffer no harm," to be sure; but this also implies that it shall receive no good unless it so please the Chief Magistrate.

Mr. Speaker, it may possibly be unfortunate, that any collision should arise between any of the branches of the Federal Government, but, Sir, if not to be encouraged they certainly ought not to be prohibited. The liberties of the people and the rights of the states are surely in as little danger from the disagreement as from the combination of the Departments of the Government to sustain each other. At all events, the legislature of a state should be the last body on earth to degrade or restrain within improper bounds, the Senate of the Union. It is the great palladium of the rights of the states—on that theatre only, do these sovereign communities meet as equals. Bring this into contempt or destroy its independence, and you rear over our heads one consolidated government, consisting of a single national assembly, and an executive chosen alike by the whole people of the Union, and limited only by the will of the great majority. The checks and balances of the system are gone, and the lines of division between the different states obliterated. Does it become us *then,* even if satisfied that the resolution of the state was erroneous by this harsh denunciation, to make war on the depository of rights so sacred? Against the present power and patronage of the executive unaided by legislative interference, the Senate cannot stand, unless armed in a righteous cause. Why then are we invoked as allies! But is there no feeling of Carolina pride which would shield *our* Senator from rebuke, even had he expressed an erroneous opinion? What is the offence with which he is here charged? That he has slept upon his post? Oh, no: it is that he was too vigilant. Possessing something of the spirit of those men, "who snuffed the approach of danger in the tainted breeze," he has given the alarm at a supposed assault on the Constitution, and rushed to the rescue. Had he, though fully convinced of the approaching attack, observed a cowardly silence, or basely cried "All's well," placed as he was, high on the watchtower of our liberties, he would have deserved the deep execration of his countrymen. And will those *then,* who, though believing this danger imaginary, admit that liberty is to be preserved only by perpetual vigilance destroy that vigilance in their own servants by inflicting degradation and disgrace? Will free men, themselves, "pardon nothing to the spirit of liberty?" Sir, men are not prone to desert the ranks of power and patronage, or incur their displeasure. It is far less difficult to float in a current than to stem its tide, and the public servant who exchanges administration for opposition must be excused at least from the motive of present reward, and should not be lightly condemned. The tendency of the selfish passions to prefer the side which dispenses offices and emolument is obvious to all; and all history will prove that far more statesmen have betrayed their trusts and basely sold the interest of their constituents by going over to the administration, than by leaving it. Beware then, how you reprove the independence of your representatives, lest you encourage them to prefer their own ease and advancement to their country's good.

Sir, I have thus far said nothing of the particular requirements which these resolutions impose. They demand of our Senator to acknowledge the error if not the falsehood of an opinion expressed on his oath. Every public servant is required to take an oath to the Constitution, in order that the great principles of justice

and liberty, which it embodies, may be kept inviolate; and whenever, by word or deed, he decides a constitutional question, the
eye of Heaven has been called to witness his sincerity, and Divine
vengeance imprecated, if he shall fail to express the honest con-
victions of his mind. Nor is this all. If it be true, that it is a
part of legislative duty, to observe the administration of the laws,
and to declare wherein they have been misinterpreted, every
legislator undertakes by his oath, to make such declaration, whenever he believes that the Constitution has been materially violated
by an executive officer. Under this high sanction, as well as a
patriotic sense of duty, was the resolution of the Senate passed,
and the vote of Mr. Mangum given. Yet, we are about to command him, to aver that this resolution is not merely untrue, but
unworthy to remain among the records of the things that once
were done. Really, Sir, it would seem to me equally proper to
direct him to vote for a resolution, asserting that none such as
this obnoxious one, of the last session, ever had passed. That
would require him expressly to tell a falsehood. This, requires
him to suppress the truth. That would ask him to declare the
non-existence of a fact, which all the world knows to exist. This
commands him to destroy the best evidence by which its existence
is proved. Is it expected or desired, that he shall obey this man-
date? Can he do it, without the lowest humiliation and infamy?
And can honor from dishonor grow? Can fame from infamy
proceed? Can we make a disgraceful requisition of him without
disgracing ourselves and the state? But these consequences must
be disregarded, and the legislative history of the country mutilated, not because, in the language of the first resolution, we shall
thereby illumine his mind "upon any great question of national
policy," or confirm and strengthen him "in time of public emergency;" but because a place may be thereby vacated. Instructions,
it would seem, should relate to future actions upon "great questions of national policy." These, however, pertain to the past,
and if implicitly obeyed can only falsify the journal of the last
session of Congress. Sir, the journal of a legislative assembly is
its autobiography—"it's life written by itself." Whether well or
ill, that which was really done should be truly noted. If the acts
which it records, be wise and just and beneficial in its consequences, it is a memorial to the honor and wisdom of its authors;
if otherwise, it confers on them an immortality of a different kind.
If the charge contained in the resolution of the Senate be untrue
and undeserved as regards the President, the imputation will only

recoil on themselves, both in the estimation of the present age and of posterity. But how futile and ineffectual are these resolutions in attaining their apparent object! The journals of the Senate have been printed and distributed in all our public libraries and have gone forth in the daily and weekly papers to the ends of the earth. Is it supposed, that by blotting out from the manuscript at Washington, that all copies will be destroyed, and this horrible resolution forgotten? We read in natural history of a wingless bird, which is hunted for its plumage, and when hard pressed by the horsemen in the chase, hides its head in leaves, and vainly supposes that its whole body is concealed. The proceeding contemplated by these resolutions, appears to me, Sir, to be founded on a like vain supposition. As well may we attempt to gather in all the leaves of the last autumn, as to destroy the notoriety which that resolution has acquired.

But, again: in what way is the "vote of expunging" to be given? On a resolution, I presume, to be hereafter introduced. And will not that resolution recite the one to be effaced, and revive its existence as often as it may be destroyed? Let us see the practical operation of these instructions. Suppose them to have passed, and that some "learned Theban" in the Senate of the United States has introduced a resolution "declaring that a resolution of the last session in the following words, to wit, etc., be expunged from the journals," (it must be recited to ascertain its identity) and that this latter resolution has passed. The journals of the previous session are brought in, and that execution may be thoroughly done upon the offending manuscript, the Vice President, by whitening or blackening, annihilates both its body and spirit. This might be considered as a not an "unsubstantial death,"—but on the next morning, when the clerk reads the new journal, the old offender is found, "alive and in full life;" and although it may "sear the eyeball" of the high functionary at whose hands it so recently suffered, it will not "down at his bidding." Thus the whole effort of this solemn letter missive from the Legislature of North Carolina to her Senator and the most servile compliance on his part with its behests, will be but to erase a resolution from one book of the Senate's journals and insert it in another. A legislative body, under our Constitution, has no right to act without recording its actions for the view of its constituents; and, like a man who walks in the snow, it cannot obliterate its footsteps without leaving others equally palpable.

But, Mr. Speaker, I deny the Constitutional right of the Senate of the United States to expunge from the journals which they have published as genuine. The Constitution declares that "each House shall keep a journal of its proceedings, and from time to time publish the same; and the yeas and nays of the members of either House on any question shall, at the desire of one-fifth of those present, be entered on the journal." Now, Sir, in the name of all the people of the state who are parties to that compact, I remonstrate against any mutilation by the Senate of that history which it has put forth to the country, as a record of its transactions. To secure the most rigid accountability and to expose the conduct not merely of the whole Body, but of every individual composing it to the public scrutiny, the searching spirit of freedom has demanded these journals to be kept. But of what avail is it, that they shall be kept and published, if at any time, even years afterwards, a Senate consisting of the same or different members, may vary or alter it at pleasure. Independently of the falsehood which might thus be interpolated, in the history of the country, what facilities for deception would it afford for apostates and demagogues? If they can expunge by instruction from us, they can do so without it; and if they can erase, it will hardly be doubted that they can also insert. Whenever, therefore, it is discovered that any measure is unpopular, the yeas and nays may be struck out on motion, though recorded years ago, so as to leave the acts of individuals entirely to conjecture; or the votes may be changed, or fictions inserted, so as to make a patriot or traitor of any public man according to the wishes and purposes of the party in power. If they can expunge the proceedings of the last session, how are they to be hindered from blotting out the proceedings of the whole administration of Washington? To guard the people from impositions and deceptions like these, the provision of the Constitution last noticed was made. It is one of the many propositions which a constitutional oath binds the conscience to maintain. But we are now required to command our Senator in Congress not merely (as I have before shown) to retract an opinion solemnly and deliberately expressed on a constitutional question, but doubly to violate his oath by an erasure of the journals. Such is the degrading dilemma in which it is proposed to place one of the most distinguished sons of the state, who has devoted no small portion of his life to her service, and whose public character constitutes a part of her moral property. When acting in masses and under party excitement, men make requirements and perform acts which their own individual honor and private judgment would condemn in others. To this house and our constituents I leave it to determine whether the proceeding contemplated by these resolutions be not of this character.

Sir, I must apologize for having detained the House thus long. I appear here not for attack, but defence—not for victory, but truth. If these humble views shall contribute anything to the better understanding of the important subjects involved in the resolutions under consideration, I am amply rewarded for the labor and attention bestowed upon them.

From M. McGehee.[62]   U.

Person, N. C., 13th. December, 1834.

Your welcome letter of the 6th inst. came duly to hand. I am not much supprised tho deeply lament the present political excitement seeing that principal is disregarded the publik good sacreficed and all produced by a set of office holders and office seekers who have but little interest beyound that of holding there office.

I am at a loss to see how to meet the difficulty in the present state of the publick mind; the people act from impulce alone. When men are reasoned into an opinian if it be rong they can be reasoned out of it, but when they are without reason and without any governing principal it seems to me that the better way is not to oppose them as it will only serve to keep them combined, when if left to them selves they will soon differ. this I think is the course that should be persewed among the people but in councils assembled as you are a position becomes absolutely necessary and I am gratified to see that you had determined to address the house.

Since Browns election I have dispaired very much but seeing that Ritchie [63] has lost his election as publick printer in Va. my

---

[62] I have been unable to identify the writer of this letter. He was probably a brother of Thomas M. McGehee of Person County, and so an uncle of Montford McGehee who wrote the memorial address on Graham, above printed.

[63] Thomas Ritchie (1778-1854), the famous Virginia journalist, editor of the *Richmond Enquirer*, 1804-1845, and *Crisis*, and of the Washington *Union*, during Polk's administration. He was a power in state and national politics.

hopes have revived for Leigh's [64] reallection; it is a matter in which I have long felt a very deep interest.

* * * * *

From Hugh Waddell.   U.

Hillsboro, Decr. 18th, '34.

My dear Graham!

Are your fingers *sore* or have you the Gout in them or is it only your heart that is sore, that you will not write me? Some time since I wrote you in answer to your kind letter & have been ever since *tri weekly* expecting to hear from you.

You should remember that being on the scene of action it is your duty to report occasionally to the Admiralty office what you have done, how you have out-manoeuvered the enemy, how you have fought your ship; what weather you have had, etc.

All this is absolutely necessary to a good officer who has been trusted with a command & I hope you have not "grown too big for your breeches," for you must remember I am one of your sovereigns & shall hold you to a strict account.

I had predicted that on the debate of the Mangum resolutions, you & Haywood would be reserved to conclude the fight & that the point was, who should have the last blow. So I see it has turned out. The Majority was smaller than I had expected; I fear the Res. will pass the Senate too.

I see there has been no report from the Committee on the Nassau affair, I shall not easily forgive "Alexander the Coppersmith" for "he hath done me a grievous wrong" as Sterne has it, in not putting you on that Committee.

I hope against hope that the Report may not be unworthy the subject.

Pray write me what you are likely to do, how party politics seem to work in regard to matters ahead, Who is to be our next President, or are we not to have another? Is there any real danger to the Supreme Court to be apprehended?

---

[64] Benjamin Watkins Leigh (1781-1849), of Virginia, a graduate of William and Mary, member of house of delegates, 1811-1813, 1830-1833, was editor of the code of 1819, delegate to the convention of 1829-1830, commissioner to South Carolina on Nullification, reporter of the court of appeals, 1829-1841, United States senator, 1834-1836. In 1836 he refused to resign upon instructions by the legislature to vote for Benton's expunging resolution, though he had, in 1811, defended the right of instruction, but with the proviso that it could not prevail when involving an act of moral turpitude.

I feel that anything from our little, quiet, dirty village, would be of little interest to you; the truth is, that except a Bill of the health of the Villagers & of the Mortality of the Hogs, whereby the aforesaid health is likely to be somewhat prolonged, there is literally nothing to state. So far is this true, that I could not have found it in my heart, much as you deserve exemplary punishment of your neglect, to put you to the expence of the postage of this scrawl, had it been necessary to remit it by mail. . . .

Mr. Swain's Inaugural was well done. What is he to do next? go to the Bar?

* * * * *

To William Gaston. U.

Raleigh, Dec. 20th, 1834.

I had the honour to receive your favour by Mr. Manly at the commencement of the Session of the Legislature. I was myself entirely satisfied on the subject of your eligibility to the bench of the Supreme Court by your letter to Mr. Devereux previously to the last session of Assembly. Your last communication is more full and I think should remove all doubt. My first impression after receiving it, was that it should be published in our newspapers, but it occurred to me that this would be supererogatory and evince an anxiety on your part which might enlist prejudice, or call out whatever of lurking hostility there may be in the country. For some time I carried it with me to the house, intending if the subject should be alluded to there to read it to them. It has not, however, been mentioned, in public, nor so far as I recollect, in private except among the gentlemen to whom I have thought proper to exhibit your letter. The only individual from whom any movement on the subject, in the Legislature, could have been apprehended, is entirely powerless and in contempt. I shall preserve your essay and, by your permission, if occasion shall require it, may in future give it general publication. In the mean time, I suggest that it will be the most proper course that the public attention shall not be called to the subject by our friends. You will not suspect me of compliment when I assure you that your appointment, to say the least, has been as generally acceptable to the public in all my sphere of acquaintance as any which has been made in the State, and that it has given increased stability to our Supreme Court. You may have seen in the Papers a notice of a Bill to reduce the salaries of the Judges. It was postponed indefinitely on the second reading, and the majority would have been much greater had not the members of the commons been absent attending the debates of the Senate on the resolutions of instruction to Senator Mangum.

Our session has been rather barren of good legislation. The Bill concerning a convention to amend the Constitution will be considered tomorrow. It will probably be again defeated.

The Resolutions to instruct are still the subject of discussion in the Senate. Messrs. Branch and Carson [65] have each occupied given a full history of private and public affairs at Washington as they were known to themselves. The Senate will pass the Resolutions by a majority of five or six. What Mr. M. will do is uncertain. He is, I think, indisposed to resign and certainly will not do so, unless advised to that course.

The Legislature will sit at least a fortnight yet. The tables are loaded with private bills to divorce, legitimate, restore to credit, etc. Mischievous as these are, I am in hopes that the Session will be brought to a close without any injurious public statute. That is the most that can be expected at present.

With assurances of the highest respect and friendly regard,

I am, dear Sir,

Your very obedt. Servt.

From James Graham.   U.

Washington, Decem. 20th, 1834.

I received yours of the 11th. inst. and I regret to learn the time of the Legislature is to be consumed in National Politicks. I fear the convention question will be over laid in the excitement of the day. I am quite anxious to see Gov Branch's speech which is to unfold some secret matters. My curiosity desires this, though I disapprove of the disclosure. Mr. Branch's position and late connection with the administration should have induced him to be silent, as any statement he may make will be regarded in the light of an accessory and therefore not entitled to full weight. Branch ought to retire from the political stage for a time. The opposition to this administration by their *violent assaults* upon near two days upon them—the latter without finishing. They have

---

[65] Samuel P. Carson.

the President have done more to sustain Genl. Jackson than his friends. There appears a total ignorance of human nature. Don't we all know if the people believe any man is persecuted they go for him right or wrong. On Thursday last the Committee of the Senate appointed to investigate the conduct of the U. S. Bank made a very long and detailed Report. The Report is exculpatory of the Bank from a great number of charges made against it. It also inculpates the Bank in several particulars. For Instance they say the Bank had a Right to defend itself but that in divers instances its operations were not only *Defensive* but *offensive*. They say likewise that the Bank ought to have accounted for the money expended under their Resolution giving the President exclusive power to expend or use money in defence of the Bank or for Secret Service. The President of the Bank withheld this information because its disclosure would present the names of some persons to the public and thereby expose them to much abuse from the press. So far as I heard the Report read I was pleased with it. I presume when printed and debated it will raise the old leven.

We have no parties here yet, they begin on the first of the new year. The number of Strangers here this Session is quite small. We will be very much confined by long Sessions every day after the first of January. I am much pleased at the unexpected Speech of Fleming [66] from Burke. I perceive from the yeas and Nays that a strong majority of the members from My District voted to Instruct Mangum. They go for what they suppose the big-pile. I wish you would look back at the Journals of last year and inform who of the members from my district voted for the new Bank. I also wish you to introduce some measure before the Legislature to prevent the circulation of Bank notes less than $5. And require the Courts to give it in charge to G. Juries. In my part of the State they pay no attention to the Law of 1827 prohibiting the circulation of State Bank notes under $5. from other states. If it be possible try and urge the convention question to a favorable termination.

*   *   *   *   *

---

[66] Samuel Fleming, of Burke County, then serving his only term in the house of commons. He made an excellent speech in opposition to instructions,

From Lawrence & LeMay.[67]   A.

Raleigh, Dec. 25, 1834.

Anxious to spread information before the public and to aid the cause of liberty and the Constitution, we take leave respectfully to ask that you will do us the favor to furnish, for publication, a copy of your speech in the H. of C. on the resolutions to instruct Mr. Mangum.

If we could get it in time to print before the adjournment of the Legislature, an opportunity of circulating it extensively, thro' the members, will be afforded.

With the highest respect and esteem,

From Hugh Waddell.   U.

Moore Fields, Decr. 27, 1834.

I recd. your very welcome letter by the mail of Wednesday, but too late to write by the return mail of that night & now do so only that I may not appear negligent.

In regard to the wish you express to know what our townsmen think you should do, on the Convention question, I beg you to make yourself perfectly easy; the course you have indicated is *no doubt*, the correct one & you will never find your constituents desiring to *instruct* you. We all agree with you & if we did not we would expect that you *must* have *some reason* for any course you might take, which when made known to us, would be amply sufficient to justify you. This is the real (not "rale") republicanism of former times; we trust our Representative, because we *know* him; if he were capable of misrepresenting us we should not have sent him. I believe I speak the united voice of your little dominion, as well as that of friendship in the foregoing.

* * * * *

Mr. Moore [68] with whom I am spending my Christmas, begs to be kindly remembered to you & says he would have written in answer to your favour to him, but he really had nothing to say & was loth to send you a blank sheet to say what he knew you believed already, viz, that he was in very sooth, your sincere

---

[67] Lawrence and Lemay were editors and publishers of the *Star and State Gazette.*
[68] Alfred Moore, of "Moorefields," Orange County, Waddell's father-in-law.

friend & wished you all the laurels which could be gathered in Legislative Halls.

I hope you will have much to tell us of the little & the great on yr return.

From Robert H. Booth. [69]   U.

Edenton, N. C., Decr. 30th, 1834.

Dear Graham,

It is with feelings of pride and pleasure but by no means of surprise that I learn the standing and influence of my old classmate and friend in the Councils of the State, especially as I am persuaded that that influence will always be devoted to the best and most elevated purposes. It is in that confidence that I am induced to trouble you with the following suggestions.

I have requested our Editor here, to send you several Nos. of his Paper containing several hasty and imperfect Essays which, amid much business occupation, I wrote on the subject of Int. Improvement. I trust you have read and considered those views. The system they point out is in my opinion the most probable if not the best that I have seen suggested and I cannot but think that if it be properly brought forward and adequately enforced it might be made *to go.* You will perceive that we have had a large town meeting & nearly unanimously requested our member F. Norcom [70] Esq, to bring forward a Bill for the purpose of having *surveys* made to ascertain the practicability, etc. of such a system; and I assure you it would afford me great pleasure to see you by the side of our friend Norcom in such a cause.

Do not despair, I pray you, of something being yet done to elevate the destiny of the State. I see that even old Montgomery [71] has so far opened his eyes and heart too as to offer a Resolution for adopting the *two fifths* principle, and whilst I do not think such a System will do for N. Carolina, yet such a movement from *such* a source is certainly a pregnant "Sign of the Times."

[69] Robert Henry Booth, of Edenton, a native of Virginia, and a classmate of Graham at the university.

[70] Frederick Norcom represented the borough of Edenton in the commons at this session.

[71] William Montgomery (1789-1884), of Orange, physician and active Democratic politician, served in the state senate, 1829-1835, and was a member of congress, 1835-1841.

By taking the position suggested you will no doubt do yourself great credit as well as the State a Service and certainly receive the thanks of

Your old friend and classmate.

Raleigh

1835

From Eliza Witherspoon.[1]   A.

Brook-Land, [Hale Co., Ala.], New Years day, 1835.

My dear Uncle

As this is new years day, and every body idle, and a continued rain prevents every thing like merriment, or enjoyment within or without door's, I have seated myself for conversing with one, who tho separated from me, is at *all times* upermost in my *thoughts,* and *affections.* The great desire I have of hearing from you, and the pleasure I anticipate in my hours of recreation, in corresponding with a much *beloved Uncle* prompts me to that pleasing duty. As arduous as composing is to me, and the reluctance with which I attempt it, yet when gratitude to an affectionate Uncle is my Theme my mind is always enclined, and my hands are allways ready.

It greatly mortifies me when I think of the time that has been suffered to elapse since I saw you, and I have not written a line. The habit of procrastinating this most important duty seems to have fastened itself, and to be growing upon me. I am entirely unconscious of the time that has entervened, (this however is no excuse), I plead guilty. If time would only delay his swifty wing at our bidding, how we would sleep away our existence in dullest appethy, forgetful of the important duties that await us. "Our years pass away as a tale that is told". Eighteen hundred and thirty four has expired, and I shall see it no more. The thought is really a serious one, that 1835 has commenced, and that 1834 has vanished like a dream.

Thinking some account of my journey might interest you, I have concluded to give you a short one. The day after I parted with you, we reached Lancaster where we remained several days with Cousin Harvey Witherspoon's family. I found them very agreeable and kind. We went from there to Camden remained there a day or two, and from there to Uncle Robert W-s., after staying a few days with them, we set out to visit some of Pa's relations, about twenty miles below, and returning to Sumterville, where Doct. Ben Witherspoon lives. Pa was taken with the billious, congestive fever, he lay 16 days confined to his bed. Several

---

[1] The daughter of Graham's sister, Sophia, who married Dr. John Witherspoon.

times his life was despared of, but fortunately he was with a skillful physician, and among kind friends. We were detained several
week in consequence of his sickness.

We left my Uncles on the morning of the 7th Nov. and reached
home on the morning of the 14th of the same month, near six
hundered miles. We returned the rout we expected through
Columbia and Augusta. Pa has not entirely recovered from his
sickness, looks much reduced. We brought out a cousin of Pa's
with us, a Miss McFadolin, quite pretty, inteligent, etc.

The family have enjoyed fine health the last summer & fall,
although the country has been more sickly than heretofore, the
Seasons very good, and fine crops of corn, and cotten. I regretted
I could not return to Grand Pa's from South Carolina, but after
Pa's sickness I found it was necessary for me to return with him,
as it is uncertain when I shall ever see my relations in that country again. Ma sometimes speaks of visiting Carrolina next Summer.
but that is very doubtful, and if she does she says I must stay at
home, but I know one thing if hard pleading will be of any
avail, every argument shall be used on my part.

We received letters from my brothers in Ohio last week, they
still continue to be pleased with their situations there. Brother
McCalla is now in Mobile, under the care of Dr. Levert of that
place, he writes to us he is recovering. he had a stroke of the palsey
last Summer, which renders him very clumsey.

I expect to visit Mobile and New Orleans the last of this month,
with my Cousin, we anticipate much pleasure, as the seasons are
generally gay at this time. Oh! my dear Uncle how much I wish
you were living in this country, where we could see you sometimes,
and surely the advantages are as great in this State as in North
Carrolina. I suppose by time you have heard of the death of Mr.
David Crawford of Mobile, a considerable opening has been made
in that *bar*. However all I ask is come an see us & judge for your
self. I have stayed pretty closely at home since my return and of
course know no news. I have been trying to make up my lost time
in reading.

I need scarcely tell you that I would be glad to hear from you,
when you have a leisure moment. I know you have a number
of persons to correspond with whose names are before mine, but
only a few lines would be a gratification to us.

From James Graham.   U.

Washington, Feb. 13th, 1835.

* * * * *

I am much pleased with your speech on Mangums Resolutions. And I think you did very well not to be a candidate for Atto. Gen'l. I incline to the opinion an effort may be made to prevail on you to offer for Congress in your district in the event Barringer declines which he will not do unless he is satisfied he cannot be elected. My advice to you is to decline at once. Don't permitt yourself to be prevailed upon to think of it at this time.

I witnessed one of the most bitter personal and political quarrels in the Senate to day I ever expect to see and hear, Between Benton & Calhoun. It was crimination and recrimination, denunciation and redenunciation. Benton was called to order, the Vice President decided he was not out of order, from which decision an appeal was taken and the vote of the majority overruled and reversed the decision of the Chair. After which Benton again proceeded. When Benton was proceeding Calhoun declared he could not say anything that he would notice. After Benton had closed his speech, Calhoun again rose and fulminated at him with great severity. The discussion arose on Calhoun's Report to curtail and correct executive patronage and extravagant expenditures. I presume Benton will challenge him but Calhoun will not notice him unless he changes his determination expressed in the Senate. They kept up the Cross fire from 1 o'clock to 5.

The opposition in the Senate are imprudent in the extreme; they have no tact, and they do not harmonize. Calhoun is restless and denounces with great energy and Boldness and has avowed in his plan there must be Revolution or Reformation, such was the enormities and corruptions of the federal government. This was a very unfortunate and unjustifiable declaration, not warranted by the facts & state of things here. Of reformation there is much need but not more than under other administrations—the post office excepted. On this Day our friend Connor made his Report on the abuses of the P. O. Department. A Counter Report was offered by the minority. They were not recd. but laid on the table and ordered to be printed. They are both so voluminous that I presume very few persons will ever know what they contain. I shall be very busy from this to the last of the Session, we sit late and early.

* * * * *

Judge White's name appears to be taking very much all through the South and Southwest. I do not feel much interest in the matter, He is a clever old cock of good mind, but he almost too homespun and east tennessee looking for that station. His friends say as soon as they return home they will get up meetings of the People for him.

* * * * *

Connor and myself have succeeded in getting *a four horse* Stage from Salisbury by Lincolnton & Rutherfordton to Ashville.

From Alfred Graham.   A.

Spring Hill Forge, February 25, 1835.

I have neglected writing so long I am almost ashamed to commence. Since my return from Tennessee I have been almost constantly here. I found the place much more out of repair than I had any Idea of And it has required my personal attention for the most part. We are beginning to get the plantation in tolerable order.

We commenced making Iron on new years Day; have made about 30,000 lbs since, Though so far it has taken most all to defray expenses, The Iron having to pay the Hands at both places and buy Provisions for both. The Furnace has been in blast since the middle of December, is doing well. Jesse Wingate and a man by the name of McGiness are the superintendants. Wingate manages very well; In fact we could not get on without him. They have made a good many Castings. John and myself had a talk about the payments lately. We have concluded to give you and Winslow Alexander Notice that you may take away 5 or 6 Tuns as soon as you can with convenience as they are getting in the way. You and him are the nearest and we thought it would sute best for you to remove them. The Iron we cannot spare much of yet but by the time you send for the Castings I think we will have part of that ready also.

On leaving Tennessee I sold Joseph the Woman and Boy I got for Henry, part Cash and part out of his Duebill. I have been trying to Buy 2 young men since, but have not yet succeeded to learn to be Hamermen again those of Fathers will be removed. I have put Joshua with Jack to learn to refine.

* * * * *

I suppose you have heard of the late Wedings in Hopewell, Rufus Reed [2] to Aunt Betsy Davidson and a Man by the name of Moore from Yorck, S. C. to Isabella Davidson. I was at the latter, we had a goodly number of people and a Dance. Mr. Williamson officiated but backed out when the Fiddle started. He would not marry Reed but attended the Marriage. James Johnson a Magistrate married him. The Relations were all opposed to this Marriage you may gess—She his sister in law with a large Family of Children.

I am so bussy here I have done nothing in that way yet, Though have seen and became acquainted with most of the Ladies here. I have attended 2 Balls since my return, one at Charlotte and 1 at Lincolnton last week. The Dutch there have really altered a great deal since I left the County for the better. Have become much more fashionable and hospitable. Father is well. He was here alnight lately. He has moved his Negroes and part of his Furniture to the Earhardt place. Has been living there since before my return here. . . .

From Thomas Lanier Clingman.[3]   U.

Huntsville, March 10th, 1835.

It has been so long since I promised to let you hear from me, that it has probably escaped your recollection, that any such promise was ever made. Making excuses however being one of those customs more honoured in the breach than the observance, I am not sure that my long delingquency would be atoned for by an apology even though it were equally long. My health is now so far restored that I am returning to my former avocations. I have been making a few speeches in the Court-house. My object however at present is only to manage a few cases, to aid me in learning the law, since I find that I acquire more practical knowledge by attending to a single case, than I should do by reading Selwyn and Chittey for a week.

---

[2] Rufus Reid, of "Mount Mourne," Iredell County.
[3] Thomas Lanier Clingman (1812-1897), of North Carolina. Educated at the university, he became a lawyer, and was at once active in Whig politics. He was a member of the commons from Surry County in 1835, and of the state senate from Buncombe in 1840, and served in congress from 1843-1845, and from 1847-1858. During that period he became a Democrat, but retained much strength among the Whigs. Elected to the senate in 1858, he served until 1861. He was a strong secessionist, and during the civil war, rose to the rank of brigadier general.

It is no part of my present purposes to settle permanently in Surry. If I should remain in the county during the present year, it will be partly with a view to give my eyes such partial rest as may prevent a return of the disease, and partly to acquire a habit of speaking without premeditation, and to become better acquainted with men by taking some share in the politics of the county. Tell me whether you think these objects will compensate me for the mental dissipation invariably attendant on political pursuits in this country. On the subject of State convention we have had some meetings, and I believe the western counties will go almost unanimously in its favor. Who will be the delegates from Orange? I have heard you spoken of as one. With respect to Federal politics, I think Mangum has nothing to fear if he stands firmly. It was my purpose to have moved a meeting to consider the subject at one of our last courts, but the weather was so unfavorable that very few of the citizens attended, and as the measure will be one of war upon two of our honorable members, it ought to be ushered in under the most favourable circumstances i. e. in May at our *political* court.

I wish you would write to me soon and tell all the news of Hillsboro. I happened purely by accident I believe, to dream last night of our beautiful friend M. P. A. and so potent were her charms (for she seemed fairer than ever) that they recalled most vividly to my sleeping fancy many scenes of the old borough. It is I think one of those places most admired at a distance; more likely to be regretted when absent than enjoyed when present. Ask Cad. Jones[4] when he is to lose his individuality and merge his separate existence in a Joinder with the fair Annie. (May all the gods and goddesses of love and beauty forgive if I have misspelled her name by inserting an *n* too much!) Miss D. too they say is going to follow her friends example; and take a worse half —and Anna C.!! What *squally* times for us single gentlemen who have not even the promise of a "fickle fair" to lean upon.

Can you give me any information concerning H. C.? I should like to know what summer breeze will kiss her cheek. Is there any probability of her attending the convention? If so, I may perchance find it convenient to be carried there by some caprice of fortune. It will certainly be a great oversight in the sovereign people if they do not make her brother nolens, volens, a member.

---

[4] Cadwallader Jones, Jr. (1813-1899), a graduate of the university, member of the commons, 1840-1842, 1848-1850. He moved to South Carolina in 1857, was a colonel in the Confederate army, and a delegate to the convention of 1865.

From Hugh Waddell.   A.

Salisbury, April 9th, 1835.

Your welcome favour was handed me yesterday & was hailed
by all your friends here with sincere pleasure; to find you so
much improved as to be able to write, was as unexpected as it
was pleasing to us. I trust you will not indulge the morbid
suggestions of your stomach, for they will be morbid for some
time to come. Take moderate exercise, but avoid of all things,
fatigue; it might be seriously injurious to you. Go out to Moorefields & see Mr. M. for a day or two at a time & do not attempt
to look into business until you feel quite restored.

I was much pleased to see that Orange turned out on the Convention question, for although the vote is small, compared with
what might have been given, yet it is more than I feared would
be done when I left home. Our people have a vis inertia, which
nothing can overcome. What ought to be done in regard to Candidates I am at a loss to advise. If men of liberal views come out
they will be immediately assailed by the demagogues & I fear
beaten in a Contest with them. Were it possible to rouse the
people in the opposite ends of the County to meet in some strength
& call out men of character it might disarm the rascals, but to go
among them & make speeches I fear will be required & this would
be too burthensome. Mr. Ruffin, yourself, Mr. Nash, Smith,[5] &
Mebane [6] will probably compose the number from which the
choice must be made, & you know what my opinions are in regard
to Mr. N.; his popularity is not what is was; though I should
be very much pleased to see him in the Convention, I should
dislike to see him defeated.

Your prospects are fairer than those of any other man who
could be run & I beg of you, if such steps are taken as to call you
out that you will not decline. You were good enough to suggest
some time ago that my name might be brought out, but this is
quite out of the question. I would not be a member were it

---

[5] Dr. James S. Smith.

[6] Either James Mebane (1774-1857), of Orange, who attended the university
briefly, served in the commons, 1798-1803, 1820-1824, (speaker 1821), and was state
senator, 1808-1811, 1828; or, more probably, Giles Mebane (1809-1899), of Orange,
a graduate of the university, who studied law under Judge Thomas Ruffin, and
became prominent in practice and in county politics. He represented Orange in
the commons, 1844-1850, and, after the county was divided, Alamance, 1854-1855,
and 1860-1861. He was a delegate to the convention of 1861, president of the senate, 1862-1865, and delegate to the convention of 1865. Moving to Caswell, he was
again state senator, 1878-1879.

matter of choice of my own; it is possible & *barely so,* that I may be before the people for the Senate & in that event my being in Convention might prejudice my hopes.

John Waddell writes me that James Campbell & himself are at Mobile & Likely to recover as the representatives of W. Simpson, a large part of the City of Mobile. Mrs. Campbell was a daughter of Simpson & her children are the only representatives; they have been offered $100,000 & declined to take it, learning that the property is worth five times that amount. Campbell will probably be in this Summer; they are lucky, if they succeed, and there seems no doubt at present.

* * * *

They will however meet treachery, perjury, etc., at every step.

From Eliza J. Witherspoon.   U.

Brook Land, April 16th, 1835.

A thousand thanks dearest Uncle for your very kind and affectionate letter, dated Feb. 4th. I need not tell you how much pleasure it affords me to be able to correspond with one I do assure feels nearer to me than Uncle. Altho' I am fully aware my letters will neither be entertaining or improving, yet the great pleasure I experience in the perusal of yours, prompts me to this pleasing task. I received a letter from Uncle Alfred the other day informing us that you had been ill. I trust ere this you are again in the enjoyment of health. I can sympathise with one that is sick, among strangers. Although you may meet with every kindness, yet there is something so endeering in the voice of a brother, Sister, or niece that is not to be found, accept with ones own relations.

I returned home a week or two ago from Mobile, where I spent six weeks very delightfully. I suppose you have heard before this of my brothers marriage, he was married on the morning of the 23d. of Feb. about 20 minutes after the ceremony was performed, we put on our riding dresses and took the Steam-boat for New Orleans. We remained there a week, I saw much to excite my curiosity as it is impossible to form a correct idea of the place until you visit it.

The weather was very bad, and we found great difficulty in getting about the City, and to add a new pleasure to the scene, we were all excessively Sea Sick, the sea was rough and we were kept out much longer than usual. in the course of two or three hours, after we left the Shore we looked as little like a bridle party as any I ever saw, there were very few persons present when the ceremony was performed, and most fortunately there were but few to witness the horrors of the Steam boat. Some of us were lying on benches, some in the berths, while others were walking the upper deck to get all the benefit of the breeze, but I will stop as I cannot do justice to the scene. We are all very much pleased with our new Sister, the old maxim you know "a new broom, etc.," but I do hope their's will continue to sweep. She is plain and unassuming, and with all very pretty, and I think will make my dear brother a good wife. They expect to set off for the North in a week or two, go up the Mississippi they expect to remain a greater part of the Summer at the Virginia Springs for his health, Tho' greatly improved, is not entirely restored. With that exception the family have enjoyed excellent health, and his, cannot be attributed to the climate.

I met with several of your old friends in Mobile. Our friend Mr. Blunt [7] tho' highly delighted with the profession of *Law,* has become very conventional of late, he was appointed to attend one in New Orleans, and expects to be sent on by the Church to Philadelphia next Summer. Doct Carter is still in Mobile and spoke very often of you, also your friend Mr. Ruffin[8] with whom I was highly pleased tho' I know him but slightly. Mobile was gay; we had a number of parties, they dance a great deal there, I became acquainted with a belle of the South, (Miss Wetten) and I believe was one of her greatest admirers. It is however thought she will marry Doct. Levert of that place, and Like all other engaged Ladies, does not receive much attention. The Theatre was also pretty good, I witnessed the performance of Power, the commedian with great satisfaction, he excels in the Irish Character. I hope my dear Uncle you will write to us shortly, as we feel very axious about you, not hearing any of the perticulars of your sickness. Ma speaks of visiting Carrolina the next Summer, if she can meet with suitable company, as it is impossible for her and Pa to leave at once, if she does not go this Summer, she will go in the fall.

It has become a settled case that I remain at home, Pa will not consent for both of us to leave him. If I should be left alone this Summer I shall feel the change very sensibly.

---

[7] Frederick Swann Blount.

[8] James Hipkins Ruffin, a brother of Judge Thomas Ruffin, now a resident of Alabama.

Our county has been gay for the last week or two, owing to the arrival of the new bride, And now dearest Uncle with all my former persuasions to induce you to visit us, I think I have a still better one in reserve for you yet, that is, I have a very charming relation here, who is spending the winter and Spring with us, I think it worth a ride from Hillsboro here to see her. I hope you will not consider it presumption in me to advise one so much older, no! I know you will not.

* * * * *

From Matthias E. Manly.   U.

Newbern, Apr. 19th, 1835.

I was much gratified to learn by your letter of the tenth inst. that your health was in a great degree restored, for I had heard that you were ill, & it had given me much pain. While I have little to live for myself, it is not so with you, and I pray God that you may long live to ornament the State & to bless your friends.

The chords which have bound me to the world are fast snapping asunder and I care little about it. This is perhaps a merciful providence as I am in bad health and may soon have in reality to bid adieu to the world and its cares.

Death I am persuaded will not now appal me since I trust it will unite me again to those whom I love better than life.

But it was not my design, as I fear I have done, to give *pain* by the disclosure of my individual feelings; I sat down for the purpose of barely acknowledging the obligations I feel for your sympathies so kindly expressed in your late communication, and of tending to you my congratulations for your recent recovery from a dangerous illness.

The Almighty has though proper to lay his hands upon me apparently in anger He has torn from me my wife—the noble, the generous, the tender-hearted. And altho it unmans me when I think of it yet I will endeavor to resign myself to his divine will & make preparation to meet her.

It is to be hoped that as a convention is determined upon that it will be composed of the best materials from all parts of the state. With all the restrictions of the bill a great deal of harm is still within the range of the convention's discrimination and depend upon it unless the convention shall be somewhat more enlightened than the last assembly was, a great deal of mischief will be done. They will mend the constitution "as the Deil mended the dog's leg by taking out a bone and putting in a stick."

Gaston & Spaight [9] will probably be sent to the convention from Craven.

Farewell

From the Philomathesian Society.   A.

Wake Forest Institute,

May 18th, 1835.

Two Literary Societies have been formed at this Institution viz. the Euzelian & Philomathesian. The object of these Societies is the same as that of similar Institutions. The Philomathesian Society is desirous to enroll your name among its honorary members. We believe that your approbation of our efforts will excite us to renewed energy in the elevated pursuits in which we are engaged.

With respect in behalf of the Society,

Jas. D. Dockery[10]   )
Peter H. Pouncey[11]   )   Committee
George Washington[12])

From Matthias E. Manly.   A.

Newbern, May 20th, 1835.

I think you expressed an intention of spending the summer in the mountains either of this state or of Virginia, in the letter which I last had the pleasure of receiving from you.

I should be glad to hear your plans more in detail & probably to join you.

[9] Richard Dobbs Spaight, Jr., (1796-1850), of Craven, graduate of the university, member of the commons, 1820-1822, 1825-1834, member of congress, 1823-1825, delegate to the convention of 1835, governor, 1835-1837.

[10] James D. Dockery came from Richmond County. He was later a student in Paris, and was a professor in the University of Alabama, a Confederate captain, and, later, a planter in Hernando, Mississippi.

[11] Peter A. H. Pouncey, of Marlborough District, South Carolina.

[12] George Washington, of Craven, a nephew of Mrs. Graham.

Such is the condition of my health that I am advised to get a little farther from the sea-shore & move about for a time.

This is the day of election.[13] Gaston & Spaight are the only persons in nomination & will therefore be elected.

Write me soon and address me at Raleigh.

From Alfred Graham.   U.

Spring H[ill] Forge, May 29th, 1835.

I was requested by Mr. Killian an acquaintance of mine near Lincolnton to write you a line and Ask the Favor of you to send him one of the advertisements relative to Allen Davies[14] Stud Horse He has a fine Mare he wishes to put but wishes to have a History of the Horse in the first place, The terms. I saw the Horse when at Hillsboro and one of the advertisements but forget the strain and Character of the Horse. If you should visit us this summer you can put one of the advertisements in your saddle-bags. Should you not do so give me an account in your Letter of the Blood and terms of Covering, etc. Killian is anxious to hear soon he would have me to write to you and Post pay the Letter. Our Friends here are all well. Father, John, and myself were all at the Celebration on the 20th May at Charlotte. There were a great many People there, a number from S. C., as well as the adjoining Counties. Governor Swain, Mangum, and Duff Green,[15] all gave speeches at the Dinner on being toasted. We Closed the business with a Ball at Hayes Tavern. A number of Ladies attended from Rowan, Cabarus, Lincoln, and Iredelle. The Miss Polks, Ferand, and Huger, from Salsbury, Miss Bar-

---

[13] For delegates to the convention.

[14] Allen Jones Davie, of Halifax, son of William R. Davie, a student at the university in 1795, member of the commons, 1806, was a noted breeder of blooded horses.

[15] Duff Green (1791-1871), journalist, politician, author, industrial promoter, a native of Kentucky, lived for a time in Missouri, where he practiced law, and served in the legislature, and edited the St. Louis *Enquirer*. He was a brigadier general in the Indian Wars, and was an ardent supporter of Jackson in 1824. In 1825 he purchased the *United States Telegraph* in Washington, and during Jackson's first administration was printer to congress, and a member of the famous "Kitchen Cabinet." With the break-up of the Cabinet, he followed Calhoun, was a moderate supporter of Nullification, warning Calhoun against the more extreme views of Hamilton and McDuffie. He supported Clay in 1832, and Harrison in 1836, and 1840. He followed Tyler in his break with the Whigs, and became a supporter of free trade. An imperialist, he favored the annexation of Cuba. He started many industrial enterprises, which were wide spread. Buchanan sent him to discuss secession with Lincoln, before the latter's inauguration. During the Civil War, he operated iron works in Alabama and Tennessee.

ringer of Cabarus, some from Yorckville, and numbers of others to tedious to tell you of. The Day passed of very well, I heard of no misunderstanding.

On the next Day they had a White Meeting, which caused a good deal of excitement. Julius Alaxander and F. Smith addressed the People. Major M'Combs was present, a Van buran man, and stated after Alaxander was done speaking and retired to the Court House, that He had stated a Dam lie with regard to the Electioneering part he had taken in the Former Presidential Election. Julius immediately struck him and a small scuffle followed, But they were soon parted. I thought at one time there would have been several squabbls among some of the more respectable People of Charlotte. Shipp and Cansellor[16] are elected members to the convention from this County.

From James W. Osborne.   A.

Charlotte, June 3d, 1835.

My dear Friend

We are just beginning to breathe with freshness and freedom from the engagements of the 20th. The Crowd has at length dispersed, business is going on in our village with its wonted energy, and the old order of things pretty much in every way restored. A full account of every thing which was done I do not doubt has reached you through the newspapers. I will only make one remark in which you may be interested. Your Father was there and I was much gratified that he seemed to enjoy the occasion so vividly. Every thing was done to make it agreeable to him as well as to all the men of "olden time" who honoured the day with their presence at the festival. Among other visitors your friend Mr. Jones was there. He has been occasionally unwell since and is yet in our village. He speaks of leaving in a few days. Swain & Mangum gave us speeches. Both of them in that way acquitted themselves with respectability. The former gentleman has gained immortal honour from his feats of wit and humour (as well as other creditable feats) at the dinner table. So far as the dinner may effect the political feeling of Mecklenburg I much fear that it will be labour lost. Parties are very violent and the friends of the administration now rallying under the flag of Van Buren are becoming more and

---

[16] Henry Cansler.

more decided. I hope however that from some benignant quarter light may yet break on our benighted country.

We had a *tolerably large* collection of ladies at the ball which was given on the evening of the twentieth. It was a *rare collection* of grace and beauty however, as we paraded with the greatest part of *that article* which is afforded by the west. In other words the gems of the land seem to have been concentrated. Of all this however my enthusiastic cousin can give you a minute detail.

In my new situation I find that my prospects are slowly but I trust decidedly improving. I purpose to take a course which may result in a reparation of the wrongs which indolence and inattention have inflicted on myself. And try to act on the maxim that the sure way to success is to deserve it.

*   *   *   *   *

From Eliza J. Witherspoon.   U.

Brook - Land, July 26th, 1835.

Although my dear Uncle is indebted to me one or two letters, I cannot for a moment think (however gratefying it may be) of expecting an answer to every letter I write him. I am fully aware the arduous duties of your avocation necessarily oblige you to be very much confined; And the few leisure moments you have to spare, that there are many whom obligation places much higher upon the list of correspondents then my own, therefore I cannot murmur.

I am often very remiss about writing myself, and I must be as lenient to the faults of others as my own.

*   *   *   *   *

. . . I expect to set out next week for the Blount Springs in the Northern part of this State, with my Father, who has had a very troublesome erruption on skin ever since his sickness last fall in Carrolina, his general health is very good, with the exception of this diseese; it resembles the nettle rash very much,—he has been advised by the Physiciens to try the effect of the Sulphur Waters.

*   *   *   *   *

The tide of emigration to this country appears to be rapidly increasing. A great many persons are here now trying to purchase lands. Judgeing from the number of persons I see here from North

Carrolina, I should think it would soon be depopulated. Judge Martin and Mr Alexander from Salisbury have lately purchased land here and I understand intend removing to Mobile. There is a good deal of excitement existing now about the Elections for Governor, Congress, Legislature, etc., but I am not enough of a Poleticien to tell you much about it. I believe it is thought this State will vote for Mr. Vanburen.

I read with pleasure the speach you sent Pa, that you delivered last winter in the Legislature. We have not heard whether you are a candidate this summer. The late disturbances in Mississippi with the slaves, have almost put my Father in the notion of selling off every thing and removing to a free State. That is I think the great objection to this country. Persons are bringing them in by hundreds. The streets of the village of Greensboro are crowded from day to day with slaves for sale. The prospects of crops this year are uncomonly fine. The season has been an unusually wet one, and quite cold, we found fires very comfortable a week or two ago. I have some gaiety in anticipation at the Springs and after I return home. My friend Miss Ross, who has been a belle in Mobile for some time expects to be married to Mr. Lightfoot the 1st of Sept. and I am to stand second best for her, a number of parties are to be given to her. She will be married at her Fathers summer residence in this county. Gossip ever on the wing, has said that Uncle Alfred has an idea of changing his situation how true this is, I cannot say. We have heard that he was addressing Miss Torrence. We feel anxious to hear the result of Uncle James Election. Major Forneys family have settled in Tuscaloosa, I have not seen any of them since they came out. Mr. Brumby is still a professor in the University.

* * * * *

From Victor Moreau Murphey. U.

Hillsborough, 6th. Augt, 1835.

To suppress any apprehension which a Letter from Hillsborough might excite I will in the offset mention that you have no cause to suspect opposition, so far as I can learn from any quarter However to be on the safe side your friends will generally put in their votes on the day of Election. I have every reason to suppose that there is not in the Town one man who desires a change in our

Representation all with whom I have conversed would discountenance any attempt in that respect.

There is however considerable excitement brewing on the Subject of the Congressional Election. The Subject is seldom mentioned without the parties becoming Clamorous & at our boarding house we had by the consent of the whole to let the Subject rest, as it frequently led to unpleasant disputes.

From the intelligence received from the different parties parts of the County & district it would be difficult to conjecture the result. My own opinions are based upon the views of General Barringer himself. I feel very confident that the contest will be a close one in this County. The latest accounts from Person are favourable for the Dr.[17] The impression seems to be that he will get a Majority of 200 votes in that Cty. Genl. B. allows him that much, but differs widely with him in the vote of Wake.

Dr. M. calculates upon receiving from 5 to 7 hundred votes. The Genl. is positive that he will not get over 200 in the County. Under these circumstances there is but little hope for Montgomery. His friends are fearful of the result. I am rejoiced to say that there is a prospect of our being relieved from the services of that worst of demagogues, Jo. Allison. Mebanes prospects are fair & I think every day becoming more so. As to the Commons no one seems to know or care any thing about the probable result.

Another dreadful calamity has befallen Judge Ruffin's family: one almost as afflicting as that which happened 12 months ago. About 3 weeks since Sterling[18] was attacked suddenly with a most violent inflammation in one of his eyes. He suffered all the agonies incident to a highly aggravated inflammation in that Organ & about the fourth day from the attack the other either from sympathy or inoculation became implicated, & I greatly fear that the consequence is permanent blindness. This fact is not positively ascertained, but every appearance argues too strongly in favour of such a conclusion. He is now here, & will I suspect soon be taken to the North. You have never witnessed any thing to equal the anxiety and apprehension of the family It has nearly exhausted Mrs. Ruffin. The Judge returned to Raleigh on yesterday to wind up the business of the Court Sterling now suffers no pain. His eyes are much inflamed & now cannot see at all. We still hope for the best though I greatly fear the worst.

---

[17] Dr. William Montgomery.

[18] Sterling Ruffin (1817-1908), never recovered his sight, bore his affliction with cheerful courage, and was immensely popular, not only in his large family connection, but with all those with whom he came in contact.

I leave that melancholy subject & touch upon one more pleasant. Miss Maria has arrived, as also Miss Julia B. They are both beautiful & gay & no doubt anxious to see you. Miss Sarah's Spectacles are I fear to be my ruin, there is a great "blow out" at Buonaparts to night in honour of Miss Julia but owing to Sterlings situation, I refrain from going as I stay with him every night. I wish you were with us. I can't sustain the character of the place and my present burthens, & without some assistance from you soon, it must sink. We have also Miss Long with us: Gov. Norwood is playing a strong game & his little bald pate saws the air continually, and should you upon your return feel the last lack of chat, old Mother Badger can supply any deficiency.

*   *   *   *   *

From Alfred Graham.   U.

Spring Hill Forge,

August 25th, 1835.

*   *   *   *   *

The Election is over. Hoke[19] and Cansler were elected by a large Majority over Monday.[20] Harry beat M. Reindhardt 64 votes for Senate. Connor beat Shipp upwards of 1400 in the Three Counties having obtained a Majority in all the Countys, this County 1016 over Shipp. I have only heard that James is elected in his district but have not heard by how much. It was believed the election would be a close one.

*   *   *   *   *

The Money that was stolen out of the warehouse which was spoken of when you were here was stolen by your Boy Abram. He broke in at the top of the Gable end and fixed up the weather boarding so that it was not discovered for some time. It is believed old Stephen and Dave put it in his head. I dont beleve he is naturally roguish. Old Steven got $5 which he gave up.

---

[19] Michael Hoke (1810-1844), of Lincoln County, educated at the Partridge Academy in Middletown, Connecticut, studied law with Robert H. Burton, and was at once successful. He had a fine intellect, was a finished and effective speaker, and possessed unusual personal charm. He and Graham were opposing candidates in a notable campaign for governor, in 1844. Graham was elected, and Hoke died before the end of the year, presumably as a result of exhaustion. His only previous political experience was as a member of the commons, 1834-1840.

[20] W. W. Monday.

From James Graham.   U.

Warm Springs, August 26th, 1835.

I arrived here two days since after comparing the Polls at Ashville. I am elected to Congress by only seven votes over Newland.
Rutherford and Burke sustained me well. Buncombe gave me a
majority of 17 Votes only. My election was very improperly connected in Buncombe with the county election, and the late members incurred much odium and lost their election by the passage
of some local Laws last winter. Durham's[21] name was withdrawn
in Haywood and Macon the day preceding the election, and he
was only run in Rutherford with a view of dividing my vote there.
Still however he got only 194 Votes in Rutherford and about
220 in the district. I lost about 100 votes in Rutherford by my
Assault on Durham and about 200 by the refusal of the Temperate
society to vote for any man who treated. Newland talks of contesting my election. I think I can show 10 votes illegal for him,
where he can shew one illegal for me. His most respectable friends
dissuade him from the effort—We have a respectable Representation in the next Legislature from Rutherford, that is A. W. Moore
in the Senate, Bedford [22] and Joseph Carson in the Commons, the
latter was nominated on Monday before the election by the People
themselves.

There is not a large company at the Warm Springs at this
time. Ashville and the Sulphur Spring are very full. . . . I have
seen no beauty in the Buncombe atmosphere this season; a good
degree of high life and great names descended to small minds.

Genl. Walton[23] died here soon after you left, and old James
Patton had the misfortune to have a large Rock that his hands
were digging at, to break loose and tumble down on him and
break both his legs—his recovery is doubtful.

I think it probable that some question touching the security
of Slavery will be agitated in most of the Legislatures of the
Southern States next winter and perhaps in Congress. If the
Fanaticks of the North are permitted with impunity to sow the
seeds of insurrection among our blacks we are in constant danger
of domestic insurrection and deadly warfare.

*   *   *   *   *

---

[21] Probably Bremen (some times called Berryman) Hicks Durham, who represented Rutherford in the commons in 1834.

[22] John H. Bedford, a member of the commons, 1834-1839.

[23] George Walton (1772-1835), a prominent man, who held many local positions, including that of postmaster, and who was a state senator, 1819-1820.

From James Murdaugh.   U.

Virginia, Portsmouth,

Sept. 7th, 1835.

I received some time ago, a letter from Doct. Thos. P. Atkinson informing me that you were the counsel engaged for Lydia, a slave manumitted by the will of the late Thomas Campbell of Nansemond County, also containing a memorandum from you for certain things to be performed, viz. to take the depositions of such persons as will prove the identity of Lydia, that she descended from the family of negroes manumitted by Campbell, or is reported in this section of county to be so descended. Also evidence to prove that Campbell's youngest child has arrived to the age of 21 years; and whether the testator in 1797 could manumit his slaves in Virginia or if any further proceedings than the probate of the will was necessary. That a copy of our Statute permitting emancipation will be required, also a copy of the will properly authenticated. That notices for taking depositions must be given in the usual way to Messrs. James Street and James L. Oberly and signed Lydia Campbell by Wm. Baird agent.

The Act of the General Assembly passed the 17th. day of Decr. 1792 permitting owners to emancipate their slaves is in the following words, "It shall be lawful for any person by his or her last will and testament, or by any other instrument in writing, under his or hand and seal, attested and proved in the County or Corporation Court by two witnesses, or acknowledged by the party in the Court of the County where he or she resides to emancipate and set free his or her slaves, or any of them, who shall thereupon be entirely and fully discharged from the performance of any contract entered into during servitude, and enjoy as full freedom as if they had been particularly named and freed by this Act." This Act was in force in 1797, the time of the death of the testator, and in the copy of the Act which you want I presume a copy must be attested by the seal of the Commonwealth, so as to give it validity in your Courts. I would beg permission to state to you, and hope I shall not be thought presumptuous in referring you to some of the decisions of our Courts, or the Court of Appeals, which will aid you in the prosecution of this suit. The negroes which were living at the death of the testator, there exist no doubt of their freedom, and the question arises, whether those born after the death of the testator, and before his youngest child arrived at age, are free or are slaves; but from an examination of the decisions of the Court of Appeals all doubt must be removed from the subject, if any exist in the construction of the will, in absence of any judicial decisions.

The first decision which seems in conflict to their freedom is the case of Maria & al vs Senbaugh. 2 Rand. Rep. page 228. "That where a testator bequeaths a female slave, upon condition that she shall be free at a certain age, and before that period arrives, she has issue, such issue are slaves."

In an examination of this case, you will find it was decided upon two principles. 1st. The mother was a slave at the time of the birth of the children, and that the condition of the children followed that of the mother (this is a rule of property but not of liberty, says Judge Brooke). 2nd. That the children of a free person bound to service, would necessarily have to be supported by the public, for the parent was not able to do so, neither was the estate of the testator bound to support them, because he had not emancipated them, and consequently it would be contrary to the policy of our Laws. But as to the 1st. principle of this decision as applicable to this case, if it has any application at all. I consider the Ancestor of Lydia was not a slave at any time after the death of Thos. Campbell the testator, and if not a slave, then she was free, and consequently her issue was free. It is clear that the right of the ancestor of Lydia to freedom occurred immediately on the death of the testator, for she was emancipated by the *Will,* and her services as well as those of the other manumitted slaves were retained for a particular time, and those services were retained for the purpose (as expressed by the testator) of raising his *children and young negroes.* Therefore the 2nd. principle in the case of Maria & al vs Senbaugh can have no application. But it is perfectly clear if the ancestor of Lydia was a slave, until the youngest child arrived at the age of 21 years, that all the children born between the death of the testator, and the arrival of the youngest child of age are also manumitted by the Will, for the testator thus writes "my will and desire is that my negro woman Pindar shall have her liberty immediately and her emancipation recorded, my will and desire is that all the rest of my *black people* should serve until my youngest child be of the age of 21 years for the use of raising of my children and young negroes, after my youngest child be of age my will is that *all my negroes should have their freedom.*"

If then Lydia was born a slave, she belonged to the estate of the testator, and is embraced under the term *all my negroes should have their freedom*, when his youngest child should arrive at age.

The following decision will be found in 6 Randolp's Rep. Isaac vs West page 652. "A master manumits his slaves at his death, and by deed directs, that they shall *serve* him as long as he lives, and at his death go free from all persons; and for himself &c relinquishes all his right and title to the said negroes, is to be construed as passing a present right to freedom, reserving a right in the testator to their personal services during his life, as a condition of the emancipation. Therefore, a child born of the emancipated females in the interval between the execution of the deed and the death of the grantor is free from its birth."

This is a case similar in point, But a decision of the Court of Appeals in 1833 in the case of Elder vs Elder's ex'or. 4 Leigh's Reports. page 252. this principle was decided "that slaves born after the testator's death and while the executor held their mothers in slavery, were emancipated. I refer you to this decision particularly as it embraces the case of Campbell's negroes, and is a complete authority in point.

I do not know where Messrs. Street and Oberly live, and therefore cannot have the usual notices served upon them, so as to take the deposition of witnesses to establish the facts necessary to show Lydia's right to freedom. The youngest child of Thos. Campbell the testator, arrived at age about 1812, and the negroes were all set free by the County Court of Nansemond, and enjoyed their liberty until 1833, when they were taken possession of by the admr., with the will annexed of Thos. Campbell decd. and divided among the heirs, and Lydia was sold.

I presume the Court will not permit the case to be tried, under these circumstances, but will grant a continuance of the cause, involving the liberty of a human being.

I shall write to Mr. Baird, the agent, and endeavor to obtain the residence of Messrs Street and Oberly so that notices may be served, and depositions taken, by the Spring Term of your Court. It is impossible to be done by the present term of your Court. Let me know what you wish to be done. I am engaged for 5 of these negroes, their case will be tried the next month. I am confident of success.

Yours Respectfully

From Calvin Jones.[24]   A.

Milton, Octr. 6th, 1835.

I am gratified at being able to-day to furnish you with the intelligence promised when I was last in Hillsborough. *Thursday
evening 15th Octr* is the time upon which we have fixed for our
nuptials. You must therefore be prepared upon coming to Caswell
Court to meet me in Roxborough on the day above mentioned.
(15th.) I trust that nothing may occur to prevent you. If Allen
Jones shall have deferred his trip until after the 15th, and if
Thomas Ashe[25] shall have returned to Hillsborough, I will thank
you to present my regards to them, and assure them of the pleasure which it will afford me to see them at Mr. Williamson's, near
Roxboro, on the occasion above alluded to.

From William H. Haywood, Jr.   U.

Raleigh, 13 Octo., 1835.

Though you and I do not *always* agree on political questions
it has never interfered with our private friendship nor with our
course upon other subjects. I take the liberty of writing to you
now on what I consider to be important *State* questions for the
purpose of inviting your attention to them & soliciting an inter-
change of opinion in order that some proper steps may be taken
in the next Legislature in time to secure final action.

1st. It is a great evil that our Superior Courts shall be wholly
lost when by reason of sickness or other accident the Judge assigned to hold them is unable to attend at the time prescribed by
law. Whilst our Circuit Judges are required to hold so many
Courts in succession this is inevitable & if it is not *now* expedient
to diminish the Circuits will it not soon be indispensible? A

---

[24] Calvin Jones (1810-1888), a graduate of the university, later moved to Tennessee. He was, for a time, professor in the University of Alabama, was chancellor of
West Tennessee, 1847-1854, and a judge of the superior court. He must not be
confused with General Calvin Jones, of Wake, who moved to Bolivar, Tennessee.

[25] Thomas S. Ashe (1812-1887), a native of Orange, a graduate of the university,
studied law under Thomas Ruffin, and settled at Wadesboro. As a Whig he represented Anson County in the commons, 1842-1843, and in the state senate, 1854.
He was a member of the Confederate congress, 1862-1864, and was elected to the
senate, but the war closed before his term began. He was the unsuccessful Conservative candidate for governor in 1868, was a member of congress, 1873-1877, and
was associate justice of the state supreme court, 1879-1887.

Judge who is in the prime of life may be able to endure the labor of a mountain Circuit, but these officers are elected for *life* and some of them must be at all times advanced beyond middle age according to all human probabilities.

And must we never be releaved from the inconvenience because we are very prudently reluctant to give up the good of a stable tenure to Judicial station? Why may not the former be remedied by reducing the physical labor of the Judge and thereby let the people enjoy the *full* benefit of this wise feature in the Constitution. It seems to me not unworthy of a remark that in the progress of a few more years these frequent delays of justice will be used with much force by the enemies of a permanent judicial tenure of office to reconcile the people to a change.

Again. I presume the amendments to the Constitution will be *ratified* by the people. If so and our present mode of compensating Circuit Judges is consistent with that provision in the Original Constn. which commands that they shall be paid "Salaries" (which I greatly doubt) then how will it be with the Constn. as amended wherein it forbids the legislature to *diminish* their salaries. Does this forbid the Legislature from reducing their pay *per Court* or does it forbid also such diminution of their labor as will by consequence reduce their aggregate compensation? Now is it not proper that the next Legislature shall *before the new Constn. goes into operation* plan this matter on such a footing as will secure to the publick a clear right to regulate the Courts and at the same time secure to the people & to their Judges the benefit of this amendment to the Constn.?

You will agree with me that great changes in the Judicial system of the State ought not to be made frequently and that they never should be hastily adopted. But I have been led since my election to the Assembly to think on this subject and though I cannot say I have made up my opinions I have been endeavoring to devise some plan of legislation that will meet the difficulties and inconveniences at which I have hinted. I hope you will give the matter some consideration and let me know your views on the subject.

Our Circuits are too large & ought to be reduced in size and consequently increased in number. Some provision might then be made requiring the Judge assigned to a particular Circuit to hold a Court or Courts within 6 Months whenever he should (by sickness or other accident) be prevented from holding a Court for a County at the regular time, notice of the time to be given by him in a manner to be prescribed by law. His place may be supplied by allotment of this duty to another Judge when he loses so many Courts that he cannot supply every omission within the 6 Mo.

What is your opinion of *locating* the Judges? Mine is not settled on the question, Tho it has been pressed upon me by Messrs. Badger and Devereaux. A new reason for it is furnished by the amendment to the Constn. which gives the Election of Gov. to the people? Perhaps I should speak more correctly if I had said the reason a fresh inducement to pervert the station is furnished by this article?

At present I incline to favor this change, but my mind vascillates & I should prefer to locate them *for a time* so as to try & leave undoubted room to return to the old practice if found to be wiser.

I know you will pardon me for writing you on this subject, though you must likewise excuse the hasty & imperfect manner of my doing so. Unless my professional brethren in the Legislature agree with me in my views or they will give theirs if we shall agree first among ourselves I am sure nothing can be done. I have not written to any others for if I do not find you agreeing with me in the belief that something ought to be done I should feel constrained to review my own thoughts before I should take any action on this subject.

I must ask the favour of an answer to this as soon as your convenience will permit you to reply.

Very sincerely your friend

From James Graham.   U.

Ashville, October 26th, 1835.

. . . I intended going through Raleigh to Washington but as my election is contested and I have numerous depositions to take I do not know when I shall pass. I feel quite confident I shall be able to shew more bad votes for Newland than he can for me, the trouble is inconceivable.

I hear some of your friends here speaking of you as the speaker of the Commons. With regard to the appointment I think you had better say to your friends If it be the pleasure of the House of Commons to confer that station upon you, you will discharge the duties as well you can: but you cannot consent to run for it if it be a mere party scuffle. I think Judge Nash can make a good

run for Judge Seawells vacancy. I think Gov. Swain is looking to
the Bench in place of Judge Martin and although he has injured
his standing among his friends still I think he can obtain the appointment—the West must have one Judge.

I think the friends of good order had better bring on all the
elections as soon as possible after the Legislature convenes so as
to avoid the party discipline and drill and with a view of abridg-
ing the length of the Session.

. . . Judge Martin appears to be delighted with his anticipations
in Alabama and I presume that climate will suit his delicate
health and I hope it may ameliorate his uneven and crabid temper.

Sam P. Carson has removed entirely to Red River and several
of the gentlemen engaged in the gold mining operations have
also removed.

Governor Swain has made a public speech to the people of
Buncombe recommending the Amendments to the Constitution.

From George Shonnard Bettner.[26]   U.

Paris, Novr. 5, 1835.

Dear Graham,

I am glad that I have a good pretext for writing to you, in addition to the very natural suggestions of my friendly feelings towards you. I am acquainted, in common with nearly all the Amer-
icans here, with an elderly gentleman, by the name of Warden,[27]
who was formerly & for a long time American Consul in this
City. Mr. Warden is a literary man, and a member of the Institute
of France, and has employed a considerable part of his life in
making a very valuable collection of books, which he is disposed
to offer for sale. Among them are a number of valuable and interesting works relating to the history of the United States, the

---

[26] George Shonnard Bettner (1801-1860), who was a class ahead of Graham
at the university, and later a tutor, became a physician in New York, and later,
in New Orleans. He was the author of "Action, or the Circle of Life."

[27] Bettner, as will be noted later in the letter, confused the name. The person
of whom he was writing was David Bailie Warden (1772-1845), diplomat, author
and book collector, a native of Ireland, educated at Glasgow, a Presbyterian
minister, and a colonel of the United Irishmen. Arrested, he was allowed to
migrate to America in 1799. He was naturalized, and in 1804 went to Paris as
secretary of the American minister, and spent the rest of his life there. He belonged to many learned societies, and was a prolific writer. The books mentioned
went to the New York State Library. An earlier collection had already been acquired by Harvard.

Southern States I believe in particular, & the West India Islands. There is a catalogue of the books published, & the title which Mr. Warden gives them is "Bibliothica Americana, or a Chronological Catalogue of Books, relating to North & South America." They comprise about 1800 volumes besides Atlasses, maps, charts, etc. There are 80 vols. fol. 381 — 4°. & 1021 in 8°, & so on. A great many of these books are rare, scarce & valuable, & Mr. W. offers the whole collection for the sum of $6000. As our State does not possess a very extensive library, & as there is, or ought to be a disposition to increase it, it would be well to make a purchase of these books. I have also written to Gov. Swain upon the same subject, and as that letter might perhaps miscarry, I have addressed you this, in hopes that you will think the subject worthy of attention, and endeavor to put things in such a train, as to have some enquiries made in regard to it. Mr. Warden's address is as follows. Baillie W. Warden No. 12 Rue Pot de Fer, St. Sulpice, Paris.

I have been in this Metropolis a few months and shall continue here several months longer. I have come to take some finishing touches in my profession, to learn the language, and to see the world. I have travelled about a great deal since I left those old solitary walls at Chapel Hill, and have had my share I believe of incidents, adventures & all such other marvellous matters which usually happen to travellers.

The sights & scenes which I witness here, are very different from what I beheld in the East & West Indies, and there are very few things in France, which would remind me of America. This is a most delightful residence, and there are so many objects here to amuse, & instruct, that it is not at all surprising that Paris is generally preferred to all other parts of the world. When I leave here, I think I shall visit Italy, England & some other parts of Europe before returning to the United States. Intending at the conclusion of my peregrinations to become a Frenchman, I think it more than probable that I shall settle in New Orleans when I go back. The opportunities of improvement in my profession are very good in this City, & you would be surprised to witness the number & extent of the Hospitals.

But what is there that would not excite your curiosity & astonishment in Paris? One may read & read forever about places & things & have no idea of them at all, unless he has seen them.

I see by the papers that your brother had a very close election. I had the pleasure of meeting him at the Virginia Springs last year. I see also that you are returned for Hillsborough. How do you like politics & law? I am happy to hear, always, of your success in both, & hope you will continue your efforts to do all in your power, to elevate & improve the poor old North State.

If I have any friends or acquaintances in your part of the world, do remember me to them. I recollect Judge Nash & his family, & I think Jno Norwood married a little girl that I used to talk love to. But these things happened a century ago, & all that I can recall to mind of your little village, is a high wooden bridge, a few romantic looking hills, & the Widow Hazle's house. Contrast these with the scenes of India—the palaces & gardens of St. Cloud & Versailles—with the Tuilleries & with the shops & shows & promenades of Paris, & verily I might believe I had another, or rather two or three existences. My address is "Care of Wells & Co. Bankers, Paris."

> I remain, Dear Graham
> Sincerely & truly
> Your affectionate friend

P. S. If you should meet with Gavin Hogg, give my Compliments to him, & speak to him upon the subject of this letter.

From J. Seawell Jones.   U.

New York, Nov. 13, 1835.

I had expected to be off for home to day, but the day being unpromising and my health being infamous, I am detained. I beg to refer you to Barringer, to peruse a letter from me to him in the matter of which I solicit your good offices.

I have completed the first volume of my Picturesque history of N. Carolina, and it will be before the public as soon as I can close some little traffic with the gentlemen of the trade. It comprises only the history of the Raleigh Colony, and is adorned with 12 plates and sixteen *vignettes* of rather an expensive character.

From Robert Hall Morrison.   U.

Near Charlotte, Nov. 16th, 12 Oclock, 1835.

In the inscrutable dispensations of God the Solemn hour has *come & gone* and our Dear Brother Alfred Graham is numbered with the dead. He died this morning at 5 oclock. I came from Bro. John's where he lay, on day before yesterday. His Sufferings were very intense. Mary has been there nearly a week.

He will be buried tomorrow morning at the family graveyard.

May God in Mercy teach us all the uncertainty of human life & the vanity of human expectations. May we my Dear Friend be enabled to prepare for that world where sorrow and separations and death shall be unknown.

I start in a few moments to attend the funeral.

Yours in haste & in much love.

From Jo. Seawell Jones.   A.

Petersburg, Va., Nov. 20, 1835.

I have just put up here for a day to get a little sleep, and find I am compelled to go by way of Shocco where I have not been for three years and where it is indispensable I should be during the next week, which is Warren Court. I beg you to look around and to get for me the office of Sec. of State, which I want purely as an enablement to historical research. I am the more *impudent* and forward in my solicitations for this post because the State is equally as much interested in the development of its history as I can be, and then I am sure the enjoyment of such an office is the only way in which an author of a history of N. Carolina can be patronised by the suffrage of the Legislature.

I have just seen the Raleigh Register and was rejoiced to see you had been run for Speaker, for although you were not elected, it is yet the best evidence of the confidence and regard of your party. Where is Barringer? Some one told me in Washington he was married. I wrote him somewhat at length from New York, not then knowing the fact. I wish him the joys of the occasion, and I wish them to you to you too—in any other quarter than New Bern where I hear we are to meet very shortly—a Phillippi to us Graham—New Bern—maybe.

By the way—as Jack Downing[28] says—"it is kinder kurous" to see how courting news does spread. You merely intend to do a little business of the sort this winter, and away the very idea spreads, first to New Bern, thence to N. York, and the other day I called in to see a lady at Mrs. Cadles boarding house, opposite Bond St., N. York, and says she to me, "Mr. Jones, do you know that your friend Mr. Graham of Hillsborough is coming to N. Bern this winter to *court* Miss—" I wont tell you her name but such is the truth, and I will tell you what else is the truth—about half a hour afterwards I was off to see about it. We will talk of this anon.

I came through Washington, dined at the White House, etc., and from what I saw and heard I predict a French war. Both the president and Secretary of State are too much excited, and if some conciliatory news does nor arrive in a week or ten days, the Message will be belligerent—decidedly. So scrub up your Musket and penknife. Write me at Warrenton.

Yours truly

P. S. My new book is creating quite a sensation. I hope The Raleigh package will arrive before the Legislature adjourns. Raleigh.

From Hugh Waddell.   **A.**

Hillsboro; Novr. 21st, 1835.

I would to God I were with you. Your letter of the 19th instant has wrought on my feelings much. Having been in the furnace of affliction I know how to sympathize with you. I feel the melancholy distinction which your letter awards me; that of being regarded by you as a sincere friend, for to none others, do we commit such sacred sorrows.

Human life is such a mystery, that we are lost in the contemplation of it; so strangely are our hopes & reasonable expectations often blasted, that we are sometimes almost driven to the *fear,* that there can be no "wise and good Governor of the world."

---

[28] Seba Smith (1792-1868), of Maine, wrote numerous books and articles, humorous and satirical, under the name of Jack Downing. He married Elizabeth Oakes. A grandson, Appleton Smith, who changed his name to Oaksmith, after a somewhat wild career at sea, settled in Carteret County, after the Civil War. He wrote poetry, essays, and letters to the newspapers, and was a most interesting person. He served in the lower house of the legislature in 1874.

This however if a true, is at best a most revolting Philosophy, for it extinguishes all incentives to virtue, & banishes "Hope," the last refuge of the wretched. I discard the suggestions of such a philosophy, & turn with ardour to a better belief. There must be *design* in removing, as there was in *placing* us here; if a design, it must be a benevolent one, for none other can be imputed to him, who even "tempers the wind to the shorn lamb." This is our only consolation, that it *must have been* for the best, or so bitter a pang had not been inflicted.

I trust in God, that this heavy affliction may not prey too much on your venerable father. He should not however, suffer himself to dwell so much on what he has lost, as on what *he has*. How few men have been blessed in their children, as he has been. And how fewer still, at his age have had so many, & so worthy, spared, to gladden his latter days.

My own wound from the loss of a dear & venerated parent, is still green. Time, my friend, is the only physician for such wounds.

I can say little to you about matters here, all seem sanguine that I shall be with you—a day more will show; but my principal gratification in going now, will be to offer in person the sincere sympathy which I feel & have here tried to express.

Adieu & believe me in sorrow as in joy,
Raleigh.

From Robert B. Gilliam.[29]   U.

Danville, Va., November 27th, 1835.

I take great pleasure in introducing to your acquaintance, Genl. B. W. S. Cabell [30] of Danville, a gentleman much distinguished in this State, for his public services and equally so in this community for his private worth. He has been deputed by the Citizens of this place to lay before the Legislature of North Carolina a memorial praying for an Act of incorporation, for a Company

---

[29] Robert Ballard Gilliam (1805-1870), of Granville, a contemporary of Graham at the university, and a close friend thereafter, served in the commons, 1836-1840, 1846-1849, 1862 (speaker, 1848 and 1862). He was a delegate to the convention of 1835, a judge of the superior court, 1863-1865, 1867-1868. He was elected to congress in 1870, but died before his term began.

[30] Benjamin W. S. Cabell, of Danville, Virginia, a graduate of Hampden-Sydney, served a number of times in each house of the legislature, was a delegate in the convention of 1829, and was a brigadier general of militia. He was an eager advocate of internal improvements.

to build a Rail Road from Weldon on the Roanoke to Evansham in the County of Wythe.

Whatever may be your views in regard to the policy of the comtemplated improvement, I doubt not, you will render Genl Cabell all possible aid, to enable him to bring the subject fairly before the Legislature; and such personal civilities as will impress him favourably with the good-feeling and hospitality of our Capitol.

From James S. Smith. U.

Hillsboro, Decb. 2nd, 1835.

I see that you have stormy times & that party promises to run high before the termination of the session. I am unable from any thing that I can learn to know whether the friends of Mr Van Buren will attempt a legislative nomination for the next presidency, But it is certain I presume that an Electoral ticket will be made out before the end of the session.

Now if the opositiotion do not use great prudence in forming their ticket defeat is certain.

We have original Anti-Jackson men, the seceders from the Jackson party, and the Nullifiers We have White men, Harrison men, & Webster men, and Clay men, & Calhoun men. Now if some plan is not fixed upon to unite all these interests defeat is certain. Would it not be well to form a ticket on the plan of the old *Murphy* ticket which gave the vote of the State to Jackson against the caucus nomination of Crawford? That ticket united all the discordant materials that then existed. I would say that the matter should be seriously considered before a final nomination should be had.

I congratulate you and all our western friends on the ratification to the amendments to the Constitution. I hope that a new era will be formed in the legislative history of the State.

I presume that before you rise you will designate a suitable candidate to fill the executive office under the new Constitution. What direction the public mind may take on this subject I do not pretend to know nor who may be a favourite of the legislature. But as I entertain an opinion on this subject which may not be common But which will influence me in my vote and in the exercise of any little influence I may possess I presume I may without any offense suggest it to you. I have then determined that I will not vote for any man under the new order of things for Governor who is a Lawyer. Do not suppose that I am going to proclaim war against you and your talented and respectable fraternity very far from it; No one who is not of the profession entertains more respect for the talents and usefulness of that body than I do. But my reasons are these: The gentlemen of the law have the exclusive monopoly of fifteen of the important offices of the State—3 Superior Court Judges, 6 Circuit Judges, the Attorney General, the Solicitor General, and 4 Solicitors—engrossing exclusively upwards of 26,000 dollars of the public revenue, with one third of the members of the legislature making 15,000 thousand dollars more. Here then is 40,000 dollars more than one half of the whole revenue of the State with all the places of Honour and profit going to one class to the exclusion of the great mass of the people.

Now I do humbly concur that there should be at least one high office in the State reserved as a reward for long services and experience in political life which should be confered on some citizen who does not belong to the profession of the law. Is not then sufficient liberty, integrity, and political experience to be found out of the legal profession to fill the executive office? I do concur that there is. Would not an executive recommendation to improve the system of the Judiciary carry home force with it and seem to more disinterested if it come from a man not of the profession?

I think then that the profession should act in this matter with a spirit of liberality in this particular. Would not such a course arrest that spirit of Jealousy that pervades the community against lawyers holding offices in the legislature—at least in some degree? Even will informed and liberal minded men will find this Jealousy for they know the great advantages that the lawyers have—their constant intercourse together—their riding extensive Circuits— and the well known Esprit du chouer of the profession, etc.

These are some of the reasons that influence my mind; they may be selfish or illiteral in the eyes of some but for my own part I think them reasonable and capable of being sustained on the soundest and most liberal principles.

I presume your session will close before the first of the new year as your term according to my construction of the ordinance of the Convention, is out then. I should think that no very important matters should be taken up during this session.

*   *   *   *   *

From Alfred Moore. U.

Hillsboro, 13th. Decr., 1835.

Some years ago, you were so good as to request my serving as a justice of peace for Orange. At that time I had other views which have been set aside by the fortunate change in my pecuniary affairs. To accident now, and to accident alone do I owe my willingness to take upon me the humble attitude of *Squire.*

You may remember, my young friend, that I served as a Grand juror last term of Orange Spr. Ct. My duty led me into the jail! —and Oh! God, my God!! what misery did I not behold? What open, shameful, unblushing fraud! what a systematic fattening on human misery. From that moment and I confess with tears which I could not keep out of my eyes, I regretted having refused your offer. There is a desperate want I plainly see of a fearless honest man on the bench.

Now, *I* have nothing to hope, or fear from the public;—the *timid, untalented, misinformed, honest,* would flock behind me and I see much good may be done—for this I yield.

It is painful to me I confess; nature will assert her claim, & my proud spirit feels and feels smartly, yet I owe duties to my country as others do, and am not to be forgiven for shrinking, because it is painful.

I pity you and every talented man in the Legislature. I well know what you have to endure from long experience. It really takes Job's patience to bear up with a sun shiny face.

From Joseph Graham. A.

Lincoln, 15 Decr., 1835.

Dear William

I recived your Letter written a few days after You had received an account of the Death of your brother Alfred. a few days after that your Brother John & his son Charles and one of the smaller Children were taken with Fever, were confined to bed for some time, but Yesterday I learn they are all convalescent, tho John has not been able yet to come up to the Furnace. She is Blowing, so far doing well, but the Forge is entirely Idle, the new log Dam put in by Alfred which was not finished will not do, supposed will have to be taken away and begun anew. the coldness of the weather and the state of Johns Health it is uncertain when that can be done. of course will make no Iron for some time. I see by the Papers that the amendments to the Constitution are Ratified, would expect the Session of the Legislature would be a short one. if this should reach you before then I would propose that the Legislature should at the expense of the State have Printed a large number of the Constitution of the United States with the Amendments and with it of the Constitution of North Carolina with the Amendments. Likewise at the last of it two or three leaves of the plainest adjudicated Cases on Constitutional Questions in the Supreme Court of the United States and Cases of the same description that have been adjudged in the Supreme Court of North Carolina, more especially such Cases as shew that powers of the Legislature is limited by their Constitutions Respectively.

The number to be printed I would propose to be equal to half the Militia in the State and at the expense of the State to be distributed to each County Court Clerk in proportion to the population in each County and delivered to all applicants on paying 12½ Cents pr. Copy. I would prefer this to giving them gratis as a number who would receive them would not or could not Read them—the Clerks could account annually for such as disposed of.

However well the people may be supplied with Copies of the Constitution near the Centre of the State, I know such supply is needed in the west. I have heard Justices of the Peace, Militia Officers and other persons of influence inquire where it might be had, and some of them Acknowledge they never had Read it. If a good Paste Board cover it might be made a School Book for boys after a certain age.

If the Clerks should not dispose of them all in Ten Years there are still some growing up would want to be supplied. . . .

From James Graham.   U.

Washington, Decm. 18th, 1835.

I have delayed writing to you some time as we have only organized and performed the melancholy office of interring 3 of our members. My man Newland is here and has presented his Petition which is referred to Com. I am told the Committee is a fair one. I have not yet been before them. I am much gratified to perceive the independent and honorable part of the House take a deep interest in my behalf, and old Ben Harden[31] of Kentucky says Newland will get *damned tired before next May*. My friends all urge me not to resign both here and at home though my inclinations are quite strong to the contrary.

I have not determined whether I may not return about the first of January or later to N. Ca. to take some depositions. In the meantime I hope you and Gov. Swain will give me the substance of the points decided in No. Ca. on Contested Elections. Must not the first notice state the grounds *distinctly* and *definitely* on which the defeated candidate charges illegality or unfairness in the election, so as to apprise me certainly of the Grounds of objection?

Must not the notice to take depositions specify the *names, residence* and defective quallifications of each person alleged to be an illegal voter so as to afford me an opportunity of sustaining the Voter and to give *him* the privilege of supporting his own Rights?

Can *hear-say* be admitted to prove how a voter voted in any case or must the testimony be from the voter voluntarily and directly given; or from some other person who *knows the fact* for instance an Inspector, or some other person who saw the Vote deposited in the Box, or any other points that may suggest themselves to you on the investigation?

A. H. Shephard [32] informed me this day Judge Martin had resigned and that his friends or perhaps his enemies wished to run his name for the Judgeship, and he consulted me on his course. I advised him not to permit himself to be used for lefthanded puposes, and he has resolved not to be Cookoed and complimented out of his seat for party purposes and has written to Raleigh that he will not accept the Judgeship. I am pleased with this act of firmness and mainly Independence. Shephard really desires the appointment but his honor will not permit him to accept it under such disgraceful motives. He likes the Gift but he disdains and damns the Giver.

When at Raleigh I advised you against the acceptance of a Judgeship. I have reflected more on that subject and I would say if you could receive it without a struggle or coming in contact

---

[31] Benjamin Hardin (1817-1852), of Kentucky, a native of Pennsylvania, was a member of the state legislature, 1810-1811, 1824, 1828-1832, 1835, a member of congress, 1815-1817, 1819-1823, 1833-1837, secretary of state of Kentucky, 1844-1847, and a delegate to the convention of 1849.

[32] Augustine Henry Shepperd (1792-1864), native of Stokes County, lawyer and active political leader. He served in the commons, 1822-1827, was a Democratic elector in 1824, a Whig member of congress, 1827-1839, 1841-1843, 1847-1851, and presidential elector, 1844.

with your immediate friends for it I think I would accept it, *after several ballotings.* I think you might be pressed to run and succeed. I would not run unless there be a very fair opportunity for success. I look upon it as a favourable position to become a good Lawyer and to stand prepared for the turns of fortune in the political changes, however consult your own views and inclinations with regard to the appointment.

Jesse Spaight [33] lies very ill here, and I think his case doubtful.

From James Graham.   U.

Washington, 22d. Decr., 1835.

The committee of Elections desire very much to see the decisions in the Legislature of No. Ca. on three points.

What construction has been given to the Act of 1796 in Haywoods Manual in relation to the notice of *Intention to contest,* *"with the ground on which the same will be disputed."* Is it sufficient to state the ground generally & vaguely; or must the ground stated be so definite and certain as to apprise the adverse party of the charges and specifications as well as the names of the illegal voters intended to the attacked and set-aside and the precincts at which they voted?—secondly If this certainly and definite object be not stated in the *first notice of Intention to contest* is it not necessary *before depositions* are taken to furnish the adverse party with the *names of the persons charged to be illegal voters and the places or precincts at which they voted?* —Thirdly what sort of testimony has been admitted and received to prove for whom an illegal voter voted? An Act of Assembly of 1800 H. M. protects the voter from answering; then can *hear say* evidence be admitted to prove for whom an illegal voter voted, or can any and what kind of evidence be received for that purpose?

When an illegal voter cannot "be compelled to discover his disquallifications as an elector," what kind of Testimony can be received to prove his disquallifications or can any or Is the Inspectors of the Election to be the final Judges? Can the *hear say* of the voter be received to disquallify him, and to change or affect his individual rights as well as the *rights of the community* and the member elected?

---

[33] Jesse Speight (1795-1847), a native of Greene County, who served in the commons, 1822; in the state senate 1823-1829 (speaker, 1828-1829); and in congress from 1829 to 1837, when he moved to Mississippi. He served in the lower house of the legislature there, and was speaker. He was a United States senator, 1845-1847.

I hope you and Gov. Swain or Judge Cammeron[34] will send me as soon as possible whatever decissions No. Ca. has made upon any of the above points in Contested elections in our Legislature as it seems the decissions in No. Ca. and the practice of that State is to have great weight in the final result of my Contested Election. I hope you will write me quickly and send me any decissions bearing on my case.

[P. S.] Genl. R. Saunders is a candidate before the President for Minister to Spain. *I know the fact I have stated.* Will he be Judge or Minister?; time will soon shew.

* * * * *

---

[34] Duncan Cameron (1777-1853), native of Virginia, who moved to North Carolina after studying law. He served for a time as clerk of the court of conference, the predecessor of the supreme court, represented Orange in the commons, 1802, 1806-1807, 1812-1813; in the state senate, 1819, 1822-1823; was a judge of the superior court from 1814-1816. He was a large planter, an active business man, was president of the state bank from 1829 to 1849. He was chairman of the committee which built the state capitol.

1836

From Jo. Seawell Jones.   **A.**

New Berne, January 1, 1836.

I have heard of some people who were so foolish as to boast that they belonged to the school of Jefferson; others I have again heard exulting in their admiration for Clay, Calhoun, or Jackson —but I—yes I, most excellent friend, am proud to say that I belong to the School of Washington—not to General George Washington, but to Miss Susan Washington of New Berne, North Carolina. I rode by her side on my way from Raleigh here; how much wouldst thou have given for my place?

Well, my dear friend, was I not too lucky in that accident? Bryan's[1] carriage broke down only nine miles from Raleigh, and I, coming quietly along in the stage all by myself, picked them up in a huddle and away we rattled. Unfortunately, however, Mrs. Bryan became very ill, and they all remained in Waynesboro. Your name is in the mouth of every lady in New Berne and I am asked at every corner If you are not engaged to Miss Washington. I always say that I am in hopes you are although I do not believe it. She asked me if you were not quizzing when you said you had never seen the Misses Gaston.

The truth is, you must marry some one or the gossips of the land will expire by exhaustion. They all quote Manly in their asservations as to your actually courting Miss Washington, and all other women expectants are laughed at for their disappointments.

Matty is mad I suppose because you did not act up to his former predictions.

Come down to New Berne, Graham, by all means, and write me next mail upon your allegiance.

Raleigh.

---
[1] Presumably James W. Bryan.

To Thomas Stamps. [2]   A.

Raleigh,

Jany. 25th, 1836.

I have had the honor to receive yours of the 17th inst., informing that I have been chosen by my brethren of the Dialectic
Society, to deliver the annual address, on Tuesday evening next
preceding the ensuing Commencement. I am too sensible of the
obligations which I owe to the Society, and too highly appreciate
this testimonial of its esteem, to decline the appointment, though
I could have wished that the call had found me in the enjoyment
of more leisure than, I fear, I shall be able to command, for
preparation.

Be pleased to communicate to the members of the Society, my
lively sense of the honorable distinction, which I have received
at their hands and the assurance of my best wishes for the prosperity and success of each & all of them, in the cultivation of
"Virtue & Science."

I tender to you my thanks for the obliging manner in which you
have communicated the request of your associates and

Am with much regard

Your Obedt. Servt.

From James Graham.   U.

Washington, Feb 7th, 1836.

I have delayed writing you for some time as I was happy to learn
from your last letter you would visit Father about this time. I hope
you have done so and that some final disposition has been made
of brother Alfred's Estate. I was gratified to learn from an intimation in your last letter that you contemplate some change in your
relations of life. I highly appreciate the name you mentioned, it
is an honored and patriotic one and presume you would do well
to preserve and secure the object in view. Delay in matters of that
kind is often attended with evil consequences. Wm. H. Haywood
is here on his way to New York; he informs me it is thought your
prospects are decidedly good and expected you would soon take a
trip to New-bern.

---

[2] Thomas Stamps, of Halifax County, Va., a graduate of the university that year,
planter.

My Contested Election is still before the Committee undecided. They refused to give me time to take any testimony after Congress met. I have however instructed my friends to proceed & take Depositions and forward them forth with to me here. I will offer them to the House and if they refuse I will offer them to the People. I still think the case is for me as now presented to the Committee, but I can make it much stronger and indeed put it beyond doubt if my testimony were all heard.

The Debates so far this Session have turned on abstract propositions and resolutions contemplating no practical legislative action. The discussions are animated and angry. Payton[3] of Ten. and Glascock[4] of Georgia have had a very violent cut and thrust debate. Payton is understood to be the Game Cock of Tennessee and he made the feathers fly out of the Georgian.

John Q. Adams has made a furious assault on the Senate with regard to the loss of the Fortification Bill and he has been *skinned alive* in both branches of Congress.

I think the opposition very indiscreet and intemperate in Debate. Wise[5] of Virginia is provoking and pouring the vials of his wrath on the Party. He takes Mr. Randolph[6] for his model. He is young and ardent with no great strenth of intellect or cultivation but he is the very spirit and soul of Chivalry. He keeps Polk, the speaker constantly on a hot gridiron.

If Genl. Dudly is going to run for Governor he should this Spring take the Halifax & Edenton Circuit & in the summer go to the West and make short patriotic Republican speeches. He must do it or he cant get on well. Let him tell Anacdotes that happened in the war when he was in the service and all's well.

If you have a thought of getting married, I think you had better decline running as a candidate this year, But if possible start some persons who will redeem Orange, tell them to live in the Range and never stop until the work is done. Bring out two men

---

[3] Balie Peyton.

[4] Thomas Glascock (1790-1841), of Georgia, lawyer, captain in the War of 1812, brigadier general in the Seminole war, 1817, Democratic member of congress, 1835-1839.

[5] Henry Alexander Wise (1806-1876), of Virginia, educated at Washington College, (now Washington and Jefferson), lawyer, active in Democratic politics, member of congress, 1833-1844. He declined post of secretary of the navy, was minister to Brazil, governor 1856-1860, Confederate brigadier general.

[6] John Randolph, of Roanoke (1773-1833), native of Virginia, educated at William and Mary, and Princeton, served in congress, 1799-1813, 1815-1817, 1819-1825, and was a member of the board of managers in the impeachment of Pickering and Chase. He was United States senator, 1825-1829, delegate to the convention of 1829, and minister to Russia, 1830.

of sense and two men of large connections and neighbourhood influence and scatter them well over the County.

I was a little unwell lately but my health is now very good. I have been but little in the gay circle this winter. I go to the large parties when the weather is not too cold but this climate requires a Sounthern man to take good care of himself.

Report and Resolutions
Orange County Whig Meeting.[7]

February 24th., 1836.

As the period approaches which is to close the official term of our present Chief Magistrate, the solicitude of the people of all America is justly excited in the choice of his successor. In the exercise of no political privilege does it behoove a free citizen to deliberate more anxiously, to scrutinize more closely, or to search more extensively for information, than in determining on whom his vote shall be bestowed for the Presidency of the United States. In our quarter of the Union, public attention has been mainly concentrated on two distinguished individuals, who are presented as competitors for this high office, between whom, in the South, at least, a selection must necessarily be made. These are Hugh L. White, of Tennessee, and Martin Van Buren, of New York. In choosing between them, a mind desirous of doing justice to both, and forming a correct conclusion for its own action, is naturally led to inquire, What claims has either upon the suffrages of his countrymen? What public services have they, respectively, rendered, either to the whole Union, or to the States to which they belong? What course of policy do they severally advocate? Where do they reside, and what are their interests, and the interests of those of whom they are most nearly connected? are they the same with, or adverse to ours? What are their political opinions, partialities and attachments, and what of advantage, or of injury, might be expected from the elevation of the one or the other?

With the early history of Mr. Van Buren we do not profess to be very familiar. He has been frequently a member of the Senate of the Legislature of N. York, has held the office of her attorney general, and also filled her executive chair. But we

---

[7] *Hillsboro Recorder*, Feb. 29th., 1836. (This newspaper was also published under title of *Hillsborough Recorder*.)

are ignorant of any important measure of state policy projected or completed by him, except the safety fund banking system, adopted upon his recommendation while chief magistrate of the commonwealth, by which the currency of the state is subjected to the control of the dominant political party, and rendered applicable to any ends which may be necessary to perpetuate their power. Among those stupendous works of improvement which everywhere pervade the state of New York, and which stand as monuments of the imperishable fame of others of her sons, we know of none which will perpetuate his memory as a statesman or public benefactor. He went into the Senate of the United States in 1822, and remained until 1828; but although the eyes of the whole nation have been constantly fixed on the proceedings of Congress, we doubt whether his most ardent admirer can point to any important act which originated with him, or to any occasion when he exhibited abilities, intelligence, or patriotism superior to his associates. Mr. Van Buren's opinions and actions in regard to national politics have been, almost invariably, of an undecided and indefinite character. He entered the stage of active manhood when the Federal and Republican parties which first divided our country yet existed, and is alleged to have been attached to the Republicans; yet he is said to have been opposed to the declaration of the late war with Great Britain, and actually supported Dewitt Clinton against James Madison for the Presidency in 1812, the latter of whom was the republican candidate. He is reported by his friends to be opposed to protective tariff duties, and to be of opinion that the federal government has no constitutional right to construct works of internal improvement within the states of the confederacy; yet his votes are recorded on the journals of the Senate in favor of an act to erect toll gates on the Cumberland road, and in favor of the tariff bills, both of 1824 and 1828, to the latter of which he gave an active and efficient support. Indeed we hardly know a public man who has filled so many high stations, whose opinions on the great questions which have divided the nation, appear to be less settled, or less generally understood. This course of neutrality, of doing nothing so positive as not to admit of variation, if not the contrary, was departed from in one remarkable instance. When the state of Missouri applied for admission into the Union upon a footing of equality with the other states, Mr. Van Buren, then a Senator in the Legislature of New York, voted for instructions to their Senators, and a request to their representatives in Congress, "to oppose the admission as a state in the union, of any territory not comprised in the original boundary of the United States, without making the prohibition of slavery therein, an indispensable condition of admission." Thus evincing a hostility to the interests of the south which destroys all claim to our support, especially at this crisis. We are aware that it is attempted to give weight to his pretensions by his nomination in the Baltimore convention in the month of May last. So far from this being a recommendation to us, it is a decided objection. That convention did not spring from the people. It was contrived and attended solely by the friends of Mr. Van Buren, many of whom held offices with large salaries under the government, and had therefore a deep personal interest in his elevation. Some of its members professed to have many constituents, others but few, and others again acknowledged that they had none. Yet by persons thus authorized, the votes of all the people of some of the states were disposed of. To say that the nomination of such a body as this was any indication of the wishes of the great body of the people, is in effect to deride their intelligence, and deny their capacity for self government. This electoral district at least, is freed from any trammels which may have been imposed by that convention. Of all the individuals who assembled there, with or without authority from the people, there was not one who even pretended that he had any commission from the freemen of this district. Nor do we know any one in the county of Orange, who had signified any wish to be represented there. The decision of that convention can therefore have no shadow of claim to authority among the people here.

In turning to the life of Judge White, we find him characterized both in public and private by the most unassuming modesty, yet the utmost firmness, decision of purpose, and consistency of action in the discharge of every duty; and if not possessed of the most specious grade of talent, certainly with the highest claims to practical wisdom. Born in the state of North Carolina, he was carried in early youth, by that spirit of enterprize which has always marked our people, to the then frontier settlements of Tennessee. Accustomed to the privations and dangers incident to a newly settled country, surrounded by savages, he acquired an energy and boldness of character, even before he reached manhood, which added to his unsuspected honesty and active patriotism, have rendered him always a favorite in Tennessee. More than once, it is said, the youthful statesman accompanied his neighbors and friends in expeditions to repel the hostile incursions of the Indians. Without the advantages afforded in the present day for education, Mr. White applied his active and intrepid mind to the cultivation of learning, and became one of the ablest advocates in his own state, one of the most able and useful members of her Legislature, and finally a Judge of her Supreme Court. But in the many posts of honor to which he was called, he never forgot those to whom he was indebted for his elevation, and has under all circumstances possessed the confidence of the people of Tennessee. When the country was involved in war, he is said to have done more to sustain that state in the efficient and honorable part which she bore in the contest, by providing the ways and means for its prosecution, and in inspiring her militia with courage, than any citizen of the state, except the General who led her armies to victory. Though known to the country as a profound judge and able statesman in his own state, Judge White had never been in the service of the nation until appointed a commissioner, under the Florida treaty, to settle the claims of our citizens on Spain. After the close of the labors of this commission, he was pronounced by his associate, Mr. Tazewell, "one of the ablest men on the waters of the Mississippi." He was elected to the Senate of the United States in 1823, where he has continued ever since. Upon the dissolution of the first cabinet in 1831, Judge White was tendered the appointment of Secretary of War, and all must recollect how generally his refusal was regretted throughout the country. Those very presses and persons who are now so bitter in reviling him, were then eloquent in his praise.

As a Senator he has uniformly supported the interests of the planting states, by an active and zealous opposition to the tariffs of 1824 and 1828; in opposing extravagant appropriations of the public money; and in endeavoring, under every change of party, to reduce the patronage and power of the Executive government within its proper limits. A statesman of firm and liberal principles, he cannot change his principles with the times. In every government there is great danger that adverse interests may arise between the tax payers and the tax receivers. The former concerned to diminish the public burthens by having no useless officers, and confining expenditure to the legitimate wants of the government; the latter living on public bounty, and interested in sustaining a multitude of offices, with large salaries. Already under our federal government there are more than fifty thousand office holders, who subsist on the public treasury, and who derive their appointments directly or indirectly from the Executive. And it also appears from official documents, that there was, at the beginning of this year, a surplus in the revenue of 20,000,000. dollars above the appropriations of last year. It must be apparent to every one that this immense revenue, which is not needed by the public wants, a large portion of which must be distributed in salaries of the appointees of the Executive, and in compensation to contractors for public employment, will, unless curtailed, render the Executive power too great for the liberties of the country. Judge White, both in 1826, and in 1836, has been in favor of reducing this overgrown power; while Mr. Van Buren, although in favor of the reduction in 1826, has of late been silent on the subject, if he has not changed his opinions.

We wish not to excite feelings of sectional hostility, but other things being equal, we deem it a safe rule in choosing a public servant, to take him who is identified with us in interest, and who in the administration of his high office cannot injure us without injuring himself, rather than one who is not bound to us by such ties. It is not to be disguised that at this time the institution of slavery is attacked in the district of Columbia by a portion of the people at the north under a claim of authority; and like attempts from the same quarter are made on our property in the states themselves, though as yet unaccompanied by a claim of constitutional power. In these circumstances, we deem it a matter of great importance to our safety and peace, to have a President who is with us on this great question. The interposition which he has it in his power to afford through the post office establishment alone, for the prevention of mischief on this subject, has been witnessed within the last year. Mr. Van Buren may not be an abolitionist, we trust he is not; but after his course on the Missouri question, it would be unreasonable to expect from him a zealous cooperation with us in resisting their nefarious attempts on our property and lives. One other consideration we deem worthy to be mentioned. North Carolina has never put forth any citizen of her own for the chief magistracy of the Union. This is the first occasion when she has had an opportunity of elevating to that office one of her native sons. Surely if he be not less qualified than his competitor, if his principles be not more objectionable, if he has rendered public services equally valuable, we shall not postpone his claim to those of any individual whatever.

Resolved therefore, That we have the highest confidence in the wisdom, firmness and unsullied purity of character of HUGH L. WHITE of Tennessee, and that we will cordially support him for the next president of the United States.

Resolved further, That we have full confidence in the ability, consistency and integrity of JOHN TYLER of Virginia, and concur in the nomination which has been made of him for the Vice Presidency.

Resolved further, That James Mebane, Dr. Strudwick and Harrison Parker, be appointed to meet the delegates who may be appointed in the counties of Granville and Person, at such time as they may agree upon, to nominate an Elector for this district.

Resolved further, That we entertain the highest respect for the public and private character, and entirely confide in the political principles of General EDWARD B. DUDLEY, of the county of New Hanover, and will endeavour to promote his election to the office of Governor of North Carolina.

From James Graham.   U.

Washington, Feb. 25, 1836.

On yesterday the Committee of Elections made a Report, the Majority five Members against me, and the Minority four members for me, that is, two Reports. The Reports are now before the House. I have asked the house to do what the Committee refused, that is to give me time to take evidence. That question is now pending. Jesse Bynum has entered the lists for Newland. On this day Wm. B. Shephard [8] scored him severely. I also handled him roughly. My friends were much gratified and told me my efforts were entirely successful and that a favourable impression had been made. I fear the zeal of my friends will somewhat injure me. They feel a very deep interest in the result. *I have the fullest confidence that I shall retain my seat* but they will move heaven and earth against me. I am resolved to pursue a straight upright, dignified course and will not turn to the right or left to lean on any party. I am governed by the old fashioned principle of Right or Wrong. I do not believe the question will be decided for a month or six weeks, and I should not be much surprised if at last it be sent back to the People. *But they cant beat me.*

[8] William Biddle Shepard (1799-1852), of New Bern. Educated at the university, and the University of Pennsylvania, he became a lawyer, and banker, served in congress, 1827-1837, and in the state senate, 1838-1840, 1848-1850.

I recd. your letter saying you would go to Newbern about this time. I am happy to hear it and hope you be rendered happy in the visit. Do not delay matters *too long* but without indecent haste terminate the matter. I am so embarrassed about this election I have not time to attend to my fashionable friends—I go to a few parties. . . . Gov. Tyler[9] will resign his seat in a few days. Leigh has not said what he will do. He ought to resign but I fear he will not.

From Jo. Seawell Jones.   A.

New Berne,

February 28th, 1836.

Are you mad? Are you cross as so,+as a little pet child once said to me, crossing her two little fingers? Why the—I will not say what—do you not write me? If you think to escape me as a correspondent by such behavior, I tell you, you are sadly mistaken. So here I come, on the old subject of love, and all its horrid, monstrous consequences. I jump "in medias res" and proclaim to you in the language of a tornado, or a Niagara, or anything else that is noisy and uproarious, that if you do not come down here *damn*— (I will curse once)—quickly, Miss W. will kick you to the other side of the room when you do come. Now Sir, be off down here, in two hours after you read this epistle, or the next time I write you I will commence as follows:

New Bern, 20th May, 1836.

"My Dear Graham

I have a splendid and gay crowd below, and rush up stairs (such a getting up stairs) merely to say to—in this short letter— that I was married about an hour since (oh, ooh, ah—gasping at being kept up so late) to the beautiful and accomplished Miss Susan Washington."

So you look out for squalls,—all that Turpentine, Cash, and all the lands, and all the Nigs, and, what is really worse than all, the lady herself,—gone, or certainly going, if you do not make haste.

---

[9] John Tyler, then senator from Virginia.

I have ruined the character of New Berne and all its male inhabitants. I have kept the whole Town in a *row*—a spree— ever since I have been here. Use up 20 boxes of Champagne, and of course have seen a good deal of real "low life above stairs," as the loveliest lady in the town told me. It has been, I might say, too gay, and still it is doomed to be still gayer, for the Misses Collins of Edenton are to be here on Tuesday, to spend a month. So I again repeat, come down, come down, from your hilly-*Boro'*. Good bye, write soon.

Outlaw[10] is here with me; sends love to you.

[*Enclosure*][11]

MISS ESTHER WAKE,

By Jo. Seawell Jones.

The city of Raleigh is the capital of the county of Wake, as well [as] of the State of North Carolina. In the year 1788 the people of the State in Convention assembled, ordained that the beautiful eminence, now crowned with the ruins of Canova's Washington and the new Capitol, should be in all future time the headquarters of the State government. It is a spot consecrated to the genius of Raleigh, and was appropriately chosen in a county founded in honor of a beautiful woman.

Miss Esther Wake was the sister of Lady Tryon, and came with Governor Tryon to North Carolina in the year 1764. She was, I have been told, at the early age of fifteen on her arrival, and during the six years of her residence in the State, she was truly and emphatically adored by all who had the distinction of her acquaintance. Even the people in their assembled majesty, bowed to the supremacy of her charms, and the Assembly of 1770 erected the county of Wake to commemorate her name. Such was the

---

[10] David Outlaw (1806-1868), of Bertie County, a classmate of Graham at the university, who did not remain to complete the course. He became a lawyer, and went into politics as an ardent Whig. He served in the commons, 1831-1834, 1854-1858; in the state senate, 1860-1861; in congress, 1847-1853; and was a delegate to the convention of 1835.

[11] The original of this document was enclosed by Jones in the foregoing letter to Graham. As it was temporarily separated from the letter, I have used an accurate copy, quoted by R. D. W. Connor in his article *"Was Esther Wake a Myth?"* in *The North Carolina Booklet*, Vol. 14, No. 4, pp. 221-224. An excellent bit of fiction, it is to be regretted that it was not finished. Another view of the matter will be found in Marshall DeLancey Haywood's discussion of the subject, in *Governor Tryon, and His Administration in the Province of North Carolina. . . .* and the question is also discussed by Dr. Kemp P. Battle, *"Is Esther Wake a Myth,"* Univ. of N. C. Mag., Nov., 1894, pp. 91-95.

influence of beauty, virtue and wit, among a chivalrous and hospitable people.

The secret history of our country is as little known as are the secret motives of the human heart. The legislator often acts from a more ignoble impulse than the pleasure of a lovely woman, and then continues to hide even this fair season under specious considerations of State policy. In the years 1767, 8 and 9, the Assembly voted sixty thousand dollars, to build a Palace for the Governor and the historian of the State will pause an age for any higher inducement for this profligacy of expenditure, than the gratification of this celebrated lady. She was ambitious enough to desire magnificent parlours and bourdoirs, wherein to receive the homage of her numerous admirers, for the Governor, previous to the building of the Palace, was compelled to provide his own establishment, which was usually rented from some of the gentlemen of the borough. The heavy taxes levied to complete the edifice, contributed to inflame the rebellion of the Regulators, and was more than any other cause, the immediate inducement of the famous battle of Allemance on the 16th. of May, 1771. But what were the horrors of war to the youthful members of the Assembly, when compared with those of a lady's displeasure? The Palace was built, the Regulators were conquered, and Miss Esther Wake was gratified.

The proverbial influence of the fair sex in matters of State was well sustained by Lady Tryon and her lovely sister, and the enthusiastic spirit of a warm-hearted people estimated even the character of their Governor by the grace, beauty and accomplishment that adorned the domestic circles of his Palace. The story of Miss Esther will serve for a beautiful episode in the history of North Carolina. Amidst the petty caucuses of a Province under the government of a subordinate military officer, it is gratifying to discover the secret source of power, even in the volition of a virtuous woman. It is better than an irresponsible cabal of intrigueing politicians and when properly watched, will but subserve the interest and honor of a people.

I have a number of private letters illustrative of the power of Miss Esther, which are almost too romantic for sober reality of historical detail. According to their authority she ruled without an effort or design, though it [is] easy to imagine that the cunning of the Governor could continue to use it for the advancement of his own interest. The younger members unquestionably yielded more easily to her known or expressed wishes from an ambitious hope of gaining her in marriage, but says Colonel John Harvey in a letter of date the 20th. of January, 1771, 'what can be said in defense of those Gentlemen of age and experience who to gratify a Governor's wife and to be sure [of] her pretty sister should vote fifteen or twenty thousand pounds to build a palace, when the people were not able to pay even their most ordinary taxes, and what is still worse, then go to war with their countrymen, to enforce the unjust law.' Isaac Edwards, the private Secretary of Tryon, in a letter to Judge Williams of date the 6th. of November, 1770, says, 'the Palace is finished, and we are in it. The Governor is much pleased with it and the ladies are now ready to give entertainments in a stile suitable to their rank and deserts. Miss Wake is in fine humor, and is every day planning her party. She has a complete set of new and splendid robes, just from home, and when she gets them on, and gets the young assembly-men in the big parlour, she can get a grant of money to build another house for herself.'

Among those who paid court to the beauty of Miss Esther was Sir William Draper, the conqueror of Manilla and the antagonist of the celebrated Junius. He was the guest of Governor Tryon in the Palace, a circumstance to which the Governor often alluded with evident satisfaction and pride. The Palace itself was dedicated to Sir William, whose name was inscribed on the vestibule, at the head of a few Latin verses of his own composition. It should have been dedicated to Miss Esther Wake, for I learn such was the original and higher destiny. Here is a letter of Sir William Draper to Sir Nathaniel Duckinfield, of North Carolina:

"Dear Sir Nathaniel—I send one of the Governor's servants all the way to your house to bear this apology for not coming myself, agreeable to your polite invitation and my own promise, I might appeal to my ingenuity and frame you a hundred excuses, which you could but accept, but the generosity of the lover, if not of the soldier, must forbid all such subterfuges. So then, My Dear Sir Nathaniel, take the truth as a great secret, I am in love, and Miss Esther Wake has graciously—" [Here the manuscript abruptly ends; the rest is lost.]

From James Graham.   U.

Washington, March 30th, 1836.

The Contested Election is now terminated and ordered back
to the People. I am well satisfied with the result. I ascertained I
had no opportunity of a fair trial here. Newland although a
White man at home has become a Van Buren man here and has
sold himself. I have become very tired of this protracted contest.

I received your letters from Newbern and Raleigh; and I am
very much gratified at the favourable result of your visit. . . . I
hope all things will go on well in the matter and don't put off
the matter. I will set out for home next week perhaps Tuesday and
will pass Raleigh and Hillsboro, but can't stop as I presume Gov
Spaight will order the Election quite soon and I must be in the
district as soon as possible.

I am writing out my speach to take home with me

From Lewis Williams.   U.

Washington, April 1st, 1836.

You will see in the papers that the seat of your Brother has
been vacated by the vote of the Van Buren party, among whom
was your redoubtable member Dr. Montgomery. Party spirit runs
higher at this time than I ever saw it before, and if our character
of standing and influence don't step forward to rescue the country from the domination which threatens us, we are undone
forever.

I do not believe the government will or can survive the misrule
for eight years longer, and I hope you and Mr. Waddell will take
the field for the August conflict. Every thing depends on carrying
Orange, Surry and a few other Counties. In Surry we have made
the best Ticket we can, and will carry it if possible by every
effort we can use.

Permit me to suggest that you and Mr. Waddell, I hope, will
be on the Ticket for Orange County. Judge Mangum tells me
that he has expectations that you will be candidates. If an united
and powerful effort is not made, the large Counties will go against
us, and that would give the Van Buren party the preponderance
in the Legislature.

If that party should beat us in August, we might as well give up the contest in November, for the impression at home and abroad in other States will be decisive against us. North Carolina is regarded by the other States as more decided against Van Buren than any other State in the South and if we should be defeated, it will be universally believed that that party is in the majority. A conclusion of this sort would be wholly destructive to our prospects every where. I hope therefore you and Mr. Waddell will be candidates and such others as will form a strong powerful ticket.

Excuse the liberty I have taken and believe me your friend truly.

From William Gaston.   U.

I have heard of your arrival in town and would call to see you but that the weather is unfavorable.

Will you do me the favour to take your dinner with me tomorrow at three o'Clock?

Truly yours.

April 3d. 1836.—

From James Graham.   U.

Washington, April 4th, 1836.

I will leave this City on tomorrow for N. Carolina. I had contemplated passing Raleigh and Hillsboro, but further reflection induces me to change that determination, and to go the upper route directly on. It is apprehended the Gov. will order an Election forthwith; and in that event I should not loose one day in getting into the district. Newland has gone on. I have remained until I could get my speech printed to put in a Box and take home in my own care. I will send you a copy as soon as it is dry enough not to blott. I wrote it out *in great haste* and had not time to correct and prune it as time is every thing with me at present.

The House paid Newland $1200 for doing nothing but make the People spend about $50,000. It is suspected he carries with him a large sum of secret service money to operate upon the People. The House utterly refused to look into the evidence, or *to decide one single proposition* submitted to them in the shape of Resolutions. And since the contest has terminated, Vanderpool,[12] one of the New York drill Sargents, has boasted of the General-Ship of his party in avoiding the single simple propositions presented, because then the trained Bands would have had to put their toes fairly to the mark and they could not have voted against me, but by giving the direct and specific propositions the *Go-by*, they left no tracks by which they could be pursued and exposed before the People, and hence the Previous Question and Gag-law was put in force to cut off all my amendments and Resolutions without any vote upon them and thereby leave not a trace behind of any action upon any proposition that could reach the merits of the Case. They sculked and dodged behind the Previous Question which covers a multitude of sins and ought to be *expunged* from the Rules of order.

A decided Majority of the Virginia Van Buren men stood by me and went against the Party. The whole case has been tried by a court of *Discretion without conscience*. It surely has been a most disgraceful exercise of Power and none but sworn Slaves to Party and tyranny could have prostituted principle and duty to such unholly purposes. It was admitted by McKay, who is devoted to his party, that Newland was but *one vote* ahead of me, *and if the House would receive and count the new testimony* that had come in after the Report of the Committee and which had been on the Table *for two weeks;* then, I was Eighteen votes ahead. But the real truth is I was 12 votes ahead of him on the old evidence independent of the new. Genl. Hawkins[13] who was one of the Committee that signed the Majority Report got up in the House and denied that he had ever consented to an important part of the Report *although his name was to it.* I said to my friends, it was a pretty fair and impartial Committee; out of the nine members, there were 4½ for me; and 4 and a ½ against me. The truth is Hawkins can scarcely write a negros pass, or read it after it is written; and when the palpable falsehoods of the Report were uncovered and exposed he winced and looked like he was taking Gaul and worm-wood; all I can say to him is, may God increase his pain. I have made no complaints but bore myself stiffly up and treated the matter with apparent indifference. No man ever had truer friends. On Saturday night they resisted the Previous Question all night long, even until day light Sunday

---

[12] Aaron Vanderpoel (1796-1810), of New York, a Democratic lawyer, who, after ten years in the state assembly, served in congress, 1833-1837, 1839-1841. He was a state judge, from 1841-1850.

[13] Micajah Thomas Hawkins.

morning, and we came nigh having a general fight and Riot. Payton gave Beardsly[14] of N. Y. the *damdest laraping* and scarcastic Scoring I ever heard from mortal man. Wise was pouring out the Viols of his wrath upon "The Party," and Bynum called him to order. Bynum said Wise should *not bully* him. No says Wise, with a most contemptuous sneer, "I would as soon Bully *a Fly*."

My friends and all the respectability of the City and District are gratified that I have escaped so well and that I have an opportunity of another Election. Newland although charged in the House with forsaking his principles and preference for Judge White before the People, and now being a Van Buren man did not deny it but sanctioned it with a nod. One of the N. Yorkers was heard to say to another, "He is a damned bungling fool; but he'll do for a soldier, for one of the rank and file." I presume he has his reward for turning his coat.

From James Graham.   U.

Greensboro, 8th. April, 1836

I am so far on my way home. I regret I have not an opportunity to see you and the more so as I presume you are going to change your situation. I am apprehensive it will be out of my power to be with you at that time if in June as you contemplate, but *If I possibly can* I will. I anticipate a great degree of hard unpleasant labour in my contest but feel quite sure of Victory, but I must be constantly on the look out. Go on with your Love affair as soon as possible and finish it.

If you intend to be a candidate in Orange begin in time [page torn] mix freely with the people, be *merry with the young men* & attentive to the old, endeavour to divide the forces against you.

From Thomas L. Clingman.   U.

Huntsville, [N. C.,], April 29th, 1836.

I have been anxious for some time past to hear from you, and should have troubled you with an epistle earlier, but that letter-writing is one of those things which like other indolent persons

---

[14] Samuel Beardsley (1790-1860), of New York, a Democrat, who, after service in the state senate, and as judge, was a member of congress, 1822-1836, 1843-1844, resigning each time before the close of his term, to become a state judge. He became chief justice in 1847.

I am constantly postponing to a more convenient season. In the present instance however there is some excuse for my not writing sooner. Having learned in the winter that you had gone "down east" to the land of dark eyes and sunny smiles, of beauty and wit and music where the head of Sapho and the heart of Haidee are combined with the *glories* of a Circassian form (it is Spring now and I have a right to be a little voluptuous in the presence of the fresh flowers, the green forests and the soft air of the Southwest) of fish, oysters, etc., which ought not to be esteemed worthy of a place on the same page with the other things named. That you should leave a land like this to return to the practice of the law, was a contingency too remote to be taken into the account.

A friend the other day informed me that he had seen you in the upper country but whether in your wanderings you had been breaking spears with brave men or hearts of fair women, he did not know. Fame with her hundred tongues has recently been so busy with your name that you may expect your friends to be looking at the head of the advertising column in the newspapers to see it announced.

Will you be a candidate this summer in Orange? From what I can learn you are the only whig whose election in that County would be pretty certain. Unless you intend to abandon politics entirely it seems to me that your interest requires that you should run this summer, for, the Congressional election coming on next year, you would, in the opinion of your friends, stand a fair chance to beat Montgomery. You are likely however to have many sins to answer for besides your own, for I am informed that one of my *honourable* colleagues, Col. Waugh[15] of the Senate, is telling the people of this county that my circular, speeches, etc., were written by you.

I was much inclined some weeks since to have left this county and settled in Rutherford or Buncombe from either of which counties I could form a much better circuit than I can do here. My friends however insist on my running again for the Assembly, and I have abandoned the intention of leaving the county for the present. In fact the attacks of my enemies have made me feel a little *bull-dogish* and I am disposed to give them another battle.

What is the news in Hillsboro? I should like to know what my acquaintances there are about. Cad Jones and his young wife are I presume still with you. There is nothing I believe so much

---

[15] Harrison M. Waugh, of Surry, who served in the commons, 1833-1834, 1860-1861, 1863-1865, 1872.

calculated disturb a bachelor as the sight of a loving and lovely couple. It makes him doubt his own infallibility, and shakes his belief in the superiority of single blessedness. After all marriages are more contagious than anything else. The sight of a single wedding is enough to turn the heads of all the young people present. As for myself I confess that the thought of these things sometimes makes me a little nervous.

Please remember me to Waddell, Jones, Murphey, and Cameron.

From Miss Abercrombie   A.

to

Susan Washington.

Philadelphia, May 5th, 1836.

Accept, dear Susan, my warmest acknowledgements for your affectionate letter and gracious invitation, you, who know the strength of my attachments, must be sensible how much pleasure your kind attention afforded me.

Would it were in my power, my beloved child, to avail myself of your kindness, but circumstances beyond my control, circumstances which can be explained only in a personal interview, entirely preclude my indulging the hope of being with you on this important this interesting occasion. But although not permitted to be present, my spirit will be with you, and my morning & evening orisons be offered particularly, in behalf of my precious Susan, on that day, when she plights her faith to one, who as the chosen of her heart's best affections, must be worthy of the trust. May God bless and sustain you in the fulfilment of the new duties which will then devolve upon you, it is a solemn obligation, but I fear not, for my dear Susan is calculated in my estimation, to add grace & lustre to any station however conspicuous.

The 8th of June will be kept by us as a jubilee, and we shall, as we are denied the high gratification of visiting you, commemmorate, at home, an event so deeply interesting to us.

My dear Martha has been in Newark nearly two weeks, & has not yet received your letter, I much fear, however, that the same causes which operate to prevent my being with you, will exclude her also, she will of course write herself.

To your beloved parents, offer my sincere regards, I know how severe the trial of parting with you must be, notwithstanding your flattering prospects; to Mr. Graham, say if you think proper, that I hope a visit to the North is in contemplation, & that I shall have the pleasure of making his acquaintance, & assuring him how very dear to my heart is *his Susan*.

I really feel unable to write on indifferent subjects, my feelings towards you, dear child, are so truly maternal.

Say for me, to the girls, what you please, and assure yourself, dear Susan, of the sincere and ardent affection of your

true friend

From James Graham.   **U.**

Rutherfordton, May 7th, 1836.

I have received yours of 22d ult. and am much gratified to learn you are to be married in June. Nothing could gratify me more than to accompany you to Newbern but my peculiar position at this time renders it impossible if I do justice to my self and friends at home and abroad. I have entered into the contest with much spirit and shall pursue it with zeal and industry untill the Election in August. I have addressed the People with Newland at Haywood, Buncombe, and Rutherford Courts. I believe in the two last Counties he is prostrate. He was publickly insulted while speaking at both places, and continually harrassed and often abused in the streets. In Rutherford I do not think He can get one hundred votes. I never received such a hearty welcome as I had here this week. I am informed in Burke also I shall do well and get a large majority. In Yancy Haywood and Macon the candidates for office are all against me, and will exert all their influence against me, but I have great confidence I shall command a large portion of the voters in those counties. I will go next week to Lincoln Court to see Father and have negro Joe sent down to you. I presume in the latter part of August will be as soon as we can do any thing to divide Alfred's Estate by which time I hope we may meet at Father's; perhaps the middle of August. Father has his new House done all but the Chimneys. I will have but a day or two to spend at Lincolnton. I must go *directly* to Burke to some Battallion Musters & keep moving until the 2d Thursday in August.

I will do all that may become a man to gain this Election, my friends are up and doing all they can and I hope to get a good ticket nominated for the Legislature in each of my 6 counties and their co operation will do much to aid me. I think you had better not become a candidate until you return from Newbern. If you do write a short circular, make it quite plain and send it freely among the people.

Judge White is gathering strength rapidly in this district and Van is going down. Since the people are informed that Calhoun, McDuffy, and Hamilton have determined to go against White they are much better pleased with him; — and since it is ascertained Van will get old Connecticut they are less pleased with him. Nullification and Federalism are all that our people are afraid of in any man.

We had a Rail Road meeting last evening to appoint Delegates to the Convention in Knoxville next 4th of July to consider the great Rail Road from Charleston to Cincinati. We entertain much solicitude and hope that the contemplated work may pass through our county. Judge Strange has been medling much in the Politics of my District I am informed. Jones treated him with great kindness. After I learned he had become the electioner of the *Apostate* Dave Newland I refused to visit the Judge on the Circuit.

A number of the Van Buren men have told me they will support me because they can't support *a turn coat.*

As soon as you are married write me again.

From Robert Hall Morrison.   **U.**

Near Charlotte, May 10th, 1836.

In the dark & trying dispensations of our Sovereign Lord the Angel of death has been permitted once more to brake the circle of our earthly friends, and our Bro. John Graham's family are sorely bereaved. Sister Betsy [16] died on yesterday, leaving many hearts to feel the desolation. I trust her Spirit has found rest and been numbered among the Jewels of Christs Kingdom.

It was a dissease of the *Liver* and has been gaining Strenth for about 7 weeks. She was resigned and anxious to depart; Was very much engaged in preparing for a better home; and very solemn & faithful in exhorting her Children & friends to prepare for death by living in the fear & friendship of God.

---

[16] Mrs. John Davidson Graham (1797-1836), nee Elizabeth Epps Connor.

May the many proofs we see & feel of the uncertainty of human life prompt us to prepare for that world, where bereavement, and sorrow & death will be known no more:

Write soon.

In great haste & much love.

From David L. Swain.   U.

Chapel Hill, 30 May, 1836.

I have heard of your misfortune, and have been thinking for some days of writing a letter of *consolation,* but have forborne upon the supposition that taking all things together, you regard the present period of your existence as rather happy than otherwise. I do not therefore address you at present for that purpose, although few persons could do so with as great propriety. In all that you now suffer, and in all that you anticipate, my experience seems several years ahead of you. You doubtless comprehend my meaning, if you do not your surgeon Doct. Strudwick can give ample explanations in the first person, and as to the second I will take the liberty to refer you to the testimony of a witness in New Bern to whom I apprehend you would give as entire credence as to all the world beside.

But to the main object of this note. You are a member of the Executive Committee and must attend the Commencement. we are new house keepers, but can manage to keep a room, and a bed sufficiently large for the repose of your family, and you will be expected to occupy it.

Present Mrs. S's and my respects to *your friends* in New Bern, and,

From George Shonnard Bettner.   U.

Algiers, Africa, June 9, 1836.

Dear Graham,

Excuse me if I interrupt your peaceful retirement by sending you a small & unexpected letter from the Land of Africa. I have been in this country now a week or two, having come hither from France. I was led here by curiosity, & must confess that I find abundant sources of amusement & entertainment. There is no city in the world like Algiers. It is built on the slope of a very steep hill, is of a triangular form, having the base on the sea. The houses are all terraced, and are all white, being made of stone & stuccoed The streets are about 4 or 5 feet wide & very densely built, & in the upper parts of the town are so steep, that they are cut into steps for the facility of ascending them. The narrow sombre streets here have a very singular aspect, but as they exclude the sun, they are no doubt well adapted to the climate. At night, even when the moon shines, they are so dark that it requires lanterns to find your way. All these moving lights at night look very droll.

As the houses are all terraced, it is the fashion to promenade on the terraces every evening at sun set. I mount my terrace regularly every day to see what is going on & to get a peep at the Moorish ladies, who are veiled up so closely, that you can see nothing but their eyes.

Juba & Jugurtha! how hot it is here! If I get out of this with a white skin, it will be more than I expect.

There are all sorts of people here, Turks, Moors, Jews, Christians, Bedouins, Arabs & some of the blackest "niggers" you ever laid eyes on. The Atlas mountains look very majestical "with their head in the clouds & their feet in the sand," They approach within 2 or 3 leagues of the town & run boldly down to the sea.

The two principal Gates of the City are called Bab-el-oued & Babasoun. The faubourg of Bab-el-oued is very interesting. Soon after leaving the gate you observe the Mausoleum or Tomb of the Seven Deys, who were all elected and massacred in one day! In some improvements which the French are making, they have now removed this monument, but they intend to restore it. Near here also are large cemeteries, Jewish, Arabian & Christian. The Garden & country Palace of the Dey, is likewise in the same vicinity, but much changed now, from what it was. At the top of the hill on which the town is built stands the Cassbah, or Palace of the Dey. It is a very extensive establishment, & it is said, that in all its various parts contains a thousand marble columns. I have been all over this & visited the Chambre a coucher of the Dey communicating with the Seraglio, I went also into the rooms where he used to keep his treasure. This Palace is much defaced already, & is now being used as a Caserne.

It is very amusing to walk about the streets here & take a view of the natives and their different costume. Like a good Mussul-

man I go very often to Mosque. In honor of the Prophet, I have
to pull off my boots & leave them at the door & go in bare-footed.
There are fine mats and carpets to walk on however, & you see
the show that is going on, the prostrations made by the worshippers, while others are sitting cross legged & chanting verses out
of the Koran. I took a ride on camel-back the other day. I strad-
dled the hump of the beast & guided him with a stick. This animal
has a most prodigious hard trot.

What is going on in North Carolina? Is the College flourishing?
I often think of the old Alma Mater & have a great affection for
her Classic Groves, Except the Palms and olive-trees here, I have
seen nothing equal to those woods anywhere. I hope the spirit
of the late venerable President, will watch over the Institution
& keep the young barbarians there in awe. I intend soon to establish a Professorship of Humanity & Civilization at Chapel
Hill, & to send there a regiment of tailors, musicians, pastry-
cooks & dancing masters in order to introduce some degree of
style, scandal & fashion into that benighted region of the world.
Make my compliments to President Anderson & his Lady and to
Professor Mitchell.

Are you bound down "in vinculo matrimonis" yet? It takes all
my time to see the world, so that I have no leisure to think of
matrimony, or of peopling the Earth, except "en passant."

I have already made a good many curious and interesting observations upon this City & Country, & shall not stay here much
longer. I shall return to Toulon, go to Marseilles & from thence
to Rome & Italy. Some affairs will then take me back to Paris,
but I shall soon go to London & England & then to the dear Land
of America, which I love continually the more, as I contrast it
with all other countries.

Remember me to all my old acquaintances in your part of the
world.

Did you receive a letter, which I sent to you some time ago
from Paris?

Ever Dear Graham, your truly affectionate friend.

From James A. King.[17]   U.

Statesville, June 15th, 1836.

I presume I may now congratulate you on what we bachelors consider the consumation of happiness here. I trust, indeed I suppose, you will have your full proportion. I am glad to perceive that you are again a candidate, you are on debateable ground & I hope that you will exert yourself to receive your election and the balance of our Ticket in the Commons. You ought not to let anything interfere so as to prevent your attention to your election, not even your *domestic* concerns; on this latter subject however I know but little & therefore I shall abstain from further remarks.

*   *   *   *

We have nothing new here. We shall give Dudly a a very large majority in the West & return a majority of Whigs to the Legislature. I have written Outlaw particularly on this subject in reply to a letter rec. from him a few days since.

Politics I find is a D_____l of poor trade & think I shall quit it after this Summer; indeed I am hardly yet a Candidate. Nothing but a Van Buren mans entering the field or a strong possibility of it will induce me to run.

You know that this county is safe and unless we are guilty of gross mismanagement there can be no danger of defeat. I do not think that there will be a Van Buren Candidate — they are making an effort to get one in the Commons — of course they will level their artillery at me.

If it should so happen that you are actually married upon the rct. of this (I have seen no acct. of it) will you present my best respects Mrs. Graham?

From Moses W. Alexander.   U.

Alexandriana, July 8, 1836.

*   *   *   *

I sold my land in Ala for which I gave $10 pr. acre for $30 pr. acre bought again for $33⅓ for 160 & for $31 — for 240 acres. My present farm possesses many advantages over that of the

---

[17] James Albert King (d. 1846), of Iredell County, who was at the university with Graham. He was a member of the commons, 1833-1836. He later moved to South Carolina, and, still later, to several states in the South.

one I sold; One half the land is Rolling, will make a heavy Crop in a Wet year, part of the Balance is very flat & will do splendid in a dry season & part sandy for situation & small field which will always open soon and yield 1000 lb. to the acre. Last winter an acre was measured in a corner of the flat land field (not better than any other piece) picked and weighed 1836 lbs. I have 130 acres planted this year have been lately informed I will make 100 Bales, which in that State average 530 lb.; some do make of 600 lb. yet sir with all this we are not to move. I could not be induced for 5 of the Best Farms in Ala. to raise my children — I may possibly tell you my greatest objection — But I cannot write it. The least objection to that country is this: Speculation is the order of the day and stalks abroad in the country untill it has entirely thrown Honesty in the Back ground & produced its concomitant to an illimitable extent viz. a want of Confidence; No Man's word is to be believed, no man's honor binds him in a transaction unless in black and white that the law will compel the fulfilment. Talk of good neighbourhoods if one exists today it is gone tomorrow. Land changes hands very often.

I must use a part of my space to congratulate your happy union with the lady of your choice I hope it will not be long untill you bring our Sister up & spend some time with us. We will be truly happy to see you.

We all greatly regret not being able to be with you on the late important pleasant hour, and may God of his infinite mercy make it to you Both an uninterrupted scene of peace, prosperity & Happiness is the prayer of your affectionate Brother & Sister.

From John Cameron.[18]   U.

Pensacola, July 8th, 1836.

Having just received intimation direct of the fact of your having cast off the slough of Bachelorism & put on the garment & priviledges of a Benedict; permit me to offer you my warmest congratulations, with my best wishes for your future welfare, together with a sincere hope that you may always have cause to look upon the step which you have taken as the most happy & fortunate occurrence of your life.

---

[18] John Cameron, son of William Cameron, and nephew of Duncan Cameron, student at the university, 1830-1831; journalist, captain in the Mexican War.

Often since my departure from the old town, have I thought with regret upon the probability of an eternal separation (at least so far as this world is concerned) from many, whose friendship & regard, while there, I prized most highly & the loss of whose society & communion, was one of the severest pangs experienced in parting.

It is more than probable that I shall here form many new associations & some new friends, but none that will ever entwine themselves around my feelings and affections, like those who are linked with all the pleasant remeniscences of my youth.

I have often in my hours of dreary solitude pictured to myself the scene of your happy rejoicings & wished that I could be a sharer in its delights. Oh! what times I would have had. Why first and foremost I would have had a congratulatory speech for the fair Mrs. Graham, as long as one of Tom Benton's Congressional thunder gusts (Heaven defend her from such an infliction I think I hear you say) and then the exuberances of literary colloquy, ready cut & dried for use two months before; which I would have poured upon the world of beauty assembled in charms there; would have placed me at once far beyond the reach of all competition in the field of gallantry, a very Magnus Apollo, a rara avis (et simillima negro que Albino) alias white nigger & second only to that Jupiter Olympus, the immortal Phlip.

Such gasconading, gallopading, serenading, lemonading such channting, ranting, enchanting, & gallanting,

> Such a bowing & blinking & wine & grog drinking
> Such a nibbling of good things & sipping of tea
> Such a squiring of Misses & wishing for kisses
> We'd have had altogether a deuce of a spree.

Oh my mouth waters at the very idea, as it rolls itself like a sweet morsel through my brain.

And who were the representatives of the land of Hog & Hominy, on the interesting occasion, with the exception always of your honorable self, as we opine that the matter in all probability could scarce have gone on without your presence. I hope that you had some one else besides Pill Norwood; his thin shanks poor fellow could not bear up under half the load of dignity which would of necessity devolve on him, & as for the quantity of good things necessary to be brought away, his lean paunch would not hold a moiety. Oh that you could have had Rory there; how sleek

& comfortable he would have looked by this time, sweet with pound cake, & big with the liquor of a thousand jugs.

I have not commenced doing any thing as yet, save reading a little, but I hope before very long to be at work & making something. There must eventually I think a very large amount of business be done in this place; those engaged in the works of internal improvement are active and sanguine of final success.

The Bank is in a flourishing condition & has been doing a fine business, for the Amt issued, & I heard the President remark the other day that had that *amt* been larger, that his profits would have been equally great in proportion.

The Railroad Company expect to have about 50 miles of their road completed, & in operation, by the winter; the rest as far as Columbus will be ready to receive freight in the course of two or three years, there will be several lateral roads, branching off to points on the Alabama River & other places all of which they will endeavour to complete as soon as practicable.

In the profession of the law, there does not at present appear to be much doing, it is in the hands of a few who contrive however to be well paid for what they do do. Judge Cameron [19] told me that a gentleman of the profession by the name of Blount (not my Lord) who has been residing in this place some six years, assured him that his profits at the last term of the Court held in this place were $1500.00 & though apparently a very clever fellow, I am sure that neither his wits or learning will ever set the bay on fire.

You will please tender my best wishes & respects to Mrs. Graham, whom although a stranger, I am determined to regard as a friend, & believe me ever

Yrs Sincerely.

I have just heard of the death of old Mr. Kirkland,[20] poor old gentleman, his loss will be severely felt by all who knew him, & his kindness and hospitality remembered long after many who made more fuss in the world shall have passed away.

---

[19] John Adams Cameron (1788-1839), a native of Virginia, a brother of Judge Duncan Cameron, graduate of the university, studied law and settled at Fayetteville. He represented the borough in the commons, 1810-1812, 1820; was a major in the War of 1812, and consul to Vera Cruz. He moved to Florida, where he became a Federal judge. He was lost on the "Pulaski," on his way from Savannah to New York.

[20] William Kirkland of "Ayr Mount," near Hillsboro, a native of Scotland, a merchant and planter.

From James Graham.   U.

Rutherfordton, August 20th, 1836.

The long agony is over and the winter of my discontent is now made glorious summer. I am elected by a majority of sixteen hundred and fourteen votes. On my arrival here last night about one hour in the night so soon as it was known I was in town the whole Village was illuminated and I was immediately conducted to a large room to partake of good wine, and the congenial shake of good friends.

The company were all intoxicated with animated animal spirits when we met; and before we parted, the lofty patriotism of the champaign, made noblemen of us all. I feel very much gratified at the result of this Election The Majesty of the People have spoken in a tone of Thunder to Congress and the Committee of discretions, without conscience.

Rutherford gave me a majority of 1007 votes and elected 1 Senator and 3 Commoners to the Legislature Burke has 3 White men in the Commons; in the two houses of the General Assembly, this District has 10 for White and 4 for Van B; last year Van Buren had 12 from this District.

I think you should be very cautious about your knee and not injure it again. Your horses I presume are kept too much in the stable, and fed too high. I feed on little grain when my horse is idle, his wind and action are better and he is more healthy and *gentle.*

On tomorrow I will set out for my plantation where I have not been since last November. It is impossible for any Member of Congress to devote much of his time to his own private business. I will return by fathers and try and sell my two small tracts in Lincoln at whatever they will bring. I will probably go on to Burke & endeavour to make sale of my Burke Land. I am desirous of converting my out Lands into active and available funds. Though I should be very happy to see you and Sister Susan at Fathers in this Month still if you do not find your lame knee able to support the Journey do not attempt it. I still hope you will be able to come up in September or October. In the mean time if you desire any thing done concerning your negroes or other matters and will let me know I will attend to it for you. I hope to pass Hillsboro and Raleigh about the middle of Nov. on my way to Washington.

Mr. Morrison has been here four days and will remain in this county another week. He informs me his own family are well, but that Dr. Moses Alexander is in bad health. My own health is very fine, indeed the good air, water, and exercise together, have given me unusual good health. Still I was anxious to have gone to the Virginia Springs but my long neglected business will not admit of my going this Season.

Give my kind respects to Sister Susan and say to her, we shall be happy to see her in sight of the Blue Mountains of No. Carolina.

From David L. Swain. U.

Chapel Hill, 26th Aug., 1836

I think it very important to the interests of the University that a convocation of those members of the Executive Committee who may have it in their power, should be held here at the shortest practicable notice. Your wife and yourself ought to come down and see us any how, and I trust that it may be convenient for you to bring her, and spend a day or two at least early in the next week. Mr. Mitchell is now writing to Judge Nash, asking him to come with you and spend a day or two at his house.

The *interior* affairs of the University seem to be progressing well enough. By the superintendent charged with the improvement of the premises, little, very little is apparently to be effected. Whether owing to his delinquency I am not prepared to say, but think it important that the Committee should have an opportunity of judging for themselves. The whole plan of improvement is yet to be settled on, and the delay of the Committee on this subject, furnishes the Superintendent with a plausible if not a valid excuse for the tardiness of his operations. This duty cannot be intelligently discharged without a particular examination of the localities, and susceptibilities of the place, upon the spot, and know, it is not only important but indispensible that you should come here.

I have many things besides these to submit to your consideration. The college buildings ought to be *insured,* and then the sooner they are burned *down* the better. The Library should be improved and a competent Librarian procured.

Considerable additions to the Philosopher apparatus should be made. So much for addition and *Reform,* none for Retrenchment.

I do not know whether Judge Nash or yourself has been retained by Thomas F. Lowry, Esq. the Deity of Chaucer hereabouts.
Be this as it may, it is essential to the existence of this Institution
that the services of Judge Settle [21] shall be secured upon the part
of the State. In addition to this we can afford to transfer to Hillsboro, or elsewhere, a small and delicate tribe of Courtezans. The
mode of transport, I submit to the more enlarged experience of
Judge Nash and yourself, and should you disagree in the premises,
I venture to advise that our *brother* Waddell be invited to attend
your Council.

Please confer with Judge Nash, and write by return mail.

Yours very truly,

I am against divers doctrines promulgated in your circular, and
claim the priviledge of a constituent to be heard upon the subject.

From Joseph Graham.   U.

August 30, 1836.

Dear William

I have Received your letter and learn with regret the situation
of your knee and the protracted time you expect to visit us and
the short time you expect to stay when you do.

I would propose that you come at such time as will least interfere with your other business & leave daughter Susan with us some
time; one of your brother Johns daughters could stay with her
here 2 or 3 weeks from whence she could visit her acquaintance,
Mrs. Gaston, stay a week or 2 at Johns, from there pass to your
sisters at Doctor Alexanders & Mr. Morisons.

Your brother James is Elected, towards the last of November
he will be passing Raleigh on his way to Washington, he could
make arrangements to take the Stage with her at Charlotte and
pass to Raleigh. Tho I have not seen or heard from James since
the Election yet I presume he would with pleasure assist in such
arrangement.

When your Uncle John[22] Returned from Philadelphia after

[21] Thomas Settle, Sr., (1791-1857), of Rockingham County, an able lawyer, who,
after service in the commons, in 1816, 1826-1829, (speaker, 1828-1829), and member
of congress, 1817-1821, became a judge of the superior court, where he served with
distinction, from 1832 until his death.

[22] Dr. John Graham (1756-1813), elder brother of Joseph Graham, born in Pennsylvania, educated at Queen's Museum, in Charlotte, a Revolutionary soldier, became
a tutor in the family of Dr. Benjamin Rush, under whom he studied medicine. He
later received the M. D. degree from the University of Pennsylvania, and settled in
Williamsburg County, South Carolina.

attending the medical Lectures in the Year 1786, a Young man in the Neighborhood who had 2 Years before suffered much with small Pox had one of his legs drawn so that it stood nearly at right angles went on Crutches, etc., he directed him each morning to strip lying on his belly and have a tea kettle with Cold spring watter poured on the affected part at the distance of 8 or 10 feet high; with this treatment in less than a month he got well, I have thought it might suit your case as you State there is a weakness in the part affected without much pain.

I have enjoyed good health, have finished my new House have resided in it several Weeks passt, have removed part of my Furniture, want the advice of some of friends how to place it (as the House is small).

My corn in the low grounds not so good on account of the very Wet season but will make plenty.

I take no News paper but a small one lately started in Linc1onton so as to have the Domestick News but occasionally Ride to the Post Office at the Furnace & Read other papers.

I have written nothing to you about your Brother Alfreds affairs as Doctor Alexander or Mr. Morison promised to inform you in what manner his affairs were settled; a Waggon which halled a part of Major Gastons Furniture from Cheraw brought a Tomb Stone for Alfred which yet lys at his House; Expect to have it put up this fall and some other Repairs made about the Family grave Yard.

I need not write any thing about Politicks but am more convinced of the necessity of publishing the Constitution of the United States and of this State as they have been amended. There is two thirds of the people in this Section of the State that do not understand the form of Government under which they live hence they are liable to be imposed on by every Demagogue; it never appeared in such glaring coulours as at the late Election. If they had the means of comprehending the Structure of the Goverment they would perform their part better.

Present my best Respects to Daughter Susan I hope to have the pleasure of seeing her at my House & further acquaintance a short time hence.

Your Affectionate Father,

From David L. Swain.   U.

Chapel Hill, 28th Sep, 1836.

Your favour of the 18th. inst. was recd. some days since. I have
not leisure at present to undertake the dissertation you propose
to me. I think that the money recd. from the Gen. Govt. should
be regarded as either a *gift* or *payment,* and should be wholly
expended in improving the internal condition of the country, by
increased facilities of transport. If I can get to the Salisbury Convention, I intend to take, and endeavour to maintain this position
before that body.

I understand that the papers of the late Judge Murphey are
in your care, & I am anxious to have an opportunity to examine
them. Mr. Bancroft [23] has forwarded to me his chapters on the
early history of the Carolinas. It has occurred to me that before
I undertake a revision, that you might be able to suggest something that would be useful to him, & I send the sheets herewith
to afford you an opportunity for so doing. He is anxious to
procure from an eye witness an original account of the battle of
King's Mountain, that shall be as graphic, and as much in detail
as practicable. I have recommended your father as the proper
person to furnish it, and have ventured to engage that he shall
undertake it. Please present my respects to the old gentleman
and unite with me in soliciting a compliance with my promise.

Are you authorized to sell Judge Murphey's papers, and if so
what is the price demanded?

Do me the favour to present Mrs. Swains and my respects to
Mrs. Graham, and tell her that though she has proved to be
rather an unsociable neighbour, we are hers and,

Yours most truly,

---

[23] George Bancroft (1800-1891), historian, diplomat, cabinet officer, a native of
Massachusetts, and generally in good standing there, although a Democrat in
politics. As secretary of the navy, 1845-1846, he was instrumental in establishing
the Naval Academy. He was minister to Great Britain, 1846-1849, and to Germany,
1867 to 1874,

From Thomas G. Polk.[24]   U.

Salisbury, No. C.,

28th Sept., 1836

On my return home with my family after an absence of several months, I found several letters addressed to me on the subject of the Address ordered to be published by the Whig meeting held in Raleigh in Decr. Last. I learnt from Outlaw that you and himself were to prepare it. If you have not yet done so, I suggest the necessity of its being done immediately. The public mind is in a good state to receive it.

It would have afforded me much pleasure to have attended the Orange Festival, and should certainly have done so, but for my absence from home at the time.

To Susan Washington Graham.   A.

Greensboro', Oct. 25th, 1836

My dear Wife.

I have concluded to send Joe to Hillsboro' to bring my sulkey that it may be repaired. He will reach there on Tuesday night—and stay next day to put the sulkey in order, for traveling—and return on Thursday. He forgot the bucket, and to put the oilcloth covers on the carriage at setting out, which I have directed him to bring with him. It may be necessary to procure a small cord in fixing the sulkey; if so he will apply to you, and please give him an order to Mr. Kirkland for one.

I found the road very fine, and ended my journey with great ease on Sunday, before sunset. At Smith's, I found Major Davie and Mr. Mebane, and we travelled thence here, the next morning by 10 oclock.

Our Court has commenced business, the cases though numerous, & some of them important, are not of very great interest except to the parties concerned.

Mr. Nash is here and quite well. He will go home at the end of the week. Mr. Scott arrived this afternoon on his way to Florida.

[24] Thomas Gilchrist Polk (1791-1867), of Rowan, eldest son of Colonel William Polk, a native of Mecklenburg, educated at the university. He represented the latter county in the commons, 1823-1826, and moving to Salisbury, sat in the commons again, 1828-1832. He was state senator, 1835-1838, and was major general of militia. He moved to Tennessee, and later to Mississippi.

Greensboro' affords no incidents in the way of news in which you would feel the slightest concern.

I had not supposed, my Dear Susan, that I would already have felt so much the loss of your society. I find going abroad to Court now, quite a different affair to what it was formerly. When not engaged actually in business, I begrudge the hours which I am forced to spend away from you. Nevertheless I maintain my usual cheerfulness, and hope that you have no difficulty in doing the like. I shall be detained here untill saturday evening, and will go then to Rockingham, but hope to be with you by the last of next week, before going to Caswell. My leg is at least as well as usual. I believe from the feeling today, I might say it is better, but will wait a little longer before I pronounce decisively on the symptoms. I will apply the brush well to it, and see what virtue there is in that by my return. If it be not better, I will resort again to the mercurial ointment.

I hope you are better of your headache, and take good care of your health. Pray remember me with kindness and accept, My dear Susan,

the assurance of my truest & fondest affection

Political Circular

THE LIBERTY OF THE PEOPLE
against
THE CAUCUS SYSTEM.[25]

To the Freemen of Orange.

Permit us to appeal to you at the present crisis, as men who prefer your country to a party. The Presidential election is near at hand, on the 10th. day of November next, you will be called to make your selection for this high and important office.

At this late period, we are aware that many have formed a settled determination in reference to that question, and whether their decision has been founded on an impartial and dispassionate review of the whole ground in dispute, or has been the offspring of mere party attachment and incorrect information, such is the pride of opinion, that they will not be convinced of their error by any course of argument. To such we know that we would

---

[25] From the *Hillsborough Recorder,* October 28th., 1836.

address ourselves in vain. But to the great body of the people, who have never seen the candidates before us for this high station, who are not involved in party politics, and who have no other design than to do right, and no interest to subserve but the welfare of their country, we will briefly state a few of the reasons why we prefer Hugh L. White to Martin Van Buren.

We presume that no candidate will be supported by an independent freeman for a place of so much importance, from mere *devotion to men;* but that whoever may be elected, will be so, merely as the instruments of the people, to effect those measures which may be deemed for the public benefit. What then, we would inquire, are the great measures which we, as citizens of North Carolina, desire to see carried out by the Federal Government?

No one can doubt, but a great majority will at once say, that the one of first magnitude is the distribution among the States of the proceeds of the *public lands.*

No candidate for some time past, has asked our suffrages for any place of legislative trust, without declaring himself favorable to such a project, and the only contest among those of every party has been, who had sustained, or would sustain it with the greatest zeal and efficiency. So decided has been the public sentiment upon this subject in our county, that no individual has been heard to oppose it. Judge White feels an equal zeal with ourselves on this subject; he not only voted for the Land Bill, but made an able speech in its behalf at the last session of Congress.

Mr. Van Buren, on the contrary, is directly opposed to this disposition of the public lands. In *April last,* several inquiries were submitted to him on public matters, by a member of Congress from the State of Kentucky; among others, "Will you, (if elected President) sign and approve a bill distributing the proceeds of the sales of the public lands among the States?" To which on the 8th. of *August last,* he replied, after stating his views at some length—"I am of the opinion that the avails of the public lands will be more equitably and faithfully applied to the common benefit of the United States by their continued application to the general wants of the Treasury, than by any other mode that has yet been suggested, and that such appropriation is in every respect *preferable to the distribution thereof among the States* in the manner your question proposes. *Entertaining these views, I cannot give you any encouragement that I will, in the event of my election to the Presidency, favor that policy.*"

This we take to be an unequivocal avowal, that a bill for the distribution of the avails of the public lands would receive his *veto* if passed by Congress;—those, therefore, who support his election, voluntarily abandon those hopes, which have been so fondly cherished by our countrymen, of getting the means of internal transport, of canals and rail roads, and of educating the poor from this immense inheritance of the people.

Another measure of great interest to us is the *distribution* of the *surplus revenue,* if a surplus shall accumulate from time to time, similar to that made by the act of the last session of Congress. The taxing machinery of the Federal government yields annually much more money than is wanted for the proper expenses of government; and this must continue to be the case until the expiration of the tariff compromise in 1842. Judge White favors the policy of dividing among the States that which is not necessary to be retained, and supported the bill of the last session, by which North Carolina, with her sister states of the Confederacy, will receive a fund of probably 30,000,000 of dollars, and her individual share will be 1,500,000 dollars,—a million and a half.

Mr. Van Buren, in the letter before referred to, expresses his ideas on this subject at too great length to be extracted in so short a paper as this; it is believed, however, that no injustice is done him when the result of his *treatise* is stated to be—1st., That he is hostile to the policy of distribution in general. 2nd., That he would have assented to the bill of the last session, *but reluctantly.* 3rd., That he does not wish it to become a precedent for future action; and that he has *fearful apprehensions* for the country from its effects. When, in addition to this, it is recollected that, with a single exception, every individual who voted against the distribution bill in either house of Congress, was his political friend, and most of them prominent *leaders* of his party, no hope of a division should like circumstances occur, can be entertained, *he* being the President. Our present limits forbid a discussion of this subject; nor is a discussion wanting.. Every man will surely agree, that when the legitimate expenses of government are paid, if the people have contributed more than is necessary for that purpose, the residue should be returned to them, rather than be kept in the Treasury, to afford employment to useless officers *for its custody,* or to furnish temptations to corrupt and unconstitutional subjects of appropriation.

A very few years since, during the administration of John Q. Adams, twelve millions was regarded as an extravagant expenditure, during the present year *forty-five millions of dollars* will be expended by the government!!! Not withstanding this enormous amount, there will be still left more than *thirty* millions at the commencement of the ensuing year, not required for the purposes of government. And yet Mr. Van Buren thinks it safest to leave these accumulating millions in the *treasury,* and entertains *fearful apprehensions* for the people should they receive a portion of them.

If there be danger in the accumulation of power—and money is power—do we not lessen that danger by dividing the power among the States, rather than by leaving it with the General Government? Liberty is not half so much endangered by the assaults of open violence, as from the covert and insidious operations of a corrupt government, (and such every government may become) in dealing out largesses and bribes from the public treasury.

A third measure of the deepest concern to us is the question of *abolition.* This we are interested in opposing by every principle of self-respect and honor, and by every duty to ourselves and to the community in which we live.

Judge White is identical with us in feeling, and in interest upon this subject, and is bound by all the ties which attach man to family, country and home, to resist the course of the abolitionists. Mr. Van Buren, on the other hand, has none of those obligations, and has evinced by his public actions that he has at least no feelings in common with us on this subject. Much has been said respecting his vote of instructions to the New York Senator on the famous Missouri question. To enable every man to read for himself, here are those instructions.—

PREAMBLE AND RESOLUTION

"Whereas, the inhibiting the further extension of Slavery in these U. States, is a subject of deep concern to the people of this state; and whereas we consider slavery as an evil much to be deplored, and that every constitutional barrier should be interposed to prevent its further extension, and that the constitution of the U. States clearly gives Congress the right to require of new states not comprised within the original boundaries of the United States, the prohibition of slavery as a condition of their admission as a state into the Union; therefore,

"*Resolved,* (if the honorable Senate concur therein,) that our Senators be instructed, and our Representatives in Congress requested, to oppose the admission as a State into the Union, of any territory not comprised as aforesaid, without making the prohibition of slavery therein an indispensable condition of admission."

Although the destiny of the American Union hung on the decision of the question in favor of the admission of Missouri into the confederacy, Mr. Van Buren and his friends in New York voted, by these instructions, against her admission, unless her citizens would submit to a constitution dictated by men living out of the limits of her territory! This vote was given in 1820—when excitement on this subject had risen to a dreadful hight, and the government was shaken to its very centre. Fortunately for the peace of the country, Mr. Van Buren's counsels did not prevail, and Missouri was admitted on an equal footing with the other states. In 1822, Mr. Van Buren had become a member of the Senate of the U. States, and then acted out the instructions he had assisted in giving to his predecessor. On a bill relating to the territory of Florida, he voted against striking out the 11th. section, as follows—

"No slave, or slaves shall, directly or indirectly, be introduced into the said territory, except by a citizen of the United States removing into the territory for actual settlement, and being at the time of such removal, *bona fide* owner of such slave, or slaves; and every slave imported or brought into said territory, contrary to the provisions of said act, shall thereupon be entitled to, and receive, his or her freedom."

Mr. King, of Alabama, moved to strike out this section, with the obvious intention of allowing the people of Florida to own slaves if they thought proper to go abroad for the purpose of purchasing them, or to buy from those who might bring them within the territory for sale.

Mr. Van Buren is recorded as voting against Mr. King's motion, and is said by the newspaper reports of that day, to have participated "briefly in the discussion" upon it, of course we suppose, against it.

With these public acts on the journals, we can hardly expect much assistance from him against abolition, unless we adopt some other mode of judging, than the old maxim that "a tree is to be known by its fruits." We know that he has asserted in a published letter, that he is now against abolishing slavery in the district of Columbia, and *in the States where it exists;* but he avows the opinion that it is constitutional to do so in the district, and is guardedly silent *as to his views* in relation to *the territories.* When we look to these facts, which are incontestible, and will not be denied by any well informed man, and when we reflect that Mr. Van Buren resides in the midst of the great body of the abolitionists, and is supported by them as the *Northern candidate,* and when we take into the estimate the well known character of Mr. Van Buren to *go with the majority* wherever he can find it, (whether right or wrong). What candid man, what man who loves his native State, and is prepared to sacrifice everything to defend her and her institutions, can lay his hand on his heart and say that he believes that these institutions would be safe in the hands of Mr. Van Buren, if the abolitionists shall succeed in carrying everything before them in the non-slaveholding States.

We do not charge that Mr. Van Buren is an abolitionist, we will make no charge so grave and so weighty unless upon full evidence of the fact. But we do charge that Mr. Van Buren is strongly supported by the great body of the abolitionists at the North.

When we reflect how natural it is for a public man to lean towards the opinions and wishes of the great body of his friends, and take in connection with this the fact that Mr. Van Buren has no constitutional scruples, and again look to his action on these subjects, we repeat the inquiry, whether any candid man could feel every thing in connection with slavery perfectly safe in the hands of Mr. Van Buren. Beware how ye trust him!

Again, Mr. Van Buren has voted for *high Tariffs,* and for Internal Improvement by the *General Government.* Judge White has uniformly opposed them.

Can any question be stated, on which it can be supposed that Judge White, if elected, would not favor our interest, and the policy we advocate, so far as his duty would permit? On the contrary, is there any measure which we can reasonably expect to effect by the election of Mr. Van Buren? As to the United States Bank, which is made a leading topic in a Van Buren address recently issued from *head quarters* at Raleigh, it is well known, and will not be denied, that Judge White has uniformly and steadily been opposed to it, in every form and shape; that he has constitutional objections to it that cannot be overruled; that he has objections on other grounds, equally insuperable. And it ought further to be stated that Judge White at no period of the existence of the United States Bank, ever coquetted with it, as did Mr. Van

Buren, when he and others so strongly solicited the establishment of a branch of it in the city of Albany, where Mr. Van Buren resides.

Many of us have no doubt observed, that the press and most zealous advocates of Mr. Van Buren seek to persuade us, that Judge White, however able, and however devoted to our best interest, cannot be elected. To this we answer that Judge White's prospects in the electoral colleges are at least equal to those of Mr. Van Buren; and, in the opinion of some of us, decidedly more promising than his. We may remark, that it is known to be a part of the policy of the party to claim every State. In which of the eight States that voted the past summer did the Van Buren party admit the probability of defeat? In none. They claimed every one, confidently; and yet the elections proved that six states of the eight are opposed to him. And where did they express a stronger confidence than in this state?

But if this were true, it would be no reason for our abandonment of a candidate who would administer the government upon its proper principles, to adopt one who would not. Should we not succeed, we would still have the consciousness of having done our duty to our country. When, however, it is recollected that the same individuals confidently predicted that General Dudley could not be elected Governor, we must be excused for not trusting to such prophecies. Others may believe it; for ourselves, we cannot suppose that the people will desert Judge White, unless we surrender up our principles in deference to men.

Published by order of the Central Committee for Orange County.

Orange County, October 27th., 1836.

To William Gaston.[26]   U.

Hillsboro, Nov. 2, 1836.

The approaching Session of the Legislature is perhaps the most important which has occurred for years and we feel that no apology is necessary for asking the advice and assistance of one who through a long life has constantly evinced an anxious and patriotic interest in whatever concerned North Carolina. But if an apology be due, we trust it may be found in the fact that there are few,

---

[26] Written in Graham's hand, and clearly of his composition.

if any, members of the body, upon whose experience or sagacity we can with any confidence rely. We fear, moreover, that the present crisis in party politics is every way inauspicious to wise legislation and that our personal attention in endeavoring to prevent evil, will leave us little time to digest or mature such plans of policy as might satisfy ourselves or meet the public confidence.

Under these impressions and deeply interested in so executing the trust confided in us, as to leave us if possible nothing hereafter to regret, we earnestly request that you will aid us with your views on the following subjects which we apprehend will occupy the attention of the Legislature and which for greater convenience we put in the form of questions.

What disposition should be made of such portion of the surplus Revenue of the U. S. as may be alloted to North Carolina? To this perhaps a preliminary question might arise, viz: whether any *permanent* plan for a disposition of this fund should be adopted, until we know the fixed policy of the Federal Gov. in regard to its continuance?

Should we at present look *only* to improving our means of Internal transport and if so, what great public works should be entitled to *primary* attention?

If other objects should share a portion of the fostering care of the Legislature, at this time, is it practicable to establish a system of common schools with well grounded hope of success?

What is the experience of other States in reference to Penitentiaries?

Should a portion of this fund be set apart for the erection of a Lunatic Asylum and should this object be postponed to either of the former?

What amendments are necessary in the Revenue system of this State?

We have to regret that this communication has been delayed so long, as not to give time for such research as you might desire, but we will not insult your patriotism by adding any regrets at the labour incident to a reply. With the highest consideration, we beg leave to subscribe ourselves,

> Your obt. servants,
> Hugh Waddell.
> William A. Graham.

Hon. William Gaston.

From John D. Graham.   U.

Elm Wood Farm, Novm. 17th, 1836.

I expect you will be informed by the western members before this letter is recd. of the death of Father he died Saturday night 8 Oclock the 12th Instant. Monday previous I Set out with him to Lincoln Court. Quite well Slep in the Same roome tuesday night. Wednesday evening Capt. Caldwell & Father went out to Major Henderson. Stayed all night; their he Complained of Cold Feet & pain in the brest. thursday come on to Lincolnton Voted and returned home. Sick that evening. Friday morning Sent for Doctor McLean who arived about 12 Oclock as he passed the Chimney coming in the House heard him fall on the Floore; found him in a fit Apoplexy; lasted only a moment; in ½ hour a Second fit. he Bleed him freely & give purgative Medicine. he sent a boy for me. I had gone 10 Miles above Beatties Ford, Iredelle Farm. Friday evening after night I arrived, found him Sitting up and walking through the Roome & talking on every subject as usual. Said he had been in a Strange way, like Sleeping but very little pain. I remained untill 3 Oclock Saturday; being Wet the night before I was very Sick he advised me to go home & take care of myself as he thought he was releaved. I Sent for William Norwood who consented to Stay all night. I arrived home about one hour before Sun Set. his boy came after me about dark. Said he was worse. as I was in bead Sick I Sent Mary Ann and Montrose, they arived perhaps an hour before he died.

Nelson Gutry Norwood Robt. Abernathy & wife was present Saturday; after I left he became worse about 5 Oclock fits on untill 8 O. at night died. when I left him he walked round the House that evening.

*   *   *   *   *

Brother James wrote me from Rutherford to Lincoln Court Stating he would be at his Farm the monday Father was buried. I Sent there for him he arived that evening at Aunt Polly M'Leans unable to come up but states on next tuesday he will meet us at Fathers late residence.

James has been Sick nearly 4 weeks Billious Fever, very bad.

*   *   *   *

From Robert Hall Morrison.   **U.**

Near Charlotte, Nov. 17th, 1836.

Once more I am called to the painful task of communicating to you the most melancholy tidings. Our venerable and beloved Father Graham has closed his earthly existence, and gone we trust to a better world!

On Monday he went to Lincoln Court. Attended to his business as usual and without complaining. On Wednesday night he was at Major Hendersons and complained Some of a pain in his breast and cold feet. On Thursday after voting he returned home. He bathed his feet and took Some warm Tea. On Friday morning he Sent for Dr. W. McLean.[27] About the time the Dr. arrived he had a paroxism of apoplexy and fell from his chair. He was lying on the floor when the Dr. came in. After taking from him a large quantity of blood he became better and talked cheerfully on various subjects during the evening. Dr. McLean & Bro. John were with him during the night. Next morning he walked about and seemed so much better that they left him about 10 oclock.

In the afternoon he was taken again & more violently. The paroxisms continued in succession until he died about 8 oclock. It was evidently apoplexy and to him unexpected for altho' labouring under the premonotory symptoms for several days, he insisted even after the first that the Dr. was mistaken and manifested no apprehensions of danger.

Mary Ann & Montrose Graham, Mr. Norwood, Mr. Abernathy, Mr. & Mrs. Guthrie & Mrs. Abernathy were present when he died. He spoke a few minutes before he died and apparently suffered but little. His funeral was attended by a large number of the neighbours and a respectable portion of the relatives.

Mary and myself had started on our way to Fayetteville to attend the meeting of the Synod, and were overtaken by a Messenger 14 miles below Charlotte. We immediately returned and made every effort to reach in time, but the grave was closed an hour or two before we arrived. Dr. Alex & Sister Violet & Bro John's family were there. Bro. James has been very sick in Buncombe. He arrived last Monday at Aunt McLean's and there received the mournful intelligence but was too weak to come up. He sent a Boy on Tuesday with a letter requesting us to meet him

---

[27] Dr. William McLean died in 1828. It is possible that the allusion was to his son, Dr. John McLean.

next Tuesday at Father's place which we expect to do. He had
the fever Several weeks, and recovers Slowly.

                    *   *   *   *

We hope to hear from you immediately. Give us freely your
counsel how to act in reference wht. you know becomes necessary.
We have many fears that Bro. James' health is so delicate tht. he
cannot go to Washington with safety to himself.

Truly we are called often & Solemnly to number our days and
prepare for death. Such visitations Should teach the vanity of
earthly objects, the emptiness of human enjoyments and the
importance of religion wh. alone can Sustain amid the trials and
afflictions of this life and prepare us for that blessed Kingdom
where Sin & Sorrow & death Shall be unknown.

We mourn a loss of no ordinary kind. Few such men have
lived; Few are called to Sigh over the grave of such a Parent.

                    *   *   *   *

To Susan Washington Graham.   A.

Raleigh, Nov. 20th, 1836.

My dearest

What language can I employ to express to you the grief by
which I am now oppressed? My venerated Father is no more!
The strongest tie which binds me to earth, (except that by which
I am united to you, thou darling of my affections!) has been
severed. When I look back on his multiple acts of kindness
towards me, his great solicitude in my behalf, when I remember
how I was literally nursed in his bosom after the premature loss
of my other parent & generously supplied in every want, how
carefully he endeavoured to instruct me in the principles of virtue
and piety, I feel the privation most sorely. A void has been created
in my heart which nothing but my consciousness of your attachment could ever render tolerable. I have as yet received no letter
from any of the family on the subject — owing to the suddenness
of the fatal event, and the passage of the stage beyond Salisbury
but twice a week there has hardly been time to communicate
the intelligence by mail. From a gentleman here I learn that he
attended the Court & election at Lincolnton on *Thursday*, returned home on friday, was taken ill on Saturday and died in the
course of a few hours afterwards. Brother James, I hope, was with

him; he must have been there soon afterwards. He has surely written me an account of it, and will be himself here, during this week or the next.

You my dearest wife, have not yet lost either of your parents. Long may they be spared to comfort & bless you. For my own part, though in the midst of bustle & company I feel that I am an isolated being. I am obliged to dry up the tear & half suppress the sigh, but the secret pangs of the heart cannot be avoided. Most heartily do I wish I was with you in New Bern or that we were again in Hillsborough or in Lincoln. To be, with my present feelings, in a crowd contending for party supremacy or the distinctions of an hour, with no bosom sympathizing with my own, is in the highest degree irksome. I received the fatal tidings last night, at Mr. Henry Jones' on my way to this place, and this is the first moment since, when I have found an opportunity to write you. Do not however suppose, my loveliest, that I am utterly without consolation in this bereavement. My Fathers life had been prolonged beyond the period usually allotted to man. He had performed many services to society, fulfilled all his duties to his family, and entertained the fullest hope of the Christians reward in the world to come. May his example by duly appreciated & followed by his children.

Mr. Bryan has been kind enough to send me your letter addressed to him, but the weather has been so unfavourable that I have not yet seen him. I left Hillsboro' on yesterday (Saturday) in company with Mr. Waddell & Mr. King of Iredell in a carriage. Poor King is in wretched health. We left him at Mr. Jones' this morning but he has since arrived in the stage. My knee, I think, still improves. I travelled in Mr. Nash's buggy with a servant to Caswell & Person Courts and drove myself home from the latter. The Court at Caswell was quite laborious & lasted untill saturday evening. A great many clergymen and others had assembled at the Convention, and I regretted that I could not stay on sunday and be present. I was obliged by the purpose of my business, & my decrepitude, to forego the pleasure of seeing Mr. Meredith.[28] I enquired through Mr. Kerr[29] however, and was gratified to learn from him that your Mother was recovering,

---

[28] Thomas Meredith (1795-1856), a native of Pennsylvania, and a graduate of the University of Pennsylvania, who became a famous Baptist minister. He was the editor and founder of the "Biblical Recorder." Meredith College was named for him.

[29] John Kerr, Jr. (1811-1879), son of the Rev. John Kerr, born in Virginia, who settled in Caswell, and represented it in the commons, 1858-1861. He was the unsuccessful Whig candidate for governor in 1852, and was a member of congress, 1853-1855.

though he was ignorant of your arrival in New Bern. The Revd. Mr. Kerr [30] was to preach the Funeral of Luther Rice [31] on Monday of Convention.

I received your brothers letter to you from N. York, and on my return from Person, your own informing me of your journey down.

I have taken a room for the present at Mrs. Taylor's but will go with you to Aunt White's when you arrive. I will be exceedingly glad to see you early, but do not hasten your departure sooner than you find convenient. I have much to say to you which I have not room nor leisure to write. I will accompany you to New Bern when you return, though I presume that the late affliction which has befallen us, will compel me to go to Lincoln in the course of the winter. It not only distresses me as a sore deprivation, but I fear, will much confuse and derange my affairs, — of all this however I shall be more able to speak when I see you.

I will call to see Mrs. White's family tomorrow, though pressed to the earth by calamity & sorrow I am still consoled by the assurance of your affection and Remain as ever

Your devoted and affectionate Husband.

From Susan Washington Graham.   U.

New Bern, Nov. 22nd, 1836.

Most deeply do I sympathize with you and heartily wish I were in Raleigh that you might have the slight consolation, which the presence of one, who you know, loves you sincerely, could afford.

Mama had invited several persons to spend the evening with Mrs. Kirkland and Mrs. Hill and I was conversing very cheerfully with the latter, when Sister handed me your letter, containing the melancholy intelligence of our dear Fathers decease. You have my dear Husband many sources of consolation and I am glad to find you disposed to draw comfort from them. Your

---

[30] Rev. John Kerr (1792-1842), a native of Caswell County, who represented a Virginia district in congress, 1813-1817. He became a Baptist minister of wide reputation.

[31] Luther Rice (1783-1836), a nationally famous Baptist minister. Born in Massachusetts, educated at Williams College, and, for the Congregational ministry at Andover Seminary, he sailed for missionary work in the Pacific, read widely on baptism on the voyage, and arrived at his destination a Baptist. He spent the next twenty years organizing the Baptists for missionary and educational work. He had much to do with the founding of Columbian College, now George Washington University.

Father's death is certainly a great loss to you but it is eternal gain to him. He lived to a good old age and has now gone, we hope, to enjoy the rest, promised to the faithful disciples of Christ. May his departed Spirit be as a magnet in Heaven to attract you thitherward. Our thoughts and affections naturally gravitate towards earth, but God in his mercy, occasionally reminds us by the departure of a dear Friend that this is not our abiding place and that we should be diligent in our preparation for the next world, where we are to be *for ever* blessed or *for ever* miserable.

I commenced writing you Tuesday night but became so faint and sick I was obliged to desist and go to bed.

* * * * *

God bless & protect you my dear Husband. May the recent afflicting dispensations of Providence induce you to meditate more frequently and more seriously upon eternity and eternal things.

Your ever devoted and affectionate Wife.

From Robert H. G. Moore.[32]   U.

Spectator Office, Newbern,
22d. Nov, 1836.

Will it be asking too much of you to furnish me occasionally with the proceedings of the Legislature? From our limited acquaintance, I confess that I am making "considerable free," as the Yankees have it; but as my friend, Mr. Bryan, has not intimated that he would favour me with a correspondence, as formerly, I am reduced to the necessity of *begging*. If the request interfere *in the least* with your arrangements or convenience, say "no" like a man, as I am very careless whether the sleepy Whigs on our subscription list hear a word of what is passing or not.

For myself, I am a Whig no more. Disgrace attaches to the name, in this State at least. I am neither more nor less than an American citizen, who wishes for his country's prosperity, and would promote it at the risk of his life; and I advise you to join "my" party.

Your family here are well. I "carried" my daughter, about an hour ago, to a party at Mr. Washington's, and I state the fact as the best evidence of the health and spirit of the family.

---

[32] Robert H. G. Moore, a native of Ireland, who came to New Bern in 1818, and established a large and prosperous school. He later became editor of the *Spectator,* a Whig newspaper.

REPORT OF
THE JUDICIARY COMMITTEE
concerning
PUBLIC and PRIVATE ACTS.[33]

The Committee on the Judiciary, who were instructed by reso-lution to enquire whether the act of the last General Assembly entitled "An Act to regulate the mode of passing private acts of the General Assembly" be applicable to the proceedings of the Legislature under the amended Constitution; and also to ascer-tain and determine what Laws are properly denominated public, and what private acts, have bestowed on the whole subject the consideration due to its importance, and

REPORT,

That they entertain no doubt as to the competency of the General Assembly of the last year, to pass the act now in question, and that the same is to be regarded as in full force, until it shall be repealed, or modified. It is one of divers laws, passed at the same session, which were conceived to be necessary to give effect to the amendments of the constitution, which had been recently sanctioned by the people, and their enactment devolved as an imperious duty on the Legislature at that time, unless clearly forbidden by constitutional prohibition. The sovereign power had ordained that "from and after the first of January, one thousand eight hundred and thirty-six" certain alterations should obtain in the constitution. Among others that "the General Assembly shall not pass any private Law unless it shall "be made to appear that thirty days notice of application to pass such law shall have been given, under such directions and in such manner as shall be provided by *Law*." This Ordinance of the Constitution was known to the Legislature of 1835 to have been adopted by the popular vote. It was also apparent to them that unless they made provis-ion by law, before their adjournment, for advertisement of no-tice in pursuance of that ordinance, that no private Law whatever could be passed by the present Legislature, until it should have made a similar enactment to that now referred and notice of thirty days should have been given, according to its terms. In

[33] From *Raleigh Register*, December 20th., 1836.

such circumstances, the propriety of the act is most manifest, if it were within the powers of the General Assembly. Your Committee believe that the General Assembly, in which the Constitution expressly vests 'the legislative authority,' have the right to pass any Law which is not inhibited by, or is not inconsistent with some provision of that instrument, or of the Federal Constitution. What clause of the Constitution, they would ask, is violated by the act before mentioned? Certainly none in the Constitution of 1776. If such an act had been passed, prior to the recent amendments by the Convention of 1835, it would unquestionably have been valid so long as the legislature would suffer it to be enforced. That convention has not only not taken away the power to enact such a law, but virtually ordained that it should be passed. It is supposed that the right to pass it is derived from the amendments, and that it could only be passed by a legislature convened under the new Constitution? It must be observed that the paragraph of the amendments, now under discussion, confers no new power on the General Assembly, but forbids the exercise of an old one, except on certain conditions.

The Legislative power of the General Assembly extends not merely to the present time and events, but may prospectively embrace any future contingency. The law in question might have provided that, in the event of the adoption of the amendments of the constitution, advertisement of application for private acts should be made for thirty days, much more when it was authoritatively announced that the amendments had been adopted, might the Legislature provide to give them practical operation. A wise law-giver will endeavor as well to prevent grievances, as administer remedies for them. To have enacted no law in reference to private acts at the last session of the Legislature, would have been to exclude any private Bill from consideration for at least the first thirty days of this session. Your committee, therefore, deem the passage of the said act to have been both constitutional and expedient.

On the other subject of their inquiry, your committee regret that their investigation had not attained more definite results, or been more satisfactory to themselves. On the one hand, they have felt that by too strict an interpretation of the term *Private Law*, much useful legislation might be prevented at the present session, whilst, on the contrary, the salutary operation of the section of the Constitution forbidding the passage of Private Laws, except on a particular condition, would be wholly abrogated and annul-

led, unless the General Assembly shall affix the proper construc-
tions to this term, and insist on its enforcement in every instance.
It can hardly be supposed that the Judiciary branch of the Government will have either the disposition or authority to look
beyond the enactments of the Legislature, to ascertain whether
they were passed with, or without, legal notice of their introduction. This clause of the amended constitution is binding,
therefore, only on the conscience of the Legislature, and is dependent upon this alone for its observance. Its true meaning is,
for that reason, to be sought with the greater diligence, and
adhered to with the more vigour. Your Committee first directed
their inquiries to the question, whether in Parliamentary language, the terms public and private acts have not a meaning in
some respects different from their legal significance. But are unable to find any authority for such difference; they have therefore
no other criteria for distinguishing between public and private
Bills, but such as are furnished by the Judicial tribunals and
legal writers, and these are far from being, in all cases, satisfactory. In some statutes, special clauses have been inserted, declaring
that those statutes shall be held and deemed to be public acts.
But this, as your committee believe, has been properly construed
not to change the character of the acts, but merely to determine
the manner in which they shall be alleged and proved in the
Courts of Justice. Whether a statute be public or private must
depend on its nature and objects. If these be private, the statute
itself cannot be public, notwithstanding the declaration of the
Legislature to the contrary; nor should the evasion be allowed
of inserting provisions of a public kind, for the mere purpose
of dispensing with the necessity of advertisement, where they do
not belong to the general scope of the particular Bill. The general description of public acts is "that they relate to the interests
of the public at large, and private, to individuals, or individuals
only." This vague description, which pervades all the elementary
books, and has by many been mistaken for a definition, affords
but an uncertain test for discrimination. Your committee believe
that the following points are settled by adjudication, or by common consent, to wit: that all acts are public,

    1st. Which concern all persons generally.

    2nd. Which affect the sovereign in any of his rights, whether
of sovereignty or property; hence any act which gives a penalty
or fine to the State, is, on that account, public.

3rd. Which concerns the officers of the State, whether civil or military.

4th. Which concern the Legislature.

5th. Which relate to trade in general, or to public highways, or navigable rivers.

And of these, some are termed public local acts, and others, public general acts, according to their respective spheres of operation. The foregoing summary may not embrace all acts of a public nature, but is supported by authority as far as it extends, and may be useful in drawing the line of distinction. Private acts, embrace all those not falling within any of the descriptions aforesaid; an attempt to define them more particularly is unnecessary. Your committee are aware that the precise boundary between public and private acts cannot, in every instance, be determined by the rules here furnished, but they are gratified by the reflection, that in the great majority of Bills there can be no question as to their character, and in any particular case where difficulty may arise on the subject, the foregoing classification may be found useful, if not decisive. To the wisdom of the House it will belong to apply them with proper discrimination, in each case in which their application becomes necessary. Your committee ask to be discharged from the further consideration of the subject.

Respectfully submitted,

December 5, 1836.   William A. Graham

From John W. Norwood.   A.

Hillsboro, Decr. 9, 1836

Dear Graham

I enclose you my Father's [34] resignation. I presume you may take the liberty of having it presented to the Legislature at such time as you may deem best.

Permit me to sympathise with you in the loss you have sustained in your venerable parent. An anticipation a few weeks since of a like affliction in my own case, has prepared my mind for fully appreciating your feelings.

---

[34] William Norwood (1767-1842), of Hillsboro, a judge of the superior court, 1820-1836.

As those who stand nearest to us by nature and affection, are removed, we must draw closer to us, our remaining relatives and friends.

[P. S.] Nothing of interest here Mr. Nash knows that this paper has been sent.

J. W. N.

Tribute to General Joseph Graham.

A Revolutionary Hero Gone! [35]

Died, at his residence in Lincoln County, on the 12th ult., Major General JOSEPH GRAHAM, aged 77 years.

When a man descends to the grave highly esteemed and much beloved by all classes of society, distinguished for arduous, faithful and efficient services as an officer of his country, and distinguished for all those tried and sterling virtues, which give a high and just claim to the most elevated rank among the benefactors of men, a due regard for excellence of character demands something more than merely a passing tribute to his memory.

General Graham was born in Pennsylvania, October 13th., 1759. His mother being left a widow with five small children, and slender means of supporting them, removed to North Caroline when he was about seven years of age, and settled in the vicinity of Charlotte. He received the principal part of his education at an academy, then taught at Charlotte, and was distinguished among his fellow students for talents, industry, and the most manly and conciliating deportment. His thirst for knowledge led him, at an early period, to become well acquainted with all all those interesting events which preceded and prepared for our revolutionary struggle. He was present at Charlotte on the 20th of May, 1775, when the first Declaration of Independence was formally and publicly made. The deep impression made upon his mind by the solemn and illustrious decisions of that day, gave good evidence that he was then preparing for the noble stand which he took during the war.

He enlisted in the army of the United States in the month of May, 1778, at the age of *nineteen years*. He served in the fourth regiment of North Carolina regular troops, under Colonel Archibald Lytle, and acted as an officer in Captain Gooden's company.

---

[35] From the *Charlotte Journal,* reprinted in the *Hillsborough Recorder,* December 9th., 1836.

The troops to which he was attached were ordered to rendezvous at Bladenboro, in Maryland. Having proceeded as far as Caswell county, they received intelligence of the battle of Monmouth, and that the British having gone to New York, their services would not be needed. He returned home on furlough.

He was again called into service on the 5th of November, 1778, and marched under the command of General Rutherford to Purysburg, on the Savannah river, soon after the defeat of General Ashe at Briar Creek. He was with the troops under General Lincoln in the trying and painful struggles against General Prevost, and fought in the battle of Stono, on the 20th of June, 1779, which lasted an hour and twenty minutes. During nearly the whole of this campaign he acted as quarter master. In July, 1779, he was taken with the fever, and after two months severe illness, was discharged near Dorchester, and returned home.

After recovering from the effects of sickness and privation, he aided his mother in the support of her family, and was ploughing in the field when he received intelligence of the surrender of Charleston, and that the British had defeated Colonel Buford at the Waxhaw, and were within forty miles of Charlotte. Instead of being deterred by the sufferings of the previous campaign, or the perils of that alarming moment, he resolved at once to leave his plough and enter the army. He was immediately appointed adjutant of the Mecklenburg regiment, and spent the summer with them in opposing and assailing the troops of Lord Rawdon.

When it was understood that the British were marching to Charlotte, he was commanded by General Davidson to repair to that place, and take command of such force as should collect there, and to join Colonel Davie. The British Army entered Charlotte the 26th. of September, 1780. General Graham was assigned the command of those troops which sustained the retreat of General Davie, and opposed Tarleton's Cavalry, and a regiment of Infantry for four miles on the road leading to Salisbury. After a heavy and well directed fire upon the British from the Courthouse to the *Gum Tree,* General Graham retreated with the men under his command, and formed on the plantation now owned by Joseph McConnaughey, Esq., and again attacked their advancing column of infantry. There his life was providentially preserved from the bursting of a gun, fired by the soldier who stood at his side, and whose arm was wounded. After again retreating, he formed on the hill above where Sugar Creek Church now stands. There, owing to the imprudent, but honest zeal of a Major White, they were detained too long, for by the time they reached the Cross Roads a party of British Dragoons were coming up the road leading from Captain Kennedy's, and after close pursuit for nearly two miles, overtook them. Colonel Francis Locke, of Rowan county, an intelligent and brave officer, was killed upon the margin of a small pond, now to be seen at the end of Mr. Alexander Kennedy's lane. Between that spot, and where Mr. James A. Houston now lives, General Graham was cut down and severely wounded. He received nine wounds; six with the sabre, and three with lead. His life was again narrowly and mercifully preserved by a large stock buckle, which broke the violence of a stroke, which to human view must otherwise have proved fatal. He received four deep gashes of the sabre over his head, and one in his side, and three balls were afterwards removed from his body. After being much exhausted by loss of blood, he reached the house of Mrs. Savannah Alexander, who yet lives near the same place, where he was kindly nursed and watched during the night, and his wounds dressed as well as circumstances would permit. The next day he reached his mother's, where Major Bostwick now lives. From that, he was taken to the hospital, and was two months recovering.

Thus, at the tender age of twenty-one years, we see this gallant officer leading a band of as brave men as ever faced a foe, to guard the ground first consecrated by the Declaration of American Independence, and when the foot of tyranny was treading it, and resistance proved unsuccessful, leaving his blood as the best memorial of a righteous cause, and of true heroism in its defence.

While the whole country was in distress, its property pillaged, its houses forsaken, and its defenseless inhabitants flying from the shock of arms, a few noble sons of Mecklenburg compelled Lord Cornwallis to designate Charlotte as the *Hornet Nest of America*.

As soon as he recovered from his wounds, he again entered the service of his country. General William L. Davidson, who had command of all the militia in the Western counties of North Carolina, applied to him to raise one or more companies, promising him such rank as the number of men raised would justify. It proved not only his energy of purpose, but great influence, that, at that difficult and hazardous period, he could raise a company of 55 men in two weeks. They were mounted riflemen, armed also with swords, and some with pistols. They supplied themselves with horses, procured their own equipments, and entered the field without commissary or quarter master, and with every prospect of hard fighting and little compensation.

After Tarleton's signal defeat at the Cowpen's, Cornwallis resolved to pursue General Morgan. At that time General Greene had received the command of the Southern Army, and had stationed himself at Hick's Creek, on the North of the Peedee, near to Cheraw. After Morgan's victory, and successful retreat, General Greene left his main army with General Huger, and rode 150 miles to join Morgan's detachment. The plan of opposing Lord Cornwallis in crossing the Catawba river, was arranged by General Greene, and its execution assigned to General Davidson. Feints of passing were made at different places, but the real attempt was made at Cowan's Ford. Soon after the action commenced, General William L. Davidson was killed, greatly lamented by all who knew him as a talented, brave and generous officer. The company commanded by General Graham was the first to commence the attack on the British as they advanced through the river, which was resolutely continued until they reached the bank, loaded their arms, and commenced a heavy five upon his men, two of whom were killed. It was supposed that General Davidson was killed by a tory who was pilot to the British in crossing the river, as he was shot with a small rifle ball. Colonel William Polk, and Rev. Mr. McCall were near to him when he fell. His body was found that night, and buried in the present graveyard of Hopewell Church.

The North Carolina militia were then placed under the command of General Pickens, of South Carolina, and continued to pursue the British as they advanced towards Virginia. General Graham, with his company and some troops from Rowan county, surprised and captured a guard at Hart's Mill, two miles from Hillsborough, where the British army then lay, and the same day were united to Colonel Lee's forces. On the next day he was in an action under General Pickens, with Colonel Pyles, who commanded 350 Tories, on their way to join Tarlton. These Tories supposed the Whigs to be a company of British troops, sent for their protection, and commenced crying "God save the King." Tarlton was about a mile from this place, and retreated to Hillsborough. Shortly afterwards, General Graham was in an engagement under Colonel Lee, at Clapp's Mill, on the Alamance, and had two of his company killed, three wounded, and two taken prisoners. A few days afterwards he was in an action at Whitsell's Mill, under the command of Colonel Washington.

As the time for which his men had engaged was expired, and the country annoyed with Tories, General Greene directed him to return with his company, and keep them in a compact body until they crossed the Yadkin, which they did, March 4th. 1781.

After the battle at Guilford, the British retired to Wilmington, and but little military service was performed in North Carolina during the summer of 1781. About the 1st. of September, Colonel Fanning surprised Hillsborough, and took Governor Burke prisoner. General Rutherford, who had been taken prisoner at Gates' defeat, and with many other distinguished citizens had been confined in custody, was discharged and returned home about this time. He immediately gave orders to General Graham, in whose military powers, and general influence he had the utmost confidence, to raise a troop of Cavalry in Mecklenburg county. Three troops of Dragoons, and about two hundred mounted Infantry were raised and formed into a Legion, of which Robert Smith, Esq., who had been a Captain in the North Carolina line, was appointed Colonel, and General Graham was appointed Major. They forthwith commenced their march towards Wilmington. South of Fayetteville, with 96 Dragoons, and 40 mounted Infantry, General Graham made a gallant and successful attack upon a body of Tories commanded by the noted Tory Colonels McNeil, Ray, Graham, and McDougal. This action took place near McFall's Mill, on the Raft Swamp, in which the Tories were signally defeated, their leaders dispersed in dismay, and their cause greatly injured. That 136 Whigs should attack and triumphantly defeat 600 Tories, headed by 4 Colonels, reflects great honor upon the bravery and intelligence of their youthful commander.

A short time afterwards, he commanded one troop of Dragoons, and two of mounted Infantry, in surprising and defeating a band of Tories on Mr. Alfred Moore's plantation, opposite to Wilmington. On the next day he led the troops in person, which made a resolute attack on the British garrison, near the same place. Shortly afterwards, he commanded three companies in defeating the celebrated Colonel Gagny, near Waccamaw lake. Shortly after this, the war was terminated in the South by the surrender of Lord Cornwallis, at Yorktown, in Virginia.

This campaign closed General Graham's services in the Revolutionary War, having commanded in 15 engagements, with a degree of courage, wisdom, calmness and success, surpassed perhaps, by no officer of the same rank. Hundreds who served under him have delighted in testifying to the upright, faithful, prudent and undaunted manner in which he discharged the duties of his trying and responsible station. Never was he known to shrink from any toil, however painful, or quail before any danger, however threatening, or stand back from any privations or sacrifices which might serve his country. To secure her liberties, he spent many toilsome days and sleepless nights—for her he endured much fatigue, and sickness and suffering, without a murmur—for her his body was covered with wounds, to her welfare he consecrated his time and treasure, and influence, during a long and unblemished life. It was not by empty words, or arrogant pretensions, but by self denying and long continued actions that he proved himself to be a friend to his country.

After the close of the war, he was elected first Sheriff of Mecklenburg county, and gave great satisfaction by the faithful and exemplary performance of the duties of that office. He was afterwards, for a number of years, a prominent member of the General Assembly, from the same county. About the year 1787, he was married to the 2d. daughter of Major John Davidson. By this marriage he had 12 children, 7 of whom have survived him. Not long after his marriage he removed to Lincoln county, and engaged in the manufacture of Iron, and for more than 40 years before his death, conducted a large establishment with great energy and prudence.

In the year 1814, when the war with the Creek Indians was raging with violence, and Generals Jackson, Coffee, and Carroll were repelling with signal bravery their ruthless aggressions, North Carolina determined to send 1000 men to aid the volunteers from Tennessee and Georgia in the conflict with those savages. General Graham's renown as an officer, and his worth as a man, commended him as the leader of the troops from this State. He received the commission of General, and was strongly solicited by the Governor of the State to accept the appointment. Although the circumstances of his family rendered his absence one of great loss and self denial, he promptly obeyed the call of his country, and marched at the head of a fine regiment of Volunteers to the scene of the conflict. They arrived about the time the last stroke of punishment was inflicted upon the Creeks by General Jackson, at the battle of the Horse Shoe; and in time to receive the submission of those they expected to conquer. Several hundred of the lower Creeks surrendered to them. For many years after the last war, he was Major General of the 5th. Division of the Militia of North Carolina.

In the year 1802 he was earnestly requested by sundry persons in the western part of the State, friendly to the better organization of the Militia, to address the Legislature on the subject, and to propose a plan for a Military Academy. The address evinced enlarged and judicious sentiments on the subject, and drew from the Assembly the following resolution:—

"*Resolved,*" That the thanks of this General Assembly be presented to Joseph Graham, Esq., of Lincoln County, for his plan of a Military Academy, submitted to the consideration of this Legislature, and that the address be printed, ten copies for each county in the State, to be delivered with the Laws and the Journals to the Clerks of the several County Courts, and by them to the Commandants of the several regiments, to be at their disposal."

His intercourse with others was marked by great dignity of deportment, delicacy of feeling, cheerfulness of spirit, and equability of temper. Men of learning and high standing have often expressed much gratification by his company, and surprize at the extent and accuracy of his knowledge. In the circle of private friendship his excellencies were strikingly displayed. He was far, very far removed from all those feelings of selfishness, vanity, suspicion, or envy, which unfit men for the duties and joys of social life. His eye was always open to the virtues of his friends. His heart was always ready to reciprocate their kindness, to sympathize with their sorrows, and overlook their infirmities. His hand, his time, his counsel, and his influence, were all at the command of those who shared his confidence, and deserved his affection.

"A friend is worth all hazard we can run,
Poor is the friendless master of a world;
A world in purchase for a friend is gain."

But there was another circle nearer to his heart, in which he was still better prepared to shine; and in which true excellency displayed is a brighter and surer evidence of worth. Justice could not be done to his character without being known in the family circle. As a Husband, a Father and a Master, those alone who were the objects of his attachment, forbearance and tenderness, could duly appreciate his conduct and demeanour.

His life was a bright pattern of those virtues which are essential to the purity and peace of society. He possessed a lofty and delicate sense of personal honor, and virtuous feeling. His presence was always a rebuke to the arts and abominations of evil speaking, profanity, and defamation. If he could not speak well of his fellow men he was wise and firm enough to say nothing. He regarded the reputation of others as a sacred treasure, and would never stoop to meddle with the private history, or detract from the good name of those around him. He felt that the sources of his enjoyment and the causes of his elevation were not to be found in the calamities, or the vices, of his fellow-men, and hence his lips were closed to the tales of slander, and his bosom a stranger to the wiles of calumny. Did all men act on the principle which governed him in this respect, a hideous train of evils which mar the purity and disturb the peace of society would cease to exist.

But General Graham did not believe, when he had served his country, his family and his friends, that his work on earth was finished. With an unwavering conviction of the truth and importance of religion, he professed to serve God, and to seek for salvation by faith in Christ. For a long period of time he was a member of the Presbyterian Church, and for ten or twelve years previous to his death, was a Ruling Elder of Unity, under the pastoral care of Rev. Mr. Adams. He cherished the most profound respect for the ordinances and duties of Christianity, and attended with deep interest and uniform punctuality upon the means of grace. He delighted much in reading the word of God, and in harkening to the instructions of the ministers of the gospel, for whom he always manifested the greatest regard. In selecting his library he proved how high an estimate he placed upon Christian instruction; and in his most unreserved intercourse with pious friends, his deep and pervading concern for *true and undefiled religion* was apparent. No circumstances would deter him from manifesting the most decided contempt for the grovelling spirit of Infidelity and irreligion.

By a life of temperence and regular exercise, with the blessing of God, he enjoyed remarkable health and vigour of constitution. On the 13th. of Oct., 1836, he made the following minute in his Day Book: "This day I am seventy-seven years of age, and in good health, *Dei Gratia.*"

As the disease which terminated his life was apoplexy, its paralyzing stroke was sudden and unexpected. He rode from Lincolnton on the 10th of November, and on the evening of the 12th. closed his eyes upon the cares and trials of a long, useful, and honorable life.

"Hope looks beyond the bounds of time,
When what we now deplore,
Shall rise in full, immortal prime,
And bloom to fade no more."

From Thomas Settle.   A.

Rockingham County, N. Ca.,

December 14th, 1836.

I received your favour of the 4th. inst. a day or two since, in
which you inform me that my name had been put in nomination
for the appointment of U. S. Senator both for the unexpired
term of the Hon. W. P. Mangum resigned & the six years succeeding. I was before the receipt of yours informed by a letter
from Mr. Reid,[36] of the fact that the night before the election
my friends had determined to run my name and by a letter from
our friend J. T. Morehead, Esqr. of the fact of my having been
run & the result of the balloting. I declare to you however unexpected as the intelligence was it shall not be disagreeable or
unpleasant to me. My nature must be changed before I can entertain towards you my worthy and generous friends any other
feelings than those of the warmest attachment and most profound gratitude. We all know that in all great contests for principal, strong exertions are to be used & sacrifices made and believing as I am sure we do, that the future liberty & happiness
of the people of this country depend on the maintenance of the
Whig principles, you must permit me to congratulate you on
your generous course in suffering yourself to be offered as the
willing victim in the late Sacrifice in the House of Commons.
You all of my acquaintances know since my appointment to the
office I now hold, I have cautiously refrained from all and every
interference in party politicks, believing it my duty to pursue
that course & that it meet the sanction of my own feelings & I
can in sincerity say to my friends that all the pride I ever felt
for political station has long since been fully gratified. I am

---

[36] David Settle Reid (1813-1891), of Rockingham County, lawyer, state senator,
1835-1842, member of congress as a Democrat, 1843-1847. Defeated for governor in
1848, he was elected in 1850, on the issue of "free suffrage," or the removal of the
freehold qualification for voting for members of the state senate, and served two
terms. He was immediately elected to the United States senate, and served until
1859. He was a delegate to the peace conference of 1861, and to the convention
of 1865.

not a candidate for any appointment or office and would be grateful to my friends if it meet their good pleasure not to run me for the appointment of U. S. Senator. I have written to Mr. Reid in answer to a letter which he wrote me in which I relieve him from all unpleasantness which he may feel on my account stating to him that I am not a candidate and authorising him as a relation to prevent my being started as one. I have further stated in reply to an enquiry or suggestion that I would not resign my present office for the appointment of Senator that it was unnecessary to express to him any determination of the course I should take as it was not in my power to say I would accept or decline.

Tell my Whig friends to cheer up & feel no mortification on my account my defeat is no indication of the defeat of our cause Our cause must and will succeed. I hope you my friends will start some one for the appointment of U. S. Senator under whose banners you may find more success than you have found under mine, no man can more ardently wish you success than I do, but I hope & believe there are many who can at this time bring you more. I am I think probably ignorant of the recent calamity to which you allude. I live as you know in an out of the way place where I get little intelligence except through the public prints & they come quite irregularly, permit me however to deeply sympathise with you in any & every calamity which has befallen you.

Give my warmest respects to our friends collectively & individually & please accept for yourself my best respects and wishes for your welfare.

I am with the highest consideration of Esteem

Your Friend.

Raleigh.

Speech on Resolution to unseat
William S. Harris.[37]

December 18th., 1836.

* * * * *

The House having resolved itself into a Committee of the Whole, the debate was opened by Mr. Graham, of Orange, in behalf of the right of Mr. Harris to retain his seat, and in opposition to the Resolution reported by the Committee. He took the broad ground that the people of any county have a right to elect, as their Representative, whom they please, whether he be a young man or an old one — a wise man or a simple one; and that it is not competent for the Legislature to vacate his seat, provided he possess the necessary freehold, and is not ineligible on account of some express Constitutional disability. Mr. G. cited several memorable cases in the legislative annals of our own State, where individuals, under the age of 21 years, had been elected as members, and served in that capacity, without any question having been raised as to their eligibility. He referred to our Revolutionary history as a period when boys sprung, almost as if by magic, into men, and expatiated on the efficient service rendered by the precocious youth of that day; and, connecting this with the fact that no qualification of *age* is prescribed by the Constitution as a pre-requisite to a seat in the Legislature, he drew the inference that the omission was not *accidental*, on the part of the framers of that instrument, but was *intentional.*— an inference strengthened by the circumstance that, a few sections further, it is expressly required that the Governor of the State shall be *thirty years of age.*

From David Outlaw.   U.

Raleigh, Decm. 18th, 1836.

You will greatly oblige me, by furnishing, at your earliest convenience, a copy of your speech delivered to day in the House of Commons.

---

[37] From *Raleigh Register,* December 20th., 1836. An attempt was made at this session of the legislature, without success however, to unseat W. S. Harris, a member of the commons from Cabarrus County, because he was not of age at the time of his election. A copy of the speech referred to has not been located, and it is probable that Graham never reduced it to writing.

I view the attempt of "the party" to vacate Harris' seat as a flagrant violation of popular rights, and I wish the facts and arguments to be spread before the community. They cannot but have a good effect.

I wish to publish the speech in the next Star.

From James Graham.   U.

Washington, Decm. 29th, 1836.

I have this day received yours of the 24th. inst. I was quite sick on my way here between Raleigh and Halifax. I came from Halifax to Garysburg, 10 miles; and there got on the Rail Road to Norfolk 75 miles; and thence up the Potomac River. I got here and took my seat on the first day.

No man ever received a more cordial reception both from the members and citizens.

Three days after my arrival I took private boarding and my health has continued constantly to improve until I am now my self again, and *in good health*. I have kept much in retirement and visited but little as yet and therefore am not deep in the anticipations of the new arrangements contemplated by the new administration.

Van Buren and his friends are apprehensive of strong and unyielding opposition from the commencement of his term, and they look to events in advance with fear and trembling. You know he received small majorities in all the States. The Senate is undergoing a rapid and unfortunate change. Talents of the highest rank are giving way and exchanged for third and fourth rate men who have Indian Rubber principles. The President, Jackson, is confined to his chamber and sees no company, it is not expected he will survive the Spring, probably not the Winter. Lewis Henry [38] is here very snugly enjoying "the spoils of Victory" or $3,500 a year. I see Henry often, he is a fine boon companion and I am gratified my State has the appointment, though I could wish service of a more elevated character had been rendered for it. Dick Johnston [39] is not quite elected by the People but

[38] Louis D. Henry.
[39] Richard Mentor Johnson (1780-1850), of Kentucky, a graduate of Transylvania, who was a member of the legislature in 1804, 1819, and of congress, 1807-1819, a colonel in the War of 1812, and credited with killing Tecumseh. Serving in the United States senate, 1819-1829, he abandoned his support of Clay, in favor of Jackson, and was defeated. He was at once elected to the house, and served to 1837, when he became Vice President, by election of the senate.

the Senate will certainly elect him vice President. Dick is dead weight to carry. He is not only a man of vulgar habits and loose morals, but destitute of talent and propriety.

Do not permit the Demagogues in the Legislature to put the surplus fund into a Bank of the State. if you cannot set it apart for Internal Improvements and free schools; then have it deposited in the State Treasury and lower your State Tax.

*   *   *   *   *

Mrs. Rencher is in Philadelphia quite sick. Rencher returns tomorrow to see her. Jesse Speight took his seat this day; he is about to remove to Missippi.

There is no hope at this Session of passing another Bill for the distribution of the Surplus Revenue. But I hope for *a vote* in Both Houses on that measure for 1838. "The Party" are taking shelter under the old Presidents Message, and the letter of the new one; unless the Tariff be reduced, no such reasons will satisfy the People.

1837

Report on Surplus Revenue.[1]

January 2, 1837.

The Joint Select Committee of twenty-six, who were appointed to inquire into the best investment of that portion of the Surplus Revenue, which will be received by North Carolina, under the provisions of the deposite act of the last session of Congress, and to whom were referred various propositions relative to such investment by both Houses of the General Assembly, have attentively considered the same; and report.

That the thirteenth section of the act of Congress, "to regulate the deposites of the public money," declared, in substance, that such deposites, in the treasury of the different states, shall be by way of loan, and not as absolute gifts.—This provision, your committee believe, should not be wholly overlooked by the General Assembly, in any disposition it may make of that portion of the public treasure which is allotted to this state. They are persuaded, nevertheless, that it should be considered and treated as a loan of the most liberal character, which the state may never be required to repay; and which, it would be most unreasonable to suppose, will be demanded by any exigency of the federal treasury for many years to come. Viewed in this aspect, it is a talent committed to the Legislature, for the proper use of which its members will justly be held accountable to their constituents and country, unless in their hands, it shall be made productive of great and lasting benefits to the people. How it can be most advantageously applied to the accomplishment of such ends, your committee have experienced much difficulty in determining. The wisdom of statesmen in former times, and in other countries, has been exhibited in devising schemes for raising the revenues actually necessary for the real or imaginary wants of government; and so novel is the spectacle of a people, not only freed from debt, but with an income vastly exceeding the necessities of government, the excess of which it is desired to invest for public health, that but little light on the subject of this reference can be derived from the history of the past.

Among the numerous plans of investment referred to them, your committee first considered the propositions of certain banking and canal companies, in New York and New Jersey, to borrow the fund due to this state, and are unanimous in the opinion

[1] From *Hillsboro Recorder,* January 20th., 1837.

that these propositions should not be accepted. The great advantage to the states, which were contemplated by the passage of the deposite act, consisted not in the receipts of interest on the sums entrusted to them; but in the renewed life and vigor which would be imparted to their industry and enterprize—their physical and mental improvement, by adding so much to the active capital within their limits. Every thousand dollars of such deposites, if used as active capital, will furnish employment to one thousand dollars worth of industry in the country where it is used. The encouragement should be given to the industry of the citizens of our own state, in preference to those of other states, so far as it can be done with the public funds, under the control of the Legislature; and that this may be done, even without the diminution of the annual profits on such funds, if invested abroad, your committee suppose, can hardly admit of question. They take this occasion to remark, that in their opinion, no one cause has militated so much against the prosperity of North Carolina, as the drain upon her capital and productive labor, which has been in progress for a series of years, and which has been accelerated within a short time. To say nothing of our contributions to the federal government; but a pittance of which has ever been expended within our limits; the large sums of money which are prodigally sent to the North to seek permanent employment in stocks, merchandize, city property, and otherwise; and to the south and south west, to be laid out in lands and slaves, have had a like disastrous effect upon her condition, though not to the same ruinous extent with the *absenteeism* of the landed proprietors of Ireland, so much complained of in that country. By a judicious use of the means now in our hands, this course of impoverishment may, in some degree, be arrested; and the ardent and enterprizing of our own people may find at home a field for their zeal and energy.

Another objection to such loans is, that the proposed borrowers are not under the control of our Legislature, nor amenable to the jurisdiction of our Courts. Your committee believe that the boon conferred by the act of Congress, was poorly worthy of our acceptance, if its only effect shall be to make North Carolina a surety to the federal treasury for the banks of other states, she receiving for such insurance only the interest on the sum thus secured, while all the advantages of the use of this vast treasure are to be enjoyed by the citizens of other states.

Your committee are also of opinion, that no portion of the public deposites should be applied in aid of the ordinary revenues, either for the support of the state government, or for county purposes. The ordinary taxes levied for these uses are far from being burthensome to the people; and by a proper adjustment of the valuation of taxable property, will yield a sum quite as great as ought to be desired. It should, moreover, be borne in mind, that those governments have been distinguished by the greatest purity of administration, and have longest preserved the blessings of liberty, in which the governing power, no matter how constituted, has been dependent for its support on annual pecuniary levies from the people. To exhaust the surplus revenue in maintaining the current expenses of government, or to fritter it away by a division among the several counties to replenish their treasures, in the manner proposed by a bill referred by the House of Commons, would be not merely to compromise the dignity of the state, but to interrupt, for a time only, the regular operation of the system of state taxation, and to disappoint the just expectations of our constituents. Your committee, therefore, return said bill to the House, and recommend its rejection.

Your committee have also been instructed to inquire into the propriety of devoting the fund in question to the establishment of a new bank, to be owned wholly by the state. A portion of them are confident in the belief that the establishment of such an institution would contravene that provision of the Constitution of the United States, which declares that "no state shall emit bills of credit;" and which they are informed has been judicially expounded to extend to any paper medium issued by a state for the purpose of common circulation. Independently of the arguments against the expediency of such a bank, which have been often urged in the discussions of this subject heretofore, your comimttee believe that no financial skill could successfully manage a bank founded entirely on a borrowed capital, demandable in certain proportions, at the pleasure of the lender; which must regulate its business according to the necessities of the federal government—the fluctuations of party politics—the appropriations made by Congress—and even the movements of individuals of that body, from motives either partizan or patriotic.

The only remaining objects of appropriation, to which the attention of your committee has been called by the direction of the Legislature, are common schools, and internal improvements.

These your committee recognize as first in importance among all the objects which now claim the patronage of the public; and but for the fiduciary character of the means in their possession, they would meet less difficulty in dedicating the whole fund immediately and irrevocably to these purposes. They, however, propose to devote it to them; while, at the same time, it shall be so invested for the present, as to be capable of recall without great inconvenience, should the state be required to refund any part of the loan. They are aware that public opinion is divided on the question, whether general education, or the improvement of the means of transportation, should be first patronized. Some of your committee were inclined to the opinion, that the whole should be expended on internal improvements; in the belief that opening new avenues to wealth, which are accessible to all classes in the community, would diffuse the means and the disposition for education to an extent almost equal to a direct appropriation for public schools; others, on the contrary, insist on claiming the whole as a school fund, as the only mode in which it can be made to benefit equally the whole population. In deference to this conflict of opinion, your committee have been induced to recommend that our whole share of the surplus revenue shall be devoted equally to popular education and internal improvements, that that part which is appropriated to education, shall be added to the fund "for common schools" now existing; and shall be invested for accumulation in bank stock, by increasing the capital stock of the Bank of Cape Fear to one million, five hundred thousand dollars; in which there shall be subscribed of the school fund before mentioned, four hundred thousand dollars; and by increasing the capital stock of the Bank of the State of North Carolina to two millions of dollars; by a subscription of the fund aforesaid, for five thousand shares in said bank.

Your committee are fully sensible of the dangers to be apprehended from an excess of banking capital; and have only consented to this mode of investment, because of a general prevalence of opinion that our present capital is too small. They propose, however, to remedy the inconveniences of an excess, should one occur, by a provision in the amended charters for the reduction of the capital stocks of both the banks, if it shall be found too great for the real demands of business. They also believe that this disposition of the addition to the school fund, can be much more economically and profitably made in the banks already in existence and in full operation, than in one owned exclusively by the state; not to mention the objections already urged to an institution of the latter character. In all monied transactions, your committee suggests that experience has generally proved that individuals having an interest in the adventure, have realized greater profits than mere agents. The proposed investments in bank may be made without any expense to the school fund, except its portion of the compensation paid to the officers of the Banks. The President and Directors of the Literary Fund, by the act of the General Assembly of 1825, will receive the dividends on the shares of that fund, and reinvest them for further increase.

The residue of the public deposites (which is estimated at nine hundred thousand dollars) your committee recommend to be added to the fund for internal improvements, and be placed under the control of the Board of Internal Improvements. That they shall proceed to loan out the same upon the terms prescribed in the bill herewith reported - that a preference shall be given in making such loans to companies engaged in constructing works for the improvement of the means of internal transportation; but that no company shall be allowed to borrow to an amount greater than one half of its capital stock actually subscribed by solvent subscribers; and that satisfactory security, either real or personal, to be judged of by the said board, shall, in all cases, be given by the borrowers. The President and Directors of the Board of Internal Improvements, are directed, whenever interest shall be received thereon, to make new loans, so as to keep the fund in a course of active accumulation. The President and Directors of the Board of Internal Improvements, have a corporate existence by the act of the General Assembly of 1819, and consist of the Governor, Treasurer, and an agent of public works, appointed by the Legislature, no one of whom receives any compensation for this service, except the last; who is entitled to pay for the time actually spent by him in public employment.

Your committee believe that it will be in the power of the Board greatly to facilitate works of internal improvement, by the adoption of the plan proposed; while, at the same time, the fund of the state will accumulate for future use. The regular business of banking requires such speedy returns of their loans, that neither rail road, canal, nor manufacturing companies can obtain from them the accommodations necessary for constructing their works. Whereas the disposition of the fund for internal improvements herein recommended, by affording longer time for payment than is allowed by legitimate banking operations, will give to them all due encouragement. Your committee have deemed it advisable that this whole fund should be placed under the control of the Board of Internal Improvements, rather than that the loans should be made by the Legislature, for the reason that but few corporations for purposes of internal improvement are, as yet, in operation in this state; and they desire that the accommodations which may be furnished by the bill before mentioned, shall be extended, whenever its terms are complied with. As the corporations which may be chartered at this session, will be of course unknown until after the adjournment, it is deemed to be inexpedient for the General Assembly to designate those to which aid shall be given, or how far it shall extend.

Your committee know full well, that many of our constituents had expected bolder measures on the subject of internal improvement, or of public education, or of both, than they have recommended—that fond hopes have been cherished by patriots in every quarter—that the state would immediately be blessed with the full fruition of those advantages for which they may now suppose that a tardy preparation is about to be made. When, however, it is recollected, that much as the subject has been agitated, even at this day, public opinion has not settled down on any great work of internal improvement, to which the public treasure should first be devoted—that no plan of common schools has yet been devised, which is capable of practical execution in every part of the state, when, moreover, it is remembered, that it is as yet uncertain whether the policy of distributing the excess of the federal revenue among the states will be repeated; and if continued, whether it will be by way of loan, or in absolute property.

Your committee presume that the present Legislature will, in some degree, deserve the gratitude of their country, if they shall so appropriate the fund confided to her, as to deepen and widen those foundations on which others may erect the superstructure of her happiness and prosperity. To carry into effect the plans herein proposed, they present the bills marked No. 1, 2, 3, and recommend that they be passed into laws.

Respectfully submitted,
William A. Graham
Chairman pro tem.

From George W. Mordecai. [2]   A.

Raleigh, 13 Jan., 1837.

I have been so closely engaged for some days that it has been out of my power to call & see you & as I am compelled to leave here tomorrow for Warrenton I shall not be able to do so before my departure. I must entrust the fate of our Bill to your management, satisfied that every thing will be done which can be consistently with your ideas of propriety. Permit me to ask your attention to another matter which is in discussion before your house and as to which I fear there may be some misunderstanding. I allude to Mr. Haywood's project, by which it seems he proposes to bestow the patronage of the Legislature exclusively on two objects of internal improvement the Wilmington & Fayetteville Roads. I was applied to some time ago, by Col. Joyner[3] to know whether we desired to *borrow* any portion of the Surplus revenue, & if so how much & on what terms. I replied that we were not now in a situation to desire a loan as the instalments had been paid in with great punctuality & the funds on hand were more than we had immediate occasion for, but suggested to him if the State refused to subscribe or adopt the two-fifth system, that then a Board of Commissioners should be established on the plan proposed by you in your report.

I had no idea of excluding ourselves from any priviledge or advantage which the Legislature might feel disposed to grant to other Rail Road Companies by way of subscription for Stock or loan at some future period & so stated to Mr. Joyner. Should therefore Mr. Haywoods project (so objectionable in many respects,) be likely to succeed, as he does not seem disposed to take care of his constituents, we must throw ourselves upon you for aid & beg you to endeavour to have our Road placed on the same footing with the others. I regret, Sir, that we are so situated as to be compelled to trouble you so often about matters which we ought to be enabled to entrust to our representative, but such is our unfortunate condition. Mr. Gales will give you all the aid he can but as he has not as much experience in Legislation as yourself, we must entrust the matter mainly to you. Raleigh.

[2] George W. Mordecai (1801-1871), a prominent lawyer and capitalist of Raleigh.
[3] Andrew Joyner (1786-1856), of Halifax, lieutenant colonel, War of 1812, member of the state senate, 1835-1852, (speaker, 1838-1840, 1846, 1848), a powerful Whig leader, deeply interested in internal improvements, and relief of the unfortunate. He was President of the Roanoke Navigation Company, and the Seaboard and Roanoke Railroad.

From David L. Swain.   U.

Chapel Hill, 20 Jan., 1837.

I have letters from Mr. Memminger[4] of the 14th. 17th. & 18th. inst. before me giving the proceedings of the General Assembly since my departure from Raleigh in connexion with the Cincinnatti and Charleston Rail Road much in detail.

I congratulate you not only on the noble triumph attained for the Country in the passage of the bill, but on the triumphant manner, in which I have the most satisfactory evidence you sustained yourself, and the State, throughout the conflict. I do not write however merely for the purpose of saying this, but mainly with a view to add my request (it should be command if I were autocrat) to that of Col. Memminger, that you will do yourself the justice, and your friends the service, to write out your speech for the press, elaborately and without delay.[5]

We will have a Freshman Class this Session of at least forty.

---

[4] Christopher Gustavus Memminger (1803-1888), of South Carolina, who had just appeared before the legislature in behalf of the proposed road. Brought to Charleston from Germany as a child, he was brought up at the Orphan House, and, adopted by Governor Thomas Bennett, was educated at South Carolina College. A member of the commons, 1836-1852, he was chiefly responsible for the beginning of a public school system in the State. He opposed Nullification, and wrote "The Book of Nullification," a pungent attack upon it. By 1860 he had become a secessionist, was commissioner to Virginia in 1860-1861, and confederate secretary of the treasury, 1861-1864. After the war, he was active in educational work, and in the development of phosphate resources.

[5] About this time, Graham's reputation for ability, sound judgment, and general effectiveness, was becoming widely recognized. The constant reference to him in the State press is part of the evidence of this. After C. G. Memminger presented the case of the Charleston and Cincinnati Railroad to the legislature at this session, Graham made a speech on the subject. The *Raleigh Star,* January 19th., 1837, thus commented:

"We have rarely heard, in the Legislature, or elsewhere, a more able or eloquent speech than that of Mr. Graham. It would have done honor to any deliberative assembly in this country. We view, with the highest satisfaction, the rapid steps by which this distinguished son of North Carolina is rising, who, we trust, is yet to adorn the national councils, and contribute thereby to elevate his native State in the scale of the Union. He is a model of what a public man ought to be, of what the public men of this country once were, uniting the highest talents with the most chivalrous and stainless honor." Apparently the speech was never printed, and is not found in his notes.

From James Graham.   U.

Washington, Jany. 29th, 1837.

I received your letter dated the day preceding the adjournment of the Legislature. I am much pleased with the principal subjects of general Legislation. Genl. Santa Anna and Almonte his secretary and interpreter have been here and have now Gone by way of Norfolk to Mexico.

Conl. Bee,[6] late of Charleston, S. C., accompanied them from Texas. He brought me a letter of introduction from Genl Pinkny Henderson[7] who is now the Attorney General of Texas. Santa Anna I saw and talked with. He is of middle size, and has the Hair and complexion of an Indian. He is an easy and accomplished man in his manners. He returns to Texas determined to assume and perform his Presidential office until his term expires in April next when he will retire from public life. He says he will recommend the People of Mexico to surrender Texas and forthwith acknowledge their Independance.

I anticipate a Revolution in Mexico whenever Santa Anna puts his foot upon the Mexican Shore.

On yesterday Van Buren resigned his seat as presiding officer of the Senate and they elected King[8] of Allabama President of that body. Benton and Walker[9] of Missippi have had an open and violent quarrell in the Senate. Walker has denounced him and his hard money scheme, told him he was striagning at a Nat and swallowing a cammel, that he was willing to use the

[6] Barnard E. Bee, who moved from South Carolina to Texas in 1835. He became secretary of state in the Lamar Cabinet in 1838, and, the following year, was appointed peace commissioner to treat with Mexico.

[7] James Pinckney Henderson (1808-1858), of Texas, a native of Lincoln County, N. C., who had moved to Mississippi in 1835. Raising a company to aid Texas, he became in 1836 a brigadier general, and attorney general of the republic. He was a diplomatic representative in Europe in 1838, but was recalled. He was later minister to the United States, a member of the constitutional convention of 1845, and governor, 1846, major general, U. S. A. in the Mexican War, and senator in 1858.

[8] William Rufus (de Vane) King (1786-1853), native of Sampson County, after attending the university, studied law, served in the commons, 1807-1809, and in congress, 1811-1816, was secretary to the legations at Naples and St. Petersburg, 1816-1818, and then moved to Alabama. He served in the convention of 1819, and was elected to the United States senate, and served to 1844. He was minister to France, 1844-1846, was again elected senator. In 1852 he was Democratic candidate for Vice President, against Graham, was elected, and died before assuming his duties.

[9] Robert James Walker (1801-1869), a native of Pennsylvania, a graduate of the University of Pennsylvania, moved to Mississippi in 1826. He was United States senator, 1836-1845, when he became secretary of the treasury. He was for a short time in 1857 governor of the Kansas Territory. He opposed secession violently, and in 1863 Lincoln sent him to Europe, charged with devising means to prevent the floating there of Confederate loans.

State Banks safe depositories of 45 millions of public monies and yet he was unwilling the General Government should take a Note from any one of these Banks for $20. Sir, says he, "I am responsible for every thing I say in this house and out of it." On tomorrow Rives will hold forth on Walkers side, and there is now an open rupture in the camp. I think Rives and Walker will take a majority of the administration Senators, but Benton will hold fast upon all the inferior men of whom there are not a few in Congress.

I think the formation of the new Cabinet will cause another rupture, there are not loaves and fishes enough to feed all the hungry swarm of Expectants who are looking ahead for office. We have no certain information yet who will fill the Cabinet, though Report says Forsyth, Woodbury, and Kendall [10] will hold on to their present appointments. Butler[11] and Dickerson[12] it is said will leave, and the War Department is now vacant. Strange manifests a disposition to talk a good deal in the Senate but they do not regard him as a strong man. He called at my room and told me he understood I had heard and believed he was electioneered against me in my district and *utterly denied it,* and I received his denial, so we are on social terms.

I hope I will be able to reach Hillsboro on my return by the 10th or 11th of March.

Rencher's wife is still in Philadelphia quite sick, and I fear she will never be well. A great crowd is expected here about first of March to witness the Inauguration of the new President.

Present my kind Respects to Sister Susan and ask her if she will not go up with us to the sale in March and see all our relations. I think you should go either to the North or Va. Springs for to cure your lameness in the Spring or Summer.

---

[10] Amos Kendall (1789-1869), of Kentucky, a native of Massachusetts, graduate of Dartmouth, had moved to Kentucky as a tutor in the family of Henry Clay. He later became an editor, and, breaking with Clay, supported Jackson. Blair brought him to Washington to edit the *Globe,* and he became a member of the "Kitchen Cabinet," and wrote many of Jackson's state papers. He was postmaster general, 1835-1840. He was a promoter of the telegraph, education of the deaf and dumb, and opponent of secession, but was a sharp critic of congressional reconstruction.

[11] Benjamin Franklin Butler, of New York.

[12] Mahlon Dickerson (1770-1853), of New Jersey, a native of New Hampshire, a graduate of Princeton, who, after serving as legislator, supreme court judge, governor, was a Democratic United States senator, 1817-1833, secretary of the navy, 1834-1838, and Federal district judge, 1840-1853.

To Susan Washington Graham.   A.

Raleigh, Febr. 12th, 1837.

My Dear Wife

I arrived here this evening in safety & health, and as I learn
that the mail is closed tonight, I hasten to write you. My journey
has been a solitary one, though the weather has been exceedingly
pleasant, and but for the recollection of what I had left behind, I
should have found it delightful. The first day I travelled the
Dover road, & found a large portion of it surpassingly bad, but
arrived before sunset at Kinston and found your brother and
family quite well. They regretted that you had not returned to
that place with me, and alleged that the expectation of Mr. & Mrs
Clark was no apology for that they had room enough for you all.
The next morning I left at nine and calling at Waynesboro to
deliver your package I saw for a few moments Mrs. Washington,
who still continues well and desires to be kindly remembered by
you.

Declining her kind request to stay for dinner (as I had still on
hand a large portion of your supplies increased by a very bounti-
ful addition from Sister Mary, I proceeded on to Mrs. Cox's, a
white house 8 miles above Waynesboro. I can't say much in the
way of commendation of it either for *bed* or *board*. This morning
I departed at sunrise, came to Smithfield for breakfast, and
reached the hospitable mansion of our excellent friend Mrs.
White this afternoon before sunset. The roads are greatly improved, and I have seldom performed a journey in winter with
less inconvenience. I have read a good deal by the way, what time
I have not been thinking of my "absent wife."

Mrs. White & the family are all well. Miss Susan will go with
me tomorrow to Chapel Hill, and I shall reach Hillsboro' the
next day. . . .

I have no time to write more as my letter must be in the office
by 9 o'clock. Yes My dear wife, write me frequently, and let me
know particularly how you are. I shall feel the greatest solicitude
to hear. Everything here reminds me of you, and I fancy that the
vacant chair at my elbow should be occupied by you. I am almost
averse to going up stairs to our room.

Farewell my dearest. Heaven's choicest blessings on you.
New Bern.

To Susan Washington Graham.   A.

Hillsboro', Feby. 17th, 1837.

My Dear Wife

After writing you from Raleigh I remained there the day following, untill eleven oclock, when I set off with Miss Susan White and after passing over a very bad road, we reached Chapel Hill at dark, spent the night with Gov. Swain, and next morning was joined by Dr. Norwood who accompanied me to this place. I have been playing the "man about town" for two days and am now seated in my old office, & have been endeavoring just now to pay off some of my long delayed debts of correspondence. I have but little society about the Hotel, indeed none, except Mr. Waugh[13] the artist from Raleigh. The town is looking as dull as ever, though several new inhabitants are said to be coming in. Mr. Waddell has sold his house (in which he did not live) to one of them, named (I believe) Spencer from Hyde County. Another has rented the White house on the way from Mrs. Hill's to Mr. Andersons. Mr. Turner has rented out his Tavern and (it is said) will occupy the house late Mr. Phillips.

Dr. Strudwick[14] has sold his Alabama plantation & negroes. Dr. Webb[15] (I suppose you know) has done the same. Mr. Cain[16] is also desirous to sell his. The South therefore seems to be losing its charms for our citizens. Col. Jones is now in that country with his son Allen; I do not know what are his views as to retaining his possessions.

Matrimony is said to be progressing with rapid strides in this quarter. Mr. Cameron[17] and Miss Hawks are certainly married. Our acquaintance Miss Nancy Graves of Caswell is also united to a Mr. Mebane of this county. Mr. Giles Mebane is promised (says Dr. Norwood) the hand of Miss Yancy of Caswell and Mr. H. Guion[18] that of a Miss C. Moore.

---

[13] Alfred S. Waugh, a sculptor.

[14] Dr. Edmund Strudwick (1802-1879), of Hillsboro, educated in medicine at the University of Pennsylvania, had a distinguished career as a physician. He was the first president of the North Carolina Medical Society.

[15] Dr. James Webb (1774-1853), of Hillsboro, a native of Essex County, Virginia, physician, and a business man with many irons in the fire.

[16] William Cain (1784-1857), of Orange, briefly a student at the university, a planter and merchant.

[17] John Cameron, hitherto mentioned, married Frances Hawks.

[18] Haywood Williams Guion (1826-1874), of Lincolnton, native of New Bern, graduate of the university, a distinguished lawyer, and a promoter of railroad development.

Wm. Cameron[19] returned from Philadelphia a few weeks ago, had quite a "blow up" with Miss Emma, and has emigrated to Alabama to endeavor to dissipate his thought in other scenes. Mrs. C. Jones Jr. has produced a daughter to "replenish the earth" —all said to be well. He has become wearied of Raleigh and has been speaking of purchasing the house, purchased by Mr. Turner[20] at Mr. Phillips' sale, or that of Mr. P. Cameron.[21]

I was waited on yesterday by the proprietress of that splendid mansion, with brick pillars in front, a few doors North of this Hotel, who offered it to me for sale, having heard that I wished to commence housekeeping, & recommended it highly as a residence for a small family. If you have a *fancy for it,* please to let me know, immediately.

The New York Courier announces, as a rumor, that Govr. Cass is to be recalled from his mission to France, and that Jo. Seawell Jones is to be his successor, and adds that altho' it is to be regretted that Mr. Cass is to be sacrificed, the new appointment will be highly acceptable to the people.

* * * * *

I find a letter here from Bro. James he will pass here on his return from Washington and will expect me to go with him to Lincoln. He gives but little news from Washington. Messrs Forsyth, Woodbury, & Kendall will retain their places in the new Cabinet, the offices of War, Navy & Attorney General, will be vacant. Dr. Montgomery of this district writes me, that he has but little hope of any one from N. C. being appointed to a place in the Cabinet, but supposes Mr. Rives of Virginia will be one of its members.

* * * * *

Be careful of your health, my dearest, & write me frequently; it seems a long time since I saw you. Be assured however of my constant kindness & affection.

My knee is as well as usual. We had rain & yesterday & the day before, previous to which it was a little painful.
New Bern.

---

[19] William Cameron (1817-1893), a physician of Hillsboro.

[20] Presumably Thomas Turner, long sheriff of Orange.

[21] Paul Carrington Cameron (1808-1891), of Orange, educated at Captain Partridge's famous school, at the university, and at Washington (now Trinity) College at Hartford, planter and businessman. He was, at the outbreak of the Civil War, the largest slave owner in the State, having nearly two thousand in North Carolina, Alabama, and Mississippi. He was an active promoter of the North Carolina Railroad, and was its president, 1861-1865. He was a state senator in 1856. His last public service was as active friend and benefactor of the university.

To Susan Washington Graham.   A.

Hillsboro', Feby. 25, 1837.

My dearest

Your kind letter enclosing two others reached me last week, and was read over and over with much delight. I presume you received mine from Raleigh on the evening you wrote, and hope that my second one from here, went to you with due speed. Judging of the pleasure with which they are read, by that afforded me by yours, I should be greatly wanting in my duty not to be punctual in writing.

Often, my dear wife, do I regret the necessity which at present separates us, & wish a speedier flight to time, or that I had earlier made preparation for your being well taken care of here. And if such be the course of my thoughts, which are filled at intervals with business or company, I am led to reflect, how solitary must be the situation of her, who for me has relinguished a large portion of society, and who by her affection for me is now secluded for a time (I trust a short one) almost from the world.

I hope your indisposition does not occur often. When reading that portion of your letter I ardently wished myself near, that I might have administered, or at least offered my poor services for your relief. Do not allow yourself to be depressed, my Love, the darkest and most tempestuous hours are e'er long succeeded by sunshine and calm.

At one oclock last Monday morning I set out in the stage for Greensboro' arrived about eleven, left there at 3 P. M. on Thursday, & reached home without accident at 2 next morning. My knee has sustained no injury from the journey, and I flatter myself is rather better in the last two weeks. Joe went to me there, on horseback, and has brought home my sulkey.

Greensboro' is still improving more than any village in this section of the State. There are at present 75 students in the "Caldwell Institute" at that place. There is, also, a female Academy which is said to flourish very well. Several new houses are going up, their steam machinery is about to be increased, and a Company from Baltimore is about to engage in mining for Copper in that County; the whole western part of the State appears to be advancing to a more prosperous condition, and the spirit of emigration is declining.

Last week I received a letter from my Niece Eliza Witherspoon of Alabama. Their family has been visited with many cases of sickness during the Autumn and Winter. Dr. W. and Sister were to set out for Carolina on the 14th. inst. and I presume will be in Lincoln before I go there. I would be highly pleased if you could go with me to see them. Eliza is promised a visit to the North with her brother and his lady, for keeping house in the absence of her parents. She expresses a strong desire to see you, and hopes she may do so in New York the ensuing summer. Says she has had many descriptions of her "new Aunt from her friends in Alabama." Dr. Alexander arrived at her Fathers while she was writing, from Mecklenburg. Dr. Strudwick & Mr. Waddell have been with me this afternoon; the former you have heard has sold his estate at the South, and has just returned from there. He is pleased with the sale of his lands, but says he wishes that he had retained his slaves & sent them to Texas. He travelled part of his way home with one of the Generals of the latter Country, who gave him a minute description of the soil and climate and stated (what is hardly credible) that the population is more industrious, sober & orderly than that of any of the Southwestern States of this Union.

No doubt is now entertained of the independence of Texas. Santa Anna will be received in Mexico with great joy, and restored to the Presidency, and he has agreed to acknowledge its independence.

* * * * *

Dr. Strudwick dissuades me from going to see Dr. Sweat, and assures me that I will eventually be well, if I will allow my limb sufficient rest. I think I will go to the North in the Summer at all events. I have undertaken some business in anticipation of going which I hope to make profitable.

Of all this when I see you; I have many things to tell you, my loveliest, which must be reserved untill we are met.

With every feeling of the warmest affection—Adieu.
New Bern.

To Susan Washington Graham.   A.

Hillsboro', March 3rd, 1837.

The Session of the Court had prevented me from writing in time for the mail, but the stage has arrived, and brought my Susan's letter of the 28th ult. and I know she will be much disappointed, should she not hear from me on Tuesday evening. Therefore I write a few hasty lines which a passenger promises to deposit in the office at Raleigh. Would that I could go with them on their destination & greet their reader wtih a cordial embrace. I have tried the life of a bachelor sufficiently long, my Love, to be surprised & wondering how I endured it formerly. My Hotel de ville has moreover been this week infested with a crowd of not the most quiet & sober citizens so that I have had rather "a vile repose." For a few years past I had supposed there was a great reformation among the people of the country in their habits of intemperance. But the observation of this week convinces me that it is a gross error. And the number of retailing shops which have recently established are likely to inebriate the whole community.

The events of the Court House would afford but little interest to you, and I have not been conversant with any thing else. I shall finish them tomorrow and hope then to be allowed to sleep more quietly than I have been doing this week. The matter of the "brick pillars" is all a jest as stated in my last, which I only mentioned on account of the supreme impudence & folly of the offer of it to me, which was done in good earnest. I have made no arrangement relative to a house & probably will not untill I see you. Mr. C. Jones Jr. is here this week and desires to buy one, as he has determined to come to this place. Judge Nash left on Tuesday and will probably be in New Bern before you receive this, though I had not heard that Miss Maria was expected to accompany him before receiving your letter. Mr. Alexr. Kirkland will set out in ten or twelve days for Mississippi; his object is to sell out his store et cet. in that country and recommence business in Hillsboro'.

* * * * *

Farewell, my dearest wife.
New Bern.

To Susan Washington Graham.   A.

Hillsboro', March 11th, 1837.

I take my seat with great willingness, to address My Susan this evening, as I have found her constantly present to my thoughts, for several days past. This being the aniversary of those delightful days of Love, which we spent together last March, & to which my memory will ever recur, with the fondest and tenderest emotions.

Being without employment this week, save in my office, I almost wish I had taken the stage at the beginning of the week, for New Bern, though I could have remained but two days with you.

My solicitude to know how you are, to be with you, and take care of you, increases every day. Do write me my darling particularly as to your state of health, and every thing pertaining to it. I shall probably leave here about this day week, 18th, for Lincoln, and return to Caswell Court 3rd of April, and hope to salute you in person on the week following. I am expecting a letter from you tonight, and another at the time I leave here. Please write me on the 23rd. to Salisbury, where I shall be, on my return about the last of the month,—And to Caswell C. H. on the 30th. to Hillsboro' on the 4th April. I will be here by the 7th or 8th.

I am exceedingly happy in saying to you, that I believe my leg is essentially better. I have been quite careful of it, but for several days past, I have walked several times back and forward across my room without even my cane. This I do, for the sake of exercise, which as it has been so long disused, must be resumed gradually. I propose therefore to engage your hand for a dance when we next meet. In the mean time, should you incline to waltz I recommend Mary as my substitute, though she may be somewhat deficient in length of arm.

At the close of the Court last Saturday, I had a visit from Mr. Mebane to inform me that he was to be married on Wednesday 8th. and he is now absent for the purpose. No one accompanied him, from here, except his brother. Dr. Norwood [22] was invited, as usual, but declined going. Miss Clancy is to be united next week to a Mr. Young of Alabama, formerly resident here. And the Dr. who you know has an eye quick to discern the evidences of such things, says he spies symptoms of a wedding about Miss C. Moore's. A gentleman who has been below reports that Miss P. Skinner is certainly to be married to Mr. Standing. I hear nothing of Miss C. Burgwyn's affair though I presume it is still on hand.

* * * * *

Dr. Montgomery, the member of Congress from this district, is said to decline a reelection. I have determined under no circumstances to be a Candidate, and have taken pains to let this be known whenever the subject has been proposed to me. Believe

---

[22] Dr. Walter Alves Norwood, of Hillsboro.

me, dearest, I would rather be with you, at our own fireside than to enjoy any honor which might attach to a membership in that body, and the idea of surrendering my profession, and leaving you for five or six months at a time, I cannot consent to.

I have today read the Inaugural address of the new President; it is quite flat and commonplace. I go out but little, scarcely at all, and have devoted this week entirely to professional matters. What time, I have not been thinking of my dear absent wife, whom I picture up stairs, in her room in the Castle, devoted to the duties of her station, & anxiously waiting the progress of time & the return of her Husband.

. . . Most ardently do I wish that time would speed his pace, and allow me again to be with you.

Be careful of your health and assured of your Husband's un-failing and devoted Love.

To My Dearest Susan.
New Bern.

To Susan Washington Graham.   A.

Hillsboro', March 17th, 1837

* * * * *

I set out in the stage at 2 tomorrow morning for Lincoln. Though pleased at the prospect of seeing again, this perhaps for the last time, all the living members of my family, I regret that a greater distance will be interposed between me and my wife. I go however with feelings tinctured by melancholy as well as joy. Ah my darling! when I have heretofore turned my face to the place of my nativity, I have been cheered by hope of again seeing the kindest of parents, and felt that I was performing an act of filial gratitude and reverence. But now I go to mingle my tears with those of my long absent brothers & sisters over his grave, to see the places, with which I have been ever accustomed to associate him, rendered desolate by the sad reality that they will know him no more. Let me not however depress you by a recital of griefs which it were perhaps criminal to indulge.

My brother James passed here last Monday night in the stage on his way from Washington. He is in fine health and spirits, was with me three or four hours and will remain in Lincoln for two or three weeks. He is again a Candidate for Congress, and does not know that he will have opposition. . . .

Our Superior Court is this week in Session and I have been exceedingly busy. My Guilford correspondent charged with Forgery was tried today, & acquited, for want of proof, that the forgery was done in Orange.

Mr. Mebane is here a blooming bride-groom. He will settle himself in the country, here, or in Caswell.

The influenza is prevailing to considerable extent in our town, but I have heard of no serious case. Mr. Kirkland will go in a few days to New York; most of the other merchants have already gone.

*   *   *   *   *

New Bern.

To Susan Washington Graham. A.

Lincoln, March 23rd, 1837.

My Dear Wife

I am again at the mansion once my Father's, but which is now bereft of his presence, and trodden by many stranger's steps. I left Hillsboro' on Saturday morning in the stage at 2 oclock, and having sent on Joe the day before, I reached Greensboro at twelve, & proceeded near to Lexington that night. I dined the next day in Salisbury, staid at the House on this side, where you & I stopped in the night last fall, and dining with Sister Mary at Davidson College, I arrived here on Monday evening in perfect safety.

All the members of our family are here except Sister Mary, whose health forbids her to come. Sister Sophia, Dr. Witherspoon and two of their sons (one a young man on his way to Princeton College) reached the Furnace on Saturday evening last. Bro. Joseph arrived from Tennessee two are three weeks ago. On yesterday our sale commenced. Bro. James and myself purchased this place, perhaps from a childish aversion to see it go out of the family. Our agreement is, that if either should desire it exclusively he may take the interest of the other at a fair valuation. I believe that we shall be able to sell it again without loss should we not desire to retain it. The negroes have all been purchased by the members of the family, chiefly by Dr. Witherspoon and Bros. John & Joseph. I bid off several, but do not expect to retain any but Joe and his family. I do not calculate however on keeping him about us unless he shall amend very much. They were all bid off at immense prices—so high that no Negro trader purchased any, except one. Today the sale will continue, & perhaps tomorrow. Some old relics of the family are not to be sold, but everything else will be exposed to sale. An immense crowd was here yesterday and some are now encamped in sight. We all huddled into the dwelling House at this place together with with crier, & clerk of sale, etc.—We shall probably finish our settlement in the course of a week, when I shall set off for Caswell, hoping to hear from my Dear Susan at Salisbury.

Dr. McLean told me yesterday, that he did not believe Mrs. Gaston would live more than a few weeks. The Maj. was here on yesterday also, & said that Mrs. G. was no better. She appears to have made a favourable impression here, and will be much regretted by the neighborhood. Judge Gaston is expected there today. Mr. Erwin[23] of Burke was here, at the sale & told me that he had received a recent letter from Mr. King,[24] dated "Charleston" and that his health was much improved.

I am writing in the midst of a room filled with a crowd and confusion, and would defer it, but that I know my Susan will be anxious to hear from me.

The Davidson College over which Mr. Morrison presides has commenced under favourable auspices. The buildings are quite respectable, and the number of students about Fifty.

I will write you again as soon as I find leisure.

Heavens richest blessings attend you.

Farewell, Yours Ever.

To Susan Washington Graham.   A.

Salisbury, April 1st, 1837.

The receipt of my Dear Wife's letter, on my arrival here tonight, impels me, late as it is, to write her at once, lest I should lose the present mail, and in my haste, has caused me to fix my date a day in advance. Two long weeks have dragged by, since I last had the felicity to hear from her, and I lost no time in despatching a servant to the post office as soon as I came.

I this morning took leave of my friends, some of them in all probability for the last time, and leaving my sulkey & horses, took

---

[23] Probably Edward J. Erwin, house of commons, 1835-1838.
[24] James A. King, of Statesville.

the stage with my Nephew John Witherspoon,[25] who is going to Princeton College. At Beatties Ford we were joined by Judge Gaston, and have all journied thence together, tomorrow morning they will take the Hack line to Raleigh, and at noon I shall set off in the Piedmont line for Caswell where I expect to arrive on Sunday afternoon. The next week I expect to spend there untill friday, when I will go to Hillsboro', and hope to go thence by the next stage, to salute my ever dear Susan. I gladly speed every moment that passes untill I behold her again. I have much to tell her, which I will not attempt to write.

My Horses & servant will remain in Lincoln, untill I return from New Bern. My negroes have been placed under an Overseer to work the plantation, where my Father lately resided.

My Brother Jos. started a few days since for Ten. Dr. Witherspoon's family left today for Alabama, by way of S. C.

I went early this week, with Dr. W. Sister S. & Brother James to Mr. Gaston's to acknowledge some deeds before Judge G.—saw there Mrs. Donaldson, Miss H. Jones etc. No one appears to entertain any hope of Mrs. Gaston's[26] recovery. The ladies who accompanied the Judge, are waiting the result of her illness, and expect to bring off her children. Her fate is much commiserated in that vicinity.

Bro James was to go today to his plantation & thence to the mountains to take another summer's Campaign for Congress— I don't know yet, whether he is to have a competitor. I carried him over the other day hoping to exhibit him to Miss E. G. as we had heard, that the Judge had arrived with his two daughters. He seems to have hopes of matrimony yet, but I fear they are distant ones. Could I but continue with Judge Gaston instead of sending this midnight scrawl to my beloved wife I should be most happy. A certainty however, that she truly loves me will console me untill we meet, which will be I hope within a week after this is received.

Mr. Wm. Ruffin[27] is about to settle here, is said to be addressing Miss Polk, and will go with me hence to Caswell.

Farewell, my Dearest Susan.

---

[25] John James Witherspoon (1818-1847), Graham's nephew, who was a lieutenant in the war with Mexico.

[26] Mrs. Alexander F. Gaston.

[27] William Kirkland Ruffin (1812-1880), eldest son of Chief Justice Thomas Ruffin, a graduate of the university. Possessed of a brilliant mind, he became a learned lawyer, but, crippled by the loss of a leg, he was unable to practice, and acquired considerable reputation as a teacher of law. Many regarded him as the equal, if not the superior, of his father, in legal learning and mental ability.

To Susan Washington Graham.   A.

Greensboro', April 24th, 1837.

My Dear Wife

I have the happiness to announce my safe arrival at Guilford
Court. I travelled in the stage from New Bern to Raleigh with
Mr. G. Carroway who was returning in all haste to Mobile to look
after a failing purchaser of his negroes. I addressed a note at
Waynesboro' to Mrs. Washington & another at Raleigh to Mrs.
White telling them of birth of our son,[28] knowing their kind
feelings towards, & their solicitude to hear of an event which
affords us so much joy. At Raleigh I merely staid one night, and
hiring a hack came the next day to Hillsboro', spent there last
Saturday, and was cordially congratulated by our many friends
on our recent good fortune. So much interest is there taken our
affairs, that the intelligence had arrived before I did. Mrs. C.
Jones, Senr., has another son, & Mrs. J. Kirkland also, (as I learn
since I left H.). I believe I have before told you of the Heirs apparent of Parson Green[29] & Mr. J. Norwood. The fulfilment of
the great command to "increase and multiply, & replenish the
earth" seems to be in rapid progress among the inhabitants of our
goodly town. I tell Dr. N. that the mountaineer beaux are at a
high premium in Athens since the appearance of my boy, and that
he had better be in haste, or the batch of urchins that has recently
come to hand will flog his, at school by and bye, as they are likely
to have the advantage of them in age as well as in size.

On the evening I reached Hillsboro' Joe arrived with my horse
& sulkey from Lincoln. I purchased a horse there, the next day, &
two others here today. I shall start him back to the plantation
with them tomorrow. He will return to Hillsboro the latter part
of May.

Mr. Hayd Guion was there last week and travelled with me
here, on way to settle himself in Lincoln. I have it now from good
authority, that he is certainly engaged to Miss C. Moore; that I
presume puts an end to her trip to Red river. Dr. Pride Jones[30]

---

[28] Dr. Joseph Graham (1837-1907), later a Confederate captain, and a well known
physician of Charlotte.

[29] William Mercer Green (1798-1887), a native of Wilmington, graduate of the
university, rector of St. Matthews Episcopal Church, 1825-1837, professor in the
university, 1837-1849, he became Bishop of Mississippi, and lived there until his
death. He was prominent in the founding of the University of the South, Sewanee,
Tennessee.

[30] Dr. Pride Jones (1815-1889), a physician in Hillsboro, a Confederate captain,
and for many years clerk of the superior court of Orange County.

is at H., a full M. D. I don't know whether he is to remain. The persons who have purchased houses there, from the low country (Mr. Waddell's & C. Phillips') have removed their families.

My friend Morgan escaped again last week at Stokes but was convicted here on yesterday of a Forgery practiced on the Bank at Salem. I arrived too late to take part in his defence,—as well as in that of a Felon from Randolph in whose behalf I had been retained. One prisoner from Rockingham was convicted at this Court of Murder, and a family Father, Mother, & two daughters are now on trial for the murder of a Son-in-law.

The accounts here from N. York are no better than when I was at New Bern. I had almost forgotten to say that I saw Miss S. W. & Ann Eliza F. at Smithfield; the latter seemed delighted to hear of the appearance of our first born and was evidently anxious to make a great many inquiries about him. How is the dear little fellow & his still dearer Mother? I seem to have been separated from them an age already.

Do write me how you both are on the 2d. May to Caswell C. H. and after to Hillsb.

Ever & truly Yours, My Dearest.

Kiss my son and present my kind remembrance to the family. New Bern.

To Susan Washington Graham.   A.

Greensboro', April 29th, 1837.

My Dear Wife

The Court is over, & most of those who have been about me during the week are gone, and I am alone in my room. My situation would readily bring to mind, my absent wife and son, had not the receipt of Sister Eliza's very obliging letter, this afternoon, presented them in full view, in their own room, which I never can forget, and to which I would gladly be transported.

Both of my brethren, the Messrs. Morehead,[31] have invited me to spend the evening at their houses, but my difficulty in

---

[31] James Turner Morehead, and his elder brother, John Motley Morehead (1796-1866). The latter, a native of Virginia, was brought as an infant to North Carolina, was graduated at the university, studied law under Archibald D. Murphey, served in the commons from Rockingham, in 1821, and from Guilford, 1826-1827, and 1858. He was governor, 1841-1845, president of the Whig national convention, 1848, delegate to the peace conference, 1861, and a member of the Confederate provisional congress. Deeply interested in internal improvements, he did much to awaken the state on the subject, and he played a large part in the construction of the North Carolina Railroad.

walking has excused me, and, although I should have been hospitably entertained, I greatly prefer to commune, even at such a distance, with my "heart of hearts." For although I have nothing to
communicate, except that tenderest affection, which you know
you possess already, still it is pleasant to linger in giving it utterance, & to contemplate the kindred feeling with which it will
be received. I have had you both before my minds eye more
frequently of late than ever, & with joy look forward to the time
when I shall see you face to face. Pray take all precautions for
your speedy restoration and omit nothing which those of greater
experience shall recommend. I was somewhat uneasy on first seeing
a letter in the handwriting of Sister instead of your own, and was
truly rejoiced to find that no more serious cause for it existed
than your weakness. Please tender to Sister Eliza my sincerest
thanks for her favour and the assurance of my highest regard. I
regret however to hear that Mother has been again indisposed, as
well as Mary, Franklin and John, but am very happy that our
dear little fellow continues well, & is so quiet and good-natured
as to give his Mother but little trouble. In this latter quality may
he long continue! What think you now of his beauty? Whom does
he resemble? Were you a painter I should insist on a weekly fac-
simile of his features. He must excell "in every great & good
qualification" to comeup to the description I give of him.

I am as well as usual, and make daily application of the decoction, which Dr. W. recommended, but perceive no particular
effect from it as yet. I shall go in the morning to Wentworth,
Rockingham C. H. in company with Mr. Morehead; the distance
is 27 miles. I sent Joe off to Lincoln on Wednesday to take the
horses I have recently purchased, with directions to return to me
at Hillsboro', three weeks hence. We shall probably finish before
the end of next week at Rockingham, and if so I will go and stay
a day or two at the Springs, and thence to Caswell by the week
following.

I have just heard that the Revd. Mr. Kerr (Father of our
friend in Caswell) who has been a candidate for Congress in the
adjoining district in Va. has lost his election.

The accounts of the pressure in New York by our papers today
are not more favourable than heretofore. No one can predict
where these distresses are to end. Bro. James' late opponent Mr.
Newland has obtained an office in Wisconsin Ter. I suppose now
there will be no opposition.

I will write you again from Caswell, though you will hardly receive the letter untill two weeks hence. "Angels & ministers of grace defend you," my dearest.

Your Ever faithful & affectionate husband.

Kiss my son for me & Present my Love to all the family.
New Bern.

From Charles L. Hinton. [32]   U.

Raleigh, May 2th, 1837.

We are anxious to hear what move you are disposed to make in Orange with regard to a Candidate for Congress.

Yourself, Mangum, Waddell, and Gales have been spoken of here. Gales tells me he cannot, the sacrifice would be more than he can bear, we have no other person in this county that has any views that way—the Candidate must come from Orange. My own opinion is it must be you or Waddell, so far as regards our political friends we should be very willing to see Judge Mangum a Candidate, but the opposition have made such exertions for the last two or three years to render him odious in this county that it would require a great effort to appease their feelings; if however you should think it advisable to start Judge Mangum, we will do our best, some of his warmest friends concur with me in this view.

We have no choice between Waddell and yourself—one of you *must* offer.

In haste,
Very respectfully.

To Susan Washington Graham.   A.

Caswell C. H.,

May 8th, 1837.

Though late at night and I am much engaged, I cannot neglect to acknowledge the letter of my Dear Wife by the mail this evening, especially as it is a hallowed day of the month in our Cal-

---

[32] Charles Lewis Hinton (1793-1861), of Raleigh, educated at the university, member of the commons, 1821-1832; state senator, 1827-1830, 1833; state treasurer, 1839-1843, 1845-1852; an ardent Whig, and a devoted friend of Graham.

endar. I am truly delighted to hear from you, particularly that you are recovering your health and strength. . . .

I arrived here from Rockingham on yesterday in company with Mr. Poindexter.[33] We had rather an uninteresting week there and adjourned the Court on Friday. I had intended to have come to the Springs & staid in the interval but accepted the kind invitation of a friend to visit him on Saturday, & came thence next day.

Our acquaintances here are all well, and make many inquiries about our son. The dear little urchin, I wish I could see him. Does he grow much and have his eyes entirely recovered?

My knee continues *no worse.* I am applying the Leopard bane; I dont know whether with much benefit or not. The season continues yet quite cool, which operates against my recovery. And it is so exceedingly dry as greatly to impair the prospects of a good crop among the farmers.

I appeared today in defence of the tutoress who whipped her pupil, of whom, I believe I told you. She was again convicted but will appeal to the Supreme Court. The Boy Sneed will be tried on Thursday; there is a full docket & we shall be here all the week. . . . The pressure[34] is about to be felt heavily in this quarter by the negro traders & their sureties, who have large sums due to them in the South which they can't collect, and who have Bank debts due here.

* * * * *

Be assured, My Love, of the faithful devotion of Your
Affectionate Husband.

From James Graham.   U.

Rutherfordton, May 8th, 1837.

I received your letter of the 27th April five or six days since and I am pleased to learn you have a fine son and that Sister Susan is doing well. I regretted to learn that you propose making *a short trip* to the North. Your lameness requires patience and perseverance, and if you go to the North for Medical aid set no limit to your return, but make a full and fair experiment of such means as may be prescribed. I think if Medical aid should not prove successful you ought to try the virtues of the Warm or

---

[33] Either Henry P. Poindexter, of Surry, member of the commons, 1818, 1820, 1840, state senate, 1825, or John F. Poindexter, of Stokes, member of the commons, 1832-1836, 1844, state senate, 1846; both distinguished lawyers.
[34] The allusion is, of course, to the panic of 1837, then in progress.

Rather Hot Springs of Virginia in August or the 1st of Sept. I think too if you would set on a table 2 or 3 times a day and swing or exercise your lame limb, the muscles and flesh of that leg would not shrink, but expand and become invigorated by exertion and use. a little *regular exercise with moderation and care* would help you.

If you go to the North I think you ought to take Sister Susan with you and go in the Stage and Rail Road. you would thereby save time and that is the common mode of conveyance in that quarter.

I have no opposition as yet and I do not know that I will have any. Gaither,[35] before I got into the district, attended 3 Courts to ascertain his prospects, but I am informed he was not encouraged and it is now said he has abandoned it. My friends were more steadfast. Gaither and his friends think I am not strong and *bitter enough* against the administration. Willis [36] and the Nullies think Nullification the *sine qua non*. Edmonston [37] and the Vanites think I do not support the administration so strong as I ought. I am apprehensive they will all give up the contest after counting the chances and the cost.

If Haywood does run in your district do start Mangum against him. I think he can beat him if he shows the people his connection with the Bank and his profits from it and so on.

I presume we shall have but little popular excitement this Summer. The pressure begins even here to be felt; all *confidence* is destroyed, and enterprise is paralized and checked. Woe be unto the man who is largely involved in Debt. If I have no opposition I will try and go to the Virginia Springs after the Election is over. Judge Pearson is quite popular with the Bar and People. He will make a first rate Judge. This is the 2d week of Rutherford Court, then comes Burke 2 weeks, and then the county courts begin on the second Monday in June at Marion and continue untill the 4th week in July at Morganton. I will attend them . . .

---

[35] Burgess S. Gaither (1807-1892), a native of Iredell, educated at the University of Georgia, a lawyer of Burke, who was active and ambitious in Whig politics. He was clerk of the constitutional convention of 1835, served in the state senate, 1840, 1844 (president, 1844), and was solicitor, 1844-1852. He was defeated for congress by Thomas L. Clingman, but served in Confederate congress, 1862-1865.

[36] Possibly Robert H. Willis, of Lincoln.

[37] Ninian Edmondson, of Haywood, member of the commons, 1821, 1823-1826, 1828-1833, state senate, 1834-1835.

To Susan Washington Graham.   A.

Hillsboro', May 20th, 1837.

My Dear Wife

Your very kind letter of the 9th. was brought to me at Person on Monday last by my friend Mr. Norwood. It was truly gratifying to learn that My Dear Susan and the pledge of our mutual love were both in good health, as well as to have the assurance renewed, that I was not forgotten by that bosom in which is garnered up almost all my affections. I have been a delinquent my Dearest in our correspondence of late, but you have by no means been infected by my example.

I returned from Person on the day before yesterday having been absent four weeks, during the two last of which I have been quite busy. The weather has been so chilly & changeable that in the last six or eight days I have contracted a violent cold, which rendered me exceedingly hoarse & uncomfortable. I have been greatly relieved by losing a large quantity of blood from my nose on yesterday, and am better today than I have been for a week. But for this, I should have had some difficulty in detaining myself here, untill the end of the County Court next week. Indeed I feel every disposition to break off for New Bern even now.

I don't believe the decoction of Leopard's bane has been of any advantage to my knee, though it is evidently improved by the change of the weather, from cold to warm, & but for the extreme severity of the spring, I believe it might have been well.

* * * * *

I travelled around this circuit with my Sulkey in perfect safety. My expectation still is to go to the North from New Bern, but am not fully resolved to do so. We must consult on it when I come, and determine what is best.

I met Judge Nash in the street yesterday, & learned that Miss Mary Simpson had come up with him. He says Miss Julia B. told him, you had "a fine boy the very image of his Father, except that he has blue eyes." I am sorry to learn from your letter that the poor little fellow has been sick, and has become lean. I have bragged him against every Boy from Dan to Beersheba, that I have seen or heard of among my friends in my travels.

* * * * *

I received a letter from Bro. James a few days since, who sends all love and congratulations to you, on the birth & name of our son. He has no opposition for Congress, and expects now that he will have none.

I am pleased to see Brother Bryan taking so conspicuous a place in the proceedings of the Merchants of New York; the distress seems to continue unabated, and must gradually reach every section of the country.

I perceive in the Raleigh papers a notice of the death of Mr. G. P. Devereux [38] at Suffolk in Va.

* * * * *

From Weston R. Gales.   U.

Raleigh, 23d May, 1837.

I see by the morning's Standard, that Montgomery has taken the fields. The Whigs are exceedingly anxious to bring out opposition, and all concur in the belief that your election would be a matter of course, if you would suffer your friends to use your name. You could get, I think, 800 votes in Wake; and I promise you, if you will consent to run, that I will attend every Muster in the county, to aid you. With you as our candidate, success *is certain;* with any other, we may be triumphant, but it will be hard work.

It is proper however, I should say, that rumor reports that you will, under no circumstances run. If this be your unalterable determination, then we must look out for some body else; for it will be monstrous, in such times as these, to permit that tool, Montgomery, to be elected.

It is perhaps known to you that my name has been spoken of, but my circumstances in life would render my entering into the Canvass suicidal, and I must positively decline the honor, whatever might be my chance of success. The only other names I have heard suggested, are Mr. Waddell, Mr. Mangum and Charles L. Hinton, of this county. I know not what the feelings of the two first are on the subject. Mr. Hinton, I know, has no inclination, but rather a positive disinclination to take the field, but I know him so well, that I feel almost certain he would consent to run, rather than Montgomery should walk over the course. In Wake County, I think he would reduce the Doctor's vote to Zero, and if Orange and Person did pretty well, he could be elected easily.

---

[38] George Pollock Devereux.

Waddell would get a much better vote in Wake than Mangum, because the latter has been so much abused here by Haywood, *ex parte,* that many persons dislike him who can give no better reason for it, than "I do not like thee, Dr. Fell."

Knowing this is the week of your Co. Court, and that you will probably come to some conclusion on the subject, I write this hasty line, *currente calamo* to say that you are the choice of Wake, if you will run; and, if not, that we are prepared cordially to support any man Orange may start, and to re-iterate my determination, from a conviction of the propriety of my course, not to be a candidate under any circumstances.

To Susan Washington Graham.   A.

New York, June 14th, 1837.

My dear Susan

I have the happiness to inform you that I arrived here to dinner today at the City Hotel & this afternoon came up to the Dr's[39] to deliver my letter, with the intention of returning again to the Hotel, and coming up tomorrow, but the Dr. and Madame have taken possession of me outright, and detained me at once.

I found them, their little daughter & Mr. Bryan quite well; the last is quite disappointed that Mrs. B. did not come with me. I have taken tea with them in company with Mr. Boyd, since which the Dr. has gone to visit patients, and the rest to hear a discourse on the great schism which has recently taken place in the Presbyterian Church in the U. S., and I am left alone to commune with my dear wife, and son; would that they were with me! I would ask nothing else for the present to be completely happy. I hope our darling son has entirely recovered from his cold, and that he will continue to grow and improve in health. Miss Elizabeth has been presented to me this afternoon, & bears in many respects a striking resemblance to her Aunt Susan. Mrs. W. kindly says to me that when I wish something to remind me of Susan that I must look on her daughter, to which I replied with not more of gallantry than truth, that if I intended to remain long in the City, I had better contrive something to make me think of her less often than I would naturally do.

---

[39] Dr. James Augustus Washington (1803-1847), Mrs. Graham's elder brother, a highly successful physician. He married Anna White Constable (1813-1894).

After leaving New Bern on Saturday I proceeded to Washington to breakfast, where I fell in company with Mr. Patton a merchant of Philadelphia an acquaintance of my family, and we travelled thence together. At Plymouth we took the steamboat at ten oclock at night for the railroad. While waiting for the Boat, who should arrive but my friend Outlaw, gallanting a buxom little lady in black—and do you think "the crittur" was not married—aye & had two children—this comes of taking a widow with a family ready provided; they were just one year behind us having been married on the 7th and were on their way to Tennessee her native country, on a visit, by way of Baltimore and the Ohio river. We travelled on together as far as that City, and I found her quite a cheerful and agreeable comrade on the journey, though I could not restrain a smile at the awkardness with which the old fellow nursed the children on board of the Boat. Her maiden name was Turner, a niece of Genl. Bryan formerly of Granville; a few years ago she married a Mr. Ryan of Bertie, and removed there with him from Tennessee, by whom she bore two children. All jesting apart, I hope Outlaw has done well, he deserves a good wife if upright character & pure honor furnishes any claim to such an one.

I slept but little on the Sound as it was rough, and reached the railroad in good time. dined at Portsmouth and took passage up the Bay at 3 P. M. In Hampton Roads we were met by a steamer from Charleston, which overloaded us with passengers, so much that there were not berths sufficient for more than half of the passengers. I slept a little on two chairs and a couple of pillows which my friend Mr. Patton was kind enough to furnish me. We met the Philadelphia boat coming out of Baltimore and reached that City on Monday afternoon, spent Tuesday there, & came over today. Young Mr. Hooper of Chapel Hill was on board the Boat from Baltimore and accompanied me thence to this City, on his way to West Point as a Cadet. I spent yesterday evening at the house of Mr. Campbell [40] a merchant of Philadelphia formerly of N. C., with whom I had some business, and who obliged me greatly by his kindness. My purpose in stopping a day at that City was to consult the Physicians in regard to my knee, about which I had almost forgotten to write anything, though it is the main subject of my visit to the North. At the request of Mr. Campbell I called in Dr. McClellan,[41] Prof. of Surgery in the new

[40] Hugh Campbell.
[41] Dr. George McClellan (1796-1847), famous anatomist and surgeon, founder of Jefferson Medical College, native of Connecticut, graduate of Yale, a pioneer in making clinical work part of the training of medical students. He was the father of General George Brinton McClellan, U. S. A., of Civil War fame.

School of Phila., and was greatly pleased with his opinion and the knowledge he evinced of his profession.

Dr. McClellan after a rigid examination assures me that there is no derangement of any thing about the joint of the knee, and that the limb is only to be cured of debility to be entirely well; this he thinks would be greatly promoted by sea-bathing, friction, etc. I was so well satisfied with this opinion that I did not call in any other physician at Philapa. In the morning I will have it examined by Dr. Aug. I inquired at Norfolk for Dr. Sweet & learned that he was not there. A man from Con'cut with whom I travelled told me that old Dr. Sweet died about 12 mos. ago, that he has a brother & sons who are bone-setters but are not reputed to be of equal skill, with him. I am satisfied that they could render me no assistance now.

*   *   *   *   *

New Bern.

From Giles Mebane.   U.

Roxboro.

June 20th, 1837.

When I saw you last in Hillsborough I said to you if any thing should happen of importance I would write you a few lines. Being at Person Court I have heard several interesting conversations upon the Congressional election in our district. There is but one opinion as to the proper & only infallible course to pursue to ensure the complete defeat of our late representative. I have received the strongest assurances that you can get a handsome majority in this county over Dr. Montgomery & never come into the county during the canvass. Messrs McGehee & Barnet [42] most confidently expect that with your name & such a circular as you may write they can and will give you a fair majority in Person. With a majority here can you not be easily elected? We do not expect your presence. Give us your name & a most excellent circular, excusing your absence by your unfortunate lameness. Let the circular be written and printed if you will by thousands where you are and sent on forthwith. This is all we desire, & will you not do this for the pleasure of your friends & a seat in the

---

[42] John Barnett, a prominent Whig, sheriff of Person County for many years, who had been in the state senate the previous session.

next *eventful* Congress? Dr. Montgomery will vainly attempt to ride into Congress upon a grand National Government Bank— Such a one as will unite "sword & purse" in the hands of the Executives—brake down all State Banks and State Governments & establish a practicul *National* Monarchy. He is in favour of such an Institution; has committed himself.

A consultation will be held this week at Chapel Hill at the Commencement to get up a candidate. Mr. McGehee will be there from this county. You will be written to by others. A large meeting could be got up to nominate you, but it is thought best not to call it; I should very much deprecate your being nominated & brought out by any meeting any where. I want your name only to be sent out by yourself in obedience to earnest and general solicitation. I will distribute 200 of your circulars in the Hawfields & beat Montgomery at Mason Hall.

Sheppard [43] is doing well in his district & will I think be re-elected.

Our Friend Sam Holt [44] is a candidate for the county court clerkship. Taylor is in a State of anxiety on the subject.

Person. 14 writs returnable at this term of the Court. There will be 40 returns in Caswell. I am not doing any thing myself in the business. Somewhat inclined to *take a hand* with Taylor and Sam Holt—being an *excellent scribe*.

I hope your knee is getting well. If so you may be with us towards the close of the campaign.

Depend upon it, a political change is going on, and now is the time for honest intelligent men (Whigs) to unite and save the country from corruption and everlasting bankruptcy. Judge Mangum certainly cannot be brought out; The trial has been made. You have the best excuse in the world for not electioneering, and committing your election to friends and patriots.

Write me at Mason Hall.

---

[43] It is impossible to say to whom he refers. There were in Congress at this time, from North Carolina, Augustine H. Shepperd, and Charles Biddle Shepard (1807-1843). The latter had just succeeded William Biddle Shepard. It probably refers to Charles, since he was in the midst of his first session. A native of New Bern, he was a graduate of the university, and had served in the commons, 1831-1832. He served in congress until 1841.

[44] Dr. Samuel Lockhart Holt (1807-1872), of Orange, a physician, who was a university graduate in the class below Graham's.

To Susan Washington Graham.   A.

New York, June 22nd, 1837.

Although I am in possession of but little that is new, as this is the regular mail day, I take my seat to communicate with my dearest Susan. The Dr. and family are quite well. I think I am improving much, still continuing the process of bathing, rubbing and salting, and walking every day a mile or two with no assistance but my cane, and sometimes not using that at all. My knee does not suffer from it, but the muscles of the foot have been so long disused that they become sore and cause me to limp. But I continue my walks notwithstanding.

The weather has been quite cool and wet ever since my arrival, which has been less favourable to my recovery. I am able to bear however so much more than I could, or thought I could when I left you that I fancy myself almost well. If you do not conclude to come on, I shall be in New Bern at all events by the middle of July, as the course of treatment I am pursuing can be applied at home almost as well as here. . . . I perceive by the Raleigh papers that the Govr. has convened his Council to advise with them, as to calling the Legislature, and am anxious to hear (as I hope to do in a day or two) what has been the result. I should dislike very much to be detained at Raleigh several weeks, independantly of being called away from here before I wish to leave.

* * * * *

. . . I went on Sunday with the Dr. to hear his clergyman Dr. Skinner,[45] but will not fail, according to your wish, to hear Mr. Williams[46] before I leave. . . .

Mr. Bryan has dissolved his partnership and is winding up the affairs of the firm, but intends, I believe, to commence business again. We will go South soon to meet Mrs. B. at Portsmouth.

The Poor of this City are suffering greatly for want of food, being thrown out of employment by the hardness of the times. There are but few persons here from the South either on business

---

[45] The Rev. Thomas H. Skinner (1791-1871), a widely known Presbyterian minister, and author. Born in North Carolina, a graduate of Princeton, he studied law, and then became a minister. He was prominent in the revival of the Union Theological Seminary.

[46] The Rev. William R. Williams (1804-1885), of New York, a graduate of Columbia, a successful lawyer for some years, he then became a Baptist minister. A man of great learning and scholarship, he acquired a great reputation as a preacher, particularly with cultured people, who delighted in his "weighty thought expressed in glowing periods." He was one of the founders of the Rochester Theological Seminary.

or pleasure. Both theatres are open, however, and a third will be ere long. I purchased on yesterday Bulwer's "Athens and the Athenians," but it has not been sent home as yet.

Do you find any leisure for reading; I hope you may, though your maternal duties are so constant, and I found the heat at New Bern so intense that I presume you can have but little either of time or inclination for books.

                    *   *   *   *   *

From John W. Norwood.   U.

Hillsborough, June 23, 1837.

McGehee and Barnett this week over at Person made me promise to write to you by express mail asking your consent to be run as a candidate for Congress. They say they have made extensive inquiries and are perfectly satisfied that you could get a majority in Person, there is there, they say, a general backing out or standing still by the party. Even Old Sandy Cunningham[47] has come over and says he will go for you. According to Barnetts account of the matter there is no one in Person who would take an active lead for Montgomery and his project of a Treasury Bank, and the fact of the removal his negroes into Florida will prevent him from exercising much influence personally. Barnett himself says he will take the field and attend every meeting of the people.

I had no opportunity myself of discussing this matter. Mangum says he was told by many intelligent persons that you could get a majority in Person.

You know more of Wake than I do, and I can add little to your knowledge of the state of things in Orange; Sam Holt is a candidate for the County Court Clerkship, which will cause a full election and Turrentine[48] says you can get a majority, without being here, and a large one if you can come on some time before the election. The desire that you should consent to be run is certainly increasing. Some days ago Col Jones said to me that some of your friends had serious thoughts of starting you without your knowledge, and wished to know what I thought of it. I told him I thought there ought to be a certainty of success before such a step could be justifiable.

---

[47] Alexander Cunningham, an elderly man of considerable influence in Person County.
[48] Sheriff of Orange.

Mangum has been nominated but will not consent to run.

If you agree to "go it" say so in a circular forthwith inclosed to me and we will see to the printing and circulation of it in Orange and Person. As to Wake, of course you would send a copy to Gales, or some other active person there, as no time is to be lost.

If you can come back by the 20 July your success I think would be certain.

* * * * *

Nothing of interest in the way of news. Judge Strange is here, he says there will be no National Bank—all Banks deserve to die —and people should come back to wooden spoons again. His speech is said to have been but common. The Imagination his subject.

From M. McGehee.[49]   U.

Person County, N. C.

27th June, 1837.

I have no doubt but you have been informed ere this that your name will be run in this Congressional district as a candidate to represent us in the house of representatives in the next Congress of the U. S.

I wish to assure you that so far as this county is concerned I think we have not entered upon it with out an investigation the result of which has been favourable and I hope warrented us in the course we have taken in common with the other Counties in our district. Altho we have not your assurance that you will serve if elected yet we go upon *faith,* that no citizen would under existing circumstances of our suffering Country refuse to serve if elected.

As your name is now before the people it now becomes our duty to adopt such means as will best suit the purpose and I wish others whome I have consulted are clearly of the opinion that you ought to write a circular as early as suits your convenience (for the earlier the better) and let them have as general a circulation as posabile both by publication in the news papers and by directing them to every voter in the district if possible.

I will further suggest to you the propriety of your addressing a private letter to my neighbour Alexander Cunningham, Esqr.,

---

[49] See note to letter from M. McGehee, dated December 13, 1834.

directed to Cunninghams Store which is my post office and should
be pleased to hear from you when ever convenient.

I can not close this letter without remarking that so far as I
have ascertained the feeling of the people they would feel indignant if you were in your circular to goad them for their blind
idolatry to a fretful old man, but it should be temperate and re-
spectfull and addressed to the patriotism of of your voters.

To Susan Washington Graham.   A.

New York, June 28th, 1837.

* * * * *

I am pursuing the same course of treatment respecting my
lameness, that I described to you heretofore. My foot has become quite sore in the instep so as to give me some pain in walking, but I still travel about considerably every day with my cane.
I have some thought of going the latter part of this week to Saratoga, and visiting on the Mohawk a Dr. Sweet (who seems to have
branched into half a dozen personages in New England and New
York since I left home.) A gentleman from Utica whom I met at
Mr. Codwise's at Tea a few evenings ago told me of several surprising cures of diseased limbs, which he had known to be cured
by this individual, whom he represents to belong to the Connecticut family.

I called today on Bishop Ives[50] who is under the direction of a
Surgeon here, but did not find him him in. . . .

I received two letters today from Hillsborough written at the
request of numerous friends in Orange and Person, urging me to
become a Candidate for Congress. I have not written a reply as
yet, & hardly know what it should be. I still think however, that
I cannot consent. It is not desirable that I should be elected, and
do not believe that it could be accomplished unless I were in the
district during the campaign. I shall probably hear further in a
day or two, and will give a definite answer.

---

[50] Levi Silliman Ives (1797-1867), a native of Connecticut, graduate of Hamilton
College, who was Episcopal bishop of North Carolina from 1831 to 1852. He was
later to become the cause of much controversy in his diocese, which ended with
his taking a leave of absence to recover from the strain caused by the accusations
that he leaned towards Catholicism, which he had formally denied just previous to
his departure, and his immediate submission to the Pope when he reached Rome.

Farewell, my wife—"thou art sweet as the smile when fond lovers meet" and "soft as their parting tear."

Kiss my Son and continue to Love me.

[P. S.] I went last Sunday morning to hear Mr. Williams preach & was quite pleased with his sermon; in the afternoon I went to hear Dr. Skinner, arriving in the morning before service commenced I went by mistake into the Sunday School on the lower floor, where Mrs. W. tells me my dear wife was formerly a teacher. . . .

To Susan Washington Graham.   A.

New York, July 3rd, 1837.

To My Susan

I am greatly disappointed my dearest in receiving no letter from you, before I set out still further to increase the distance between us. Your letter of the 14th ult. four days after I left home. is all that I have had since our separation. In a letter received by Mr. Bryan the day before he left us, it was stated that no letter from me had then reached New Bern. If so, you will have full employment for some afternoon, for I have written, I think twice every week since my arrival, commencing with the night I set foot on this island. The mails must be exceedingly deranged, or the post masters very negligent.

I am continuing the same course of treatment with my knee, but am not sure that it is much improved. This day I set out for Saratoga, and will probably go to see Dr. Sweet who is not far from there. Bishop Ives informed me on Friday that Dr. Sweet was in the City, and I immediately went in search of him, but he had just gone in the Boat for Albany. He was returning from Philadelphia and staid but a day here, will return in the course of two weeks on way to Delaware. I could see him then but wish to drink the Saratoga waters for a few days, and am impatient to return to the "jewels of my heart." My present course of treatment I can apply as well at home with my Dear Wifes assistance as I can here. Dr. Washington thinks that the secret of Sweet's skill consists in frictions, and that his bone setting is in most cases deceptive. He advises me to see him, but I will not suffer any violent operation from him without the approbation of a physician. Bishop I. is under the care of Surgeons here, and also consulted Sweet, two of them concur in opinion with Sweet that his shoulder is yet out of place, the others hold the contrary. He intends to yield to the latter for a short time longer & unless relieved will submit to the remedy of Sweet. He concurs in the present mode of treatment which he says (by violent frictions) will relax the muscles and shew that the shoulder is not reduced; this Sweet relieved Miss Sneed of N. Bern but is not the same who operated on Mr. Collins.[51] I have some curiosity but can't say that I have great faith in his remedies.

I hope to return to the City in a week from this time, and will let you know the result, if not by letter, in my own proper person, in a week more. Unless you make your personal appearance here, or write to me that you will come soon.

I have written to my friends in Hillsborough expressing the hope that they will not nominate me for Congress, and presume that will end the matter. Success in my absence cannot be expected, and if elected my plans so far as formed, would be wholly deranged.

* * * * *

Since I commenced writing I have received a letter from Person stating that my name is now before the people as a Candidate for Congress, But still hope that the other counties will not fall in with the arrangement. I feel however the more anxious to get home in consequence of it, & know what is going on. The Dr. & Mrs. W. send love to you; they seem so happy with their little "bairn" that I long to lay eyes on my Dear Jos. again.

Present my love to all, and believe me yours in truest affection. New Bern.

To Susan Washington Graham.   A.

Balston Spa, July 5th, 1837.

My Dear Wife

I promised to write you as soon as I reached New York again, but as I am alone in my room this evening & in a strange place, I will earlier indulge myself in the pleasure of communicating with you, the more especially as I have material enough for an interesting letter to one who loves me so truly. I left N. Y. on the evening

---

[51] It is impossible to determine whether the reference is to Josiah Collins (1768-1839), of Edenton, a native of England, merchant, manufacturer, and planter, or to his son Josiah Collins (1808-1863), of Edenton and of "Somerset Place," Washington County, planter and active business man.

of Monday the 3rd. in the Steamboat for Albany, reaching the latter place to breakfast next morning. I there learned that Dr. Sweet had left the day before for his residence. I proceeded by railroad to Schenectady, where I was informed that he lived about fifteen miles from there & near the railroad on which I was. Accordingly I kept on, & found him at Amsterdam near which is his residence. He accompanied me to my room at a Hotel and before I commenced undressing pronounced my "hip out of place;" this I knew to be untrue. He however insisted & said, contrary to the evidence of my senses, that the thigh of the injured limb was longer than the other. The injury, he said, was in the hip, but the knee and ancle joints were both "twisted." My confidence in him was of course, at once destroyed. He said that the remedy for my case was to roll the bones into joint after bathing the limb with a mixture which he had. I inquired if it would be painful or would require me to be confined for a while. He said the pain would not be very great, and there would be no necessity for confinement, that he would begin by resetting the hip, and thence go downwards. I was satisfied the idea of setting bones, as he described, was mere nonsense, and if there was any virtue in his application, it must consist in his bathing and rubbing. However I had taken the trouble to visit him and had a moderately strong hip, I concluded to submit to his experiment, intending to stop him if the pain should become too great. He heated his mixture consisting of sassafras oil, alcohol, etc., slightly, and rubbed the limb, and after turning it about in a few contortions which gave no pain (or very slight) he pronounced that the hip was in place. He then went to the knee, bent the leg inwardly untill it was somewhat painful, and then turned the arch and foot in divers ways, cracked all the toe joints, and pulled the other leg, saying it was contracted, & it was necessary to bring them both to the same length. He wetted bandages in his mixture and put them around the hips knee and ancle. The first being, as he said, to keep the hips in place. He gave me two vials; one containing "essences of cordials" to be mixed with alcohol and salt, for bathing the limb, twice a day, and the other "mixture of oils to relax stiffened muscles." I need not say to you that I regard his whole procedure as the merest quackery, and although the injury under which I labour is a matter of most serious concern, it required all my philosophy to keep from laughing in his face; that he may be able to set bones when broken or disjointed I have no doubt, and that his course of frictions with stimulating liquids may be beneficial in restoring the circulation is also probable. But seeing "with how little wisdom the world is gulled" he makes a dislocation of every case, and thereby magnifies his skill. He is the same who cured Miss Sneed, as he told me, but not Mrs. Cox, and is evidently much gratified at the extension of his fame. He goes far and near from New England to the Mississippi in his business. I would not detract from his professional reputation, which is high with many intelligent persons here as well as elsewhere. But give you the particulars of my interview and observation, not desiring to impair the faith of others, in which, not infrequently has been their cure, as I believe. He advises exercise, rubbing with his alcoholic mixture, & occasionally with the marrow of the bone of a ham, these I shall follow, as I have no doubt of their propriety.

Getting through with him, I hired a conveyance to this place, which I reached yesterday at sunset. Finding here Mr. J. Collins of N. C. & forming other acquaintances I believe I will not go to Saratoga but return to N. York in a day or two. Dr. Sweet visited me here today, and thinks every thing in a good way. I am glad to think I am not injured by his operation, & hope the residue may be serviceable. I have been thus minute, because I knew you would wish to know what was his mode of treatment.

How is my Dear Son? Kiss him for me and say Father will come to see him soon, probably by the last of next week.

My Ever Dear Susan, Adieu.

[P S.] I expect Dr. Aug.[52] will have a hearty laugh at my expense when I relate to him my interview with Sweet. There is pleasant little company here. With my Wife and son I don't know where I should be happier. The Water is very good.

I would be glad if you would prepare to leave New Bern soon after I arrive. The summer is advancing, and it may be unsafe to remain much longer. Mr. & Mrs. Bryan will hardly have left for New York before my return. I recd. your last letter the day before I left the City. There is great delay in the Mails. Can we not prevail on Sister Eliza to go with us to Hillsboro' if Mother comes North?

---

[52] Dr. Washington.

Editorials on Congressional nomination.

Raleigh Star.

July 12, 1837.

We are highly gratified to learn from the subjoined slip from the office of the *Hillsborough Recorder,* that WILLIAM A. GRAHAM, Esq., of Orange, has, in compliance with the pressing solicitations of his fellow citizens in many parts of the district, consented to become a candidate to represent this district in the next Congress. It will be seen that he has been nominated by two public meetings held in this county; and the nomination will, we doubt not, be enthusiastically responded to in every quarter of the district. It has already been hailed with heartfelt joy and satisfaction whereever the information has been received.

Mr. Graham is one of the most talented, upright and patriotic sons of North Carolina. He possesses the highest qualifications for public station. The marked ability and faithfulness with which he has represented the people of Orange in the State Legislature, prove him worthy of any trust; and if the people of this district would be represented in the national councils by a man who would reflect honor upon them and upon the State, in whose judgment, knowledge and principles they could safely confide; who would command respect and influence in Congress; who would, in his able and efficient labors in that body, ever scorn to play the partisan or the demagogue; and who would pursue, with singleness of purpose, and unflinching firmness and energy, the public interest, if, we say, the people would be represented by such an individual, they will rush to the polls in August, and bestow their suffrages upon WILLIAM A. GRAHAM, of Orange. Let those who know him best, be active in urging his claims, and let those who are less informed on the subject, inquire into his character. It will bear the most rigid scrutiny. Let them examine. The tongue of slander dare not, cannot say aught against it. In public & in private he has lived above reproach. If the people will open their eyes to the dangers which threaten them—suffer themselves to be convinced of the imperious necessity of calling into public service, in the present emergency, the best talents, virtue and patriotism of the country, his election is certain.

Let every sincere friend of our Republican institutions do his duty.

Hillsborough Recorder

July 14, 1837.

William A. Graham. The nomination of this gentleman, in opposition to Dr. Montgomery, has been eagerly responded to in various portions of this county, and we find there is a fixed determination among the whigs to strain every nerve to secure his election. They know that he is "honest, capable, and faithful to the Constitution," and that the times require sound hearts and strong heads in the Councils of the Nation. Mr. Graham, it is true, is at the North, where he has gone to seek surgical advice for an injury received by him last summer. He will probably return some time this month, in time to visit some portions of the District. But suppose he does not, and that he is unable to address any portion of the people? This constitutes no reason why the whigs should not rally as heartily in his support, as though he were here, contesting every inch of ground. As a party, the whigs go for *principles,* not *men,* and they have selected Mr. Graham because he is identified with their principles, and because, present or absent, he is the same inflexible Patriot, the same dignified gentleman, the same enlightened Legislator, and the same pure, incorruptible citizen. No advantage can be taken of this absence to circulate slanderous reports against him, because the blamelessness of his life defies these ordinary weapons of partizan warfare. We therefore, say to our whig friends in Orange and Person, do your duty, and, in the hour of trial, Wake will not prove recreant. If ever there was a time when the lover of his country had cause for exertion, now is the time. The Whigs of Pennsylvania have just set us a glorious example; let us not follow, but eclipse it. If we fail, we can still console ourselves with having done our duty, but, if we triumph, we shall achieve a victory which will inspirit the friends of the Constitution throughout the Union.

Acceptance of Nomination for Congress.[53]

July 14, 1837

We are authorized by a letter just received from WILLIAM A. GRAHAM, esq., to announce that he has yielded to the earnest solicitations of his friends, and has become a candidate to represent the Freemen of this Congressional District in the next Con-

[53] *Hillsboro Recorder,* July 14th., 1837.

gress of the United States. Mr. Graham, it is well known, is now laboring under the effects of an injury, received some months since, and has found it necessary to visit the North for his restoration, and is now in the city of New York. Mr. G. is expected to return some time before the election, and a circular expressive of his views will be published in a few days.

The circumstances under which this worthy gentleman has consented to become a candidate, require that his friends should be vigilant and active in his behalf, and what his sterling merits cannot effect, they should strive, with weapons of truth to carry. It is supposed that, with proper exertion, a majority will be obtained for him in Wake and Person; and if he can *divide* with the Dr. in Orange, (for the honor of the county we could hope for a majority,) the result must be favorable to the friends of reform.

Our country is now writhing under the effects of an 'experiment' upon the very vitals of commerce and trade—we mean the currency. The nostrum administered in its once healthy state has but reduced it to the sad condition of the unfortunate Italian. And shall we permit folly and inexperience further to experiment upon the depreciated and wasted constitution? By the distress which has been brought upon thousands of our merchants and farmers of the North and West and South-west by the wretched condition of the unemployed mechanics and manufacturers, by the sufferings of the destitute laborers, who have been deprived of the means of obtaining daily subsistence; let us conjure you to discountenance the operatives of quacks and impostors; and fly to that which wisdom would prescribe, and which our own experience has proved to be perfectly adapted to our wants. Let this district, then, assist in the glorious work of expulsion; let us drive the experimentalists from their work of death, and supplant them by men of tried wisdom and virtue. Mr. Graham's talents and worth are well known to the people of the district, and what we might say would fall far short of his real merits. We all know that he has wisdom to discern our interest, and we do know that he has honesty to strive for it.

Then let us be vigilant and active. The honor of the district calls for it—the interest of the county requires it—and our own individual interest strenuously demands it.

Campaign Circular.

July 25, 1837.

To the Freemen of Wake, Orange, and Person Counties.[54]

Fellow Citizens: I take this method of offering my services as a candidate to represent you in the House of Representatives of the next Congress. Many of you were pleased to request this at a much earlier period, and but for a necessity which I deemed absolute that I should be absent from the District, during the greater part of the summer, I would, though with great reluctance, have yielded to this invitation. Knowing and approving that custom which has long prevailed, and which requires the candidates for public station to appear in person before the people, and exhibit their views of public affairs before the election, and being unable on my part to comply with it, I left home supposing that all thought of my nomination had been abandoned. I have since learned however, that my fellow citizens in various parts of the District many of whom I have not the honor of a personal acquaintance, have with the knowledge of my absence insisted upon presenting my name to the people. For this generous manifestation of their confidence I entertain the liveliest gratitude, and should I be the choice of the District will endeavor to repay it by faithful and devoted service. Whilst I have no disposition to intrude on the public attention I am not insensible I trust to any of the duties of a citizen and do not feel at liberty to withhold my assent from the offer which has been so feelingly made. Whether it will prove acceptable to the majority with whom rests the election must remain to be determined so far as I am concerned by the unbiased suffrages of the voters themselves.

The late period which I returned to the state allows me no time for canvassing the District even if I were capable in any degree of affecting public opinion. The present condition of our financial affairs is well calculated to awaken anxiety and call for the most serious and patient attention from every citizen: not as partisans with minds already made up, but as patriots desiring nothing so much as the welfare of the country. Our public monies amounting to many million dollars have been paid into Banks which are unable or unwilling to repay the Government. No portion of it at present is repaid in gold and silver and much it is feared will never be repaid at all. Bank notes, which constitute by far the largest portion of our currency are no longer convertible into specie. Exchanges are destroyed so that it is difficult if not impossible to make remittances from one part to another of our country, to carry on the necessary commerce between them and the foreign nations. Many of our merchants and other citizens both the judicious and prudent as well as the reckless and speculating have suddenly and unexpectedly both to themselves and others become insolvent. Pecuniary confidence between man and man has been greatly abridged and in many places destroyed. The great staple productions of the country have fallen in price and agricultural as well as mechanical labor meets with insufficient reward. Our immediate section of country from its interior position as well as other causes is happily exempt in a great measure from the calamities which oppress others; but no section can long escape unless a remedy be speedily applied; and every section is interested in the safe keeping of the public monies, the soundness of the circulating medium, the facilities of domestic trade, and the prosperity of our foreign commerce.

I shall not attempt to trace the causes of these things or to censure any as agents in their production. The evils are of sufficient moment to call for the union of all patriotic minds to remove them: suffice it to say that whatever may have been the origin of the disease, the remedy (so far as remedy is possible) can be looked for only from the general government. Accordingly the President has convened Congress at an early date. But what shall Congress do? How can they best provide for the collection and safe keeping of the public treasure: for equalizing exchanges and reviving commerce, for making bank paper, so far as it circulates equal to gold and silver or else to cease from circulation entirely. These are questions for the whole American people. Shall it be by the destruction of all the banks? Congress can do this if it would. The State Legislature claim the power to allow and to establish banks under a great variety of modifications, and no one of the 26 as far as I know has failed to exercise it. Shall it be by the issue of treasury drafts redeemable with gold and silver at the public treasury? I do not perceive how that would better the exchanges, or the qualities of the bank paper of the state. It failed also as a measure of finance when tried by Mr. Dallas the Secretary of the Treasury under Mr. Madison. He therefore withdrew his objections to the incorporation of a National Bank and recommended its establishment. Shall it be by a bank to be carried on by the Government on its own fund between the times of their collection and disbursement?

This would be found difficult in practice and would so greatly enlarge the powers of the executive as to give it undue weight in the Government.

Whether the President will recommend to Congress any specific plan of relief, I know not. Should he do so, it will be entitled to deliberate and impartial consideration. I regret that it is not now before the country, that I might in this communication signify my approval or dissent; on a subject upon which those with better means of information and longer versed in fiscal affairs appear to be at a loss. I must needs speak with diffidence; and but for your right to know even the inclination of my mind, I might without impropriety be silent until every plan was fully developed. As yet, however, I perceive no safer guide than experience: that a National Bank both that chartered under Gen. Washington, and under Mr. Madison, was highly beneficial in collecting and transmitting the public monies and in equalizing exchanges: that after the first few years of their existence their paper was equal to gold and silver in all parts of the Union, and in many foreign countries, thereby preventing the exportation of specie; and that the latter contributed greatly, if it did not solely cause the resumption of specie payments by the State Banks, then, as now, almost universally suspended, I believe are facts demonstrated by our history—these were benefits. It was said on the other hand that they were dangerous to liberty and guilty of improper practices for which they ceased as National institutions. I am aware of the danger of monied power and if such a corporation cannot be so restricted as to be imcapable of wanton injury either to the public or individuals, it should not be allowed. But the legislative power must be lamentably impotent if it cannot fashion the creation of its own creature so far as to render it accountable to the law for its conduct and punished if not prevent its abuses. I believe Congress has the Constitutional power to establish a Bank and I at present perceive no measure better calculated to relieve our distresses.

I have been thus explicit in the statement of my present impression because if elected I wish to be at liberty to support such measures as the best interest of the country may require, after a due consideration of all. Should this be the incorporation of a Bank, I assure you it would proceed from no personal or partisan zeal: from no particular love for banks, but a conviction of public benefits. I could never, however give my consent to such an institution unless such guards as would prevent all abuses which could be foreseen. To avoid all misconstruction of motives, I take the liberty to state that I have never been either a stock share holder or debtor in any bank whatever: the only interest I had in them is in common with every other citizen, that their notes shall be at all times convertible into Specie, and therefore equal to it. It is known to many of you that I did not concur in the election of the present Chief Magistrate; and should a competitor be presented whom I may prefer, I probably shall not do so at the next election. I will endeavor nevertheless whether in public or private life, to do justice to his measures and should deem myself altogether unworthy of your confidence were I capable of opposing any measure on account of the source from which it sprung. My first wish is that the country shall be well governed rather than it should be governed by any particular set of men. My opinion in relation to the public land, the distribution of the surplus revenue, the repeal of the Treasury circular, and the wanton interference with our rights in the attempts at abolition by the people of other states, I presume are sufficiently known to require no notice here.

With this imperfect exposition of my sentiments, I cheerfully leave the result with you, perfectly satisfied whatever it may be.

Your fellow citizen,

William A. Graham.

Raleigh, July 25, 1837.

From Mary G. Morrison.

[Davidson College], August the 7th, 1837.

*   *   *   *   *

Our first examination took place last week We had A very large collection; there was a greater display of welth and show then I have ever seen in in this part of country. We have 68 students. Thare was an address delivered to the 2 socityes by Major John Beard[55] of Salisbury. Our infant College has sucseeded so far with greate satisfaction. We will for some time labour under

---

[55] John Beard, of Salisbury, editor of the *Carolina Watchman,* an influential figure in the community, state senator, 1826.

grate disadvantages for want of more bildings. Our chapple is up
to the second story and will bee finished in the corse of a few
months. And have commenced 2 more dormiterrys which will
make 5 in number. There is a good many more applications for
next session.

May the Lord bless you both And when he has done with you
on earth May he receive you to himself is the Prayer of

Your affectionate sister.

From Charles L. Hinton.   U.

Graham   827
Wake
Montgomery   797
                  ——
                  30

You find that your vote in this County equals my expectations
when I see you, I am afraid to hear from Orange & Person. If you
should be elected I want you to attend two Barbecues in Wake,
one in the neighbourhood of Rosses the other at Hortons before
you go to Congress, the people are anxious to see you.

We believe if you could have shewed yourself in Wake we would
have given a majority of 300. Do write me by next mail.

In haste

From Charles Manly.[56]

Raleigh, 12 Aug, 1837.

My dear Graham,

It *may* be that you will receive a dozen letters today communicating the same intelligence & it may be that one half relying on
the other may send you none at all. I have concluded therefore
to have the pleasure of informing you that the correct vote of
Wake ascertained from the Shff: is for Graham 849, Montgomery

[56] Charles Manly (1795-1871), native of Chatham County, lawyer, reading clerk
of the commons, and chief clerk for more than twenty years. He was clerk to
commission on claims under Treaty of Ghent, Whig elector, 1840, secretary and
treasurer of the university, 1821-1849, 1851-1868, governor, 1849-1851.

792, Majority 57. We regard this under all the circumstances as a very great achievement.

We have it in contemplation to have *two large gatherings* of the people before long in different parts of the County where *you must attend,* not for the purpose of glorifying in an empty Whig triumph, but that they may see you and become acquainted with you and your principles. It will have a great effect in *future* however the election may have eventuated now. You will there be no candidate for their votes & they will believe what you say. The people want light. They have heard heretofore from the stump only one side.

When will you be at liezure to attend at Eagle Rock in the lower part of this County? Can you on Saturday of your County Court? We must have it before Fall Circuit begins.

Write to me to Pittsboro tomorrow. We are waiting very impatiently to hear from Orange & Person.

From James Graham.

Rutherfordton, August 15th, 1837.

* * * * *

I am told my negroes and overseer have been sick and I fear he will not incline for that reason to stay another year with me. If so I shall be much embarrassed before I leave in my farming arrangements.

The vote here has been quite thin as we had no opposition for Congress or either of the Clerks.[57]

I have not heard a word yet from your District. I hope however you have been successful. I am at a great loss to know how long Congress will set, and cannot make my arrangements at home to suit my business.

There is a great advantage in getting to Washington early so as to make choice of and appropriate a good seat to one's self.

J G

McGinnis has no waggon to haul his corn or gather his crop. You should get one soon as he must have one.

---

[57] In most of North Carolina at this time, politicians always wanted contests for candidates for local offices, because the voters generally were much more interested in them, than they were in those further removed from them, and turned out voters to vote.

From James W. Bryan.

Steamboat Kentucky,

Sept. 1, 1837.

The melancholy event which has occurred in the death of Mr. Washington, brought us all back to No. Carolina again, and we shall, God willing, reach Newbern on Sunday evening next. I think I express the honest sentiments of my heart when I declare that I have lost my best friend. My intimate Conexion with Mr. Washington[58] for the last three years endeared him to me very much and I am oppressed with the same melancholy feelings which the loss of my own father alone could excite.

Cousin Betsy is quite melancholy and seems to grieve much that she left home although Mr. W. urged her to do so. Ann is sorely grieved indeed and suffers very much. All make great exertions to sustain themselves under the truly afflicting dispensation.

* * * * *

John and myself were to have formed the first of this month with Mr. Washington a commission House in N. Y., but this occurrence has put an end to that project & is a lamentable lesson of the uncertainty of human life. I was winding up my affairs for that purpose. This event closes my conexion with N. York and compels me to abandon all idea of removing from N. Ca., Exclusive of the weighty objection that Mrs. B. is unwilling to reside in N. Y. & her Mother insists on her returning to our State. I am however compelled to return to close my affairs and will only remain in N. C. this trip about a month.

George Washington is with us, and it would be a most gratifying and consoling event to all for Cousin Susan to visit Newbern forthwith.

If you cannot leave your Circuit you might get some one to accompany her down. Whilst we were satisfied that your worldly affairs would be improved by your remaining at home, yet we were exceedingly sorry on many accounts that you did not succeed in defeating Dr. Montgomery; if you had have been brought out a little earlier there could not have been I think the slightest doubt of your success, but it is a matter that should cause you no regret, on the contrary your juxtaposition with Such a man

---

[58] John Washington (1768-1837), the father of Mrs. Graham and Mrs. Bryan.

has made your merits more obvious and given you a very enviable notoriety abroad.

I left the Dr's family all well and both of them satisfied and highly gratified with the apparent and obvious certainty of our increase of lineal descendants; be fruitful & multiply & replenish the earth seems to be a very favorite & pleasing Scriptural duty in this world.

We have had Steamboats loads of Members of Congress along with us & all believe that a Treasury Bank is all that will be seriously attempted.

Rhode Island has gone for the Whigs; the members elect started the next day for Congress after the Election.

The Steamboat is rocking, pitching, & rolling at such a rate that you must have "optics keen" indeed if you can decypher this miserable scrawl.

I had almost been induced to go to Albany this winter, but as I had not permanently settled in N. Y. and was winding up, etc., I abandoned it.

I think I shall lead quite a quiet life for some time, although I believe I shall return to the Bar as soon as my business will permit me so to do.

Give my love to Cousin Susan and Kiss your littke boy for me. Say to her that Ann has been intending to write to her every day until the news reached her of her father's death, which has rendered her unfit for everything.

Let us hear from you both soon.

From William Kimbrough.   U.

Memphis, Sept. the 5th, 1837.

I wrote to you sometime since and directed my Letter to Washington presuming You would be Ellected to Congress and would have left home before a letter Could reach You.

I now write to You by the request of my Sister to inform You of the unpleasant information of the Death of Col. Joseph Graham,[59] Your brother. he died on the 18 of last month with a Slow Feavor which continued on him for nearly the whole time of his sickness; he was confined to his room 18 days; he was attended

---

[59] Joseph Graham, Jr. (1797-1837), Graham's brother, who moved to Memphis in 1828, and became the first sheriff of Shelby County. He married Sarah Kimbrough, sister of the writer of this letter.

by two Doctors of the highest Standing and took medicin in the first of his disease without any difficulty but in the last Stage of his Sickness he would not take any medicin at all. He professed Religion and was perfectly resigned to his fate, said he knew he should soon leave this world and that he was willing to die and recommended his family in the hands of the Lord.

His wish to Sister Sarah was that You and Your Brother James Should have the mannagement of his Children and in as much as he made or asked her if she would be willing for You to take the mannagement of the children, She wishes one of you to come out soon as convenient and if possible to be the Children's Guardien as she thinks it was Col. Graham's wish. There will not I fancy any person administer on the Estate before we can hear from You. there is Several Thousand dollars of notes now in the hands of Seth Wheatley a Lawyer for Collection which of course will have to stop till there is an administrator which you know. You will pleased write to Sister or to my self as soon as You get this. Come out if You posibly can and give Sister Sarah such advice as You think best. by attending to this You will confer a favor on a Broken harted Widow and a friend.

From James Graham.   U.

Washington, Sept. 17th, 1837.

On yesterday I received a letter from Tennessee written by "Buckley Kimbrough" the brother of Brother Joseph's wife, and by it learn our Brother Joseph died on the 18th. day of August of the billious fever. The afflictions of Providence have fallen recently upon our family with peculiar distress. The ways of Providence are unsearchable and past finding out, and we his dependant creatures must submit to the decrees of Heaven and our own sure destiny. Mr. Kimbrough in his letter says brother Joseph in his illness requested if he should die, that *you* and *I* should have the management of his children. His wife appears anxious that we should do so . . .

I have written Brother John to see Dr. Harris and see if they can procure some person to go to Tennessee by the 17th. of Nov. (the day when the Hire is out) and bring into No Ca Anna Eliza's negroes.

I hope your health is improving and that you will be careful not to expose yourself, or to venture too much upon your strength before you acquire it. When your health is good your constitution requires a good deal of *regular exercise* so as to through the Bile to the surface and do not derange or obstruct the Pores of the Skin. The Flesh Brush or the Bath, (either Spring water or tepid) should be often resorted to. Eat simple food which agrees with your stomach and is easy of digestion. A wine glass full of French Brandy made in weak Toddy just before Dinner will strengthen you.

I anticipate *no Relief* to the Country at this Session. Tomorrow Calhoun is to speak and declare his sentiments on the Currency and the *Message;* at this time he is shrouded in darkness, and no one knows how he will go. I believe we shall adjourn towards the last of October. If so I will go home.

* * * * *

The debates in both branches will be very animated and quite interesting from this to the last of the session—Discussion will do much good to the Country. . . .

[P. S.] Jo Seawell Jones is here at Gadsbys Hotel. He lives in high stile and keeps a private or rather public Parlour, and *sees everybody!* He seems quite familiar with all parties and I suspect he is looking for an office. He says Gov. Dudly had appointed him to attend the Flat Rock in Buncombe next month where he is going on behalf of N. C.

Mr. Van Buren has fitted up the Presidents house in *princely stile.* He will have a much stronger support among the Members in favour of the hard money system than I anticipated, though I do not believe this Session will adopt it. I had no conception of the great number of small Bills (shinplasters) and individual notes that were circulating here. Gold & silver is unknown except to Members of Congress & Brokers.

Dr. Montgomery, I am told, has let go his Bank of Government paper and goes strongly for the *Hard Money.* There are many strangers here to hear the war of words to commence tomorrow.

From William Montgomery. [60]   U.

H. R., 27th. September, 1837.

* * * * *

We Move on Slowly Here, We are now discussing the Bill in the House that We got out of the Committee last Night after 10 days

[60] William Montgomery was, of course, his late successful competitor for a seat in Congress.

discussion there, to postpone the payment of the Fourth Instalment of the act of June 1836. to the States, the payment is postponed until 1st January 1839. With a proviso that the 3 First
instalments shall not be called For until Further orders, the Senate has passed a Resolution to adjourn on the 9th next Month.
We Cannot git of then, We May in 2 weeks, not Sooner. There is
a Strange Spliting up among parties Here. Mr. Calhoun goes for
the Late Message and the Strong probability is that the South will
soon be acting again together, Govnr. Branch was Here and declared in Favour of the doctrines of the Message. He was invited
and dined with the president. Mr. Rives and Mr. Talmage [61] Has
a Small party that Seemes to be Seperated to themselves.

Things are putting on a Better appearance in N. York Specie
is Down to 4½ per cent and Several Banks Has Resumed payment.
We Confidantly Hope and Calculate on Better times Soon,

Do write Me Soon,

Yours,

With great Regard.

From Paul C. Cameron.   U.

Fairntosh, Orange, Saturday morn,

Sept. 30, 1837.

I am just making preparations, to leave this, on a visit to my
poor brother and the family at Raleigh, and in answer, to your
application, for the use of my house, I have only time to say, that
I do not think, that I can with propriety *let* it to you, as I have
heretofore *refused* it to others. An improper construction, might
be placed, upon such a disposition of it, and that too by individuals,
between whom and myself, the kindest relations exist. I doubt not,
you will properly appreciate my motive.

Most sincerely do I sympathize with you, in the many losses,
you have been called to sustain, in a number of your *near* and *dear*
relatives. But you have much to comfort and sustain you under
these trials.

It is only within a few months, that *I* ever felt that "Luxury of
Grief" so happily described by a gifted and melancholy poet.

---

[61] Nathaniel Pitcher Talmadge (1795-1864), of New York, a graduate of Union
College who, after service in the legislature, was elected to the United States senate,
and served until 1844, when he was elected governor. He was a Democrat.

528   N. C. DEPARTMENT OF ARCHIVES AND HISTORY

Anne [62] is not with me, at this time on a visit to her friends on Haw River, whence I shall betake myself immediately after my return from Raleigh, if Mrs. Roulhac [63] will vouchsafe her permission.

To Mrs. Graham I beg you to present me in proper terms—and to *little "Jos"* I would offer a kiss, if *she* would permit me. I have never seen him, but doubt not, he is a very "kissable" little fellow.

Very truly your friend,

From James Graham.   U.

Washington, October 1st, 1837.

* * * * *

You mentioned to me you thought you were giving Maginnis too much; you pay him high but if you think of working your hands up there, I do not think you can do better, and if *he is not soon employed by you* he will be employed by some other person.

I think Congress will adjourn about the 20th of this month (October) and I may or may not go home according to the lateness of the day of adjournment. My wish is to go if I have time to attend to my business at home.

Calhoun is now identified with Benton and Co; his party (the Nullifiers) will generally go with him. Preston and Thompson [64] stand firm, and will not follow. Rives and Talmage, have both made speeches, and able ones, in favour of their old instruments the State Banks; King [65] of Georgia has made the *ablest speech* made in Congress this Session, altho' Clay and Webster have spoken. I will send you King's speech so soon as it is published. The Bill to postpone the 4th. Instalment of the Surplus to the States passed by 118 to 106. It is postponed to Jany., 1839.

It is not expected by any one here that the fourth installment will ever be paid to the States. Postpone means then to *repeal* the

---

[62] Anne Ruffin, (Mrs. Paul C.) Cameron, the daughter of Judge Thomas Ruffin.

[63] Catherine Ruffin (Mrs. Joseph B. G.) Roulhac, the eldest child of Judge Ruffin.

[64] Waddy Thompson (1798-1868), of South Carolina, graduate of South Carolina College, lawyer, member state legislature, 1826-30, major general of militia, advocate of Nullification. He served in congress from 1835 to 1841, as a Whig, and was minister to Mexico, 1842-1844.

[65] John Pendleton King (1799-1888), of Georgia, native of Kentucky, lawyer, United States senator, 1833-37, when he resigned. He was later a judge, president of the Georgia Railroad, delegate to the convention of 1865.

Law. Mongomery at first voted against the Bill but at last *voted for it*. The Bill was passed by the destructives and nullifiers their new Allies. The funds of U. S. are now in the State Banks. They are now *unavailable* to U. S. but available to the States in which they are.

I think Calhoun and the Nullys going over to Van will dam him and his administration. They live to destroy.

There is more talent in this Congress than the last. I have little hope that we will give any real Relief to the People.

From Thomas Ruffin.   U.

Allamance,

October 2nd., 1837.

If I could bring myself to part from The Hill [66] to any person, upon any terms, it would gratify me extremely to dispose of it to yourself. But my attachment to the place is very strong, the more so, as a brother's dead body, and those of direct descendants are interred there, and, moveover, in case of my death, I take it for certain that Mrs. Ruffin would prefer it for a residence before all other situations.

These considerations have heretofore induced me to refuse twenty-five hundred dollars for the property; which, as a price, I cannot but acknowledge to have been ample. In point of feeling my disinclination to part from it is not at all weakened either by time or separation. I must therefore decline your proposal; which I assure you I do both respectfully & reluctantly. Mrs. Ruffin, I believe, would almost agree that *you* should have our favorite place; and, as the means of fixing you to your liking, and near us, the motive with us all is very strong to let you have the matter, according to your choice. But, upon the whole, I trust you will find that you can select other situations nearly as agreeable to yourself, from which the present proprietor can part without a pang. At any rate, I confide in your well tried regard to excuse me upon this occasion—especially as you will perceive that I have not thought myself at liberty simply to return a naked refusal of your offer, but have thought it due to both of us to accompany it with the real reasons which influence me—the force of which I doubt not you will fully appreciate.

---

[66] Later "Burnside," the Hillsboro home of Paul C. Cameron.

Circumstances have of late allowed to us so little of each other, that, if matters should continue as they have gone on, we shall be almost strangers. I hope you will call when passing in the course of your circuits. That, at the least, though when my family shall again get into a state to accommodate our friends, Mrs. Ruffin and I would be yet more obliged if you and Mrs. Graham would spend some time with us.

I am, with sincere regard,

Your friend and obed't Serv't

From Joseph W. Evans. [67]   U.

Chapel Hill,
October 11th., 1837.

Dear Sir:

I am proud to communicate to an individual for whose character and talents I entertain so profound a respect, this result of an election which was held at the last session of the Dialectic Society.

We deeply regret the occurrence which prevented your compliance with a similar request on a previous occasion; & fondly hope that no circumstance will prevent your addressing the Society on Tuesday night, preceding the next Commencement.

Very respectfully,
Yours,

From James A. King.   U.

Statesville, Octr. 21st, 1837.

* * * * *

I spent a good part of the Summer in Va. at the Red Sulphur Springs, and think that my health in all respects has been much improved. I now think that the complaint with regard to which I was very uneasy at one time has been entirely overcome. I have therefore determined without further delay to resume the practice of my profession either here or in Ala. or Miss., If should be pleased with the prospects there. My principal reason however for going there if I should go is that I have had for a few years

---

[67] Joseph Washington Evans, of Cumberland, president of the Dialectic Society at the university.

some negroes in the Ten District who have been doing me but little good. I am advised besides that the climate of that country would suit me & that the prospects for doing business in our profession are decidedly better than here.

It is true that to Miss. especially there are many very strong objections. the Structure of their Judiciary for instance; but after all in these times of general misrule and disorder I don't know if we are to have a continuance of them, that it is right or necessary to be very fastidious as to our locality; so far as I am concerned at least I believe that I shall not give myself much trouble with reference to that matter, and again I believe it may be said that no man of feeling ever quits N. C. but with deep regret—so it will be with me if I should *depart the realm.*

I should like to know from you what your views are on this subject. I think a year or two since that you were not definitely determined whether you would make a permanent settlement in this State. I could wish, especially if I remove myself to be in the same State with you at least.

If you stay in N. C. I suppose you will have to supercede the illustrious Dr. M. from your district. If you have any inclination that way you certainly ought, as from all learn, in another contest there can be no doubt of your success.

Of politics in all their ramifications for some time to come I have taken leave.

In this part of N. C. the administration is certainly loosing ground. It has at last hit the people in a very vulnerable point— the pocket. There are few who indulge in golden dreams; they have ascertained to their sorrow that it was but a dream at best.

I should like very much to visit your part of the State but I fear that I can not do so conveniently at this time.

If I should go South I expect to be in this State next Summer.

* * * * *

I remain very
Sincerely your friend

To Susan Washington Graham.   A.

Greensborough, Oct. 21st, 1837.

My Dearest Wife

The mail leaves this morning, and I suppose you think it time that I should write you. I would have done so earlier but for the pressure of my engagements. We have had quite a busy week, and the Court will sit untill the latter part of the week. I wish the business were of such a character that I could afford you any amusement by its detail, as I have had time to think or converse of but little else.

I shall endeavour to get home by Thursday evening and presume that you will have made your arrangements to set off the next day. I have purchased no horse as yet, having seen none to suit me, but am to have one brought in on Monday, which, from description, I believe may answer.

Please write me by the earliest mail as to the condition of the one at home. I rather fear for you to undertake the journey with him, even if he shall greatly improve. Should I not be with you before Thursday please pack up our furniture &c ready to be left, and your trunk for traveling.

Should it continue as warm as it is now, I think you would prudently defer your visit for a week or two more. It is here exceedingly dry, there having been no rain at the time of the late storm with us. You have no doubt seen in the last Papers that that storm caused a wreck of the Steam Boat between Charleston & New York near Ocracoke bar, with the loss of more than one hundred lives. [68]

Several members of Congress have passed here on their return home in the two last stages. Today Mr. Calhoun, Judge White and others of distinction dined in the village but I did not see them. I hope Brother James will be here by the next stage as I am anxious to see him in relation to the affairs of myself and of brother Joseph's family.

*   *   *   *   *

There is a family of Italians performing divers feats of agility, etc., for evenings entertainment of the public here. I have not been to see them, as I cannot readily submit to be "crowded & bored with elbow points" to gratify my curiosity.

Greensboro continues to improve rapidly in new and ever elegant buildings. The cotton factory has been doubled, a large Brick Building has been erected for the "Caldwell Institute," and the Methodists are putting up buildings for an extensive female seminary.

---

[68] The steamship "Home" left New York on October 7th., and went aground off Sandy Hook that afternoon, but was floated off by high tide. Two days later, in the midst of a violent storm, she was beached about six miles from Ocracoke Inlet, and nearly a hundred persons, mostly women and children, were drowned.

A furnace for smelting Copper has lately been put in operation not far off, the ore of which abounds in this County. I saw
today a specimen of the melted ore, not quite purified, which appears to promise large profits to the miners.

How is my Dear Boy and Wife? Would that I could now see
them; One hour of their society is worth a whole week of the
scuffle and excitement of a Court.

Pray preserve your healths & be assured of my love.

    With every feeling of affection,

                  I am, My Dear Susan,

To Susan Washington Graham.   A.

            Hillsboro', Nov. 10th, 1837.

My Dear Wife

I am unexpectedly here, having finished the business of Caswell Court earlier than I expected. Mr. Norwood & myself came
half way yesterday evening & arrived to dinner today. Though
I had quite a cold ride on the day I left, the weather has been
charming ever since untill today, when it rains nearly all day. I
reached "High rock" before sunset on Sunday evening & Rockingham C. H. early on Monday. The engagements of the Court
being ended, I went to dinner on Saturday to the Rockingham
Springs, and remained a day, found the extent of accommodations
for lodgers quite improved, and still an excellent table. The day
following I reached Caswell C. H. There has been recently a
great religious excitement there, and preaching for ten or twelve
days in succession. A young Baptist Clergyman named Wilkes,
who was there during the time, baptized the youngest daughter,
Louisa, of Col. Graves [69] & married her the same day. He had
been engaged to her Sister who died last Summer, and resides in
Georgia. My kind landlady, Mrs. Graves, inquired very affection-
ately for you, and expressed a great desire to see our Boy.

I was very busily engaged during my absence, especially for the
last week and feel somewhat fatigued. I have two days to rest before going to Person however, and if my Dear Wife and son were
only here, I should be quite refreshed in that time. I have driven
down to Mrs. Palmer's and shall occupy my old office, after it has

---

[69] Probably Barzillai Graves, a well-known citizen of Caswell, a member of the
commons, 1813, 1818-22, 1832, state senator, 1814-15.

been somewhat cleansed; on my arrival it afforded a very good miniature of the "Augean Stable." I was strongly tempted to stop at Mrs. Hill's, but suppose I would have found it quite as desolate there, as here, since the departure of those who, for the time, constituted it my home.

I was greatly relieved on receiving your affectionate note from Smithfield at Yanceyville; for I seriously doubted whether our injured horse would be able to perform your journey. I marked your progress with the setting of each sun, And as I watched his descent, clear & bright, from the yard at Lenox Castle on Saturday, congratulated myself that my loved ones had been favoured with a pleasant week for travel, and had probably now reached their destination.

* * * * *

The Diavolo family were again at Rockingham & Caswell, and are to be here, and at Raleigh soon. I postponed going to their exhibition untill Caswell Ct. and was then so busy that I could not.

* * * * *

New Bern.

To Joseph W. Evans. [70]   U.

Hillsboro'

Nov. 11th 1837.

I have had the honor to receive your polite letter, informing of my election to address the Dialectic Society on Tuesday preceding the next Commencement. Having been before honored by a like appointment, and feeling a deep sense of the obligations due from me to the Society, I was unwilling to decline untill I ascertained that my acceptance might be again attended with disappointment. Duties which have recently devolved on me, and which I can by no means neglect, will probably compel me to be absent from the State, during the months of June & July next. Of this I am not at present certain, but I so much expect it that I am not at liberty to make any engagement to the contrary.

I beg of you to assure the members of the Society of my gratitude for their good opinion which has been twice so flatteringly manifested, and to declare to them that no difficulty which is not

---

[70] Joseph Washington Evans (d. 1854), of Cumberland County, a graduate of the university.

insuperable, should prevent me from fulfilling (though I am conscious very imperfectly) the task which their kindness has imposed.

For the flattering manner in which you have been pleased to communicate their wishes, I return my sincere acknowledgements.

                    I am high respect,
                                De Sir, Your Obed^t. Servt.

To Susan Washington Graham.   A.

                                    Hillsboro', Nov. 22, 1837.

My Dear Susan

I have not written you as often as I intended since your departure, but I do not know that you are in any thing the loser thereby as very little has occurred worthy of communication.

I went last week to Person, and having an unusually short Court, returned by the middle of the week. Not being particularly engaged for Guilford I have declined to go there at this term and am finishing off one odd job and another which I may find to have been heretofore neglected. I have been therefore generally seated in my office rummaging over books and papers. The town affords no amusements to call one out, and but for the recent scandal about a certain Mons. Ducoight who was here last Summer, I believe many would perish of actual exhaustion. He (you have no doubt heard, as bad news never fails to spread rapidly) is reported to have made an attempt to take the life of his wife, and has been driven from Edenton by public indignation.

                    *   *   *   *   *

I was very glad to learn by your letter on Saturday night that you had reached New Bern in safety, though I regret exceedingly the exposure of Joseph to the measles, & Whooping Cough. I hope you will spare no pains to prevent his taking them, though it would seem to be inevitable.

How is the dear Boy? I did not suppose I would miss his company so much as I do. If you do not write regularly and let me know how you both are—and be well, I fear I shall have to come after you soon.

After the Court here next week, I shall go directly to Lincoln, probably in the Stage. My present impression is that I will continue to farm there the next year. I hope to sell my lands however, and to arrange a good deal of unfinished business that I have there, as well as to make a new contract with my overseer, and provide for a sale of the present Crop. I shall be absent two or perhaps three weeks. My business at the Supreme Court will require me to stay two or three weeks in Raleigh, where I hope to be the second week in January—the first I shall be in Caswell.

*   *   *   *

Mr. William Anderson is a Candidate to fill the Professorship of Languages in the University, vacated by the resignation of Mr. Hooper. [71] I wish him success.

You have probably learned from the newspapers that young Henderson [72] of Lincoln who killed Hoke [73] has been convicted of manslaughter only. I rejoice at it for the sake of his parents, who have always been fast friends of mine.

The Intelligence of the New York elections has come over us like the fall of manna on the Israelites. The remotest corners of the Union appear to be in ecstasies by reason of it. I have before me the last Recorder and would send it herewith, but it is so absolutely barren, that you would not be compensated for opening it.

Kiss my Boy and present my Love to all.

[P. S.] You will excuse this most villainous paper, on which I write on account of my negligence in sending a servant & not going myself to select it.

Mons. Diavolo & his *"interesting family"* are to perform here next week; they are now at Raleigh.

You have now my Dear some leisure for reading which I hope you improve. I expect this week to receive 2nd Vol. of Davis' Life of Aaron Burr, which I shall peruse with much interest. It is expected to contain much secret History never before developed.

Again Farewell, my ever Dear Wife.

G.

---

[71] William Hooper (1792-1876), a native of Wilmington, grandson of William Hooper, signer of the Declaration of Independence, graduate of the university, where he served as tutor, studied theology at Princton, and, becoming an Episcopal minister, was rector in Fayetteville, 1822-25, when he became a professor at the university. He became a Baptist minister, and was one of the founders of Wake Forest College. He went to Furman University in 1838, was professor in South Carolina College, 1840-46, when he became president of Wake Forest. Resigning two years later, he taught and preached until his death.

[72] Logan Henderson.

[73] Marcus Hoke.

From James Graham.   U.

Raleigh, Nov. 30th, 1837.

I am here on my way to Washington and came by Pittsboro.

I presume you will go up next week as you are looked for. Just do as you think will suit your own convenience in working or not the Earhart place. Your negroes have suffered some for clothing and shoes. If McGinnis stays with you tell him he must not bring any Hogs or Colts to the Earhardt place, as he now has both and I believe against your agreement with him. He has a good corn Crop. I think you might hire out one of your negroes, and still have enough of hands to work that place. I have made arrangements with Brother John to lease the plantation for me if you do not take it. I have not been able to hear anything yet of Brother Franklin's negroes; Thompson you know has gone for them. I desire them to be hired out at Christmas for one year. I have told David Reinhardt to go on and sell all brother Joseph's Iron & Castings as fast as possible, so as to try to make his Land and Iron & Castings pay the sum due on his note.

* * * * *

To Susan Washington Graham.   A.

Hillsborough, Decr. 2nd, 1837.

My Dearest

Your two last letters informing me of the illness of our dear child have inspired me with the most melancholy apprehensions —so much so that unless I hear from you by the mail this evening you may expect to see me along with this. It is now Saturday evening near sunset, & I had made all preparation (the Court being closed) to start tonight for Lincoln. My business there indeed imperatively requires it, but should I not hear that Joseph is better before I go, I shall spend the time there with but little satisfaction. I hope therefore that the mail will bring me intelligence that that he is better. Indeed, had your last arrived one day earlier, so as to enable me to reach New Bern this evening I would have gone on Thursday.

If be better, my darling, I know you will omit no care in protecting him and preventing a relapse.

I am so much hurried that I have no time to think or write. Should I not come down I will write you as soon as I get sufficient leisure. And I hope you will write me to Salisbury, by the middle of next week.

*　*　*　*　*

I would be exceedingly glad to be at the funeral of your venerable Father but I am apprehensive that it will be out of my power.

The sun has set & my letter must go to the office.

Be assured, my Dearest, of my love.

Kiss my poor sick Boy.

Ever Yours, My Dear

New Bern

To Susan Washington Graham.   A.

Vesuvius Furnace, Lincoln,

December 16th, 1837.

My Dear Wife

*　*　*　*

Arrived at Hillsboro' in the night & departed before day; was told by Mr. Palmer that Maj. Davie had purchased Mr. Anderson's House, and C. Jones, Jr., had exchanged with Mr. Spencer for the late residence of Mr. Waddell. Old Mr. Phillips is expected to return about Christmas. At Salisbury I hired a conveyance, as the stages did not meet, and on Tuesday evening about 8 oclock reached Davidson College where I found Mr. Morrison's family quite well, & delighted to see me.

On the next day I went with Sister Mary to see a relative & met two maternal Aunts whom I had not seen before for many years. A violent snow storm commenced while we were there, and it now lies four or five inches deep on the ground.

I went yesterday to my plantation and found all well except one of the negro women. They have made an excellent crop of corn, and I hope to have near a thousand bushels for sale. I committed an error in not placing more stock there, as the hands could easily have raised their own supplies of meat. By failing to arrive earlier I have lost my overseer, who, saving a few faults, has perhaps done better than any I could get. Another will be here this morning to see me, and if I agree with him I will work the place another year. It is an excellent plantation for grain &

stock, & I don't know but what I may accept Bro. James' offer to purchase it.

My business will probably detain me here untill the last of next week, and then my good friends in Mecklenburg will hardly excuse me if I return without going to see them. I must at all events get to Hillsboro a few days before Caswell Court 1st Jan., and after that I shall go directly to Raleigh. I will write you again however before I go to Caswell. I have sent for divers individuals to meet me here today to propose sale of land & several other matters of business, after which I will go down with brother John to his house on the river. He has been here ever since I came. His Furnace is now in blast and requires much of his attention here . . .

How is my poor Boy? I have not seen a child since I left but has reminded me of him. I hope you will take especial care to prevent his getting the Whooping cough.

Farewell thou darling of my heart.

Division and Value of Slaves   U.
belonging to John Washington.

In obedience to an order of the Court of Pleas and Quarter Sessions for the County of Craven, on the petition of Elizabeth Washington, and others, the widow and next of kin of John Washington, deceased, authorising and appointing us Commissioners to divide the Negro Slaves of said John Washington, deceased, among the widow and next of kin of said deceased, we proceeded to execute said order at the Egypt plantation in the County of Craven, on the 27th. day of December, A. D. 1837, and after viewing and valuing said slaves, do allot, divide and set them apart to the widow and next of kin of the said John Washington, deceased, according to the petition filed for said division at the November term, A. D. 1837, of said court as follows, viz:

No. 1		No. 2.	
To Elizabeth Washington, the following slaves, viz:		To Jno. C. Washington, the following slaves, viz:	
Old George	$50.	Nancy	$375.
Nathan	600.	Hester	300.
Caroline	400.	Sheppard	275.
Betty	300.	Haywood	200.
Sally	100.	Harriet	150.

Louisa	250.	Windsor	600.
Ben	300.	Prince	600.
Frank	200.	Henry	200.
Hannah	375.	Jacob	725.
Charity	325.	Zilpha	350.
Mima	225.	Kizziah	200.
Amy	350.	Suckey	150.
Stephen	200.	Amanda	125.
Jim	600.	Chloe	375.
	———	Harriet	100.
	$4275.		———
			$4725.

No. 3.

To James A. Washington, the following slaves, viz:

Peter	$375.
Charles	600.
Peter	300.
Siddy	375.
Maria	250.
Ted	200.
Dinah Collins	375.
Eleanor	200.
Betsey	150.
William	150.
Sam	75.
Beck	375.
Frank	250.
Kitty	350.
Jefferson	300.
	———
	$4325.

No. 4.

To Eliza H. Grist, the following slaves, viz:

George Grace	$725.
Silvy	375.
Shade	550.
Eli	425.
Green	450.
Adam	550.
Affy	50.
Mary	375.
Horton	325.
Elias	400.
Silvy	250.
Squire	280.
Morris	200.
Tom	125.
	———
	$5080.

No. 5.

John C. Washington trustee of Ann M. Bryan

Clara	$250.
Madison	600.
Lemuel	400.
Isaac	450.
Dinah	250.
Charles	550.

No. 6.

To William A. Graham & wife, Susan S. Graham, the following slaves, viz:

Alfred	$600.
Leah	375.
Caesar	450.
Rose White	225.
Barbara	375.

Dicey	250.	Sally	375.
Argent	150.	June	250.
Richard	150.	Ben	300.
Martha Ann	50.	Ann	150.
Henderson	300.	Richmond	450.
Moses	525.	Jim (little)	450.
Calvin	450.	Willis	400.
William	450.	Harriet	300.
Rose Allen	175.		
			$4700.
	$5000.		

No. 7.
To George Washington the following slaves, viz:

Fanny	$375.
Sarah	200.
Milly	200.
Mima	150.
Henry	175.
Mark	125.
Simon	600.
Aleck	600.
Grice	475.
Peggy	150.
Maryella	375.
Dilsy	300.
Jack	350.
Nancy	150.
Dinah	325.
Julia	250.
	$4800.

No. 8.
To Mary A. G. Washington the following named slaves, viz:

Charity	$375.
Needham	150.
Frank	75.
John	600.
George	600.
Patience	375.
Obed	300.
Nicey Ann	175.
Jeanette	125.
Hannah	75.
Cely	375.
Mary	200.
Betsey	375.
John	525.
Phil	425.
	$4750.

The value of all of the slaves we estimated at Thirty Seven thousand, six hundred & fifty five ($37,655) as will appear by reference to the amounts affixed to their respective names above, which would entitle each one of the next of kin & distributees to a share in & to said slaves in value of $4706.87½. We therefore direct and adjudge, in order to equalize the said division that share No. 5—allotted to John C. Washington, trustee of Ann M.

Bryan, pay to share No. 1—allotted to Elizabeth Washington—
two hundred & ninety three dollars & twelve and half cents
($293.12½), and that share No. 4—allotted to Eliza H. Grist—
pay to share No. 1—allotted Elizabeth Washington—one hundred
and thirty eight dollars & seventy five cents ($138.75) and also
that said share of No. 4—allotted as aforesaid,—pay to share No.
6—allotted William A. Graham & wife—six dollars and eighty
seven & a half cents ($6.87½), and also that said share of No. 4
pay to share No. 3—allotted to Dr. James A. Washington— the
sum of two hundred and twenty seven dollars & fifty cents
($227.50), and that share No. 2—allotted to Jno. G. Washington,
—pay to share No. 3—allotted to James A. Washington— the sum
of eighteen dollars, twelve & half cts. ($18.12½) and that share
No. 7—allotted to George Washington, pay to said share No. 3—
allotted to James A. Washington—ninety three dollars and twelve
& half cents, ($93.12½) and also that share No. 8—allotted to
Mary A. G. Washington—pay to said share No. 3, set apart as
aforesaid to James A. Washington, the sum of forty three dollars
and twelve & half cents ($43.12½). We further find that among
the said slaves of which the said John Washington, dec'd, died
possessed and which are distributable among his widow and next
of kin, viz: Elizabeth Washington, John C. Washington, James
A. Washington, Eliza H. Grist, John G. Washington, trustee of
Ann M. Bryan, William A. Graham, and wife Susan, George
Washington and Mary A. G. Washington, there are the following
named slaves, viz: Aaron, Sall & Jinny, all of whom are so aged
and infirm as to be utterly worthless & valueless, and must necessarily be a tax upon, and expense to the estate of the said John
Washington, for their maintenance & support for the residue of
their lives—but the widow and next of kin, having agreed among
themselves to make provision for their comfortable support, we
have deemed it inexpedient to incumber or tax any of the shares
with them, and have not therefore, divided them.

Given under our hands and seals this 27th. day of December,
1837.

		(——)
A copy of Division of)	John Harris	(Seal)
Slaves belonging to the)		(——)
Estate of John Washington,)	John T. Lane	(Seal)
		(——)
dec'd. Report of Commissioners.)		

To Susan Washington Graham.   A.

Raleigh, Decr. 20th, 1837.

My Dear Susan

I am here I presume contrary to your expectations, and with much inconvenience to myself. I reached Hillsboro' on Tuesday night last, not in "thunder lightning & in rain," but in a deep and obstinate snow, the second one that I encountered on the way.

Learning that the Board of Trustees of the University were to meet on yesterday, and being under great obligation to my friend Wm. E. Anderson for his many kind offices, I could not forego the duty of friendship in endeavouring to advance him to the Professorship of Ancient Languages.

The Board met yesterday afternoon, there being many candidates before it, among others Mr. Burke of New Bern. On the first ballot a Mr. Fetter [74] of Flushing, Long Island, was chosen; no others being voted for, but him & Mr. Anderson. He is highly recommended, and although his appointment did not receive my support, I hope he may do well.

I left Lincoln more than a week ago and visited my Sisters and some other friends in Mecklenburg whom I had not seen for several years. They made many kind inquiries concerning you, and insisted that I should by all means bring you to see them next summer. I was detained near two days in Salisbury by the failure of the stages to meet, in company with Mr. Conner on his way to Washington. He has been detained at home by sickness.

Bro. John left Lincoln while I was there for Raleigh via Hillsboro' in company with Revd. F. Nash. [75] He staid two days at Hillsboro', and left here on yesterday before I arrived, so that I have not seen him since he left home.

I have engaged a new overseer on my plantation and made arrangements for working it another year. I was in Hillsboro' so short a time that I did not procure a house. . . . I believe I cannot do better at present than to take Mr. Spencer's,—(formerly Mr. Waddell's), which is for sale or rent. He having bought other lots and being about to erect a Hotel, I should not expect to keep

---

[74] Manuel Fetter (1809-1888), a native of Pennsylvania, educated at Columbia, where he served as professor before coming to the university. He was dropped from the faculty when the "carpet-bag" government came into power in 1868.

[75] A son of Judge Frederick Nash, a Presbyterian minister, who was a student at the university for three years. He was in Lincoln County for some years.

it, but it may serve our present purpose. There are four rooms, 3 having fireplaces, all on the ground floor, besides an office in the yard with 2 rooms, a large garden & about 3 acres attached. I can't say I like it, But may take it temporarily. I would be glad to learn from you what furniture we shall want, and will take the earliest measures to procure it.

You have probably heard of the marriage of Dr. W. Cameron to Miss E. Moore; it was a small party and rather a melancholy one, owing to the affliction of the family. Also Mr. D. B. Hooper[76] to Miss Hooper at Chapel Hill. Miss Charlotte Jones of Pittsborough is to be married about this time to Mr. Wm. Hardin, a widower with many children. I learn from Govr. Swain that Mrs. White's family are well. I may run down to see them before I go out today. The stage will carry me to Hillsboro' tonight, and tomorrow I go to Caswell, shall return here about Monday the 8th. of Jany. to the Supreme Court. If you find any friend coming up about the 15th, I would be glad for you to come then, if well. I do not wish you, my Dearest, to travel alone, and if no one is coming I will go for you. My business will detain me here two weeks at least. I long again to see you and my dear Boy; driven about as I have recently been, back and forth, and in all companies, I have often turned my thoughts to those whose society & comfort is my greatest delight.

Pray be careful of your health and continue to me the affection of your pure heart.

---

[76] John de Berniere Hooper (1811-1886), a native of Brunswick, graduate, tutor, and professor of the university, who married a daughter of Dr. William Hooper.

INDEX